HRAC

JUL   2023

Life, Liberty, and the Pursuit of Happiness

LIFE, LIBERTY, AND THE PURSUIT OF HAPPINESS

Britain and the American Dream

WITH BENJAMIN FRANKLIN—WILLIAM STRAHAN—
SAMUEL JOHNSON—JOHN WILKES—
CATHARINE MACAULAY—THOMAS PAINE

PETER MOORE

Farrar, Straus and Giroux
New York

Farrar, Straus and Giroux
120 Broadway, New York 10271

Printed in the United States of America
Published simultaneously in Great Britain by Chatto & Windus and in the
United States by Farrar, Straus and Giroux
First American edition, 2023

Image on title page and part openers: Philadelphia viewed from the great tree at
Kensington, under which the Treaty of Shackamaxon was signed in 1682; from
the Miriam and Ira D. Wallach Division of Art, Prints and Photographs: Prints
Collection, the New York Public Library (1801); https://digitalcollections
.nypl.org/items/510d47d9-7b30-a3d9-e040-e00a18064a99.

Library of Congress Cataloging-in-Publication Data
Names: Moore, Peter, 1983– author.
Title: Life, liberty, and the pursuit of happiness : Britain and the American
    dream / Peter Moore.
Description: First American. | New York : Farrar, Straus and Giroux, 2023. |
    Includes bibliographical references and index.
Identifiers: LCCN 2023001279 | ISBN 9780374600594 (hardcover)
Subjects: LCSH: Enlightenment. | Political science—Great Britain—
    Philosophy—History—18th century. | United States—Civilization—
    Influences, British. | American Dream. | Philosophers—Great
    Britain—Biography.
Classification: LCC B802 .M643 2023 | DDC 194.1—dc23/eng/20230328
LC record available at https://lccn.loc.gov/2023001279

Designed by Patrice Sheridan

www.fsgbooks.com
www.twitter.com/fsgbooks • www.facebook.com/fsgbooks

1   3   5   7   9   10   8   6   4   2

To Thomas

The natural flights of the human mind are not from pleasure to pleasure, but from hope to hope.

—SAMUEL JOHNSON, *RAMBLER* NO. 2, MARCH 24, 1750

Contents

HAPPINESS (1771–1776)

Cast of Principal Characters

BENJAMIN FRANKLIN (1706–1790): Philadelphian printer, diplomat, and "electrician"

WILLIAM STRAHAN (1715–1785): Scottish-born London printer, merchant, and politician

SAMUEL JOHNSON (1709–1784): English man of letters; author of *A Dictionary of the English Language*

JOHN WILKES (1725–1797): English politician and pamphleteer

CATHARINE MACAULAY (1731–1791): English historian and political activist

THOMAS PAINE (1737–1809): Anglo-American journalist and writer

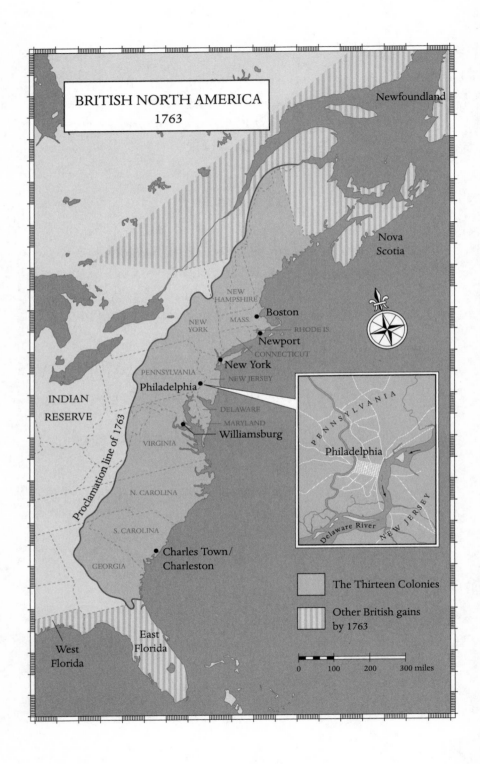

BRITISH NORTH AMERICA
1763

Newfoundland

Nova
Scotia

NEW
HAMPSHIRE

NEW
YORK

MASS.

Boston

RHODE IS.

Newport

CONNECTICUT

New York

PENNSYLVANIA

NEW JERSEY

Philadelphia

INDIAN
RESERVE

DELAWARE

MARYLAND

Williamsburg

VIRGINIA

Proclamation line of 1763

N. CAROLINA

S. CAROLINA

Charles Town/
Charleston

GEORGIA

PENNSYLVANIA

Philadelphia

NEW JERSEY

Delaware River

West
Florida

East
Florida

The Thirteen Colonies

Other British gains
by 1763

0   100   200   300 miles

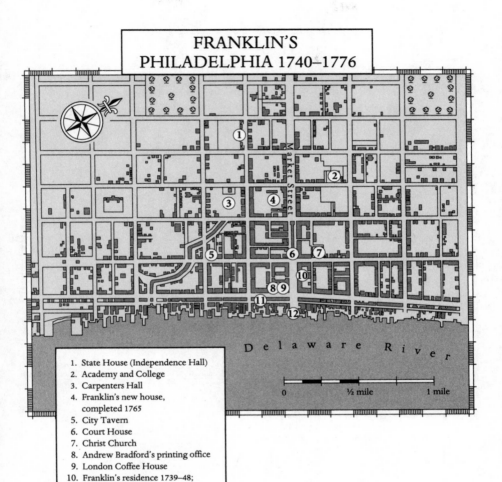

FRANKLIN'S
PHILADELPHIA 1740–1776

Market Street

Delaware River

0   ½ mile   1 mile

1. State House (Independence Hall)
2. Academy and College
3. Carpenters Hall
4. Franklin's new house,
   completed 1765
5. City Tavern
6. Court House
7. Christ Church
8. Andrew Bradford's printing office
9. London Coffee House
10. Franklin's residence 1739–48;
    printing office, 1739–52;
    Post Office 1739–52
11. Crooked Billet Tavern
12. Market Street Wharf

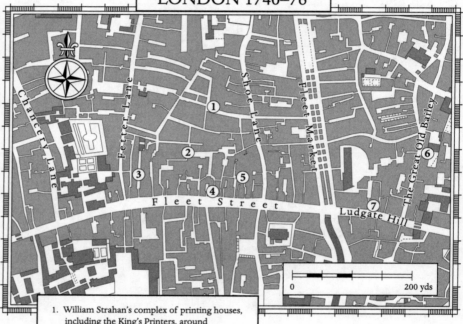

STRAHAN'S
LONDON 1740–76

Chancery Lane

Fetter Lane

Shoe Lane

Fleet Market

The Great Old Bailey

Fleet Street

Ludgate Hill

0   200 yds

1. William Strahan's complex of printing houses,
   including the King's Printers, around
   Little New Street
2. Samuel Johnson's house at 17 Gough Square
3. Dryden Leach's printing shop, 1763
4. William Strahan's first printing house, Wine
   Office Court
5. William Faden's printing shop,
   Peterborough Court
6. Approximate location of Richard Balfe's
   printing shop, 1763
7. Approximate location of George Kearsley's
   bookshop

Life, Liberty, and the Pursuit of Happiness

Prologue

THE FOURTH OF JULY

BRITAIN FIRST DREAMED THE Enlightenment dream, but it was America that made it happen. To be precise, it made it happen at about ten thirty in the morning of Thursday, the Fourth of July, 1776.[1] On that day fifty or so delegates from thirteen of the British American colonies came to a vote on adopting the amended text of the Declaration of Independence. Of these, all but New York, who pleaded for more time, assented. Inside the Pennsylvania State House, where the Second Continental Congress was taking place, a little piece of bureaucratic theater ensued. It is not recorded but it is easily imagined. The document was attested by the slender, dark, Irish-born secretary Charles Thomson. It was then passed along to be authorized by the imposing figure of John Hancock, the Boston merchant who was serving as the president of Congress. As Hancock's hand flourished and his quill scratched across the paper, the umbilical cord that had connected colonial America to the mother country for more than a century and a half was cut.

Memories of that occasion would remain with the text's principal author for the rest of his life. Ten days before his death—he died with impeccable timing on July 4, 1826—Thomas Jefferson recalled the "host of worthies, who joined with us on that day, in the bold and doubtful election we were to make for our country, between submission or the sword." It was a happy reflection, Jefferson acknowledged, that half a century on, the wisdom of their actions had been borne out. The Declaration turned out to be a signal, "arousing men to burst the chains, under which monkish ignorance and superstition had persuaded them to bind themselves, and to assume the blessings and security of self-government." Ever since that day, Jefferson added, "all eyes are opened, or opening, to the rights of man."[2]

There was no such clarity as the sun rose over the Delaware on July 4, 1776. That morning was refreshingly cool in Philadelphia. As Jefferson left his lodgings on Seventh and Market Street for the short journey to the State House, temperatures were yet to nudge into the seventies. As for the business of the day, Jefferson, like everyone else, knew what was coming. The great confrontation had taken place three days earlier, on July 1, when the faction opposed to independence—led by the Philadelphian lawyer John Dickinson—made one last, impassioned plea for caution. The thirteen colonies, united or not, were wretchedly vulnerable. In New York, a mighty British fleet was expected any day, and when they arrived they would find their opponents without money, allies, or munitions. To go to war against Great Britain in such circumstances, Dickinson starkly put it, was "to brave the storm in a skiff made of paper."[3]

Dickinson was answered by John Adams, the delegate from Massachusetts, whose tireless advocacy for independence had made him the star of Congress. Adams was a man who perfectly conformed to Edmund Burke's description of American lawyers as "acute, inquisitive, dextrous, prompt in attack, ready in defence, full of resources."[4] Over the past months Adams had done as much as anyone to bring the issue of independence to a head. As he rose in reply to Dickinson on July 1, a spectacular summer storm broke. With the debates inside the State House wreathed in secrecy, no record of Adams's words would be preserved for posterity. But those who witnessed his speech considered it to be the finest of his life. Adams argued with resolve, and with touches of brilliance. He made the case for courage. A tense vote on independence followed the next day. The issue was decided.

Attention then transferred to the wording of the Declaration. It was nearly a month since June 11, when Jefferson had been appointed to a body—later solemnized in history as "the Committee of Five"—charged with preparing the document. The as-yet unwritten Declaration's chief purpose was the setting out of the colonies' rationale for separating with Britain, should that be their decision. Still something of a stripling among the other delegates at thirty-three, Jefferson had hitherto appeared as a brooding, silent, relatively untested member of Congress. But as a Virginian he had the advantage of being a representative of the most populous and influential colony, and ever since his pamphlet, *A Summary View of the Rights of British America* (1774), he had been marked out for his perceptive mind and lucent, supple prose.

After his appointment to the committee, Jefferson was delegated—seemingly by Adams—the task of preparing an initial draft. This was no easy assignment. So much had been said during the past decade. So many claims and counterclaims. Jefferson's challenge was to marshal all the years of collected experience into a single text: one that would function both as a legal indictment that clarified the crimes of the past, and as a piece of philosophy that pointed the way to a beckoning future. To achieve this Jefferson would need to find a persuasive mode of expression, but at the same time he had to take care not to overextend himself. He could not stray beyond the ideas that had already been expressed in Congress.

Jefferson met this challenge in sparkling style. From its opening sentence, "When in the course of human events it becomes necessary for a people to advance from that subordination in which they have hitherto remained,"[5] his words flowed with what the historian Carl Lotus Becker has termed "that felicitous, haunting cadence which is the peculiar quality of Jefferson's best writing."[6] When Adams first read the draft, he found himself "delighted with its high tone, and the flights of Oratory with which it abounded."[7] Some parts of the preamble were then tightened or fortified by Adams and Benjamin Franklin, who were also on the Committee of Five. Together they also scrutinized Jefferson's list of twenty-four distinct charges against King George III, before the draft was submitted for consideration.[8] Then Jefferson's agonies truly began. Words, phrases, entire paragraphs were picked over, quibbled at, or struck out as Congress sought to find a balance that was palatable to all.

By the morning of July 4, with about a quarter of his initial draft deleted, Jefferson's miseries were at an end. Perhaps the tall, rangy Virginian enjoyed a morning stroll to the State House, along Philadelphia's clean, cobbled, regular streets. Or perhaps, like the gentleman that he was, he rode his horse. We do not know. We can only be sure that at about breakfast time, Abraham Clark, a delegate from New Jersey, was confiding in a letter home that a declaration, "I expect, will this day pass Congress. It is nearly gone through, after which it will be Proclaimed with all the State and Solemnity circumstances will admit. It is gone so far that we must now be a free independent State, or a Conquered Country."[9]

Several items of business lay before Congress that morning. Adopting the amended text of the Declaration was second on the list. So it was that in mid-morning a fair, handwritten copy of the text was produced. It was presumably a single sheet of standard crown paper, fifteen by twenty inches, but one that, as Jefferson with his tidy, quantifying mind might have calculated, would reduce the size of the British Empire by around 400,000 square miles. This crucial document in the history of the United States is now missing, presumed destroyed. But we can just about catch sight of it in our mind's eye, the words flowing along in Jefferson's suave, schoolmasterly hand.

Much of the emotive language—on slavery, on King George— had been scratched out during the previous days. But the most flourishing phrase of all had survived, with only minimal adjustment, to the end. This was a trio of nouns that appeared in the second sentence, nouns that grew rhythmically and enchantingly in length. These words were destined one day to become an evergreen mantra for politicians and a shorthand for that ideal we call the American Dream:

Life, Liberty, and the pursuit of Happiness.

OVER THE PAST QUARTER millennium, this felicitous line has become world-famous. In America itself it is part of secular scripture. It is carved into the white imperial marble of Jefferson's own memorial in Washington, D.C., and it is inscribed on porcelain enamel panels inside the caverns of Mount Rushmore. Every Fourth of July, readers of the *New York Times* can read the words in the paper's annual Independence Day issue, and on countless other days theater-goers can hear the phrase delivered with irresistible style in Lin-Manuel Miranda's hit musical *Hamilton*:

Life, liberty, and the pursuit of happiness
We fought for these ideals we shouldn't settle for less.[10]

There is a winning clarity here. So much is evoked with such little language. In a phrase of just seven words, Jefferson, it seems, has captured the unique purpose and energy of the American Revolution. To hear these words is to be instantly transported back to that founding moment, a seemingly simpler time before all the traumas and antagonisms of our current age; a time when all that existed was an inspiring vision written on a piece of paper in Philadelphia.

But just as Jefferson's line has had the most vibrant of afterlives, it has a captivating pre-history too. Many have noticed that several weeks before the Declaration's appearance, in the Virginia Declaration of Rights, a lawyer called George Mason laid claim to the "inherent

rights" of the "good people of Virginia," among which were "the enjoyment of life and liberty, with the means of acquiring and possessing property, and pursuing and obtaining happiness and safety."[11] Nor
were such thoughts confined to America. In Britain, in the 1750s and
1760s, Samuel Johnson made repeated use of the line "the pursuit of
happiness,"[12] while his rival, the republican historian Catharine Macaulay, dwelt in her own political pamphlets on the "virtue, liberty,
and happiness of society."[13] Other instances abound, from as far back
as John Locke's "life, liberty and estate,"[14] which featured in his *Two
Treatises of Government* in 1689, right through to the parting words
the Scottish printer William Strahan wrote to his estranged friend
Benjamin Franklin in July 1775. "I wish," Strahan signed off in terms
that seem prophetic to us now, "the Liberty and Happiness of all our
Brethren with You."[15]

There are patterns of thought here, similar to those the Harvard
professor Bernard Bailyn identified in *The Ideological Origins of the
American Revolution* (1967). Detecting these patterns, Bailyn argued,
was vital if one was to unlock the subtle codes of the revolutionary
era. For despite appearances, the revolution was no straightforward
affair. No white American colonist before 1774 could honestly claim
to be oppressed. In the colonies there was almost total freedom of
speech and freedom of conscience. The colonists could trade without
many restrictions, they were spared several of the taxes that were
levied on their English counterparts, and they made much of their
privileges as freeborn Britons—privileges that entitled them to a
range of legal protections, from Habeas Corpus to the right to trial
by jury. There was no Bastille on the banks of the Delaware, no Star
Chamber on Broadway. Indeed, for much of the century the colonists generally wanted more of Britain than less of it. "We have often
wished," wrote William Franklin, the royal governor of New Jersey,
to a London friend, "that we could put Great Britain under sail, bring
it over to this country and anchor it near us."[16]

This is a playful line but it is one that conveys an important message. As Bailyn demonstrated in his Pulitzer Prize–winning study, and as we tend to forget today, the relationship between Great Britain and her American colonies in the pre-revolutionary years was complex. Rather than being repulsed by an overbearing parent, the colonists were often in awe of a nation they considered uniquely special. It is easy to see why. For the first seventy-six years of the eighteenth century, it was Britain that was generally regarded as the glamorous, revolutionary nation. It was the English, after all, who had thrown off two tyrannical monarchs in the previous century, obtaining for her people a spectrum of rights virtually unknown any-where else in the world. The most satisfying and enduring of these episodes, and the one that truly gave Britain its glossy, modern sheen, was the Glorious Revolution of 1688, when James II and his Catholi-cism were chased out of the kingdom. The following year a Bill of Rights was passed, curbing the Crown's power, preventing the levy-ing of taxes without Parliamentary consent, banning the keeping of a standing army during peacetime, and ensuring the free election of political representatives. These were some of the privileges enjoyed uniquely by British citizens, a place where people loved to speak of their Parliament as the greatest assembly in the world.

So it was that for much of the eighteenth century the colonists gazed east, much as we look to the west today, toward a land of lib-erty. It was commonly held that it was there, in Great Britain, that the purest, most exhilarating and fulfilling form of life was to be experienced. This was the kind of life that was written about in the periodical essays and novels, magazines and newspapers: the kind of enlightened life that was being lived by philosophers like Isaac New-ton, wits like Joseph Addison, adventurers such as George Anson and the prosperous, buccaneering merchants of the City of London. It was the kind of life people wanted to experience for themselves, and it was the kind of life that was worth defending if it ever came under sustained attack.

In the 1760s, as Bailyn showed, this is precisely what the colonists believed was happening. From their distant position, an ocean's width away from the hub of political power in London, they detected what they interpreted as an artfully laid plot against their liberty. The plot, Bailyn wrote, "transformed the meaning" of their struggle. It converted them from zealous partisans into unruly rebels, whose burning ambition was to protect the privileges and liberties they believed were being snatched away. The conviction that such a plot existed "added an inner accelerator to the movement of opposition." Whether the conspiracy was real or not was less important than the fact that the colonists thought it was. This belief "could not be easily dispelled: denial only confirmed it, since what conspirators profess is not what they believe; the ostensible is not the real; and the real is deliberately malign."

> It was this—the overwhelming evidence, as they saw it, that they were faced with conspirators against liberty determined at all costs to gain ends which their words dissembled—that was signalled to the colonists after 1763, and it was this above all else that in the end propelled them into Revolution.[17]

The conspiracy against liberty that Bailyn identifies is a familiar one to historians of the eighteenth century. It centers on political events in Westminster in the years following the accession of King George III in 1760 and the Treaty of Paris in 1763. Key to it are the taxes that were laid by the British Parliament on the American colonies in the years 1765 and 1767. The astonishing story of John Wilkes played a vital role too. The colonists followed Wilkes's dramatic career obsessively, and in it they found proof of what they suspected. A tyrannical cabal absolutely was attempting to destroy the liberties that set Britain apart. It was of the utmost importance that they oppose any attempts to execute the same scheme in America. In this way the revolutionary dynamic was set. The channel of events was put into a course that would flow toward the Pennsylvania State House on July 4, 1776.

TODAY THE LINE "LIFE, Liberty, and the pursuit of Happiness" is strongly associated with the events of the Fourth of July. But over the years I have come to think of it as having a broader meaning; one that should not be confined to a single moment in time. For contained in that phrase is so much revealing history. "Life" gives us not only Locke's theory about a person's "natural right" to biological life, but something that meant just as much to figures like Jefferson at the time. This was the "Enlightenment" life, that questing, expansive, and empowering form of existence that arose in a distinctive (and morally suspect) form in Britain during the first half of the eighteenth century. "Liberty" is a word that captures better than any other the political strife of the 1760s that shattered the harmony between the colonies and the mother country. "Happiness," meanwhile, is an aspiration that drives to the core of what the delegates in 1776 were striving to achieve. Some of them were utopians; others were gritty pragmatists. They were all, however, motivated by the pursuit of an ideal identified by the historian Darrin M. McMahon as "a radical new force during the Age of Enlightenment."[18]

Contained within this line, then, is a compelling, unfolding story: Enlightenment Britain; the political crisis; a dream of something better. This is the story I tell in this book. To make sense of a history that is complex, I have abandoned the overarching narrative to focus instead on a number of significant, mainly British participants, whose involvement in the events of their time is often underplayed. Among them are the impetuous politician John Wilkes; the formidable man of letters Samuel Johnson; the republican historian Catharine Macaulay; and the ruthless polemicist Thomas Paine. All these, as we shall see, thought just as long and hard about life, liberty, and happiness as Thomas Jefferson did.

But at the heart of this story are two other men. One, Benjamin Franklin, is universally known today as a Founding Father and arguably the greatest American that ever lived. The other, William Strahan, is only remembered by a tiny few. The friendship between the two, however, is one of the most extraordinary of the time. It is a friendship that reveals more about that most complex and significant of events, the American Revolution, than just about any other.

Life

(1740–1759)

One

A NEW MAN

ON DECEMBER 11, 1740, as the first snow of winter fell in the city of Philadelphia, Benjamin Franklin released the most thrilling issue of his newspaper in months. It was days like this that printers relished, when they had a story to turn heads and ignite conversation. But for Franklin, the printer and proprietor of the *Pennsylvania Gazette*, this excitement was tempered by anxiety. Because for all the drama of his front-page story, he knew that tucked away inside the paper was something far more explosive.

That December Franklin was a month shy of his thirty-fifth birthday. He was an instantly recognizable figure in the raucous streets around his Market Street print shop. He stood at a modestly tall five feet nine inches, had golden brown hair, deep-set hazel eyes, and, although often hesitant or reticent in conversation, he was decisive in action. As he flitted between Market Street and the Pennsylvania State House, where he oversaw political proceedings as Clerk of the Assembly, he gave off a faint air of prosperity. He wore a silk-lined coat in the winter months, along with Holland shirts that ruffled at the sleeves. These flashes of affluence, conspicuous enough in a co-lonial society that was highly alert to such details, still fell short of true refinement. To study Franklin more closely was to see he was a working man. He was bull-necked. His chest and shoulders were powerful from years of heaving type cases and working the press. Although he was now edging into middle age, people could still just about glimpse the athletic boy who, long before he was known for anything else, was known for his skill as a swimmer in the turbulent waters of Boston Harbor.

That childhood in Boston was now almost two decades behind him. He was born in 1706, the youngest son of a tallow chandler, Josiah Franklin, and his second wife, Abiah. His youth was spent within the confines of the family—working first as his father's assistant, later as his brother's apprentice—in the austere culture of Puritan New England. Few of Franklin's contemporaries in Philadelphia knew much of this. Like so many in the boisterous young city, he had simply appeared one day in 1723 at the riverside, unkempt, disoriented, and, as he later remembered, with no more than "a Dutch dollar and about a Shilling in Copper" to his name.[1]

Seventeen years later, many of those who had seen Franklin enter Philadelphia for the first time—a scene he would later brilliantly recount in his *Autobiography*—had vanished from the streets, carried away by the transience of life in the colonies. But while scores had died, failed, or left to start anew, Franklin had prospered. His talent and drive marked him out from the start. He forged friendships with most of the ingenious figures of the city, like the book-loving Joseph Breintnall and the self-taught mathematician Thomas Godfrey. Soon after his arrival no less a man than Pennsylvania's governor, Sir William Keith, took notice of him. It was he who encouraged Franklin to cross the Atlantic to London for what turned out to be a formative eighteen-month stay in 1725–26. Apart from this one interlude, however, Philadelphia had always remained his home. By 1740, seventeen years after his arrival, he was established as a prominent citizen in the boisterous, expanding, and fiercely competitive city, thickly enmeshed in its business and politics.

Anchoring Franklin to the center of the city's everyday life was his newspaper. He released the *Gazette* on Thursdays, beneath the tagline "*Containing the freshest Advices Foreign and Domestick.*" That week he had got hold of a delicious front-page story for his readers. It was told in a series of letters that had been written four months earlier in the Irish town of Nenagh. They described a horseback pursuit across rural Ireland. The chase had begun when a notorious band of robbers, the Kellymount Gang, "well mounted and armed," had been seen crossing from County Kilkenny into Tipperary. Catching the scent, twelve "young and stout Fellows" had vowed to run them to ground. "Never was there a Pursuit so vigorously carried on for the Time," one letter affirmed. The hunt had extended over a vast region, from the meadows of Queen's County to the banks of the Shannon. It included two white-knuckle shootouts, one up a "black Mountain" near a hill called Devil's Bit.[2] Coming mere months after the highwayman, Richard "Dick" Turpin, had been executed at York, this was enthralling copy. For Philadelphia's sizeable community of Irish immigrants, in particular, it was a cocktail of adventure and nostalgia that could hardly be bettered.

Newspaper stories like these acted like portals. They were mechanisms that temporarily carried readers away from their isolated position on the fringes of the Empire, back to the Old World where they could, for a moment, feel the damp Irish breeze on their cheeks. This was something new and exciting. For all human history the bounds of life had been narrow. Life had been experienced in the parish and, when necessary, explained in the church. Newspapers altered this. With their rise, a kind of vicarious experience had emerged. A reader in Philadelphia could pick up a newspaper and find themselves a fly on a wall inside the court of George II, or aboard a fighting frigate in the Channel, or gazing at the gallows in an English county town.

Following an emerging formula, which appealed to a readership that was hyper-sensitized to news from the Old World, Franklin prioritized the best British and European stories by placing them at the start of his four-page paper. The later parts were reserved for domestic news, notices of runaways, inventories of newly arrived ships, and advertisements for land sales. It was in this section of the newspaper, on December 11, 1740, that Franklin inserted a piece that, in an understated way, eclipsed his lead story. It was written by Franklin himself. His eight hundred words were crowded into a single column in small type. "THE Public has been entertain'd for these three Weeks past," it began, "with angry Papers, written expressly against me, and publish'd in the *Mercury*."

> The *two first* I utterly neglected, as believing that both the Facts therein stated, and the extraordinary Reasonings upon them, might be safely enough left to themselves, without any Animadversion; and I have the Satisfaction to find, that the Event has answered my Expectation: But the *last*, my Friends think 'tis necessary I should take some Notice of . . . [3]

For those who knew Franklin, this was curious from the start. Throughout his career he had established a reputation for reserve. New acquaintances were often perplexed by this, finding him a difficult person to read. Unforthcoming in private, Franklin had taken equal care not to embroil himself in public disputes. However much enflamed by injustice, he had come to the conviction that forbearance was almost always the best way. It was an ethos that Franklin not only adhered to himself, it was one he propagated over and again to readers of his bestselling *Poor Richard's Almanack*:

> He that lieth down with dogs, shall rise up with fleas.
>
> ———
>
> It is better to take many injuries, than to give one.
>
> ———
>
> None preaches better than the ant, and she says nothing.[4]

But for a few weeks at the end of 1740, Franklin was provoked out of this pose. For all its charms, Franklin knew that Philadelphia, the "City of Brotherly Love," was a ruthless place. It was a place, as Franklin decided, where even the ant must occasionally take a stand.

BY 1740, THIRTEEN BRITISH colonies existed along a narrow, continuous strip on the eastern coast of the North American continent. Their establishment had been the work of the previous century. Beginning as nothing more than vulnerable beachheads, held by a determined few, each of the colonies had gradually broken free from their enclave origins. By the 1740s they stretched several hundred miles inland. In this time, justified by the charters that they carried from the King of England, the settlers had built towns and roads, and established farms, all the time pushing farther and farther into lands that for tens of thousands of years had been home to the Indigenous American peoples. Few were troubled by this. Instead, more than a century after the first wooden houses were constructed at Jamestown in Virginia, the settlers retained a romantic sense of mission. This was a sensation that was equally felt by the preachers of Boston, the merchants of New York, and the planters of Virginia.

Regional stereotypes such as these were well established by the 1740s. But behind them lay thirteen complex colonial worlds that operated in their own distinct ways, with their own particular hopes and concerns. They were all united, however, by the bond they continued to share with Great Britain. This was a foundational relationship that was both structural and emotional. It was often described, then as now, in terms of a mother and her children. It is an appealing image but it is one that needs to be qualified. If Britain was the mother, then she was something of an erratic one. Often distracted by her own domestic cares and more interested in financial growth than anything else, she had never quite got around to defining the limit of her children's freedom.

While the colonies were indulged to some extent—being nourished by British trade and held together by a framework of English
law—they were generally left alone to deal with their own problems.
The colonists broadly liked this dynamic. It allowed them to grow
without too much intrusion from London, while at the same time
they knew that if any great problem appeared they could send petitions across the Atlantic to the king. These, however, rarely elicited
a quick reply. The news took anywhere between one and two months
to travel between America and Britain and, thanks to the prevailing
winds, it usually took even longer to come back. Even when a petition arrived in Westminster it was rarely dealt with quickly. By the
1740s there was really only one word that made the British establishment, either at St. James's or in the Palace of Westminster, sit up and
think hard about America. That word was "France."

This was the second vital aspect of the colonial dynamic. For
as much as the colonies cherished their founding bond with Great
Britain, they shared a distrust of the ancient enemy. The French, as
everyone well knew, had their own designs on the North American
continent. And while the British colonies had been growing on the
Atlantic coast, far away, inside the boundless interior, the French had
been making charts, building forts, and striking treaties with peoples
like the Odawa or the Abenaki. The anxiety the colonists felt in 1740
could be understood by simply glancing at a map. Surrounding the
British colonial strip to its north and west lay an enormous territory
known simply as New France. In recent years, apprehensions concerning this had become muddled up with something else. The 1730s
had been filled with territorial and trade squabbles with the other
great European power, Spain. There had been differences concerning the newest and southernmost of the colonies, Georgia, and there
had been confrontations in the Caribbean. These spats had ripened
into formal war in 1739, and due to the *Pacte de Famille* between King
Philip V of Spain and his Bourbon nephew, Louis XV of France, es-
calation was feared. To those who lived in British America, it seemed

as if the long-anticipated contest for supremacy on the continent was soon to begin.

The Province of Pennsylvania was situated in the middle of these British American colonies, tucked away from the Atlantic coast behind New Jersey. There was something special about this place. Founded on the basis of a charter that had been granted on March 4, 1681, sixty years on it remained, along with Delaware and Maryland, one of the few proprietary colonies,* and it retained the utopian aura of its founder. William Penn was a remarkable figure. Described by one historian as being a mix of "courtier and sectarian; saint, schemer, and scholar,"[5] he was the wealthy son of an English admiral who had the vision of creating "a free Colony for all mankind."[6] Penn's project was a response to the religious strife that had riven English society in the seventeenth century. A convert to the new Quaker sect, he had seen at first hand the need for a place where a person's freedom of conscience was guaranteed. When Charles II had given him lands in the New World in lieu of debts owed to his father, Penn set about establishing a society where no one was to be injured on religious grounds and where everyone was welcome so long as they believed in one Christian God.

Penn named this experimental colony "Pennsylvania," or Penn's Wooded Country, and he had decided that "a green country town" was to lie at its heart.[7] He engaged an English surveyor called Thomas

---

* Over time different types of colony had evolved. There were royal colonies "governed directly by the Crown through a governor and council," chartered colonies "governed by royal charter without direct interference from the Crown," and proprietary colonies, which were governed by a proprietor who had been awarded a charter by the monarch to govern with "the fullest prerogatives of government." Many of the thirteen east-coast colonies that existed in 1740 were founded in the seventeenth century as proprietorships. As they developed, most converted into Crown colonies as the British monarchy sought to concentrate power. In addition to this grouping, Britain had around a dozen other colonial possessions in the New World. These included Nova Scotia and Newfoundland in the northeast of the continent, as well as Caribbean islands like Barbados and Jamaica.

Holme to realize this vision. Having crossed the Atlantic, Holme had started work in 1683. It was at precisely this time that Isaac Newton was beginning his *Principia Mathematica*, three thousand miles away at Trinity College in Cambridge. Newton's masterpiece and Holme's *Portraiture of the City of Philadelphia* were entirely different works, but they were both expressions of the same emerging culture. They conformed to a central tenet of Enlightenment thinking: that order was Nature's first law. Holme's streets were not haphazard. They did not twist and turn outward from a cathedral or a castle. Instead he designed a grid of intersecting streets that slotted into an area, two miles by one, between two rivers. A few avenues and a central square were Holme's only flourishes. Philadelphia's allure was not only its tolerance; it was also its regularity. In the coffee houses of London, this "green country town" was soon being talked of as a beacon of rationalism: an enlightened settlement in a land filled with space and promise.

Set beside the broad Delaware, roughly eighty miles upstream from the Atlantic Ocean, and opening out onto fine, fertile lands, Philadelphia's potential was easy to see. Letters back to Europe spoke of charming creeks, vast apple orchards, and the huge pigs that roamed the nearby woodlands, fattening themselves on fallen peaches. Whether this was propaganda or not, by 1740 people knew at any rate that Philadelphia now ranked among the largest settlements in the colonies. Where seventy years before the Lenape had hunted deer in woodlands and panthers were to be found prowling among whortleberry bushes, there now stood civic buildings and churches. A Quaker aristocracy controlled the politics and mercantile affairs of the town, whose inhabitants, owing to Penn's insistence on religious tolerance, also included Anglicans, Episcopalians, Presbyterians, Lutherans, and Catholics. While many, like Franklin, had family ties to England, there were others with links to Scotland, Ireland, and Sweden, and, especially in what was called the "back country," there were communities from Germany and Holland. More elusive in the archives, but visible everywhere, were slaves of African origin. They had formed part of Philadelphia's social fabric since its earliest years and, by 1740, comprised around a tenth of its population.[8]

Any of these people could be found in 1740 milling together on Holme's little network of streets. While by European standards Philadelphia remained a modest size—its population of ten thousand was still only around half of that of Bristol—its handsome, brick-built State House, under construction since 1732, and elegant Christ Church added touches of refinement. Commerce was brisk too. Situated at the center of British America, on the post road that ran for a thousand miles between Boston and Charleston, it was a natural hub. Outside Franklin's printing shop on Market Street flowed a constant stream of traffic. There were rowdy parties of sailors with their broad trousers, scarlet waistcoats, and pigtails, Quakers in their beaver hats, gentlemen with swords hanging at their sides, hawkers, maids, and stevedores, hauling goods from the riverside to the open-air stalls of the bustling Jersey Market.

While the stream of faces was ever changing, Franklin's New Printing Office remained a constant feature of this lower stretch of Market Street. It was here, aged twenty-two, in 1728, that he had first set up his press. By 1740 his business had developed substantially. It was now something that is best imagined as an upstairs-downstairs operation. While Benjamin oversaw the printing upstairs, on the ground floor his wife Deborah stewarded a general store. Often marginalized in the Franklin story, Debby's contribution to the family's success was substantial. She kept the accounts, served customers, and, with each passing year, enhanced the range of stock for sale. A trip to Franklin's on Market Street meant more than a chance to buy a *Gazette* or stationery, like quills, paper, and inkstands. Visitors could also pick up tea leaves and goose feathers; luxuries such as chocolate; watches and telescopes; and Franklin specialities like the family's very own Crown Soap.

While paying for any of these, customers could hear the creaks and groans of the press. More often than not these were signs that a fresh issue of the *Gazette*, produced weekly since Franklin had taken control of the title in 1729, was on the way. But in the autumn months it might also have been the sound of the bestselling *Poor Richard's Almanack* going into print. One of Franklin's chief ambitions in his early days in business had been to successfully enter the almanac market. It was here that the best and surest money was to be made. Almanacs were pocket-sized, cheaply bound, and filled with practical details for everyday use, like the phases of the moon, calculations of the tides, or prognostications of the weather. Simply written and practical, they were hugely popular. For many of the working people in colonial America—farmers, builders, smiths, and sailors—an almanac was the only kind of book they owned apart from a Bible.

After several aborted attempts, Franklin had launched *Poor Richard's Almanack* at Christmas 1732. In many respects it was a conventional performance, with its content structured around the months of the year and enlivened with little verses and predictions. But a clever ploy made it stand out. As a young boy in Boston, Franklin had been besotted with the daring and creativity of writers like Jonathan Swift, Richard Steele, and Joseph Addison. From all of these Franklin borrowed elements to create a persona that was irresistible to his readers. "Richard Saunders" introduced himself in the debut *Almanack* as a humble country man, who passed his nights gazing up at the stars and toying with his philosophical instruments, which his long-suffering wife Bridget derided as his "rattling-traps."[9] Once he had divined his predictions for the next year, Saunders, or so the pretence went, then transmitted them to Franklin in Market Street for printing.

Polite and gentle, Richard Saunders was an easy man to like. But what Philadelphians loved most about him was his dark humor. In his first tenderly written preface, Saunders casually predicted the sudden death of his chief rival in the almanac trade, a man named Titan Leeds. "He dies," Saunders wrote, "by my Calculation made at his Request, on Oct. 17, 1733, 3 ho., 29m., P.M., at the very instant of the ♂ of ⊙ and ☿."[10] Such audacity was unprecedented in the colonial almanac trade, and it elicited the expected response from Titan Leeds, who declared himself at the first opportunity to be very much alive. In response, he attacked this Richard Saunders as "a false predicter, an ignorant, a conceited scribbler, a fool, and a lyar."[11] With everything going perfectly to plan, Franklin seized his opportunity to twist the knife one more time. He replied:

> Mr Leeds was too well bred to use any man so indecently and so scurrilously, and moreover his esteem and affection for me was extraordinary: so that it is to be feared that pamphlet may be only a contrivance of somebody or other, who hopes, perhaps, to sell two or three years' Almanacks still, by the sole force and virtue of Mr Leeds' name.[12]

What Franklin knew, but most of his readers did not, was that this whole episode was an almost perfect replication of an infamous hoax perpetrated by Jonathan Swift in London a generation before. Franklin, though, could hardly have expected it to go as well as it did. Saunders's temerity thrilled readers so much that the first number of *Poor Richard's* sold out instantly. Its readership had continued to expand ever since, so that by 1740 it was selling a remarkable ten thousand copies a year right across the colonies, from the windswept north to the sunny south.

This success had provided Franklin with an unexpected opportunity. His initial aim was to make money out of the title, but seeing the extent of its reach, he had begun to sense other possibilities. With the colonies still so young and lacking a unified identity, Franklin realized that *Poor Richard's* provided him with a platform which he could use to spread his ideas about how an "American life"—which Franklin thought of as a life of the colonists' own making, constructed inside the safety of their own property—might be lived. "I consider'd it as a proper Vehicle," he reflected, "for conveying Instruction among the common People, who bought scarce any other Books."[13] Franklin disseminated this "instruction" through pithy, often funny maxims that he sprinkled throughout the pages.

Great talkers, little doers.

———

Nothing but money, is sweeter than honey.

———

The worst wheel of the cart makes the most noise.

———

Where there's marriage without love, there will be love without marriage.

———

Early to bed and early to rise, makes a man healthy, wealthy, and wise.[14]

Poor Richard's and the *Gazette* might have been Franklin's best-known publications, but his press was more often than not busy with other work. These were the bonds and counterbonds, bills of sale, apprentice indentures and promissory notes: the documents that were the cogs and gears of the Georgian world. Franklin really was, as the writer Jill Lepore has genially put it, "a jack-of-all-pages."[15]

ONE OF FRANKLIN'S GREAT advantages in business was his strategic mind. He had a natural ability to step back from the emotion of a situation so he could better interpret it with logic. This talent equipped him well for chess, a game he played with single-mindedness from youth. He wrote revealingly about the chain of thoughts that passed through his mind when a game was in process. "If I move this piece, what will be the advantage of my new situation? What use can my adversary make of it to annoy me? What other moves can I make to support it, and to defend myself from his attacks?"[16]

Franklin's cool strategizing made him a difficult character to read. But for those with the sharpest eyes, there were signs during the late summer of 1740 that something was being planned in the Market Street shop. The most conspicuous evidence of this were the visits of a local conveyancer called John Webbe. Webbe is a hazy figure to us today. Little can be said for sure of his life apart from the fact that he was "Scotch Irish," a name given to those who had migrated from the northern part of Ireland. Where people came from mattered. Those, like Franklin, who could trace their family back to England were esteemed in the colonial caste system. "To be an Old England-man," Franklin recalled, "was, of itself, a character of some respect, and gave a kind of rank among us."[17] By contrast the Scots Irish endured a low reputation. People considered them to be wild, uncouth, and untrustworthy, and the *Gazette* abounded with stories of Irish runaways and petty criminals. Franklin, however, was clearly more disposed to Webbe. He was an educated man with an interest in politics who had contributed several pieces to the *Gazette* over the years. In late 1740, Franklin had decided to make him into something more.

The project he had in mind was an attractive one. With the *Gazette* on a steady footing, *Poor Richard's* going well, and his finances healthy, Franklin had decided that the time was ripe to take on the latest and most exciting form in journalism. Sometime in early 1741 he planned to release America's first-ever magazine. Until a decade before, "magazine" had been used exclusively to denote a military storehouse. But in 1731, playing on the idea that words were weapons, a London printer called Edward Cave had converted the term for a new use. Cave's title, the *Gentleman's Magazine*, was billed as a storehouse of ideas. At forty pages long, it was longer than a newspaper, and with twelve monthly issues, it was more regular than an almanac. Opening Cave's magazine, readers could enjoy a range of the best weekly essays; pieces of poetry; snippets of news; lists of notable births, deaths, and marriages; the prices of goods at the Exchange; and a catalog of recently published books. All of this, carefully selected and edited, was distilled into one elegant publication, and one, Cave estimated, that spared his readers the task of sifting "200 *Half-sheets per Month*."[18]

Due to the sheer amount of work involved, people expected Cave's project to fail within months. But there turned out to be something attractive about magazines. Soon Cave was selling between two and three thousand copies every month, and demand increased with every passing year. Central to this success was the format. With a month to prepare each issue, Cave was able to compile a publication of breadth, quality, and style. In an age that still lacked a central body of reference works, these characteristics were appealing. Readers began to treat his magazine as an authority. They would thumb through it to check a date or a name or to settle an argument. To this authority, Cave added innovation. Each year he pioneered a new journalistic technique. He ran poetry competitions, immersive historical essays, original features on scientific discoveries like electricity, and cleverly disguised (to avoid the official censor) records of Parliamentary debates. His latest innovation had come just one year earlier, in 1739, when a range of original woodcut maps appeared alongside a feature on the complex geography of Crimea and Ukraine.

Franklin, who had spent a formative eighteen months working in London's printing houses as a young man, loved the *Gentleman's Magazine*. Years later he would affirm that, despite its many imitators, it had "always been, in my Opinion, by far the best."[19] The contents were excellent enough, but Cave had added to them an air of aspiration. While the loaded term "gentleman" featured prominently in the title, the magazine was not exclusively written for the monied few who sauntered around St. James's in their elegant attire. Instead it was a title that could be picked up by a successful merchant in the city, or a clever apprentice who wanted to animate his mind with knowledge. This was a characteristic Franklin admired. He had long rooted his own identity in what he called the "middling sort." These were the industrious, practical people who, to his mind, were the heartbeat and future of colonial America. They were the people with whom he had established clubs and collaborated on civic projects ever since he had been in Philadelphia. Now they were the prospective readers he had in mind in late 1740 as he entered into discussions with John Webbe about producing an American magazine.

Webbe was vital to Franklin's plan because there was no way he could compile the magazine himself. Over the previous years, Franklin had taken on a growing number of official posts. In 1736 he secured the role of Clerk of the colony's Assembly, a position which gave him "a better Opportunity of keeping up an Interest among the Members."[20] The following year he was appointed to an even more desirable office. As postmaster for Pennsylvania he had taken overall responsibility for storing, sorting, and delivering all of the letters— both foreign and domestic—that passed through the colony. These responsibilities came on top of Franklin's other professional and civic commitments. To add to them the challenge of compiling a magazine was a step too far.

Webbe presented a solution to this problem. He was a tolerably good writer with a curiosity about politics, and he was seeking a challenge. Although he was certainly no Edward Cave, the pool of suitable literary men in Philadelphia was not large. A series of meetings was held, and discussions developed into an agreement. The magazine, it was decided, was to be a joint venture. Webbe was to oversee the editorial content while Franklin was to assume responsibility for production and distribution. Franklin had settled on a cover price of fifteen shillings for an annual subscription. This was substantially more than the ten shillings he charged for the *Gazette*, but it reflected the costs of production and superior quality of the contents. As to profits, Franklin was to reap 75 percent of the proceeds from the first two thousand copies sold. Should the magazine sell more than that, the excess would be evenly split between the two of them.

This is how things stood in the autumn of 1740, when all of Franklin's carefully laid plans came crashing down. The astonishing, enraging moment arrived in the first week of November when his

bitter rival, the printer Andrew Bradford, produced an advertisement for a magazine of his own. This three-page "plan" was carried
in Bradford's newspaper, the *American Weekly Mercury*. To complement
the *Mercury*, the ad revealed, this new production was to be called the
American Magazine. It was to be a monthly compendium of "publick
affairs," or "A PUBLICK THEATRE . . . on which the most remarkable
Transactions of each Government may be *impartially* represented."[21]
Although the plan was signed by Bradford, by now Franklin surely
knew the worst of it. Not only had he been outmaneuvered by his old
rival, Franklin had also been double-crossed. For the editor of this
American Magazine was to be one John Webbe.

"THREE MAY KEEP A Secret, if two of them are dead," Franklin
wrote in *Poor Richard's* in 1735.[22] It was a maxim he would often have
cause to reflect on in Philadelphia, where business dealings were no-
toriously knockabout. But there was something especially maddening
about Webbe's treachery in 1740. Franklin channeled his outrage into
an announcement of his own. He answered the ad in the *Mercury* at
the first opportunity, in the *Gazette* of November 13. He revealed to
his readers that he, too, had been planning to print a magazine. In
fact, Franklin's *General Magazine* would be released *before* Bradford's
American Magazine, "*In* January *next*." He elaborated:

> This MAGAZINE, in Imitation of those in *England*, was long
> since projected; a Correspondence is settled with Intelligent
> Men in most of the Colonies, and small Types are procured,
> for carrying it on in the best Manner. It would not, indeed,
> have been published quite so soon, were it not that a Person, to
> whom the Scheme was communicated in *Confidence*, has thought
> fit to advertise it in the last *Mercury*, without our Participation;
> and, probably, with a View, by Starting before us, to discourage
> us from prosecuting our first Design, and reap the Advantage of
> it wholly to himself.[23]

Having revealed the depth of Webbe's treachery, Franklin announced his price. Abandoning the original idea of selling subscriptions at fifteen shillings a year, he revealed that the magazine would be sold for just ninepence an issue. Franklin would also make "considerable Allowance to Chapmen who take Quantities." For a man so prudent, it was this decision, more than anything else, that revealed the pitch of his rage.

What happened next was extraordinary even by the vehement standards of the time. After a weekend's brooding, by the Monday morning Webbe had decided that rather than visit Franklin to settle their differences in private, he was going to use the *Mercury* as a forum for putting Franklin on public trial. Always happy to see Franklin abused, Andrew Bradford gave Webbe all the space he wanted.

Webbe's polemic was printed under the title "The Detection." It amounted to a coruscating, intensely personal assault on Franklin's character. He described Franklin as a man of malicious temperament who had gratified this vice by "blackening the Reputation of a private Person." In the face of such a provocation, Webbe wrote, he had a civic duty to respond. If he did not defend himself then it was likely Franklin would, as he described it, "not stop at this single Instance of spitting his Malignity from his Press, but be incouraged to proceed in making use of it as an Engine to bespatter the Characters of every other Person he may happen to dislike."[24]

Franklin's method of smearing his opponents, Webbe elaborated, was sly. Rather than state his name directly, before outlining his accusations, Franklin had preferred to peddle insinuations relating to "a Person." To Webbe this was a cowardly, dishonorable formulation of language. Indeed, it was

> by far the most mischievous Kind of Lying; for the Strokes being oblique and indirect, a Man cannot so easily defend himself against them, as he might do, if they were straight and peremptory. There is something too more mean and dastardly in the

Character of an indirect Lyar than a direct one. *This* has the Audacity of a Highwayman, *That* the Slyness of a Pickpocket. Both indeed rob you of your Purse, and both deserve a Gibbet; but, were I obliged to pardon either, I could sooner forgive the *bold* Wickedness of the one, than the *sneaking* Villainy of the other.[25]

Having dealt with Franklin's tone, Webbe progressed to his argument. He conceded that Franklin had "communicated" a desire of printing a magazine. But what of that? "If that were a Consequence," he reasoned, "then Mr. Franklin has only to *offer* himself as a Printer of Books or Pamphlets to every Man that he thinks has a Talent for Writing, and they shall from thenceforth be restrained from publishing any Thing without his Consent." As it was, talks between Webbe and Franklin had progressed into an agreement. But after contemplating the terms, Webbe had seen how much they were ridiculously weighted against him. Having determined that Franklin was trying to exploit his labor, he explained, "I thought my self, on these Discoveries, even supposing there were no grosser Frauds yet behind to mention, acquitted from my Engagement." He rounded off:

Of what Composition, then, is the soul of that Man, who, having contrived to make a Property of his Friend, will afterwards charge him with a Violation of Trust, and *coolly* and *deliberately* endeavour to murder his Reputation in the *most publick Manner*, on which his Livelihood, tho' not in the Capacity of a Magazine-Writer, entirely depends.[26]

Webbe's "The Detection" was printed in Bradford's *Mercury* on November 20. To support his argument, he included a transcription of Franklin's rough notes for the magazine contract, and as an added titillation, the *Mercury*'s readers were promised "the Remainder of the *Detection* in the next." At a glance, it was a devastating performance. Webbe laid Franklin bare as a grasping, craven, domineering, and untrustworthy businessman. But closer inspection showed a flimsiness to his argument. If Webbe's intention was to refute Franklin's claims, then had he not achieved the opposite? He had admitted that Franklin had approached him about the magazine first, and confirmed that he had subsequently broken his contract by carrying his idea to Bradford.

Whatever the case, the weeks that followed were as uncomfortable for Franklin as they were lively for the readers of Philadelphia's newspapers. Incapable of letting the matter lie, Webbe renewed his assault with greater vigor over three consecutive issues. Abandoning his idea of a "detection," he instead ran line by line through Franklin's advertisement for the *General Magazine*, treating his plan with scorn and sarcasm. Finding similarities between his and Franklin's "*ideas*," he likened his plight to that of the Roman poet Virgil, who, having written some elegant lines in honor of Caesar, had been amazed to discover a mediocre poet called Bathyllus claiming them for his own. Even by Webbe's standards this was high-flown stuff. For weeks Franklin chose not to answer. His only public comment came in characteristic style. In the newly launched *Poor Richard's Almanack* for 1741, readers were provided with another maxim. "If you would keep your secret from an enemy, tell it not to a friend."[27]

While he remained tight-lipped in public, privately Franklin was furious about Webbe's treachery. Rather than having the long winter months before him, during which he could experiment with designs, plan print runs, and ensure the quality of the copy, he now had the irritation of a competitor and the stress of a deadline. Worst of all was the prospect of being outdone by his old rival, Andrew Bradford. For years Franklin and Bradford had loathed one another. This dislike could be traced all the way back to the first days after Franklin's arrival in Philadelphia. Then, young and penniless, Franklin had called at Bradford's print shop in search of work. He had ended up lodging with Bradford for a time and found him to be an unscrupulous operator, content to spy on rivals and steal ideas. Not only was he devious, to Franklin he reeked of privilege. Andrew was the son of William Bradford, one of the first printers in all the colonies. Raised in the trade with all of his father's plum contacts, Andrew had been able to establish himself unopposed. He had launched the *Mercury* as Philadelphia's first newspaper, been appointed postmaster, and pocketed all the fat governmental contracts, printing the laws, proclamations, and minutes of the Assembly. By the time the young Franklin knocked on his door in 1723, Bradford was established: connected, wealthy, and secure.

In his *Autobiography*, written decades later, Franklin's dislike of Bradford was still palpable. He derided his skill as a printer, branding him as "very illiterate."[28] He characterized Bradford's *Mercury* as "a paltry thing, wretchedly manag'd, no way entertaining."[29] Any profit Bradford accrued, Franklin intimated, came more from cronyism than ingenuity. For years Franklin whittled away at Braford's inky fiefdom, charming away the official contracts, building up the *Gazette* as a serious competitor to the *Mercury*, then wresting control of the almanac market with *Poor Richard's*. In 1737 Franklin struck what everyone knew to be the decisive blow. That year, in somewhat mysterious circumstances to the people of Philadelphia, he replaced Bradford as postmaster for Pennsylvania. This position brought only a token salary, but it carried prestige and gave Franklin control of the postal riders who carried not just letters, but also newspapers and almanacs to readers across the colony. He had marked his elevation by updating the *Gazette*'s imprint so that it read, tauntingly to his rival: "Printed by B FRANKLIN, POST-MASTER."

It is not hard to see why Bradford, stung by this series of reversals, took his chance for revenge. Now well into his fifties, Bradford's interest was more in acquiring land and property than it was in literary innovation.[30] But in his print shop on Front Street he had most of the equipment needed to produce a magazine, and with Webbe in his pocket, he had the perfect means of annoying his rival. Indeed, Webbe turned out to be an unexpectedly useful attack dog. Throughout November and into December he continued to claw away at Franklin's reputation. Was it not interesting, Webbe suggested, that Franklin had refused to reply to any of his pieces? According to all rules of logic, "Facts *so stated*, and NOT DENIED, are, according to a *universal* Rule of judging, CONFESSED; and therefore Mr. Franklin's Silence is the *highest* Justification I can desire."[31]

Webbe then, unwisely as it turned out, made a further allegation. Franklin was not only dishonorable as a businessman, he was vengeful too. Webbe revealed that since his elevation to the office of postmaster, Franklin had abused his position infamously by preventing the postal riders from carrying copies of Bradford's *Mercury*. This was behavior especially calculated to damage a rival business. After so many charges, personal and professional, it was this that finally brought Franklin's silence to an end.

THE QUARREL OF LATE 1740 came at a poised moment in Franklin's life. He had come so far since that October morning seventeen years earlier when he had clambered out of a boat at Market Street Wharf and gazed at Philadelphia for the very first time. Now he was financially secure and socially connected. He was intellectually stimulated by the Friday evening meetings of his Junto or "Leather Apron" Club, which he had formed together with most of his "ingenious" acquaintances in 1727, "for mutual improvement,"[32] and he had acquired enough power to be able to propose and put into action projects for benefitting the community. But equally, as the new decade began, there was an undercurrent of unfulfillment. Now in his late thirties, Franklin was experiencing the sensation of time slipping past, of the melting away of his chances to truly make a mark on the history of the times.

These were unsettling thoughts. Franklin had long known that he possessed superior qualities of mind and all his business success was objective proof of this. But as yet he had no lasting legacy. He owned very little property, and since the loss of his beloved son Frankie, who had died from smallpox in 1736, aged just four, it was unclear who would succeed him in business. Also frustrating was the fact that he remained stuck outside the sphere of the true elite. Franklin knew the great men of the colony. Many of them visited his shop, and with some his relationship stretched further. James Logan, the city's pre-eminent scholar, was one such person. He lived in style at a grand house to the north of the city, where he kept one of the best collections of books in the colonies. Logan thought enough of Franklin to allow him to browse his library, but along with excitement, his visits there must have been shaded by discontent. The books might have been accessible, but the world to which Logan belonged—the world of ideas, of politics, of science, of philosophy—remained out of reach for someone who, after all, remained just a provincial printer.

When Franklin started out twelve years before, an honest tradesman was all he wanted to be. He took care to cultivate his persona. He dressed plainly, kept away from the taverns, made sure that he was seen pushing his wheelbarrow, piled with papers, around the dusty streets. This was, as he later explained in his *Autobiography*, a calculated performance, intended to fix his identity as a humble but industrious artisan. Franklin's plan was successful. It brought him custom, and this made him prosperous. But as he had grown more affluent, his identity had become problematic. As a tradesman, Franklin belonged to the ordinary class of workers. Such people might be industrious, they might even be ingenious, but as they spent their lives in the unvarying drudgery of practical work, those in the highest ranks of society did not believe them capable of elevated thinking. Their minds, the old prejudice held, were too obedient and too busy to engage with the deep, abstract demands of politics, philosophy, or science.

And yet these were the fields Franklin felt himself powerfully drawn toward. As the 1740s began, he was already puzzling over a problem that would preoccupy him for much of the next decade. If he was to fully realize his potential, then he would have to dismantle the very identity that he had so carefully cultivated. Could he somehow transition from an artisan into something more refined? Something that gave him more leeway to influence events? In Market Street in December 1740, wearing his leather apron, with his blackened fingers, harassed by the cares of business and derided by John Webbe as being "a *meer* Printer,"[33] the idea of joining the true elites on their own level was too ludicrous to express. In colonial America, as in the mother country, each individual knew their place in the rigid hierarchy. This system was informed by categories like nationality, race, gender, and family pedigree. There were nuances too, with some professions among the low and middling classes being seen as more respectable than others, and as many gradations among the ranks of the gentry. But at its most simplistic, as the historian Gordon Wood has pointed out, the essential distinction within colonial society was between two opposing groups: the aristocracy and the ordinary. This was the most important and fundamental of all social divisions. As Wood explains it:

> So distinctive and so separated was the aristocracy from ordinary folk that many still thought the two groups represented two orders of being. Indeed, we will never appreciate the radicalism of the eighteenth-century revolutionary idea that all men were created equal unless we see it within this age-old tradition of difference. Gentlemen and commoners had different psyches, different emotional makeups, different natures. Ordinary people were made only "to be born and eat and sleep and die, and be forgotten."[34]

Franklin might have embraced his ordinariness when he first set up as a printer—and much later he would proudly cultivate the story of his magnificent rise from the obscurity of his birth in Milk Street, Boston—but in 1740 it had become a source of discomfort to him. Although as a printer he was part of a new and dynamic profession, which conferred on him a powerful ability to shape and engage in culture, in itself the trade was still considered unrespectable. A New York printer, writing at this time, reflected that no family "of Substance would ever put their Sons to such an Art."[35] This was a verdict Franklin was forced to feel every time he climbed the steps to his press room.

Another mark of Franklin's ordinariness, and one he felt deeply, was his birth. Despite the fact that he was of English heritage, he was nonetheless one of seventeen children, and the youngest son at that, born to a candlemaker. In Philadelphia, the best he could do with such a background was to keep quiet about it. In colonial America as in Europe, the advantages of belonging to a good family could never be underestimated. To be successful while lacking "Hereditary Honour" was to risk being derided as a "new man," "an upstart," or "the first of his family." In an essay printed in London in 1739, a journalist explained how pervasive the prejudice was:

> I have known a Fox-hunter preferred in a Treaty of Marriage, because his Grandfather had been a General: And a Fellow that could not spell his Name, to a Man of Learning with equal Fortune, because the former had had a Lord Chancellor of the same. It is common for a Lady to have more Regard to the Arms she is to have on her Coach, than to the Companion she is to have in it.[36]

In 1740, then, Franklin was undistinguished by trade and birth as well as his marriage to Deborah, who for all her practical qualities, could never quite be considered "polite." And yet one day Franklin hoped to find a way into more elevated circles. How he could achieve this was a riddle. One thing, at least, was plain. To advance in the Georgian world, Franklin would have to be mindful of his character. Everyone knew that good character was the hallmark of a true gentleman. Such people were honorable, patriotic, genial, altruistic, and true. They were the kind of people who would help a friend in need, who would be magnanimous when wronged, who would be fair in business and would rally to a collective cause. What they absolutely were not was the type of person who would renege on business deals or who would hatch schemes in private to ruin their rivals.

John Webbe knew this very well. He had spent time with Franklin over the previous months and perhaps during their meetings he had sensed his ambition. Webbe also likely knew, because most Philadelphians did, that Franklin's was far from being the unblemished life. There had been whispers. As a young man he had a habit, as Franklin's biographer Carl Van Doren described it, of going to women "hungrily, secretly, and briefly."[37] These moonlight assignations had long since come to an end, but gossip continued to trail him. Who, for instance, was the mother of his son William? The boy, aged about ten in 1740, was an acknowledged and cherished part of the Franklin household, but few then (and none today) knew exactly where he came from. For his critics this was the behavior of a rascal, and one moreover who, in a world of believing and practicing Christians, was hardly ever to be seen inside a church. And what of his common-law marriage? Deborah's first husband may have vanished, but he had never been certified dead. Then, worst of all for those who had come to regard Franklin's activities with an air of suspicion, was his enthusiastic membership of the Freemasons. What was this new and secretive society? Was it not just another of Franklin's dishonorable ways of getting ahead?

From his very first "Detection" in the *Mercury*, Webbe played on such doubts. He framed his pieces as exposés that sought to show the people of Philadelphia a different man to the sagacious, hard-working printer they thought they knew. The Franklin that emerged from Webbe's descriptions was a sly, unkind, embittered man. Webbe claimed to have experienced this for himself in his dealings with Franklin, but for anyone wanting further evidence there was his malicious behavior as postmaster. What better proof of his character could there be than this? Secret orders forbidding riders from even carrying copies of his rival's newspaper? Surely this was the work of a power-hungry upstart, rather than that of a community-loving artisan.

It was this accusation that Franklin knew he had to answer. On December 11, he decided to set the record straight. It was true, Franklin owned, that he had forbidden the post's riders from delivering any copies of Bradford's *Mercury*. But this was not something of his own doing. He was only acting on direct orders from above, in fact orders that had come from none other than Alexander Spotswood. This was a name everyone knew. For decades Spotswood had been a high-profile figure in American society, serving most notably as lieutenant governor of Virginia. On his death six months earlier, he had been mourned as one of a pioneering generation of settlers. In his last years Spotswood had served as Postmaster General of America. It was in this capacity that he had come into contact with Andrew Bradford.

Spotswood had considered Bradford lazy. His accounts were always wretchedly late, and whenever Spotswood asked after them he was met with "trifling Excuses *and* fallacious Promises." The Postmaster General had first decided to punish Bradford by removing him from office. But even after this—a move that had resulted in Bradford's replacement by Franklin—he had failed to turn in the necessary papers, leaving a chasm in Pennsylvania's bookkeeping that stretched all the way back to 1734. Exasperated, Spotswood had written to Franklin telling him that Bradford's behavior was "no longer to be born with." It deserved to be checked with "*some Mark of my Resentment.*"[38] So it was that Spotswood had ordered Franklin to prohibit Bradford's *Mercury* from being carried by the riders as a punishment. To prove his case, Franklin had Spotswood's letter printed in full in the *Gazette*.

This was a delightful turn in the story for those who had followed the saga over the past month. What had begun as a personal quarrel about a piece of business between Franklin and Webbe had developed, as the best stories do, into a tale that sucked in others: first Bradford, then Spotswood. Where, readers could only wonder, would it lead next?

Over the following week the weather turned cold. Inside Franklin's shop the mood was tense. As the winter closed in, a period of labor as intense as any Franklin had ever known lay before him. He had promised readers his magazine in little more than a month, and he had to keep his word. As he began the process of compiling materials for the *General Magazine*, the air grew sharp and icy. Soon brisk flurries of snow were falling over Philadelphia, from a gloomy, threatening sky.

Two

THE RACE

THE BITTER WEATHER CONTINUED as the month wore on. On December 15, the Schuylkill River, just to the west of Philadelphia, froze fast. Meanwhile plates of ice three inches thick were seen floating down the Delaware. By the twentieth, these had locked and fused between the harbor and the New Jersey shore. Then, after dark on Christmas Day, temperatures plunged. The next weeks were filled with a succession of snowy days and frosty nights. By the beginning of January, Philadelphia's streets were forbidding places. The ice now extended past Front Street to the quays, wharves, and jetties of the riverside. In more remote areas, in the woods, plains, and valleys of rural Pennsylvania, snow lay deep.

When he had first come to inspect his newly chartered lands in 1682, William Penn found his colony's climate to be not unlike the south of France. He wrote home reporting that the air was sweet and clear, the sky serene, often without a cloud. But Penn soon learned that nature was capricious at the place he had chosen for his "Holy Experiment" in religious toleration. Thick fogs and mists could descend or foul vapors rise from the rivers and creeks with perplexing speed. Summers were breathlessly hot. Most testing of all, though, were the terrible winds that gusted from the north-west. They carried to Pennsylvania the cutting chills of the Canadian Great Lakes. During winter the air was "dry, cold, piercing and hungry,"[1] quite different to the grim, damp, black winters of England.

It was this north-westerly wind that set in during January 1741. It brought a spell of cold that surpassed everything anyone had ever known. The snow fell for hours at a stretch. The nights of January 6 and 7 were, by common agreement, estimated "to be the coldest Days we have had these many Years."[2] From south of Philadelphia, at a property called Yates's Houses, came the news that a large black bear had appeared in the yard "and quarrelled with the dog."[3] Though it was trailed and shot, people were left with the disquieting thought that the cold was driving wild animals into their civilized spaces. With the roads clotted in snow and ice, supplying the city was becoming troublesome too. The best remaining route ran straight across the frozen Delaware to the New Jersey shore. By early January scores of sleds were shuttling back and forth over the ice each day, carrying wood, coal, and bread.[4]

As they slid toward Philadelphia, they passed the outlines of abandoned vessels in the harbor: their masts and spars frosted white, their hulls entombed in the ice. A minute more and they were skimming across the waterline and coming to a halt on Market Street. There, as the drivers rubbed whatever warmth they could into their hands, glancing up through the snow they might have seen the glow of a fire through the upstairs window of Franklin's New Printing Office.

INSIDE, THE TASK THAT confronted Franklin was uniquely challenging. Three great difficulties confronted him. The first was the formidable size of the magazine project, which involved a combination of creative, technical, and physical demands. Second was his insufficient workforce. Over the years he had constructed a trusted team of workers, which in early 1741 included Joseph Rose, Olaf Mallendar, and James Parker. But they were laboring men, unsuitable for the editorial role Webbe had left vacant. There was no way around it: Franklin was going to have to compile the magazine himself. The last of his difficulties was the weather. Intense cold created a range of maddening problems for a printer. But looking out at the snowy streets in January 1741, Franklin knew that it was something that he could not escape.

There was, at least, the excitement of a new project. The *General Magazine*, however, was not just another printing venture. It was Franklin's first chance for years to engage directly with British journalistic culture, the very kind of literary work that set the coffee shops of the Strand and Covent Garden abuzz. For Franklin, this was something rare and exhilarating. To truly understand a person, Napoleon Bonaparte would observe some years into the future, to truly know what their dreams and fears are, it is vital to know what the world was like when they were twenty years old. On Franklin's twentieth birthday, in January 1726, he was living in Duke Street, off Lincoln's Inn Fields, in the vibrant heart of London.

There were few places on the planet as exciting as London at this time. While still distinguished by its grand and ancient allure, the city had nonetheless undergone something of a modern makeover. From buildings across the capital's skyline fluttered the Union Flag with its bold combination of reds, whites, and blues that together captured the unity and confidence of the new kingdom, Great Britain.* Beneath the rooftops, the London streets buzzed with life. For sev-

---

* Acts of Union were passed by the English and Scottish parliaments in early 1707. The first article of both of these provided that "the Two Kingdoms of England and Scotland shall, upon the First Day of May next ensuing . . . and for ever after, be United into One Kingdom by the name of *Great Britain*." These acts recast the political map of the British Isles. The ancient kingdoms of England and Scotland were dissolved, and the parliament in Edinburgh was abolished. Henceforth Scots were to be represented politically by forty-five members of the House of Commons and sixteen peers in the House of Lords. The origins of the Union Flag (which was already being called the "Union Jack") stretch further into history. Versions of it can be traced back to the time of the Union of the Crowns of England and Scotland in 1603.

eral generations, since the Great Fire of 1666, the northern bank of the River Thames had been a noisy building site. The crooked, charcterful buildings of the medieval city were replaced with refined, geometrically precise constructions like George Dance's imposing Mansion House and Sir Christopher Wren's St Paul's Cathedral with its magnificent dome. In the shops, standardized weights and measures were being introduced to help regulate the sale of goods, while outside, signposts were erected, helping people to navigate their way through the chaos.

Also promising to guide people safely through the maze of life were the scores of newspapers and periodicals that could be found piled high in coffee houses and taverns. These too had their roots in the mid-seventeenth century, when pioneering newsmen like Marchamont Nedham created titles such as *Mercurius Britanicus* or *Mercurius Politicus* to champion his political causes. By the opening decades of the eighteenth century, the number of these "public papers" had proliferated greatly. Strolling into Button's Coffee House, Covent Garden, Franklin could browse news sheets like the *Courant*, *Gazette*, *Daily Post*, or *Post-Man*, or hear the verdict on the latest literary essays. These essays were almost all written in a manner that sought to emulate the style and success of the great *Spectator*. Produced in a fabled whirl of creativity fifteen years earlier, this had been the work of two society wits, Richard Steele and Joseph Addison. Filled with insight, memorable characters, and humor, the *Spectator*'s essays established a new standard in literary culture. For those of Franklin's generation, Addison and Steele were the Lennon and McCartney of their time.

Addison, in particular, was a favorite of Franklin's. The *Spectator*'s essays captivated him when he "chanced upon" them as a boy in Boston, and stepping inside Button's, he would have experienced the thrill of knowing he was inside an establishment that was founded by the great wit himself. In fact it was here, around a decade before, that Addison had famously arranged for a lion's head to be hung up on the wall. The face of the creature was purposely fierce. Its mouth was open, showing rows of glistening teeth. In an early attempt at reader-generated commentary, people were invited to drop their written contributions into the lion's mouth for consideration. "I intend to publish once every week," Addison explained, "'the roarings of the lion,' and hope to make him roar so loud as to be heard all over the British nation."[5]

Addison's lion at Button's was a powerful symbol of the print culture that was shaping London at this time. A week could be lit up by the appearance of a devastating political essay. A poet could be demolished by a coruscating review. This was the cultural environment that created such ruthless writers as Jonathan Swift and Daniel Defoe. And as they experimented with innovative satires and novels, stories from across Europe appeared in an endless stream in the daily papers. They told of coups in Constantinople and mighty fleets at Cadiz, the glittering court of Louis XV in Versailles, and the construction of palaces in St. Petersburg. For some this torrent was overpowering. In a funny and memorable edition of the *Tatler* in 1710, Addison lampooned a new eighteenth-century character: the news addict. Addison's satire featured in a story he narrated about a man he called the "Political Upholsterer." Outwardly this upholsterer seemed an asset to his community. Londoners saw him in the early morning bustling through the city streets, apparently engaged on "Matters of Importance." At length, however, Addison divulged the truth.

> He had a Wife and several Children; but was much more inquisitive to know what passed in *Poland* than in his own Family, and was in greater Pain and Anxiety of Mind for King *Augustus's* Welfare than that of his nearest Relations. He looked extremely thin in a Dearth of News, and never enjoy'd himself in a Westerly Wind. This indefatigable kind of Life was the Ruin of his Shop; for about the Time that his Favourite Prince left the Crown of *Poland*, he broke and disappear'd.[6]

By the time of Franklin's arrival in London in 1725, a neologism had been invented to describe those, like the "Political Upholsterer," who had lost all sense of proportion in this information age. They were derided as "*quidnuncs*," from the Latin for "what's now?" or "what's the news?"[7] Their appetite for print was unquenchable, and soon after his arrival, Franklin joined the profession that supplied it. Franklin earned his living as first a pressman and later a compositor in a succession of London's busiest printing houses. As such he was able to boast that he had played his own part in this grand literary moment, as he worked on the production of a range of enchanting titles, from accounts of voyages to urbane works of poetry and philosophy. On one particularly exciting occasion, Franklin was even involved in a new edition of the *Spectator* itself.

Here in London was the best place to experience a new form of modern life. It was a form of life—colorful, progressive, daring— that people knew only existed because England had fought her way through the horrors of the previous century. That experience, everyone knew, had been testing, but it left the British people with a unique and precious inheritance in the form of their political constitution. This was something that Britons were taught to love. It was not, as we tend to think of it today, a formal written document. Instead, trying to capture its essence, the writer Henry Fielding likened it to a human soul, something "*invisible and incorporeal*," that existed beyond the sum of its physical parts. Better still, Fielding thought, the constitution resembled the perfect harmony that was produced by the "proper Composition of the several Parts in a well tuned musical Instrument."[8]

The active parts that mattered when it came to the constitution were the collected laws of the kingdom, the institutions that provided legislative and executive authority, and the customs, manners, and habits of the people that had formed over time. For most Britons, and particularly the Whigs who supported Robert Walpole, the constitution was something that had been centuries in the making in

England (which is one reason it was more often called the "English constitution") and that had been perfected in recent years. As well as Magna Carta of 1215 and the Bill of Rights of 1689, the Whigs were equally proud of 1714, the year King George I arrived in Britain to become the first Hanoverian monarch. This was the point, one constitutional expert has contended, "at which the Crown ceased to govern through its ministers and ministers began to govern though the Crown."[9] This was very much as the Whigs saw it at the time. What other nation, after all, could claim to have balanced the monarchical, aristocratic, and democratic forms of government in such delicate measures? Where else were there general elections every seven years? Which rival nation had secured for its citizens privileges like Habeas Corpus? For the Whigs it was clear that Britain had perfected a political formula: one that balanced order and freedom, fairness, and opportunity. As such they considered their constitution one of the greatest accomplishments in human history.

These were the Whigs who held sway during Franklin's time in London. As the political order had stabilized under Walpole's leadership, so Britain seemed to be experiencing a cultural flowering. Franklin toured the playhouses, sifted through bookshops, and befriended philosophers. Once he was very nearly introduced to Sir Isaac Newton himself. While he was mostly happy to remain a wide-eyed observer, on occasions he did move toward center stage. Of all the incidents during his time in London, he would retain a particularly fond memory of the occasion when, while overtaken by a burst of youthful bravado, he decided to demonstrate the swimming skills he had learned as a boy in Boston. Franklin leapt into the Thames at Chelsea and swam downriver, past Westminster Abbey, the Palace of Westminster, and Somerset House on the Strand, "performing on the Way," he remembered, "many Feats of Activity both upon & under Water, that surpriz'd & pleas'd those to whom they were Novelties,"[10] until he arrived in triumph at Blackfriars.

*   *   *

IT IS TEMPTING TO freeze in time that moment at Blackfriars, as Franklin pulled himself out of the turbid water with a grin of delight. It is a powerful image because it symbolizes the dynamism and freedom Franklin experienced in London. This was a mode of life entirely different to what he had known as a boy. Massachusetts had had its homely charms, but the people's concerns there were the concerns of earlier times. God remained the pivot around which all of life revolved. In Boston, people commonly thought of themselves as being participants in a divine project, in which the Creator of the Universe was taking a particular interest. As the historian Philip Dray has explained, settlers in New England believed themselves to be inhabiting an enchanted landscape, "a place of dark, impenetrable forests, vengeful thunderstorms, portentous comets, witches, and ghosts."[11] As such, Franklin spent his childhood Sundays listening to preachers like Cotton Mather hold forth about doctrines such as the Eternal Decrees of God (the teaching that all the particulars of life were preordained according to a Grand Plan), a belief Franklin thought "unintelligible,"[12] or that some people were God's chosen ones, or that God would curse the souls of those who rejected the Gospel.

In New England such dogmas were central to the way people understood the world. God rode in people's hearts and peeped over their shoulders. London was an escape from this. In the theaters of Covent Garden, the shops of the Strand, and the taverns of Fleet Street, it was possible to experience a deterministic attitude toward life. Here, for better or worse, an emerging generation of culturally alert Britons were beginning to see themselves as masters of their own destiny. A young man could strike out alone in business, write a poem, or dive into the river for a swim. What the consequences of these decisions might be and what those who took them hoped to achieve was a different matter, but the point remained that people were increasingly looking to themselves rather than God when they decided how best to act.

At twenty, Franklin sensed this. He even flirted with atheism, the ultimate freedom, when he produced an impulsive (as he would later consider it) pamphlet, which called into question the existence of God, the human soul, and the afterlife.[13] The "good life," as he came to understand it, the life that was truly worth living, was about potential and progress, not doctrines and dogma. Voltaire, the French man of letters who was also visiting London at this time, thought much the same. Had Oliver Cromwell lived in the 1720s and not the 1650s, he reasoned, he would not have troubled himself with war and beheading his king. "He wou'd be a wealthy city trader, and no more."[14]

Franklin left all this behind in July 1726 when he stepped aboard the *Berkshire*, an Atlantic packet bound for America. London had laid a strong claim to his heart, but there was still something in Philadelphia that attracted him more. In all Franklin's life this was among his boldest moves. Had he remained in London, with his skills and work ethic, it is quite possible that he would have thrived as a printer. For all its youthful promise, Philadelphia had little to offer in comparison. There was no library for self-study, no academy for educating the young, and as Franklin later recalled, there was not even a decent bookseller's in the colonies south of Boston. While London was crammed with fine Baroque and Palladian buildings, in Philadelphia, not many decades had passed since the settlers had lived in caves on the banks of the Delaware and Pennsylvania had been one great forest. Franklin was nonetheless filled with a yearning for America. In his voyaging journal he recorded that when he caught sight of his native continent again, his eyes "were dimmed with the suffusion of two small drops of joy."[15]

Philadelphia may have paled in comparison to London in many respects, but when it came to future potential, Penn's "green country town" was arguably a rival to the British capital. Franklin knew the advantages of its geography, on the banks of a deep river with a vast continent stretching out behind it. While this setting would fuel its growth long into the future, its culture had yet to be defined. The

Quakers might have provided Pennsylvania with its first character, but there was still scope here, for someone with drive and talent like Franklin, to shape attitudes and distinguish himself. Indeed, once established there would be opportunities for him to introduce to Philadelphians the ideas that had so excited him in London. This is precisely what he did. Shortly after his return, Franklin founded his Junto Club with those "who hoped to improve themselves." Four years later, in 1731, he suggested the creation of a lending library, which soon opened for its fifty or so subscribers as the Library Company of Philadelphia. As Franklin's biographer Nick Bunker has pointed out, the initial list of books he drew up for the library "can fairly be described as remarkable." There was "no theology, no sermons—certainly nothing by Cotton Mather—no fiction, no drama, no metaphysics."

> Of course the Library Company wanted the complete works of Addison and Steele; perhaps because Franklin was tired of people borrowing his set of *The Spectator*. But most of all they wished to have modern history, geography, astronomy, and science. Textbooks of geometry, a teach yourself guide to Newton's calculus, and a treatise on conic sections: that was the sort of thing.[16]

What Franklin was striving to achieve here, at the Junto Club and in the scores of political, moral, and scientific essays that peppered the pages of the *Gazette* throughout the 1730s, is not difficult to see. He was trying to unite his twin passions: colonial America and the Enlightenment culture of Britain. Just as he was eager to convey "Instruction among the common People" with *Poor Richard's*, he wanted to illuminate the minds of his progressive-minded peers, to show them the exciting, rewarding form of life that was emerging and was increasingly available to them. Due to the demands of his business, his ability to do this was constrained for many years. But by the 1740s the time had come to take a confident step forward. Impatient for progress, Franklin believed that the opening phase of the colonies' development was complete. This had been a time of drudgery, when the colonists were consumed by the challenge of building settlements and infrastructure, roads and harbors. Now, as the new decade began, Franklin decided that the time had arrived to "cultivate the finer Arts, and improve the common Stock of Knowledge."[17]

The *General Magazine* was to be an important part of this process. Franklin knew that if it could only be set up effectively, it could be a powerful way of communicating ideas to the most receptive, culturally attentive listeners in the colonies. The magazine would appeal to the sort of boy he had been in Boston twenty years before: bright, ambitious, outward-looking. It would be crammed with the most fashionable essays by the best English writers on everything from politics to geography and science. It was to be a breeze of brisk British air on the east American coast.

AS JANUARY BEGAN, FRANKLIN found himself in a delicate position. With Webbe gone, everything depended on him. In the advertisements he had run through November and December, the usually cautious Franklin had been bellicose. He tempted prospective readers with a magazine freighted with content, with eight distinct sections in all, including:

> Extracts from the Votes, and Debates of the Parliament of *Great Britain*.
> The Proclamations and Speeches of Governors; Addresses, Votes, Resolutions, &c. of Assemblies, in each Colony.
> Essays, controversial, humorous, philosophical, religious, moral or political.
> A concise CHRONICLE of the most remarkable Transactions, as well in *Europe* as *America*.
> Course of Exchange between the several Colonies, and *London*; Prices of Goods, &c.[18]

All told, a single edition of Franklin's *General Magazine* was to run to tens of thousands of words. Whether Franklin could deliver on these promises was uncertain. The magazine he had advertised to his readers seemed as long and varied as the *Gentleman's Magazine* itself. But Cave's success was grounded in his position as an insider. His offices were at St. John's Gate, Clerkenwell, a stroll from the bookshops of Paternoster Row, almost equally close to the coffee shops of Covent Garden or Fleet Street and not far from the center of political power in Westminster. It was easy for him to follow fashions and pick up rumors. In contrast, three thousand miles and a vast ocean separated Franklin from this world and the creative energy that sustained it. Franklin knew this. He also knew Cave had a team of writers around him to convert his ideas into finished literary materials. Among these were poets like Richard Savage, classicists such as Elizabeth Carter, and a man called Johnson who, it was rumored, was able to produce sparkling prose on just about anything. When preparing a new issue, Cave drove his subordinates hard, often prevailing upon them to work "from twenty-four to fifty hours at a stretch, and even on Sundays, to get copy ready."[19]

How Franklin intended to emulate any of this in four weeks at Market Street remained an open question. As he had explained in his advertisement in the *Gazette,* some progress had already been made. He had acquired, for instance, the small-letter Brevier type the previous summer, which allowed him to fit a large amount of text onto a page. He had also opened correspondence with "Intelligent Men in most of the Colonies,"[20] who, in time, he hoped would help supply him with original and lively homegrown pieces too. But with the roads all blocked, communication with anywhere outside Philadelphia was halted. Franklin can only have looked out with gloomy eyes on the snow that fell on the city from morning till candlelight on January 8. All the while the north-west wind continued to blow. Hints of Franklin's discontent can still be viewed in the archive. Issues of the *Gazette* in January are printed in uncommonly large type, an old trick for reducing the workload. At the same time, Franklin dropped the advertisement for the magazine that had run in the *Gazette* since November. This was a subtle acknowledgment that his magazine was not going to be ready as planned. As he set to work sourcing the thousands of words of copy, his workforce—Rose, Mallendar, and Parker—were left to dread the job that was coming their way.

Printing might have been considered a lowly trade, but it was reasonably paid and it had the allure of being a growing, fast-paced industry. On fine days, with the soft Pennsylvanian sun slanting in through the windows, the work could even be seen as an attractive blend of mind and body. The compositor would stand at the type cases, scanning the handwritten copy. As his eyes raced along the lines, his fingers would dart to and fro, locating pieces of type by touch, fetching them out and then—*click, click, click*—dropping them into the composing stick. The work was a chain of deft, fluid movements between the capital letters that were lifted from an upper case, and regular characters, spaces, and punctuation pieces that were taken from the lower. Once a stick was filled with arranged type, it would be emptied into a wooden frame called a galley. Here sentences, paragraphs, and, at length, entire columns of distributed type would accumulate to create finished "formes" that were ready for the press.

To the unprofessional eye, a printing press, the machine that dominated Franklin's press room, seemed a cumbersome instrument. It not only consumed a vast amount of space, it was also awkwardly shaped, looking something like a heavy table jammed inside an empty door frame. But to printers such a press was a thing of beauty. Its frame was made of fine, seasoned oak so that it would never warp. It was polished from top to bottom, and its ironwork was oiled every day. It stood a shade taller than Franklin himself, at just beneath six feet, and each of its components had a distinct, expressive name. There was a cap at the top, hind posts at one end, and a spindle in its center. For it to operate smoothly, the whole superstructure had to be harmoniously aligned. The upright panels called "cheeks" had to be absolutely vertical. The carriage that intersected them had to be perfectly horizontal. The feet that planted the machine on the floor had to be sturdy enough to absorb the jolts that vibrated through it for hours upon hours, day after day.

It took two men to operate the machine. One had to continuously beat the upper surface of the forme with ink; the other had to operate the lever that brought the press down onto the sheet of paper as it was drawn through in a carriage. Ever the improver, over the years Franklin had scrutinized each discrete part of this process. He experimented with different papers and inks, seeking brightness, contrast, and durability. Quality was one thing, but productivity was always his central aim. The goal was a steady, repeatable rhythm. To rush was to risk a series of disasters: smudges, blotches, and misalignments. Yet to fuss and fiddle over every page was to fall infuriatingly behind. While techniques and materials could be perfected, the weather was one element that could not be controlled. And it was cold that printers loathed the most. It could freeze paper and type solid so that even the business of starting work became a heroic battle. Thereafter the compositor would have to struggle along with numbed, unresponsive fingers, while in the most extreme cold the whole machine might seize up completely.

It was conditions like these that Franklin and his pressmen faced in Market Street during the early weeks of 1741. The only consoling thought was that Bradford's workers would be experiencing the exact same troubles on Front Street. Meanwhile Philadelphia's readers crowded around their fires expectantly. Soon they were all going to find out which of the two would issue their magazine first: the venomous Mr. Webbe or the clever Mr. Franklin?

AS THE MONTH WORE on, the scale as well as the intensity of the cold weather became plain. Letters arrived from New York describing the massive chunks of ice that had come floating down the East and Hudson rivers, feeding the harbor until it was a mass of jostling bergs. Similar tales came from Boston. The streets where Franklin spent his earliest years were covered by a carpet of ice that stretched into the bay and out to sea. Tents had been erected on the Charles River "for the Entertainment of Travellers,"[21] who experienced the strange sensation of sleeping on the water. The cold stretched south too. From the town of Lewes at the mouth of the Delaware came a report that Franklin printed in the *Gazette*, that "'tis all Ice towards the Sea as far as Eye can reach."[22]

It was the end of January before temperatures rose. But with such a volume of snow having fallen over the Pennsylvanian landscape, this only instigated a new disaster. As the upper reaches of the Delaware thawed, a great, clumsy, tumbling mass of ice was propelled downstream until it came to rest at a bend ten miles north of Philadelphia, near Trenton. The *Gazette* reported that icy debris was strewn on the bank, frozen mounds twenty feet high, so "that in some Places the River is turn'd out of its Bed, and flows over the low Lands, doing great Damage."[23]

But even this turned out to be only a brief reprieve. Days later the north-west wind returned and snow was again driving down in the Philadelphian streets, returning them to the state they had been in for much of January. In Market Street the work went on regardless. Ever since Christmas, Franklin had been absorbed by his objective, and at last, at the beginning of February, there were signs that all the effort had been worth it. On February 5, he ran a short, triumphant advertisement in the *Gazette*:

Next Week will be published,
(To be continued Monthly)
The General Magazine,
AND
Historical Chronicle,
For January, 1741.
Printed and Sold by B. FRANKLIN.[24]

Whatever optimism Franklin felt at printing this notice was short-lived. The same day the *Mercury* released a competing ad, informing customers that the *American Magazine* was also set to be issued the following week. As to the particular day the *Mercury* was not specific, but for Franklin the enraging prospect of being overtaken by Webbe must now have seemed very real.

Thursday, February 12, Franklin's promised day, came with no sign of the magazine, just a note in the *Gazette* amending the expected date to "*Monday next*."[25] This final delay was to be fatal. For down on Front Street there was news from Bradford's. The printing of the *American Magazine* was complete and it was almost ready for release. So it was that on February 13, 1741, John Webbe and Andrew Bradford launched the very first magazine to be produced in America. When they sold their first copy in the snowy Philadelphian streets, they became the first in a line that would extend down the centuries to such luminous titles as the *New Yorker*, *The Atlantic*, and *Vanity Fair*. Trailing just a few days afterward, on February 16, came Franklin's *General Magazine*. The occasion brought some satisfaction. In her ledgers, Deborah recorded the visits of several prominent citizens who came to Market Street to pick up a copy of the much talked-about "magaseen." Among them were the wealthy Quaker merchant Israel Pemberton, the lieutenant governor George Thomas, and most excitingly of all, one of William Penn's sons, Thomas Penn, who bought six copies.[26] These visits were some consolation. But for Franklin, someone who prided himself on being first, the feeling was bittersweet at best.

Reading through the *American Magazine*, Franklin would have instantly seen how Webbe and Bradford had done it. They had favored pragmatism over all else. Rather than establish a visual identity of their own, they had copied the *Gentleman's Magazine* in every way: the type, the arrangement of design elements, the position of the woodcut on the opening page, the division of the content into two columns. It was as if Bradford's pressmen had somehow got hold of Cave's template formes and filled them with different type. But Franklin did not have to study the *American Magazine* for long to see that comparisons ended here. It was a slim production, at just forty-two pages. The opening eight were entirely given over to an enlarged reprint of Webbe's initial "Plan," the piece that had first run in the *Mercury* at the beginning of November. Thereafter there were transcripts of debates in the colonial assemblies of New Jersey, Pennsylvania, and Maryland and a garrulous piece in Webbe's usual bombastic style about the "miracle" that was underway in Pennsylvania. For a cover price of one shilling, three pennies more than the *General Magazine*, it was not quite the glittering chronicle of enlightenment that Franklin had envisaged.

Franklin had taken far more pains over his own magazine, which was announced on its title page by a huge woodcut depicting the Prince of Wales's coronet with its three dashing plumes. This swashbuckling appeal to patriotism stood at the head of a magazine of seventy-six pages, with seventeen distinct sections running to some thirty thousand words. With almost the whole compilation overseen by Franklin alone, it must rank as one of the most tremendous outpourings of energy of his entire career as a printer. This was an impressive feat, but as a literary production it still fell somewhat short. Its contents were for the most part more useful than entertaining, and for its first fifty pages the *General Magazine* plodded through proceedings, proclamations, and acts before it arrived at the sections with more zest. Among these was the reprinting of a sprightly poem entitled "Admiral Hosier's Ghost," some snippets from the papers, and a roundup of international events—the liveliest item of which recorded the death of the Holy Roman Emperor, Charles VI, who had died after eating "Mushrooms stew'd in Oil."*,27

---

* This event, which would have seemed whimsical to readers of the *General Magazine* in early 1741, would turn out to have much more significance. Charles's death was exploited by the neighboring French, Prussians, and Bavarians as an opportunity to challenge the Hapsburg dynasty to which he belonged. The result was the War of the Austrian Succession. Voltaire would write of Frederick's death, "ce plat de champignons changea la destinée de l'Europe" (Voltaire, *Oeuvres complètes* [Paris: Garnier, 1883], p. 48).

Exhausted by the effort, Franklin still managed to issue a new edition of the *Gazette* the following Thursday, but once again signs of the strain were shown by his reliance on large type. It was only then, with the huge task finally behind him, that Franklin at last had the opportunity to attend to an outstanding piece of business. Few people had ever injured him as John Webbe had. He had betrayed his trust, defamed him publicly, and ruined his chance to launch a long-cherished project as carefully as he had wanted. Perhaps Franklin was already counting the cost of his association with Webbe in pounds, shillings, and pence. For a while he had let Webbe's aggression pass in silence, but by February he had decided to take his revenge. Just as Webbe sensed Franklin's vulnerabilities, Franklin knew Webbe's. He knew him to be a deeply insecure man who was jealous of others and uncomfortable in his Scotch-Irish identity. To exploit this, Franklin fell back on a favorite old trick: an anonymous letter to the newspaper.

Anonymous letters were a common feature of newspaper columns at this time. In the days before journalism had established op-eds, they were a way to express public or expert opinion. Sometimes arguments would play out over the course of several issues or even months, with correspondents sparring over the question of the day or answering an antagonist. This is just what Franklin did to Webbe in February 1741. Introducing himself as a member of the Irish community in Pennsylvania, he claimed to know Webbe—a man who "*has always been shy of us his Country-Folks*"—very well. He described how Webbe had often sought to conceal his identity by pretending to come from another nation altogether. This was a shameful strategy, and one doomed to failure, for Webbe was branded on the tongue with a "*great Brogue*," an indelible characteristic, which forever betrayed him as a "Teague."[28]

Here was a slur intended to wound. For a generation since the English writer John Dunton had published his *Teague Land: or A Merry Ramble to the Wild Irish* (1698), the term had been cruelly and casually applied as a stereotype to describe the uncouth, backward Irish.

Almost as lamentable as Webbe's accent was his ability as a writer. Arguing that "*Nonsense in Prose is not quite so agreeable as in Verse,*" Franklin set anonymously to work, converting Webbe's latest *Mercury* piece into something quite, *quite* different. It began:

> *ARRA Joy! My monthly* Macasheen *shall contain Sheets four,*
> *Or an Equivalent, which is someting more;*
> *So dat twelve Times four shall make fifty two,*
> *Which is twice as much as fifty two Newsh-Papers do:*
> *Prishe shingle* One Shilling: *But shubscribe for a Year,*
> *You shall have it sheaper, at de shame Prishe, Honey dear:*
> *And if you will but shubscribe to take it de Year out,*
> *You may leave off when you pleashe, before, no doubt.*[29]

PHILADELPHIA'S LONG ISOLATION CAME to an end on March 14, when a sloop and a ship successfully picked their way through the ice to the harbor. With the trees in blossom and spring not far off, their appearance altered the mood in the city. Other vessels would soon be following these first: three-masted West Indiamen, heading for Willing Wharf; brigs filled with beaver skins and linseed from Boston; snows loaded with bales of Virginian tobacco or sacks of Carolina rice. Once again, Philadelphia was stirring into life.

From the countryside came news of a different kind. The weather had forced many people to the brink. West of Philadelphia, in Lancaster County, the snow had stood three feet deep for weeks on end. Great numbers of the "back Inhabitants" had been left to fend for themselves on scavenged deer carcasses, taken from "the Swamps or Runns about their Houses." As one report ran:

> Many Horses and Cows are dead, and the greatest Part of the
> Gangs in the Woods are dead; that the Deers which could not
> struggle through the Snow to the Springs are believed to be all

dead, and many of those which did get into the Savannahs are also dead, ten, twelve and fifteen being found in the Compass of a few Acres of Land.[30]

Other rumors suggested that even the Lenape, whose affinity with nature and ability to endure hardship was known to far outstrip that of the colonists, had been challenged by the cold. Reports filtered back that they were predicting a scarcity of deer and turkeys for the years ahead. Such news served to remind the colonists how vulnerable their communities were. A hard winter was nearly enough, it seemed, to drive them to ruin. This was a reflection to make Franklin's obsession with British literary culture look misguided. In Market Street even he must have been weighing the wisdom of launching a magazine. Did he really have the apparatus to produce something like this? Were there enough interested readers in the colonies? Did people really have time to engage in cultural and scientific debates as they did in the coffee houses of Covent Garden?

Theorizing was one thing, but in the meantime, unless Franklin wanted to lose face, he had to continue with the interminable business of getting the *General Magazine* out every month. This left him busier than ever during the first half of 1741. He ran pieces on the escalating war between Britain and Spain in the Caribbean, articles about the evangelical preacher George Whitefield, along with poems and accounts of the latest colonial projects. Beyond this, Franklin tried to position the *General Magazine* as a reference work, filling it with chronological lists of the kings, queens, and emperors of Europe. All this created a flutter of interest, but never much more. For all his doughty toil, the *General Magazine* was undercut by a deeper failing. Unlike the *Gazette* or *Poor Richard's Almanack*, the *General Magazine* never developed a strong identity. There were no jaunty, teasing prefaces. There were none of the amusing fables or the anonymous letters that featured in the *Gazette*. Looking back from a distance of nearly three centuries, the *General Magazine* seems an appropriate title for a publication that never really found its distinctive voice.

At least Franklin could take heart from that fact that he outlasted Webbe's *American Magazine*. That folded in April 1741, after just three editions. Through sheer persistence Franklin went on with his own magazine until the summer. It was then that Philadelphia was hit by its second natural disaster of the year. This came with a ship of German immigrants: a fatal malady that caught hold in the riverside streets and thereafter worked its way around the city. Remembered as "the Palatine Distemper,"[31] it caused many to flee Philadelphia in fear of their lives. A cynic might claim that it also provided Franklin with the opportunity to cease publication of a title that had already cost him enough trouble and money.

There was, though, one longer-lasting legacy of the *General Magazine* and the bitter winter of 1741. At about that time, Franklin started to sketch out designs for an improved fireplace. Those found in the city up until that point, he believed, were poorly constructed and were just as good at filling rooms with smoke as heat. A design for what would later become widely known as the "Franklin Stove" would soon afterward be advertised in the newspapers.[32] The experience of spending days in the pressroom in the freezing temperatures of early 1741 was, doubtless, one that Franklin did not wish to repeat.

THE BANKS OF THE Schuylkill River were considered to be Philadelphia's finest setting. Here, far away from the bustle of Market Street and the harbor, people could wander through grassy meadows and oak groves that abounded with wildflowers, right to the banks of the river. In the summer, swimmers would push out into the water, further animating a scene that was also filled with boating parties and fishermen casting for sturgeon and catfish in the shallows. Had Benjamin Franklin's been the conventional colonial life, then he may well have ended up living here, in a handsome brick house of his own construction with a fine garden filled with apple and peach trees.

To many people this was precisely the direction that Franklin seemed to be heading in as the 1740s marched on. His printing business continued to become more profitable and extensive as the years passed, with partnerships in New York and South Carolina, and connections to paper mills in Williamsburg and Wissahickon. When his old rival Andrew Bradford died in November 1742, Franklin was left as indisputably the preeminent printer in Pennsylvania and even, perhaps, in all the colonies. Approaching forty, wealthy and active, it was surely only a matter of time before Franklin exchanged his leather apron for something more comfortable. These were thoughts that, doubtless, had occurred to him and Deborah too. But for all his exterior success, something continued to gnaw at him as he returned to the New Printing Office, day after day.

There were several causes of Franklin's discontent. A constant worry was the future of his business. It was hard to avoid the reflection that had his son Frankie not died in 1736, he would have been a growing boy by now, ideally placed to succeed him. As it was, the future of the business was far from clear. Young William Franklin had shown no interest at all in the printer's trade. This meant that there was no prospect of Benjamin retiring, which in turn meant there was no chance of him escaping his identity as a "mechanical man," the slur Webbe had used against him. Though he was prominent and respected in Philadelphian society, it seemed as if Franklin had reached the point beyond which he could scarcely hope to rise. The difficulties of his situation were made all the clearer by the presence of his neighbor, a young man named James Read.

Franklin was fond of the boy he knew as "Jemmy." He was the son of one of his wife Deborah's relations and had moved into the house next to the Franklins along with his mother, after the early death of his father, a merchant called Charles Read. There was so much in Jemmy to remind Franklin of himself. He was clever, bookish, and ambitious. Best of all he had spent time in London, having also crossed the Atlantic when he was about twenty. Only in one way were the two sharply divided. While Franklin came from obscurity, Jemmy Read was distinguished by birth. Before he died, his father had served as Mayor of Philadelphia and Supreme Councillor of Pennsylvania. His family were also linked by marriage to some of the most respectable figures in the province. One of his aunts was married to the scholar James Logan. Another was the wife of Israel Pemberton, the affluent Quaker merchant. All this enhanced the young man's social status. By the time that he was setting out on his career in the law in the 1740s, the name "James Read, Gentleman" was beginning to appear on official documents in the city.[33]

For Franklin, who remained in the subservient role of Clerk of the Pennsylvania Assembly, the advantages Read enjoyed over him were obvious and quite possibly irritating. It was out of their friendship, however, that something quite unexpected arose in the summer of 1743. During his time in London, Read had come to know a young printer, William Strahan. After Read's return to Philadelphia, the two remained in touch, in the hope they might be able to do some business together. In July 1743, Read heard from Strahan, who had written to ask a favor. Strahan was interested to know whether there was encouragement to be found in Philadelphia for a potential migrant. One of his workers, a printer called David Hall, had expressed a wish to sail to the colonies, and he was seeking advice on his behalf. "He understands his Business exceedingly well, is honest, sober and Industrious to the last Degree,"[34] Strahan affirmed.

Read naturally passed the letter to Franklin, who read it through. On July 10, 1743, Franklin replied.

PHILADA. JULY 10. 1743

Sir,

Mr Read has communicated to me part of a Letter from you, recommending a young Man whom you would be glad to see in better Business than that of a Journeyman Printer. I have already three Printing-Houses in three different Colonies, and

purpose to set up a fourth if I can meet with a proper Person
to manage it, having all Materials ready for that purpose. If
the young Man will venture over hither, that I may see and
be acquainted with him, we can treat about the Affair, and I
make no doubt but he will think my Proposals reasonable; If
we should not agree, I promise him however a Twelvemonths
Good Work, and to defray his Passage back if he enclines to
return to England,

I am Sir, Your humble Servant unknown,

B. Franklin[35]

Franklin did not yet know it, but this letter would establish two of
the most important relationships of his life. The first was with David
Hall, an ambitious printer who was everything that John Webbe was
not. The second was a friendship of a far greater magnitude. Strahan
was already a tradesman of repute, and in 1743 he was at the start of a
career that would propel him into a position of tremendous power and
wealth. Franklin, always on the lookout, sensed his chance. Here was
a wise, ambitious, and connected businessman who might do for him
what the *General Magazine* had not. If all turned out well, then Strahan
could provide Franklin with that most elusive thing: a pathway to the
highest plains of Enlightenment London.

Three

NORTH STAR

ON THE MORNING OF July 4, 1744, London was abuzz with excitement. After a fortnight's breathless reporting in the newspapers, the day had finally arrived when the treasure captured from the Spaniards in the South Seas by Commodore George Anson was to be brought to the Tower.

The whole spectacular story had broken three weeks earlier. Anson, the commander of a squadron of Royal Naval ships, had been sent into the vast and poorly charted ocean that lay between America and China to harry Spanish shipping. Anson's voyage in the South Seas had lasted for almost four years. During that time his sailors faced tremendous hardship—scurvy, foul weather, constant food shortages. Hundreds of them had died by April 1743, when Anson found himself off the Chinese coast. There he settled on a plan to intercept a Spanish treasure galleon with his sixty-gun, fourth-rate warship, the *Centurion*. Anson knew the galleon was due in Manila, and he cruised out into the ocean in the hope of finding it. On June 20, 1743, Anson's men caught sight of their prize and gave chase. Realizing that there was little hope of escape, the captain of the galleon, the *Nuestra Señora de Covadonga*, broached to and cleared her guns. There ensued a dramatic engagement of an hour and a half, "within less than Pistol Shot."[1] In that time, the forty-gun Spanish ship was crippled by the ferocity of Anson's assault. Its masts and rigging were shot to pieces, cannon fire holed the galleon at the waterline, and more than 1 in 10 of her 550 men were killed. In comparison, by the time the Spanish admiral struck his flag, just two of Anson's men were dead.

The war with Spain had been lurching on since late 1739. In that time, the news of any naval triumph over the Spanish had been enthusiastically chronicled in the British press. There was nothing, however, to rank alongside what Anson had done. His intrepid victory on such a distant ocean was compelling enough, but what added disbelief to the excitement was the contents of the galleon. The *Nuestra Señora de Covadonga* was indeed "the prize of all the oceans." When taken, it was revealed by the papers, she had been carrying 1,313,843 pieces of eight, 35,682 ounces of virgin silver, and assorted items of plate.[2] This was a haul so vast it was difficult to comprehend. It computed to about two pieces of eight for every single Londoner. In mid-June, Anson had completed his voyage, which ended up being a full circumnavigation of the globe. As the *Centurion* dropped anchor at Spithead, the ramifications of what had happened were being absorbed in Whitehall. It took days to unload the treasure at Portsmouth, but by the start of July it had been transported sixty miles inland to the village of Putney on the southern banks of the Thames.

On Saturday, July 4, 1744, the treasure that had been seized in the azure China Sea was prepared for the final stage of its epic journey, through the green English fields. After breakfast on Putney Common, a train of thirty-two wagons set off, the first of which was draped in a Union Jack, which had been symbolically placed over a Spanish ensign. At the head of the cavalcade strode the *Centurion*'s officers, swords drawn, with the rest of the ship's company behind, guarding a total cargo of 298 chests of silver, 18 of gold, and another 20 barrels of gold dust.[3] They crossed Putney Bridge, passed the market gardens of Fulham, and made for the fashionable expanse of Hyde

Park. There they were met by kettle drummers, French horn players, and trumpeters, who conducted them along Piccadilly, past the royal palace of St. James's, and into Pall Mall, where George II's youngest son, the Duke of Cumberland, and daughters, the princesses Amelia and Caroline, greeted them.[4] To Britons who were increasingly inclined to think of themselves as modern-day Romans, it was a sight to savor. The parade, as several newspapers pointed out, was like an ancient triumph, with Anson playing the part of a Pompey or a Caesar.

On wound the wagons through that summer afternoon, to music and the beat of drums. The wealthy watched from their town houses in St. James's. The shopkeepers peered out of their shopfronts as the procession made its way east along the Strand. The merchants in the City of London saw it last: their eyes drawn instinctively toward the chests of money rather than anything else. Soon, as they well knew, the procession would reach the gates of the Tower of London, where the Royal Mint was based. There the Spanish gold was to be loaded into furnaces and, at a temperature of over a thousand degrees centigrade, melted down into Great British coins.

FOR THOSE WHO WATCHED the procession pass by, the treasure stood as tangible evidence of Britain's changing place in the world. For centuries Old England had been an isolated island nation on the rim of Europe, peripheral to the continent's important events. Great Britain, however, was of a quite different character. Rather than constrained, feudal, and godly, it was outward-looking, restless, and concerned, most of all, with the business of making money. This was the brisk, mercantile culture that was championed at all costs by the Whig administrations of Robert Walpole and now Henry Pelham and that Franklin had experienced during his years in London. Voltaire saw it too. He approved of Britain's devotion to trade, believing it fueled a virtuous circle. As people grew richer, Voltaire reasoned, they were lifted out of dependency. With this enhanced degree of freedom they had more leeway for commerce. Trade and that most celebrated thing, "liberty," were thus intimately connected. Over time the interaction of these two forces had started to have a broader effect, "whence arose the grandeur of the State," and by this means a distinctive mode of life had arisen in Britain, where the people loved liberty more than anywhere else. It was such a contrast with Voltaire's own country:

> In *France* the title of marquis is given *gratis* to any one who will accept of it; and whosoever arrives at *Paris* from the midst of the most remote provinces with money in his purse, and a name terminating in *ac* or *ille*, may strut about, and cry, Such a man as I! A man of my rank and figure! And may look down upon a trader with sovereign contempt; whilst the trader on the other side, by thus often hearing his profession treated so disdainfully, is fool enough to blush at it. However, I need not say which is most useful to a nation; a lord, powder'd in the tip of the mode, who knows exactly at what a clock the king rises and goes to bed; and who gives himself airs of grandeur and state, at the same time that he is acting the slave in the anti-chamber of a prime minister; or a merchant, who enriches his country, dispatches orders from his compting-house to *Surat* and *Grand Cairo*, and contributes to the felicity of the World.[5]

Almost exactly a hundred years before Anson's treasure had rolled through London, England had been tearing itself apart at the Battle of Marston Moor. A century on, this battle must have seemed a distant, almost parochial event to those inside coffee houses like Garraway's on Exchange Alley. Instead of battles, royal blood, and human souls, the chatter in such places was more likely to revolve around business opportunities or geopolitics. Some merchants looked across the Atlantic to the West Indies or American plantations for their money. Others were lured east. Much of the focus in the 1740s was on the rising fortunes of the East India Company. What opportunities awaited the

Company, the gossip ran, now that the wealthy Mughal Empire had collapsed? As to what the monarch, King George II, thought of all this, few people really cared. Gone were the days when the Crown governed everything, and in comparison with what had preceded them, the Hanoverians had shown themselves to be mild rulers. "No lurking, mischievous STUART," as one journalist would put it, dare "interfere in the management of public business."[6]

These were the attitudes of the City merchants and Fleet Street tradespeople who looked out at Anson's treasure wagons on July 4, 1744. Among such people, almost certainly, was the young printer William Strahan. It is a vividly imagined scene. Strahan—slender, dark-haired, blue-eyed, a tricorn hat, angled against the glare of the summer sun—leaning against the narrow opening to Wine Office Court as Anson's procession rolled along the street in front of him. Wine Office Court, an enclosed alleyway that jutted off the northern side of Fleet Street, was home to Strahan's printing business. For a young man keenly invested in the fortunes of the British Empire, the sight of such treasure yards from his door was not a thing to miss. This was one of the most exciting stories since the days of Drake or Raleigh. It can only have left Strahan wondering what it meant for him.

And yet for all the excitement, for Strahan the summer of 1744 was shadowed by sadness. Two months before that July day, Strahan had bid farewell to his oldest friend, David or "Davie" Hall, who had sailed for Philadelphia. In a life defined by movement and change, Hall had been one of the few constants for Strahan. They had served their apprenticeships under the same master in Edinburgh. After coming to London they had lived and worked together again. Strahan had always admired Hall's character, which mixed easy cheerfulness with serious application. He always remembered how Hall had shared his apprentice wages with his frail parents, despite only earning a "small Pittance." Afterward, when Strahan had set up his own printing house, Hall had been the best of his employees with his "constant and unwearied" effort.[7] Now he was gone.

Hall's decision to migrate might have been saddening, but it was understandable. Over the last decades, the lure of travel had grown as the bookshops had filled with exciting accounts of voyages and travels. For Hall, the colonies had a powerful appeal, and of them all, Pennsylvania held a particular charm. As well as being known for its tolerance and regularity, pamphlets printed in Europe and circulated widely had advertised its "delicate, pleasant, and wholesome"[8] climate. They had spoken of a landscape of golden meadows and bucolic creeks where frogs croaked and flying squirrels leapt from tree to tree. Unlike in some parts of America, Penn was said to have developed amicable relations with the Indigenous tribes,* adding social harmony to the natural beauty. These reports, for readers like Hall, were charged with romantic power. Migration was no longer simply a means of escape. Instead it was an adventurous opportunity in itself.

These were thoughts that played in many minds. But Hall's interest in America was able to take practical shape thanks to Strahan's transatlantic connections, in particular the friendship he had forged with James Read. Read was a refreshing character. He had none of the coarseness that was stereotypically connected with those from the colonies. Instead he was educated, commercially minded, and well

---

* Much was made of William Penn's friendly disposition toward the Native American tribes. In the 1770s, Benjamin West would produce a striking history painting that depicted the signing of the Treaty of Shackamaxon in the shade of a great elm tree in 1682. The treaty was signed by Penn and Tamanend, chief of chiefs of the Lenape nation, and it asserted that the settlers and Indigenous people would live in perpetual peace. By the 1730s, though, the optimism of this vision was fading. In a notorious episode in 1737 called "the Walking Purchase," Pennsylvanian officials defrauded the Lenape and Munsee out of as much as a million acres of land in the Delaware and Lehigh Valleys. The detail of this related back to one of the deeds from the 1680s, which stipulated that the tribes had agreed to the sale of the amount of territory a man could walk in the space of a day and a half northward of the settlement of Wrightstown. To exploit these terms to the maximum, a misleading map was produced, while the fastest runners were sought in the colony. Starting on September 19, 1737, one of them managed to cross around sixty miles in the agreed time. This episode left a bitter legacy.

connected. When Hall began to talk about America, for Strahan the obvious thing was to write Read a letter soliciting advice. The reply that had returned from Market Street, signed by his "humble Servant unknown"[9] was unexpected and intriguing. Philadelphia might have been more than three thousand miles away from London, but already in Fleet Street people were beginning to hear the name "Franklin." As Strahan would soon tell a friend, he was someone whose "Fame has long ago reached this Part of the World."[10]

Reading Franklin's letter, Strahan's excitement grew. Franklin's offer—guaranteed work, the prospect of some kind of partnership agreement if all went well, and the price of his return voyage home otherwise—was handsome indeed. Plans for Hall's departure went ahead over the winter of 1743–44. Strahan supplied Hall with a loan and several cases of fashionable Caslon type so he could immediately start work when he arrived. In the spring of 1744, Hall had bid his old friend farewell, gathered his belongings, and left.

The months that followed were anxious for Strahan. A transatlantic crossing was a risky affair at the best of times, but that summer brought acute dangers. While the war against Spain continued to simmer in the Caribbean, a larger and more complex conflict had burst into life on the European continent. The death of the Holy Roman Emperor Charles VI in 1740 triggered a dispute over who should succeed to the throne of Austria. Britain was drawn into this quarrel, which pitted against each other two ancient and formidable dynasties, the Hapsburgs and the Bourbons. Britain's decision to support the Hapsburg claimant, Maria Theresa, who was the daughter of Charles VI, led in a circuitous way to a declaration of war by the French on Great Britain at the start of 1744. Ever since, there had been rumors of a French invasion, and during the months that led up to Hall's departure, the papers were filled with stories of skirmishes in the Channel. For Hall, these reports carried extra menace. When his ship, the *Mercury Galley*, eventually sailed from Devon, she was escorted by four bomb ketches, which saw her safely into the Atlantic. Meanwhile, in London, the likelihood of disaster remained so high that Strahan found it difficult to insure Hall's passage. The premiums, he wrote, were rising by the day. Even with the paperwork complete he was left to fret, half-expecting any day to receive news that Hall had been "nabbed by the French."[11]

But in September, as quickly as could be hoped, news reached Wine Office Court of Hall's safe arrival. Apart from a persistent case of jaundice, his voyage had gone smoothly. Philadelphia, however, was not the tranquil utopia Hall had anticipated. A French attack was anticipated here too, and everywhere the atmosphere was nervous and belligerent. As he had explored Market Street and the riverside jetties, he was greeted with the sight of fortifications being installed. Picking up copies of Franklin's *Gazette*, he read appeals for "Gentleman Adventurers" who were needed to serve in the colony's infant navy. "My countrymen," Hall wrote, swiftly adopting a note of patriotism, "are doing all they can to make the French repent the war, having this week sent out four very fine privateers, one of them in all respects fitted out as well as one of His Majesty's twenty gun ships and, I believe, better manned."[12]

Of more immediate concern was Franklin's behavior. Having been so encouraging before Hall had sailed, in their first meetings the postmaster had seemed guarded and non-committal. Hall was left fretting that he had sailed halfway around the world on a false promise. Unsettled, he wrote to Strahan frequently over the winter and into the spring of 1745, asking for counsel on how best to proceed. Were the connection with Franklin not to work out, Hall wondered, would it be a good idea to open a coffee house on Front Street instead? Doing so would allow him to re-create some of the buzz of London on the banks of the Delaware. Strahan's reply was a study in prudence. He acknowledged the merit of the idea, but cautioned Hall to be careful. Failure was easy in the colonies. The wisest course was to stick at printing, the profession he knew, and in the meantime to "cultivate a good Correspondence with all the honest and creditable People you can."[13]

If things still did not work out, Strahan reminded Hall that a job remained open for him in Fleet Street where he now had two presses constantly busy. As well as taking on work from booksellers, Strahan had tentatively started to print some titles for himself too. His first experiment in this new line was a pamphlet, which, Strahan told Hall, had already earned him "a Dozen pounds." There were other projects pending, so if, after a winter of life in the colonies, Hall was still not settled, "*remember what I say to* you, I advise you by all means to return to Old England." "I don't doubt," Strahan added, "but I can do something for you at any time that will make it worth your while, in a Way perhaps you don't think of."[14]

Reading these letters feels like eavesdropping on a warm and intimate relationship. Strahan plays the role of elder brother. He is curious but wary of Hall's choices. He admonishes him to remember the responsibility of his debt and he consistently emphasizes the central point that an honest character is the bedrock of everything. He sends Hall little luxuries: sets of pens, the latest copies of the London magazines, a fine new hat, a ruffled shirt. Sometimes his letters take a more playful turn. "Are you like to get married yet?" he pries. "Surely the Girls are (some of them at least) tolerable?"[15] As for himself, Strahan goes on, his family continues to grow. In suitably mercantile style he tells Hall that he has another child, "upon the Stocks," adding cheerfully, "I believe I must send some of them to America to help to people some Colony there."[16]

These letters are a window into an intimate relationship between old friends, but a third individual gradually becomes more present as the months pass. Strahan's interest in Benjamin Franklin is inescapable. To begin with he, too, shows caution. "I dare say he will deal honourably by you,"[17] he writes to Hall in March 1745. But at the same time flights of fancy begin to creep in. Soon he is asking Hall to "Remember me in the kindest manner to Mr. Franklin and his Spouse." Hearing that Franklin and Deborah now have a daughter who is almost the same age as his own little girl, Rachel, he insists that a message is passed on to two-year-old Sally. "Her Husband," Strahan refers to his son William, "is this Day five Years old, and a brave thriving Fellow."[18]

It was not long before Strahan was speaking of Franklin in the handsomest terms. "You will," he wrote to Hall, "I dare say, have all the Reason in the World to like him; for he seems to me, by his Manner of writing to have a very good Heart, as well as to be a Man of Honour and Good Sense."[19]

STRAHAN WAS NOT YET thirty when Hall sailed for Philadelphia. Despite his youth he had already established himself as a fast-emerging name in London's printing trade. He had arrived in the capital in the mid-1730s from Edinburgh and started off working as a journeyman for old William Bowyer the printer on the south side of Fleet Street. Back then he worked chiefly as a compositor, building galleys for works like Defoe's *Tour Thro' the Whole Island of Great-Britain* or Swift's *Political Tracts*. Strahan lasted around two years with Bowyer before he left the security of an established business and the comfort of fourteen shillings a week to strike out alone.[20] The printing market was growing at that time. For a hard worker like Strahan, with a bright mind and a diligence that is instantly visible to anyone who examines his scrupulously written ledgers today, there was chance enough. He set up shop at Wine Office Court, across the alleyway from the Cheshire Cheese tavern on Fleet Street, and had soon taken on a contract for the bookseller Thomas Longman. By the time David Hall left for the colonies, he was already secure, with a pile of ready cash and even greater hopes for the future.

Strahan was enough of a businessman to realize that while Hall's departure was sad, it also presented him with an opportunity. In London, where publishing was more developed than in the colonies, printers usually took on jobs for the booksellers. While it was possible for printers to be both the producer and the seller, to do so was to risk upsetting the clients on whom they relied. As Strahan told Hall in his letters, he had dabbled in printing a pamphlet for himself, but this was as far as he was prepared to go in the London market at the moment. When it came to the colonies, though, there were no such considerations. He knew that if Hall succeeded in establishing himself in Philadelphia, then in the future he might be able to print books to export to him. In the short term, meanwhile, he could at least act as Hall's book buyer in London: finding copies in the shops of Little Britain and Paternoster Row and sending them on, with a little profit, to Philadelphia. Hall would be the vital link in this chain, but a hundred times better than Hall would be Franklin himself. Unlike Hall, Franklin was established. He understood the readers of Philadelphia. He knew their tastes and had their trust.

But there was also cause for caution. Was America really a wise place to do business? Weren't the colonies bedraggled outposts on the outer fringes of civilization? Bookshops and schools of learning there were few and far between. In fact, many people thought of Americans as being borderline barbaric. In 1729, Jonathan Swift had played acidly on this stereotype in his pamphlet, *A Modest Proposal for Preventing the Children of Poor People from being a Burthen to their Parents or the Country*. In this he proposed the eating of small children as a solution to the food shortages in Ireland. Although the Irish were the central targets of Swift's satire, the colonists came out of it badly too. Swift's "pamphleteer" claimed to have been given the idea by a "knowing *American* of my Acquaintance in *London*." This man informed him "that a young healthy Child, well nurs'd, is at a year old, a most *delicious*, *nourishing*, and *wholesome* Food, whether *stewed*, *roasted*, *baked*, or *boyled*; and I make no doubt, that it will equally serve in a *Fricassee*, or a *Ragoust*."[21]

In a society where xenophobia was rife, this picture of the backward colonists was easy to embrace. Strahan, however, knew more than the average Briton. He had met the impressive James Read, and he was on terms with a man called Peter Collinson who could tell him much more. Collinson traded as a woolen draper in Gracechurch Street in the City of London, but his real passion was for botany. In his drive to find the most interesting exotic plants, he had forged relationships with like-minded individuals in Philadelphia, and in particular with a Pennsylvanian outdoorsman called John Bartram, who conducted perilous journeys toward the frontier to collect plants for him. From Collinson, Strahan could see America's promise for himself. The packages he received from Bartram were not the product of a backward society. Instead, neatly labeled and utterly beguiling, they were tangible evidence of what was at least the beginnings of an inquisitive and enlightened culture.

Now Franklin had appeared in Strahan's life, bringing more evidence of American ingenuity. In his first letter Franklin described a printing business that was both established and expanding. Nothing could have been calculated to impress Strahan more. Over the following months an intriguing succession of letters reached Wine Office Court from Market Street. They described Pennsylvania in enticing terms. It was not the land of ill repute skeptical Britons thought it. Franklin's New Printing Office stood on a bustling commercial thoroughfare at the center of a flourishing city. It had a lending library stocked with books by thinkers like Robert Boyle, which operated under the strict management of a board of directors.

As Strahan was digesting all this, in the early autumn of 1744 something even more striking arrived. "I send you per this Ship a Box," wrote Franklin in an accompanying note, "containing 300 Copies of a Piece I have lately printed here."[22] The piece in question was an entirely new translation of an old classic: Cicero's *Cato Major, or his Discourse on Old-Age*. As Franklin had hinted, the book, which was infused with the eloquence and glamour of ancient Rome, was a *bona fide* Philadelphian performance. Cicero's text had been translated by James Logan, and the production was executed with grace and flair by Franklin. The title page blended black and red ink in harmonious and striking combination. The text was elegantly arranged. The binding was sumptuous. *Cato,* Strahan would have immediately recognized, was a statement: an object that fused together the best qualities of the Ancients and Moderns. In his preface, Franklin expressed his hope that this book was "a happy Omen, that *Philadelphia* shall become the Seat of the *American* Muses."[23]

Strahan must have been one of the very first people in Britain to have the privilege of examining it, and he can only have been filled with admiration. One book did not make a culture, but it could certainly demonstrate potential. And if Philadelphia was a cultural project, then Franklin had made it plain to Strahan from the very start that he wanted him to be part of it. "I have long wanted a Friend in London," Franklin confided in one of his earliest letters to Strahan, "whose Judgment I could depend on, to send me from time to time such new Pamphlets as are worth Reading on any Subject (Religious Controversy excepted) for there is no depending on Titles and Advertisements. This Favour I take the Freedom to beg of you, and shall lodge Money in your Hands for that purpose."[24]

To a twenty-first-century mind, this arrangement seems a relatively straightforward one. In the 1740s, though, the infrastructure for international trade was haphazard. For a book to travel from London to Market Street, it first had to be located in one of the bookshops, most likely those around St. Paul's or Paternoster Row. Then transport had to be arranged in one of the packets that crossed to Philadelphia. Due to the weather, these ships only traveled between the spring and autumn equinoxes, and even during the summer the voyages would be freighted with risk. Books were coveted items. On a crossing, one or two—or more—might vanish into the pockets of light-fingered sailors. They were vulnerable to water damage, too. A careless captain, an unlucky wave, or a leaky hold might ruin an entire consignment. A terrifying thought was that a vessel might be lost altogether. This was a nightmarish scenario that could wipe away months of earnings, or even bring about bankruptcy. Perhaps the only thing worse than a ship being lost was the prospect of its being seized as a prize by the Spanish or the French, with a crate of books ending up on sale in the markets of Paris or Madrid.

For a man like Strahan, who kept abreast of every farthing that passed through his business, these were concerns indeed. But even if the books did arrive safe in Market Street, the worries did not end there. In the Georgian world, money was in short supply and there was very little to regulate or safeguard capital flows. The cost of a crate of books could easily surpass £100. With Franklin at such a distance, he had no option but to buy these items on credit and then wait for the promised bill of exchange to settle the balance. For all that Franklin appeared an impressive character, and for all Philadelphia seemed a city of promise, Strahan knew this was a gamble. Later he would experience the pain of a trading relationship gone sour when James Read refused to honor a bill of over £130. Strahan would plead and threaten, but Read's debt would never be paid.[25]

But in 1744, as Franklin's first letters were delivered to the door of Wine Office Court, the situation was poised. Franklin, ten years Strahan's senior, was the older and more established of the two. Yet Strahan operated in a far more advanced market, and Franklin needed his help to access it. As such one has to read Franklin's early letters to Strahan as delicate, calculated attempts to gain his confidence. His language is brief and purposeful. He adds dashes of detail here and there that suggest his business acumen ("The Life of Du Renty, charg'd at 6s. per Doz. has *Price stitch'd Four pence* under the Title Page. Is there not some Mistake in the Charge?" he inquires[26]), and he keeps a constant tally of his debts, tracking the passage of his bills of exchange as they make their journeys across the Atlantic. By November 1744, the first £20 Strahan extended to Franklin had been serviced, and one of the most significant transatlantic capital flows in early American history was established.

The letters were not solely about business. "We have seldom any News on our Side the Globe that can be entertaining to you on yours,"

Franklin wrote modestly at the time of Hall's arrival in 1744. "All our Affairs are *petit*. They have a miniature Resemblance only, of the grand Things of Europe. Our Governments, Parliaments, Wars, Treaties, Expeditions, Factions, &c., tho' Matters of great and Serious Consequence to us, can seem but Trifles to you."[27]

To illustrate his point, Franklin mentioned the loss of one of Philadelphia's ships, a twenty-gun sloop, that had recently been fitted out as a privateer to harry the French. A fault in her design had led to a disaster when she capsized in the Delaware. A hundred men had drowned, and the people of Philadelphia had responded with the sort of horror that could only be matched in Britain if "Fifty Sail of the Line"[28] were destroyed in an all-out battle.

As well as military matters, Franklin kept Strahan informed of Hall's activities as he settled into his new life in Philadelphia. At other times he enticed Strahan with gossipy asides that revealed the grit and grain of life at the far side of the world. Having sent *Cato* to London, he now wondered whether Strahan would be interested in another curiosity. Franklin proposed to send him an account of a treaty that was currently being brokered between the colonies of Virginia, Pennsylvania, and Maryland, and the "united Five Nations of Indians." Franklin's offhand reference to "those Barbarians"[29] captures something of his attitude toward the Indigenous people at this time, but the offer suggests that he had sensed something important. Strahan, Franklin seems to have gathered, was drawn to politics. Franklin might have been tipped off by Hall that Strahan liked to study political debates, to scrutinize the personalities that were involved, and to untangle the complexities of a situation. In the years ahead this shared obsession with the political world would bind Franklin and Strahan together.

From the letters that have survived, it is clear that the two printers fell swiftly, effortlessly, into friendship. Books and trade, though, were never far from either's mind. In the hope of staying ahead of his competition, Franklin encouraged Strahan to send him copies of the

very "best Newspapers and Pamphlets constantly"[30] as well as titles
from the bookshops. Most of all, Franklin sought practical works. The
first crates packed for Market Street contained three dozen copies of
The Young Man's Companion; a guide to arithmetic by a schoolmaster
from Bedford; a dozen copies of Elisha Cole's old English Dictionary,
"containing many Thousand of Hard Words"; and an assorted mix of
grammars, vocabularies, and guides, as well as six copies of *Aesop's
Fables* in Latin.

Within a year, with their friendship blossoming and plans expanding, Franklin's requirements had changed. He was no longer exclusively interested in practical works. "I would not have you be too
nice in the Choice of Pamphlets you send me," he told Strahan. "Let
me have everything, good or bad, that makes a Noise and has a Run;
for I have Friends here of Different Tastes to oblige with the Sight
of them." He had heard that a new copy of Pope's collected works
was to be issued, and if there was anything from James Thomson the
Scottish poet, Strahan was to send it right away. "That charming Poet
has brought more Tears of Pleasure into my Eyes than all I ever read
before. I wish it were in my Power to return him any Part of the Joy
he has given me."[31]

Finding his theme, Franklin went on:

> Your authors know but little of the Fame they have on this Side
> the Ocean. We are a kind of Posterity in respect to them. We
> read their Works with perfect Impartiality, being at too great a
> Distance to be byassed by the Fashions, Parties and Prejudices
> that prevail among you. We know nothing of their personal
> Failings; the Blemishes in their character never reach us, and
> therefore the bright and amiable part strikes us with its full
> Force. They have never offended us or any of our Friends, and
> we have no Competitions with them, and therefore we praise
> and admire them without Restraint.[32]

*   *   *

IN FRANKLIN, STRAHAN HAD found a kindred spirit. They were not only temperamentally suited but also bound together by a shared faith in Britain's future. From Wine Office Court, Strahan could see right before him the same questing, front-footed culture that Franklin had experienced two decades before. And like Franklin he could just about imagine where this culture might lead: toward a society where the population was freer and better educated; a society filled with opportunities, where the people lived longer and happier lives.

As book merchants, Franklin and Strahan were a part of the social machinery that moved people toward this bright, beckoning world. But Strahan knew progress was not assured. In his Edinburgh childhood, when the Leith customs officer's son played games on the steep wynds that led up the hill toward the ancient castle, he was not called "Strahan" at all, but William Strachan, and his boyhood home was a place suspended between worlds. To the south, England called, a land of potential and progress. To the north, however, beyond the River Tay, the landscape rose and coarsened into what was considered a "melancholy country," filled with dark hills and heaths, that were

> often obscured by misty weather; narrow vallies, thinly inhabited, and bounded by precipices resounding with the fall of torrents; a soil so rugged, and a climate so dreary, as in many parts, to admit neither the amusements of pasturage, nor the labours of agriculture; the mournful dashing of waves along the friths and lakes that intersect the country; the portentous noises which every change of the wind, and every increase and diminution of the waters, is apt to raise, in a lonely region, full of echoes, and rocks, and caverns.[33]

In 1715, the year of Strahan's birth, an army of Highlanders had come out of these hills. These were tall, ferocious men, bound together by clan loyalty, who spoke "Erse" (Gaelic) and were armed with broadswords. Their aim was the restoration of the Stuarts to the British throne and the undoing of the Glorious Revolution. The rebellion caused panic. Growing up in the years after its suppression, Strahan grew used to people talking of the divided worlds: the land of kin, fealty, and hierarchy to the north, and the land of freedom to the south. By the time he had completed his apprenticeship at twenty-one, Strahan and his friend Davie Hall had decided where their allegiances lay. They had left Edinburgh and taken the high road to England.

London's lure was always strong. Some years before, a chronicler called Edward Chamberlayne had artfully explained "that in most Families of *England*, if there be any Son or Daughter that excels the rest in Beauty, or Wit, or perhaps Courage, or Industry, or any other rare Quality, *London* is their *North-Star*, and they are never at rest till they point directly thither."[34]

This was true for the 1730s, too, though now it was equally a destination for the Scots as the English. A generation later another Scottish migrant, James Boswell, would set down a memorable description of his arrival in London. He found himself "all life and Joy" when he reached Highgate Hill and got a clear view of the capital. Filled with a powerful sensation of possibility and wonder, Boswell recounted some words of Addison, burst into song, "and," he wrote, "my Soul bounded forth to a certain prospect of happy futurity."[35]

There were perils aplenty in the city, but there was a steadiness in Strahan's character that protected him from early disaster and enabled him to establish himself. In July 1738, two years after his arrival, Strahan married Margaret, daughter of the Reverend William Elphinston, an Episcopalian clergyman from Edinburgh. This is one of the few known facts from Strahan's early years in London, but it is a revealing one. It shows him just as keen to embark on a family life as he is ambitious to set himself up in business. It also connects him to the community of Scottish expatriates. This was a crucial platform for Strahan. Apart from the Elphinstons, Strahan also benefited from the friendship of the Edinburgh-born bookseller Andrew Millar, who kept a fashionable store on the Strand. It was a familiar story. A generation after the Acts of Union, the Scottish seemed to be everywhere in London. Some, like Millar or Strahan, were tradesmen. Others were working their way into powerful posts in the army, as politicians or lawyers. While this provided new arrivals like Strahan with a support network, it also earned them the time-worn prejudice of Londoners who derided them as nepotistic arrivistes. While people begrudgingly allowed the Scots to be "very fit for business," they were equally thought of as "intriguing, cunning, tricking" and lacking any "honour or conscience."[36] Such suspicions, in turn, generated something else. In their desire to fit in, to prove their loyalty, many Scots in London became the most zealous of Whigs and the greatest champions of Empire.

This was not enough, however, to dispel the prejudices of the English. Indeed it remained an article of faith in British politics that if bad things happened, they usually had their roots in Scotland. The Hanoverian dynasty might have ruled Britain for three decades, but in the north the old Jacobite cause lived on, with many important families hoping for a return of the deposed house of Stuart. This saddled the Scots with suspicion. Were these "North Britons" who formed such a prominent part of London's parliament, its law courts and its economy, true and honest subjects of King George? Or were they a dangerous, insurgent force, devoted friends of France and firm upholders of the Catholic faith, biding their time and awaiting their chance? A Strahan could Anglicize his name and fly the Union Jack and cheer in Piccadilly as Anson's treasure wagons trundled past, but was all this anything more than a performance?

By the early 1740s, the Jacobite cause seemed pretty much spent. Its figurehead, James Francis Edward Stuart, or "the Pretender" as the Whigs called him, had been born a prince of England and heir to the throne in 1688, but within months his father had been overthrown and his long, peripheral life as a royal exile had begun. Since then he had been an irritation for the Hanoverians and a diplomatic bargaining chip for the French and Spanish. But as the Pretender aged, his capacity for troublemaking had waned. Then, in the summer of 1745, something unsettling happened. As well as receiving letters from Franklin in Philadelphia, Strahan was also absorbing worrying news from the north.

In the July 1745 issue of the *Scots Magazine*—another title created in imitation of *Gentleman's Magazine*—there was a line to catch Strahan's attention. "There have lately been several rumors, of some designs upon Scotland or Ireland by the pretender's eldest son."[37] The son in question was Charles Edward Stuart. Born in Rome and raised a Catholic, he had a different energy to his father. He had studied the conflicts of the past decade, too, and they had given him an insight into modern methods of war. With his father's encouragement and financial support from France and Spain, the timing seemed ideal for an attempt of his own.

By mid-August Strahan knew there was substance to these rumors. A letter, written in Edinburgh on the thirteenth, addressed the story cautiously. "In the present Hurry of Affairs," it explained,

> many Reports must be expected, but it is not judg'd proper to insert them all without better Authority than has yet reach'd us: However, to satisfy our Readers in some measure, the common Report goes, that about 2000 Men are landed in Lochabar, or in some of the Western Islands, and that a Fleet of 50 or 60 Sail has been seen off the Isle of Skie. Whatever be in these Reports, it is certain the Government are now fully appris'd of the Designs of our Enemies, and are taking all proper Measures to render them abortive. This Day Colonel Gadiner's [sic] Dragoons march'd for Perth by Way of Stirling, whither also General Cope is about to set out.[38]

In the absence of clear intelligence, a frenzied mood took hold in London. At first this centered on a desire to accurately know the size of the rebel force and whether they were armed with broadswords or artillery. Reports trickled in. It became clear that the Jacobite army was substantial, that the prince had taken Edinburgh and defeated the king's army at Prestonpans. It was said that "many Persons of Figure and Distinction" had joined the rebel army, that "they had Plenty of Money, Provisions and warlike Stores,"[39] and that they were not satisfied with victories in the north, but were determined to march into England. By November London's newspapers were filled with extracts of letters, written by northern gentlemen. One from Berwick explained that "We have been here for some Time in the utmost Confusion, expecting the Highlanders to attack us every Day."[40]

Faced with a situation that bore similarities to 1660, when an army from Scotland had marched south to restore a Stuart to the throne, people looked to the press for clarity and leadership. A long article printed in the *Scots Magazine* in October depicted the revolt as a fortifying event. "The Romans never appeared so truly Roman by acquiring victory, as they did by resenting defeat," it cajoled.

> There is in a brave people, such as the *Romans* were, and such as I hope the *English* now are, a solidity, by which, instead of *breaking*, they *rebound* from a fall. The spirit which our countrymen has shown since a recent disgrace [the Battle of Prestonpans], does them more honour than ever they could have acquired by a partial success against a naked, needy, desperate crew. We are told of certain little noxious animals, which it is not at all difficult to destroy once you catch hold of them, but 'tis ten to one that they don't bite you while you are endeavouring to seize them. Our highland enemies are somewhat of this kind: they have had their *snap*, and, it must be owned, we have been confoundedly bit; but it is now more than probable their success will be fatal to themselves alone.[41]

As such the rebellion yielded an opportunity. It both brought people together and presented a chance to draw an old, dangerous poison. This, indeed, was the process that began in the months that followed. The newspapers tracked the story. Having reached as far south as Derby, the invasion stalled. An army led by the Duke of Cumberland was sent in pursuit. By spring the Jacobites had retreated all the way to the north-east of Scotland, and the armies finally came face-to-face at Culloden, near Inverness. News of Cumberland's spectacular victory reached London on April 23, 1746, St. George's Day. Cumberland's seven thousand men had routed a Jacobite force of six thousand, who had fled and scattered into the hills.

The reports of the victory shattered the tension of months. Boisterous crowds began to assemble in the streets. It was a time for any so-called North Britons to keep out of sight. For two young Scots, however, this was not an option. Alexander Carlyle and Tobias Smollett were in a coffee shop as the news arrived. Years later, when writing his *Autobiography*, Carlyle retained a powerful memory of that day. He remembered peering nervously out of the coffee house with Smollett and seeing the people working themselves into a "perfect uproar of joy." Both he and Smollett had appointments to keep, so they decided to edge into the street, keeping side by side. Finding the mob "riotous," they were forced to hide in an alleyway. There they removed their wigs to conceal their status and drew their swords. Before they moved again, Smollett cautioned Carlyle "against speaking a word, lest the mob should discover my country and become insolent, 'for John Bull' says he, 'is as haughty and valiant to-night as he was abject and cowardly on the Black Wednesday when the Highlanders were at Derby.'"[42]

TWO MONTHS LATER, ON July 5, 1746, shortly after sunrise on a Saturday morning, an express rider dismounted outside the New Printing Office on Market Street in Philadelphia. The letter he was carrying contained the first account of Cumberland's victory to reach America. Although the week's *Gazette* had already been printed, Franklin instantly ordered his pressmen to find a way of covering this breaking news story. The single sheet "SUPPLEMENT to the *Pennsylvania Gazette* No. 916" was issued later that day. It conveyed the "undoubted Intelligence":

> That the DUKE OF CUMBERLAND gave an intire Defeat to the Rebels on CULLODEN *Mure*, in a bloody Action, which lasted from Seven to Ten o'clock that Morning; in which the Earl of *Kilmarnock* and Lord *George Murray*, &c are Prisoners; and the PRETENDER'S Son was also taken Prisoner in Lady *Mackintosh's* House, about Two Hours after that.[43]

Just as it had in London, this report would instigate a series of "great Rejoicings" in Philadelphia, where the return of the Stuarts was a dreaded prospect. For months people across colonial America had been left to fret about such a possibility. What would it mean for them? Would entire territories be ceded to France? Would America be filled with political migrants and fugitives as it had been after 1660? The report printed by Franklin's press on July 5 dispelled all of this.

Franklin himself had particular reason to celebrate the return of political stability. The combination of war with France and the rebellion had produced such inflation in shipping costs and insurance premiums that he had been compelled to pause his book trade. More disquieting for him was Strahan's silence. For months in 1745–46, his letters to Wine Office Court had gone unanswered. At length Franklin had started to worry that his new friend had been cruelly snatched away. Disease and accidents were common features of life. But at a moment filled with such anti-Scottish feeling, there was the additional possibility that Strahan had been involved in some violent episode. By the spring of 1746, Franklin's concern had grown considerably. "I have had no Line from [you]," he wrote, "since that dated June 1745, which, with your equal Silence to our Friends Hall and

Read, made me apprehend that Death had depriv'd me of the Pleasure I promis'd myself in our growing Friendship."[44]

If Strahan was indeed gone, then at least Franklin had Hall for
solace. Although he had been wary at first, Franklin had grown to
respect Hall. He noticed in him many of the same virtues—industry,
honor, ability—that Strahan possessed. Franklin's first thought had
been to set Hall up in Barbados, along similar lines to his partnerships with printers in South Carolina and New York. Plans for Hall's
establishment had been made in the summer of 1745—materials
were sourced and a location scoped out—but as the date for his departure neared, Franklin felt a strange "Reluctance" to part with the
Scottish printer. Seeing how well Hall managed the press room in
Market Street, he opted to keep him close for a little longer.

Franklin and Hall doubtless pondered the meaning of Strahan's
silence and the state of his health. But they need not have worried.
Across the Atlantic in Wine Office Court, life was going on as pro-
ductively as ever. In fact, as others had submerged themselves in
reports of the rebellion, over the spring of 1746 Strahan had been
quietly applying himself to business. In particular, that spring he had
become involved in a hugely ambitious literary project. People had
long relied on old, substandard English dictionaries; plans were continually mooted to produce something better, only to be abandoned.
In the 1740s, however, talk among London's booksellers had begun
again. The time had come for a completely original, comprehensive, and authoritative reference work. To reduce the risk of financial disaster, a consortium of booksellers had been assembled. One
was Strahan's Scottish friend Andrew Millar, and it was presumably
through him that he had been approached with a view to printing the
work. It was to be a logistical challenge of the highest magnitude,
but for Strahan it was just the opportunity he had been awaiting. The
project would provide him with stability for months, perhaps even
years to come.

With the booksellers agreed and a printer engaged, only one thing was wanting. This was a figure of sufficient erudition and application to compile the materials. One of the booksellers, Robert Dodsley, had someone in mind. This was Samuel Johnson, one of Edward Cave's writers for the *Gentleman's Magazine*. Johnson was a man with a rare facility for language and a phenomenal memory, who had the ability to write with poetic flair at astonishing speed.

On June 18, 1746, a fortnight before the news of Culloden reached Philadelphia, at the Golden Anchor Inn in Holborn, Johnson signed a contract to compile the dictionary. Although he did not appreciate it yet, Strahan found himself uniquely connected to two of the great geniuses in all Western history: Benjamin Franklin of Philadelphia and Samuel Johnson of Lichfield.

Four

SPARKS

BY 1747, THREE YEARS had passed since David Hall had joined the *Mercury Galley* and set sail for Philadelphia. As the months and seasons rolled by, Strahan knew that the prospect of his friend returning was dwindling. Hall's regular letters told of a steady professional life at Franklin's, where he was now installed as foreman of his press room. There was something else too. Hall had found a girl. Mary or "Molly" Leacock was the daughter of a pewtersmith and shopkeeper who lived around the corner from Franklin's on Second Street. Mary and her sister Susannah were considered "the ranking belles"[1] of the city, highly sought-after for dances, boating parties on the Schuylkill, or picnics at Windmill Island. Jemmy Read had already married Susannah. Now a match looked likely between Davie and Molly.

This was happy news. But the idea of Hall's life moving so decisively forward was also something to put his friend into a ruminative mood. More than a decade had passed since they were both apprentices at Mossman and Brown's printing house in Edinburgh. Memories of the morning climbs up the Royal Mile to the shop on Craig's Close in the shadow of the castle were still vivid. Even then it was clear to Strahan there was something singular about Hall. He possessed "none of the Levity so common to that Stage of Life." He had a firmness, Strahan decided, a streak of seriousness and dependability that ran deep in a character that was otherwise "chearful, easy, and social."[2]

These traits indicated that a bright future lay ahead of Hall. The apprenticeship years were commonly considered to be vital in the formation of character. It was at this time that the sober, honest, and diligent boys would start to catch the eyes of their elders, while the lazy and thoughtless ones would gain bad reputations. Little incidents during these years could have an enormous effect on the course of a working person's life. This idea, of behavior and its consequences, lay at the heart of a series of prints by William Hogarth that appeared in the autumn of 1747. By this time Hogarth was firmly established as one of the leading artists of the day. He was known, best of all, for his series of narrative paintings that examined the fortunes of colorful figures in Georgian society: the beau, the rake, the prostitute. In his latest work, *Industry and Idleness*, Hogarth charted the fortunes of two young apprentices, Francis Goodchild and Tom Idle.

In the opening scene Hogarth shows Goodchild and Idle at a Spitalfields silk-weaver's, where they work at neighboring looms. From here the apprentices' stories diverge dramatically. Tom Idle's tale is one of squandered opportunities. Caring little for his work, he fritters his time away. At length he is turned out of his master's house. Lost to polite society, Idle is portrayed in ever-worsening circumstances, keeping increasingly desperate company. His sad tale approaches its inevitable conclusion when he is convicted of a capital crime and sentenced to death. Hogarth's last picture of Idle has him manacled inside a cart that rolls toward the gallows at Tyburn. The scene is filled with raucous London life. The crowd heaves and jeers and hoots. Idle, whose failing was to treat life as nothing more than mindless entertainment, has become mindless entertainment himself. Hogarth leaves the final, dismal scene to the imagination.[3]

To underline his moral, Hogarth arranged his illustrations cleverly. Each step of Tom Idle's story is interspersed with a scene from

Goodchild's life. From the very first plate he shows a brightness in
Goodchild's face. While Idle moons about nearby, Goodchild is a
paragon of productivity. Soon after he is pictured with the same focus inside a church, singing lustily as part of the congregation. So far
this was a conventional depiction of Protestant virtues. But Hogarth
adds a modern twist. As his master's favorite, Goodchild is promoted
from the loom to the counting house. Shortly after he marries his
master's daughter. The final two plates picture Goodchild in respectable old age. One shows him presiding over a spectacular feast in
an extravagant hall as part of his responsibilities as one of the sheriffs of London. The other is titled "THE INDUSTRIOUS 'PRENTICE,
Lord Mayor of London." In it, Goodchild rides through London's
streets in a golden carriage. Just as the crowds gathered to jeer Idle at
Tyburn, they congregate for Goodchild, too. But rather than pity or
scorn, they come to cheer. A vast crowd mills and jostles about his
coach. Faces peep from every window. The whole is a riot of sound
and energy, of the kind that must have accompanied George Anson's
procession through the capital in July 1744.

Hogarth's series caused a stir when it was published. As one Londoner wrote:

> WALKING some Weeks ago from *Temple-Bar* to *'Change* in a pen-
> sive Humour, I found myself interrupted at every Print-Shop by a
> Croud of People of all Ranks gazing at Mr. *Hogarth's* Prints of *Indus-
> try and Idleness*. Being thus disturbed in my then Train of Thoughts,
> my Curiosity was awakened to mingle with the Croud, to take a
> View of what they seemed so much to admire. Mr. *Hogarth's* Name
> at bottom was sufficient to fix my Attention on these celebrated
> Pieces, where I found an excellent and useful Moral discovered
> by the nicest Strokes of Art to the meanest Understanding.[4]

This was true. The moral was simple enough: good conduct has good
consequences. Franklin himself would typically sharpen this senti-

ment in one of his famous aphorisms: "Human felicity is produc'd not so much by great Pieces of good Fortune that seldom happen, as by little Advantages that occur every Day."[5] Goodchild was the very personification of this. Yet as Strahan would have seen in the print-shop windows, Hogarth's pictures carried a deeper meaning too. For the prints to work, as a tool for modifying behavior, people had to believe the story was plausible. Who in the past century would have thought a silk-weaver could become Lord Mayor of London? Sure enough, Thomas Wolsey might have been born a butcher's son, and Thomas Cromwell, according to legend, may have started out as a blacksmith's boy, but these were outliers: individuals of outstanding gifts. Hogarth's Goodchild, however, has scarcely any genius about him. His most notable quality is his "industriousness."

Industry and Idleness stands as evidence, then, that it was increasingly common for people to move upward through the social ranks to become one of the "better sort." And not only was such an elevation possible, it was also desirable. At the start of Hogarth's series, as Goodchild sits at his loom, he has little capacity for pleasure. His life is one of mechanical drudgery. His face is devoid of expression. But as his fortunes rise so does his level of happiness. When he stands by his master in the counting house there is a shine of satisfaction on his face. This shine breaks out into a smile as he marries the master's daughter. Embedded in Hogarth's series is a powerful message, one that links social mobility, power, material wealth, and happiness. Any thinking person can gauge Goodchild's motive when he stands for sheriff and later puts himself forward to be Lord Mayor of London. He is pursuing a greater state of temporal happiness.

Strahan, with his shrewd, analytical eye, would have absorbed all this. He could also enjoy the cheering reflection that Goodchild's tale matched his own in many particulars. Strahan had risen from apprentice to master. His marriage to Margaret, the clergyman's daughter, brought him respectability, and children and work had come his way.

As he liked to say, "he never had a child born, that Providence did not send some increase of income to provide for the increase of his household."[6] His story, too, was far from over. As 1747 drew to a close, he was approaching an exciting but daunting moment in his life. Strahan was now comfortably wealthy. With working and living conditions cramped in Wine Office Court, the time was coming to expand into larger premises. During the months ahead, Strahan would dismantle his press and move to a new location at 10 Little New Street, a few minutes' walk to the north. Here there was room for more presses, more workers, and greater projects. The future for William and Margaret Strahan and their children looked rosy indeed. And the news that kept arriving from Philadelphia was every bit as good.

ABOUT THE TIME THAT Hogarth's *Industry and Idleness* was published in London, far away in Philadelphia, Benjamin Franklin was standing in an artist's studio. He wore an elegant chestnut wig. His face was dusted with rouge. His body was wrapped in a midnight-green velvet coat. To gaze into Franklin's face in this, the most unfamiliar and one of the most compelling of his portraits, is to see a mix of defiance and discomfort. His self-consciousness is understandable. This was his coming-out portrait, and it was a risky affair. Painted on his retirement from trade, it captured a moment of transition. As anyone who saw the portrait would immediately have known, Franklin was abandoning the leather-aproned class in which he had rooted his identity for decades. He was embracing a new identity: that of a gentleman.

In the great game of eighteenth-century life, this was the boldest move. Almost all gentlemen were born into their rank. They had rich family histories, independent sources of wealth, and no need to toil with their hands from morning till night. They sat in separate pews in church, socialized in different spaces and in different ways. Like plants that grew in richer soils, the gentry were thought to possess something distinctive in their fiber. Not just something different, but something objectively and fundamentally better than was found in the common stock of ordinary people.

For years Franklin had quietly rebelled against this mode of thinking. As a boy in Boston he had regarded the scholars at Harvard with a mix of envy and contempt. In his very first published writing— the pseudonymous "Silence Dogood" essays that were printed, when Franklin was just sixteen, in his elder brother's newspaper, the *New-England Courant*—he had seized the chance to lampoon the foolish, ignorant young men the college was turning out. They were hardly of a superior mind, he suggested; rather they knew "little more than how to carry themselves handsomely, and enter a Room genteelly."[7] In contrast, Franklin's loyalty had been with the artisan class to which he belonged: the smiths, printers, chandlers, tailors, apothecaries. It was with these that he had lived in London and it was with them that he formed his Junto Club "of mutual improvement,"[8] when he returned to Philadelphia in 1727. In those days Franklin's attitude was pretty much that which had been so memorably expressed by Oliver Cromwell during the Civil War: "I had rather have a plain russet-coated captain that knows what he fights for and loves what he knows, than that which you call a gentleman and is nothing else."[9]

It is hard to pinpoint when Franklin's attitude started to change. Perhaps his faith in the middling sort was shaken by the failure of the *General Magazine*; there being too little interest among them to support even a single literary magazine. Or maybe it was his gradually increasing proximity to those of greater means. For years now, for instance, he had been visiting James Logan and browsing his magnificent library at Stenton. But Logan's attitude toward Franklin, while somewhat encouraging, had its limits. His support for Franklin's projects was often lukewarm, and he believed the colonial population to be, in general, "too ignorant to be scientifically engaged."[10] Maybe, too, the emergencies of the recent wars had made Franklin painfully aware of his limitations. There was one terrifying moment, in 1747, when French and Spanish privateers attacked trading vessels on the Delaware, just twenty miles downriver from Philadelphia. Franklin was as alarmed as everyone by the news, which drove him to write the pamphlet *Plain Truth*. Although this included his rallying cry, "we, the middling People, the Tradesmen, Shopkeepers, and Farmers of this Province and City!,"[11] he knew that ultimate political power, the power to achieve things and effect change, rested with the elite.

Considerations like these, perhaps allied with a deeper sense of his own destiny, drove Franklin into a dilemma familiar in twenty-first-century culture. How does one transform oneself into something new, into something entirely different, and into the thing one really believes oneself to be? In Franklin's portrait by Robert Feke, ideas like these seem to be playing through his mind. As ever, Franklin has choreographed his performance carefully. Anticipating the scorn he would face if his transformation was too bold, Franklin has chosen to wear a conservative blend of muted greens and browns. His status as a "New Man" is suggested by the background, which shows a broad sweep of the Pennsylvanian landscape, filled with hills, clouds, and sky. The sun is rising. Here, the portrait seems to say, is a new man in the New World at the start of a new day.

Franklin was right to tread carefully. He knew deep down that he was spectacularly underqualified for this change. He was a man with little hereditary honor, who had no formal schooling, who had always lived in rented accommodation and had, for the past two decades, toiled for his living among the ordinary classes. Unlike Francis Goodchild, he had never married his master's daughter to be welcomed by his new family into a fine town house. Instead, Franklin was married to Deborah Read, who was rarely invited to accompany her husband when he was asked to dine with the great figures of the city. Although his shift in status had been gradual, he understood that sitting for a portrait dressed in the costume of a gentleman was a very public act. Georgians took great glee in knocking down people like him. They were derided as impostors, social climbers, subversives. Such tags may well have haunted Franklin at this time. As he wrote in the 1746 edition of *Poor Richard's*, "The Sting of a Reproach, is the Truth of it."[12]

The second half of the 1740s, then, were delicate ones for Franklin. In a society as ruthless as colonial Pennsylvania, he risked being ostracized by both the class he was leaving as well as the one he was trying to join. What Deborah made of the process is unrecorded, but to have a husband so set on changing his identity must have brought its challenges. Looking at Feke's portrait, she could either have felt proud of his accomplishments or perplexed by his actions. Whether she needed it or not, the painting was confirmation that Franklin would not be retiring to a sleepy life by the banks of the Schuylkill. There was more, much more, that he wanted to do.

While the portrait captured the decisive moment of visual transformation, Franklin's modification progressed in a series of careful steps. David Hall's arrival was central to this. With a skilled and trustworthy deputy, Franklin was finally able to remove himself from the strain of manual work. As Hall moved into his old home in Market Street, Benjamin and Deborah, their children William and Sarah, and a number of newly acquired slaves—another indicator of his social standing—moved to a quieter part of town. There he began to act in ways appropriate to his new station in life. In 1748, he was elected to the city council. The following year he was appointed a justice of the peace, and he started to agitate for a series of social reforms. All of this helped boost Franklin's gentlemanly credentials, but nothing inflated his reputation as an extraordinary citizen quite like his embrace of science.

Franklin's drift toward science has often been interpreted as a natural blossoming of his inner character. Shorn of the cares of the working life, his mind was at last free to expand and settle on the teasing problems of Nature. There is certainly truth in this, but Franklin's scientific work must be seen also in the light of his efforts

to acquire social status. For while Franklin lacked the birth credentials of a gentleman, science provided him with a different way of
distinguishing himself. Due to the time that experimentation took
and because it usually required access to specialist books and apparatus, science had come to be thought of as a refined activity. Moreover, especially through stories of Sir Isaac Newton's recent work
on gravity and motion, the persona of the "natural philosopher" had
come to have a distinct social cachet. When Voltaire visited London
in the 1720s, for instance, he found Newton "the subject of every
one's discourse,"[13] in spite of the fact that very few people actually
comprehended what it was that he had done.

From time to time the glow of British science was experienced
in Philadelphia. Logan had had a letter extracted in the *Philosophical
Transactions* of the Royal Society in 1735, when he sought to explain
why forks of lightning should appear "crooked and angular," instead of
falling directly to earth.[14] The city's botanist John Bartram also experienced the thrill of having several papers—one on the arrangement
of rattlesnakes' teeth, another on a curious wasps' nest—accepted
for publication in the *Transactions*. Bartram owed this success to his
connection to Peter Collinson, the woolen draper and botanist. Collinson was one of the earliest enthusiasts for American science, and
Franklin could see how Bartram's local reputation had been enhanced
by this international friendship. Bartram was no more refined than
Franklin was. But he had something few others could match. He had
a powerful link with the intellectual center.

Franklin must also have realized that he was temperamentally
suited to the rigors of scientific work. For years in Market Street, he
had fiddled with his printing press, with recipes for ink and methods
for producing paper, accumulating practical skills. He had the knack
of noticing things too. When returning from England to America in
1726, for instance, he kept a voyaging journal that was filled with
descriptions of the marine life, the fluctuations of the atmosphere: of
rainbows and eclipses and the currents that tugged beneath the ship's

hull. This habit endured when he was back in Philadelphia. Franklin filled pages of the *Gazette* with stories of thunder gusts, lunar eclipses, and lightning strikes.

> From Newcastle we hear that on Tuesday the 8th instant, the lightning fell upon a house within a few miles of that place, in which it killed 3 dogs, struck several persons deaf, and split a woman's nose in a surprizing manner.[15]

For years Franklin had been too busy to investigate the second half of this story. Just what was surprising? What had really happened? If these questions had bothered him then, now the moment had come for him to engage with them. At last a gulf of time was opening up before him. He both wanted and needed to distinguish himself. And as so often happened during Franklin's life, at just the right moment something unexpected turned up. This time it was a package sent from London by Peter Collinson. It contained the latest news about electricity.

THE ANCIENT GREEKS HAD noticed that something peculiar happened when pieces of amber, the translucent resin of long-dead trees, were rubbed together. A strange attractive quality seemed to arise so that the amber could draw other light objects toward it. Out of the Greek for amber, "ēlektron," developed the word "electric," which was used by the English polymath Sir Thomas Browne in the 1640s to describe objects that could be charged into a magnetic state by friction. In the years after Browne, people started to call this power "electricity," though no one in the age of Newton, Hooke, or Boyle had the slightest idea what it was.

Had Franklin investigated electricity during his London years in the 1720s, he would have learned that people knew little more about it then than the Greeks had thousands of years before. Only a few tentative discoveries had been made. People had noticed that electricity was present in several other objects in addition to amber, and they had studied the kind of materials the electrical force was able to disturb—feathers, chaff, or leaf brass. To show this power in action, some enthusiasts had developed "electrical machines." These peculiar-looking contraptions usually involved a pole that was skewered through the center of a glass globe. When a handle was fastened to one end of the pole, it was possible for an operator to spin the globe and create an electric force or atmosphere. While this looked impressive, much the same effect could be obtained by rubbing a glass tube with something like sheep's wool. Indeed, it was while doing just this in the spring of 1729 that a man called Stephen Gray began a remarkable series of experiments.

For many years Gray had been a peripheral figure in London's scientific community. He was known for his flair for grinding lenses and his association with John Flamsteed, the old Astronomer Royal. By 1729, though, most of those who knew him would have reasoned that Gray's contributions to natural philosophy were at an end. Now in his sixties, he lived in retirement, an old man among the scholars at the Charterhouse in London. Here, one day, Gray decided to investigate the properties of an electrified glass tube. In a series of progressive experiments, Gray discovered that the "electric virtue" was not confined exclusively to the glass, but that it could be passed on (that is, conducted) to other materials. Gray's discovery came through a mixture of luck and instinct. While fiddling with his glass tube, he picked up a piece of cork that happened to be nearby. He plugged this into one end of the tube. Next, Gray bored a hole through an ivory ball, then mounted it onto a stick that he pushed into the cork. Once he electrified the tube, he was intrigued to see that the ivory ball—at the far end of his eccentric apparatus—was able to attract and repel a feather. Equally interesting was the fact that it seemed to be able to do so with the same force as had the glass tube.

From this moment onward, Gray's obsession was to find out how far the "electric virtue" could travel, and which materials would best conduct it. By the time that his work was detailed in a paper for the

Royal Society, he had achieved the astonishing feat of passing electricity through 886 feet of packthread, "at which amazing distance," one bemused journalist wrote, "it will impregnate a ball of ivory with the same virtue as the tube from which it was derived."[16] This was a detail to tantalize. But what made Gray's discoveries of 1729–30 irresistible to the scientific community was the disclosure that during the course of his research he had electrified a human being.

The person in question remained nameless. But Gray revealed it was a boy of eight or nine years old, presumably one of the pupils at the Charterhouse. Gray had arranged for the boy to be suspended horizontally in his chambers, with a length of "hair-line" under his breast and thighs. He then electrified his glass tube and held it to the soles of the boy's feet. At the same instant a piece of leaf brass—a whisper-thin sliver of metal—was "attracted to the Boy's Face with much Vigour." It rose, Gray wrote with a mixture of surprise and triumph, "to the Hight of eight, and sometimes ten Inches."[17]

Ever since, scientific showmen had sought to exploit electricity's potential for performance. Soon the idea of the electrical show was established in Europe. These usually took place after sunset so the white light of a spark could cut dramatically through the darkness. The flashes were always too quick for even the keenest of eyes, but the smell that lingered acted powerfully on the audience's imaginations. Some said the stench reminded them of oil of vitriol; others that it was like phosphorus. More intrigue was generated by the choreography. Some repeated Gray's "dangling boy" experiment, which became a cherished parlor trick. A German professor called Georg Matthias Bose, meanwhile, pioneered more sensational acts. In one favorite part of his performance, Bose would select a pretty girl from the audience and invite her to accompany him on stage. He would then ask her to stand on an insulated stool while an assistant charged her body with electricity. Once she was primed, the men in the audience would be invited forward for a kiss, but as they leaned in toward her lips, sparks would dart out, sending them scurrying away.

Bose's tricks were quickly replicated by others, thrilling audiences across Europe. The demonstrations were so enchanting because they seemed to expose, for a fraction of time, the secrets of Nature. In some ways this was similar to what Newton had achieved with his work on gravity in the generation before. But while Newton focused on the exterior world—the universe of planets and stars—electricity was a force that seemed to arise from within. As one writer reflected, "Electricity became all the subject in vogue, princes were willing to see this new fire which a man produced from himself, and which did not descend from heaven."[18]

There was detail here to stir Franklin's interest in several ways. His zest for empirical science was one thing. Also interesting was electricity's connection to polite society. The sort of people who were attending electrical performances in London, Paris, or Berlin also enjoyed a night out at the theater or a stroll in the pleasure gardens at Vauxhall or Ranelagh. A feature on electricity, printed in *The Gentleman's Magazine* in April 1745, listed the members of European royal houses who had fallen for the charms of the science. Among them was the Governess of the Netherlands, the Margravine of Brandenburg, and the Duke and Duchess of Gotha, who "had a course of lectures on electricity read to them by a professor."

> The *Hanoverian* ladies of quality did yet more, they procured machines, and try'd the experiments themselves, and electricity took place of quadrille. Even *Poland* itself, which is not accounted very polite, was not insensible to these wonders of nature. The grand chancellor of *Poland*, Zaluski, had an electric machine brought to him, made by his order, from *Leipzig*.[19]

These words featured in the article that fell into Franklin's hands toward the end of 1746 or early 1747. For years before Franklin's connection with Strahan was forged, Peter Collinson had acted as the London book-buying agent for the Library of Philadelphia. Every year a package assembled by Collinson would arrive from London, generating a flutter of excitement among the library's hundred or so members. In this year's consignment, Collinson had included a sixpenny pamphlet called *Acta Germanica*, inside which was a brief overview of the state of electrical science. Collinson had put something else inside the crate too: something exceptionally exciting and, as Europeans were at that time discovering, really quite dangerous.

Soon Franklin was writing personally to Collinson, to acknowledge his "kind present of an electric tube, with directions for using it." The tube's arrival "has put several of us on making electrical experiments," Franklin explained, "in which we have observed some particular phaenomena that we look upon to be new." Promising to describe these further in due course, Franklin signed off:

> For my own part, I never was before engaged in any study that so totally engrossed my attention and my time as this has lately done; for what with making experiments when I can be alone, and repeating them to my Friends and Acquaintance, who, from the novelty of the thing, come continually in crouds to see them, I have, during some months past, had little leisure for any thing else.[20]

Franklin was still a working printer in Market Street at the time Collinson's package arrived. It is tempting to picture him sitting quietly at his desk, eyeing the strange glass tube and running a finger down the list of instructions as Hall and the pressmen bustle in the background. Like Newton picking up a prism or Christiaan Huygens gazing through a telescope for the first time, this was a powerful moment of encounter in the history of science.

It was also a potentially lethal one. Until the mid-1740s, those wanting to use electricity had only been able to do so by "exciting" it: either manually by rubbing an object, or mechanically with the aid of a machine. The apparatus Collinson had sent to Philadelphia, however, changed all this. Once prepared, the glass tube or jar was capable of containing electrical power for use when required. The science of what was happening remained barely understood. But preparing one of these jars or tubes was simple enough if the steps were followed. First it was important to wrap the glass in tinfoil. Then it was filled with water. Iron filings were dropped inside, and a wire was poked through the lid. One of the first to tinker with such a contraption was Pieter van Musschenbroek, a professor at the University of Leiden in the Netherlands. Casually touching the wire, Musschenbroek received a shock so powerful it can still just about be felt today by anyone who reads the letter he composed afterward to a friend in Paris. He wrote of the "new but terrible experiment, which I advise you never to try yourself, nor would I, who experienced it and survived by the grace of God, do it again for all the kingdom of France."[21]

Of course, Musschenbroek could not have written anything more calculated to encourage others to replicate his work. Getting wind of the "Leyden jar," Johann Heinrich Winckler, a professor of ancient languages at Leipzig, assembled a device of his own. Soon he was producing massive, potent sparks. "They can be seen (even in the Day time)," Winckler wrote, "and heard at the Distance of fifty Yards. They represent a Beam like Lightning, of a clear and compact Line of Fire; and they give a Sound that frightens the People that hear it." The effects of the sparks on a person, he revealed, were equally profound.

> It put my Blood into great Agitation; so that I was afraid of an ardent Fever; and was obliged to use refrigerating Medicines. I felt a Heaviness in my Head, as if I had a Stone lying upon it. It gave me twice a Bleeding at my Nose, to which I am not inclined. My Wife, who had only received the electrical Flash twice, found herself so weak after it, that she could hardly walk. A week after, she received only once the electrical Flash; a few Minutes after it she bled at the Nose.[22]

Others put the Leyden jar to other use. In Paris the Abbé Jean-Antoine Nollet enthralled the court of King Louis XV by using the jar to deliver simultaneous electric shocks to people standing in a circle. Nollet asked the first and last person to touch the inner and outer part of a Leyden jar. The instant they did, everyone in the circle leapt into the air. One of Nollet's demonstrations involved a circle of no fewer than 180 soldiers. On another occasion, in a lively union of the spiritual and scientific worlds, Nollet performed the same trick on several hundred monks. Electrical fever crossed the Channel too. Around the time Collinson's crate arrived in Philadelphia, accounts of electrical experiments were being regularly received by fellows of the Royal Society. In December 1746, they heard that a Mr. Baker had successfully electrified "a Myrtle tree, of between 2 or 3 Feet in Height, growing in a Pot, at the Seat of the Duke of *Montague* at *Ditton*." Montague had watched at a safe distance, seeing "Streams of fine purple Fire" issue from the branches.[23]

There is a similar puckish quality to stories of Franklin's earliest electrical work. Once he had mastered the use of the Leyden jar, there was nothing to stop him and a group of like-minded friends from performing the same tricks in provincial Philadelphia as a fellow of the Royal Society might in the universities of England. Indeed, Franklin's distance from the established centers of science in London gave him the ability to work with freedom and a spirit of adventure. Stories from this time are among the most vibrant of any in Franklin's life. Electricity parties were organized by night, so that Philadelphians could watch as sparks flew from electrified objects. There were circle charges like Nollet's; bells were made to tinkle; barrels of rum were set alight; and on one fondly remembered occasion Franklin even electrified a portrait of King George II so the golden frame around his head shone with electric life.

Within a short span of time, Franklin achieved a proficiency with electricity that by 1748–49 surpassed that of anyone else in the colonies. He could now claim membership of an entirely new kind of social order, one that did not fit neatly into traditional divisions between the "better" or "meaner" sort. It was an international fellowship of philosophers and thinkers.

There might have been a playfulness to Franklin's electrical work, but from the start he treated the subject seriously. Methodical in his ways, Franklin observed and documented everything he did. He was soon beginning to doubt the received wisdom that electricity was a force that could be excited within objects. Instead, one of his first realizations was that electricity was everywhere and that rather than appearing or disappearing as commanded, it was actually transferred from one object to another. Sometimes, he realized, there would be a great imbalance between the amount of electricity in one object and another. One might have too much, and another too little. When these objects were placed in proximity, a spark or shock would be generated as electricity jumped from one to the other. To explain this imbalance with greater precision, he coined the contrasting terms positive and negative to describe different types of electric charges.

Following this discovery, which was unknown to European science, Franklin was able to start picturing a new physical system, with electricity sometimes remaining inside an object, but at other times flowing from one to another in search of balance. His discoveries began to accumulate:

1. THAT it is a real *Element*, intimately united with all other matter, from whence it is *collected* by the tube, or sphere, and not *created* by the friction
2. That tho' it will fire inflammable bodies, itself has no sensible heat
3. That it doth not, like common matter, take up any perceptible time in passing thro' great portions of space
4. That bodies replete with this fire strongly attract such as have less of it, and repel such as have an equal quantity

5. That it will live in water, a river not being sufficient to quench the smallest spark of it
6. That, contrary to other matter, it is more strongly attracted by slender sharp points, than by solid blunt bodies[24]

Wondering whether there was practical use for any of this, Franklin decided to investigate whether electrifying objects or animals could have any beneficial effects. While many birds died, the results did not suggest anything obvious. Everything Franklin did, though, was written down for the benefit of fellow "electricians" in Europe. Between 1747 and 1749, Franklin sent a series of letters detailing his research to Collinson in London, who, in turn, shared them with others in London's scientific community. Very soon whispers began, of the curious experiments that were being undertaken by "a Gentleman in Philadelphia." It was just the description Franklin would have relished.

In the spring of 1749, Franklin wrote again to Collinson. He had decided that the best time for electrical research was in the winter, when the atmosphere was damp. With the hot Philadelphian summer coming on, it was time for a rest.

To put an End to them for this season somewhat humorously in a Party of Pleasure on the Banks of SchuylKill, (where Spirits are at the same Time to be fired by a Spark sent from Side to Side thro' the River). A Turky is to be killed for our Dinners by the Electrical Shock; and roasted by the electrical Jack, before a Fire kindled by the Electrified Bottle; when the Healths of all the famous Electricians in England, France and Germany, are to be drank in Electrified Bumpers, under the Discharge of Guns from the Electrical Battery.[25]

AS THE MID-CENTURY NEARED, the study of electricity was more than just a science. It was a symbol of the new kind of dynamic, exhilarating form of human life that was beginning to emerge. Most people, to be sure, continued on in their old ways. Their lives were dictated, as they always had been, by the rhythms of the seasons and the teachings of the church. But for a growing few, a different kind of human existence was becoming possible. This was a life that mixed ambition and pleasure, involved more risk but promised more reward. The electrical spark was a powerful emblem of this. To see a darkened theater lit up by a flash of electricity was more than just pure drama. It was to witness a force of nature being changed from its latent to its active state. For some—like Franklin and Strahan, Collinson or Hall—a parallel process was at work in the social world, on both sides of the Atlantic. People's lives were being animated, their spirits were being charged, their potential was being unlocked. They were being set free.

It was this belief that bound Franklin and Strahan together. For years now the flow of letters had continued between Philadelphia and London, their tone a mix of earnestness and affection. Franklin would always begin with requests for books or news. But he always reserved a paragraph toward the end for domestic asides. One running theme was his plan to visit London so that he could meet Strahan in person and see the city he had left twenty years before. Deborah Franklin and Margaret Strahan had struck up a parallel friendship, and the four of them relished the prospect of a meeting: of dining at Strahan's in Little New Street, or visiting the theater at Covent Garden. Enticing as these ideas were, the plans had not yet matured. Franklin's civic commitments created a barrier that was proving too difficult to navigate. In a letter to Strahan in October 1749, he again left his friend in suspense. "I have not laid aside my intention of seeing England," Franklin explained, "and believe shall execute it next year, if nothing extraordinary occurs, in which your conversation is not one of the least pleasures I propose to myself."[26]

He did, however, have other news. The 1740s were not only a transformational decade for Franklin himself; the city around him had evolved too. Ten years ago, Philadelphia still had much of its frontier feel. Among the newly arrived migrants like Hall were many who could recall the earliest days of the colony, when a few dwellings huddled on the edge of the Delaware and Thomas Holme's hopeful grid of streets was little more than that. During the 1740s, though, most of those with memories of the primitive settlement had died, and Philadelphia had progressed into a new phase of growth. To the west of the city, settlers and farmers had probed farther into the landscape, generating new tensions with the Indigenous people. Traffic on the river had increased too. While the war with France and Spain made people nervous, it had also catalyzed trade. The city's growth had been strong and steady. Its population had grown from an estimated ten thousand in 1739 to more than thirteen thousand by 1750.

Franklin was one of the beneficiaries. Much later on, reflecting on this period of his life, he would admit he had "on the whole abundant Reason to be satisfied with my being established in Pennsylvania."[27] The partnership terms he agreed with Hall were generous, and they left him with an income of around £600 a year, a sum that would continue to come his way until the mid-1760s. But with his new position in the hierarchy, Franklin felt the pressure of new responsibilities. Having set himself up as a leading citizen, he wanted to redouble his efforts to be a useful member of the community. For, while he had achieved a personal ambition, there was still so much to be done for Pennsylvania as a whole.

An old itch, in particular, still bothered him. A key motivation for launching the *General Magazine* was to educate those around him. The magazine was to be a vehicle of ideas; a cultural forum on which Americans could nourish their minds. This was a noble idea, but years after the quarrel with the long-vanished Webbe, nothing had yet been achieved. Indeed, in the 1740s Franklin had suffered another failure, when his attempts to establish an "American Philosophical Society" petered out. Although he had been convinced that enough "Virtuosi" or "ingenious Men" existed to support such a body—modeled on Britain's Royal Society—events had, just as with the magazine, proved him wrong.[28]

In his letter to Strahan, Franklin divulged his latest solution to this problem. He had long been irritated by the fact that Philadelphia did not have an educational establishment of its own. The sons of the gentry were forced to either rely on private tutors, or suffer what Franklin termed "the hazard" of leaving the city altogether for Harvard, or William and Mary, or the new College of New Jersey about eighty miles away in Newark. Ever since his failures with the *General Magazine* and the American Philosophical Society, Franklin had been thinking about a different approach. If the older generation of colonists were not to be relied upon, then the focus should naturally shift toward the next. He had arrived at the conclusion that the time was right for him to push forward a project to establish a school or academy in Philadelphia. Unlike the *General Magazine*, this was not to be a private venture that was poorly resourced and full of risk. Instead, Franklin felt confident to propose a community-funded civic enterprise, grounded in altruism instead of entrepreneurialism.

Franklin's campaign had begun in August. He asked Hall to print an anonymous letter that introduced the project on the first page of the *Gazette*. Franklin's letter was subtle, persuasive, and elegant. After a statement of intent and an appeal to colonial pride, he included the translation of a letter by the Roman imperial governor Pliny the Younger to his friend Tacitus. Pliny had met a boy in his native Como who was forced to travel to Milan for his education. He was shocked by this. "Where can they be placed more agreeably," he asked Tacitus, "than in their own country, or instructed with more safety, and less expence, than at home, and under the eye of their parents?"[29]

It turned out that Franklin's anonymous letter was just the prelude to a more complete performance. Soon after, he produced an unsigned pamphlet called *Proposals Relating to the Education of Youth in Pennsilvania*. In it Franklin invited his readers to picture their ideal academy. It would be in a spacious house that was situated either in the center of Philadelphia or in the countryside nearby. The exact location was not critical, but the availability of outside space was. The academy would open out onto the broad Pennsylvanian landscape, or would have its own garden, orchard, meadow, and fields. Inside the house would be an excellent library, and the classroom would be furnished with globes and mathematical and scientific apparatuses. The walls would be covered with maps depicting all of the known geographies of the world, while the scholars would also have access to instructive "Prints, of all Kinds, Prospects, Buildings and Machines."[30]

The student population would be made up of boarding and day scholars, and the management of the school would be given to a rector, "a Man of good Understanding, good Morals, diligent and patient, learn'd in the Languages and Sciences, and a correct, pure Speaker and Writer of the *English* Tongue." Under his superintendence, the scholars would divide their time between the classroom and the open air. To keep their minds supple, Franklin argued, it was important they remain active in body as well as mind. They would be "frequently exercis'd in Running, Leaping, Wrestling, and Swimming, &c."[31] So animated, they would be ideally primed for the central business of learning. In a rousing passage, he affirmed:

> As to their STUDIES, it would be well if they could be taught *every Thing* that is useful, and *every Thing* that is ornamental: But Art is long, and their Time is short. It is therefore propos'd that they learn those Things that are likely to be *most useful* and *most ornamental*. Regard being had to the several Professions for which they are intended.[32]

It was at this point that Franklin departed from traditional ideas of education. Once inside their classroom, the scholars would be guided on an educational journey by the tutors. There would be a little formal study, especially with regard to handwriting, grammar, and pronunciation, but otherwise the flow of ideas was to be organic. History was to be the keystone subject. When studying the force of oratory, for example, in the time of Ancient Rome or Greece, the tutor could seize the opportunity to branch off into an explanation of language and its use. When examining the downfall of empires or nations, the students would be perfectly primed to study political philosophy and the importance of civil order. It was all to be inter-connected and harmonious. For instance: "While they are reading Natural History, might not a little *Gardening*, *Planting*, *Grafting*, In-oculating, &c. be taught and practised; and now and then Excursions be made to the neighbouring Plantations of the best Farmers, their Methods observ'd and reason'd upon for the Information of Youth?"[33]

All this was rooted much more in Franklin's belief in human potential than it was in the traditional forms of education, where the emphasis lay much more on refining the students. In short, Franklin was proposing an enlightened academy. His instincts were practi-cal and his inspiration came chiefly from a number of English and Scottish pedagogues, like John Locke, George Turnbull, and David Fordyce. The kind of scholar to emerge from this establishment would be physically strong and mentally equipped. They would not be too polite or too worthy to hold a trowel or push a wheelbarrow. Nor would they have had their minds shadowed by God. As one recent academic has pointed out, "As a document in American edu-cational history, Franklin's *Proposals* is remarkable for what it did not include: religion."[34] Apart from a fleeting mention that talked gener-ally about the "usefulness" of religion to society, there was hardly any spiritual dimension to Franklin's proposal at all. His objective was to prepare students for the demands of this world, not the next.

Franklin sent a copy of his *Proposals* to Little New Street for in-spection in October 1749. Instinctively he knew that Strahan, the front-footed, practical man of business, would approve. Strahan, like Franklin, was convinced of the merits of this new, modern, enlightened life. The same, however, could not be said of everyone. Indeed the man who would become the greatest critic of the progressive cause, in both Britain and colonial America, was someone Strahan was getting to know well. By the late 1740s, one of his closest working relationships was with Samuel Johnson. Several years had passed by now since the contract for a dictionary had been signed, and during that time Strahan had watched as Johnson's efforts in lexicography lurched uncertainly forward. The demands of the project were enormous, but they had not stopped Johnson involving himself in other literary pursuits. Recently he had had one of his plays performed at Drury Lane and almost simultaneously had produced a long poem that had captured the attention of the town.

The poem was titled *The Vanity of Human Wishes*. It was composed in imitation of one of the famous satires by the Roman poet Juvenal, something Johnson had done before. From its panoramic opening lines,

> LET observation, with extensive view,
> Survey mankind from China to Peru;
> Remark each anxious toil, each eager strife,
> And watch the busy scenes of crowded life . . . [35]

it revealed the author to be someone who was thinking deeply about the human condition. But where Franklin focused on potential and projects, Johnson was far more cautious. Life was a perilous journey, Johnson argued, and in our quest for the things we most desire—wealth, celebrity, long life, beauty—we could easily go astray. The poem contained a warning:

> Unnumber'd suppliants crowd Preferment's gate,
> Athirst for wealth, and burning to be great;
> Delusive Fortune hears th' incessant call,
> They mount, they shine, evaporate, and fall. [36]

Franklin had once asked Strahan to send him anything "that makes a Noise and has a Run," and so, it seems, Strahan did at the end of 1749 with *The Vanity of Human Wishes*.

As Strahan was examining Franklin's *Proposals* in London, Franklin was reading Johnson's poem in Market Street. *The Vanity of Human Wishes*, the first work published under Johnson's name, spoke of a world agitated into motion. Migrants were leaving their homes, tradesmen were changing their statuses, "projectors" were launching schemes, colonies and companies were trampling the old orders underfoot. Very soon Johnson would write much more about this in his periodical the *Rambler*, a work that Franklin would also help bring to America. For now, though, Franklin excerpted several portions of *The Vanity of Human Wishes* for reprinting in *Poor Richard's Almanack*. In doing so he became the first person to print the writing of Samuel Johnson in America.

Five

THE *RAMBLER*

IN ITS EDITION FOR May 1750, the *Gentleman's Magazine* printed an enticing piece of scientific news. Contained in a letter, entitled "A *curious Remark on* ELECTRICITY; *from a Gentleman in* America," the piece revealed that a hitherto unexplained characteristic of "electrical fire" had been observed. In the letter the author explained that he had created a rod, with a sharpened point at one end, with which he had been able to "draw" electricity out of a substance. He went on: "The doctrine of *points* is very curious, and the effect of them truly wonderful: and, from what I have observed on experiments, I am of opinion, that houses, ships, and even towns and churches may be effectually secured from the stroke of lightening by their means."[1]

Readers had already been introduced in January to this Philadelphian gentleman who was occupied with electrical experiments. This latest dispatch suggested that he had made a significant step forward. Electricity had long been considered a plaything. But here was a hint, perhaps even more than a hint, that it might actually have some practical value. Equally fascinating was the author's implicit connection between electricity and the even more mysterious phenomenon of lightning. To the careful reader, it seemed he was claiming that electricity and lightning were one and the same thing.

This was the kind of claim that was certain to elicit a response from London's intellectual community. Almost immediately, on June 9, one arrived. It came in one of the new periodicals that, ever since the days of the *Spectator*, had made it their business to scrutinize current affairs. The essay was not an overt critique of the news from Philadelphia. Rather it was a meditative piece on the danger posed by science to human society. The current rage for natural philosophy, the author contended, was yet another instance of the distractions that were filling the modern world. What was happening now was actually an inversion of the celebrated work of Socrates. Two millennia before, the great philosopher "drew the wits of Greece, by his instruction and example," turning them away "from the vain pursuit of natural philosophy to moral inquiries," directing their thoughts away "from stars and tides, and matter and motion," to "the various modes of virtue, and relations of life."[2]

Nowadays, the writer claimed, people were picking up their bad, pre-Socratic habits again. As an example, he gave the story of a man named Gelidus. A "man of great penetration, and deep researches," Gelidus was cool and rational, shrewd and diligent. With a mind perfectly suited to the demands of the "abstruser" arts, burrowed deep in Gelidus's psyche was the conviction that it was his particular destiny to solve problems "by which the professors of science have been hitherto baffled." To fulfill this mission he spent his days sequestered away in the highest parts of his house where none of his family were allowed to enter. Even when he came down to eat or to rest, he remained in such deep thought that he scarcely noticed those around him. Gelidus walked about, the writer explained, "like a stranger that is there only for a day, without any tokens of regard or tenderness."[3]

Written in the present tense, this was a story to provoke. Was this "Gelidus" (a word that in Latin means "icy") a complete invention? Or was the name merely a veil for a contemporary figure, perhaps one of the Royal Society fellows who gathered in Crane Court? While this remained ambiguous, Gelidus's story was vividly told:

> He has totally divested himself of all human sensations; he has neither eye for beauty, nor ear for complaint; he neither rejoices at the good fortune of his nearest friend, nor mourns for any publick or private calamity. Having once received a letter which appeared to have been sent by sea, and given it his servant to read, he was informed, that it was written by his brother, who, being ship-wrecked, had swum naked to land, and was destitute of necessaries in a foreign country. Naked and destitute! says Gelidus, reach down the last volume of meteorological observations, extract from the letter an exact account of the wind, and note it carefully in the diary of the weather.[4]

In these two publications, the *Gentleman's Magazine* for May 1750 and the *Rambler* No. 24 of June 9, 1750, we can see, in the closest historical proximity, a division of perspectives. The subject in question was the merits of the modern, enlightened life. The two views pitted wit against learning, vision against skepticism, ingenuity against caution, liberalism against conservatism, and—to put it in personal terms—Benjamin Franklin against Samuel Johnson.

WILLIAM STRAHAN CAME TO know Johnson at about the time he opened his correspondence with Franklin, five years earlier. Whereas Franklin was an easy man to like, Johnson was a more forbidding character. In an age that prized politeness as a virtue, his appearance and his manners were all to the contrary. At around six feet, Johnson was physically imposing, and by the 1740s the sight of his broad, shambling frame in the narrow alleyways around Fleet Street was a familiar one. At closer quarters his appearance was even more startling. People were struck by the "immense structure of his bones"[5] and the livid scars that crossed Johnson's neck and face—the remnants of a childhood infection of scrofula. Johnson's mannerisms were unsettling too. His body seemed possessed, with constant jerks and starts. Then he had a way of "twirling his fingers and twisting his hands."[6] Few forgot their first encounter with him. Once, when William Hogarth was looking through a window, his attention came to rest on a man, "shaking his head, and rolling himself about in a strange ridiculous manner." Hogarth, though a brilliant student of character, concluded that this must surely be "an ideot."[7]

A few minutes in Johnson's company, however, were enough for anyone to discover that he was nothing of the sort. Johnson, the son of a bookseller from Lichfield in Staffordshire, was as erudite as anyone. Indeed, Victor Hugo's lucent line "He never went out without a book under his arm, and he often came back with two,"[8] could have been written expressly for him. And Johnson was not just clever, he was respected and connected too. He had come to London, Dick Whittington–style, to seek his fortune, with his Lichfield friend David Garrick, now the popular actor-manager of the Drury Lane Theatre. Edward Cave of the *Gentleman's Magazine* depended on him entirely. Even the great Alexander Pope rated him a rare talent, praising Johnson's visionary poem "London" on its appearance in 1738. Many others, like his new printer, William Strahan, admired him too. But equally people knew they had to tread carefully around him. Johnson had an uneasy temper, and if challenged he could flare unexpectedly. Some stories had already passed into legend. There was the time when he felled an impertinent bookseller called Osborne with a folio Greek Bible. Or the occasion, in his younger days at Lichfield, when he found a man sitting in his seat after the interval at the theater. When this intruder refused to budge, Johnson scooped up the man and the chair, throwing them headlong into the pit.

Vignettes like this were often cast in comic terms. Likewise, stories about Johnson's relationship with his wife Elizabeth or "Tetty"

were filled with levity. Their marriage was, everyone knew, an unusual one. It had grown out of a "strange romance" in the early 1730s
between the young, awkward Johnson and Tetty, a vivacious widow
from Birmingham who was almost twice his age. This age gap was
enough to generate comment on its own. Anecdotes of Johnson and
Tetty were eagerly swapped, many of them filled with what one biographer has called "a vein of high, and sometimes cruel, sexual comedy."[9] This, along with the jibes about his physical appearance, was
something that Johnson had long had to endure. Behind the mirth lay
a more complicated story: of an affectionate but challenging marriage,
of a life that to Johnson himself seemed full of struggle and shame. For
years as he sought to establish himself, he had lived apart from Tetty
in wretched circumstances. In the years immediately following his arrival in London in 1737, he had been so poor that he was often forced
to write in the dark for lack of candles. Sometimes he was homeless
altogether, and spent the nights pacing the streets and squares of the
capital until the sun rose and the coffee houses opened again.

By the time Strahan came to know him in 1746, the worst of this
was behind him. With a good advance for the dictionary, Johnson
had been able to establish Tetty and himself in a handsome, three-
story building on Gough Square, just around the corner from Wine
Office Court and close to Strahan's new printing office on Little New
Street. This proximity was not accidental. As the dictionary was such
an enormous project, it was useful for Johnson to be near Strahan
so they could communicate effectively.* Out of this closeness a relationship had formed. At first it was more pragmatic than affection-

---

* Good communication between a writer and a printer was essential. The courts and
alleyways around Fleet Street were often filled with errand boys, known colloquially as
"printers' devils," picking up copy for their masters or running page proofs back to the
author. The relationship between Strahan and Johnson concerning the *Dictionary* was
especially important. The job was far too big to be set in one go. Strahan had nowhere
near enough type for this. Instead the *Dictionary* had to be produced piecemeal with the
setting, proofing, and printing being done in short order to allow for the recycling of
the type.

ate. Johnson, wanting to stay well out of the way of the consortium of booksellers who were impatient for the dictionary, made use of Strahan as something like a proto–literary agent. Strahan collected money on his behalf and passed messages between him and the booksellers. Occasionally, too, Johnson would call at Little New Street for breakfast or conversation, and legend has it that he liked to pause in the courtyard outside Strahan's house and "in moments of abstraction," hug a lime tree.[10]

It was in informal settings like this that Johnson really thrived. He loved company, and sitting down with Strahan gave him the chance to churn over the political or literary subjects of the day. A conversation with Strahan about Franklin's electrical work in Philadelphia may well have been the spur for the *Rambler* No. 24 in June 1750. It was, after all, just the kind of thing to catch Johnson's attention. He was temperamentally attracted to science for its novelty and creative potential. Stories would later be swapped about Johnson's interest in chemistry, with friends calling around to find his chambers perilous with fizzing vials or "fierce and violent" flames.[11] Electricity, too, caught his imagination. When he came to define the word in his *Dictionary*, he, suggestively, added an additional snippet of descriptive detail:

ELECTRICITY. *n.s.* [from *electrick*. See ELECTRE.] A property in some bodies, whereby, when rubbed so as to grow warm, they draw little bits of paper, or such like substances, to them. *Quincy.*

Such was the account given a few years ago of electricity; but the industry of the present age, first excited by the experiments of *Gray*, has discovered in electricity a multitude of philosophical wonders. Bodies electrified by a sphere of glass, turned nimbly round, not only emit flame, but may be fitted with such a quantity of the electrical vapour, as, if discharged at once upon a human body, would endanger life. The force of this vapour has hitherto appeared instantaneous, persons at both ends of a long chain seeming to be struck at once. The philosophers are now endeavouring to intercept the strokes of lightning.[12]

This entry betrays Johnson's curiosity. The whole entry is underpinned by a sensation of almost childlike excitement. Over the years, Johnson had sought to guard against this temperamental enthusiasm. Electricity was certainly an attractive field of study, but was it anything more than the fashion of the day? Investigating it might occupy someone for a day or even a year, but was it enough to sustain a lifetime's work? Johnson was unsure. Throughout his life science had been an ascendant force in society, with Isaac Newton as its figurehead. "His countrymen honoured him in his life-time," wrote Voltaire, "and interred him as tho' he had been a king who had made his people happy."[13] Many had attempted to make Newtons of themselves, in subjects from chemistry to geology, and Johnson had watched suspiciously. A person could be driven to anything in pursuit of knowledge. To satisfy their curiosity a philosopher might be driven to morally dubious actions, such as vivisection, a practice Johnson detested. Natural philosophers, too, would often neglect their families or their Christian duties, because their minds were so utterly fixed on solving a problem or finishing a piece of work. The result was a proliferation of Gelidus-like characters: people with absent minds and vacant eyes, who were as much a product of modern Britain as those *quidnuncs* who sacrificed their existences to chasing the daily news.

Perhaps this distraction would be acceptable, Johnson pondered in one of his later essays, if the success of their work was assured. But the march of knowledge was slow, and most inquiries failed in the end. Johnson gave the Royal Society as an example of this. It had been established with pomp and expectation on the Restoration of Charles II in the last century, but when examined with a cold eye, how many of their promises had come true?

The society met and parted without any visible diminution of the miseries of life. The gout and stone were still painful, the ground that was not plowed brought no harvest, and neither oranges nor grapes would grow upon the hawthorn. At last, those who were disappointed began to be angry; those likewise who hated innovation were glad to gain an opportunity of ridiculing men who had depreciated, perhaps with too much arrogance, the knowledge of antiquity. And it appears from some of their earliest apologies, that the philosophers felt with great sensibility the unwelcome importunities of those who were daily asking, "What have ye done?"[14]

This was no vendetta against science. Johnson's thinking was broader than that. He was suspicious about modern, enlightened society. Yes, it was true that great progress had been made over the past century. Not far from where he lived in Gough Square, he could gaze out at handsome new buildings like the Mansion House or he could stroll to Surrey over Westminster Bridge. Then there was the growth of the colonies in America and the huge wealth generated by the East India Company. But this was mercantile, scientific, or imperial progress. Johnson was more interested in the question of *moral* progress. In his early years in London, he had to fight to survive. He had lived in terrible lodgings in streets filled with abandoned children, gin-soaked delinquents, diseased prostitutes, and desperate debtors. The modern world might be exciting for some, but for others it was a nightmare. In 1746, the year Johnson signed his dictionary contract, a writer called James Burgh produced a pamphlet called *Britain's Remembrancer: or, the Danger Not Over*, which spoke of the nation as being filled with: "luxury and irreligion . . . venality, perjury, faction, opposition to legal authority, idleness, gluttony, drunkenness, lewdness, excessive gaming, robberies, clandestine marriages, breach of matrimonial vows, self-murders . . . a legion of furies sufficient to rend any state or empire that ever was in the world to pieces."[15]

In Johnson's eyes the greatest villains were the Whigs. Over the last forty years, since the arrival of the house of Hanover, they had monopolized political power in Britain. Under leaders like Robert Walpole and now Henry Pelham, they had both stabilized and thoroughly corrupted the system. People knew that when the general election came around every seven years, a ruthless political operation would stir into life. Seats would be bought, voters would be bribed, candidates would be forced into rotten boroughs, and power would once again be secured. While the corruption was bad, to Johnson the Whigs' political principles were even more loathsome. With their belief in the importance of trade, their taste for any idea that would foster commercial growth, and their disregard for ancient traditions, Johnson thought they acted with a high-handed disregard for that thing he called, in one of his favorite phrases, "the living world." As James L. Clifford, an astute reader of Johnson's thought, explained it:

> Whiggery to Johnson meant an easy optimism, a bland acceptance of fashion, a willingness to experiment and tamper without absolute certainty of improvement, a sophistical use of theory instead of a realistic approach to the ills of mankind. Whiggery to him meant a negation of principle, where ends justified means. This spirit showed itself in many ways—the callous adoption of any policy if it brought large increase of wealth to the nation. Wars of conquest or stealing lands from savages might be excused if England prospered financially. Expansion of overseas business had become the *sine qua non*. Yet, as Johnson later wrote, "Trade may make us rich, but riches, without goodness, cannot make us happy."[16]

Here was a word, "happy," around which so much of Johnson's writing revolved. Had the advances of this new, enlightened age actually generated more happiness? To Johnson's mind it had not. He believed that while progress could benefit some, it was important to see the wider story. The East India Company, for example, might be generating profits and filling the shops of the Strand with spices and silks, but it could only do this by exploiting native populations in distant lands. Even something as thrilling as the spectacle of George Anson's treasure wagons rolling through the City of London needed to be challenged. Yes, he had brought terrific riches home from an astonishing circumnavigation, but at what human cost? Had not thousands of sailors perished on the voyage, of hunger and scurvy, and in the most desperate of conditions? In the *Rambler* No. 19, printed just a few weeks before his attack on natural philosophers, Johnson argued:

> Though the world is crowded with scenes of calamity, we look, for the most part, upon the general mass of wretchedness with very little regard, and fix our eyes upon the state of particular persons, whom the eminence of their qualities marks out from the multitude; as, in reading an account of a battle, we seldom reflect on the vulgar heaps of slaughter, but follow the hero, with our whole attention, through all the varieties of his fortune, without a thought of the thousands that are falling round him.[17]

It was important, Johnson felt, that the rage for progress be challenged. A revealing line in his *Plan for the Dictionary*, which Strahan printed in 1747, unwittingly captured this conviction. "All change," he affirmed, "is of itself an evil, which ought not to be hazarded but for evident advantage."[18]

AS WITH FRANKLIN, TO understand Johnson's attitude toward life, it is useful to look at his experiences at the age of twenty. In September 1729, Johnson was a student at Pembroke College, Oxford. His life until this point had been set on an upward trajectory. During his boyhood in Lichfield, everyone had known him for his dazzling mind and for his tenacious memory that could produce lines of poetry on demand. It was a source of local pride when he had secured a place at one of the great universities. On the eve of his departure, Ann Oliver, who had taught Sam at her dame school, gave him a present of some gingerbread, telling him he was "the best scholar she ever had."[19]

The episode ended disastrously. With his father unable to afford his fees, Johnson was forced to leave Oxford after thirteen months without completing his degree. Returning to Lichfield, he suffered an almost total breakdown. There followed a period of gloom and dejection during which some friends worried he was on the brink of suicide. It was in the black months after his departure from Oxford that Johnson began to manifest the violent tics that were to affect him for the rest of his life. In later years he could rarely bring himself to talk about the experience of these years. Johnson had risen out of provincial obscurity almost to the point of being admitted into the highest, politest, most respectable circles in British society, only to have it cruelly snatched away.

Seventeen twenty-nine, the year of Johnson's psychological breakdown, also witnessed another significant, and possibly related, event. Toward the end of his spell in Oxford, he picked up a book called *A Serious Call to a Devout and Holy Life*, written by William Law, a reclusive Cambridge-educated curate with an unstinting attitude toward religious practice. Throughout his boyhood, Johnson's Christianity had never been pronounced. Like most Britons he went to church, said his prayers, and took communion on a Sunday, but he had never reached any point of profound engagement. Law's book changed this. It was written in earnest and was addressed to just such a middle-of-the-road Anglican as Johnson. The story of what happened next is told by James Boswell in his celebrated biography. Johnson had taken up Law's book, expecting it would be dull, as such titles usually were, "and perhaps to laugh at it." But Johnson "found Law quite an over-match" for him.[20] The book's central message was introduced on its first page. People were apt, Law argued, to mistake instances of devotion for actual devotion. Prayer was a case in point. People would say one in public or private, then, thinking their religious duty was fulfilled, they would forget God until, at length, the time for another prayer arrived and he would rise in their minds again. This, Law wrote, was not true devotion:

> He therefore is the devout man, who lives no longer to his own *will*, or the *way* and *spirit* of the world, but to the sole will of God, who considers God in every thing, who serves God in every thing, who makes all the parts of his *common* life, parts of piety, by doing every thing in the name of God, and under such rules as are conformable to his Glory.[21]

Law's message struck Johnson hard. It was a message that continued to vibrate in his mind after he left Oxford, and it shaped his attitudes thereafter. Law's effect was twofold. Johnson was unsparing in his appraisal of his own moral behavior, experiencing deep sensations of guilt and inadequacy. Equally, his hostility toward modern, progressive, Whiggish society, which edged Christianity out in favor of other concerns, intensified. This marginalization of religion in his contemporaries' lives was not only the consequence of direct challenges from philosophical movements like Deism—which held that while God was responsible for Creation, he was now mostly an absent figure—but also came about by subtler means. A merchant might be too busy with his business to go to church on a Sunday, a natural philosopher too deep in his studies to find time to pray. Franklin, who was guilty on both counts (the best stretch of churchgoing Franklin ever achieved was "five Sundays successively"[22]), was typical of the kind of figure Johnson disdained. Had Johnson read his proposals for the Philadelphia Academy in 1749, he would have considered the absence of religion a moral crime.

All of this lay deep inside the writer that Strahan came to know in the 1740s. Strahan, a careful reader of character, knew that Johnson was a strange compound. He had a rebellious streak, yet at the same time he was devout. He could be bright with humor and ambition, but at other times sunk in the gloom of melancholia. Depressive episodes had continued to afflict him ever since his Oxford days, and another struck following the publication of *The Vanity of Human Wishes* in 1749. In response, a group of Johnson's friends established a social club that met weekly at a well-known beef-steak house called the King's Head on Ivy Lane, near St. Paul's Cathedral. One of the members, John Hawkins, recounted that this quickly became the favorite part of Johnson's week, where he would spend hours "in a free and unrestrained interchange of sentiments, which otherwise had been spent at home in painful reflection."[23]

The Ivy Lane Club's nine members met on Tuesdays. They were a mix of writers, doctors, merchants, and booksellers, and one can imagine them turning over politics or news or discussing the latest book or pamphlet. Perhaps, too, they discussed the letters that Peter Collinson was receiving from Philadelphia about electricity. Of his friends in the club, Johnson was fondest of a young physician called Richard Bathurst. Bathurst shared Johnson's Tory politics, and there was a vitality to him that Johnson found refreshing. "My *dear dear Bathurst*," he would later recall, "whom I loved better than ever I loved any human creature."[24] In exchange for his youthful spirit, Bathurst experienced Johnson at his eloquent, expressive, conversational best. Having eaten a solid supper and ordered up several bottles of lemonade: "Johnson was, in a short time after our assembling, transformed into a new creature: his habitual melancholy and lassitude of spirit gave way; his countenance brightened; his mind was made to expand, and his wit to sparkle; he told excellent stories; and in his didactic style of conversation, both instructed and delighted us."[25] It is an appealing picture: the convivial club jump-starting Johnson's gloomy mind. The gatherings, though, did more than simply rally his spirits. They were also a creative stimulus that set him on a path toward an entirely new literary project.

Throughout his life, Johnson stuck to the belief that humans were at their best and most content when they were employed. To remain still, either physically or mentally, was to risk seizing up. "The business of life is to go forward,"[26] he would declare. Action produced action and in time generated momentum. Even if this activity did not create anything worthwhile in the short term, it had a value in and of itself. It was easier, in Johnson's opinion, to transfer momentum from one job to another than it was to conjure it out of nothing. So it logically followed that a busy person had more chance of finishing a task before someone else who had to begin from a standing start.

Thoughts like this had an added meaning for Johnson at the start of 1750 because he was confronting a problem with his dictionary project. He was four years into the daunting commission. Fired with ambition, Johnson had initially thrown himself into the work. But by now progress had stalled, and over the last year, he had come to the sickening conclusion that he had made a false start. Much of the methodological work was insufficient and needed to be undone. Not only had time been squandered, but a great deal of the money he had taken as an advance in 1746 had gone too. Faced with the prospect of another painful failure—one to outdo perhaps even the Oxford experience—Johnson needed to find ways to supply himself with a new and regular source of income. The natural move would have been to visit Edward Cave to see if there was any work to be had at the *Gentleman's Magazine*. But, instead, seemingly encouraged by John Payne, a bookseller who was one of the Ivy Lane Club, Johnson decided to try something more ambitious. He would produce a series of bi-weekly essays.

Nearly forty years since Addison and Steele's time, the periodical essay remained one of English literature's most popular forms. Year in, year out, new titles continued to appear in the *Spectator* style. The essays would be written from the point of view of a pseudonymous central character, who would mask their identity beneath that of a familiar archetype: an "entertainer," a "wanderer," a "senator." They would be observant, insightful, and short. Challenging readers with their wit, they operated like little secular sermons, never demanding more than ten or so minutes at a time. While entertaining, it was their ability to engage with readers at a deeper level that struck people from the start. During the *Spectator*'s initial run, the writer John Gay had written breathlessly to a friend, telling him that:

> It is incredible to conceive the effect his writings have had on the Town; how many thousand follies they have either quite banished or given a very great check to! how much countenance, they have added to Virtue and Religion! how many people they have rendered happy, by shewing them it was their own fault if they were not so! and, lastly, how entirely they have convinced our young fops and young fellows of the value and advantages of Learning![27]

Johnson was no more than an infant when these words were written, and like Franklin, he had grown up in awe of the celebrated periodical writers. In 1750 there were reasons to think that he could add to the tradition. Everyone recognized the quality of Johnson's prose. It was as balanced, grand, and sweeping as one of Wren's buildings and just as recognizable. Johnson's erudition, too, suggested that any periodical he composed would bristle with modern and classical allusions. Best of all, perhaps, was Johnson's ability to write quickly. Once he was engaged on a piece, words poured out of him at an astonishing pace—it was once said that written material flowed out of Johnson "as *correct* as a *second edition*."[28] All this was encouragement enough for a trio of booksellers and printers, including John Payne and Edward Cave, to agree to pay two guineas for every issue of a new periodical series. On Tuesday, March 20, 1750, the first issue of the *Rambler* appeared.

In the opening numbers of the *Rambler*, Johnson dwelt at length on the problems of setting out on new projects: of mustering the energy, clarifying the vision, and avoiding overcommitment. One of the greatest perils, he explained in No. 2, was hope. Hope created danger, because humans had a natural tendency to live, as he described it, "in idea." "The mind of man is never satisfied with the objects before it," he reflected, "but is always breaking away from the present moment, and losing itself in schemes of future felicity."[29] There was a logic, Johnson observed, behind this. As life was "gradual" and "progressive," to power themselves along, people "must always discover new motives of action, new excitements of fear, and allurements of desire."[30] This process, argued Johnson, extended onward throughout a person's life into infinity. He described this pattern, in a paragraph that concluded with one of his most elegant aphorisms. "THE end, therefore, which, at present, calls forth our efforts will be found, when it is once gained, to be only one of the means to some remoter end, and the natural flights of the human mind are not from pleasure to pleasure, but from hope to hope."[31]

While this was a timeless insight into human nature, Johnson suggested that it was particularly applicable to the society in which he lived. The Fleet Street neighborhood teemed with projectors and philosophers, speculators and schemers. These were people obsessed with "futurity," the utopian vision of a better world. Like little Quixotes, their behavior made them conspicuous, and in turn, it made them a frequent subject of "raillery to the gay, and of declamation to the serious."[32] But rather than laugh or chide as many other periodicals did, Johnson turned the focus on himself. "PERHAPS no class of the human species," he wrote, "requires more to be cautioned against this anticipation of happiness, than those that aspire to the name of authors."

> A man of lively fancy no sooner finds a hint moving in his mind, than he makes momentaneous excursions to the press, and to the world, and, with a little encouragement from flattery, pushes forward into future ages, and prognosticates the honours to be paid him, when envy is extinct, and faction is forgotten . . .[33]

Johnson claimed to be "yet but lightly touched with the symptoms of the writer's malady," but in examining himself he was encouraging his readers to do the same. It was necessary, he suggested, for people to reflect on the power of their own fantastical imaginations—of the exciting prospect of a new job, of a journey or the value of a new purchase—to see how they too placed far more emphasis on the promise of tomorrow than the certainty of today. The trick, Johnson argued, was not to do away with hope. Rather it was to know the potency of its appeal and to guard against the disappointments that it might well bring.

CAUTION AGAINST THE MODERN world's obsession with the future was a theme that ran through early issues of the *Rambler*. "IN futurity," Johnson warned in No. 8, "chiefly are the snares lodged, by which the imagination is intangled. Futurity is the proper abode of hope and fear, with all their train and progeny of subordinate apprehensions and desires."[34] This was the *Rambler*'s voice from the start: grave and profound, elegant and complex. The prose style was no doubt the first thing to strike new readers in the spring of 1750, but almost as plain was the fact that this writer had a provoking insight into the human mind. The early essays confronted topics like:

> Retirement natural to a great mind. (No. 7)
> The fondness of every man for his profession. (No. 9)
> The duty of secrecy. The invalidity of all excuses for betraying secrets. (No. 13)
> The folly and inconvenience of affectation. (No. 20)

As for himself, Johnson enjoyed the freedom of the form and, particularly, the fact that it allowed him to write anonymously. This reminded him of an observation of the Italian courtier Castiglione: "A mask confers a right of acting and speaking with less restraint, even when the wearer is known to the whole company."[35]

For the moment, Johnson's mask was still in place, and from behind it, he wrote with such conviction that it took some bravery to oppose him. His treatment of *"passionate men"* (No. 11), for instance, was typical.

> Their rage, indeed, for the most part, fumes away in the outcries of injury, and protestations of vengeance, and seldom proceeds to actual violence, unless a drawer or link-boy falls in their way; but they interrupt the quiet of those that happen to be within the reach of their clamours, disturb the course of conversation, and interrupt the enjoyment of society.[36]

Those who wasted their days in a passion were categorized as irritants, along with those fools who spent their life chasing celebrity. "APPLAUSE and admiration are by no means to be counted among the necessaries of life," he wrote in No. 20, "and therefore any indirect arts to obtain them have very little claim to pardon or compassion."[37] Later in the series he would return to this idea in one of his most memorable statements: "When once a man has made *celebrity* necessary to his happiness, he has put it in the power of the weakest and most timorous malignity, if not to take away his satisfaction, at least to withhold it."[38]

These arguments connected with a broader theme that was present in the *Rambler* from the start. This was the shortness of time. Only a small portion of it is given to us, Johnson emphasized over and over again. Realizing this was of vital importance, because humans were much better at conceiving ideas than performing them. It was as the old adage said: *Ars longa, vita brevis*, "art is long, and life is short." In No. 8, he presented his readers with a scientific image to illustrate how much time people frittered away:

> It is observed by modern philosophers, that not only the great globes of matter are thinly scattered through the universe, but

the hardest bodies are so porous, that, if all matter were com-
pressed to perfect solidity, it might be contained in a cube of
a few feet. In like manner, if all the employments of life were
crowded into the time which it really occupied, perhaps a few
weeks, days, or hours, would be sufficient for its accomplishment, so far as the mind was engaged in the performance.[39]

Like Montaigne in his famous essays a century and a half before, Johnson sought to provide his readers with a variety of tricks by
which they could steel themselves against pitfalls like these. To help
keep people's attention rooted on the present moment, in No. 17 he
recounted the story of an Eastern monarch, who had kept a member
of his household whose duty it was to call out, "every morning, at a
stated hour; 'Remember, prince, that thou shalt die.'"[40] The purpose of
this was not simply to call the prince's attention back to the present
moment, it was also to fill him with a sense of urgency.

By the time of the cautionary story of Gelidus the natural
philosopher, in No. 24 on June 9, 1750, the Rambler's readers had a
strong sense of the writer's method. The essays would often open
with the issuing of a statement, which would then be dismantled and
interrogated—a process one historian has likened to "turning a
thing upside down and shaking the nonsense of out it."[41] While there
was plenty of example, allegory, and instruction in the Rambler, there
was little overt religion. Instead the essays were underpinned by a
bedrock of Stoicism and the ancient Greek ideal of ataraxia—the quality of mental quietude or unperturbedness.

In No. 20, Johnson put his philosophy into visual form, making
use of a vibrant story that he had come across during his days of
working on the Gentleman's Magazine. In the winter of 1739–40,
readers of the magazine were thrilled by the reports of a magnificent
ice palace that had been built at St. Petersburg, in the time of Tsarina
Anna of Russia. "The state of the possessor of humble virtues," he
wrote, "to the affecter of great excellencies, is that of a small well

built cottage of stone, to the palace raised with ice by the empress of Russia; it was for a time splendid and luminous, but the first sunshine melted it to nothing."[42]

Such lines were admired by early readers. One, an old Philadelphian friend of Franklin's called James Ralph, spoke of the *Rambler* being the work of a writer "blessed with a vigorous imagination, under the restraint of a classical judgment, and master of all the charms and graces of expression."[43] Despite this, sales were modest. By the time of No. 24 in June 1750, only around five hundred were being bought each week, even though at twopence the cover price was cheap. This was a low circulation by the standards of the most popular periodicals and only a fraction of what Addison and Steele had achieved with the *Spectator*. The worry for his publishers was that, despite all his talent, Johnson as a periodical essayist did not quite work. By convention, periodicals were nimble and accessible. Few would apply these descriptions to Johnson. For his critics he was a saturnine moralist with a tendency to overthink and brood,* whose prose style was so sophisticated that his thoughts had to be unraveled like mathematical equations.

None of this troubled Johnson. From the beginning he had a clear idea of what he wanted to achieve. The *Rambler* was to be serious and profound, and before he started Johnson had decided to omit subjects he considered "local or temporary,"[44] to concentrate instead on the timeless issues faced by humans. In itself this was a critique of modern society's fickleness. This feature connected with another quality, that was strongly apparent to readers in both Britain and, as we shall see, America, but which is not so obvious today. This was the sense of foreboding that ran through the essays. They are filled with examples

---

* Over the years Johnson's friends, as well as his enemies, would often accuse him of over-philosophizing life—something that only generated more misery. One such was the lawyer Oliver Edwards. In his *Life*, Boswell records the charming occasion when Edwards teased his friend, "You are a philosopher, Dr Johnson. I have tried too in my time to be a philosopher; but, I don't know how, cheerfulness was always breaking in."

of characters such as Gelidus: people corrupted by their passions and by the vices of the societies in which they lived.

Worries about Britain's moral health were growing in the mid-eighteenth century. The years of the *Rambler* (1750–52) were the years of Hogarth's *Gin Lane* and Henry Fielding's *Enquiry into the Causes of the Late Increase of Robbers*, works that conveyed a sense of moral sickness. And if virtue was abandoning Britain, then what did that mean in the long run? As the young Boston lawyer John Adams would shortly argue, virtue and liberty were powerfully connected. "Liberty can no more exist without virtue and independence than the body can live and move without a soul."[45] For proof of this, people only needed to look to the history of Ancient Rome. The story of the fall of the republic in the first century BC was one all educated people knew. And best known of all was the history of the political convulsions that surrounded the rise of Julius Caesar. The future dictator grew up in a Roman society that had descended into luxury, scheming, and venality. It all seemed eerily familiar.

The English clergyman and writer Conyers Middleton drew this parallel explicitly in his *Life of Cicero* in 1742. "On the *Barbarity* and *Misery* of our *Island*," he wrote in a thoughtful aside,

> one cannot help reflecting on the surprising Fate and Revolutions of Kingdoms: how *Rome*, once the Mistress of the World, the Seat of Arts, Empire and Glory, now lies sunk in Sloth, Ignorance and Poverty; enslaved to the most cruel, as well as to the most contemptible of Tyrants, *Superstition and Religious Imposture;* while this remote Country, anciently the Jest and Contempt of *the polite Romans*, is become the happy Seat of Liberty, Plenty, and Letters; flourishing in all the Arts and Refinements of Civil Life; yet running perhaps the same course, which *Rome* itself had run before it; from virtuous Industry to Wealth; from Wealth to Luxury; from Luxury to an Impatience of Discipline and Corruption of Morals; till by a total Degeneracy and

Loss of Virtue, being grown ripe for Destruction, it falls a Prey
at last to some hardy Oppressor, and, with the Loss of Liberty,
losing every thing else, that is valuable, sinks gradually again
into its original Barbarism.[46]

Many shared Middleton's worry that Britain's moral regression would
lead to political and economic catastrophe. Johnson's *Rambler* could,
therefore, be viewed as a cautionary work, an effort to ward off disaster before it happened. This belief can be detected in the publicity
poem Edward Cave inserted in the *Gentleman's Magazine* in July 1750:

> *Proceed Great* Rambler, *and with manly fire*
> *War against crimes, and still make Guilt retire,*
> *Till the detested Fiends shall shun the light,*
> *Sunk in the shades of their primeval night.*[47]

While some continued to grumble about Johnson's style (the
Marchioness Grey complained to a friend that "every paper is full of
so many hard words as really break my teeth to speak them"),[48] others realized that the *Rambler* was not to be judged as just another in
the endless train of periodicals. To the mind of Walter Jackson Bate,
a twentieth-century biographer of Johnson, the *Rambler* transcended
that familiar form. Instead its lineage could be traced back to the
Greek aphorists, the book of Ecclesiasticus, the Renaissance human-
ists and authors like Montaigne and Bacon. Blending together all of
these subtle influences, in the *Rambler* Johnson created something
entirely his own.

Indeed, the essays were so uniquely Johnson's that his efforts to
conceal his authorship were bound to end in failure. The actor David
Garrick, who knew Johnson and his ways as well as anyone, was
among the first to suspect "the Rambler's" true identity. By August
1750, Edward Cave knew the game was up. In a letter to his fellow
printer Samuel Richardson, Cave confirmed that "Mr Johnson is the

Great Rambler, being, as you observe, the only man who can furnish two such papers in a week, besides his other great business."[49]

JOHNSON'S "GREAT BUSINESS" WAS, of course, the *Dictionary*. But in 1750, he was confronting a case of ambition colliding with reality. That June day, four years back, when the contract was signed at the Golden Anchor Inn was beginning to feel a long time ago. Almost as distant was the release of the *Plan for a Dictionary of the English Language*, a clever pamphlet that Strahan had printed for the booksellers as a way of drumming up subscribers. Despite occasional flutters of optimism (in the February 1749 issue of the *Gentleman's Magazine*, one "W.S.," almost certainly Strahan, inserted an advertisement informing the readers that a dictionary was "now in great forwardness"[50]), by the time of the *Rambler*'s appearance, not a single sheet of printed copy had been produced.

For someone as orderly as Strahan, this was cause for anxiety. A minute's walk from Little New Street, in Gough Square, Johnson was overworked, emotionally fraught, and short on the money he desperately needed to support not only himself, but an increasingly frail Tetty, who spent much of her time unwell in bed. Indeed, his finances were in such a parlous condition he was said at the time to have been unable to pay his milkman. At this crucial point in the *Dictionary*'s creation, Strahan played a decisive role. He knew it was futile to pick battles with Johnson. Had he marched to Gough Square to confront him, there was every chance that he might suffer the same fate as the unfortunate Mr. Osborne. Instead Strahan decided to cajole Johnson, counsel him, and shield him from the impatient booksellers. Strahan was now wealthy enough to spare him some cash when necessary. He also developed a scheme whereby Johnson would receive a guinea on acceptance of every printed sheet. Johnson respected his printer for this and learned to appreciate him for more than just his business flair. Strahan took care to proof Johnson's copy. Several times this led to improvements. "What you tell me I am ashamed never to have thought on," he admitted after Strahan had tidied up one of his drafts. "I wish I had known it sooner. Send me back the last sheet; and the last copy for correction."[51]

Managing the process remained a delicate business. In November 1751, Strahan was forced into the role of go-between, when he was obliged to send Johnson a letter on behalf of the booksellers hinting that they were on the point of cutting off his funding. The reply which came back from Johnson was charged with the heat of a thousand suns. In it he reiterated his position: "That my resolution has long been, and is *not* now altered, and is now *less* likely to be altered, that I shall *not* see the gentlemen partners till the first volume is in the press, which they may forward or retard by dispensing or not dispensing with the last message."[52]

In his press room, nearby in Little New Street, these were uncomfortable moments for Strahan. Should the dictionary fail, then it would be a loss for him as well as Johnson. Indeed, for Strahan, such a public failure, on such a scale, would be unprecedented. Ever since he had started out, his printing business seemed charmed. The proof of this success was tangible. At Little New Street he had seven presses at work every day, sunrise till sunset, and even those were insufficient to cope with the commissions that streamed in. In one of his letters to Hall in Philadelphia, Strahan was buoyant. "I have, and am likely to have," Strahan confided, "as much Business as I can possibly do." Now was the time to be brave. He was eyeing a set of six neighboring buildings that belonged to the Goldsmith's Company. His idea was to demolish these and to have an entirely new building—forty feet square, two stories high—erected on the site. This would cost Strahan £500—as much as a gentleman might earn in a year. "But," as he pondered in his letter to Hall,

> it will render my Habitation exceedingly commodious, for I shall have room for 4 more Presses, and Compositors in proportion, with Ware-house-Room, etc, and a pretty piece of

Ground to add to my Garden besides. In short, when it is finished, which will be about Christmas, my House and Garden will stand upon a Spot of Ground near 90 feet square, and be beyond Dispute the largest and best Printing-house in Britain.[53]

Strahan could take even more satisfaction from the progression of Hall's own career. By now reports of Hall's "prosperous Business" were making their way independently back to Little New Street. These delighted Strahan, but he was even more pleased to hear of the "esteem" Hall was held in by other Philadelphians. Receiving such news, he wrote, "gave me a Pleasure not to be described, and was a Cordial to my very Heart."

Hall had not yet been in the colonies a decade, but through his connection with Franklin he had flourished to become Philadelphia's leading printer. He now managed the entire operation at Market Street, and should he live to see out the partnership agreement with Franklin, then he would have the right to buy the entire business. It was quite a feat for the two Scots boys. Strahan was soon to have the largest and best printing house in the capital of Britain; Hall might soon have the greatest on the whole continent of America. Their success was unquestionable, but for Strahan sadness still lingered. "Lord, what a pleasant Day should we have, were we met in Britain!," he wrote wistfully in 1752. "The very Thought of it almost fuddles me." Knowing that such a reunion was unlikely to happen, he took, without quite knowing why, solace in something one of their old friends used to say: "The Sea that runs up to Philadelphia also runs up the River Thames."[54]

Strahan and Hall's achievements were impressive, but they were nothing when compared to what was happening to their mutual friend. Franklin's reputation had grown astonishingly throughout 1750 and 1751. The "extracts from a gentleman in Philadelphia" that Collinson had passed to the *Gentleman's Magazine* were followed by a more developed treatise, *Experiments and Observations on Electric-*

ity, Made at Philadelphia in America, which Edward Cave printed in April 1751. Ever since that sparkling book's appearance, Franklin had become a celebrity, as well known in Europe as any American. *Experiments and Observations* laid out Franklin's theoretical discovery, as Joseph Priestley would afterward put it, that "electrical matter was not created but collected by friction, from the neighbouring non electric bodies." This was captivating enough. But what really elevated him to mythic status was the practical application of what he had learned. As he had set out in his letter to Collinson, Franklin had shown that pointed rods had a "wonderful" ability to draw electricity from a substance. Combining this observation with his conviction that lightning was another, more potent form of electricity, Franklin had conceived of something that became known as the sentry-box experiment.

> On the top of some high tower or steeple, place a kind of sentry-box big enough to contain a man and an electrical stand. From the middle of the stand let an iron rod rise and pass bending out of the door, and then upright 20 or 30 feet, pointed very sharp at the end. If the electrical stand be kept clean and dry, a man standing on it when such clouds are passing low, might be electrified and afford sparks, the rod drawing fire to him from a cloud. If any danger to the man should be apprehended (though I think there would be none) let him stand on the floor of his box, and now and then bring near to the rod the loop of a wire that has one end fastened to the leads, he holding it by a wax handle; so the sparks, if the rod is electrified, will strike from the rod to the wire, and not affect him.[55]

Before Franklin had the opportunity to conduct this himself, it was performed, in the spring of 1752, by a series of Frenchmen. The first, Thomas François d'Alibard, managed to draw electrical fluid out of a Parisian cloud with a fifty-foot rod on May 10. A week later the experiment was repeated in the French capital, and in July it was undertaken in England. In between, it seems that Franklin performed the terrifying feat that would pass into scientific legend, when, according to his own account, he climbed the tower of Christ Church in Philadelphia while a summer storm raged overhead. From the top of the tower Franklin flew a kite into the clouds, and soon after sparks jumped from a key that he had fastened to a length of silk insulating string.

Franklin sent news of this to Collinson in October 1752. Franklin's thrilling letter was passed around London's scientific community and doubtless reached the ears of Samuel Johnson too. Perhaps the news would have been enough for Johnson to concede that Franklin's work was of more than "local or temporary" value, although he was not the kind of person to admit an error. Indeed subtle attacks on Franklin had resurfaced throughout the *Rambler*'s run. "He that is growing great and happy by electrifying a bottle," he wrote in No. 118, "wonders how the world can be engaged by trifling prattle about war or peace."[56]

This time, however, there was no chance of a response. By the time news came of Franklin's success, the *Rambler*'s run had ended. In its final number, Johnson bid farewell to his readers in frank terms. Whatever the "final sentence of mankind" was going to be, he wrote, "I have at least endeavoured to deserve their kindness." As well as his observations on human nature, Johnson pointed out that he had "laboured to refine" the English language, "to clear it from colloquial barbarisms, licentious idioms, and irregular combinations."[57] All this, while writing on topics ranging from grief and hope to procrastination, celebrity, ambition, and anger, Johnson had certainly done. No longer was his name known only to a select few in Fleet Street. It was becoming increasingly mentioned across the country and even as far away as colonial America. Among the titles Strahan packed for Philadelphia in the summer of 1752 was a six-volume edition of the *Rambler*, perhaps the first copies to ever cross the Atlantic.

For his part, Strahan had a unique glimpse into both Franklin's and Johnson's minds. In Johnson he could clearly see genius, but he could detect hypocrisy too. He must have thought that Johnson's opinions about the delusion of hope were a bit rich, coming from a man who had locked himself up in his garret for years on end, having agreed to undertake the greatest literary project of all. When Johnson satirized Gelidus, he could almost have been laughing at himself.

This had crossed Johnson's mind too. In the *Rambler* No. 14, Johnson wrote:

> NOTHING is more unreasonable, however common, than to charge with hypocrisy him that expresses zeal for those virtues, which he neglects to practise; since he may be sincerely convinced of the advantages of conquering his passions, without having yet obtained the victory, as a man may be confident of the advantages of a voyage, or a journey, without having courage, or industry, to undertake it, and may honestly recommend to others, those attempts which he neglects himself.[58]

INDEED, LIKE GELIDUS, JOHNSON'S personal relationships had suffered due to his habit of hatching schemes and obsessing over projects. The most strained of these was with his wife. When he and Tetty had married, in 1735, they had been free and modestly wealthy. Tetty had come into "a small family fortune" of £600 after the death of Henry Porter, her first husband—quite enough to set the couple up in Staffordshire for many years to come. It was not long, however, before this was whittled away. Much of the money went on a school Johnson established at Edial, outside Lichfield, which soon failed. Thereafter Tetty was left alone for months at a stretch, following her husband's decision to set out for London and to try his fortune as "an adventurer in literature."[59]

Tetty soon followed Johnson to the capital, but their time together was challenging. Now in her fifties, Tetty had to adjust to a rowdy, dirty urban environment. She was often separated from her husband, too, while he worked on pieces for Edward Cave in a succession of dismal garrets around Fleet Street. By the time the *Dictionary* contract had been signed and money finally came into their hands, it was already too late. There had always been deep affection between the couple, and Johnson would always insist to friends that it was "a love-marriage"[60] on both sides. But by the time Tetty entered Gough Square she had been worn down by the events of the last decade.

Those who encountered her over the next six years saw a sharply different person than the younger, gregarious Tetty, who dressed well, ate heartily, and loved company. According to the recollection of Robert Levet, one of Johnson's lodgers, in her last years she was "always drunk and reading romances in her bed, where she killed herself by taking opium."[61] John Taylor, an old school friend of Johnson's, was even more unsparing. "She was the plague of Johnson's life," he declared, "abominably drunken and despicable."[62] During the exhausting years of the dictionary project, Tetty escaped the damp and noise of Fleet Street whenever she could, retreating to the outlying village of Hampstead, which was known for its healthy atmosphere. Her withdrawal, emotionally and physically, left her sensitive husband even more vulnerable.

Strahan, like everyone else, heard whispers of all this. As Johnson's friend he would have felt the jolt, in March 1752, of the distressing news that reached him from 17 Gough Square. Tetty Johnson was dead.

Six

ESCAPE

JOHNSON'S GRIEF SHOCKED EVERYONE who knew him. With Tetty gone he was unmoored. For a time he shunned all company and work and "grew almost insensible to the common concerns of life." To escape the haunting atmosphere of Gough Square, Johnson would leave the house after dusk to walk the streets of London. One of Tetty's companions, Mrs. Desmoulins, remembered that "this for many a lonesome night was his constant substitute for sleep."[1] Johnson later told one of his own friends, the poet Thomas Warton, that ever since Tetty's death he had seemed to himself "broken off from mankind; a kind of solitary wanderer in the wild of life, without any direction, or fixed point of view: a gloomy gazer on a world to which I have little relation."[2]

Stories began to circulate about Johnson's anguish as he watched Tetty being placed in her coffin, and how he had uncharacteristically been driven to drink. To one friend, Mary Hyde, it seemed as if Tetty's death had precipitated a second loss. Gone, too, was the youthful Johnson: the lean, lank, bony writer who used to stride purposefully around Fleet Street. Very soon, after the funeral, he seemed much older. Worried about Johnson's ability to withstand the distress, his friends started to think of ways to help him recapture his spirits. One idea seems to have emerged from the Ivy Lane Club and, particularly, Johnson's friend Richard Bathurst.

As so often in cases of painful bereavement, people looked beyond the grief-stricken individual to the environment they lived in. Gough Square, they all knew, had the aura of a shrine. Its rooms were filled with tangible reminders of Tetty's life—pictures, books, crockery, and clothes. A good step toward helping Johnson would be to make a change. In the days immediately after her death, Bathurst made a suggestion to Johnson. About a fortnight later, the front door at Gough Square swung open and in walked a ten-year-old Black boy called Francis Barber. Just four years before, this boy had been a slave in Jamaica. Now his extraordinary journey had brought him to this extraordinary place.

IT IS IMPOSSIBLE TO know just when Johnson first heard about Francis Barber. Perhaps it was on one of those Tuesday evenings in Ivy Lane, when, sitting beside Richard Bathurst with his lemonade before him, Johnson learned that a boy had been brought back to England from the family's plantation in Jamaica. Bathurst was not the kind of character to share this news without comment. Like Johnson he was a forthright Tory. "He hated a fool and he hated a rogue and he hated a *Whig*,"[3] Johnson later recalled. Another of his dislikes was the practice of slavery. Bathurst had been born in Jamaica in the early 1720s and raised in what he described in unequivocal terms as an "execrable region."[4] At about the age of sixteen, in 1738, he had left the island, to study medicine at Peterhouse, Cambridge, and despite his family ties he had little interest in ever going back.

While all of Bathurst's London friends were struck by his vehemence on this point, to some of them at least it must have been puzzling. Ever since a fleet dispatched by Oliver Cromwell had seized Jamaica from the Spanish in 1655, it had been considered the prize of England's Caribbean possessions. More than four thousand square miles in extent, rich, green, and fertile, the idea of the warm Atlantic waters lapping at its shores was an inviting one to many in the British capital.

Along with natural charm, there was economic opportunity on the island too. Over the past two or three generations, people knew that the wild Jamaican landscape had been cultivated by settler families who had turned the soil to a specific and very profitable use. By 1750 the island was, alone, the source of 42 percent of Britain's sugar imports. A series of plantations now spread out in a patchwork across Jamaica, from north to south, east to west. One of these had long belonged to Richard Bathurst's family, but in the summer of 1749, at around the time the Ivy Lane Club started to meet, the news reached him that the family's plantation had collapsed. Johnson, who was seeing plenty of the young physician at this time, recorded his response. "My dear friend Dr Bathurst," Johnson recalled, "declared he was glad that his father, who was a West-Indian planter, had left his affairs in total ruin, because having no estate, he was not under the temptation of keeping slaves."[5]

Bathurst's father, who, from his rank in the island militia, was known as Colonel Bathurst, had arrived in Britain in 1750. His life as a planter had ended, but he had brought one living reminder of it across the Atlantic with him. This was a former member of his indentured workforce. As Johnson was starting out on the *Rambler*, Colonel Bathurst was easing himself into London life—something that was alien to him too—while trying to find a place in British society for this boy. One of the colonel's first acts was to get him baptized. For most English subjects, this was a conventional rite of passage, which usually took place shortly after birth. For the seven- or eight-year-old boy, however, it was a ceremony powerfully invested with meaning. It not only brought him into the Christian fold, alongside other worshippers across the country, it also amended his status in a possibly significant way. A year before he had been a chattel slave. But what was his legal standing once he disembarked in Britain? And what would it be now that he was a baptized member of the Church of England?

In the 1750s there were no straightforward answers to these questions. But while the law remained unsettled, the belief was widespread (especially among slaves) that baptism equaled freedom.[6] This, then, was a significant move by Colonel Bathurst that could be interpreted as his giving the former slave his liberty. Whether this was his intention or not, what is certain is that the boy left the ceremony with a new name. He was now "Francis Barber," and the colonel had more plans for him yet. In 1750 young Francis was sent far to the north of London, to a school in the village of Barton, near Richmond in the North Riding of Yorkshire. He stayed there for several years, but by 1752 Francis had returned south and was living with the colonel's son, Richard Bathurst. It was then that Tetty died and the idea was formed to place him with Johnson at Gough Square.

As an aid for Johnson's recovery, this was a shrewd move. While everyone knew that Johnson was an intimidating intellectual who was prone to depressive spells, many also recognized the streak of childlike playfulness in his character. When at ease he would entertain friends with feats of physical prowess, leaping over chairs, rolling down hills, or challenging rivals to spontaneous running races. Johnson was a perfect example, his friend Oliver Goldsmith thought, of Montaigne's observation "The wisest men often have friends with whom they do not care how much they play the fool."[7] By the 1750s, too, Johnson was becoming known for his propensity for befriending younger people. The most famous of these would turn out to be James Boswell, but there would be many others too: Charlotte Lennox, Hester Thrale, Bennet Langton, and, of course, Bathurst himself. Johnson was at ease as the older, dominant character in these friendships, playing the role of weathered sage that came naturally to him. He also benefited from his younger friends' buoyant energy, which contrasted so sharply with the temperamental gloom he always tried to escape. Another favorite youngster was the society wit

Topham Beauclerk, who had a particular gift for drawing out Johnson's silliness.

Once, when in a churchyard with Beauclerk, Johnson had lain
down on a gravestone to rest his legs. Beauclerk had amused Johnson with the observation "Now, Sir, you are like Hogarth's Idle Apprentice."[8] Another time, in later years, when Beauclerk was walking
home in the early hours after an evening's drinking, he was seized by
the idea of waking Johnson. With a friend, he "rapped violently" on
Johnson's door to see if he would like to join them on a "frolic" around
the town:

> At last [Johnson] appeared in his shirt, with his little black wig
> on the top of his head, instead of a nightcap, and a poker in his
> hand, imagining, probably, that some ruffians were coming to
> attack him. When he discovered who they were, and was told
> their errand, he smiled, and with great good humour agreed to
> their proposal: "What, is it you, you dogs! I'll have a frisk with
> you." He was soon drest and they sallied forth together.[9]

This nighttime "frisk" progressed "in joyous contempt of sleep" from
Fleet Street to Covent Garden, to another tavern, and finally ended
with breakfast at Billingsgate. Tales of the escapade thrilled Johnson's
friends. They could picture the merriment, with the impish, care-
free, spontaneous Johnson cantering gleefully through the streets.
This inner character was something they knew could be roused with
just a little art. And it was with this in mind that Bathurst, another
of Johnson's younger friends, thought that the presence of a boy in
Gough Square might brighten his mood.

There was a second, equally powerful reason to think that Johnson would welcome Barber. Ever since his financial position had improved in the 1740s, Johnson had gone to unusual lengths to support
the vulnerable or those who, as it was said, were not in the "common
run."[10] This predilection—arising partly out of his personality, but

also without doubt from his life experiences—had already brought several peculiar characters to Gough Square in recent years. One was the Yorkshire-born physician Robert Levet. Described by Boswell as a silent man, of "a strange grotesque appearance" and "stiff and formal in his manner,"[11] visitors to Gough Square often encountered him as a brooding, unexplained presence.

Johnson, however, had no complaint with Levet's ways. He admired his medical knowledge, despite the fact that most of what he knew had been learned "through the ear." Described as "an obscure practiser in physick amongst the lower people," Levet would often be out on his wandering rounds. Sometimes he would return in an alcoholic daze. But Johnson made allowances for this. He knew that while Levet's patients were often poor, they usually had the means to pay in kind with drink. Believing he deserved some payment for his time, Levet, perhaps a little too often, accepted the gift. Excusing his friend, Johnson held that Levet was "perhaps the only man who ever became intoxicated through motives of prudence."[12]

Along with Levet in Gough Square was a Welsh lady called Anna Williams. In her mid-forties in 1752, she was bright, inquisitive, and orderly, traits that should by rights have guaranteed her a steady life. But Williams had been the victim of circumstance. The source of many of her woes was her father, whose zest for natural philosophy and determination to solve the problem of calculating longitude turned him into a character not unlike "Gelidus." For many years Anna lived with him in the Charterhouse buildings that were also home to the electrical pioneer Stephen Gray. At length her father's irascible temper led to both his and his daughter's eviction. Left destitute, their situation was further aggravated by physical disability. Having suffered from the early onset of cataracts, Anna was completely blind by the 1750s. Hearing of their plight, Johnson proposed they lodge with him until their circumstances improved. Anna would remain an almost continual presence for the rest of Johnson's life.

Robert Levet and Anna Williams both found distinctive roles

within the Gough Square household. In the mornings Levet would sit silently beside Johnson, filling his mug with tea. Williams meanwhile conquered her disadvantages to the point that she was able to assume the role of housekeeper. Both middle-aged and serious, neither Williams nor Levet were capable of filling Gough Square with any great gaiety. But Colonel Bathurst's boy was a different matter. In 1752, he was in the advanced years of childhood, suggesting he was independent enough to be able to run errands for Johnson and to be of practical use about the house. As Francis Barber's biographer, Michael Bundock, has pointed out, there was a further, deeper reason for Johnson to feel a bond of affinity with Francis:

> Johnson's strange looks and manner were often the subject of ridicule, and the terms of such comments are revealing of how he was perceived: he was "monstrous," "barbarous," "a savage." This was exactly the language used by many travel writers at the time to characterise the inhabitants of countries which were not "civilised," particularly people of African origins—such as Barber.[13]

Barber's arrival added a fascinating new element to Johnson's unusual household. Just how those first weeks went in the spring of 1752 it is impossible to know. Johnson remained plunged in misery. Williams, meanwhile, suffered a further disappointment when a long-awaited operation on her eyes failed to restore her sight. Complicating this fraught emotional environment further was the dictionary project. Six years after the contract was signed, the booksellers' patience was now growing thin. With work on the *Rambler* at an end, all of Johnson's energy had to be channeled in the one thing that he had to do.

We can picture Johnson in his garret in 1752, perched on the ancient three-legged stool that, legend has it, was his favorite spot. Johnson was an untidy worker. He raced through books with his lead pencil, marking up words, phrases, and passages, then stacking them up in perilous piles as they awaited their turn for transcription. The pace at which Johnson worked and the way he irreverently handled the books led the writer Henry Hitchings to liken the garret at Gough Square to "a sort of backstreet abattoir, specializing in the evisceration of books."[14] As these were gutted, a parallel process was whirring inside Johnson's mind. What did this word mean? Where did it come from? How can I best describe its essence? With increasing speed, Johnson's celebrated definitions continued to come:

> PATRON, n: One who countenances, supports or protects. Commonly a wretch who supports with insolence, and is paid with flattery

> POLITICIAN, n: 1. One versed in the arts of government; one skilled in politicks. 2. A man of artifice; one of deep contrivance

> QUONDAM. [Latin.] Having been formerly. A ludicrous word

> TRANCE, n: An ecstasy; a state in which the soul is rapt into visions of future or distant things; a temporary absence of the soul from the body[15]

For a long time this has been our vision of Johnson at work on his great dictionary, a labor that Walter Jackson Bate, quondam Lowell Professor of the Humanities at Harvard University, ranked "as one of the greatest single achievements of scholarship, and probably the greatest ever performed by one individual who labored under anything like the disadvantages in a comparable length of time."[16] One part of the scene, though, remained missing until the 1990s. An analysis of the surviving materials has proven that another individual was also present in the garret of Gough Square.

Bundled together with a mass of preparatory notes were a number of slips marked with a boy's handwriting. They carried the words "antigue/an," "England England," and "Francis Barber."[17] What these slips of paper show is that Francis Barber had climbed the stairs and was there in the garret too. Barber's business was not defining words, but something even more profound. He was defining just who *he* was.

GOUGH SQUARE WAS A world of daily routines: of creaking floorboards at daybreak; of silent breakfasts; of comings and goings at the front door; of the waft of Johnson's favorite pies rising up from the kitchen in the late afternoon. Williams, Levet, and the rest of the household revolved around Johnson like planets orbiting their sun. This was entirely different from what Francis Barber had known during the first eight years of his life.

In those childhood years he was woken at daybreak in a thatched hut on the Orange River estate in Jamaica. One of 150 slaves on Colonel Bathurst's plantation, his life back then was similarly demarcated by routine. There had been half an hour for breakfast and two for dinner. For the rest of his time, sunrise to sunset, he had worked in the fields with the slave gangs. These, as one historian has described it, roamed across the island plantations like "slow moving armies,"[18] who hacked away at the swaying sugar plants, cropping the cane close to the ground, stripping it back and bundling the stalks for collection. As a child he would have been spared the tough physical work of slashing at the cane, but from the time he was able to walk he would have been put to use: following the steps of older slaves with a woven basket, gathering stones and rubbish and pulling out weeds.

Unlike Gough Square, where the atmosphere of the house might be colored by the passing of the seasons, a pressing deadline, or Johnson's temporary absence, there was little variation to this routine on Bathurst's plantation. A sultry climate continued all the year round, with little fluctuation in the daily temperature or hours of sunlight. Occasionally a ferocious storm might sweep in from the Atlantic, but otherwise the sense was one of time stopped. Any slave seeking to disturb the rhythm endangered themselves. Overseers monitored everything: instructing, chivvying, reprimanding. But Barber had most likely seen far worse. The slave-drivers always came to the sugar fields with a whip or an oak stick in their hands. A legal system was supposed to constrain their behavior—pro-slavery writers in Britain would make much of the law that stipulated that no overseer was to inflict more than ten lashes of his whip at a time, for example, unless the slave's owner was present; or that the owner who gave more than thirty-nine strikes should face a penalty of £5. But the violence was difficult to police.

Casual thrashings were commonplace. Masters could inflict even more pain by having lime juice, salt pickle, or bird pepper rubbed into wounds. These were the consequences of minor infractions like talking back or avoiding work. Much graver punishments confronted those who threatened retaliatory violence, stole from the stores, or tried to run away. They might be shackled sweltering in the stocks for hours on end. Others had their ears cropped, their nostrils slit open, and their cheeks branded. Given the numerical imbalance of the white and Black populations—in 1730, for instance, a total of 443 whites controlled a population of more than seven thousand slaves in one parish, Westmoreland, on Jamaica—paranoia fueled ever more violence.[19] The evidence of this neurosis was plain for all to see. In 1750, shortly after Bathurst and Francis left Jamaica, a slave had pulled a knife on a white man. Soon overpowered, the slave was instantly hanged from a nearby tree. The hand which had held the knife was cut off at the wrist and his body was left to rot.[20]

This was not an isolated incident. Indeed it was the kind of response the slaves had come to expect from their masters should they challenge their authority. Many slaves knew no other life than this, having been born into bondage on the lands they were forced to farm. But such were the conditions on the plantations—the grinding intensity of the labor, the inadequacy of food, and the absence of medical care—that mortality rates were high. To replenish the numbers, more and more slaves arrived every year, with around seventy thousand Africans arriving in Jamaica in the 1740s. Some of these came from other Caribbean islands, but most had endured the horror of the Middle Passage across the Atlantic. Timing their arrivals between November and February, so they were well placed to appeal to plantation owners ahead of the sugar harvest, thirty or so slave ships would arrive in Jamaican waters every year.

For those inside the ships, this was a wretched time. Having first, as Barber's contemporary Olaudah Equiano put it, "fallen victims to the violence of the African trader," and "the pestilential stench of a Guinea ship,"[21] for an average of around £30 each the slaves would then be bought for resale by Kingston factors like Thomas Hibbert.[22] According to one calculation, of a hundred Africans who were taken prisoner in the interior, about half would have died before they passed into the factor's hands. Almost another 50 percent of those who survived the voyage would perish in the months after arrival, as the weakened slaves confronted new diseases. By the time their "seasoning" was complete, just thirty of the original hundred would have survived to see plantations like Bathurst's.

The Bathurst family had come to Jamaica at around the time that William Penn was embarking on his own transatlantic project. As Penn surveyed the banks of the Delaware, the Bathursts secured a grant from Charles II for lands on the upper lip of the Orange River, north of Kingston. For seventy years the family lived on their estate, surrounded by a few buildings, some livestock, and fields of sugar cane. At 2,600 acres, all told, the Bathurst estate was reasonably large, and it would have sounded impressive enough to traders in the City of London who could have computed it as seven times the size of Hyde Park. The family's status also seemed rather elevated, with the master in the 1740s styling himself as "Colonel Bathurst," a member of the island militia and an established part of the plantocracy. Appearances, however, were deceiving. The colonel's title was more honorary than earned, and for all the size of his lands, the Orange

River estate was unfavorably located, ranging over rocky hills and exposed to the storms and showers of the northern coast.

This was the place that, presumably, was the childhood home of the boy that Johnson later knew as Francis Barber. We know little of Barber's early life. Neither the colonel nor his son left an account, and nothing survives from Johnson himself. Scholars have nonetheless managed to throw light onto Barber's early biography in recent years.[23] For among the papers recording the sale of the Orange River estate in 1749 is one that contains several captivating details. It confirms that while the buildings, the equipment, sugar, molasses, and slaves were to be sold, four individuals were to be kept back. One was described as a "mulatto child of Colias." Then there was a man named Shadrach and a woman named Nancy. Along with these was "a negroe boy named Quashey." Of these four, Francis Barber, given his skin color and age, can only have been one.[24]

Quashey is a revealing name. To connect it with Francis Barber is to connect him with far deeper histories. Many slaves came to have multiple identities. Olaudah Equiano, author of the well-known memoir, is an example of this. During different phases of his captivity, he was given various names. On a slave ship he was Michael, whereas on a Virginian plantation he was Jacob. Later a different master called him Gustavus Vassa after an old Swedish king. "When I refused to answer to my new name," he explained, "it gained me many a cuff; so at length I submitted."[25] It was only in later life that Equiano was able to reclaim his African identity. Other slaves had different names foisted on them by their masters: Cato, Caesar, or Pompey were common, filled with resonance of ancient Rome, while others like Joe or Jack were Anglicized derivatives that contained subtle links to day names in the Akan language of Ghana: Joe from "Cujoe" (Monday) or Jack from "Quack" (Wednesday). In the name Quashey, also often recorded as Quashe, the Akan language survives almost intact, since "Kwasiada" denoted Sunday, and Quashey was a name frequently given to babies born on that day.

As with Equiano, the boy who arrived at Gough Square in 1752 would be distanced from all of this. Just why Colonel Bathurst decided to bring him back to Britain is a question that invites speculation. Perhaps Quashey had some sort of favorite status. Maybe he had featured in some significant episode. Perhaps the colonel was discharging a promise. All that can be said for certain is that at seven or eight years old he was separated from any family and friends he may have had in Jamaica and carried across the Atlantic to England. Soon after, in an environment completely alien to anything he had ever known, he was taken to a church for his baptism and his reappearance in the world as Francis Barber.*

This was a bewildering series of events to confront a young boy. Equiano provides the best source for a parallel experience. On arriving in Falmouth from the plantations, he wrote, "every object I saw filled me with new surprise."[26] He gazed at the people with their white skin and their strange technologies like clocks and watches, and was perplexed by the sight of snow. This environment would, if anything, have seemed even more unusual to Barber. Within months of leaving Bathurst's Orange River plantation, he was in the seething, stinking, restless heart of London. Not long after that he was displaced yet again, to a school in rural Yorkshire with its blustery north winds, oak woods, hawthorn hedgerows, and chiming church clocks. All the time Barber was hugely conspicuous by the color of his skin. This was a sensation Equiano confronted too. In Guernsey he befriended a five-year-old girl called Mary.

---

* In itself the experience of being taken inside a church would have been novel for Barber. From the seventeenth century onward, little attention was given to fostering Christianity among the enslaved population in the Caribbean islands. Much later, in 1800, only twenty Anglican places of worship existed across Jamaica to serve a population of around four hundred thousand. One historian has estimated that only three hundred worshippers regularly attended divine service on Sundays—a statistic to raise Johnson's ire. As such, it is unlikely that Barber had ever entered a church before his arrival in Britain. For more, see Robert Worthington Smith, *Slavery and Christianity in the British West Indies*, p. 173.

I had often observed, that, when her mother washed her face, it looked very rosy; but when she washed mine it did not look so; I therefore tried oftentimes myself if I could not by washing make my face of the same colour as my little play-mate (Mary), but it was all in vain; and I now began to be mortified at the difference in our complexions.[27]

During his time in Yorkshire it is unlikely that Barber encountered any other Black people. This was not the case in London. In the riverside neighborhoods of Wapping, Shadwell, and Limehouse, with their transient, international flavor, sailors, and porters could be found from everywhere from China to Peru. While the greatest concentration of Black Londoners was here, there were several thousand others living in other parts of the capital who looked very much like him. The eighth plate of Hogarth's *Industry and Idleness*, for instance, shows a Black man serving drinks at a dinner in the Guildhall in the City of London. His presence is unremarkable. He is scarcely noticed by the dignitaries who are lost in their food and conversation. Others could be found in domestic service, and many served as sailors on merchant or military ships.

It was through this world that Barber walked in April 1752 to reach Gough Square. Aged about ten, the boy had already lived one of the most unlikely of lives. Now he was entering one of the most significant homes in the history of English literature. For Richard Bathurst, "giving"—an ambiguous word—Barber to Johnson was a transaction easily enough understood. It was a way to distract Johnson from his grief and to help recharge his spirits. For Barber himself, this would not have been so obvious. Nor did the development make sense to many of Johnson's practically minded friends. One, John Hawkins, was left in wonder. "The uses for which [Barber] was intended to serve this his last master," he wrote, "were not very apparent, for Diogenes himself never wanted a servant less than he seemed to do."[28]

*   *   *

THE SPRING OF 1752 was a confused time in Gough Square. As Johnson contended with his grief and sought to find the vitality to push forward with the dictionary, he simultaneously had to form a plan for the young boy who had come into his care. When he married Tetty in 1735, she had been forty-six years old, and there was never any real prospect of their having children. And yet in 1752, as a direct consequence of her death, Johnson was propelled into the nearest relationship to fatherhood that he would ever have.

The terms of the relationship between Johnson and Barber, however, remained unclear. How Johnson acted over the months that followed is therefore instructive. Soon after Barber had settled, Johnson started looking for somewhere where he could continue with his education. For a writer of slender means this was a challenge, and Johnson's first attempt to place Barber at a poor school in nearby Blackfriars was frustrated when he contracted smallpox on his first day. Once recovered, Barber did not return to this school, but Johnson's efforts were not at an end.

Next he enrolled Barber at a writing school, run by his friend Jacob Desmoulins, at Orange Court, Castle Street, near Leicester Fields.[29] This was fifteen minutes on foot from Gough Square, climbing the hill of Fleet Street before passing under the Temple Bar and traveling the length of the Strand to the church of St. Martin-in-the-Fields. For a boy whose life had been so monitored and confined until so recently, the exhilarating sensations evoked by the sight of the shop windows, the stream of noisy traffic, the steps of the playhouses, and the doors of handsome buildings can scarcely be imagined. The Orange River in Jamaica and Orange Court in London really did belong to two different worlds.

It seems likely that there is a link between Barber's education at Desmoulins's writing school and the scraps of paper discovered among Johnson's dictionary notes. Perhaps Francis was practicing his letters or showing Johnson what he had learned. If this was the case, then they would surely be a source of pride. Johnson may have been a supporter of the marginalized, but there was something particularly powerful in Barber's case. At least Anna Williams and Robert Levet had been given opportunities. Barber's beginning was starkly different. His was a history of the kind of displacement Johnson had written about as far back as 1738 when he attacked the merciless march of European colonization in his poem "London":

> Has Heaven reserved, in pity to the poor,
> No pathless waste, or undiscover'd shore?
> No secret island in the boundless main?
> No peaceful desert yet unclaim'd by Spain?[30]

This was an attitude at odds with the popular mood. While most people thought of the world as a place of excitement and opportunity, where territory could be taken and fortunes could be made, Johnson was already meditating on the consequences. The mania for imperial expansion, he knew, could drive people into immoral action. The Atlantic slave trade was an example. The English had long been involved with this trade, but since the end of the War of the Spanish Succession in 1714, supported by terms agreed at the Peace of Utrecht, this participation had intensified. By the time that Johnson reached adulthood, Britain was established as the most prominent of the trading nations. Every year hundreds of slave ships would set out from the ports of Bristol or Liverpool for the coast of West Africa. Once there they would spend months scouring the region, gradually filling their holds with hundreds of human victims, before they turned west into the Atlantic for voyages that have been described as "a floating nightmare of human filth and degradation."[31]

As all this took place at a remove from Britain, it was always possible for people to simply ignore it. Others sought to justify the trade. Some pointed out that it was an ingrained feature of all human societies. A different argument held that it was permitted in Scripture, as a practice condoned by the Old Testament and nowhere forbidden in the New. As the trade grew throughout the century, new racist theories gathered currency. One of these, which can broadly be termed "the degeneracy theory," held that while all the peoples of the world had been created equal, the condition of some had sunk due to environmental, educational, or political factors. Black Africans were considered to be among these sunken people.

Another argument carried an even more virulent form of prejudice. The idea, known as "polygenesis," claimed that the different races of the world were different species that came from distinct acts of creation. For those who held to such a view, Black people were not seen as being human at all. This was no marginal theory. One who at least flirted with it was the famed enemy of intolerance David Hume. In an essay, *Of Natural Characters*, revised in 1753, Hume wrote: "I am apt to suspect the negroes and in general all other species of men (for there are four or five different kinds) to be naturally inferior to the whites."[32]

Such thinking not only justified the slave trade in African people, but it even allowed some extreme pro-slavery propagandists to claim that they were undertaking some benevolent act:

> A slave in his own country, he is still a slave in the West Indies; but his means of happiness are considerably increased. In Africa his life was held cheap, and at the absolute disposal of his master; he could have nothing like property, was probably contemptuously treated, wretchedly fed, and often punished as severely as in the islands. In the West Indies his life is protected; food, clothing and assistance in sickness and old age are secured to him by benevolent laws.[33]

However ludicrous these justifications seem to the twenty-first-century eye, they were embraced by many at the time because they assuaged guilt and legitimized participation in what was unquestionably a profitable business. But not everyone was convinced. The formal abolition movement began only later in the century, but privately people were already expressing their distaste at what Britain was doing. This disgust was sometimes expressed in unexpected quarters. A fascinating recent discovery has shown that while Barber was learning penmanship under the tutelage of Jacob Desmoulins at Orange Court, not far to the west of London at Kew, the Prince of Wales was writing anti-slavery essays.

A tall boy, serious and dignified, the young George had been set on a course of essay writing by his tutor, John Stuart, the Third Earl of Bute. As the prince studied the craft of government and the perils of power, he had produced a two-hundred-page manuscript for his mentor, titled "Of Laws relative to Government in general." In it George expressed his belief that "Slavery is equaly [sic] repugnant to the Civil Law as to the Law of Nature," and he opposed the pro-slavery arguments for "the European traffic of Black slaves," arguing that the "very reasons urg'd for it will be perhaps sufficient to make us hold this practice in execration."[34]

As the young prince scratched down these words for Bute, ten miles away in Gough Square, Johnson was thinking much the same thing. But while the prince grappled with slavery in abstract terms, as something that, for now, remained an intellectual question, to Johnson it was something far more real. Barber had been intended as a comforting presence for Johnson. Perhaps Bathurst had imagined him amusing his master by chasing the cat or helping him by running copy around to Strahan's. But it seems that Barber's influence was more profound. He arrived at a crucial juncture in Johnson's intellectual life. The early 1750s was both a time when he was on the verge of securing his literary reputation with the publication of the *Dictionary* and a moment when he was thinking deeply about the fundamental questions of human life: about the consequence of actions, about the duties that one human has to another, and about the best way to acquire and sustain happiness.

In these years when Barber was a boyish presence in Gough Square, Johnson's attitudes toward European colonialism and the exploitation of Indigenous populations were sharpened. Writing of Jamaica in 1756, for instance, he described the island as being "a place of great wealth and dreadful wickedness, a den of tyrants and a dungeon of slaves."[35] In the same year, when he was sent a review copy of a newly published map of North America, he responded in equally strident terms. The map was drawn by Franklin's Philadelphian friend Lewis Evans, and it was intended to encourage Britons to support a new wave of settlement in the massive Ohio Valley. "It will very little advance the power of the English to plant colonies on the Ohio," Johnson stated in a review filled with skepticism and suspicion. How could sending Britons to settle lands at unimaginable distances, at the expense of those who already lived there, increase the happiness of anyone?[36]

By the late 1750s, Johnson's views on European expansion were well known. In the *Idler*, an essay series he began in 1758, he wrote several times about the exploitation of Indigenous people during the Age of Exploration. In No. 81, he characterized colonial operations in Canada as being initially concerned with the eradication of the native people with "the sword and the mines," before the focus shifted to the business of supplying "their place by human beings of another colour."[37] Continuing this theme a few essays later, in No. 87, he reminded his readers that "of black men the numbers are too great, who are now repining under English cruelty."[38] Around the same time, in an introduction he contributed to a book of voyages, *The World Displayed*, Johnson wrote at greater length about the dreadful consequences of the encounters between Indigenous people and Europeans who were aflame with "the infection of enterprise."[39]

One episode particularly caught his imagination. This was the moment when the fifteenth-century Portuguese explorers sailed southward along Africa's Gold Coast. Here Johnson relied on a work by the French Jesuit writer Joseph-François Lafitau, who in 1733 had jotted down a lively story relating to the moment of first contact. The "natives," Lafitau explained, had "gazed with astonishment on the ships when they approached their coasts, sometimes thinking them birds, and sometimes fishes, according as their sails were spread or lowered; and sometimes conceiving them to be only phantoms, which played to and fro in the ocean."[40]

To this, Johnson appended a view of his own.

> Such is the account given by the historian, perhaps with too much prejudice against a negroe's understanding; who though he might well wonder at the bulk and swiftness of the first ship, would scarcely conceive it to be either a bird or a fish; but having seen many bodies floating in this water, would think it what it really is, a large boat; and if he had no knowledge of any means by which separate pieces of timber may be joined together, would form very wild notions concerning its construction, or perhaps suppose it to be a hollow trunk of a tree, from some country where trees grow to a much greater height and thickness than in his own.[41]

Johnson then recounted how the Africans were murdered "in wanton merriment," by the Portuguese, "perhaps only to try how many a volley would destroy." He concluded:

> We are openly told, that they had the less scruple concerning their treatment of the savage people, because they scarcely considered them as distinct from beasts; and indeed the practice of all the European nations, and among others of the English barbarians that cultivate the southern islands of America [the West Indies] proves, that this opinion, however absurd and foolish, however wicked and injurious, still continues to prevail. Interest and pride harden the heart, and it is in vain to dispute against avarice and power.[42]

These paragraphs are as useful a glimpse into Johnson's mind as any in the 1750s. They show him in classic pose, rooting for the underdog. The Africans looking out at the Portuguese ships are not feeble creatures of little understanding who are awed by European technology. Instead they are rational humans, reckoning with a sight they had never seen before. Indeed if anyone is deluded, it is the European settlers. "Interest and pride" really has prejudiced their minds.

There is a connection here between Johnson's description of the fifteenth-century Africans and his decision to persevere with Barber's education. He both accords the dignity of human status and remains firm in his belief that they have the ability to progress. Through his years with Barber in Gough Square, he would have a constant, tangible reminder of the damage that could be caused by expansionist overseas projects. When such schemes involved the exploitation of a group of people, as was certainly the case in British America, they were all the worse.

THIS WAS LIFE IN the 1750s: boisterous, expansive, confident, unstable; charged with potential but undercut with a seam of moral weakness. Even at the time people knew they were living at a loaded moment in history, when the old ties of parish and church had been loosened, when luxury and corruption had intensified along with the social and economic progress. Franklin, in one of his letters to Peter Collinson in 1753, touched on this. As a devoted lover of the country, its laws, customs, and liberties, Franklin had been troubled to read in the papers that Britain was growing increasingly morally degenerate. This filled him with a feeling of jeopardy. "I know you have a great deal of Virtue still subsisting among you," he wrote, "and I hope the Constitution is not so near a dissolution, as some seem to apprehend." But should the worst happen, Franklin speculated, and Britain sink as Rome had:

> Should this dreaded fatal change happen in my time, how should
> I even in the midst of the Affliction rejoice, if we [in America]
> have been able to preserve those invaluable treasures, and can

invite the good among you to come and partake of them! O let not Britain seek to oppress us, but like an affectionate parent endeavour to secure freedom to her children; they may be able one day to assist her in defending her own.[43]

As Franklin was writing in earnest to Collinson, in Little New Street, Strahan's worries were beginning to subside. A practically minded man, Strahan's focus over the past few years had not been fixed on the fate of Great Britain but rather on the success of Johnson's dictionary. At the time of Tetty's death, the project was years behind schedule and Strahan close to despair. But after Barber's arrival, Johnson settled into a productive pattern. By April 1753, the first volume, covering the letters "A" to "K," was in print, and Johnson was able to carry over the momentum into the second and final volume. By April 1754 this, too, was almost complete. Exactly a year after this, in April 1755, the London papers were able to announce the news:

A DICTIONARY of the ENGLISH LANGUAGE: in which the Words are deduced from their Originals, and illustrated in their different Significations by Examples from the best Writers. To which are prefix'd A HISTORY OF THE LANGUAGE, and a GRAMMAR. By SAMUEL JOHNSON, *M.A.*[44]

From the moment the first copies went on sale, Johnson's reputation was made. It was a work, one of Johnson's friends, John Hawkesworth, asserted, "written with the utmost purity and elegance."[45] With war once again seeming imminent between Britain and France, people were quick to compare Johnson's individual achievement against the combined efforts of the French Academy. Johnson, Hawkesworth pointed out jubilantly, "alone has effected in seven years what the joint labour of forty academicians could not produce to a neighbouring nation in less than half a century."[46]

In the same moment, Strahan's reputation was made too. He had long been a rich man, but now he would be talked of in distinguished terms as the printer of Johnson's *Dictionary*. This feat confirmed his position in polite society—a position that was only bolstered when it was discovered that, as well as knowing Johnson, he was on the warmest terms with Franklin, the ingenious natural philosopher from Philadelphia whose work on electricity and lightning had changed the way people viewed the world. This made Strahan an enviably connected man. The idea of him inviting Johnson around for a breakfast at Little New Street before a letter arrived at his door from Benjamin Franklin is one to tantalize the mind. Strahan's relations with the two men were very different. Temperamentally and politically he was a much closer match with Franklin, whom he still longed to meet. With Johnson, the friendship, if it can be rightly described as such at this point, was of a much more professional nature. Whatever the case, Johnson rated Strahan highly. Surviving documents from his time working on the *Dictionary* show that he relied on him totally, trusted his editorial instincts, and often turned to him at moments of crisis.

The publication of the *Dictionary*, however, did not mean that Strahan was quite free of Johnson's personal disasters. Unlike Franklin, who was by now very wealthy, Johnson's finances remained parlous. He was troubled by debts several times in the late 1750s, and on at least one occasion he appealed to Strahan after being locked up in a debtor's prison. Johnson dealt with these episodes with the equanimity of one who had endured a precarious life for two decades. Another episode, though, upset his mental balance much more. It began in late 1756 and concerned the young boy, Francis Barber.

By this point Barber had been living with Johnson for four years. In that time he had stopped attending the writing school, instead settling into the role of Johnson's valet. This, at least, was how Johnson viewed Barber's place in the Gough Street household. Barber, however, seems to have understood their arrangement differently. Scholars have recently asked an important question about Barber's status during the years 1752–56. If he was brought into Britain as a slave by Colonel Bathurst and then effectively given to Johnson, what did that make him? The law in Britain did not allow for the keeping of slaves, and it would be bizarre to think of Johnson as being a slave owner. But as far as Barber was concerned, and as his actions demonstrated, he did remain the living property of Colonel Bathurst, at least until the latter's death in late 1756. As the terms of Bathurst's will declared, "I give to Francis Barber a Negroe whom I brought from Jamaica aforesaid into England his freedom."[47]

After four years in Gough Square, where he had to endure Johnson's and Levet's eccentricities and Anna Williams's earnestness, Barber was ready to take Bathurst's will at its word. One day in late 1756, he left the house and did not come back. When he found that Barber was gone, Johnson was shaken. "You will think I forget you," Johnson wrote to a friend in the autumn of that year, "but my Boy is run away, and I know not whom to send."[48] Strahan doubtless heard about Johnson's search for Barber, and given his relish for scouring the papers, he would surely have noticed an advertisement that was placed in the *Daily Advertiser* in early 1757: "WHEREAS Francis Barber, a black Boy, has been for some Months absent from his Master, and has been said to have lived lately in Wapping, or near it: This is to give him Notice, that if he will come to his Master, or apply to any of his Master's Friends, he will be kindly received."[49]

It is a quirk of history that in the summer of 1757, Barber was not the only young Black man to be enjoying his freedom in Britain. At the same time Barber had left Gough Square and was rumored to be living on the banks of the Thames in the East End, another young enslaved person, called John King, had left his master in equally abrupt circumstances. As with Barber, a similar ad was placed to assist in the hunt. It explained that King was wearing "a good Hat with a Silver Button and Loop, an old blue Frock and Waistcoat much worn and dirtied, Leather Breeches, and spotted Worsted Stockings."[50]

Although he was careful to conceal his own identity, this advertisement was placed in the press by a famous Philadelphian. King was one of the two slaves Benjamin Franklin had brought to London to serve him.

Franklin's arrival in London signals a new phase in an unfolding story. Over the next two decades he would spend most of his time in the British capital: two decades during which some of the fears for Britain that Franklin expressed in his letter to Collinson would be realized. Historians now refer to these years as "the years of crisis,"[51] and one of the figures most responsible for the coming strife was, as it happens, someone Johnson was forced to approach in his search for Barber. This man was called John Wilkes.

Wilkes was clever, witty, and, as far as Johnson was concerned, a paragon of moral degeneracy. A Member of Parliament, who was a highly connected figure in the Whig political establishment, Wilkes was rumored to pass his days drinking, whoring, and writing lewd satires. Johnson had himself been a victim of Wilkes's wit. On the *Dictionary*'s publication Wilkes had leaped on Johnson's dubious claim that "H seldom, perhaps never, begins any but the first syllable" of a word, responding gleefully: "The author of this remark must be a man of quick *appre-hension*, and *compre-hensive* genius; but I can never forgive his *un-handsome be-haviour* to the poor *knight-hood*, *priest-hood* and *widow-hood* . . . I do not wonder at so great a Scholar's disregarding a *maiden-head*, but should he dare to treat the God-head with neglect?"[52]

Learning that Barber had joined the Royal Navy, Johnson was advised to solicit help from Wilkes. He did so grudgingly, using the Scottish writer Tobias Smollett as an intermediary. Johnson made it clear that Barber was "a sickly Lad of a delicate frame, and particularly subject to a malady in his Throat which renders him very unfit for his majesty's Service."[53] These appeals seem to have borne fruit, for Barber was discharged from the navy soon afterward.

Johnson, however, could not bring himself to be grateful. Indeed,

Smollett told Wilkes that he had "heard nothing of his acknowledge-ment" for the favor. On the contrary, Smollett said he had read a card Johnson had written complaining about Wilkes. What this card said is a matter for the imagination. But if Johnson was wary of John Wilkes then his foresight was justified. There was something devil-ish in his personality; a strong current of mischief and bravado that was too impetuous and daring for a Stoic like Johnson to tolerate. But even if Johnson detected any of this in 1759, he could not have foreseen the havoc the Member of Parliament for Aylesbury was poised to wreak. Over the decade to come, Wilkes would upend British politics. And as the story of "Wilkes and Liberty" played out in Britain, its effects would spill over and animate a parallel crisis in colonial America. The world Franklin and Strahan knew, the lives they thought they were going to live—all of this was about to vanish forever.

Liberty

(1762–1768)

Seven

SCRIBBLERS AND ETCHERS

ON AUGUST 23, 1762, a summer breeze blew east along the English Channel. At Portsmouth, the largest port on England's south coast, this was the worst wind for those wanting to cross the Atlantic. For one passenger it was particularly frustrating. Benjamin Franklin had been in Portsmouth for a fortnight, waiting for the packet ship *Carolina* to sail. But deciding that the weather had set in, the ship's chief officer, Captain Friend, ordered his passengers to disembark once again. Having clambered dejectedly down the gangplank, Franklin's mood was at least brightened by a letter that was waiting for him on shore. He opened it and found that it was from his great friend William Strahan.

It was apt that a letter from the Scotsman should catch Franklin just before he sailed for Philadelphia. During the five years of Franklin's London stay, Strahan had been an almost constant presence. Indeed it was a note of Franklin's own to Strahan that could be said to have opened this period all those years before. "Our Assembly talk of sending me to England speedily," Franklin wrote in early 1757. He primed Strahan to "look out sharp, and if a fat old Fellow should come to your Printing House and request a little Smouting,* depend upon it, 'tis Your Affectionate Friend and humble Servant."[1] Strahan must have read this with skepticism. For years Franklin had made similar promises. In the end, though, the trip was always put off, due to some civic commitment or his wife Deborah's "invincible Aversion to crossing the Seas."[2] This time was different. In July 1757, to Strahan's delight, Franklin did materialize in London. There was no Deborah, of course, but he was accompanied by his well-turned-out son William.

Franklin and William had taken lodgings with a Mrs. Stevenson in Craven Street, near Charing Cross. They were soon happily established, close to the center of political power in Westminster. This was appropriate, for Franklin had come to Britain on official business. As he had hinted to Strahan, his task was to petition the proprietor, Thomas Penn, on behalf of the Pennsylvanian Assembly. Seventy-five years after its founding, the Penn family remained the colony's proprietors but recently their relations with the Assembly had soured. The crux of this quarrel was a question of governance and, particularly, taxation. The Assembly wanted to tax all land in Pennsylvania equally, but the Penns refused to allow levies to be raised on their own estates.

Franklin's task was to point out the unfairness of this and, hopefully, find some remedy. It was not an easy task. Although he was a seasoned operator, Franklin had never before confronted anything like Westminster's political machine. Progress came at glacial pace. His commission did, at least, provide him with funds and a sense of purpose. It left Franklin with plenty of free time too. And while the Penn family regarded Franklin as a troublemaker, many in London cared much less about his political assignment. Instead they were ea-

---

* "Smouting" is an antiquated word that was already obscure enough in the 1750s to be left out of Johnson's *Dictionary*. It was a slang term used by printers denoting "part-time or irregular work."

ger to meet the inspired American who had been awarded the Royal Society's prestigious Copley Medal in 1753, "on account of his curious Experiments and Observations on Electricity." Ever since that date, or so it seemed, wherever Franklin went, stories of his achievements arrived before him.

In Britain, Franklin lived the sort of life that he dreamed about in his younger days. He spent winter nights in bright conversation with scientific friends at club meetings or at dinners in London. When the days lengthened and the capital emptied out for the summer, Franklin took the opportunity to explore Great Britain more widely. Along with William he researched their family history in Northamptonshire. Franklin also headed north to Scotland, where he gazed over the great landscapes of lochs and hills and met the philosopher David Hume. Then there were the invitations to committees; the audiences with nobles; and the honorary degrees from the universities of St. Andrews and Oxford. These allowed him to amend his identity once again. From "Benjamin Franklin, Gent.," he evolved into "Dr. Franklin," a wise and benevolent, if slightly unusual, older man. Indeed, it was as Dr. Franklin that, on May 1, 1760, he crossed paths with the future Dr. Johnson at a society meeting in London. This is the only occasion when Franklin and Johnson were recorded as being in the same place at the same time. Suggestively, neither mentioned the event in their private or public papers.[3]

Equally suggestively, Franklin did not seem in a hurry to return to Philadelphia, where Deborah and his daughter Sally waited for him. Instead he was content to remain in the Stevensons' household, where, in particular, he grew close to his landlady's clever young daughter Polly. The girl was of a similar age to Sally, and she impressed Franklin with her inquisitiveness. Franklin gave Polly little lessons in the sciences, and in time the two developed a delightful relationship. Beyond Craven Street, Franklin grew close to a group of Royal Society fellows, consolidating his friendship with the botanist Peter Collinson and forging a new one with the physician John Pringle.

None of his friends, though, were as close as Strahan. After their lengthy correspondence, they must have met with some trepidation. But, as it turned out, the printers got on as well in person as they did on paper. Strahan in particular felt a buoyancy, a brightness, a sense of heightened animation in Franklin's company. He admired Franklin's mind and recognized his talents, but he also appreciated the way he conducted himself. He never found Franklin too busy or haughty to listen to others, even "those of inferior Capacity." Instead, he saw in the Philadelphian a striking emotional intelligence. It allowed him "to level himself for the time to the Understandings of his Company, and to enter without Affectation into their Amusements and Chitchat."[4] For Franklin's part, he found "Straney," as he affectionately called him, a paragon of British good sense, humor, and industry.

In 1762, when the time came for Franklin's return to America, Strahan was shattered. Knowing no one else who could truly comprehend what he felt, Strahan decided to write a letter to his old friend David Hall in Philadelphia. Of Franklin, he explained:

> As for myself, I never found a Person in my whole Life more thoroughly to my Mind. As far as my Knowledge, or Experience, or Sentiments of every kind, could reach his more enlarged Sagacity and Conceptions, they exactly corresponded with his; or if I accidentally differed from him in any Particular, he quickly and with great Facility and Good-nature poured in such Light upon the Subject, as immediately convinced me I was wrong. It would much exceed the Bounds of a Letter to tell you in how many Views, and on how many Accounts, I esteem and love him, or how much and how universally he is esteemed by all who know him here. Suffice it to say, that I part with him with infinite Regret and Sorrow. I know not where to find his equal, nor can the Chasm his Departure leaves in my Social Enjoyments and Happiness ever be filled up. There is something in his leaving us even more cruel than a Separation by Death; it

is like an *untimely Death*, where we part with a Friend to meet no more, *with a whole Heart*, as we say in Scotland.[5]

Strahan had said the same to Franklin himself. On a memorable occasion in March 1760, Strahan spent a whole evening trying to convince Franklin to settle permanently in London. "He was very urgent with me," Franklin afterward wrote to Debby. Central to Strahan's proposals was a marriage between William Strahan, Jr., and their daughter Sally. "In point of Circumstances," Franklin, ever the businessman, ruminated, "there can be no Objection. Mr. Strahan being in so thriving a Way, as to lay up a Thousand Pounds every Year from the Profits of his Business, after maintaining his Family and paying all Charges."[6]

But even as he was writing this, Franklin knew there was little hope of tempting his wife and daughter across the Atlantic. The family was too closely tied to Philadelphia, and Deborah's horror of a voyage was too much to overcome. One day his London life would have to end. This end came in 1762, accelerated by an uncharacteristically foolish blunder. Throughout Franklin's stay, Britain had been fighting a war against France. In 1760, the British Exchequer had released a little over £26,000, an enormous sum of money, to cover Pennsylvania's wartime expenses. As representative of the colony in London, Franklin took control of the money, which he soon afterward invested in government annuities. While this was a perfectly legal thing to do, it nonetheless involved risk. A nightmare followed. Instead of the anticipated peace, the war in fact expanded. In consequence the ministry's credit had tumbled. By February 1762, when Franklin's broker shifted the last of his toxic stock, his total loss exceeded four thousand pounds. It was vital Franklin return to Philadelphia to explain himself.

On August 10, 1762, Franklin said his farewells to friends in London. Strahan found the departure difficult. In his letter to Hall, he described the event as a "melancholy Occasion": a parting that was "the more bitter and agonizing, as it is likely to be *endless*."[7] Franklin felt a similar sadness. Replying to Strahan from Portsmouth, he wrote:

> I cannot, I assure you, quit even this disagreeable Place without Regret, as it carries me still farther from those I love, and from the Opportunities of hearing of their Welfare. The Attraction of *Reason* is at present for the other Side of the Water, but that of *Inclination* will be for this side. You know which usually prevails. I shall probably make but this one Vibration and settle here for ever.[8]

HAVING FINISHED HIS LETTER, Franklin was left to brood. Portsmouth, as he had suggested to Strahan, was not a place he liked. He had grown used to the fashionable streets of London. Portsmouth was seedy by comparison. Its cobbled High Street was lined with noisy taverns, shabby lodging houses, and military outfitters. The restless mood in the streets contributed to Franklin's apprehension about the voyage ahead. Once the *Carolina* left the safety of the harbor, she would soon be in the English Channel and at the mercy of enemy ships.

The war with France was now entering a seventh year. It was a confused conflict: desperate, sprawling, and complicated. At its heart, however, was a grand contest for imperial domination between two ancient European rivals: France and Britain. On paper this was an unequal match. France's population of twenty-five million was twice that of Great Britain's; its army was correspondingly larger too. Britain, though, had a bigger navy, and this was a huge logistical advantage in a war that involved fighting across the four quarters of the world.

Portsmouth was as good a place as any to make sense of it. As he waited for the wind in 1762, Franklin might have reflected that it was just outside the arms of the harbor, in the Solent, that the wretched Admiral Byng had been court-martialed and executed early in the war, in 1757. Very few people believed Byng deserved such an end—his crime was a failure to aggressively pursue the enemy during the loss of the Mediterranean island of Minorca—but his death did have an effect. No one wanted to share his fate. In fact, people wanted the absolute opposite. To be in the British military, one had to be cool, clinical, and resolute. As Admiral Boscawen famously put it, "Never fire, my lads, till you see the whites of the Frenchmen's eyes."[9]

The people of Portsmouth had seen many great fleets assemble at the Spithead anchorage over the years that followed: the transports that sailed up the St. Lawrence to victory in Canada; the towering ships of the line that had chased the French fleet in among the terrible rocks of Quiberon Bay in Brittany. These stunning achievements in 1759 had firmly turned the course of the conflict in Britain's favor, and they had made heroes of men like General Wolfe and Admiral Hawke. While the military leaders carried out the daring assaults across the world, in Westminster William Pitt was seen as the man of iron who made it all possible. Pitt was a figure of legend. It was said that his nose resembled an eagle's beak, that there was a glint in his eyes that bespoke a strange power. He was known, most of all, as a magnificent orator, who could "by turns drop honey or distil venom."[10] All this may have seemed like excitable hagiography, but at the time many people believed it. In 1761, when Pitt's chariot approached St. Paul's Churchyard during the lord mayor's Show: "At every stop the mob clung about every part of the vehicle, hung upon the wheels, hugged his footmen, and even kissed his horses. There was an universal huzza; and the gentlemen at the windows and in the balconies waved their hats, and the ladies their handkerchiefs."[11]

And by this time Britain had one more hero too. While Pitt plotted in Westminster and Wolfe climbed the slope toward the Plains of Abraham, in India a belligerent commander named Robert Clive had been conducting a series of ruthless engagements on behalf of the East India Company. In the summer of 1760, Clive had returned to Portsmouth in the *Royal George*, along with a staggering personal fortune of £300,000. Besides the victories in Canada and off the French coast, Britons were left to absorb the extraordinary fact that one of the most profitable regions on the planet lay completely under their control.

For Franklin, as for any patriotic Briton, this was a time of huge excitement. And while her influence had grown abroad, the country had been refreshed from within by the accession of a new king. The opening of a new reign was always a vibrant time, but there was something in the figure of young George that kindled particular enthusiasm. According to Horace Walpole, society gossip and youngest son of the old prime minister, George was "not a wild, dissipated boy, but good-natured and cheerful."[12] Although naturally shy, he was described as being "tall, and full of dignity; his countenance florid and good-natured; his manner graceful and obliging."[13]

Franklin had been present in September 1761 for the coronation of the twenty-three-year-old George III, the youngest king since Edward VI in the 1540s. The whole event was seen as an expression of George's personality, and Franklin was impressed. To be leaving Britain in the earliest phases of his reign was an irritation. A new era was beginning, and for Franklin, who loved to be at the center of things, this was not the time to be sailing away to a life on the margins. More galling still was the fact that Franklin's political fortunes had turned. Five years before, on his arrival, for all his scientific celebrity, he had been written off by the Penn family as someone who "will be looked very coldly upon by great People."[14] No one could say the same in 1762, because there had been an astonishing political turnaround.

For several generations, British politics had been dominated by a Whig oligarchy. The most significant politicians tended to come from one of a handful of key families—the Walpoles, Pelhams, Cavendishes, and Grenvilles. These ruled in concert with the Hanoverian monarchs who had so far accepted their reduced position in Britain's political system. In consequence, politics had long been stable, but as the length of the Whig supremacy had increased, so had the degree of corruption. Posts, offices, seats, sinecures were often sold off or presented in return for favors that helped to prop up the status quo. Sir Robert Walpole had been the grand master of this, and in the 1760s his *modus operandi* was continued by the neurotic, scheming, and fabulously wealthy Duke of Newcastle. Now in his sixties, Newcastle's ability to manage the Members of Parliament was almost as admired as his political longevity. Since 1724 he had held one high political office or another, and throughout the years of war he had continued to head the ministry, in which he was known as the "Minister of Numbers" while Pitt was the "Minister of Measures."[15]

As long as this endured, Franklin had little hope for change. The politicians he had to petition on behalf of the Assembly were too entrenched, too compromised to listen to a lone American voice. But with the young king's accession, the old Whigs' grip on power was weakening. Indeed, the great wave of political change that was soon to break over Westminster could be traced back to a rainy day at the races in Egham, Surrey, more than a decade before, when John Stuart, Third Earl of Bute, was invited by Frederick, Prince of Wales, to make up a fourth at cards. Bute was a Scottish nobleman of some pedigree. He had been educated at Eton and the University of Leiden, and, while still young, he had married Mary Wortley Montagu, the only daughter of a former ambassador to the Ottoman Empire. In the 1740s, however, Bute was not established in London society, and the story was later told that in his younger days he was too poor to keep a carriage of his own. But Frederick liked Bute. He appointed him one of the lords of his bedchamber, and he had become an established part of Frederick's household by the time of the prince's sudden death in 1751. As a result of this, his young son George became heir to the throne. And as Frederick's widow, Augusta, the Dowager Princess of Wales, contemplated her son's future, she turned for emotional support and intellectual guidance to a man she very much liked: Lord Bute.

Franklin would have heard the stories along with everyone else. The prince was devoted to Bute; the two of them spent afternoons and evenings at the royal residence at Kew in deep conversation. Later in the century, Thomas Jefferson would single out this moment as one of the prime causes of revolution. He believed that in George's "Tory" education he could glimpse the "seeds of war."[16] Here Jefferson was not quite right. If anything, the kind of relationship that existed between Bute and the prince more closely resembled what Franklin had advocated in his promotional pamphlet for the Philadelphia Academy.

In George's private quarters the two discussed the role of kingship, the history of English laws, customs and liberties, economics, religion, the value of freedom of speech, and questions of deportment. It is likely, too, that George picked up his relish for horticulture from Bute, an avid gardener. All told, the tone of the prince's lessons was progressive and enlightened, and an intimate bond developed between the two. In the decade between 1756 and 1765, the prince wrote at least 340 letters to Bute, and he solicited his advice on everything. "I have already lived long enough," he wrote to Bute aged twenty-one in 1760, "to know you are the only man I shall ever meet with who . . . at all times prefer[s] my interest to your own."[17] Later that year, when he heard that his grandfather, George II, had collapsed and died, the first thing George did was to write to Bute. "A most extraordinary thing" has just happened, he revealed to his friend.[18]

It had long been seen as inevitable that George would bring Bute into government when he became king. During the early part of Franklin's time in London, this prospect was troubling those in power. As a countermove against Bute, rumors were put about that his influence had come as a result of an affair he was conducting with the prince's mother. There was talk of a connecting door between Bute's chambers and Augusta's bedroom at Kew, a door that would creak at night. In the hands of two such people, the young prince was but a pawn. Horace Walpole summed up the gossip with his usual élan. George had long, he wrote, lain under the influence of "a passionate, domineering woman, and a Favourite without talents."[19] This was most likely nothing more than cruel whispering, but events in the aftermath of the new king's accession added credence to the rumors. Within days George had Bute made a privy councillor. Shortly afterward, Bute was maneuvered into the influential position of Groom of the Stole, which ensured their close personal connection would continue. Not long after that, Bute was elected to the House of Lords as one of the representative peers for Scotland.

The political agitations did not stop here. As Bute's position was being formalized, a number of Newcastle's placemen were relieved of their offices. Then, following the cracks, came the great fissure. William Pitt had long been considered a keystone of British politics. But in the summer of 1761, he found himself oddly isolated. Pitt's problem was the tremendous cost of the war. The king, who had been taught by Bute to regard debt as a moral sin, was eager to confront the matter by opening peace talks with the French. Pitt opposed this violently. Rather than curtail the war, Pitt had quite another idea. He had long been suspicious of the intentions of Spain, due to their *Pacte de Famille* with France. Though it had long been neutral, in 1761 Pitt received intelligence that suggested the Spanish were preparing to enter the conflict. In response, in the autumn, Pitt demanded Britain issue a preemptive declaration of war. When his colleagues refused to back him, Pitt resigned in disgust. In an instant the Pitt–Newcastle partnership was shattered and a gaping hole emerged at the center of British politics. The historian Kate Hotblack characterized the shock people felt. It was, she wrote, "as if a department of State had gone out of office."[20]

The king was generous to Pitt, presenting him with an annual pension of £3,000 and granting a hereditary peerage to his wife, Hester. But George could afford to be magnanimous. Now Pitt was gone, the path for high office was opening up for Bute. When Newcastle, isolated and elderly, resigned in the spring of 1762, the king called for his man, known to all as "the Favourite." While there was a sense of inevitability about Bute's elevation, people were left to gaze in wonder all the same. In less than two years King George had broken the Whig oligarchy that had governed Britain for over a generation. Now Bute, a Tory, and a Scottish Tory at that, was in charge. This had ramifications for everyone, but it held particular significance for Franklin. Bute, with his interest in natural philosophy and especially botany, was an associate of two of his friends: John Pringle, the physician, and the botanist Peter Collinson. Unexpectedly, the chandler's boy from Milk Street in Boston found himself with that magical quality in the Georgian world, "interest." He was now connected to the most powerful political figure in the whole British Empire.

Although Franklin would not like to be reminded of the fact in years to come, he was an admirer of Bute. In both Craven Street and in his Philadelphian home he had portraits of him on full display. Such a public statement was understandable, for Bute was the kind of man who had the ability to change Franklin's life. Sensing his chance, Franklin spent his final summer in London putting his influence to work. Lobbying efforts had gone forward in June and July, and by the time Franklin arrived in Portsmouth, a staggering development in his family fortunes was about to take place. William Franklin, who had arrived with his father in 1757, with little more idea than reading law and gaining admittance to the bar, had, over the course of several letters, convinced Bute of his character and his "long Acquaintance with the Management of public Business in the Colonies."[21] As such at the beginning of September, in just a few weeks' time, he was to be appointed royal governor of New Jersey. And Franklin's ambitions were not satisfied yet. Before he left London, he wrote again to Bute. This letter was carefully calculated to please. Franklin passed on several hints to Bute about ways to preserve gunpowder. He also issued a promise. Once safely home, both he and William would comb the beaches for shells for Lady Bute's collection.

Franklin had lived in the political world long enough to know a pretty shell from an American beach could carry significant political capital. What positions might come his way in the future was something to ponder as he sailed across the Atlantic. But for all his hope, there was reason to worry too. Bute's position was unstable. While the king's support was firm, Bute had many enemies at Westminster. Some were already referring to him as a "Northern Machiavel," and shortly after Pitt's resignation the previous November, the public's mood toward him had been expressed when his coach was pelted with dirt as he rode to a dinner with the lord mayor. Bute had taken the precaution of hiring George Stephenson, well known as the "one-eyed fighting coach-man," but even so, as the crowd closed in, he had only been saved from a confrontation by the intervention of a party of constables. The mob was a threat for Bute, but his greatest enemies remained the members of the displaced Grenville faction, such as Pitt and his scheming brother-in-law, Lord Temple. Both of these had ceded power to him, and both remained furious. Their irritation was inflamed by the drive for peace with France. In May, as Bute was establishing his own ministry, Pitt had declared to Parliament:

> I am convinced this country can raise 12, 13, 14 or even 15 million the next year: I know it without seeking information from bundles of papers and accounts. The only question is whether grievous and permanent as that tax must be, it is not to be preferred to the perpetual dishonour of the nation, the aggrandisement of the enemy, and the desertion of your allies, all which tend to an inglorious and precarious peace.[22]

So the lines were drawn. Pitt and Bute were viewed as opposites: one was a hawk, the other a dove; one was a Whig, the other a Tory; one an Englishman, the other a Scot. As ever, the quarrel was fought out in print. The paper war began when Pitt's ally, Lord Temple, began to fund an anti-Bute weekly called the *Monitor*, edited by his personal lawyer, Arthur Beardmore. Bute responded by bankrolling a pro-ministerial journal of his own. The *Briton* appeared the week that Bute kissed hands with the king. It was edited by Smollett, the popular Scottish writer, whose engagement by Bute seemed an astute move. Provoked by this, Temple reacted swiftly. A week after the *Briton* appeared, yet another journal was launched. In an obvious parody of Smollett's title, this one was called the *North Briton*.

Franklin must have flicked through the *North Briton* with half a frown and half a smile. The author, as one reader put it:

> attacked [Bute] with such intrepidity, and seasoned his satire with such a poignancy of wit, that it was instantly admired and bought up, by people of all ranks. His stile was masterly and elegant, his wit and satire truly classical, always exceeding keen, and very seldom gross, which operated incredibly upon the minds of the people. His facts were *always* genuine, and incontrovertible; which gave the paper a character of veracity. His doctrines were strictly constitutional, and his arguments too strong to need any other assistance to convince the public, who were betraying its interests.[23]

The *North Briton* was the kind of journal the young Franklin would have admired. It was irreverent, daring, and nimble. For the older Franklin, however, it was a more perplexing read. Throughout the summer it appeared every Saturday, with contents that grew increasingly wild and uncouth. Just who the author was, no one yet knew. But as the wind turned at Portsmouth and Captain Friend invited his passengers to board the *Carolina* one last time, Franklin may well have left the country with a reflection. Nothing could continue for long the way the *North Briton* had begun.

UNTIL A FEW WEEKS earlier, the solution to the riddle of the *North Briton*'s authorship could have been found just twenty miles to the north of Portsmouth in the city of Winchester. John Wilkes had been billeted there in his capacity as colonel of the Buckinghamshire Militia. Though by no means a military man, Wilkes had been drafted into a wartime role that he relished. In his rich red coat, he was able to play the part of a soldier—drilling troops and guarding a small number of French prisoners of war. These duties, however, were far from onerous, and they left him with ample time for his entertaining side project.

Knowing Wilkes was a gifted writer, Lord Temple had approached him earlier in the spring with his plan for an anti-Bute journal. It was a spontaneous idea, but it turned out to be a very good one. Wilkes's manner of writing, jaunty and wry, was ideally suited to the job. Every Saturday since, a new *North Briton* was printed in London. First in the coffee shops and later in the county towns as it traveled with the post, readers came to love the forceful, satirical attacks on Bute. Vitalized by the success of the journal, Wilkes left his barracks at the beginning of August to spend the rest of the summer in his parliamentary constituency at Aylesbury.

In 1762, Wilkes was in his late thirties. He was a familiar figure in London's political circles, with his prominent lantern jaw, thin face, and right eye that pointed perturbingly inward. Such features, along with the fact that some of his teeth had started to fall out, left Wilkes with a somewhat startling appearance. He remembered once being told that his face should not be exposed to pregnant women. Like Johnson, though, those who took the time to talk with him were soon repaid for their efforts. There was never any gloom about Wilkes. By contrast his personality sparkled and shone in conversation. Edward Gibbon, who met him at the Winchester camp, was struck by this. In his journal he reflected that he had "scarcely ever met with a better companion." Wilkes was a man of "inexhaustible spirits, infinite wit, and humour, and a great deal of knowledge," Gibbon decided, qualities that seemed all the stranger when set beside the other things that were known about him. Wilkes was, Gibbon went on: "a thorough profligate in principle as in practice; his character is infamous, his life stained with every vice, and his conversation full of blasphemy and bawdy. These morals he glories in—for shame is a weakness he has long since surmounted."[24]

Raised as a gentleman, educated in Leiden, and brought into the House of Commons as a supporter of Pitt in the 1750s, Wilkes had until 1762 been just another middling politician at Westminster. He had drifted between town and country and made sure he voted the right way when required. Estranged from a wife whom he had married early and never loved, he was known—if he was known at all—for his rakish personal life. He spent money carelessly and ran thick with a dissolute set of noblemen, politicians, and hangers-on who were rumored to meet at Medmenham, an abandoned monastery in the Buckingham countryside, for alcoholic and sexual orgies. Wilkes was happy to confess his sins. Once, when offered tobacco, he was reputed to have replied: "No thank you. I have no small vices."[25] He would, however, have taken issue with Gibbon's picture of him as an abandoned rake. Wilkes saw himself more as an Epicurean; an educated gentleman who lived with a sense of freedom in terms of thought, religion, and sex.

While the question of whether Wilkes was a libertine or a rake could be argued out over a bottle of claret, the undeniable fact was that his lifestyle cost him huge amounts of money. Getting into Parliament alone required thousands of pounds in bribes. His lifestyle thereafter— which included a fine Westminster town house—far outstripped his means. By the early 1760s, Wilkes knew that the only real way of rescuing his appalling financial situation rested with his political connections. As he was enmeshed within the powerful Grenville faction, headed by Pitt and Temple, he always had some hope of a cozy sinecure or, more glamorous still, a lucrative posting overseas—over the years he had petitioned for appointments to offices like the governorship of Canada. Most recently Wilkes had set his heart on a position at the Board of Trade. None of these attempts had amounted to anything, however, and when Pitt and Temple resigned in the autumn of 1761 his chances of preferment seemed at an end.

Had that been the end of it, Wilkes would have melted away into obscurity, and the entire history of the decade to come would have been different. But instead Temple decided to use Wilkes as a strategic weapon against Bute. Given Wilkes's talents he was a natural enough choice, and he had the additional benefit of being friendly with the greatest satirical poet of the day. Charles Churchill, huge, hefty, and awkward, was in physical terms a complete contrast to Wilkes. But like Wilkes he was in his thirties, separated from his wife, dreadful with money, and bent on a life of pleasure. When the two first crossed paths in 1762, their bond had been instant. Whether Temple had noticed this growing friendship, or it was just lucky timing, Wilkes and Churchill were soon working in league on the *North Briton*.

Each acted as a catalyst for the other. Their remit was broad but their target was specific. Temple wanted them to inflict as much misery on Bute as they possibly could, and he was happy to cover the costs. Wilkes and Churchill immediately began to scheme. Like Johnson and Franklin, they had grown up under the influence of the great periodical writers, and they knew all of their tricks: the anonymous narrator, the fictional readers' letters, the use of historical allusions, satire, imposture, and mimicry. Their very first idea was mischievous. The title *North Briton* was selected not only in reply to Smollett's *Briton*, but also because it allowed them to tap into English prejudice against the Scots. Bute's nationality was an inherent weakness in political terms. Worse still for the Whiggish English, his surname was "Stuart," which could hardly be more unfortunate.

With all this in mind, Wilkes and Churchill decided to annoy Bute by writing under the persona of a tone-deaf, gleeful "North Briton," a period term for someone from Scotland. Everything was designed to rile and amuse English readers:

> I thank my stars, I am a *North Briton*; with this almost singular circumstance belonging to me, that I am "*unplaced* and *unpensioned*": but I hope this reproach will soon be wiped away, and

that I shall no longer be pointed at by my sneering countrymen. (*North Briton* No. 1)

I Cannot conceal the joy I feel as a *North Briton*, and I heartily congratulate my dear countrymen on our having at length accomplished the great, long sought, and universally national object of all our wishes, the planting of a *Scotsman* at the head of the *English* Treasury. (*North Briton* No. 2)

The EARL OF BUTE (with triumph be it spoken) is now at the head of affairs, and there is nothing which we may not, which we ought not to hope for from the favour and patronage of our worthy *Countryman*. (*North Briton* No.4)[26]

This sly technique conferred an instant notoriety on the *North Briton*, which encouraged the duo even more. The creative process worked something like this. Wilkes would sketch out pieces, according to the news of the week or the whim of the moment. He then forwarded his draft to Churchill, who polished the prose and added flourishes of his own. The completed copy was then sent to London, to William Richardson (nephew of Samuel the novelist), who printed the *North Briton* for the bookseller George Kearsley, who sold it at his shop on Ludgate Hill for twopence halfpenny. Among this were several discrete steps. Temple's money kept the machine running, and a lawyer named William Johnston would run his eyes over the copy to check for any libel. The dukes of Newcastle and Portland were also said to be involved, although if they were, they took care to keep their distance.

Due to the provocative nature of the *North Briton*, involving a lawyer was a necessary precaution. But for their part Wilkes and Churchill were relaxed about the threat of prosecution. Both were careful to conceal their involvement, and for a libel to be proved, authorship had to be established. The most vulnerable of all of them was not Wilkes, Churchill, or Temple, but Kearsley, the publisher, whose name appeared on the front of each Saturday's edition. Not anticipating the kind of writing he would be putting his name to, Kearsley began to fret as the first copy came in. A month after the debut edition, he voiced his complaints. Wilkes responded, "You may be assured that your apprehensions as Publisher, are not well founded . . . I have a very good opinion of your judgment, but here you are certainly more timorous than there is any occasion to be."[27]

In fact, Kearsley was merely being sensible. The issue that had unsettled him was *North Briton* No.5, in which Wilkes drew a malicious parallel between Lord Bute and the fourteenth-century warlord Roger Mortimer. Mortimer was an infamous figure in English history. He was known for having seduced the queen, allegedly murdered King Edward II, and driven England into a state of desperate tyranny. "O may Britain never see such a day again!" the "North Briton" had reflected, "when power acquired by profligacy may lord it over this realm; when the feeble pretentions of a *court minion* may require the prostitution of royalty for their support."[28] Entertaining as such a skit was, Wilkes was dancing on the edge here. Everyone knew it. Even Churchill had winced. "The paper of the third [*North Briton* No. 5, July 3] will never be forgotten, and you will never be forgiven, as it is universally ascribed to you," he cautioned. "I desire you to take great care of your health, and still more of your life."[29]

By August it seemed Churchill's anxieties had been unfounded. While Temple had cautioned Wilkes to take care, no one had confronted him. Indeed, Wilkes believed, there was nothing for him to worry about at all. In his mind, Hanoverian Britain was a very different country to Stuart England. Back then he might have been pilloried or hauled in for questioning, or worse; there had been traitors' charters, and the king's messengers had swept the capital's streets for underground printers. But no printer had been executed in Britain since John Matthews in 1719, and in the years since, Wilkes thought, a free press had become an essential part of British life.[30] He had opened the first number of the *North Briton* with these words:

> The *liberty of the press* is the birth-right of a BRITON, and is justly esteemed the firmest bulwark of the liberties of this country. It has been the terror of all bad ministers; for their dark and dangerous designs, or their weakness, inability, and duplicity, have thus been detected and shewn to the public, generally in too strong and just colours for them long to bear up against the odium of mankind.[31]

In fact, rather than heed Temple's warnings, Wilkes broadened his range to include attacks on anyone who could be seen as supportive of Bute's ministry. As Franklin was sailing from Portsmouth, Wilkes was busily assaulting Samuel Johnson. Having already teased Johnson over his *Dictionary*, he spotted an opportunity for more fun when the papers carried the news that the lexicographer had accepted a royal pension of £300 a year for services to literature. Johnson had never been fond of the Hanoverians and had long prided himself on his independence as a writer. By accepting the pension he had compromised himself. Ruminating on this, Wilkes had leafed through a copy of Johnson's *Dictionary*. As he explained in *North Briton* No. 12, he found a number of instructive definitions. One he thought worth bringing to his readers' attention related to the word "favourite," which Johnson had defined as "*a mean wretch, whose whole business is by any means to please.*"[32]

There was better to come:

> The word *pension* likewise has of late much puzzled our politicians. I do not recollect that any one of them has ventured a definition of it. *Mr Johnson*, as he is now a *pensioner*, one should naturally have recourse to, for the truest literary information on this subject. His definition then of *pension* is, *an allowance made to*

any one without an equivalent. In England it is generally understood to
mean pay given to a state hireling for treason to his country.[33]

This was Wilkes at his best: incisive, fearless, sarcastic, suggestive.
It was just the kind of material to amuse the *North Briton*'s growing readership. For while Smollett's *Briton* had only ever sold in the
hundreds, Wilkes and Churchill were now read by thousands each
week. Quite by accident, Wilkes had found his vocation as a political agitator. "Give me a grain of truth," he wrote with characteristic
brio, "and I will mix it up with a great mass of falsehood so that no
chemist will ever be able to separate them."[34]

As the summer ended and September began, Wilkes made plans
to leave Aylesbury for his town house in Great George Street, in the
heart of Westminster. Before he was called back to the militia's camp,
he wanted to catch up on the latest political gossip. One thing in particular had caught his attention. After Johnson had been pensioned off
by Bute, rumors were flying that another leading cultural figure had
gone the same way. Wilkes had known William Hogarth for years.
They belonged to a dining society called the Beefsteak Club that met
in Covent Garden. Now, however, it was said that Hogarth had been
approached by Bute to launch an attack on Wilkes and Churchill.

Arriving in London, Wilkes learned the truth of this. On September 7, Hogarth had released a dramatic new work, crammed with
political detail, entitled *The Times*. In it a fire burns furiously along
a row of houses, while a team of firefighters battle against the odds
to extinguish it. Leading the efforts is King George III himself, who
stands on top of a plinth in full armor with a gushing fire hose in his
hand. Meanwhile a group of kilted Scotsmen and English sailors rush
with buckets to keep the water flowing.

Others, though, are not being so helpful. Standing high on a pair
of stilts, with a millstone reading "3000 £ per annum" around his
neck, William Pitt pumps a pair of bellows at the flames. And farther
away, in a building called the Temple Coffee House, two figures peep

out of the garret window. Both hold hoses, but instead of pointing them at the fire, they direct their jets unhelpfully toward the king. Their faces are shining with glee. As Wilkes must instantly have known, these were the faces of himself and Charles Churchill.[35]

DRAMATIC THOUGH IT WAS, Hogarth's *The Times* ranked second in interest in September 1762 to the news that John Russell, the Duke of Bedford, had set off for Paris to formally open negotiations for peace. Bute and the king, it seemed, had got their way. After almost seven years of fighting, the war seemed to have run its course.

To Wilkes, as to all Pitt's allies, this was grave news. But on September 10, Wilkes's attention was tugged away from politics. He had spent the afternoon out in town. Arriving home at Great George Street about five o'clock, he found a note waiting for him. Written in an urgent tone, it came from the household of Lord Talbot, the Lord Steward. This was ominous. According to the note, one of Talbot's servants, a Mr. Secker, had called at his house three times without success. Secker's letter informed Wilkes that if he did not receive a reply that day he would return again at nine the following morning. By the time Wilkes finished this brief note, he must have guessed what lay behind it.

Talbot was an old-timer on the political stage. Over the past year, however, he had become more significant than ever before. In his capacity as Lord High Steward he had played a prominent part in George III's coronation: walking directly before the king in the procession to Westminster Abbey, carrying the golden crown of St. Edward with its twinkling diamonds, emeralds, rubies, and sapphires. After the six-hour ceremony had concluded in the abbey, a "coronation festival" was held in Westminster Hall. At dusk on an early autumn day, the ancient hall had an enchanting atmosphere. It was illuminated by three thousand wax candles, and everyone that mattered was present: "our crowned heads, and almost the whole nobility, with the prime of our gentry, [all] most superbly arrayed, and adorned with a profusion of the most brilliant jewels . . . To conceive it in all its lustre," wrote one eyewitness, "I am conscious that it is absolutely necessary to have been present."[36]

For Talbot, though, this was an anxious rather than an aesthetic experience. Before the coronation banquet began, his role was to position himself on horseback at the head of the king's table. This task had its perils. The gloom, the din, the gaze of a thousand eyes, and the smell of roasted venison were all quite enough to panic or distract a horse. To combat this, Talbot had spent some time in Westminster Hall with his "very fine brown bay," rehearsing the moment. All this was to no avail. As the first course was served, Talbot attempted to make his horse walk backward away from the king's table. This maneuver was crucial if Talbot was going to keep his face toward the royal presence, as etiquette required. The command turned out to be too much for the horse. Instead of walking backward in a straight line, it progressed, as Wilkes described it, "like the great planet in *Milton, danc'd about in various rounds his wand'ring course. At different times, he was progressive, retrograde, or standing still.*" This was more Don Quixote than Sir Lancelot. The Duke of Cumberland was said to have had a fit of giggles, and yet more etiquette was breached when other diners burst into a round of spontaneous applause. Horace Walpole had merrily likened the scene to a slapstick at Bartholomew Fair.

Talbot, unsurprisingly, had not found the episode quite so amusing. Wilkes, however, had. In the twelfth issue of the *North Briton*, he made the playful suggestion that Talbot was as deserving of a ministerial pension as Johnson:

A politeness equal to that of lord TALBOT's *horse* ought not to pass unnoticed. At the coronation he paid a new, and, for a *horse*, singular respect to his sovereign. I appeal to applauding multitudes, who were so charmed, as to forget every rule of decency, and to *clap* even in the *Royal* presence, whether *his*, or his *lord's* dexterity on that day did not surpass any courtier's. Caligula's *horse* had not half the merit. We remember how nobly *he* was provided for. What the exact proportion of merit was between his *lordship* and his *horse*, and how far the pension should be divided between them, I will not take upon me to determine.[37]

Having spent August in Aylesbury, Wilkes had remained out of Talbot's reach. But now he was back in Westminster, it seemed that the Lord Steward wanted to have a word. Wilkes dashed off a quick reply to Talbot's note. A response soon came back to Great George Street. By now it was clear that Talbot was furious about the passage in the *North Briton* No. 12. He demanded to know whether Wilkes had written it. This question put Wilkes in a tricky position. To admit his authorship was to expose himself to accusations of libel. Furthermore, if the news got out that he admitted to writing one paper, then the inference was that he had a hand in the others. Wilkes decided to respond with a mix of caution and threat. "I must first," he wrote to Talbot, "insist on knowing your Lordship's right to catechise me about an anonymous paper. If you Lordship is not satisfied with this, I shall ever be ready to give your Lordship any other satisfaction becoming me as a gentleman."[38]

This reply, which Wilkes sent round to Talbot's town house in Mayfair that night, was shockingly inflammatory. The threat was embedded in the final line and, particularly, in that suggestive word "satisfaction." Was Wilkes really offering to fight Lord Talbot in a duel? Duels did happen from time to time. They were seen as an extra-legal device by which disputed points of honor could be settled. One way to prove one's right to be considered a gentleman, so the logic went, was to risk everything to defend it. Sometimes situations could escalate alarmingly quickly. One news story in 1760 described the almost unbelievable confrontation between two intimate friends, an officer and a doctor:

> casually meeting together in the Coffee House, the Doctor with a small Stick struck the Officer a gentle stroke over the Shoulder, on which the Officer struck his Antagonist a gentle Blow over the Legs, upon which the Doctor asked him if he was in earnest, to which he replied only in a Joke; Words then ensued, and the Doctor insisted on Satisfaction, notwithstanding the earnest intreaties of the Major; after which the Doctor was run through the Body, and died in a few Hours, but declared to several Gentlemen that he was the Aggressor, and that he forgave him.[39]

Wilkes's letter of September 10 raised the possibility of a similar confrontation. Perhaps Wilkes was seeking to silence Talbot with the ultimate threat, but if this was his tactic, it did not work. Furious letters followed Wilkes from London down to his camp at Winchester. Over and again Talbot demanded an answer to the same question. Was Wilkes the author of the *North Briton* of August 12? When it became absolutely clear that no answer was forthcoming, Talbot told Wilkes that he had no other option but to assume that he had written the paper. "Your Lordship has my free consent to make any conclusions you think proper," Wilkes replied, "whether they are well or ill grounded; and I feel the most perfect indifference about what they are, or the consequences of them."[40] Their correspondence at an end, a location was selected, a date was picked, and seconds were chosen. On Tuesday, October 5, Wilkes and Talbot were to meet at the Red Lion Inn, twenty miles outside of London at Bagshot in Surrey. No one was to know in advance.

Bagshot was a coaching village on the Portsmouth road, filled with inns and cottages, and conveniently out of the way for a private transaction of this nature. On the appointed date in early autumn, Wilkes arrived at the Red Lion with a Mr. Harris who was to act as his second. Were things to go awry, then it might soon be Harris's job to convey Wilkes's cold body back to London or Aylesbury, but Wilkes did not seem troubled. He had spent the previous night with the "jovial *Monks of St Francis*"[41] at Medmenham Abbey, where he had been up drinking till four in the morning. At least, Wilkes thought, he had the chance to sleep off the hangover, for he believed that Talbot had agreed to sup with him that night and that their duel was to take place the following morning. Arriving at the inn, Wilkes discovered that this was not the case. Meeting Talbot's second, Colonel Berkeley, he was told that it was Talbot's firm intention to fight that night.

Berkeley then took Wilkes through to meet Talbot. A dramatic scene ensued. The Lord Steward was in "an agony of passion." Neglecting the usual pleasantries, he immediately accused Wilkes of injuring him and insulting him—and that he was not used to being either injured or insulted. The questions tumbled out. Why had Wilkes done it? Was he the author of the *North Briton* of August 12? Talbot was determined to know. Confronted with this barrage, Wilkes sought to keep calm. He repeated the line he had established in his letters. By what right, he asked, did his lordship catechise him about a paper that did not bear his name? While Talbot searched for an answer, Wilkes reminded him that, while he was not equal in rank with a Lord Steward of the Household, he nonetheless remained "a private English gentleman, perfectly free and independent," which he held "to be a character of the highest dignity."[42]

It was clear now that events had reached an impasse. Wilkes was never going to provide Talbot with his answer. Understanding as much, Talbot reaffirmed his desire to fight at once. At length, Wilkes agreed, on condition that he could first settle some outstanding business. He promised Talbot that this would take up very little time and that they could fight directly after. As to weapons, it was Talbot's choice. Wilkes had brought "both sword and pistols." An emotionally fraught hour followed, as Wilkes composed his letters and Talbot loitered nearby in a state that was described as "half frantic." When Wilkes asked for the door to his room to be locked so that he could progress in peace, Talbot "became quite outrageous." In Wilkes's words, he

> declared that this was mere *butchery*, and that I was a wretch who sought his life. I reminded him, that I came there on a point of honour, to give his Lordship satisfaction; that I mentioned the circumstance of locking the door, only to prevent all possibility of interruption, and that I would in every circumstance be governed, not by the turbulence of the most violent temper I had ever seen, but by the calm determinations of our two seconds, to whom I implicitly submitted. His Lordship then asked me, if I would deny the paper. I answered, that I neither would own, nor deny it; if I survived, I would afterwards declare, not before. Soon after he grew a little cooler, and in a soothing turn of voice said, I have never, I believe, offended Mr. Wilkes; why has he attacked me? he must be sorry to see me unhappy. I asked, upon what grounds his Lordship imputed the paper to me? that Mr. Wilkes would justify any paper to which he had put his name, and would equally assert the privilege of not giving any answer whatever about a paper which he had not; that this was my undoubted right, which I was ready to seal with my blood. He then said he admired me exceedingly, really loved me; but I was an unaccountable animal—such parts! but would I kill him who had never offended me?[43]

Soon after Wilkes's letters were finished and sealed, the combatants picked up one of the large horse pistols Talbot had brought. A coin was then tossed to see which of the seconds was to give the order to fire. This came down on Wilkes's side. All the preparations at an end, the party of four left the inn. It was dark by now, and the little garden the four men entered was illuminated by moonlight. The distances were then paced out. Eight yards lay between John Wilkes and Lord Talbot. They stood with their backs to one another. After a pause, Harris called "fire." The men wheeled round and both shot at the very same instant. Neither bullet hit.

Without a pause, Wilkes lowered his pistol. As he walked toward Talbot, he spoke the words his opponent had risked his life to hear: "I wrote the *North Briton*."[44]

WHEN NEWS OF THE duel at Bagshot reached London, it caused a sensation. Wilkes did not even have the trouble of telling the tale himself, as Colonel Berkeley had been so impressed at his behavior that he had gone right round London, repeating the wondrous story for all who wished to hear.

"The affair of Ld. Talbot still lives in Conversation," Churchill wrote to Wilkes on October 23, "and you are spoken of by all with the highest respect."[45] Reading this, Wilkes knew what he meant. While Talbot had been lost in an ungovernable passion, he had displayed throughout the *sang froid*, the ironic detachment that was the mark of a gentleman. This was the kind of deep inner character that could only rarely be exhibited. He had shown moral courage. For this he was richly rewarded. At the Beefsteak Club, Churchill told him, everyone was asking after Wilkes's health. As for Wilkes himself, he was celebrating his social triumph in quite a different way. "A sweet girl," Wilkes replied to Churchill, "whom I have sigh'd for unsuccessfully these four months, now tells me that she will trust her *honour* to a man who takes so much care of his own."[46]

That autumn was a time of triumph for Wilkes. As well as silencing Talbot, he hit back against Hogarth in a venomous issue of the *North Briton* in which he characterized the artist as a greedy, craven figure: "Gain and vanity have steered his light bark quite thro' life," Wilkes wrote. Though he certainly did have talents, Wilkes depicted him as a fading force reduced to stealing ideas from others to remain relevant. "I have observed for some time," Wilkes explained, in words that Hogarth would not forget, "his *setting sun*. He has long been *very dim*, and almost *shorn of his beams*. He seems so conscious of this, that he now glimmers with *borrowed light*."[47]

All this was an entertaining sideshow for the political class, but people's real attention lay on the fate of the peace talks between Bedford and the wily French minister, the duc de Choiseul, at Fontainebleau, outside Paris. For the month since Bedford's departure speculation had been rife. What kind of a peace was he likely to broker? How could he possibly make sense of such a messy global conflict?

At the start of November everyone found out. On the third, news reached London that a preliminary treaty had been signed. The details of Bedford's agreement were fascinating. At last Britons could see just what the years of fighting had been for. Bedford, it turned out, had compromised. While he had forced France to surrender all claims to Canada and had confirmed the return of Minorca, he had ceded the valuable island territories of Guadeloupe and Martinique in the Caribbean. The city of Havana, too, which had so recently and thrillingly been seized from the Spanish, was also to be exchanged. To defray the British for Havana, the Spanish had ceded Florida.*

This was geopolitical horse-trading on an unprecedented scale. In a scratch of Bedford's pen, almost all the maps of the Americas would have to be redrawn. In London, such a rush of news was dif-

---

* So began the interesting and often overlooked history of Florida as one of Britain's American colonies. After the Peace of Paris was ratified in 1763, the region was split into two political units: East and West Florida. These colonies, being younger, enjoyed a better relationship with the mother country than their thirteen neighbors to the north. They never really joined the formal opposition to colonial rule, and when news of the Declaration of Independence reached them, in August 1776, there was fury, and effigies of John Hancock and John Adams were hung in the trees of St. Augustine Plaza.

ficult to digest. A row, inevitably, soon broke out. Had Bedford been too soft? Had he really given up Havana? What about the immensely valuable fishing rights off Newfoundland? The rumor was spread that Lord Egremont, the new secretary of state for the Southern Department, had flown into a passion in the king's closet during a debate about Bedford's terms. Leading the opposition, though, was the *North Briton*. Week after week it railed against Bedford's imbecility. To stress his point, Wilkes provided a visual depiction of the balance of Bedford's exchange:

Guadaloupe	
Mariegalante	
Desirade	
Martinique	
Right of fishing and curing on Newfoundland	
St. Peter	
Miquelon	MINORCA
Pondicherry, and all their settlements in the East-Indies	
Goree	
Belleisle	
St. Lucia	Three Neutral Islands[48]

But against all Pitt's opposition and the public's disgust was the settled will of King George and Lord Bute. Having decided the war was too costly, peace was their first priority. To ensure Bedford's treaty was passed by Parliament, Bute recruited one of the most effective and ruthless political operatives of the day. Henry Fox, soon to become Lord Holland, was a Westminster veteran. In the run-up to the opening of Parliament in mid-November, Fox worked his way through the Members. He wanted their vote. What he needed to find out was their price. According to one of Wilkes's associates, the bookseller John Almon, Westminster came to resemble a market stall:

> The royal household had been increased beyond all former example. The lords and grooms of the bedchamber were doubled. Pensions were thrown about indiscriminately. Five and twenty thousand pounds were issued in one day, in bank notes of one hundred pounds each. The only stipulation was, *Give us your vote*. A corruption of such notoriety and extent had never been seen before. There is no example, in any age or country, that in any degree approaches to it.[49]

While the MPs were bought off, opposition writers were suppressed. To quiet Wilkes, Fox suggested that he might be made governor of Canada. This was tempting, but Wilkes refused. Elsewhere, stronger tactics were enforced. In early November, a general warrant was signed by Halifax for the apprehension of those connected with the anti-ministerial *Monitor*. This type of warrant was frequently used because it permitted limitless speculative searches of suspects' properties, without having reasonable grounds for arresting a particular person. The author, Arthur Beardmore, was among those detained by a veteran "messenger" called Nathan Carrington—"a Person very Conversant in Affairs of that sort"[50]—as was a writer called John Entick, whose property was turned upside down by a detachment of such messengers. At the same time another general warrant was composed for the authors and printers of the *North Briton*. Although this was never executed, a copy of it was shown to everyone connected with the title. One, William Richardson, the printer, quit immediately.

Within a month, Fox's job was done. Although Bute's coach was stoned in the streets, and he was forced to travel in disguise under the protection of a detachment of guards, his objective had been achieved. In late 1762, George III's "glorious peace" sailed through Parliament, though an odd peace it turned out to be.

Eight

NO. 45

THE "NORTH BRITON'S" PERSONALITY changed as the months passed. Whereas he was originally a comic creation, expressly designed to irritate Bute, he came to be something more profound and symbolic. The humor, the tricks and hoaxes, remained, but increasingly these were mixed with a more serious strand of writing. As MPs auctioned their principles off to the highest bidder, the "North Briton" defined himself by contrast. He was a horrified onlooker, the champion of political freedom, the defender of English liberties. He was a writer who still carried the ideals of 1688 in his heart. In December, as the peace treaty was easing through Parliament, propelled by Crown money, Wilkes began one number with a dreamy passage reminiscent of Addison and Steele's "Spectator" and his ghostly wanderings about the city.

> ALMOST every man I meet looks strangely on me—some industriously avoid me—others pass me silent—stare—and shake their heads—Those few, those very few, who are not afraid to take a lover of his country by the hand, congratulate me on my being alive and at liberty—They advise circumspection—for,

they do not know—they cannot tell—but—the times—Liberty
is precious—fines—imprisonment—pillory—not indeed that
they themselves—but—then in truth—God only knows—.[1]

Passages like this were freighted with emotional power. Its central message, that "Liberty is precious," struck a note that resonated. People talked of English liberty as a rare and fragile thing. Broadly, it meant freedom from tyranny. More distinctly, people thought of it as the right to live with some independence, within a legal system that protected them from the malignant reach of arbitrary power, in a property of their own possession that was safe from intruders. This last point was a deeply important one. As William Pitt would soon express it in an admired speech in the Commons, "The poorest man may, in his cottage, bid defiance to all the forces of the Crown. It may be frail; its roof may shake; the wind may blow through it; the storm may enter, the rain may enter, but the King of England may not enter; all his force dares not cross the threshold of the ruined tenement."[2]

As well as knowing what it was, people knew where it came from. English liberty had materialized out of the wild woods of Saxony a thousand years before, to be carried across the sea to the island of Britain. Often attacked in the years that followed the Norman Conquest, when tyrannical kings snatched at the ancient freedoms of the Saxon communities, it had nonetheless survived to be fortified by Magna Carta. It had endured another series of "formidable, violent and bloody"[3] assaults in the days of the Stuarts. The triumph of the seventeenth century was that so far from being destroyed, the old English liberties were instead renewed by the Glorious Revolution.

Wilkes knew the potency of this story. He knew that the English loved their liberty, and considered it to be the spirit force that allowed them to live happier lives than the harassed subjects of despotic regimes. But liberty was more than a birthright. It was a responsibility, and it was the task of each generation to preserve it for the next. It only took a single despotic ruler like Charles I to wrest away people's rights. It was this anxiety that Wilkes began to play upon as the *North Briton*'s run continued. Rather than being merely a vehicle for anti-government jibes, it began to portray itself as a bulwark of English liberty, something that stood in opposition to the autocratic instincts of a power-hungry favorite and a venal Parliament.

Here Wilkes was exploiting a powerful idea at a primed moment. As 1763 began, people were still getting the measure of King George III. While the young monarch had impressed everyone during his coronation—nobody, wrote one onlooker, "ascended the throne with so much grace and dignity"[4]—his behavior during the previous year's peace negotiations suggested that he was happy to interfere with Parliament to get his way. This was a worrying sign. But while this was so, in portraying the "North Briton" as a voice of moral purity, Wilkes was being hypocritical. For years he had been an en-thusiastic participant in the political system he now attacked. In the general election of 1754, for example, when he stood as a candidate in the constituency of Berwick-upon-Tweed on the English–Scottish border, he spent thousands of pounds buying up votes. In a more elaborate tactic, he even went so far as to bribe the captain of a vessel transporting his opponent's voters from London to "mistakenly" land them in Norway. Although Wilkes had lost on that occasion, he understood the rules of the game well enough to triumph in Ayles-bury the next time around. Those who knew he was behind the *North Briton* might have reminded him about this, but Wilkes was not the type to fret over the consistency of his arguments. His focus was solely on being an effective weapon against Bute, and in the early months of 1763, as Pitt hemmed and hawed on the sidelines, the *North Briton* remained just that.

The venom of Wilkes's writing was displayed at its best in the *North Briton* No. 38, which appeared on February 19. In this issue, Wilkes employed one of Franklin's favorite techniques: the fictional letter. But rather than inventing a humorous persona, Wilkes instead wrote from the perspective of one of the most inflammatory characters in the kingdom. James Francis Edward Stuart, the "Old Pretender," had lived for years in exile in Rome. In the *North Briton No. 38*, Wilkes claimed to have intercepted a letter written by him that was intended for his fellow Scotsman Lord Bute. "Dear COUSIN," it began,

> WE have heard with infinite satisfaction of the most promising state of our affairs, not only in our *antient* kingdom of *Scotland*, where, indeed, our interest has always been deeply rooted in the hearts of our subjects, but likewise in *England*, where, till of late, we have never been able to entertain any well-grounded hope of recovering our just claims, and regal rights. Every thing, through your benign influence, now wears the most pleasing aspect. Where you tread, the *thistle* again rises under your feet. The sons of *Scotland*, and the friends of that great line of the *Stuarts,* no longer mourn. We have had the truest pleasure in hearing of the noble provision you have made for so many of our staunch friends, and of the considerable posts, both of honour and profit, which you have bestowed on them. We no less rejoice at this than at the *proscription* you have made of our inveterate enemies, the *Whigs*, and the check you have given to that wicked *revolution spirit,* as well as to the descendants of those who have impiously opposed our *divine, hereditary, indefeasible right.*[5]

This was sharp satire. In Little New Street it could hardly have made comfortable reading for another son of Scotland. Like Wilkes, William Strahan had been watching events at Westminster closely. In one of his regular letters to Hall in Philadelphia, he confirmed that "a great many Removals have been made in most of the Public Offices . . . Almost all the Duke of Newcastle's Friends have been expelled, which has given a general Alarm." With Henry Fox hugely empowered after his services to the king during the last Parliamentary session, circumstances were "pretty much into the old Channel of Corruption," he sighed.[6]

As Whitehall was cleansed of these old, entrenched figures, Bute, with Fox's support, was seeking to build a fresh ministry with new faces. The problem he encountered, however, as Wilkes instantly comprehended, was a lack of talent. With so many of the able and experienced public figures attached to the Whig factions Bute wanted to remove, he was forced to recruit characters of dubious ability. To Wilkes's mind the most risible of Bute's appointments had come the previous year when one of his old drinking companions, the rakish ringleader of the Medmenham Monks, Francis Dashwood, was appointed as Chancellor of the Exchequer. To Wilkes this was unbelievable. He had watched Dashwood "puzzling all his life at tavern bills"; now he had been "called by Lord Bute to administer the finances of a kingdom above an hundred millions in debt."[7]

In March, Dashwood delivered his first budget to Parliament. He was nervous and performed poorly. Later, according to Walpole, Dashwood admitted his failure. "People will point at me in the streets," he reflected, "and cry: There goes the worst Chancellor of the Exchequer that ever appeared!"[8] For Wilkes, despite their friendship, it was an opportunity not to miss. He tore into Dashwood, depicting him as an exemplar of ministerial incompetence. At one point in his speech, Wilkes related, Dashwood argued, "*that he was not for an EXTENSION of the excise laws, but for an ENLARGEMENT of them.*"[9]

Beneath the buffoonery lay still greater concerns. As part of a drive to replenish the treasury after almost a decade of war, Dashwood announced that a tax was to be levied on cider. Wilkes sensed this was a dangerous move. Cider-drinkers had a particular profile. They were nearly all English, predominantly members of the rural poor, and almost totally excluded from the political franchise. To burden such a group with their own tax was foolhardy. Wilkes opened No. 43 with a quote he had triumphantly recalled from Cicero: "A duty is imposed upon our very apples, and I confess that great sums of *money* may be raised by the tax, as well as great murmurings."[10]

ONE NOTABLE FEATURE OF Wilkes's character was his ability to compartmentalize. To him his political and private lives were separate things, and it was no trouble for him, for instance, to deride Hogarth or Dashwood in the *North Briton* on a Saturday, then dine with them at the Beefsteaks on Sunday. He had this same attitude toward France. Whereas for years it had been one of his political targets due to the war, he nevertheless admired it as a place of cultural riches, intellectual inquiry, and pleasurable delights.

This stance was bound up with Wilkes's affection for Europe as a whole. At eighteen his parents had sent him to study at the University of Leiden in the Dutch Republic. After a childhood spent in the domineering atmosphere created by his Presbyterian mother, this was a release indeed. In Leiden, Wilkes first tasted true freedom. In the smoky boarding house run by Madam van der Tasse, in the homeland of the Whig hero William III, he spent evenings discussing the political systems of ancient Greece and Rome. On walks by the Rhine he debated the nature of life with other students, including Paul-Henri Dietrich, later to become famous as the Baron d'Holbach, talking about human purpose, free will, and atheism.

For Wilkes the Treaty of Paris might have been a political abomination—he caustically described it as being like the Peace of God, "as it passeth all understanding"[11]—but it also presented him with an opportunity. As the Channel was now open, he judged the time to be ripe for a trip to the French capital. This would both provide him with a short break from writing and British politics, and give him the chance of taking his daughter Polly to the Continent for the first time. Polly was thirteen years old. Very bright, curious about the world, and utterly devoted to her father, Wilkes regarded her as being the only good thing to have come out of his ill-starred marriage. Always indulgent, Wilkes wanted his daughter to experience the same rich culture he had himself encountered in the 1740s. In late February, soon after the treaty was signed, Wilkes hurried across the Channel to meet a potential governess. A month later, with the arrangements finalized, he left the *North Briton* in Churchill's hands and sailed for France once again, this time with Polly by his side.

They found Paris crammed with "Gentlemen and Ladies from all Parts of England,"[12] all of them taking advantage of the chance to travel. After a little sightseeing, Wilkes left Polly with her tutor, Madame Carpentier, then turned for home. He found the separation a strain. All the way back to Calais he was shrouded in gloom, a mood made all the worse by a fall from his horse. But then, as he sat there in the sea breeze with the gray waters of the Channel stretching out before him, something happened to wrest his mind away from family matters. Wilkes knew his correspondence was being monitored by governmental spies, so he was careful not to disclose too much. But he did allow himself one candid line in the letter he hastily wrote to Polly. "A gentleman just arriv'd from England tells me," Wilkes explained, "that Lord Bute is entirely out."[13]

Wilkes sailed back toward Dover in suspense. When he left England there had been rumors about Bute's position. He had seemingly been suffering from stress brought on by the continuous criticism, speaking of "black ingratitude" and complaining that "In my opinion the Angel Gabriel could not at present govern this country."[14] Also, after a period of dormancy, Newcastle was once again on maneuvers, holding a lavish dinner for his Whig friends. "When the news of this union reached the Favourite," one journalist reckoned, "he began to entertain thoughts of retiring."[15]

These thoughts were stiffened by threats of physical violence. The previous months had seen several unsettling incidents in London's streets. In one particularly nasty episode on his way to the lord mayor's dinner in the City, Bute's coach was attacked and his guard chased away. But was this enough to make him resign? Wilkes was left with this question as he headed home. "And if he had gone then was Pitt poised to return?" If this was the case then surely he was to be rewarded for his efforts. While others had been intimidated by Bute's influence and Fox's methods, Wilkes had continued undaunted. As he declared in the *North Briton*, "Fear is the proper companion of guilt only; and I have not yet learned to call a sincere and uniform love of my king, and my country, by that name."[16]

Over the next days in Great George Street, Wilkes caught up with the news. It was true. Bute had gone. It was said that he was so worn down by the demands of office that he was now recovering in the spa waters at Harrogate. Dashwood had stepped down, too, meaning a complete change at the top of government. But any optimism that Wilkes felt was soon dispelled when he heard that Pitt was not going to return. The king, unenthusiastic about that prospect, had turned instead to a trio of Bute's supporters. Two of them were veteran political operators: the earls of Halifax and Egremont. The biggest winner in the reshuffle, however, was George Grenville.

Serious-minded, clever, and diligent, Grenville was someone that Wilkes knew well. In earlier times he had been an ally, a central component of the Grenville faction—the brother-in-law of William Pitt and the younger brother of Wilkes's patron, Earl Temple. Over the last year, though, Grenville had been happy to serve in Bute's administration. This transfer of loyalties was not appreciated by Pitt or Temple, but it did speak to Grenville's cold ambition. A charmless man who could bore colleagues rigid in debates, no one had imagined that he had the ability to actually lead government.* But with nowhere else to turn, the king had asked him to form a ministry.

---

* Grenville's ability to bore colleagues in the Commons is encapsulated in one of the best-known stories about him. Several years later, Grenville delivered a long harangue in the chamber about the state of the public finances. During this, Lord North, leader of the administration, fell asleep. Thinking this disrespectful, one of his colleagues nudged him, just as Grenville was remarking, "I shall draw attention of the House to revenues and expenditures of the country in 1689." Hearing this, North exclaimed audibly, "Zounds, Sir, you have woken me up a near one hundred years too soon."

All this was maddening to Pitt, Temple, and Wilkes. It was bad enough to see Grenville, a loathed turncoat, in the highest office, but another thought taunted them too. Was Bute really gone, or had he merely stepped back to pull the strings from the shadows? When Pitt and Temple managed to acquire a draft copy of the speech the king was about to give at the close of the Parliamentary session, it confirmed their suspicions. All Bute's policies were to be continued.

It was later said that it was after Wilkes happened to overhear the furious Pitt and Temple raging about this that he felt compelled to act. Others have argued that it was Pitt who instructed Wilkes to launch his attack on Grenville. Whatever the case, on April 23, St. George's Day, three days after the king delivered his speech, the *North Briton* No. 45 appeared. It was a typically trenchant attack on the political elite. While Wilkes was careful to direct his venom at what he called "the *minister's speech*,"[17] it was otherwise a blistering performance. It was, he declared, the "most abandoned piece of ministerial effrontery ever attempted to be imposed on mankind"; a speech "not to be paralleled in the annals of this country," that not merely contained "an infamous fallacy," but it was one that prostituted "*the honour of the crown*."[18]

When narrating the sequence of events that ensued, historians have usually supposed that George Grenville was the one whose patience snapped. In fact orders came from even higher. On April 25, Halifax wrote to Charles Yorke, the Attorney General, and Fletcher Norton, the Solicitor General, explaining that he had been commanded by the king to refer No. 45 "to your most attentive Consideration." They were to deliver their verdict, as quickly as possible, "how far, and under what Denomination of Guilt, the Author, Printers and Publisher of this seditious Paper may be liable to Indictment and Prosecution."[19]

On April 27 the lawyers replied in private, confirming, "We have taken the said Paper into our Consideration, and are of Opinion, that it is a most infamous and seditious Libel."[20] With this ascertained, the decision was taken to silence Wilkes by prosecuting him to the fullest extent of the law. So began, as one contemporary termed it, "such a series of singular and extraordinary transactions, as perhaps are not to be equalled in the annals of any civilized nation."[21]

FOR FIVE DAYS AFTER the publication of No. 45, Wilkes's life went on as before. In his house on Great George Street he drafted some copy for the forty-sixth number of the *North Briton*. This issue, Wilkes had decided, was going to focus on religion. In one of its first moves, Grenville's ministry had announced that May 5 had been appointed as a day of thanksgiving to God for the recent peace. To Wilkes this was more cynical politicking. "RELIGION is now made a political state-engine," his draft started, "to serve the vilest and most infamous purposes of an abandoned minister, or of a wicked and corrupt administration." This thanksgiving was, if considered coldly, a "most daring insult on the common sense of mankind."[22]

Wilkes knew that these words would sting in Whitehall. The "abandoned minister," of course, was Bute. He may have left London, but Wilkes wanted to stress his continued presence in political decision-making. And even if the thanksgiving had nothing to do with Bute, then at least the insinuation would irritate Grenville. At this point Wilkes seems not to have foreseen any ill consequences to such an attack. Grenville might well have been as annoyed as Bute, but that would make little difference. Not once in all the eleven months that the *North Briton* had been in print had his name appeared anywhere on it. Libel was the danger he faced, and for it to be proved someone would have to betray him. So far his network had remained quiet. But even if his identity was exposed, Wilkes knew he had been careful with his language. He had a knack for subtlety, for insinuating a point rather than stating it baldly. Beyond this Wilkes enjoyed another special layer of legal protection. As a Member of Parliament he could only be apprehended in three very specific instances. He had to have committed a felony—a murder, an assault, or a kidnapping—or instigated a breach of the peace, or, most unlikely of all, been guilty of treason. On all these counts, Wilkes considered himself safe.

It was with surprise, then, that in the morning of Friday, April 29, Wilkes heard the news about an old acquaintance of his, a printer called Dryden Leach. The night before, Leach had been in bed at his home in Crane Court off Fleet Street, when a number of the king's messengers rapped at his door. Over the next hour a shocking scene played out. Everyone was ordered out of bed, even though it was the middle of the night and Leach's infant child lay "dangerously ill." On suspicion of being connected with the *North Briton*, Leach, his servants, and his journeymen printers were all arrested and his papers carried away for inspection. This was extraordinary. Leach's involvement in the *North Briton* was so minor as to be almost inconsequential: he had printed a single number the previous November as a last-minute favor for Wilkes. If the ministry wanted to apprehend the people involved with the *North Briton*, why did they not first arrest the publisher George Kearsley? After all, it was his name that appeared on the title page each week.

This anomaly was not to linger long. The messages reaching Wilkes from Crane Court were soon joined by others coming from Ludgate Hill, where Kearsley's bookshop had been raided at sunrise. The story was much the same. There had been a knock at the door. Kearsley had opened it to a brace of messengers who invaded his property, turned everything upside down, and seized all of his papers. When Kearsley asked the chief messenger, a man named Watson, to show him the warrant on which he was acting, Watson told him to be quiet and insisted upon his immediate obedience.

The reports were alarming. Wilkes, always more of a warm idealist than a cool student of the law, was outraged. He knew that no one, not even the king's own messengers, could storm in and ransack a person's house without a warrant signed by a justice of the peace. As far as he was concerned, too, no warrant could be issued unless strong evidence, given under oath, had first been collected. Had someone betrayed him? Wilkes needed to speak with Leach and Kearsley himself, who he soon discovered were being held at one of the messenger's houses on Crown Street, north of Charing Cross. Wilkes hurried there. At the door he found that the house belonged to a messenger called Robert Blackmore, a congenial figure. If Wilkes was worried that he was going to be arrested himself, Blackmore showed no such intention. Instead he invited Wilkes into the room where the detained men were being held. Here Wilkes was able to study the copy of the warrant that had been used to arrest both Leach and Kearsley. It read:

> These are in his Majesty's name to authorize and require you (taking a Constable to your assistance) to make strict and diligent search for the Authors, Printers and Publishers of a Seditious and Treasonable paper, intitled the North Briton, Number XLV Saturday April 23rd 1763 printed for G Kearsley, in Ludgate Street London, and them, or any of them having found to Apprehend and Seize, together with their Papers and to bring in Safe Custody, before me, to be Examined concerning the Premises and further dealt with according to Law. In the due Execution thereof all Mayors Sheriffs Justices of the Peace Constables and all others his Majesty's Officers Civil and Military and loving Subjects whom it may Concern are to be aiding and assisting to you as there shall be Occasion. And for so doing This shall be your Warrant. Given at St James' the twenty sixth day of April 1763 in the third year of his Majesty's Reign.
>
> Dunk Halifax[23]

This clarified many mysteries. Until now it was unclear which issue of the *North Briton* had instigated the action. It could have been any number of them, and Wilkes himself was bemused to find that it was No. 45, which he reassured Kearsley was "a very innocent paper."[24] But there was more here to worry him. Most noticeable was the signature beneath. Halifax's name confirmed that this was a matter involving the most powerful politicians in the land. More disturbing was the use of the word "treasonable." This was a word that conjured up chilling enough images in itself. But it was more significant than that. Under a charge of treason, Wilkes lost his protection of privilege.

Whatever anyone would ever say of Wilkes, he was certainly a man of great courage. Whereas many people in his situation would flee, he decided to meet the ministry's intimidation with a counter-move of his own. To his mind there were problems with the warrant. Did Halifax, a politician, have the authority to issue such a legal document? Had a constable been present at Leach's and Kearsley's as was required by law? On what sworn evidence had the warrant been granted? Moreover, Wilkes considered there to be a deeper problem with the document. It specifically referred to No. 45, an issue he knew had absolutely nothing to do with Leach. The ministry's informants had clearly made a grave error here. Their misidentification of the printer had caused them to apprehend not only one wrong man, but by the sound of it almost the whole of Leach's workforce. All this on the strength of a warrant that bore Kearsley's name alone, and thereafter spoke only in general terms of "authors, printers and publishers." How could such a document be used in England to deprive an individual of their liberty?

Wilkes's strategy soon emerged. First he wanted to release his associates from what he considered to be illegal imprisonment. One of the most famous acts in English history offered a way to achieve this. By going to either the Court of the King's Bench or the Court of Common Pleas at Westminster, Wilkes could obtain a writ of Habeas Corpus, which demanded a prisoner be brought before the court so that the conditions of their detention could be examined. But then an idea still more exciting occurred to Wilkes. The events of the morning, he realized, were, among other things, an attack on the freedom of the press. What better way to respond than by ensuring that the next issue of the *North Briton* was published as usual the following day? Could there be a more powerful symbol of English liberty than that?

Ever since the threats of the previous November, the *North Briton* had been printed by a low-profile figure called Richard Balfe, whose premises were hidden delightfully up a series of steps behind, of all places, the law courts at the Old Bailey. If Wilkes could get his draft copy of No. 46 to Balfe that afternoon, then he would be able to triumph over the ministry the following morning. Around midday Wilkes put his plan into action. He found Balfe and told him to set to work immediately, ordering him to send a proof copy at five that evening. Returning to Crown Street and his old friend Leach, Wilkes spent the rest of the day in great good humor. Blackmore, the messenger, soon discovered that rather than it being a mere social call, Wilkes and Leach were holding something of a party inside his house. As the evening of April 29, 1763, wore on, he was left to listen to the sound of wine bottles opening, of the raising of toasts and the singing of songs.

It was approaching midnight when Wilkes left Blackmore's. He stumbled down St. Martin's Lane, through Charing Cross, and along Whitehall toward home. As he entered Great George Street he found some messengers waiting for him. Later they would recall that Wilkes was "very much in Liquor."[25] Holding a wine bottle in his hand, he swaggered toward them, promising to "serve" with his sword any of them who tried to take him. Opting against a confrontation, they let the MP for Aylesbury pass, and watched him disappear inside his house. So events stood primed as the bells of St. Margaret's struck twelve and welcomed in April 30, 1763, which Wilkes would always afterward call "that memorable day."[26]

SOME YEARS LATER, CHARLES DICKENS would write evocatively about the appearance of London's streets in the hour before dawn. "There is an air of cold, solitary desolation about the noiseless streets," he reflected in his *Sketches by Boz*, "which we are accustomed to see thronged at other times by a busy, eager crowd, and over the quiet, closely-shut buildings, which throughout the day are swarming with life and bustle."[27] Dickens relished that delicately poised moment, shortly before sunrise, when "the drunken, the dissipated, and the wretched have disappeared; the more sober and orderly part of the population have not yet awakened to the labours of the day, and the stillness of death is over the streets."

It was at such a time, "in the sombre light of daybreak," that John Wilkes awoke on Saturday, April 30, 1763. He usually had cause to look forward to Saturdays, when the *North Briton* was published. But this day, Wilkes immediately sensed, was bound to be different. Had he not resisted the messengers the night before, he would already be in custody along with Leach and Kearsley. Wilkes knew this, but there were other things he did not know. He could not be sure whether Balfe had completed the print run for No. 46. He also did not know what had become of the messengers. He did not know, too, that at that moment three of them were moving into position outside his house. John Money, the leader of the trio, had taken a position at the west end of Great George Street, by St. James's Park. Robert Blackmore, Wilkes's acquaintance from the previous day, was guarding the eastern opening of the street at Whitehall. A third messenger, James Watson, was covering another exit, which led into St. Margaret's Churchyard.

Inside his house Wilkes pulled on his scarlet coat, his jack boots, and his three-cornered hat. With Kearsley in custody there was no one to distribute No. 46 of the *North Briton*, so his driving purpose was to reach Balfe's print shop to see what was happening there. It was possible Balfe had already been taken up too. If so, his task would be to secure the manuscript copy of No. 45 and destroy any other evidence that remained. Having dressed, Wilkes opened his door, stepped out into the street, and turned left toward Whitehall. This was his first stroke of fortune. Instead of Money or Watson, Wilkes met the pliable Blackmore. This morning, as the night before, Blackmore seemed in awe of Wilkes, who confidently held out his hand to greet him. A brief exchange took place. Wilkes promised Blackmore that he needed to visit a friend in the Temple—London's legal quarter—but that by nine o'clock, he would be back "to breakfast" with them at Blackmore's house.

With this Wilkes hurried on, leaving Blackmore to explain himself to his colleagues. Around an hour later, at eight o'clock, Wilkes appeared at the Old Bailey. The sight that greeted him was disheartening. Balfe's door had been forced and was now boarded up. It seemed that he, too, had been visited by the messengers. Searching the area, Wilkes managed to rouse one of Balfe's journeymen who had somehow evaded arrest. Wilkes implored this man, John Williams, to help him enter Balfe's print shop so he could see if any finished copies of No. 46 were inside. Requisitioning a bricklayer's ladder, Williams clambered up and got into the press room through a window. Inside, the great machine stood silent and abandoned. All the papers seemed to have been taken away. But the journeyman noticed that the form, filled with arranged type, was still in place. Williams first tried to run a few sheets off. But whether for lack of paper, help, or time, he soon abandoned this plan. Instead he attempted to carry it down the ladder to Wilkes. This was too ambitious. Halfway down, it fell, sending lead type scattering across the street.

The instant the letters collided with the ground, Wilkes's shrinking hopes of printing No. 46 that day were gone for good. By midmorning he had left Balfe's and the Old Bailey and was seen strolling back down Whitehall toward Great George Street. For the messengers, at least, this was welcome news. Since Wilkes had vanished at sunrise, they had been in a state of panic. Blackmore had been scolded for letting Wilkes slip away, while the riverside wharves and jetties were frantically scoured for any sign of him, or any word that he might have escaped down the Thames.

John Money, the chief messenger, was particularly fraught. He knew that Kearsley, the publisher, had given Wilkes up during the course of his interrogation the previous afternoon. Kearsley's collapse was understandable. He had been personally interrogated by the earls of Egremont and Halifax, the two secretaries of state. This would have been a stiff test for anyone. Halifax was a suave and sharp Old Etonian who had held many political offices over the years. Egremont, though, had an even keener interest in the affair. He had been thickly involved in the peace negotiations over the last year and had every reason to loathe Wilkes. A sour man, a member of an old Tory family, Egremont was considered "more proud than able."[28] As soon as he had Kearsley's evidence, which was soon reinforced by more from Richard Balfe, he had issued a verbal order for Wilkes to be arrested at once. Daunted by the prospect of apprehending Wilkes while drunk, Money had let him pass the previous night. This morning, again while Money was in command, he had talked his way free again. Seeing Wilkes back on Great George Street, then, came as a huge relief.

Wilkes's keen, strategizing mind, however, was already plotting his next move. He considered the harassment he had faced monstrous. This was no longer simply about the freedom of the press. If these messengers were truly going to arrest him, then it had become a question of civil liberty. As he explained himself:

On my return from the city early in the morning, I met at the end of Great George-Street, one of the king's messengers. He told me that he had a *warrant* to apprehend me, which he must execute immediately, and that I must attend him to lord Halifax's. I desired to see the *warrant*. He said it was *against the authors, printers, and publishers of the North Briton, No.45,* and that his verbal orders were to arrest *Mr Wilkes*. I told him that the *warrant* did not respect me: I advised him to be very civil, and to use no violence in the street, for if he attempted force, I would put him to death in the instant; but if he would come quietly to my house, I would convince him of the illegality of the *warrant*, and the injustice of the orders he had received. He chose to accompany me home, and then produced the GENERAL WARRANT. I declared that such a *warrant* was absolutely illegal and void in itself, that it was a ridiculous *warrant* against the whole English nation, and I asked why he would serve it on me, rather than on the lord Chancellor, on either of the secretaries, on lord Bute, or lord Corke, my next door neighbour. The answer was, *I am to arrest Mr Wilkes.* About an hour afterwards two other messengers arrived, and several of their assistants. They all endeavoured in vain to persuade me to accompany them to lord Halifax's. I had likewise many civil messages from his lordship to desire my attendance. My only answer was, that I had not the honour of visiting his lordship, and this first application was rather rude and ungentleman-like.[29]

As Wilkes's later testimony shows, he was not overawed by the events. Instead he was calm, polite, and assertive, and out on the street he made one very clever move. Rather than let the messengers detain him on the public highway, he invited them inside his house. "Come go along with me home," he said, "and let us have some Breakfast."[30] The belief that an Englishman's home is his castle is one that can be traced back to at least the sixteenth century. In truth, in 1763 and in the cold eyes of the law, this was no more than an appealing fiction, but it was an idea that carried substantial emotional weight. There was an important difference in the British mind between sweeping a suspect off the public highway and arresting him in his property. Already suspicious of the written warrant and shocked to hear it had been issued along with a "verbal" one, Wilkes decided that it would be better to confront the messengers inside his own home.

The scenes that followed inside Great George Street that morning were, by turns, dramatic, fraught, playful, and farcical. Once the door was closed behind them, Wilkes asked to see the warrant, and having looked over it declared, "This Warrant is nothing to me neither will I Obey it."[31] He then called for breakfast, politely refusing all the while to be arrested. John Money—seeing that this would not be a straightforward affair—left for Halifax's house, which as it happened was only a few doors away on the very same street. Amid the commotion, Wilkes managed to dash off a series of notes asking friends to help. Unluckily the first person to saunter through the door was someone he did *not* want to see:

> While some of the messengers and their assistants were with me, *Mr. Churchill* came into the room. I had heard that their *verbal* orders were likewise to apprehend him, but I suspected they did not know his person, and by presence of mind I had the happiness of saving my friend. As soon as Mr. Churchill entered the room, I accosted him, *Good morrow, Mr Thomson. How does Mrs Thomson do to day? Does she dine in the country?* Mr. Churchill thanked me, said she then waited for him, that he only came for a moment to ask me how I did, and almost directly took his leave. He went home immediately, secured all his papers, and retired into the country. The messengers could never get intelligence where he was.[32]

An assortment of other visitors followed over the next two hours. The most notable of these was Lord Temple, who assured Wilkes that a writ of Habeas Corpus had already been applied for in the Court of Common Pleas at Westminster. Meanwhile the ministry's patience was beginning to wane. Money had returned from Halifax's with renewed spirit, but Wilkes continued to resist arrest. By now his manner was becoming firm. He told Money that he had "Entered his house without his leave" and "desired [they] would Immediately Quit it, that it was the House of a Member of Parliament, and that he should stand up for the Privilege of Parliament."[33] At this point Robert Wood, an undersecretary to Egremont, arrived to reinforce the messenger's authority. Then, at about midday, a constable called Robert Chisholme appeared with two assistants. "I was then threatened with immediate violence, and a regiment of guards, if necessary," Wilkes remembered. At length, in the early afternoon, seeing that further resistance was futile, Wilkes handed his sword to Chisholme.

As the sword changed hands, Wilkes told the constable that if he had come at one or two in the morning, "he would have shot the first Man that entered the House and with that Sword that I now give you would I have spilt the last drop of your Blood."[34] He then demanded that each of those involved in his arrest write their names on a piece of paper (thirteen names were signed). Finally satisfied, he walked out of his house, climbed into a sedan chair, and was carried the comically short distance to Halifax's house, under full guard.

Here Wilkes was shown into a great apartment that overlooked St. James's Park. Waiting for him at a table were Halifax and Egremont. Wilkes would never quite have it in him to dislike Halifax, whom he considered a polite but corrupted minister. His loathing for Egremont, however, was total. He recalled how Egremont received him with "a supercilious, insolent air."[35] The interrogation began with questions about his relationship with Kearsley and Wilkes's knowledge of the *North Briton*. Wilkes, as he put it himself, "did not find myself disposed to gratify," resolving that "at the end of my examination all the quires of paper on their lordship's table should be as milk white as at the beginning."[36]

> Lord Halifax then, "desired to remind me of my being their prisoner, and of their right to examine me." I answered, "that I should imagine their Lordship's time was too precious to be trifled away in that manner; that they might have seen before I would never say one word they desired to know;" and I added, "indeed, my lords, I am not made of such slight, flimsy stuff;" then turning to lord Egremont, I said, "could you employ tortures, I would never utter a word unbecoming my honour, or

affecting the sacred confidence of any friend. God has given me firmness and fidelity. You trifle away your time most egregiously, my lords." Lord Halifax then "advised me to weigh well the consequences of my conduct, and the advantages to myself of a generous, frank confession." I lamented "the prostitution of the word, GENEROUS, to what I should consider as an act of the utmost treachery, cowardice, and wickedness." His lordship then asked me, "if I chose to be a prisoner in my own house, at the Tower, or in Newgate, for he was disposed to oblige me."[37]

It had been a day rich in drama that had been acted out on the very margins of English law. With Wilkes refusing to answer Halifax's question—instead he "made a few remarks on some capital pictures" that were hanging in the room—the secretary of state decided to have him sent to the Tower. As this transfer was being authorized, one final piece of legal chicanery took place. The writ of Habeas Corpus that Wilkes had awaited all afternoon had by now been granted. A message arrived from Westminster Hall, but at Halifax's it was rendered worthless due to a technicality. The writ had been made out to Robert Blackmore and James Watson, the two messengers who had held Wilkes while he was in his home at Great George Street. By late afternoon he had now passed out of their care, into the custody of Halifax and Egremont, and then into that of the constables who were charged with carrying him through London's streets to his place of detention. Believing themselves to have outpaced the writ, the secretaries of state found themselves able to ignore it.

Before he left Halifax's, Wilkes told Halifax and Egremont that if he lived to the first day of the next session of Parliament, "he would Stand up in his Place and acquaint the House of the whole proceeding."[38] This was a threat he would come to regret. Meanwhile, as Wilkes headed toward the Tower, where he had been ordered to be kept under "close guard"—a more restricted form of imprisonment—a thorough search was being made of his house on Great George Street. Papers were pulled out of drawers and carried away in sealed bags; locks were picked and cabinets broken open. Lord Temple, who was present, later said that it was a scene "too barbarous an act for any human eye to witness."[39]

SIX WEEKS LATER, ON June 14, in the fading light of an early summer's day, Benjamin Franklin gazed out across the Hudson River as his ferry crossed from the Jersey shore. Before him lay Manhattan Island with its rich green landscape of woods, hills, and meadows. At its southernmost tip stood the bustling city of New York with its teeming waterfront and the unmistakable outline of Fort George, a landmark that could be picked out by anyone from the huge Union Jack that flapped in the harbor breeze.

Franklin had every reason to be in good spirits. He had spent the day in Elizabeth Town with his son William, whose appointment as New Jersey's royal governor had been marked by a lavish dinner given by the local corporation. How his fortunes had changed, he must have reflected, in the forty years since he had made this very journey in reverse in 1723. Back then he was near penniless and traveling south, away from his family. Now, heading northward, he was wealthy, respected, and renowned. He was perhaps the best-known American in the world. Before him, instead of uncertainty, he now had clear objectives. He intended to spend the summer of 1763 on a tour of the northern colonies: meeting officials and checking roads in his capacity as America's deputy postmaster. For someone who loved to travel and relished the art of improvement, an exciting time lay ahead.

A week of cheerful social calls, meetings, and dinners had passed since Franklin left Deborah in Philadelphia. The mood in the colonies was buoyant. News of the signing of the Peace of Paris had at last made it across the Atlantic. The existential threat from France had finally been lifted from the British colonies. Franklin had signaled his own satisfaction in a letter to Strahan in early May. "I congratulate you sincerely on the signing of the Definitive Treaty," he wrote,

> which if agreable to the Preliminaries, gives us a Peace the most advantageous as well as glorious, that was ever before obtain'd by Britain. Throughout this Continent I find it universally approved and applauded; and am glad to find the same Sentiments prevailing in your Parliament, and the unbias'd Part of the Nation. Grumblers there will always be among you, where Power and Places are worth striving for, and those who cannot obtain them are angry with all that stand in their way. Such would have clamour'd against a Ministry not their particular Friends, even if instead of Canada and Louisiana they had obtain'd a Cession of the Kingdom of Heaven. But Time will clear all Things, and a very few Years will convince those who at present are misled by Party Writers, that this Peace is solidly good, and that the Nation is greatly oblig'd to the wise Counsels that have made it.[40]

Indeed, since Franklin's return to America his social standing had been enhanced by the general knowledge that he, after his years in London, had the ear of those "wise Counsels." William's appointment was evidence of this, and as a result everyone wanted to see him. His first day in New York was a testament of his status. In the morning he was received by the colony's governor, General Robert Monckton. This was followed by a call on General Amherst, one of the heroes of the last war. In the evening he dined with the fabulously wealthy Lord Stirling, a member of New York's old elite. It was a dizzying day, and Franklin had plenty of news for everyone. His voyage back to Philadelphia had been pleasant. Captain Friend had called in at Madeira, and Franklin had been impressed by the landscape and its bountiful crops of corn, grapes, apples, peaches, oranges, lemons, plantains, and bananas. Supplies of all these were stowed away in the little convoy of ships that sailed with the *Carolina*. Sailing in a convoy,

Franklin decided, was much better. As the weather was fair and the ships sailed in close company, it was easy for passengers to "visit from Ship to Ship" for dinner. It was like "travelling in a moving Village, with all one's Neighbours about one."[41]

Ever since he had arrived back in Philadelphia in November, Franklin's life had gone on enjoyably. Despite his long absence he had found his wife content, his daughter Sally was "grown quite a Woman," and his friends were "as hearty and affectionate as ever." In February William and his new wife—"a very agreable West India Lady"—had returned from London too. Franklin had been delighted by his son's reception in New Jersey. "A River only parts that Province and ours," Franklin explained, "and his Residence is within 17 Miles of me, so that we frequently see each other."[42]

There was only one truly discordant note for Franklin. This was a rumor, published in the *Pennsylvania Gazette* shortly before his departure, explaining that Bute was about to be replaced as prime minister by the Duke of Devonshire. Although Hall, who had now edited the paper for fifteen years, had no more information than this, he had thought the report—which dated to the end of March—was worthy of being included among the London news. With the summer coming on and more European ships arriving in the American ports, it would not be long before this gossip was substantiated or, as Franklin hoped, proved false. As it was, two days after his arrival in New York, a letter bearing a quite different story sailed into the harbor.

This Day Mr Wilkes Member of Parliament for Aylesbury, Writer of the North Briton, is sent to the Tower, by Warrant, for treasonable Practices (In other Words, for libelling the Government): In the said North Briton the King's Speech is attacked and treated with unreserved Freedom; and the Warrant sets forth that he has endeavoured to sow Sedition, and alienate the Affections of his Majesty's Subjects.

It will make a terrible Noise, and no Doubt the City will

be all on Fire upon the Occasion; Lord Chief Justice Pratt has granted a Habeas Corpus, and Mr Wilkes is to be brought on Monday to get Bail, if he can obtain it. He refused to apply to Lord Chief Justice Mansfield, as being a Scotchman. I do not imagine that ever Party Spirit carried People to greater Excesses, or was more violently agitated. It is probable Mr. Wilkes will remain in the Tower till the Parliament meets.[43]

There was material in these two brisk paragraphs to captivate. The colonial newspapers had long obsessed over English stories, but never in living memory had they carried news of a Member of Parliament being incarcerated inside the Tower. It was as if time had collapsed. Instead of news from Georgian Britain, were they getting reports from the Elizabethan Age? Just who was this John Wilkes? What had he written that had been so offensive? The answer to this question was provided four days later when, owing to the "very great Curiosity of the Public" and the "repeated Applications of a great Number of our Readers," No. 45 of the *North Briton* was reprinted in its entirety by the *New York Gazette*.[44]

For almost all Americans, No. 45 was the first they had ever heard of the *North Briton*. For them, regardless of what they thought of the peace, there was something marvelous in the audacity of this John Wilkes. It was beyond intrepid to confront the king and government as he had. Franklin's view, however, was quite different. Having a better sense of British politics, he understood the volatility of the situation. At almost the same time as news of Wilkes's arrest, confirmation arrived of Bute's resignation. For Franklin this was a desperate blow. The day the *New York Gazette* printed No. 45 across its front page, Franklin decided it was his responsibility to defend Bute's reputation in the colonies. He wrote a letter, since lost, to his partner Hall, cautioning him against printing No. 45 in the *Gazette*. Instead, he asked him to run a spirited vindication of Bute, which he had originally read in the *Gentleman's Magazine*, at the earliest possible opportunity.

This was about all that he could do, apart from fret to friends in private letters. To the watchmaker John Whitehurst, Franklin wrote:

> The Glory of Britain was never higher than at present, and I think you never had a better Prince: Why then is he not universally rever'd and belov'd? I can give but one Answer. The King of the Universe, good as he is, is not cordially belov'd and faithfully serv'd by all his Subjects. I wish I could say that half Mankind, as much as they are oblig'd to him for his continual Favours, were among the truly loyal. Tis a shame that the very Goodness of a Prince should be an Encouragement to Affronts.[45]

To Strahan, Franklin displayed more emotional vulnerability. He felt cut off from London, he confessed, alienated from the forum of great events.

> I expected when I left England, to have learnt in your Letters the true State of Things from time to time among you; but you are silent, and I am in the dark. I hear that Faction and Sedition are becoming universal among you, which I can scarcely believe tho' I see in your public Papers a Licentiousness that amazes me. I hear of Ins and Outs and Ups and Downs, and know neither why nor wherefore. Think, my dear Friend, how much Satisfaction 'tis in your Power to give me, with the Loss only of half an Hour in a Month that you would otherwise spend at Cribbidge.[46]

Although Franklin would have to wait some weeks for a letter from Little New Street, news about the Wilkes affair came more briskly. Every ship brought a fresh development. At three thousand miles' distance, people were learning names they had never heard before—Wilkes, Leach, Kearsley, Balfe—along with the street plan of the Old Bailey and Westminster. In the *Gazette*, Hall charted every step. First came Kearsley's release, for behaving with "great Candour," and Wilkes's incarceration in the Tower. Then there was news of a succession of cases in the Court of Common Pleas, where Wilkes had defended himself as a champion of English liberty. This, he told Chief Justice Pratt, was "the governing Principle of every Action of my Life . . . For this," Wilkes added, "I have been imprisoned, sent to the Tower, and treated with a Rigour YET unpractised, even on Scotch Rebels." The *Gazette* reported his speech in full:

> But however these Ministers may now strive to destroy me; whatever Persecutions they are now mediating against me; yet to the World I shall proclaim, that Offers of the most advantageous and lucrative Kind have been made to seduce me to their Party, and no Means left untried to win me to their Connection: Now, as their Attempts to corrupt me have failed, they aim at intimidating me by Prosecution; but as it hath pleased God to give me Virtue to resist their Bribes, so I doubt not but he will give me Spirit to surmount their Threats, in a Manner becoming an Englishman; who would suffer the severest Trials, rather than associate themselves with Men who are Enemies to the Liberty of this Country. Their Bribes I rejected, their Menaces I defy; and I think this the most fortunate Moment of my Life, when I appear before your Lordship, and this Court, where Innocence is sure of Protection, and Liberty can never want her Friends and Guardians.[47]

No Pennsylvanian who read these words could have guessed that Wilkes was a weak, hesitant speaker. There was little of the great Pitt in his oratory. But in this age of printed news, this mattered less. Instead people were left to gaze at the text in wonder. An additional item explained that great numbers of noblemen had traveled in their coaches through the City to visit Wilkes in a display of support. This was only a foretaste of what was to come. On May 7, after a procedural delay of a week, his case was finally heard in full in the Court of Common Pleas. By now Wilkes had had a chance to collect his thoughts. He invoked Magna Carta and derided the government's actions as resembling a "Star Chamber Tyranny." His speech would be long remembered:

> FAR be it from me to regret that I have passed so many more Days in Captivity, as it will have afforded you an Opportunity of doing, upon mature Reflection, and repeated Examination, the more signal Justice to my Country. The Liberty of all Peers and Gentlemen, and what touches me more sensibly, that of all the middling and inferior Classes of People, who stand most in Need of Protection, is in my Case this Day to be finally decided upon: A Question of such Importance as to determine at once whether English Liberty be a Reality or a Shadow.[48]

This was enough to convince the court. Wilkes was discharged, with Charles Pratt ruling that his arrest had violated his Parliamentary privilege. As the verdict was announced, three great huzzahs were given. Having reclaimed his freedom, Wilkes had made the short, triumphant walk back to Great George Street. A crowd estimated to be ten thousand strong joined him, waving their hats in the air, shouting out "Wilkes and Liberty." Once home, he flung open an upstairs window to salute his supporters, who "returned with three fresh cheers." Something strange, it was clear to every American reader, was happening in London. For as long as everyone could remember, politics had been a particular pastime for a particular kind of person. Advancing to real prominence meant gaining influence with the tiny set of grandees—perhaps as few as thirty people in the whole kingdom—who really mattered. In May 1763, Wilkes abandoned this approach. Instead of the Duke of Newcastle or the Marquis of Rockingham, Wilkes was drawing his support from the mass of ordinary people in London and beyond.

This shift in allegiance was too much for many of his peers. It was easy to see him as a sellout, a turncoat, and a destroyer of social norms. For this, Wilkes was hated. Beyond Westminster, though, people were left to ponder the unsettling elements of his case. In Philadelphia as in Exeter or Lichfield, the talk was of how high-handed the secretaries of state had been. No sworn evidence had been collected before Wilkes was arrested. A general warrant had been signed by Halifax that had justified the seizure of a man in his own house and the confiscation of his possessions. Worse still, this had not been undertaken in the heat of a moment; rather it was part of a cold, premeditated plot. In Philadelphia, a place that was already developing a reputation as a nursery of bright lawyers, this was procedurally alarming. Was this not more reminiscent of those *lettres de cachet* used by the king of France against his political opponents?

The more people read, the worse it seemed. Apart from the general warrant that had been used to imprison Wilkes, there was the verbal order Egremont had issued to "enter the house, and break open the door, of a Gentleman, a Member of Parliament, at the dead and silent hour of midnight; to drag him out of his bed, seize his person; to break open his most private repositories, and carry away all his papers." This was scandalous. "Could any man have believed," demanded one pamphleteer, "that such a thing could have been attempted in this country?"[49] The messengers had wisely ignored the verbal order, preferring to bide their time until the following morning. But had they entered his bedroom, would Wilkes have been within his rights to kill the intruder? Would he have been charged with murder? Or if Wilkes had been killed himself, "at whose hands would his blood have been required?" These dilemmas were mercifully avoided, but the fact remained that Wilkes had been carried off to the Tower, leaving his house undefended, free to be "ransacked and plundered;

my most private and secret Concerns divulged." As the government seized his possessions, his character was assailed with "every vile and malignant Insinuation, even of High Treason itself." Even writs of Habeas Corpus were evaded. As Wilkes had demanded, was English liberty a reality or a shadow?

Thanks to the *Gazette*, Philadelphians were able to study all of the relevant documents themselves, including a complete transcript of the bill committing Wilkes to the Tower, which Hall printed on July 14. The story promised to run for longer yet. Once Wilkes was released, his trial for libel remained pending. Wilkes himself, however, was undaunted. The ships that came up the Delaware in June and July brought news of his response. While the secretaries of state debated whether it was wise to shift Wilkes's prosecution to the Court of the King's Bench, Wilkes had acted nimbly. To retrieve his seized papers he had applied for a warrant to search Halifax's and Egremont's homes. This was inevitably refused, but Wilkes's reputation was enhanced, as it was when, in July, he issued proceedings against the secretaries of state for the colossal damages of a reputed £50,000 each. Meanwhile, to keep his political voice alive, Wilkes had set up a printing house in Great George Street where he was busily producing new material for his growing number of supporters across the country.

Once again, Wilkes could be accused of hypocrisy. While he complained so loudly about the raid on his home at Great George Street, he failed to mention the fact that on April 30 he had, by his own admission, conspired to break into Richard Balfe's printing shop. As Balfe stated in his interview, he never once gave Wilkes, or John Williams or whoever it was that climbed the ladder into his press room, permission to do so. But nuances like this escaped the papers and certainly did not reach Franklin's eyes as he traveled on his circuit around the northern colonies. What was clear, though, was that just a year after his departure from Portsmouth, British politics had imploded. The idea of the strife in London, just yards away from his room at the Stevensons', unsettled him.

For the best account of what was happening, he waited for Strahan's reply. It eventually materialized in the early autumn, and for Franklin, it made for further dismal reading. At the start of July, a series of suits, brought by the wrongly arrested printers, had been brought before the Court of Common Pleas. The compensatory damages were enormous, Strahan explained, running into thousands of pounds for trespass, assault, and false imprisonment. They "seem intended to mark in the strongest Manner," Strahan added, the court's "Contempt of the Government." All this had put Wilkes, whom Strahan considered "the most profligate of Men," into the highest of spirits.[50]

More disappointing still for Franklin was Strahan's analysis of the cause. Having watched the episode unfold, he blamed Lord Bute. "I am sorry to tell you," he wrote, "that my Countryman has shewn himself altogether unequal to his high Station. Never did a Ministry, in our memory, discover so much Weakness. They seem to have neither Spirit, Courage, Sense, nor Activity, and are a Rope of Sand."[51] Indeed, the situation within the country had changed enormously. Wilkes had become a focal point for a wider spectrum of grievances, from annoyance at the corrupt political system to anger with the terms of the Peace of Paris, which was said to have squandered a strong hand. Already "45" was becoming a rallying slogan for disenchanted Britons. It was dissent in shorthand, evoking not only the forty-fifth number of the *North Briton*, but also and more ominously the year 1745 and the Jacobite rebellion.

While writers disliked the suppression of free speech and those in the City of London grumbled at the end of a profitable war, discontent extended into the country too. One of the major causes was Dashwood's Cider Tax. This had been unpopular from the start. Unsurprisingly the greatest resistance had come from the orchard counties like Worcestershire, Herefordshire, and Dorset. Everything about the Cider Tax was hateful. It was a tax on the poor, a tax on the English, a tax on enjoyment. Collecting the excise was also hazardous. It meant tax inspectors were forced to brazenly search inside private houses, just as the government had done to Wilkes. As one petition to the king put it, the tax was "a Badge of Slavery upon your People."[52] Out in the shires, a coach had been seen chalked with the slogan: "Liberty, Property, no Excise, and ready Money."[53]

Another report from Britain made it into the *Gazette* in early July. It told the story of the thanksgiving day, May 7, the date Wilkes had attempted to ridicule in the unpublished *North Briton* No. 46. It was both rich and foreboding in its detail:

> On the thanksgiving day here, scarcely three of the churches out of fourteen had their bells ringing; and over most of the church doors hung Apples dressed up in crape, with this inscription; "Excise the first fruits of Peace." About 6 o'Clock a procession began in the manner following: 1st, A man riding on an Ass, and on his back this Inscription; "From Excise and the Devil, good Lord deliver us." A string of apples in mourning, was hung round the ass's neck, which was supported by 30 or 40 men, each having a white wand, with an apple at the top of it, also in mourning. Next came a cart, with a gallows fixed in it, and the plad figure hanging by the neck. After that followed a cyder hogshead with a pall over it, carried by six men in black cloaks; on the pall was a number of escutcheons, with inscriptions to the same effect as those above-mentioned. The whole was accompanied by some thousands of people, who proceeded hallooing and shouting thro' the principal streets of the city; and at night a bonfire was prepared in which they cast the figure, and burnt it.[54]

Nine

INFAMOUS

AFTER THE QUIET SUMMER months, the autumn of 1763 saw Westminster stir back into life. By the beginning of November, an atmosphere of poised anticipation filled the bustling network of streets that lay between St. James's Park and the River Thames. With Parliament due to be opened in little more than a week, members of the Commons and Lords were crowding back to town. "This meeting," wrote one newspaper expectantly, "in all probability, will be the greatest, and the disputes, perhaps, the warmest, ever known."[1]

Wilkes remained the central point of focus. Ever since his release from the Tower in early May, he had been bellicose. Over the summer he had instigated a series of cases against the government relating to the manner of his arrest. He had also converted one of the upstairs rooms at his Great George Street house into a press room so that he could continue to communicate with the readership he had established during the *North Briton*'s run. All the time Wilkes was looking forward to the opening of Parliament. This would give him a formal opportunity to lodge his complaint about the government's behavior. While this was certainly a moment to seek redress, some of Wilkes's friends were also urging caution. Some thought that the government was planning some kind of move of their own. High-level meetings were said to be taking place at Halifax's. What was being discussed there was anyone's guess. The only thing everyone could be certain about was the fact that Egremont would not be involved. Much to Wilkes's disappointment, the secretary of state had died suddenly in August. "A scoundrel trick. I had form'd a fond wish to send him to the Devil, but he is gone without my passport,"[2] Wilkes remarked on hearing the news.

At the time of Egremont's demise, Pitt very nearly returned to power. Approaches were made, talks had happened, but the king and the great war hero were unable to agree terms. This obliged George to turn back to Grenville, pacifying him with the words "Let us not look back, let us only look forward; nothing of that sort shall ever happen again."[3] Bruised by the affair, the young king nonetheless had call to be relieved. At least he did not have to deal with a Whig like Pitt on a daily basis. Grenville may have been irritating, but he was better than the alternative. Instead of Pitt, another familiar figure was drafted back into government. Lord Sandwich was an old political beast. Wilkes knew him socially from the Beefsteaks and the gatherings at Medmenham, where he was said to be one of the most abandoned of Dashwood's dissolute friends.

It was during this suspenseful lull before the opening of Parliament, when all the talk was of Wilkes, Grenville, and Pitt, that an entirely new and surprising name abruptly appeared in public life. In the first week of November, the papers were filled with notices for a new book, *An History of England, from the Accession of James the First*, by Catharine Macaulay. This was intriguing. A number of similar histories had been released over the past decade: one by Hume, another by Smollett. No one, though, imagined a woman would make a contribution to the genre. "THE History of England by a Lady," wrote the *London Chronicle* on its publication, "seems such an extraordinary phænomenon, that every one eagerly asks the reasons of its appearance."[4] Inflating curiosity further was the vehemence of Macaulay's introduction, which the *Chronicle* found compelling enough to print in full in its edition of November 3–5. It began:

> I think it incumbent on me to give the Publick my reasons for undertaking a subject which has been already treated of by several ingenious and learned men. From my early youth I have read with delight those histories that exhibit Liberty in its most exalted state, the annals of the Roman and the Greek republicks. Studies like these excite that natural love of freedom which lies latent in the breast of every rational being, till it is nipped by the frost of prejudice, or blasted by the influence of vice.
>
> The effect which almost constantly attends such reading, operated on my inclinations in the strongest manner, and Liberty became the object of a secondary worship in my delighted imagination.[5]

Here, it was clear from the outset, was no watery or saccharine history. Macaulay, whoever she was (and no one yet knew), was obviously politically inclined. Having stressed her admiration for the Roman Republic, she compared that classical ideal with the miserable reality of Georgian Britain, a country "where luxury has made a great progress," and where the "doctrine of slavery" practiced by tyrannical rulers "finds so many interested writers to defend it by fraud and sophistry." Macaulay then launched an attack on the political class. Too many of them, she argued, were deficient in education. Sent off to public schools, where they learned little more than a smattering of Latin or Greek, they gained no appreciation of the divine precepts of liberty embedded within these noble languages. Having learned little more at university, she continued, the nation's elite progressed to the last part of their education in "what is called the tour of Europe":

> that is, a residence for two or three years in the countries of France and Italy. This is the finishing stroke that renders them useless to all the good purposes of preserving the birth-right of an Englishman. Without being able to distinguish the different natures of different governments, their advantages, their dis- advantages; without being able to comprehend how infinitely they affect the interest and happiness of individuals, they grow charmed with every thing that is foreign, are caught with the gaudy tinsel of a superb court, the frolic levity of unreflecting slaves, and thus deceived by appearances, are rivetted in a taste for servitude.[6]

These arguments, combined with the timing of the book's ap- pearance, generated a ripple of excitement in the title and its author. With Parliament about to open, a contested issue at hand, and a great deal of introspection about civil liberty and the British constitution, Macaulay's prose acquired a strange power. Like "the North Briton," Macaulay placed herself outside the sordid world of connections, in- terest, and money. If anything the author's sex helped even more by distinguishing her from those involved in the business of politics. Be- ing a woman, she could not possibly have any ambition for herself. Added to this was novelty. A woman had never written in this manner in this genre before. But Macaulay was unapologetic. "If the execution is deficient, the intention must be allowed to be meritorious; and if the goodness of my head may justly be questioned, my heart will stand the test of the most critical examination," she wrote.[7]

People did not need to read further than Macaulay's introduction to know that here was a bright, compelling new voice. What no one yet knew was how much this lady would be a central figure in the public debate over the years to come. In a man's world, Macaulay's would be a distinct voice. And in November 1763 she had chosen a dramatic moment to start to speak. Not far from Macaulay's home on Jermyn Street, a plot was being concocted in the fashionable streets of Westminster and the chambers of St. James's Palace. A group of some of the most powerful men in the country had decided that the time had come to take their revenge on John Wilkes.

WILKES HAD SPENT THE summer in Paris with Polly. Only in September had he traveled to London to prepare for the new session of Parliament. Ever since, the government had watched his every move.

> *Monday, October 31st*, 1763. Mr. Wilkes went out this morning at half an hour after ten o'clock to Mr. Belenger's in Hedge Lane, and stayed half an hour, from thence home to dinner. Mr. Leach, the printer, came at two o'clock, and stayed an hour and a half. We have not seen Mr. Wilkes since.
> *Tuesday, November 1st*. Mr. Churchill came to Mr. Wilkes this morning at nine o'clock, and stayed an hour. Soon after, Mr. Beardmore, the attorney, came, but did not stay. We have not seen Mr. Wilkes this day.[8]

The reports continued day after day. They listed the names of every MP who called at Great George Street, and they tracked Wilkes as he made his way across town to see Humphry Cotes, his solicitor, or to Vauxhall where Charles Churchill was lodging. They also kept an eye on the pressmen who, on November 6, spent the evening "busy composing" in Great George Street. As the days passed, the details grew. On Sunday, November 13, two days before Parliament was due to open, the spies followed Wilkes to St. Margaret's Church, where he attended the morning service. After lunch they tracked him through a busy list of social calls: at the French ambassador's, at MPs' houses in Curzon and Dover Streets, and, finally, at Temple's.

Wilkes thereafter returned to dine at Great George Street, before he doubled back to Curzon Street to meet with George Onslow, MP for Surrey and, suggestively, the son of the old speaker of the Commons. "From thence," the day's report concluded, "he went home, and we have not seen him since."[9]

The account of Wilkes's activities was then forwarded, as it was every day, to Philip Carteret Webb. Most governments throughout history have found use for a figure like Webb. While his official title was Secretary of Bankrupts, he operated in a more amorphous manner. Webb was someone who knew things. He untangled things. He knew how to fix things. Aged about sixty in 1763, he was well regarded in Westminster for his knowledge of the law and his ability to devise tactical solutions to political problems. The latest problem was Wilkes. Ever since the *North Briton* first appeared, the ministry had been unsure of how to counter him. In despair they had turned to Webb, and he had set to work at once.

Along with Charles Yorke and Fletcher Norton, the ministry's two senior lawyers, Webb was involved in the issuing of the general warrant. He was there throughout Wilkes's arrest. He was present in Great George Street, rifling through the drawers and cabinets for evidence. He flitted in and out of the chamber while the secretaries of state had interrogated Wilkes, and, so it was said, it was on Webb's advice that the writ of Habeas Corpus had been ignored. Webb had even followed Wilkes to the Tower, where he supervised his incarceration and monitored his visitors. Wilkes considered Webb "the most infamous of all the tools of that administration."[10] Walpole echoed this assessment. He thought Webb "a most villainous tool and agent in any iniquity."[11]

Webb was certainly ruthless, but over the spring and summer of 1763, the idea was left to fester among those in government that he had also been heavy-handed. At the heart of the matter was a question of law. General warrants had been issued regularly by secretaries of state since the Glorious Revolution, to legitimize the search for rebels or runaways and, most often of all, the suspected authors, printers, and publishers of lewd or libelous papers. But one had never been used before to apprehend anyone as tenacious as Wilkes. Webb and his colleagues Yorke and Norton seem not to have considered what might happen if someone challenged the legal status of these warrants. And that was precisely what Wilkes did.

First Wilkes had protested against his treatment in the public papers. Then he took his grievances to law, filing suits against the king's messengers and encouraging the other printers to do the same. In early July one of Dryden Leach's journeymen, a man named Huckle, had his complaint of trespass and false imprisonment heard before Chief Justice Charles Pratt in the Court of Common Pleas. Pratt had sided with the printer. He observed that the warrant was flawed because it did not include Huckle's name and because it was issued in the absence of any sworn evidence. Huckle left the court with £300 in damages, much to Webb's dismay. Forty-nine people all told had been taken up on the same warrant. The cost of compensation, simple mathematics suggested, might exceed ten thousand pounds. To Wilkes's mind, the sum might be greater still. In a letter to Temple, he crowed, "The City are warmly my friends, and talk of 20,000*l.* damages to me. The Administration are stunned, and poor Webb is really an object of compassion."[12]

For Webb this was professionally embarrassing. But this was only the start of it. A stream of pamphlets had flowed from the presses over the summer, packed with incontrovertible evidence of the ministry's malicious treatment of its political opponents. To ignore a writ of Habeas Corpus was seen in England as a desperate crime and more the behavior of a medieval baron than an enlightened politician. Many also felt that Wilkes had been cruelly handled during his confinement in the Tower. There, under Egremont's orders, he was kept under close guard, which meant he was denied visitors and the use of writing materials.

In a nation where liberty was considered a sacred cause, this was unacceptable. If an MP could be thrust into such a situation, what protection existed for anyone else? While the public blamed a rotten government for Wilkes's treatment, in Whitehall it was known that Webb had been at the center of the decision-making. And, for all the risks the ministry had run, what was there to show for it? Wilkes remained at large. The costs were enormous. Every opposition writer in London was emboldened, and Wilkes's voice was amplified beyond all measure. The print shops were full of his likeness, "45" had become a rousing slogan, and songs to "Wilkes and Liberty" were sung on every street.

> *WHEN* Scottish *Oppression rear'd up its d—n'd Head,*
> *And* Old English *Liberty almost was dead;*
> *Brave WILKES, like a true* English *Member arose,*
> *And thunder'd Defiance against* England's *Foes,*
> *O* sweet *Liberty! WILKES and Liberty!*
> *Old English Liberty, O!*[13]

To those who had wanted Wilkes gone—Grenville, Halifax, Bute, the king—Webb must have seemed more like a bungler than a fixer. But in the face of all this embarrassment, Webb did have one consolation. The ministry might have been operating outside the law on April 30, but it had at least taken maximum advantage of the opportunity. Webb had been at the center of this. Those who saw him inside Great George Street, personally directing the hunt for evidence, remarked on the incredible "zeal" with which he had worked. He had flung open every drawer and cabinet, throwing piles of papers into bags. When some drawers failed to open he had called for a locksmith. Later Wilkes made the claim that he had been plundered, as if he had suffered a burglary. For once he was not exaggerating.

Whatever heat he was now feeling, Webb's diligence had at least borne fruit. Sifting the mass of confiscated documents, he discovered one that was truly incriminating. This was a manuscript of an obscene poem entitled *An Essay on Woman*. On the face of it, this was just a harmless piece of juvenilia. It was written years before by Wilkes and an old drinking companion (now dead) called Thomas Potter. The poem, composed for the amusement of friends, parodied Alexander Pope's famous *Essay on Man* line for line, exchanging his noble observations on the human spirit for bawdy in-jokes, double-entendres, and scandalous insinuations about establishment figures like the Bishop of Gloucester. A fully worked-out piece, the poem came replete with a title page featuring a drawing of a phallus beside a ten-inch rule, as well as an advertisement and a design. Wilkes and Potter had gone to great lengths to grossly distort Pope's cherished masterpiece:

An Essay on Man (Pope)	**An Essay on Woman (Wilkes & Potter)**
AWAKE, *my St JOHN! leave all meaner things*	AWAKE, *my Fanny,*
To low ambition, and the pride	*leave all meaner things,*
of Kings.	*This morn shall prove*
	what rapture swiving
	brings.
Let us (since Life can little more	*Let us (since life can*
supply	*little more supply*
Than just to look about us and to die)	*Than just a few good*
	Fucks, and then we die)
Expatiate free o'er all this scene	*Expatiate free o'er that*
of Man;	*lov'd scene of Man;*
A mighty maze! but not without	*A mighty Maze! for*
a plan . . .	*mighty Pricks to*
	scan . . . [14]

At twenty pages and littered with profanities, the poem would have filled up a lively half hour's reading for Webb when he examined it in early May. While it certainly contained material that any judge would condemn as libelous, it was nonetheless useless to Webb in its current form. The libel laws depended on the printing of a work, an act which signified publication. Wilkes had not done this; in fact, he had anticipated the danger. Soon after his arrest, Wilkes placed an advertisement in the *Public Advertiser*, stating that:

Speedily will be published,
By PHILIP CARTERET WEBB and LOVELL STANHOPE, Esqrs,
AN ESSAY on WOMAN[15]

Webb could read this ad in one of two ways. It was either a taunt, or perhaps a precautionary device to shield Wilkes against any underhand attempt of Webb's to have the poem printed himself.

Apart from this, little else of material value had appeared from the raid at Great George Street. Webb, irritated and embarrassed, was left to brood on his misfortunes over the summer. Indeed, his mood was aggravated further when he learned that Wilkes was bringing a suit against him for illegally entering his property. Given what had happened in the other cases, Webb's prospects in court did not look good. But then, quite out of the blue, in late July news reached him of an unexpected development. One John Kidgell, chaplain to the Earl of March, made contact. Kidgell had some information that he was eager to pass on. When the two men finally met, Webb heard the first version of a quite fantastical story.

BY JULY IT WAS common knowledge that Wilkes had set up a printing shop in his home. His central idea was to produce a collected volume of the *North Briton*, and with his old friend Dryden Leach's help, he installed two machines and employed some pressmen, despite knowing nothing about the art of printing. Wilkes's management of his new establishment was erratic. As the collected volume of *North Briton* essays had been delayed due to the ongoing legal cases, various occasional jobs had been summoned up to give his men something to do.

It was at this point that Wilkes made a foolish blunder. Thinking of his old parody of Pope, he reasoned that as he had his own printing press he might as well run off a dozen or so copies of the poem for the amusement of friends. Wilkes did not believe this constituted an act of publication as he had no intention of selling the work. In any case, to protect himself he swore his men to secrecy. Then, a few days into the job, Wilkes changed his mind again. With just a small fragment of the poem printed, he decided the time had come to begin on the *North Briton*. Several new pressmen were taken on to help speed the production. One of these was called Samuel Jennings, who arrived knowing nothing about *An Essay on Woman*.

Soon after he started, Jennings was "going to his work in the Morning as usual," when he spotted "a piece of paper on the Ground which contained about eight pages." He had heard some talk from the other pressmen about "a piece of work [that] was carrying on with all the privacy possible," and with this in mind he picked it up and examined it. Its language was so striking that it instantly caught his eye. He took it home, showed it to his wife, and thought no more of it. His wife, however, was of an economical temperament. The following morning she used the printed sheet "to hold a Little Butter," which was part of Jennings's food for the day. This package of "Radishes & Onions with Bread & Butter" Jennings took with him that evening to the Red Lion Inn, Jermyn Street, where he met a friend called Thomas Farmer, for supper.[16]

Farmer was a compositor who worked at a printing shop in Peterborough Court, off Fleet Street. As they ate, Farmer noticed the sheet of paper. In particular his interest was caught by "the Peculiarity of the Subject," and he asked Jennings what it was and how he had got hold of it. Jennings told Farmer it was part of a work "carried on in a Private Manner" at Great George Street.[17] Curious, Farmer asked Jennings if he could borrow it. Wanting to share his find with friends, the next morning Farmer took the paper to the printing shop where he worked, which belonged to a Scotsman called William Faden. Soon Faden's pressroom was buzzing with chatter. Wanting to know what the matter was, Faden took the paper and studied "the Extraordinary Nature of the Contents." John Kidgell, an acquaintance of Faden's who happened to be visiting Peterborough Court at the time, was given the paper too. Horrified at the contents and deducing that it was Wilkes's work, Kidgell decided to take it to the one person in the world Wilkes would have wanted it to be kept from: Philip Carteret Webb.

In the four months since that fortuitous July day when Kidgell called to see him, Webb had considered how best to deploy this unwieldy weapon. He had immediately realized that this was proof of publication and that Wilkes could now be prosecuted for libeling a figure as eminent as the Bishop of Gloucester. He might have been reckless in April, but Webb was determined to be more careful this time. Over the summer and into the autumn, a plan to destroy Wilkes had been hatched and nurtured. Everyone who hated Wilkes came into league: Grenville, Halifax, Sandwich, the lords temporal and spiritual, and even King George himself. "The continuation of Wilkes's impudence is amazing," wrote the king, "when his ruin is so near."[18] Wilkes might have escaped once, but this time Webb took great care to ensure that the stone walls of Parliament would close around him. As the Rev. John Kidgell wrote darkly in a letter to Webb on November 10, "the Hour of Attack approaches."[19]

A LITTLE AFTER MIDDAY on November 15, Wilkes left Great George Street for the Houses of Parliament. It was a short walk, barely more than a few minutes to the ancient building he knew so well, with its great vaulted roof adorned with carvings of angels in flight. Wilkes joined his fellow MPs as they filed through to the Lords to hear the king, who had come to Parliament in his gold coach.

There was little new in the king's speech. George proclaimed the peace as the restoration of "publick Tranquillity" and then reminded the politicians of the need for strict economy in light of the country's "heavy Debts." There was just one line toward its close to catch the ears of astute listeners. The king mentioned what he considered a "licentious Spirit, which is repugnant to the true Principles of Liberty, and of this happy Constitution."[20] His speech at an end, the king departed and Parliament split into its two Houses for the opening debates to begin.

The chamber of the House of Commons looked like an old chapel, with its rows of benches, covered in green cloth, rising up like choir stalls along either side. On the floor of the House was a broad table, on which a scepter was placed when a session began, and where a pair of clerks sat recording the speeches of the day. Behind the clerks rose the speaker's chair. Like a small pulpit, it was the focal point for the debates.

As the benches filled up, Wilkes had a chance to collect himself. The sight around him was rich and varied. It was almost unheard of for all five hundred members to attend in the same sitting. But that day the Commons was "the fullest known for many years."[21] In Georgian times the MPs were generally younger than in later years, with many of the representatives under thirty. Many of these were refined gentlemen, others were army and naval officers, and a great number gave off a distinct air of the provinces. They wore spurs on their boots, thick greatcoats, and wizened tricorn hats. By custom the members kept these hats on until they wished to ask a question. When they did, they would stand and remove them with a flourish as they tried to catch the speaker's eye.

Wilkes understood all these conventions well. He also knew that there was a vital importance in timing. To speak first was to set a tone and to steer a conversation. Over the past few weeks he had made several visits to the house of the speaker, Sir John Cust, during which he had the chance to ask questions on points of procedure. In particular Wilkes wanted to know how he could "secure precedence over all other business for a statement of his case."[22] Wilkes's plan was simple. He had come that day with a copy of a speech that he planned to read, complaining of the government's attack on his Parliamentary privilege. Desperate not to be outflanked, he did not even wait for the swearing in of the new members to be completed before he stood and begged leave to bring a complaint.

Immediately there was a response. At the center of the Treasury bench, the front bench to the speaker's right, was Grenville, the prime minister. Wearing court dress as custom dictated, Grenville stood and opposed Wilkes's motion as a breach of order. The prime minister also announced he had a point to make himself. He told the House that he had in his pocket a message from the king. This news, in turn, prompted an intervention from William Pitt, who countered that "the privileges of the house were sacred" and that the Crown had no "right to interfere." As a Member of Parliament had been insulted, Pitt argued, "it was a duty they owed to themselves to have that insult redressed; and that as the complaining member had made his motion first, it was undoubtedly his right to be heard before any other business was proceeded on."[23]

At moments of contention like this, attention, then as now, turned to the speaker. John Cust was still fairly new in post. He had reluctantly succeeded the long-serving Arthur Onslow two years earlier and had yet to attain his predecessor's command over the House. The Duke of Newcastle, who had been prime minister on Cust's appointment, rated him "a sort of plodding orderly man,"[24] but the reality was worse. Cust had little of Onslow's fiber, and his grasp of parliamentary practice was loose. These factors, which were of little consequence on most occasions, would have more profound consequences this day. For a while Cust allowed the argument between Pitt and Grenville to play out. He then, after working through some trifling business, allowed the House to move to a vote that determined whether Wilkes could bring his complaint immediately. Here Wilkes suffered his first and most serious disappointment. His motion failed by 111 to 300. As Wilkes sat down, Grenville was invited to read the king's message to the House.

The letter was purposeful, and Grenville, a skilled parliamentarian, delivered it crisply. It explained that the king had issued an order to "apprehend and secure" John Wilkes since the last session of Parliament closed, as he had received evidence that he was the "author of a most seditious and dangerous libel."[25] While he was aware that Wilkes had been discharged from custody by the Court of Common Pleas, he noted that he had declined to appear and answer to his charge at the Court of the King's Bench. Given this, Grenville explained,

> his Majesty being desirous to shew all possible attention to the privileges of the house of Commons, in every instance where they can be supposed to be concerned; and, at the same time, thinking it of the utmost importance not to suffer the public justice of the kingdom to be eluded, has chosen to direct the said libel, and also copies of the examinations, upon which Mr Wilkes was apprehended and secured, to be laid before the house, for their consideration.[26]

Wilkes sat silent and aghast. Ever since the Hanoverians arrived, it had been a settled convention that the king would operate only through the agency of his ministers. What he was doing here seemed a classic case of interference. It was the kind of act that all true Whigs should instinctively resist as Pitt had done. But for Wilkes, there were more pressing concerns. He knew the king loathed him. Not long ago he had told Temple, "I hear from all hands that the King is enraged at my insolence."[27] Now George was inviting the House of Commons to assume its ultimate authority and to act very much like a court of appeal to a judgment that had been passed elsewhere. This was the kind of thing that may occasionally happen in the Lords, but never in memory had the Commons been used in this way. Had Cust not sat in the speaker's chair, had the members not been so pliant, and had the message come from someone with less gravitas than the king, the direction may well have been disregarded. But as it was, the MPs, like Cust, complied.

The chamber transformed from being a place of debate into one that resembled a court of law. An address of thanks was voted to the king, then Grenville started to read the examinations of Kearsley and Balfe. Meanwhile Wilkes was left in shock. There was nothing he could do to halt proceedings. His best hope lay with his greatest supporter. Pitt demonstrated his willingness to fight. But despite his repeated and tenacious objections against the proceedings and, later, the wordings of the charges laid against Wilkes, it was all to no avail. After hours of debate the Commons passed a motion by a majority of 273 to 111. It stated:

> That a paper intitled *The North Briton*, No. XLV, is a false, scandalous, and seditious libel, containing expressions of the most unexampled insolence and contumely towards his Majesty, the grossest aspersions upon both houses of parliament, and the most audacious defiance of the authority of the whole legislature, and most manifestly tending to alienate the affections of the people from his Majesty, to draw them from their obedience to the laws of the realm, and to excite them to traitorous insurrections against his Majesty's government.[28]

The opening part of their plan complete, a subsequent move was then initiated to have No. 45 symbolically burned at the hands of the common hangman. Throughout all this, Wilkes sat in silent despair. One by one his enemies rose to revenge themselves for his abuse of them in the *North Briton*. The most uncomfortable moment came when the secretary to the treasury, an associate of Webb's called Samuel Martin, confronted Wilkes about a passage in the *North Briton* No. 40, which had described him as "the most treacherous, base, selfish, mean, abject, low-lived and dirty fellow that ever *wriggled* himself into a secretaryship."[29]

Having remembered the line with unsurprising clarity, Martin observed that, "A man capable of writing in that manner without putting his name to it and thereby stabbing another in the dark, is a cowardly rascal, a villain, and a scoundrel."[30] Martin knew this was dangerous language. But Wilkes sat stock-still as he spoke it. At the time, some MPs thought that Wilkes was rattled. Others explained Wilkes's reticence as yet another example of "that honest indignation and exaltation of mind so peculiar to himself, and so superior to those cringing, cowardly betrayers of the rights of the people." It was the early morning before Wilkes was invited to bring his own complaint. By then it little mattered.

By that time, too, Wilkes probably knew the worst of it. While one old friend, Grenville, had assaulted him in the Commons, another, Lord Sandwich, had been equally brutal in the Lords. Not long after the king's speech had ended, as Wilkes sat waiting for his chance to catch the speaker's eye, Sandwich had sprung his own trap. During the preceding months, Webb had been hunting down each of the printers who worked for Wilkes. From them, at length, he had managed to acquire a full printed copy of *An Essay on Woman* along with testimony about the circumstances of its production. In the Lords that day, Sandwich took the opportunity of reading the poem out before the most eminent audience in the kingdom.

Wilkes would have heard the anecdotes along with everyone else. One lord apparently sat with his fingers in his ears. Others roared in mock-horror for more of the verses to be read. The Bishop of Gloucester, the greatest victim of the satire, was the most offended of all. He had, according to Walpole, "foamed with the violence of a Saint Dominic; vaunted that he had combated infidelity, and laid it under his feet; and said, the blackest fiends in hell would not keep company with Wilkes, and then begged Satan's pardon for comparing them together."[31] Wilkes's character was in tatters, his humiliation complete.

When Wilkes arrived home at Great George Street that night, he did not go to bed. Instead, he wrote a letter. Of all the many things that crowded in on his mind, the slur from Samuel Martin shone out. Wilkes composed a short response to his assailant:

> Sir,
> You complained yesterday, before five hundred gentlemen, that you had been *stabbed in the dark* by the North Briton, but I have reason to believe you was not so much in the dark as you affected and chose to be. Was the complaint made before so many gentlemen, on purpose that they might interpose? To cut off every pretence of ignorance as to the author, I whisper in your ear, that every passage in the North Briton, in which you have been named, or even alluded to, was written by
> Your humble servant,
> John Wilkes[32]

A reply to this was not long in coming. A little before noon the following day, Martin called personally at Great George Street. Wilkes was out, visiting Cotes, but Martin had a letter in his pocket that he asked the servant boy to deliver to his master. In it Martin noted Wilkes's admission. He had more to say too. "I must take liberty to repeat that you are a malignant & infamous scoundrel, & that I desire to give you an opportunity of shewing me whether the epithet of cowardly was rightly applied or not. I desire that you & I may meet in Hyde Park immediately, with a brace of pistols each, to determine our difference." Martin would, he told Wilkes, wait by the ring in the park, "so concealed that no body may see them, & I will wait there in expectation of you one hour."[33]

Having delivered his letter, Martin strode up Bird Cage Walk to Hyde Park, where he "touched the rail" of the ring at twenty-two minutes past twelve. The ring was a crowded, bustling location. It was built more than a hundred years earlier, during the reign of Charles I, as a place for members of the royal court to ride out in their carriages. A century on, it was an established social space where the rich and the fashionable would spill out of Mayfair or St. James's to ride or walk in the fresh air. Martin was in no mood for such diversions. He paced up and down under the trees on the east side of the ring for "a considerable time." Just after one o'clock, he saw Wilkes approaching "pretty fast" from the direction of Grosvenor Square gate. Wilkes apologized to Martin for keeping him waiting and then the two of them left the shade of the trees and the chatter of the people, and started to walk toward the north wall of the park in search of "a more private place." Each had a pair of pistols buried inside his coat.

This was nothing at all like the Red Lion at Bagshot. Feigning a "friendly & earnest" conversation as they made their way across the park, the two men scanned their surroundings for a quiet spot. Somewhere out of sight. As they walked, Wilkes began to sense that this was a rash undertaking. There were no agreed rules. There were no seconds. No time had been spared for preparation. Martin, meanwhile, seemed completely at ease, both emotionally and practically. He suggested they stand back to back, walk half a dozen paces, and then turn to fire. When Wilkes suggested they exchange pistols, to remove any chance of subterfuge, Martin refused, saying he "saw no reason why each should not use his own." Martin described what happened next, in an emotionally charged "memorandum" he composed directly afterward.

> When we approached pretty near to a rail, which divides the Park at a low watry place, Mr W. proposed this to be the spot; which Mr M. agreed to. They both stooped under the rails, and being gott on the other side, Mr W. again proposed to change

a pistol on each side, & Mr M. assenting Mr W. laid both his own pistols upon the grass & desired Mr W. to make his choice which he did & desired Mr M. to make his choice which he did & laid down one of his pistols upon the ground, taking up one of Mr Wilkes's. Mr W. immediately desired to have that pistol of Mr M. which he had kept in his hand, when he put down the other upon the ground. Mr M. immediately complied with this request. Mr W. thereupon took up two pistols from ye ground—one which was his own & the other which was Mr W's. They then parted from each other, not more (I believe) than six paces each.

As Martin wheeled around he was shocked to see that Wilkes was "stooping towards the ground" and it looked as if he was "examining the priming" of one of the pistols. Before Martin had chance to fire, Wilkes appealed to him, "Stay a little, I am not ready."

"I will stay till you are ready," Martin replied.

At this Wilkes stood upright. The men pointed their pistols at each other. Martin said, "Now, Sir," and both fired "nearly at ye same instant."

As the smoke rose, it was clear that both had missed. This was the point at which the duel had concluded at the Red Lion, shortly to be followed by a glass of claret and a burst of notoriety. This time it was to be different. Each tossed away his spent pistol. They had used their own weapons for the first exchange. Now they were to use each other's.

Martin saw Wilkes take a few brisk steps forward, with his remaining pistol leveled toward him. At this, Martin retreated a few paces. He then "presented" his second pistol and fired. At the same instant Wilkes tried to do the same, but his weapon "snapped" without discharging its bullet. As he lowered his own pistol, Martin watched as his opponent threw his weapon "immediately upon the ground."

Unbuttoning his surtout, frock, and waistcoat, Wilkes pulled away the fabric to expose a gaping wound. As he pressed his hand to his body, Martin saw that "a large patch of blood" had already collected on his shirt "about the middle of his belly."

"I have killed you," said Martin.[34]

CATHARINE MACAULAY WAS STILL only thirty-two years old. A slender lady, quite tall, with delicate features and oval face. It was her eyes, however, that caught most people's attention. According to one friend, a Mrs. Arnold, they were as "beautiful as imagination can conceive, full of penetration and fire."[35] In 1763 she lived with her husband, a wealthy and respectable Scottish physician called George Macaulay, in a fine town house at the junction of Jermyn Street and St. James's, off Piccadilly. Had she glanced out of her front window in the early afternoon of November 16, she might have caught sight of a wounded gentleman stumbling along in the arms of a servant, down the slope toward Pall Mall. There, with the blood oozing through the man's clothes, the retreating figures hailed a sedan chair, which vanished into St. James's Park.

Over the next fortnight, Macaulay, like everyone else in London, was left to pore over the news that came out of Great George Street. Quickly, word spread that Wilkes had been dangerously wounded in a duel with Samuel Martin. It was a murky affair. People were soon evaluating Martin's conduct, and their verdict was unsparing. If he was so offended by the North Briton No. 40, which had been published all the way back in March, then why had he waited eight months to make his complaint in such a public forum?

Reports filtered out, too, that Martin had insisted the duel be fought with pistols, whereas by the rules of honor, the choice should have been Wilkes's to make. And what of the pistols? Hadn't Wilkes's second shot failed? Wasn't that Martin's pistol? As for himself, Martin was not around to hear these questions. He had fled for safer ground on the Continent. Perhaps this was a wise move. It was not long before other stories were circling. One was that he had spent the weeks leading up to the opening of Parliament practicing at target with his pistols in the countryside, "Sundays not excepted." This brought Martin a derogatory new nickname in London: "The Targeteer."[36]

Had Wilkes died in such circumstances, it would have seemed more like an assassination than anything else. But the news from Great George Street was encouraging. The day after the duel, Wilkes underwent a delicate operation to remove the ball from his body. It seemed that it had deflected off one of his coat buttons, entering his body through the belly and coming to rest in his groin. The procedure was a success. More encouraging was the news that a fragment of Wilkes's coat had been retrieved from the wound along with the ball, removing the peril of infection. In the days that followed, Wilkes's condition was the principal interest of the papers. He was reported to be in constant pain, but slowly recovering. The chief focus of trouble now was not his wound, but news from Parliament.

Regardless of his physical state, the formal efforts to destroy him were continuing. The government tabled a motion to strip the protection of privilege from members accused of libel. This was pushed through the Commons by King George's childhood friend Frederick, Lord North, the Member of Parliament for Banbury, who helped it achieve a majority of 258 to 133. The Lords then continued the Commons' work, approving all the pending motions against Wilkes and the *North Briton*. On hearing this the king was said to be "in great spirits, and greatly pleased with the success." A date of December 3 was set for No. 45 to be burned by the common hangman, and the expectation was that Wilkes would be stripped of his position as an MP shortly thereafter. Politics never being a sentimental profession, news came up from Buckinghamshire that canvassing was already underway in Aylesbury. If this was not disquieting enough for Wilkes, his misery was compounded when he heard that his greatest ally, William Pitt, had deserted him after hearing about *An Essay on Woman*. In a passionate speech Pitt denounced Wilkes as "the blasphemer of his God, and the libeller of his King," declaring, he had "no connexion with him."[37]

For Macaulay the shameful events in Parliament during the past month were sadly predictable. When the critical time had come, the members had betrayed their principles and the interest of the nation to side with a powerful king. Some MPs had been overawed by the might of the Crown; others had thought more of their own prospects. Not enough of them had stood up for the hard-won British liberties that were being sacrificed as both Wilkes and the *North Briton* were expelled from public life. For Macaulay this was no great surprise. Men, she believed, were more given to corruption than improvement.

This conviction had arisen out of years spent reading seventeenth-century histories, when the Stuarts with their lust for power had driven England twice to revolution. Time and again, men—often bright, able men—had been corrupted by public office. Power, she saw, was a consuming force. It was, as the Commonwealthman John Trenchard had described it, a force that, "warms, scorches, or destroys, according as it is watched, provoked, or increased."[38] In the first volume of her history, Macaulay dwelt on the story of Sir Francis Bacon, King James I's Lord Chancellor. Bacon, Macaulay reminded her readers, "was a fine scholar, and deep philosopher," yet he, like so many, had become "a servile instrument for supporting arbitrary measures."[39] Bacon had been prosecuted and disgraced. And if someone like him had succumbed, with all his talents, then why should we be surprised when ordinary members of Parliament did the same?

These were the kind of speculations on human nature Macaulay had long turned over. Born Catharine Sawbridge into a prominent Kentish family, after her mother's early death she had been brought up in a country house on the Downs, with little expectation that she would be anything other than a conventional Georgian lady. Her father, bereaved and absent, left her to grow up in the care of a Mrs. Fuzzard, an indolent governess who taught her nothing. When the

Bluestocking Elizabeth Montagu, who had been a neighbor in Kent, heard that "Kitty Sawbridge" had produced a history book, she wrote in bafflement to her brother: "If she took her sentiments from her Father, & her language from Mrs Fuzzard it must be an extraordinary performance."[40]

But Catharine had possessed one great advantage: her father's library. Later when people came to speculate on how a young girl had acquired so much knowledge without anyone suspecting, they could only conclude that it had come in the long, solitary hours of self-study, when she "rioted in intellectual luxury" surrounded by books.[41] Quietly, very much as Franklin had, Catharine started with volumes of the *Spectator*, before she progressed to deeper studies. Here, the story was told, "she dwelt with delight and ardour on the annals of the Greek and Roman republics. Their laws and manners interested her understanding, the spirit of patriotism seized her, and she became an enthusiast in the cause of freedom."[42]

As it turned out, Macaulay's book was indeed extraordinary, although not in the sense that Elizabeth Montagu had anticipated. After its introduction was carried in the *London Chronicle* at the start of November, it became one of the most sought-after books in town. On the 30th, the philosopher and author Thomas Hollis recorded in his diary that he had finished Macaulay's first volume. "The history is honestly written, and with considerable ability and spirit; and is full of the freest, noblest, sentiments of Liberty."[43] A few days afterward, Horace Walpole wrote a note to a friend, enquiring, "Have you read Mrs. Macaulay? I am glad again to have Mr Gray's opinion to corroborate mine that it is the most sensible, unaffected and best history of England that we have had yet."[44] Lord Bute heard about it too. One of his cousins sent him a note. "What is this McCaulay history? I saw in the newspapers an extract of a preface that seemed to me to be the rhapsody of a crazy head."[45]

As these sentiments were being expressed privately, the book received a full public appraisal in the *Monthly Review* where its style was praised for being "so correct, bold, and nervous." The reviewer, charmed by the appearance of a history book by a woman, a hitherto unknown novelty, was so taken by *A History of England* that he felt it challenged his perception of nature. No one could read a work like this and believe any longer that thinking was "confined to those who wear beards." Nevertheless, he believed, projects like this did not come without their dangers:

> Intense thought spoils a lady's features; it banishes *les ris et les graces*, which form all the enchantment of a female face. Who ever saw Cupid hovering over a severe and studious brow? and who would not keep at awful distance from a fair one, who looks with all the gravity of a Greek professor? Besides, severe thought, it is well known, anticipates old age, makes the forehead wrinkle, and the hair turn grey; nay, we are not sure, whether in time, it may not perfectly masculate the sex: for we read of one Phatheusa, the wife of Pytheus, who thought so intensely during her husband's absence, that, at his return, she had a beard grown upon her chin.[46]

Such words, however bizarre to a twenty-first-century eye, capture the inherent lure of Macaulay's book at the time. But the *History* was not attractive for the author's sex alone. The timing of its appearance, at the height of the Wilkes affair, was crucial. As people read news of the votes in the Commons or heard of Sandwich's betrayal in the Lords, they could find a sort of abstract analysis in Macaulay's writing. Parliament was only acting in 1763 as it had done so many times before in the Stuart Age. In this sense, the *History* was more than a novel piece of literature. It was a warning.

The reviewer for the *Monthly Review* realized as much. He relished the way Macaulay exploded the reputations of both Queen Elizabeth ("The vices of this Princess were such as could not exist with a good heart, nor her weaknesses with a good head")[47] and King James I ("the virtues he possessed were so loaded with a greater proportion of their neighboring vices, that they exhibit no lights to set off the dark shades")[48] and was determined to expose the corruption which was staining Georgian politics. In a triumphant passage, she told the story of Sir John Savile, an opposition MP, who had successively been promoted by James I until he finally received a peerage. Savile's story, Macaulay wrote, "was the first instance of that practice of buying-off individuals; which, in the hands of succeeding Monarchs, has silently and surely effected what James and his son in vain attempted by clamour and violence."

In response, the writer for the *Monthly Review* simply stated: "If this passage needed a comment, this is not a time to make it."[49]

SATURDAY, DECEMBER 3, WAS the date appointed for the burning of No. 45. Around noon on that dark winter's day, people began to gather at the Royal Exchange. From the start there was a febrile mood in the streets. Wilkes had often written to Temple during the buoyant summer months, boasting of the support he had in the City, where people were "almost unanimous in the great cause of liberty."[50] The Exchange, standing in the fork between Threadneedle Street and Cornhill, was the focal point of the City. It was an unlucky location, as the ministry would soon realize.

It was later said that the misfortunes of the day were "not a little Encouraged" by the presence of many well-to-do people, who crowded at their windows or leant over their balconies and "made the Air resound with their Clappings" whenever the people below showed any sign of defiance.[51] This mass of people was roundly described as the greatest mob that had been seen in London for a long time. At half past twelve, they began to hiss in the most murderous manner as two men appeared, one carrying a large bundle of sticks, another a lighted link. Had there not been a ring of constables guarding the wood, they would have been dashed away, but instead those defending the scene managed to press the crowd back until the dignitaries started to arrive. First to appear was Alderman Thomas Harley MP, one of the sons of the Earl of Oxford, but the horses which drew his carriage were so frightened by the noise that they halted at a distance and refused to approach.

At this, Harley, who had been appointed to oversee the burning, clambered out of his carriage and began to read the motion condemning the *North Briton*. He was drowned out by jeers from the crowd. "They were armed," Walpole wrote, "with that most bloody instrument, the mud out of the kennels," and "they hissed in the most murderous manner."[52] Having done his best, Harley stepped back and the *North Briton* was placed onto the link, but "just as it began to Blaze,"[53] the crowd surged and knocked it to the floor. Seeing it was too dangerous to proceed, Harley retreated to his coach, as the mob, encouraged by those above, broke into open battle with the constables.

Many injuries were sustained in the confusion that followed. The glass windows of Harley's carriage were beaten in, leaving a bloody gash across his face. Full of angry life, the rioters roamed the capital's streets all that afternoon. At nightfall they parodied the day's events with a bonfire of their own at Temple Bar. Instead of a copy of No. 45, they burned a large jack boot and a petticoat, which Walpole called "the mob's Hiero-glyphics for Lord Bute and the Princess Dowager."[54] Hundreds were said to have watched the flames dart and flare through the December sky. Hearing this, the king was said to be "much disturbed and exasperated."[55]

For Wilkes, who had been humiliated in front of the entire political class, this was solace indeed. From this moment onward, he would never forget where his greatest source of support lay. While so many of his friends had deserted him, in the City of London and among the traders of England, he remained a hero without compare. Better news was to follow a few days later, when the Court of Common Pleas finally heard the case relating to the seizure of his papers on April 30, which Wilkes had brought against the undersecretary of state Robert Wood. Once more Chief Justice Pratt oversaw the arguments, and again he found in favor of Wilkes, ruling that it had been illegal to enter his property and to seize his papers. These violations were compensated by £1,000 in damages.*

Receiving all this news in Great George Street, Wilkes was nonetheless coming to a resolution. London had become too dangerous a place for him. It was now abundantly clear that Grenville, the king, and a range of powerful others were determined to reduce him to nothing. More disquieting was the discovery of an assassin outside his door. A Scottish soldier, livid at the insults given to his native people in the *North Briton*, had vowed to avenge what Wilkes called "the old Berwick grudge."[56] With the Commons also demanding he return to the chamber to give evidence on the libel charge, Wilkes decided that his time was up. On December 23, the spies who had watched his home for months saw him being helped out of his front door and into a waiting carriage. In seconds Wilkes was gone. The next day he was sighted at Canterbury, where he arrived in "the utmost Haste" at the Fountains Inn in a chaise and four. "About Half an Hour after," a newspaper report explained, "came an Officer in his Regimentals, and on being told Mr. Wilkes was gone forwards, hurried after him."[57]

Reaching Paris, Wilkes was left to brood on the events of an extraordinary year. He had acquired as great celebrity as anyone in the land, but it had come at a huge cost. His reputation was tarnished, his

---

* The battle over the legal status of general warrants was not quite over yet. After Wilkes and the printers' victories in the Court of Common Pleas in 1763, challenges continued. The government appealed one of the printers' cases in the Court of the King's Bench, England's highest criminal court, in 1765. There Lord Mansfield, the Scotsman Wilkes had done his best to avoid in April, concurred with the ruling of Charles Pratt (now Lord Camden) in the Court of Common Pleas. Wilkes regarded the defeat of general warrants as one of his greatest achievements. The most legally significant of the cases that arose out of the general warrants affair of 1763–64 was that of *Entick v Carrington* in 1765. For more on the lasting significance of this case, see Lord Justice Sedley's Denning Lecture, "New corn from old fields: Ministerial government, history and the law" (2012).

finances were woeful, and the campaign against him was not finished yet. In the months following his flight, he listened helplessly to developments at a distance. First came the news that he had been expelled from the House of Commons. On the heels of this, in February, came his trial in absentia for the two charges of libel. Unsurprisingly he was found guilty on both counts.

The ministry continued to pursue their vengeance to the limit. In August the sheriff of Middlesex read a proclamation outside the door of St. Margaret's Church in Westminster, just yards away from his house in Great George Street. It demanded Wilkes present himself at the Court of the King's Bench. As he did not comply, on November 1, 1764, the court pronounced a sentence of outlawry against him. This was a bitter, devastating blow. Outlawry was a status filled with medieval resonance: of Robin Hood and William Wallace, who in legal terms were said to bear a *caput lupinum*, a "wolf's head," because they were considered the "most pernicious animal that infested the kingdom."[58]

While outlawry meant something different in the eighteenth century to what it had in the thirteenth, it remained a ruinous thing. Wilkes now lay outside the protection of the law. He could not own property, and while he could not be killed with impunity—as had previously been the case—were a sheriff to see him in the street then he could simply be served with a writ of Capias Utlagatum. Then, in theory, he could be hauled to jail where he would be left to languish forever. To Wilkes, and his remaining friends, it was clear there was no way back. Even his case against Lord Halifax, whom he had been pursuing for damages after his unlawful arrest, was halted as Wilkes had no legal rights. Despite all, he sought to maintain a sunny outlook. "If I stay at Paris," he told his solicitor Humphry Cotes, "I will not be forgot in England; for I will feed the papers, from time to time, with gall and vinegar against the administration."[59] It was the best he could do.

*   *   *

WILKES MAY HAVE GONE but in Britain people were left to come
to terms with the events of the past few years. The story of one is
instructive.

John Horne was a Cambridge-educated clergyman who, since
1760, had held the living of New Brentford, seven miles outside
London. Like all Englishmen Horne had been raised with a love of
the constitution, and as he watched what happened in 1763 he was
aghast. "The image of Mr Pitt seemed to have haunted his dreams;
the wrongs of Mr Wilkes to have broken his slumbers," it was later
recorded. Seeing the treatment these figures had received from opponents like Bute, Grenville and Egremont, Horne grew suspicious
that "a regular plot" had been laid by the ministers for the destruction
of the constitution. Whether King George himself was spearheading
this plot was uncertain, but by the time of Wilkes's flight to France,
Horne had "anticipated the time, when, like Denmark about a century before, and Sweden at a subsequent period, the liberties of Great
Britain were to be laid prostrate at the feet of a young, artful, and
ambitious monarch!"[60]

Writing about this decades later, Horne's biographer, Alexander Stephens, stressed the vital importance of this conviction to his
subject. "This suspicion, however strange and unaccountable it may
appear to some, [Horne] cherished until the day of his death," Stephens wrote. "And this ought to be considered as one of the secret,
but powerful springs, by which all the actions of his future life were
actuated."[61] As Wilkes was being erased from polite society, Horne
was abandoning hopes of ecclesiastical preferment. Instead of a quiet
career in the church, Horne had decided to "vindicate the liberties
of his country, or suffer as a martyr in their defence." He started to
produce songs in defence of Wilkes, something Horne followed with
"squibs, puns, paragraphs, letters and essays" that spoke of Britain
as a sunken nation. Soon he produced a daring pamphlet titled *The
Petition of an Englishman*, filled with simmering prose. In language
that was arresting, if somewhat unusual for an ordained minister of

266 LIFE, LIBERTY, AND THE PURSUIT OF HAPPINESS

the Church of England, Horne mimicked what he presented as the goverment's sinister inner voice:

> Squeeze out, therefore, the eyes that presume to pry into your
> mysteries and intrigues of STATE or LUST.
> Slit the nose that dares to smell a RAT.
> Wring off the ears and root out the tongues, that listen to, or
> whisper the words—LIBERTY and LAWS.[62]

Horne's actions were extreme ones. But many others, in more subtle ways, were similarly touched by the Wilkes affair. One who was energized by all the talk of liberty was Catharine Macaulay. In 1764, still a novelty, she channeled her thoughts about contemporary politics into the second volume of her history. As Wilkes lay low, Horne plotted, and Macaulay wrote, the spring of 1764 turned into summer and then autumn. And as another winter came on, an advertisement appeared in the *London Chronicle* for December 11. It informed its readers, "On Monday evening last, the ingenious and much-esteemed Dr Benjamin Franklin, arrived here from Philadelphia."[63]

Ten

NEWS-WRITERS

ON THOSE CHARGED NIGHTS in the Commons, when Wilkes was an obsession and the ice of Grenville competed with the fire of Pitt, had a member of the House glanced up toward the gallery, they would often have seen William Strahan's keen eyes gazing down on them. Strahan was drawn to politics. From the public gallery, he could study the subtle shifts of power. During early 1764, as the ministry's project to destroy Wilkes reached its climax, Strahan had been there day after day. It was not just personal curiosity that tempted him to Parliament. While in the gallery he took care to record the proceedings. These notes were put into his letters to David Hall in Philadelphia, which were then distilled into copy for the *Gazette*. This made Strahan perhaps the first transatlantic political correspondent, and it also meant that readers of the *Gazette* were as well informed about British politics as anyone in colonial America. In 1764, Franklin wrote to Strahan, encouraging him with his journalism. "Your Political Letters are Oracles here," he explained. "I beseech you to continue them."[1]

After Franklin's return in late 1764, he would sometimes accompany his friend on trips to the gallery. Away from his place of work,

Franklin noticed, Strahan would become meditative. Once as they sat in silence, Strahan had been struck by a thought. No two journeymen printers in his knowledge, Strahan whispered to Franklin, had met with such success as they had. He was right. By the mid-1760s, Franklin was the most distinguished American in Britain. Strahan, meanwhile, had arrived in Franklin's estimation "at the head of [his] profession."[2] Strahan no longer had to walk the mile from Parliament to Little New Street. A rich man, he was now drawn home in his own carriage, just as the now long-dead Edward Cave of the *Gentleman's Magazine* had once been.

In his brick house on Little New Street, recently enlarged with stabling, Strahan could relax in the company of his family. Apart from his second son, George, who was away at University College in Oxford, and his elder daughter Rachel, who had married an apothecary called Andrew Johnston, the remainder of Strahan's family were still at home with him and Margaret. This included his youngest, Peg (named after her mother), who was now a girl of fourteen, and the boys William Jr. and Andrew. Both of these were men now, and useful employees at his printing shop, just across the street, where eight or nine presses clicked and clacked from eight till eight, six days a week.

Strahan still printed for booksellers like Andrew Millar and Thomas Longman as he had in his very earliest days. Over the years, he had sent them some of the greatest works of the age, from Johnson's *Dictionary* to Hume's *History of England* and novels like Tobias Smollett's *Roderick Random*, Sterne's *Tristram Shandy*, and Goldsmith's *Vicar of Wakefield*. With titles like these in his catalog, Strahan was no longer obliged to cast around for jobs. The best writers came to him.

There had been a degree of diversification over the years, too. Since 1749 he had printed the *Monthly Review*, the first title expressly devoted to the reviewing of new books. An even more regular source of work came in 1757 when Strahan started to print a thrice-weekly evening paper called the *London Chronicle*. This had been launched with aplomb, the introduction specially composed by Johnson himself. Fancying himself as a newspaper man, Strahan had put money into the title, making himself the principal shareholder and exercising editorial power when he wished. On his appointment as the royal governor of New Jersey, for instance, William Franklin wrote anxiously to Strahan, asking him to frame the news in a particular way. Due to Strahan's contacts, the *Chronicle* soon gained a reputation for the quality and timeliness of its reporting. Conservative and courtly in its outlook (the *Chronicle* never had much time for Wilkes), its standing is reflected in Boswell's account of Johnson's boisterous nighttime ramble with Topham Beauclerk. Getting wind of the story, Garrick warned his old friend, "I heard of your frolick t'other night. You'll be in the Chronicle."[3]

On March 24, 1765, Strahan celebrated his fiftieth birthday. It was a chance to gaze back over all the successes and to make some sense of his personal story. He was no longer a mere printer, but a central component in a vibrant literary network: a fixer, an energizer, and an organizer for harassed writers like Johnson. Others knew him more as an editor, polishing up and condensing their copy before it went to press. Indeed, Strahan could make the singular claim that he had, over the years, tidied up the prose of not only Samuel Johnson but David Hume and Laurence Sterne. In years to come he would do the same for Adam Smith and Edward Gibbon, who once remarked that thanks to Strahan, "many blemishes of style," previously invisible in his manuscript of *The Decline and Fall of the Roman Empire*, "were discovered and corrected in the printed sheet."[4]

Strahan, though, was always one for future projects rather than past reflections, and by 1765 he was plotting his next move. Having already secured half the patent for producing law books, which were printed at a Law Printing House some distance from New Street, Strahan next set his mind on becoming the official printer to the University of Oxford. Beyond this was something that was even more ambitious. This was to acquire part of the patent for the

King's Printer, which would bring him the monopoly for producing all the official acts and proclamations made by Parliament. As ever, one of the first to hear of Strahan's latest plan was one of his oldest friends. Twenty years had now passed since Hall had left Wine Office Court for Philadelphia, but the flow of letters between the two had not ceased. They wrote to each other as frequently as once a month, and Hall in particular would bristle at any extended spells of silence. Their letters always opened with business. Like Franklin before him, Hall depended upon Strahan to send crates of books for the Market Street shop. According to one scholar's calculation, around £18,000 worth was dispatched between 1760 and 1772.[5] This was such a colossal amount that it ensured that Hall's shop was one of the best-stocked in all the colonies.

But there was more to Strahan and Hall's relationship than this. Only Strahan's side of the correspondence survives, but it demonstrates the affection the two men continued to hold for one another. With Hall, Strahan was unrestrained. He worried about his wife Margaret's "old bilious Complaint" and expressed his hope that she would improve in the waters at Bath. He talked with pride about his new grandchildren, born to Rachel and Andrew Johnston, "the most charming engaging Creatures you ever saw."[6] Strahan shared with Hall plans for jaunts into the country and for nostalgic trips back home to Scotland, and he often signed off with the cozy line: "Remember us all to your Fire-Side."[7] This fireside remembrance was, by 1765, the best Strahan could hope for. Both knew that they were unlikely to meet again. "I am very sorry you seem to give me so little Hopes of seeing you in England once more," he wrote, "but I do not wonder at your Attachment to a Country where you have now past so great a Part of your Life."[8]

Strahan could at least reflect that while he had lost one friend to Philadelphia, he had gained another in return. His relationship with Franklin was as warm as ever. For Franklin, Strahan was a kindred spirit: someone whose judgment he valued and whose company he loved. For Strahan, Franklin was a man above all others. Although his scheme to unite the families with a marriage between William Jr. and Sally had come to nothing, Strahan still wanted to keep Franklin close. The image of the two men together, watching, whispering, churning over the ramifications during debates in the House of Commons, is one of the enduring visions of the times. It freezes a picture of the two printers—both capable, both calculating, both dynamic—watching the fault lines develop; noticing before anyone else the cracks that would soon become a chasm.

ON MAY 15, AN ARTICLE ran in the *Public Advertiser* that would have caught Strahan's attention. Although it was obviously something more, it masqueraded as a letter from a reader. Titled "The Duke of York's Travels," it satirized the recent avalanche of reports concerning the movements of George III's younger brother. If these reports were true, the piece pointed out, the Duke of York was poised, simultaneously, to embark on a dizzying range of activities. He would, in the next weeks, be appointed to command a fleet in the Mediterranean and another in the Channel. He would sail in a yacht to Copenhagen and ride in a coach around the Duchy of Brunswick. Without pausing for breath he would cross the Atlantic to North America, where he was to "range the Continent," and "go a Wood-hunting with the Cherokee Kings." All that remained, the letter rounded off, was for the Duke to set off, "up the Ganges to call upon the Nabob, and then advance and pay a Visit to the Great Mogul, and afterwards sail for China, and go up to see the Grandeur of the Court of Pekin."[9]

Although the letter-writer's identity had been concealed beneath the pseudonym "the Spectator," Strahan could spot Franklin's prose at a distance. He was familiar with his friend's methods too. During Franklin's previous visit Strahan had occasionally placed veiled contributions from him in the *Chronicle*. Letters to the press were a recognized journalistic device, and they remained one of Franklin's favorite tools for influencing public opinion. Now that Strahan had editorial influence in a London paper, Franklin made the most of the opportunity. To begin with, this meant humorous articles that were intended to make gentle points. But during his two years in Phila-delphia, Strahan noticed the tone of the pieces Franklin sent him to publish had grown increasingly strident. This was a reflection of what was happening in Pennsylvania. Where once it had been famous for its tolerance, the province's politics had grown poisonous. At the heart of the quarrel was a battle of factions. On one side was the Penn family's "Proprietary Party," which defended the status quo. On the other was the Assembly Party or "Old Ticket," led by Franklin. The Assembly Party sought a change in the colony's status. Annoyed by the Penn family's chartered tax privileges, which they believed were unfair, Franklin's party wanted George III to take Crown control of the colony. The articles and pamphlets he sent to Strahan before his return in 1764 had been in support of this end.

These pieces revealed a different, more anguished Franklin than Strahan had previously known. From William Franklin, Stra-han heard that Pennsylvania was "in a state of Anarchy,"[10] and when Franklin did reappear in London at Christmas 1764 he seemed drained and wounded. Strahan soon heard the story for himself. Franklin had spent much of the year being ruthlessly attacked by his political opponents. The governor of the colony, John Penn, had written that "there will never be any prospect of ease and happiness, while that villain has the liberty of spreading about the poison of that inveterate malice and ill nature which is deeply implanted in his own black heart."[11]

Penn's assessment, full of loathing though it was, seemed mild beside some of the other venomous broadsides he had to withstand. Franklin was described as a man of turbulent soul; a plotter; a man delirious with rage, disappointment, and malice. Catharine Macau-lay had characterized Francis Bacon as a gifted philosopher with a dangerous thirst for power; it was in similar terms that one of his staunchest critics, an eloquent young Philadelphian lawyer called

Writing the Declaration of Independence, 1776, by Jean Leon Gerome Ferris. An idealized twentieth-century depiction of the fascinating moment in June 1776 when Thomas Jefferson (right) presented his draft to the sitting Benjamin Franklin and John Adams. (Library of Congress)

ABOVE: *Arch Street Ferry, Philadelphia*, by William Birch. Life in eighteenth-century Philadelphia was always at its most exuberant along the banks of the Delaware River. It was not far from here that Benjamin Franklin famously stepped ashore for the first time in 1723. (Library Company of Philadelphia)

LEFT: *Thomas Jefferson*, by Mather Brown, 1786. This is the earliest known likeness of Jefferson, and it catches something of the youthfulness that struck his fellow delegates in 1776. (National Portrait Gallery, Smithsonian Institution)

John Adams, by John Trumbull, 1793. Brilliant and restless, John Adams was the star of the Second Continental Congress.
(National Portrait Gallery, Smithsonian Institution)

Benjamin Franklin, by Robert Feke, circa 1746. This stiff and formal portrait of Franklin was made at a crucial juncture in his life, when he was trying to escape his identity as a "leather apron man" and forge a new one as a gentleman.
(Harvard University Portrait Collection, Bequest of Dr. John Collins Warren, 1856)

A Man Called William Strahan, unknown artist, circa 1765. Starting from nothing, William Strahan built the greatest printing business in London. He worked with many of the leading writers of the age, but his firmest friendship was with Benjamin Franklin. (Yale Center for British Art)

Northumberland House, London, attributed to William James, circa 1759. This view looks across Charing Cross in central London. Straight ahead lies the Strand, which leads eventually to Fleet Street. (Yale Center for British Art)

Samuel Johnson, by James Watson, after Joshua Reynolds, 1770. This print is based on a candid painting by Reynolds. It shows Johnson's poor eyesight and awkward mannerisms. There is also a strong sense of his intellectual force and capacity. (Yale Center for British Art)

The Idle 'Prentice Executed at Tyburn, by William Hogarth, 1747. Hogarth's moral stories enjoyed great popularity in the mid-eighteenth century. In this depiction of the execution of "Tom Idle," he shows the deadly consequences of immoral behavior. (Metropolitan Museum of Art)

The Industrious 'Prentice Lord Mayor of London, by William Hogarth. While Idle dies at Tyburn, his fellow apprentice, the dutiful "Francis Goodchild," becomes Lord Mayor of London. Goodness, Hogarth suggests, is the way to happiness. (Metropolitan Museum of Art)

The Glorious Defeat of the French Fleet under the Command of Marshal Conflans, print made by Peter P. Benazech, circa 1759. Victories like that of Admiral Edward Hawke at Quiberon Bay in 1759 carried Britain toward triumph in the Seven Years' War. (Yale Center for British Art)

Portrait of William Pitt the Elder, by William Hoare, 1754. While military leaders like Hawke or General James Wolfe carried out daring assaults across the world, in Westminster Pitt was regarded as the man of iron who made it all possible. (Metropolitan Museum of Art)

Portrait of a Man, probably Francis Barber, Manner of Sir Joshua Reynolds. This intriguing portrait is a student copy of an original by Sir Joshua Reynolds. Opinions differ on whether it truly shows Francis Barber, the ex-slave who came to live with Samuel Johnson in 1752. (Tate)

George the Third King, print by William Woollett, circa 1763. As Britain emerged victorious from the war with France, the country was reinvigorated from within by the accession of King George III. He was considered to have a graceful and obliging character and to be devoted to duty. "The Glory of Britain was never higher than at present, and I think you never had a better Prince," wrote Franklin from America. (Yale Center for British Art)

Benjamin Franklin, by David Martin, 1767. This portrait captures Franklin in a classic pose, deep in thought at his writing desk. During the 1760s and into the 1770s, he spent considerable time in such a situation, composing letters to America and working on his rich journalistic and scientific pieces. (© 2023 White House Historical Association)

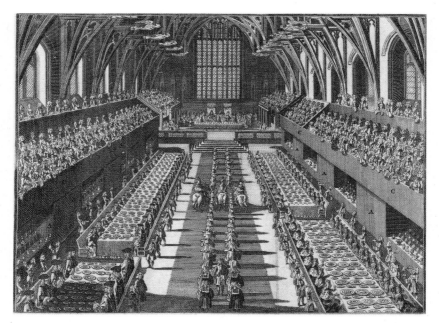

A Perspective View of the Inside of Westminster Hall, unknown artist, 1761. For some the coronation of George III was an anxious affair. One mishap led, in time, to a duel between the Lord High Steward and the member of Parliament for Aylesbury, John Wilkes. (Yale Center for British Art)

The Times, by William Hogarth, 1762. After the accession of George III, British politics descended into factionalism. This dramatic illustration by Hogarth framed the divisions. John Wilkes can be seen upstairs in the Temple Coffee House pointing his hose at the king, who is fighting the fire. (Metropolitan Museum of Art)

John Wilkes, Esq., by William Hogarth, 1763. After his arrest and incarceration in the Tower of London in the spring of 1763, Wilkes achieved fame in both Britain and the American colonies. Many regarded him as a champion of liberty, while others considered him a dangerous subversive. In this vicious print, Hogarth depicted Wilkes as a gentleman with the face and soul of a devil. (Metropolitan Museum of Art)

John Wilkes ("English Liberty established or a Mirror for Posterity"), printed for John Lee, 1768. Despite the efforts of the establishment to silence Wilkes, he mounted an extraordinary political comeback in the spring of 1768. In the colonies, "Wilkes and Liberty" became a popular cause célèbre. (© National Portrait Gallery, London)

The House of Commons, engraving by James Fittler, 1804. Although from a generation later, this engraving depicts the old chamber that witnessed the political convulsions of the 1760s, from the Wilkes Affair to Grenville's Stamp Act. (Yale Center for British Art)

The Repeal, or the Funeral of Miss Ame-Stamp, published by Carington Bowles, 1766. By the mid-1760s the colonists were beginning to suspect that there was a British plot to deprive them of their liberty. Two of the great villains, Grenville and Bute, appear in the center of this histrionic print, which was issued upon the repeal of the Stamp Act in 1766. (Metropolitan Museum of Art)

The Boston Massacre, engraving by Paul Revere, 1770. This depiction of the violence in Boston in March 1770 was circulated widely in the months that followed. One copy of this famous engraving reached one of the patriots' great London friends, the republican historian Catharine Macaulay. (Metropolitan Museum of Art)

A gathering at Joshua Reynolds's house, engraving by W. Walker, 1848. Johnson famously told Boswell that "a tavern chair was the throne of human felicity." In this print Johnson is the center of attention at one of his treasured club nights. (Wellcome Collection)

A View of Matavai Bay in the Island of Otaheite, 1776, by William Hodges. This view of Tahiti, with its dreamy light and enchanting landscape, was primed for a Western audience who had grown deeply interested in the question of human happiness. (Yale Center for British Art)

ABOVE LEFT: *Porcelain figure of Catharine Macaulay*, Chelsea Factory, circa 1775. This graceful figure depicts Macaulay as the successor of Sydney, Hampden, Milton, and Locke. The stand bears the inscription "Government a Power Delegated For the Happiness of Mankind Conducted by Wisdom Justice And Mercy." (Metropolitan Museum of Art)

ABOVE RIGHT: *Samuel Johnson*, by Joseph Nollekens, 1777. Macaulay's 1775 pamphlet in support of the colonists prompted Johnson to issue his even more strident critique, *Taxation No Tyranny*, just a few months later. (Yale Center for British Art)

An Exact View of the Late Battle at Charlestown, June 17th, 1775, by Bernard Romans, circa 1775. This rare and panoramic early American print depicts one of the first confrontations of the revolution. (Metropolitan Museum of Art)

Benjamin Franklin, by Joseph Siffred Duplessis. In 1775 Franklin returned to Philadelphia and formally joined as a delegate to the Continental Congress. To Strahan he wrote, "You and I were long Friends: You are now my Enemy, and I am, Yours, B. Franklin." (National Portrait Gallery, Smithsonian Institution)

Thomas Paine, mezzotint by James Watson, 1783. This print of Paine, made at the end of the war, shows him secure and at ease. This was not the case when he first arrived in Philadelphia in 1775. "When my country, into which I had just set my foot, was set on fire about my ears, it was time to stir. It was time for every man to stir," he wrote. (National Portrait Gallery, Smithsonian Institution)

The Declaration of Independence, Philadelphia, July 4, 1776, mezzotint by H. S. Sadd after J. Trumbull. Within half a century, many events from the revolutionary era had passed into formal history. Here, John Trumbull depicts the moment the Committee of Five presented the Declaration to Congress in the summer of 1776. (Wellcome Collection)

John Dickinson, had derided Franklin. He was, Dickinson conceded, "a great luminary of the learned world." But, he went on, "Let him still shine, but without wrapping his country in flames. Let him, from a private station, from a smaller sphere, diffuse, as I think he may, a beneficial light; but let him not be made to move and blaze like a comet to terrify and to distress."[12]

In Philadelphia, where news of Wilkes's campaign against Bute and Grenville had been so thoroughly reported, it seemed as if the virulence of Westminster politics had crossed the Atlantic and taken root in Market Street. Just as Bute was assailed as being a creature of tyranny, so was Franklin. Just as Bute's private life had been fair game for his critics, so was Franklin's. One pamphlet, entitled *What is Sauce for a Goose is also Sauce for a Gander*, accused Franklin in turn of mistreating his patrons, of assuming others' merits in philosophy, of begging titles, of thirsting after greatness, and of raising William, his bastard son out of a "hand maid" called Barbara.[13] Aiming to silence the anonymous attacks, one of Franklin's friends felt compelled to offer a challenge in the newspapers. John Hughes proposed to pay £10 to the Pennsylvania Hospital for every charge against Franklin that was substantiated to the satisfaction of an impartial person. "But this challenge," William Franklin told Strahan in a letter from New Jersey, "they were afraid to accept . . . The malice of the Prop. Party against my Father on account of his wanting to bring about a change of Government is beyond all bounds. They glory in saying and doing things to destroy his character that would make even Devils blush."[14]

The campaign against Franklin was successful inasmuch as he lost his seat in the assembly elections of October 1764. His Old Ticket party, however, had retained overall control. In the fiery political climate, the assembly had pushed through a formal petition against the Penn family, and they had again selected Franklin as the colony's agent and gave him the task of returning to London to formally present it to the king. It was on these terms that Franklin had left Philadelphia and Deborah yet again in November 1764. His return passage across the Atlantic was fast and tempestuous, and within little more than a month he was once more sitting in Mrs. Stevenson's parlor in Craven Street. Over the months that followed, Franklin's friends watched his spirits rising. For Strahan the surest sign that Franklin's mood was improving was the merry satirical piece about the Duke of York's travels in the *Advertiser*.

It soon became apparent, though, that Franklin's "Spectator" letter was more than a chance for a little fun. A week after its appearance, a second anonymous letter followed in the same newspaper. On the face of it, this piece, titled "'A Traveller': News-Writers' Nonsense," was a riposte to the first. It opened with a defense of journalists. By reporting rumor, it held, journalists were merely providing the reading public with the material they desired. The speculative reports were beneficial in many other ways too. They fueled conversation and provided opportunities for readers to discuss the wider context. They might use an article as a catalyst to learn geography or to test their political knowledge. These were things that filled otherwise tedious hours. In fact, the writer elaborated, instead of being credulous, if anything the reading public had become too skeptical. "Formerly every Thing printed was believed," the writer pointed out, "because it was in Print. Now Things seem to be disbelieved for just the very same Reason."[15]

No one who knew Franklin as well as Strahan did could read this letter without suspecting that there was a deeper game at play here. This second piece was as plainly Franklin's as the first. But what was he up to? After starting in such sober, reasoned terms, the letter detailed a variety of facts about North America that were both surprising but, the author affirmed, "certainly true." The tails of American sheep, for example, were so laden with wool that each one had to be placed on a four-wheeled cart to "keep it from trailing on the Ground." Those fools who did not believe this were the same kind of people who did not believe that New York was a center for silk spinning, or that thousands of cannon were cast in the ironworks of

Quebec each year, or that a cod and whale fishery was soon to be launched in the Great Lakes.

> Ignorant People may object that the Upper Lakes are fresh, and that Cod and Whale are Salt-water Fish: But let them know, Sir, that Cod, like other Fish, when attacked by their Enemies, fly into any Water where they think they can be safest; that Whales when they have a Mind to eat Cod, pursue them wherever they fly; and that the grand Leap of the Whale in that Chace up the Fall of Niagara is esteemed by all who have seen it, as one of the finest Spectacles in Nature![16]

Disbelieving such reports, the letter concluded, was the newest disease to infect the British mind. Therefore it was important to make a stand against the misplaced skepticism of "Mr Spectator" and to stand up for news writers who, for sixpence an article, provided intelligence that was not only useful to "Coffee-house Students in History and Politics" but also to the "infinite Advantage of all future Livies, Rapins, Robertsons, Humes, Smollets, and Macaulays, who may be sincerely inclin'd to furnish the World with that *rara Avis*, a true History."[17]

Reaching the end of this nimble piece of Swiftian satire, Strahan would have understood Franklin's point. At a time of aggressive imperial expansion, many minds remained clouded by ignorance. Britain might now be overseeing an empire in the East and West, but the average person knew almost nothing in detail of the world that they were attempting to govern. When it came to America, for instance, Britons had a general sense of the country's vast expanse, but there was a vagueness when it came to anything beyond that, let alone the fine details. What was the landscape like? What about the culture? Years of publicity pamphlets, encouraging migrants to colonial settlements like Philadelphia, had also seeded some strange ideas. Americans might still be frequently stereotyped as bumptious provincials, but there were also exaggerated views of the continent's prosperity. One letter, written by a Briton to a friend in New York, had been reprinted in the London papers the previous year:

> The Report of your Gaiety and Luxury has reached your Mother Country; and they infer from thence your Opulency, which is further confirmed by the extravagant Expences of your Youth sent here for Education, and therefore you are well able to bear Part of the Expences your Defence has cost the Nation; and can you blame them for such a Conclusion? Is it not natural to infer it from the Premises?[18]

This neatly captured a mood that had become widespread since the Peace of Paris. America's defense had cost enormous sums during the last war, and it was one of the key factors behind the worrying rise in the national debt, which had more than doubled from £55 million before the war to £132.6 million by its end. Given all this, wasn't it fair that the colonists help to replenish the treasury now the war was over? One person who thought so was the prime minister, George Grenville. After Dashwood's resignation as chancellor in April 1763, Grenville had combined the two great offices. With peace secured, Grenville's chief objective had been to rescue Britain from its parlous financial state. The first of his efforts to prize money from the colonies came in the spring of 1764 with the introduction of a sugar tax. By the start of the following year, he was planning his next move.

As someone who was emotionally and financially involved in the colonies, Strahan watched closely as Parliament's attitude toward America became more assertive. One of the first acts to trouble the colonists was a proclamation in the autumn of 1763 that the whole North American continent west of the Appalachian Mountains was to be reserved as land belonging to the Indigenous peoples. This ruling seemingly confined the colonists to their narrow strip along the Atlantic coast, and in America the news was received with frustration. With the sugar tax following so soon after, Strahan saw that Grenville's ministry was willing to test the colonists' patience. This made him nervous. Strahan liked King George. He considered him "one of the best Men breathing,"[19] but he was not convinced by the ministers who served him. Writing to Hall, he summarized affairs. Lord Bute, he explained, "the man he loves best, and has most confidence in, is unhappily altogether unfit to take the Lead in this Country." Grenville, his replacement, was little better. Strahan thought him obstinate and overbearing and derided him as a "financier" who was too quick to hurtle into complicated economic schemes.[20]

Two decades of friendship with Franklin had taught Strahan much about the American state of mind. He knew the people prized their connection to Britain, but he also understood that the colonial system had been allowed to develop in a way that muddled independence and subservience. When it came to matters of war and foreign policy, the colonies were keen to stand alongside Britain. Indeed they had played an active role in the fight against France. In domestic matters, however, they liked to tend their own gardens. Taxes were a case in point. Although Strahan believed, as just about everyone did, in the principle of Parliamentary sovereignty that had been established in the seventeenth century,* he knew the custom had been for the colonists to raise their own taxes through their own legislatures. Grenville was not troubled by this. In his mind it was very clear. If Americans wanted British troops to protect them during a war, then they could expect British taxes to follow in times of peace.

---

* Sovereignty can most simply be explained as being "the right to have the last word." William Blackstone's *Commentaries on the Law* (1765) stated the classic Whig conception of Parliamentary sovereignty. "There is and must be in all [forms of government] a supreme, irresistible, absolute, uncontrolled authority, in which the *jura summi imperii*, or the rights of sovereignty, reside . . . [In England the] 'sovereignty of the British constitution' was lodged in Parliament, the aggregate body of King, Lords, and Commons, whose actions no power on earth can undo."

It was with these thoughts in mind that Strahan read about Grenville's new policy for a stamp tax in America. This was a pet policy of Grenville's, and the prime minister was said to be "besotted" with the idea. In the opening months of 1765, despite lobbying from Franklin, the act passed through Parliament without opposition. This was surprising because the terms of the act were quite something. From November 1, a royal stamp would have to be borne on a vast range of printed materials—legal documents, administrative papers, diplomas, bonds, articles of apprenticeship, dice, cards, newspapers, almanacs, and pamphlets. To Grenville this was a broad but fair levy on a people who had been generally spared over the years. It was hoped the tax would raise around £50,000 a year, which would cover around a quarter of the expense of stationing British troops on the continent.

But for Strahan there were points of concern. Apart from the ideological difficulties of such a thing, the practical challenges were huge. He knew, from years of experience, how stressful it was to run a transatlantic business. He had only succeeded because Franklin, and then Hall, had been trustworthy partners, but even then it had been a continuous battle. Now the government was proposing to establish an infinitely more complicated system on a much greater scale. How was this ever going to work? Who were going to be the stamp officers? How was the paper to be stamped? Who would prosecute those who did not comply? To Hall he later reflected,

> You must know I am one of those who have from the Beginning looked upon this Affair as of the most serious Nature. I am truly sorry that such a Law was ever thought of, because it has given Birth to much Dissention between the Colonists and the Mother Country, and hath raised a Ferment which I am afraid will never entirely be laid.[21]

In the spring, as Franklin's pseudonymous pieces were running in the London press, the ships carrying American stamps were moored in the Thames. As for what was happening in the colonies, Strahan could only imagine.

DURING HIS YEARS IN Market Street, David Hall had seen vast changes. In the 1740s the town still had a frontier rawness, with its dusty streets and buccaneering characters. There were only a handful left now who could recall the early days of the colony. By 1765 Philadelphia was established as the largest settlement in British America. In recent years the bustling thoroughfares by the harbor had been paved, the wooden stalls of the Jersey Market had been cleared and replaced by permanent brick structures. A hospital had been founded, and transport links had been improved. There was now a choice of ferries for those wanting to cross the Delaware to New Jersey, and timetabled services existed for the three-day coach journey to New York.

Hall had reported on many of these developments in the *Gazette* over the preceding years. In that time his clientele had become increasingly affluent too. It was now common to see merchants wearing silver buttons on their coats. Others marked their status with a variety of wigs—dress, scratch, or cut—while the better-off ladies had taken to wearing hooped dresses, some of which were so extravagant that they were obliged to pass through shops' doors sideways, like a crab. Hall had done his best to cater for such people. As well as the *Gazette*, books, and printing supplies, visitors to his store could buy watches, penknives, spectacles, or choose from a lively collection of prints, among which featured portraits of King George and his new wife, Queen Charlotte, the dukes of York and Cumberland, and William Pitt. In a city that was increasingly culturally aware, these were desirable objects. Glancing out of his window, Hall no longer just saw barrows and carts jostling for space on Market Street. Now there were sedan chairs, chariots, and at least three coaches. Down at the harbor, merchants, gentlemen, and sea captains met at the London Coffee House, the social and mercantile hub of the bustling city, where they sipped their drinks and conducted business around the hissing urn.

Hall's own days remained rooted in the New Printing Office by Pewter Platter Alley. This might have been hard and repetitive work, but the terms he had negotiated with Franklin brought him the kind of security many other colonials could never acquire. On the foundation of a steady job, Hall had been able to construct a settled family life. Along with his wife Molly, there was now a new generation of children with familiar names: David Hall, Jr., William Strahan Hall, Deborah Franklin Hall. For all these there was money enough for little luxuries like summer excursions to Reading, where hot days could be spent paddling in the local rivers or fishing for trout.

In Philadelphia, meanwhile, there was a close-knit group of friends. One was Deborah Franklin, who had recently moved into a new house farther up Market Street. This property was a testament to her husband's successes, and it was intended for their retirement. Since Franklin had left for London, Hall had been keeping an eye on Deborah. "I am oblig'd to you for calling so often at our House," Franklin wrote to Hall from London, "and doubt not a Continuance of your Friendly Offices towards my little Family, which need them more than ever, as we have now more Enemies."[22]

Over the years Hall's relationship with Franklin had been good. The two managed to balance cordiality and respect. In letters they remained stiffly professional as "Mr. Franklin," and "Mr. Hall," but enough trust existed between the two for Franklin to leave Hall in editorial control of the *Gazette* and allow him to get on with the printing work as he wished. For his part, Hall accepted his status as Franklin's junior, and was content to tolerate the odd intervention. But an important date was approaching. According to the terms signed in 1748, at the beginning of January 1766, their partnership agreement was due to expire. Hall would then have the right to purchase all of the printing machines and materials. It was a moment

Hall had looked forward to for years. After the longest of all apprenticeships, at the age of fifty, at last he was going to be his own man.

In the summer of 1765, this excitement was marred by events.
First of all the buoyant wartime economy, encouraged by Westminster's willingness to pump resources into the colonies, had faded. As
trade slackened, there came a series of bankruptcies, of people who
were in "no way Suspected." This was ominous, but worse was anticipated. Ever since the Peace of Paris, news from Westminster was
greeted anxiously. The politicians who had come into office since
the king's accession seemed, from all reports, more intrusive and
assertive than their predecessors. The Cider Tax and the Wilkes affair were both evidence of this. And there was something particular
in the arrest, imprisonment, and persecution of Wilkes that created
disquiet. The colonists were left to wonder whether Bute, Grenville,
and the king really were the faithful guardians of the British constitution and liberties they professed to be. And now it seemed the
government had a new target. The same Parliamentary session that
had dealt with Wilkes had passed the Sugar Act, and more legislation
designed to curb America's freedom was rumored. There was talk of
a so-called Quartering Act that would oblige the colonies to provide
accommodation and sustenance to redcoat soldiers.

Worse were the whispers about a stamp tax. By the late spring
the climate of nervous expectation had developed into something
more belligerent as news arrived confirming that Grenville's Stamp
Act had passed into law. From November onward, the colonies were
going to be subject to Grenville's elaborate, extensive, and inescapable
scheme. The stamps in themselves were innocuous-looking things.
Each was like a miniature coat of arms, with a crossed sword and
scepter covering a royal crown, above which, in confident capitals,
was emblazoned the single word AMERICA. The amount of tax levied
would depend on the document, but every single stamp symbolized
one and the same thing: that a sum of money had been extracted from
an American pocket and transferred to the British treasury.

Hall had more reason than most to be gloomy. Franklin had confided in a letter that the tax would "affect the Printers more than anybody."[23] The *Gazette*, he warned, would have to be printed on paper bearing the penny stamp. For longer pamphlets, a shilling stamp was required. Another of Hall's revenue streams was affected too, as a separate two-shilling duty would be payable on every advertisement that ran in the *Gazette*. As the tax was so entirely new, people were still struggling to digest its details. Would it be levied only on an ad's first printing? Or would the rate have to be paid every time an ad appeared? Then there was the issue of the stamps themselves. As there had not been time to establish stamp offices in the colonies, Grenville had decided to send pre-stamped paper from London. But what did this mean for the local paper mills? Were they to be sacrificed to Grenville's policy too? And what about the quality of the paper the government was going to send? What condition would it be in after a transatlantic voyage? In an exasperated letter on June 20, Hall confirmed to Franklin, "It certainly will hurt the Printers and Paper-makers in an extraordinary Manner."[24]

Having waited so long to become his own man, Hall was now faced with the prospect of his dreams being dashed due to one hamfisted piece of policy. In fact, it was worse than that. For as well as suffering the effects of the tax, he was simultaneously at risk of being seen as an agent of the Crown. Due to Franklin's political connections, Hall had inherited what in ordinary times was the plum job of printing all the royal proclamations in Pennsylvania. But now this task was not so congenial. That summer he had the unenviable responsibility of both producing and selling the official text of the act. As such the New Printing Office became a natural focus for discontent. This seemed unfair. Unlike Franklin, Hall had never wanted to be involved in politics. During his time editing the *Gazette*, he had carefully kept himself out of the kind of scrapes Franklin often experienced, and throughout that summer he maintained this policy, refusing to print any pamphlet that attacked the British government.

In his letters Franklin approved of Hall's desire to stay above the fray. But to others this stance looked different. Where did Hall's loyalties truly lie?

For a man unused to public scrutiny this was an uncomfortable situation. Hall decided that it was best to keep his head down and think practically. To beat the November deadline, Hall had *Poor Richard's Almanack* for 1766 printed five months early. Otherwise he remained anxious. Throughout the summer he wrote frequently to Franklin, telling him subscribers were "leaving off" the *Gazette* fast. They were being driven by principle as much as by financial concerns, with many of them warning Hall they would not pay anything "towards that Tax they could possibly avoid."[25] Soon, Hall told Franklin, he expected only a small rump of readers left.

In these letters Hall's usual deferential air toward Franklin wavered. Undercutting everything was a feeling of frustration. Wasn't it convenient that Franklin's interest in the printing house was ending as the industry was about to collapse? Aggravating this was Franklin's silence. No letters arrived from London during the early part of the summer, and as time passed, Hall's faith started to falter. "I should have been glad if you could have done anything to prevent the Stamp Act," he wrote to Franklin, "as nothing could have contributed so much to have *removed the Prejudices* of many of the People against you."[26]

From Hall, such a statement was telling. Ever since the fiery exchanges of 1764, Philadelphia had remained a place divided. One of the central points of discussion was Franklin's character. Whose interests was he representing in his capacity as an agent in London? The colony's or his own? Who stood to benefit if Pennsylvania did become a Crown colony? Was Franklin setting himself up to become a royal governor like his son? Sensing an opportunity, Franklin's enemies in the Proprietary Party decided that it was in their interests to oppose the Stamp Act in public. They described it as a foretaste of things to come if the colony were to be taken over by the king.

The Assembly Party, led by Franklin's ally Joseph Galloway, had no eloquent response to this. Franklin's reputation was damaged further when the enraging news arrived that he had managed to secure the appointment of John Hughes—his friend and former landlord who had recently defended him in the newspapers—as the colony's stamp officer. This development gave credence to the idea that Franklin was colluding with Grenville. Some of Franklin's enemies went further, suggesting that he had actually had a hand in framing the act.

Even Hall was left to wonder. In August a letter from Franklin finally reached Market Street. Rather than being reassuring, however, it had a moody, belligerent undercurrent. Franklin told Hall that all of his lobbying had failed and that his hopes for repeal were delayed until the next Parliamentary session. His advice was prudence. While he expected the subscriptions to drop a little, "perhaps a tenth Part," the shortfall could be recovered by demanding ready money instead of credit, and by raising the *Gazette*'s price proportionally.[27] Such homespun wisdom was familiar enough to Hall, who had spent enough time with Franklin to know his methods, but they were utterly inadequate for the crisis at hand.

By August reports of spontaneous protests against the Stamp Act were arriving in Philadelphia from across the colonies. "We are all in a Ferment here," Hall wrote to Franklin on September 6. Reports had come from Boston, where Lord Bute and Andrew Oliver, the Massachusetts stamp officer, had been hung in effigy, and the building intended for the stamp office pulled down. Oliver had reportedly resigned his post out of fear, as did the stamp officer in Rhode Island soon after. When their counterpart in New Haven, Connecticut, refused to step down, a mob threatened to demolish his house if he failed to surrender the stamp materials as soon as they arrived. More news was coming out of Virginia and New York, and, Hall explained:

> In short, there seems to be a general Discontent all over the Continent, with that Law, and many thinking their Liberties

and Privileges, as English Men lost, or at least in great Danger, seem Desperate. What the Consequence may be, God only knows; but, from the Temper of the People, at Present, there is the greatest Reason to fear, that the Passing of that Law will be the Occasion of a great Deal of Mischief.[28]

By now Hall's exasperation at Franklin was overtaken by something more like panic:

For as the Time of the Law taking place draws nearer, the more the Clamours of the People increase against me, for my Silence in the Paper; alledging, that as our Gazette, spreads more generally than all the other Papers put together on the Continent, our not Publishing, as the Printers of the other Papers do, will be an infinite Hurt to the Liberties of the People. And I have been told by many, that our Interests will certainly suffer by it; nay, Hints have been given, that in Case of the Peoples being exasperated I must stand to the Consequences. So that how to Behave, I am really at a loss, but believe it will be best to humour them in some Publications, as they seem to insist so much upon it.[29]

Hall was left half-wishing that Franklin was at his side, for counsel and reassurance; and half-relieved that he was away from danger. "The Spirit of the People is so violent against every One, they think has the least concern with the Stamp Law, and they have imbibed the Notion, that you had a Hand, in the framing of it, which has occassioned you many Enemies."[30]

By now it was clear that a small spark was all that was needed to ignite Philadelphia's mob. This spark came sailing up the Delaware on September 16. The vessel was commanded by the same Captain Friend who had carried Franklin home in 1762. Everyone expected the stamped paper to be on board, but instead they got something else. Friend's packet brought the surprising news that Grenville's government had fallen. Jubilation ran through the streets. That evening, from his window in Market Street, Hall would have looked over a scene that was unlike anything he had witnessed before. Bonfires were burning. A restless crowd was gathering outside the London Coffee House. They were bent on a reckoning with the stamp officer, John Hughes. Shortly after nightfall the mob started to heave and jostle as it began to move westward from the river. The people jeered and shouted as they headed up Market Street, in the direction of Benjamin and Deborah Franklin's handsome new house.

IN CRAVEN STREET, FRANKLIN was shaken out of his complacency by a trio of anguished letters from Philadelphia in early November. One from Hall spoke of the "Consequences" he was likely to suffer for not opposing the Stamp Act in print. More fraught were the dispatches from Hughes. Rather than a coherent letter, Hughes had written a series of snapshots, capturing the terror of his situation on successive days in September:

> Sept. 8: You are now from Letter to Letter to suppose each may be the last that you will receive from your old Friend, as the Spirit or Flame of Rebellion is got to a high Pitch amongst the North Americans; and it seems to me that a Sort of Frenzy or Madness has got such hold of the People of all Ranks, that I fancy some Lives will be lost before this Fire is put out . . .
>
> Sept 10: Our Assembly met yesterday, and this day a Majority of 15 against 14, were for sending a Committee to New-York, to meet the Committee of Boston on the 1st. of October, where they insinuate there will be Men sent from every Colony, in order to unite, and become, as they express it, *like a Bundle of Rods*, alluding to the Fable of the Old Man and his Sons . . .
>
> Sept 12: Our Clamours run very high, and I am told my House shall be pull'd down and the Stamps burnt. To which I

give no other Answer than that I will defend my House at the
Risque of my Life . . .

Sept 16: in the Evening. Common Report threat[ens] my
House this Night, as there are Bonfires and Rejoicings for the
Change of Ministry. The sober and sensible Part of the People
are doing every thing towards being in Readiness to suppress a
Mob if there should be any Intention of Rising. I for my Part am
well-arm'd with Fire-Arms, and am determin'd to stand a
Siege. If I live till tomorrow morning I shall give you a farther
Account; but as it is now about 8 aClock, I am on my Guard,
and only write this between whiles, as every Noise or Bustle of
the People calls me off.[31]

While Hughes's dispatches made for horrifying, if compulsive,
reading, even they could not compete for emotional intensity with
the letter Franklin received from Debby. Like Hughes she had spent
the terrifying evening of September 16 barricaded inside her home.
Joined by a cousin and one of her brothers, and anticipating a siege,
they had sent for a number of guns. Soon one of the rooms had been
transformed into a "magazine." In the plain and phonetic style Franklin knew so well, Debby went on:

I ordored sum sorte of defens up Stairs such as I Cold manaig
my self, I sed when I was advised to remove that I was verey
shuer you had dun nothing to hurte aney bodey nor I had not
given aney ofense to aney person att all nor wold I be maid uneasy by aney bodey nor wold I stir or show the leste uneseynis
but if aney one Came to disturbe me I wold show a proper re-
sentement and I shold be very much afrunted with aney bodey.[32]

The moment these letters reached Franklin in London was one of
the most significant of his life. For years Franklin had prided himself
on his political instinct: on an ability to see the bigger picture and

to chart the safest course. It was clear in November 1765 that these skills had failed him. While he remained an ocean away in his comfortable London lodgings, his family, business partner, and political allies had all been left utterly exposed thanks to his myopia. They were all safe, as it turned out, but this was thanks to luck as much as anything. Had a small circumstance been different, had someone recklessly fired a gun, or a window been shattered, then things might have been very different indeed.

Recognizing all this, Franklin sat down to write a consoling letter to his wife. "I honour much the Spirit and Courage you show'd, and the prudent Preparations you made in that Time of Danger."[33] This was followed by a note to Hall. "Assure yourself," he wrote, "nothing can be falser than the Reports you mention that I had even the least hand in framing the Stamp Act, or procuring any other Burthen on our Country."[34] Realizing how badly his reputation had been damaged, and how suspicions about his conduct had been left to fester, Franklin knew he needed to clarify his position in public. To do this, he turned to Strahan, who was ideally placed to help.

A week after writing his letters to Deborah and Hall, something significant appeared in the *London Chronicle*. Preceded by a note from a figure signing himself "W. S."—certainly William Strahan—came a series of letters that contained "the sentiments of two Gentlemen of acknowledged abilities and integrity upon a subject which is of the last consequence to the peace, safety, union, dignity, and stability of the British Empire."[35] Significantly the letters dated from earlier in the summer. The first of them, written by Franklin to a contact in Philadelphia, demonstrated his disapproval of Grenville's tax and his efforts to combat it. The letter was filled with rich poetic imagery, and it remains to this day one of Franklin's most lucid and memorable:

DEPEND upon it, my good Friend, every possible step was taken to prevent the passing of the Stamp Act. But the tide was too strong against us. The nation was provok'd by American claims of independence, and all parties join'd in resolving by this act to settle the point. We might as well have hindered the sun's setting. But since it is down, my Friend, and it may be long ere it rises again, let us make as good a night of it as we can. We may still light candles.[36]

Eloquent as it was, this was in fact a setup for a second, equally appealing letter that laid out for British readers the American point of view. This was written by Franklin's Philadelphian friend Charles Thomson. Responding to Franklin's point about independence, Thomson stressed,

There never was any mention of the colonies aiming at independence, till the ministry began to abridge them of their liberties. I will venture to affirm, and to you I can appeal for the truth of what I say, that history cannot shew a people so numerous, so far removed from the seat of Royalty, who were so loyal, so attached to their King, and who at the same time had such true sentiments of liberty, as the British American Colonies. How long this will continue God knows.[37]

Those in the colonies, he went on:

cannot bring themselves to believe, nor can they see how England with reason or justice could expect, that they should have encountered the horrors of a desert, borne the attacks of barbarous savages, and, at the expense of their blood and treasure, settled this country to the great emolument of England, and after all quietly submit to be deprived of every thing an Englishman has been taught to hold dear. It is not property only we contend for. Our Liberty and most essential privileges are struck at: Arbitrary courts are set over us, and trials by juries taken away: The Press is so restricted that we cannot complain: An army of mercenaries threatened to be billeted on us: The sources of our trade stopped; and, to compleat our ruin, the little property we had acquired, taken from us, without even allowing us the merit of giving it; I really dread the consequence.[38]

The *Chronicle* letters with their introduction by Strahan ran in the paper of November 16. For months the British public had read reports of angry mobs and burning houses. Here was a different type of voice from America: impassioned, reasoned, and persuasive.

The letters also marked an important moment for Franklin. They showed him bringing his old skills as a writer and editor to a new political problem. He had done this before, on occasion. But until this point Franklin had never waged a sustained paper campaign in Great Britain on behalf of one of his political causes. That December, and into January of 1766, using Strahan's influence at the *London Chronicle* and other contacts at the *Gazetteer and New Daily Advertiser*, he combatted the anti-American invective in the British press with a series of clever pieces of his own. None of these were printed under Franklin's name. Instead, using instincts acquired long ago, he deployed one pseudonym after another: "F. B.," "N. N.," "Homespun," "A Friend to Both Countries." With Franklin an active participant in the political conversation, an important old hurdle came tumbling down. As Edmund Burke would once put it, "there is a parenthesis of three thousand miles of ocean between the beginning and the end of every sentence we speak of America."[39] This was no longer the case.

His anonymous newspaper pieces turned out to be only a prelude for an even greater performance. In Westminster the reaction to the news from America had been varied. Strahan was in the Commons in January when Grenville stood to give "a long, confused, violent, inflammatory Speech, highly censuring the Behaviour of the Colonies in regard to the Stamp Act, calling it downright Rebellion."[40] But the majority of the MPs, Strahan told Hall, were more measured.

They wanted to hear the arguments, rather than condemning the colonists "unheard." To better understand the reaction, the House of Commons devoted several sessions in mid-February 1766 to an examination of experts. On February 13 it was Franklin's turn to give evidence. It was an unusual situation. For once Franklin was not insinuating in the newspapers. He could not hide behind a pseudonym. Standing in the same chamber that had not long before seen the debates about the peace and the quarrels over Wilkes, he had no choice but to speak *in propria persona*. "What is your name, and place of abode?" His answer was stark. "Franklin, of Philadelphia."[41]

Franklin had prepared as carefully as ever. During the days before he had sought out friendly members, who he asked to supply him with useful questions. The first of these was a man called James Hewitt, the MP for Coventry. Hewitt opened the inquiry:

HEWITT: Do the Americans pay any considerable taxes
            among themselves?
FRANKLIN: Certainly many, and very heavy taxes.
HEWITT: What are the present taxes in Pennsylvania, laid
            by the laws of the colony?
FRANKLIN: There are taxes on all estates real and personal,
            a poll tax, a tax on all offices, professions, trades
            and businesses, according to their profits; an
            excise on all wine, rum, and other spirits; and
            a duty of Ten Pounds per head on all Negroes
            imported, with some other duties.
HEWITT: For what purposes are those taxes laid?
FRANKLIN: For the support of the civil and military
            establishments of the country, and to discharge
            the heavy debt contracted in the last war.[42]

Fourteen friendly questions were put to him before one of Grenville's supporters took their turn. "Are not the Colonies, from their circumstances, very able to pay the stamp duty?" "In my opinion," Franklin replied, "there is not gold and silver enough in the Colonies to pay the stamp duty for one year." To evade the central question of whether the colonists were denying Parliament's right to tax them, Franklin relied on the distinction between "internal" and "external" taxes. This was a new theory, which divided domestic "internal issues" from broader "external" ones. In this conception Parliament was within its right to lay duties on imported commodities, as people could choose whether to buy these or not. But by its nature an "internal tax" that was forced upon the people without their consent was an arbitrary move that deprived the people of their rights, so therefore might be opposed.

Before long Grenville was on his feet himself:

GRENVILLE: Do you think it right that America should be protected by this country, and pay no part of the expence?

FRANKLIN: That is not the case. The Colonies raised, cloathed and paid, during the last war, near 25,000 men, and spent many millions.

GRENVILLE: Were you not reimbursed by parliament?

FRANKLIN: We were only reimbursed what, in your opinion, we had advanced beyond our proportion, or beyond what might reasonably be expected from us; and it was a very small part of what we spent. Pennsylvania, in particular, disbursed about 500,000 Pounds, and the reimbursements, in the whole, did not exceed 60,000 Pounds.

GRENVILLE: You have said that you pay heavy taxes in Pennsylvania; what do they amount to in the Pound?

FRANKLIN: The tax on all estates, real and personal, is Eighteen Pence in the Pound, fully rated; and

the tax on the profits of trades and professions,
with other taxes, do, I suppose, make full Half a
Crown in the Pound.[43]

Grenville had sought to corner Franklin with detail, but his strategy was misguided. As a small tradesman, and one moreover who
obsessed over marginal profits, Franklin could answer questions like
these without trouble. Numbering 174 questions, all told, Franklin's
examination went on for three hours. Throughout he was sure-footed,
confident, and steadfast in his advocacy of the colonial cause. By the
time he stood down he must have known it was a triumph. Grenville's
replacement as prime minister, the Marquis of Rockingham, told a
friend several days afterward that "he never knew Truth make so great
a Progress in so very short a Time."[44]

This verdict was echoed by Strahan. Ever since November,
Strahan had watched in admiration as Franklin sought to argue the
American case. "He is forever with one Member of Parliament or
other," he told Hall, "endeavouring to impress them first with the
Importance of the present Dispute; then to state the Case clearly, and
fully stripping it of every thing foreign to the main Point; and lastly,
to answer Objections arising from either a total Ignorance, a partial
Knowledge, or a wrong Conception of the Matter."[45] Strahan put
Parliament's willingness to engage with the subject down to Franklin's burst of energy; the task had employed him, "with very little In-
terruption, Night & Day."[46] Strahan had not been there on February
13 when Franklin was examined, but he heard enough to be able to
tell Hall that he had thrown "more Light upon the Subject than all the
other Informations they had put together . . . You cannot conceive
what Impression his Replies made on the House," he explained,

and with what strength of Argument he display'd the Justice
and Necessity of an immediate and total Repeal, as well as the
Folly and Inexpediency of ever making such a Law, while the

American Assemblies were always ready, when ever called upon, to contribute to the Support of the British Government, to the utmost of their Power, and even beyond their Ability.[47]

All this happened at a testing moment in Strahan's personal life. On November 24, soon after Franklin received the letters from Deborah, Hall, and Hughes, Strahan's eldest daughter, Rachel, had died "after an illness of only three days." Shocked, Strahan wrote to Franklin at once. "Oh! my dear Friend!" the reply came back from Craven Street,

> I never was more surpriz'd than on reading your Note. I grieve for you, for Mrs. Strahan, for Mr. Johnston, for the little ones, and your whole Family. The Loss is indeed a great one! She was every thing that one could wish, in every Relation. I do not offer you the common Topics of Consolation. I know by Experience how little they avail; that the natural Affections must have their Course; and that the best Remedy of Grief is Time. Mrs. Stevenson joins her Tears with mine. God comfort you all.[48]

The fact that Strahan turned to Franklin at this moment of crisis, and that he responded in such terms, emphasizes the nature of the relationship between them. During the months that followed Strahan had the opportunity to repay the kindness. He not only supported his friend in his newspaper campaign, but after his appearance in the Commons he made use of his connections to help Franklin clear his name in America. After pestering the Clerk of the House for a transcript of Franklin's whole examination, by Easter he was writing to Hall, telling him he would send this as soon as he had it. This would be sufficient, Strahan knew, to "for ever silence his Enemies with you."[49] Congratulating Hall on the end of this "grand Affair," Strahan believed it was high time that the ministry took the opportunity of settling America's political status. "I consider British Subjects in America as only living in a different County, having the self-same Interests, and entituled to the self-same Liberties of every kind," he wrote. "Our Interests are, and ought to be, mutual and inseparable. The Strength, Opulence, and Security of us all depend upon our strict and intimate Union."[50] And he elaborated the idea on another occasion in tantalizing terms:

By much the most satisfactory and most honourable for both sides, as well as the most salutary, safe, & beneficial for the whole British Dominion, would be to unite us together by an incorporating Union, in the same manner as Scotland was in 1707, and allow the Colonies to send Representatives to our Parliament. This would completely answer every good purpose to both Sides, and cement us, by insensible Degrees, in so complete a manner, as would forever put it out of the power of any foreign Potentate or internal Cabal, to separate us. By this very Means was Wales long ago, and Scotland more lately, so firmly united to the English Crown, to the amazing Aggrandizement of this Island, which but for this had long ago become a Province to France, or some other Continental Power.[51]

In Philadelphia the mood was jubilant. When the captain of the brig carrying the news of the repeal reached the London Coffee House, a bowl of punch was immediately prepared and a festival spontaneously began. "All was joy and hilarity," recalled one citizen.[52] The streets were illuminated, bonfires were lit, barrels of beer were opened for everyone to enjoy. A feast for three hundred was given the next day in the State House gallery. An even larger celebration followed on June 4, the king's birthday. That day hundreds gathered in a grove on the banks of the Schuylkill. As they ate they gazed out to the water where the barge *Franklin* was festooned with Union Jacks. For Hall, finally his own man, it was sparkling copy for a newspaper he at last owned himself. The best story of all, though, he reserved for a small group of associates. During the summer of 1766, Hall would read sections of Franklin's examination aloud to admiring friends. It was not until September, when Philadelphia was once again preparing for elections, that he finally went to print with the pamphlet that would transform his business partner's reputation in America. *The Examination of Doctor Benjamin Franklin, Before an August Assembly*, showed Franklin standing firm against the British government. No one who read the transcript could ever again doubt where his true loyalties lay.

That summer much more clamor was made about the total repeal of the Stamp Act than the passing of a different piece of legislation, the Declaratory Act, which became law just one day later. The Declaratory Act was a defensive piece of law-making, passed by a bruised Parliament, that reaffirmed Westminster's right to pass laws across the empire. None of Strahan's ideas about Parliamentary representation for Americans, however, were acted upon. As for Franklin himself, he emerged from the experiences of 1765—66 a changed man. Until now his enthusiasm for Great Britain, her customs and her manners, had been unbounded. But after the Stamp Act crisis he began to regard the mother country's attitude rather differently. For some the shift was hardly perceptible. But for those who knew him well like Strahan, the reconfiguration was clear enough. The combative, anonymous pieces in the newspapers continued to come. Franklin took care, too, to ensure that these were transmitted to friends across the Atlantic for reprinting in the colonial press. In addition, people began to spot Franklin in surprising places. He was even said to have attended Catharine Macaulay's Tuesday salons at her house in Berners Street, off the Oxford Road.

MACAULAY WAS NOW IN her mid-thirties. Over the past years she had undergone a change in status, from single-minded author to a mother with family responsibilities. Macaulay had relished this. "There never was," one acquaintance reported, "a more affectionate wife, or more tender mother."[53] Yet this harmony had not lasted long. A year after their daughter, Catharine Sophia, was born in 1765, her husband George had died. Perhaps it was the emotional weight of these events that drove her to leave the house in St. James's and move to a quieter part of the town.

Berners Street, situated on the northern fringes of Westminster, not only had a calmer atmosphere, it was more conveniently located. Just ten minutes in her "fashionable" sedan chair brought Macaulay to the library at the British Museum, one of the finest centers of learning in Europe. At Berners Street, meanwhile, in her new capacity as a wealthy widow, Macaulay set about establishing a household to befit her celebrity status. She had her rooms furnished with blue silk damask fabrics, cabriole chairs, luscious carpets, and mahogany tables. Adding to the fashionable allure (as well as to Macaulay's reputation as someone who quite enjoyed luxury herself) was "a well-chosen Collection of Pictures by several admired Masters."[54]

For an emerging generation of freethinkers and foreign visitors, Macaulay became, in the words of Walpole, "one of these sights" they were "carried to see."[55] She was spoken about as "a most agreeable Lady," whose "conversation is of the same kind with her writings, and though she plays at cards and talks of different subjects," she always returned to politics, which was the subject that absorbed her most of all. In the eyes of one, she was "quite a phenomenon . . . She has studied the nature of government so as to make herself perfectly mistress of it."[56] Much of this learning was indeed done at the British Museum, and a delightful story about Macaulay in the museum's library dates to this time. When she asked to browse the correspondence between King James I and the Duke of Buckingham, the librarian told her that "many of them were wholly unfit for the inspection of any one of her sex." He then proposed he select a few for her to study. "Phoo," replied Macaulay, "a historian is of no sex," and then she "deliberately read through them all."[57]

Tuesday was the day for gatherings at Macaulay's house for the "mutual friends of Liberty." On those days people like the writer Thomas Hollis, the philosopher Richard Price, and guests including James Boswell or even Franklin himself would gather to eat ice cream, sip from bowls of chocolate, and talk of politics. There was a radical edge to these conversations. Could a monarchist be a true friend of liberty? Should the system of hereditary honours be abolished? Why did Oliver Cromwell turn his back on the principles of the English Revolution? As well as discussing history and theory, people would exchange political gossip. Years after his fall, rumors continued to swirl that Bute was choreographing events from behind the curtain. One of Macaulay's friends even held that he wanted to become king. Another argument was that Bute, in league with Grenville, had formed a scheme "to send Bishops to America and absolutely enslave that country."[58] As tales like these were passed around, Macaulay was said to preside over the proceedings with "the air of a princess," as two servants in laced liveries flitted to and fro in constant attendance.

This description of her, by Hollis, might have been ironic given the nature of the gatherings. But it did show how she was seen: as an ethereal, detached presence in the grimy political world. This was an image Macaulay played upon. A 1766 reprint of the first volume of her *History* included a pictorial frontispiece that showed her in profile in the dress of a Roman matron, with her hair coiffured, a golden necklace draped around her neck, and her head surrounded by a frame of laurel leaves. To open her book was to cleanse and fortify the mind. As one recent historian has put it, "Macaulay's story of the Stuarts was a sort of historical mirror in which her contemporaries could watch villains of the present take on the odious form of villains of the past."[59] In a world which forbade women from playing active roles in politics, Macaulay had discovered a form that enabled her to shape opinion. In some ways, too, being a woman actually helped. No one interfered with or shut down her political salons at Berners Street, however inflammatory the conversation.

Regardless of her family circumstances, Macaulay's productivity continued to increase. Following the debut of her *History* in 1763, a second volume had followed in 1765, a third in 1767, and a fourth was now in production. Nor was she restricting herself to the seventeenth century. After years of studying Spartan law, Roman politics, and Epicurean philosophy, she was eager to print her own ideas about what a truly enlightened society should be. She sketched its parameters in a compelling letter of 1767. It would not be ruled by an interfering king like George III. In fact, there would be no monarch at all. Instead it would be a free republic, governed, as in Ancient Athens, by a democratic system. The apparatus of state, Macaulay explained, would tessellate together. Executive power would lie between two "orders." There would be a Senate of no more than fifty, "to prevent the confusion which usually springs from assemblies too numerous."[60] This would ensure wisdom. Alongside this would be a larger "House of the People" of about 250. Both of these would have a third of their members replenished by annual elections, meaning that every three years there would be a complete rotation. The House would source new representatives from the mass of the people, while new senators would be drawn up from serving members of the House.

Motion was central to Macaulay's system. Like the components in one of James Watt's engines, the machinery of state would always be moving. New representatives—uncorrupted, energetic, public-spirited citizens—were to be the fuel in this system, which was always subject to disorder if the movement should ever stop. "Let no member," wrote Macaulay, "of either the senatorial or representative body, be capable of re-election under the space of three years." In this way no tyrant could accumulate power, as Sulla, Pompey, or Caesar had in Rome. "The remedy of a dictator," too, she wrote, "should never be made use of, but in the most desperate cases."

All this might seem ambitious, Macaulay acknowledged, but when compared with existing forms of government in Europe, which had lately produced despots such as "Lewis the Fourteenth" in France or "Harry the Eighth" in England, it was surely an improvement. "Of all the various models of republics," Macaulay reiterated, "it is only the democratical system, rightly balanced, which can secure the virtue, liberty and happiness of society."[61]

Eleven

A SEVEN-YEAR LOTTERY

BY CHRISTMAS 1767 THE newest and most prestigious of buildings in Strahan's New Street complex was almost complete. The King's Printing House was an elegant three-story townhouse, built from brick and fitted with neat rows of broad sash windows. To add a touch of refinement and suggest the precision work that was going on inside, a large, graceful clock had been integrated into the outer brickwork. This looked out over an enclosed courtyard that gave onto the street, which visitors entered through an iron archway. Flanked by a run of railings and two oil lamps, the archway was a work of tasteful craftsmanship. As the ironwork rose and joined, it split into the recognizable form of the royal crest. Fleet Street may have been some distance from Westminster and St. James's, but here, as the coat of arms proclaimed, was a building infused with all the majestic power of the Crown.

Since printing had begun to formalize as a trade in the sixteenth century, the Crown had awarded specific patents that gave the holders a monopoly over printing certain kinds of books or documents. Over time many of these had lapsed, but one, known generally as the "King's Printer," had survived. It gave the holder the exclusive right to produce Bibles, books of Common Prayer, proclamations, statutes, and injunctions. The patent was usually awarded for long periods, and over the years, the Crown had made up shortfalls in its finances by selling it well in advance. Therefore the patent that was due to come into force for the years 1770 to 1800 had actually been granted in 1716 and, in the Georgian way, had since passed between private hands like a rare and desirable bond. Knowing the old patent was almost exhausted and that the next inheritor, a man called Charles Eyre, knew nothing about the printing trade, Strahan had approached him in 1766 with a proposal. Within a year Strahan had secured his prize. For a payment of £5,000 he acquired a third share of the patent for the next thirty years. In that time Eyre was to pay him £300 a year to manage all the practical business. As Strahan told Hall:

> This is an Affair of Consequence, which at this time a'day I should hardly think of imbarking in, but that I have Sons in the Business to succeed me. The Gentleman, however, with whom I am to be connected, as well as every Circumstance attending it, is extremely agreeable. And you know it is the most repu-table part of our Trade in Britain, which is some Allurement to invite one to be concerned in it.[1]

When the agreement had been struck in 1766 the assumption had been that Strahan would occupy the old premises in Blackfriars, where the King's Printing House had been situated for a century. But Strahan had, as ever, better ideas. With funds to spare, he reasoned that it was far more convenient for the printing to be carried on at a newly built property on Little New Street. Work had commenced in 1767. "It will be an excellent house," Strahan enthused to Hall, "every way more commodious than that in Blackfriars."[2] By Christmas 1767 Strahan could look out of his parlor window at the latest addition to his little empire. As soon as the old patent expired, the King's Printing House would begin operations.

While this all boded well for the future, there remained enough to occupy him in the present. At his private printing house, the presses continued to work at the limit. One of his steadiest sources of work was the *Chronicle*. The paper was now a decade old and firmly established as one of London's finest, bristling with intelligence and color. Released on Tuesdays, Thursdays, and Saturdays, it was designed to synchronize with the country post, and people in the shires had come to depend on it for the latest political, social, and economic stories. As 1768 began, there was plenty for Griffith Jones, the editor, to report. The most pressing story was the weather. The first weeks of January brought a dramatic spell of cold. Out in the countryside roads were buried by the drifts and the landscape was blanketed white. In the capital the Thames froze and reports held that the river remained unnavigable for fifteen or so miles, all the way to Gravesend.

Stories rippled back to Little New Street, of nightwatchmen and river boys being found frozen solid at sunrise. Elsewhere many of the capital's poor were said to be on the brink. For a long time the price of bread had been high and the cold made the situation acute. In early January a party of guards was ordered to march out of the Tower to confront a riotous body of weavers in Spitalfields. Arriving at the scene, the guards had been surprised to find the weavers carrying "old swords, sticks, and bludgeons." Some were so furious that they struck the soldiers, who, went the report, "were obliged to return the same in their own defence."[3]

There was something ominous in such stories, but for Strahan a deeper source of disquiet continued to be the news from America. After the repeal of the Stamp Act, there had been hopes of refreshed colonial relations. Further cause for optimism came with William Pitt's return to frontline politics. Pitt was a known friend to America. In a celebrated moment during the Stamp Act crisis, Strahan had told Hall, "without communicating his Intention either to Friend or Foe, to one of the Ministry or one of the Opposition, he came unexpectedly into the House on the first Day of their Meeting, and made that famous Speech in your Behalf."[4] Pitt's speech had been one of his finest. It included the unforgettable line that "Americans are the sons, not the bastards of England!"[5]

Although Strahan had not been sure whether Pitt's motives were as pure as he portrayed them, he had most certainly done the colonists what he called "essential Service." Copies of the speech, like the transcript of Franklin's interrogation, were circulated across the Atlantic, with some of the staunchest committing his words to heart. The return of the war hero to power, after the undistinguished ministries of Bute, Grenville and the Marquess of Rockingham, was therefore an exciting thing. Strahan regarded Pitt as "the only Man, that can at present extricate us from our present and more immediate Difficulties," although he admitted to uncertainty about his manner. Pitt's superiority over his colleagues stretched to such lengths, Strahan told Hall, that he was emboldened "to treat the whole House upon several Occasions, in the Course of the Session, like a Parcel of School-boys."[6]

And then, at the very moment of his return, Pitt managed to ruin his public standing by accepting an earldom from the king. This move, which transformed him from plain William Pitt into the stately Earl of Chatham, was viewed as an abandonment of principle for a man who had built an identity around being "the Great Commoner." Thomas Gray, the poet, branded it, "the weakest thing ever done by so great a man."[7] In one foolish blunder, Chatham had both alienated his supporters and removed himself from the House of Commons. Now a peer of the realm, Chatham would henceforth speak from the more sedate benches of the House of Lords, much weakening his ministry in the lower house.

Reduced in popularity, Pitt was also strangely enfeebled in body. From 1766 onward, Chatham's physical and mental state became precarious. Something, it was clear to everyone, was wrong with him. In public his ailments were ambiguously spoken of as being a "protracted illness," which in reality seemed a mixture of gout and depression. The consequence was that Pitt was almost totally absent from his post, leaving a void at the top of politics. With Pitt giving no direction, continuing problems like America and the national debt fell to others. One who tried to confront both was the new chancellor of the exchequer, Charles Townshend.

Townshend was known as a "dazzling orator and an amusing but unreliable man,"[8] and in May 1767 Strahan had sent Hall an overview of a long, "fine" speech he had given in the Commons. In this he spoke suggestively about "drawing some Aids from America," which clearly meant more taxation. But he argued that it "should be as little as possible burthensome" to the colonials.[9] Rather than one blunt tax, like Grenville's Stamp Act, Townshend talked of duties on imports of wine, oil, and fruit, as well as levies on china, paper, tea, and painter's colors. While Grenville dismissed these measures as "trifles," others were worried that so soon after the Stamp Act, they would stir up the same resentment once more.

This was indeed what had happened. When news of the Townshend Duties arrived in the colonies, the response was furious. By Christmas 1767 Britons were reading in the newspapers about clamorous meetings in Boston's Faneuil Hall where resolutions had been adopted banning the import of goods. At the same time the Bostonians declared their intention to produce taxed items like glass and paper for themselves. This challenged the convention that America was the source of raw materials and Britain the home of manufacturing.

In London especially, this was a development that did not go down well. This time it was not just the hardliners like Grenville who expected obedience from the colonists, but also the moderates who had realized in 1766 that the Stamp Act was a badly conceived policy. The Townshend Duties were light, and as they were dispersed across a range of commodities, Americans had more scope to avoid them if they wished. If this was not good enough, then what would be?

Anti-American sentiment reigned in the newspapers, where colonials were branded as "diggers of pits for this country," "lunaticks," "sworn enemies," and "false," "ungrateful," "cut-throats."[10] The ministry responded in its own way by creating the new post of Secretary of State for the Colonies, and appointing Wills Hill, the First Earl of Hillsborough, a more forceful figure than Lord Shelburne, who had previously been responsible for America.

Both Strahan and Franklin were unnerved by this. The situation, if anything, was more serious than in 1765. In response Franklin delivered a speech to a group of MPs, explaining the rationale behind the Americans' attitude. Strahan judged this so elegantly argued that he arranged for it to be printed, three thousand words in all, in the *Chronicle* for January 5–7. The article was addressed to Strahan as the "PRINTER OF THE LONDON CHRONICLE," and the pseudonym he used, F+S., suggests the depth of the collaboration between the two. The piece was characteristically clear and persuasive. To conceal his own opinions, Franklin used the literary device of assuming the colonists' point of view, in order to better understand their mode of reasoning. His argument concluded:

> For notwithstanding the reproaches thrown out against us in their public papers and pamphlets, notwithstanding we have been reviled in their Senate as *Rebels* and *Traitors*, we are truly a loyal people. Scotland has had its rebellions, and England its plots against the present Royal Family; but America is untainted with those crimes; there is in it scarce a man, there is not a single native of our country, who is not firmly attached to his King by principle and by affection. But a new kind of loyalty seems to be required of us, a loyalty to P[arliamen]t; a loyalty, that is to extend, it is said, to a surrender of all our properties, whenever a H[ouse] of C[ommons], in which there is not a single member of our chusing, shall think fit to grant them away

without our consent; and to a patient suffering the loss of our privileges as Englishmen, if we cannot submit to make such surrender. We were separated too far from Britain by the Ocean, but we were united to it by respect and love, so that we could at any time freely have spent our lives and little fortunes in its cause: But this unhappy new system of politics tends to dissolve those bands of union, and to sever us for ever.[11]

For Strahan, who remained invested emotionally and commercially in America, this unrest was disturbing an otherwise settled life. Since Rachel's death in 1765, the family's circumstances had moved on. His eldest son, William, had entered into partnership with him, and his youngest, Andrew, was taking on more responsibilities in the pressroom. George remained in Oxford, but he was doing well and had secured a fellowship. As Strahan explained in a letter to Hall in February 1768, his daughter Peg, too, was ready to fledge. She was "almost ready for a Husband," Strahan judged, "and will, if I mistake not, make a very good wife."[12]

By now the cold, acrimonious winter was almost at an end. With the longer days and better weather came hopes for brighter news. One event, everyone knew, was bound to dominate public life over the next months. The old Parliament, elected after the king's accession in 1761, had nearly run its course. This meant that at any moment a general election might be called. This always heralded a period of rancor, drama, exuberance, and devilry. But the election of 1768 was destined to cause even more of a commotion than usual.

For Strahan the biggest worry was the scores of "Nabobs" who had returned to Britain having made vast fortunes in India, "by Rapine and Plunder, in most Cases attended with the most shocking Instances of Barbarity."[13] Around thirty or forty of these were going to secure seats in the forthcoming Parliament, he wrote to Hall on February 13. But unknown to Strahan there was someone else who was destined to upset British politics far more than any of these. For hidden in a Westminster house not far away was John Wilkes. He had stolen back into the country, and he had picked his moment well.

FOUR YEARS HAD PASSED since Wilkes had been bundled out of his front door in Great George Street and into a coach bound for Dover. Back then his prospects had seemed incomparably gloomy. His political campaign had left him physically wounded, socially isolated, legally exposed, and almost bankrupt. Such comprehensive ruin would have been sufficient to crush just about anyone else for good, but Wilkes had somehow managed to retain his old gaiety of spirit. While Parliament and the colonies began to quarrel in 1764, Wilkes had been enjoying the social life of Paris. Later, when his funds had started to dry up, he had left France for Naples in the company of his mistress, a sensual, mesmerizing Italian beauty called Gertrude Corradini whose sexual appetite left Wilkes in a state of wonder. In Naples, Wilkes had lived the life of the libertine in exile, infatuated with Corradini and equally enamored with the classical landscape around him. Here he had met the young lawyer and socialite James Boswell. Despite the aggravating fact that Boswell was Scottish, Wilkes had taken an instant interest in him. Together they explored the Neapolitan streets and climbed the storied slopes of Vesuvius, chattering all the way. Charmed, Boswell afterward wrote of Wilkes in a letter to Rousseau:

> All theories of human nature are confounded by the resilient spirit of that singular factionary [Wilkes], who has experienced all the vicissitudes of pleasure and politics without ever having suffered a moment of uneasiness. He is a man who has thought much without being gloomy, a man who has done much evil without being a scoundrel. His lively and energetic sallies on moral questions gave to my spirit a not unpleasant agitation, and enlarged the scope of my views by convincing me that God

could create a soul completely serene and gay notwithstanding the alarming reflection that we all must die.[14]

Wilkes may have dabbled in airy philosophy, but he missed the grit and grain of daily politics. In March 1766, back in Paris, he complained to his lawyer Cotes about his "entire ignorance" of public affairs. He had only the gossip of the French coffee houses to go on, and the news was not encouraging. A story was doing the rounds that his old patron, Temple, had abandoned his principles and joined with "Lord Bute, the maker of the infamous Peace of Paris; the Duke of Bedford, the signer of it; Lord Halifax, the friend of General Warrants; Lord Sandwich, the worst character in the nation; George Grenville—what shall I call him?"[15] Far from London, Wilkes had the "mortification" of hearing this rumor twenty times a day, but he had no idea whether or not it was true. He remained as ignorant, he told Cotes, as he would have been had he acted on the invitation he had recently received to travel to America.

Wilkes did not disclose anything more about this invitation, but it must have been a tempting one. After the Stamp Act, he could be guaranteed a warm welcome as a champion in the fight against tyrannical forces. But Wilkes's feelings about America were lukewarm at this point. "There is a spirit little short of rebellion in several of the colonies,"[16] he had told his brother Heaton in 1765. Neither Boston, New York nor Philadelphia was a strong enough lure for Wilkes, whose mind remained fixed on a return to Britain.

In 1766 and 1767 he made several surreptitious visits to London, but each time found little encouragement in his bid to secure a royal pardon. One of his biggest obstacles was one of his oldest friends. Wilkes had been devoted to Pitt during his younger years. Despite the manner of their estrangement in 1763, Wilkes always considered Pitt to be his greatest hope of rehabilitation. When Pitt returned to power in 1766, Wilkes thought his time had come. He hurried back across the Channel, only to find that Pitt would have nothing to do with him. Retreating to Paris, Wilkes channeled his anger into a fiery pamphlet that attacked his former patron's honor. In Wilkes's view, in transforming from William Pitt into Lord Chatham, his old ally had been strangely altered.

> He was indeed long the favourite character of our countrymen. Every tongue was wanton in his praise. The whole people lavished on him their choicest favours, and endeavoured by the noblest means, by an unbounded generosity and confidence, to have kept him virtuous. With what anguish were we at last undeceiv'd! How much it cost us to give up a man, who had so long entirely kept possession of our hearts! How cruel was the struggle! But alas! how is he changed? how fallen? from what height fallen? His glorious sun is set, I believe never to rise again.[17]

Wilkes's polemic appeared late in 1766. It was copied, syndicated, and spread right across Britain. Coming at a time when Chatham's reputation was in decline, the affair had quite the opposite effect on Wilkes. In Paris he received admiring letters once again, along with one from his brother that described Chatham's response to the pamphlet. "I hear he is so provoked and storms so much," he wrote, "his friends talk of its having had the effect on him of driving him mad."[18] Wilkes gleaned another thing from the episode too. It seemed that his popular support remained. If there was a time to exploit this, it was during an election. Wilkes calculated that in 1768 he would have a unique chance of making a comeback. On February 7 of that year he boarded a ship bound for Dover. As ever he waved away the cautions of friends who advised prudence. "What the devil have I to do with prudence?" Wilkes blustered. "I owe money in France, am an outlaw in England, hated by the King, the Parliament, and the bench of bishops, pursued by the courts of law, the ministers, &c &c. What do you talk to me of prudence for? I must raise a dust or starve in a jail."[19]

Wilkes, however, was acting on more than just daring. Always reckless with money, by the end of 1767 the loans he had drawn during his exile were nearly due. Confronted by the prospect of financial ruin, he had struck a bargain with a London publisher to produce a history of England, in the same vein as Macaulay's. But the advance for this came nowhere close to clearing the shortfall. It was obvious to Wilkes that he had to find a way to radically improve his affairs. Returning to London was a brave move, but it was one of the very few available to him. He knew the dangers that awaited him. After the disgrace of 1763, he had been almost totally abandoned by the political community. He had no hope of any support from them. His legal status as an outlaw was an even greater worry. At any moment in Britain a sheriff could serve him with a writ of Capias Utlagatum, upon which he would be seized and confined until he could be brought before the court. Beyond this was the separate matter of his private debts. As a debtor he ran the possibility of being taken up at a moment's notice and thrown into the Marshalsea Prison.

These were no small worries, but Wilkes met them with a plan that was so utterly brazen that it is hard to think of anyone else who would have attempted it. Once the old Parliament was broken up, he decided to offer himself as a candidate in the election. This tactic had two advantages. First, the audacity of the move would mobilize his supporters, and the more popular support he could gather, the more difficult it would be for his enemies to apprehend him. The second was less certain but even more exciting. If he could succeed in getting himself elected, then he could—in theory—regain all the privileges of a Member of Parliament. In legal terms it was not clear whether he could actually be elected to the Commons as an outlaw (although there had been precedents to suggest that he could). And if he did somehow manage, then it was equally unclear what his rights would be. Wilkes's plan would test English law. To succeed he would need courage, support, and, just as importantly, a great deal of luck.

After arriving in London in February, Wilkes lay low in a house in Westminster. He adopted the name "Osborn" and corresponded with a tight group of old friends including the printer Dryden Leach. As he waited, he had time to consider one big question. Which constituency should he target? There were 558 seats in the House of Commons. In essence, Wilkes needed to win just one. But for the plan to work, the choice of seat had to be right. He was not likely to be successful, for obvious reasons, in one of the forty-five Scottish seats. Nor, as Wilkes wanted to present himself as a champion of English liberty, could he bribe his way to victory in one of the rotten boroughs like Old Sarum, where a handful of bribed electors would decide the result. He needed a high-profile constituency, which would fuel his newspaper campaign, with an electorate sizeable enough for him to make inroads with the small proportion of uncommitted voters. The more votes he could get, the stronger would be his moral authority. Ideally, too, the constituency should have a low bar of entry and a large quota of seats. For a time Wilkes toyed with the idea of standing for the City of Westminster. By March, however, he had moved his ambition eastward, to the City of London.

Those who heard whispers of Wilkes's plan would instantly have seen the merit of it. The City was the seat of commerce. It was a place of ambitious tradespeople and far-sighted merchants, who firmly believed in the twin virtues of trade and liberty. Ideologically, for Wilkes, this was fertile ground. In 1763 the City had been "warmly his friends" during his contest with Bute, and five years on he had every hope that they might embrace him again. There were other enticements too. Ever since the days of King Henry III in the thirteenth century, the City had returned four members to Parliament, giving Wilkes a wider target of seats. Admission for candidates, too, was not going to be troublesome. Candidature was not determined by property, but by the membership of one of the City's livery companies. So long as Wilkes could persuade one of them to allow him to join, then he was free to submit his name before the eight thousand or so voters.

By early March speculation was rife in the papers that Parliament was due to be dissolved any day. There were other rumors too. "We hear that a celebrated Outlaw is at the Moment actually in the Kingdom," went one.[20] On Friday, March 4, this report was confirmed when Wilkes dispatched a servant and a note to Queen Charlotte's levee, formally requesting a royal pardon and proclaiming himself to be a victim of malevolent "former ministers" who had employed "every wicked and deceitful art" against him.[21]

For Wilkes this was the crucial moment. Were the king or the nominal head of the ministry, the Duke of Grafton, determined to stamp him out, a sheriff might well have been sent to arrest him. None appeared. This hesitation provided Wilkes with his chance. On the tails of his request for a pardon he released another public letter. This was addressed "*To the worthy Liverymen of the City of London.*" In it he confirmed his intention to stand as a candidate. "The chief merit with you, Gentlemen," he explained, "I know to be a sacred love of liberty, and of those generous principles, which at first gave, and have since secured to this nation, the great charter of freedom."[22]

The following Thursday, March 10, Parliament was at last prorogued. The next day a royal proclamation followed, dissolving Parliament and ordering the elections to begin. "The Cry of *Wilkes and Liberty* is beginning to be re-echoed in our streets," Strahan wrote in bemusement to Hall. "I cannot think he will by any Means succeed; Yet it is impossible to say what the Folly of the lower Class of Liverymen (by much the majority) may accomplish. But whatever the Event may be, I shall ever consider the Choice of such a Man to be a lasting Disgrace to the City of London."[23]

ONCE THE ELECTION WAS in progress and his presence in the country was confirmed, Wilkes abandoned all caution and walked about as publicly as he could. In part this was to evade his private creditors, few if any of whom would be brave enough to apprehend him on a London street. He had a second motive too. Wilkes was one of the first politicians to fully understand and manipulate the power of the press. His experiences in 1763 had been his apprenticeship. He had fed news writers with stories. He had leaked transcripts of speeches to printers, and he had mastered the art of the public spectacle, turning mundane episodes into moments of histrionic theatre. Five years on he had lost none of his skill. By making himself as conspicuous, as interesting, and as accessible as he possibly could, he ensured that he soon became the most compelling story in town. In 1768 Wilkes dominated what is now called the attention economy. Scarcely a newspaper appeared without his name in it.

Eighteenth-century elections ran to a quite different rhythm than those of today. While we are accustomed to the idea of months-long national campaigns that conclude on a polling day, Georgians knew a far messier and more fragmented system. In many constituencies voting would begin within days of the old Parliament being dissolved. In tightly managed seats the process would be quickly concluded, with the favored candidate often having his election rubber-stamped without having the trouble of visiting the constituency or speaking with the voters.

While such MPs viewed the electoral period as a time for relaxation, for others it was very different. For those standing for competitive seats where the outcome was hard to predict, an election was an exhausting and financially bruising time. This made cautious souls like Franklin wary of them. In a letter written that March he described them as being like "a seven Years Lottery . . . tho'," he added ruefully, "all that have Tickets should not get Prizes."[24]

To acquire the prize, candidates in such seats were expected to lavish time, attention, and a good deal of roast beef and Madeira wine on their voters. Often this process would commence long before the election actually began, and it would continue until the moment the poll books closed. Wise voters would conceal their intentions for as long as possible. This inflated their importance as elections ran on. It was not unusual for tight races to tumble onward for days or even weeks, with running totals being kept and the tactics growing increasingly wild. These contests would often only finish when one candidate had amassed an unconquerable lead or his rival lost heart or ran out of money. With hundreds of contests taking place simultaneously, it was difficult to keep track of what was happening at a national level. All told, a Georgian election was a brawling, exhausting, drunken, elaborate, underhand, theatrical performance with 558 contrasting storylines. In 1768, the story that demanded everyone's attention was John Wilkes's.

The opening week of Wilkes's campaign was exhilarating. The day after the dissolution he attended a dinner at the King's Arms tavern, Cornhill, where "a great number of the Nobility and Livery of the City of London" had come to meet him. This was more than Wilkes could have hoped for. The gossip, too, was that people were sanguine about his chances. In the coffee houses, sums of five, ten, and fifteen guineas had apparently been put down on Wilkes's victory. At the same time news slipped out that a Privy Council meeting had been held in Westminster, at which it had been decided to leave Wilkes at large for now. With the authorities remaining timid, Wilkes's plans went forward. He now had to be admitted as a liveryman into one of the City's guilds. Wilkes was no craftsman, but he had nonetheless managed to join as a freeman of the Joiners' Company, a body who were so enthusiastic to welcome him as a member that they presented him with a "Box of the Heart of true English Oak."[25]

This administrative hurdle crossed, Wilkes was free to concentrate on the campaign. His strategy was clear. He intended to present himself as the champion of English liberty and as a victim of tyrannical ministers. In the City, where the ideal of liberty was cherished as much as anywhere, he thought that this might just be enough to propel him into one of the top four places. The forces ranged against Wilkes, however, were considerable. Six others had already announced their candidacy for the City, and most of them had spent months or even years building their voter base. Among Wilkes's opponents were some of the most powerful politicians in the land.

Thomas Harley, who had been terrorized by the mob during the burning of *North Briton* No. 45, was one. Harley was the current Lord Mayor of London, and alongside him were two former holders of the office: William Beckford and Sir Robert Ladbroke. Another standing was the fabulously wealthy American merchant Barlow Trecothick. These alone were enough to fill the quota of seats. Whether Wilkes could overturn any of them at such short notice was doubtful.

The poll opened at the Guildhall on Wednesday, March 16, when Wilkes joined the other candidates on the hustings. After all the noise, this was a time to take stock. "Contrary to all Expectation," wrote one Londoner in a letter that would soon be published in Philadelphia, "a Spirit" had been "quickly infused into the lowest Class of People" by Wilkes's campaign. It was these people—day laborers, porters, journeymen—who were there at the Guildhall that day. "Real mob," one witness called them. When it was his turn, Wilkes addressed the crowd with "more Coolness, and Presence of Mind, than could have been expected from one who was acting so bold a Part."[26]

> I stand here, Gentlemen, a private man, unconnected with the great, and unsupported by any party. I have no support but you: I wish no other support: I can have none more certain, none more honourable. If I have the happiness, Gentlemen, of being returned to parliament by your favour, I shall be ready to pay the greatest deference to the sentiments of my constituents on every occasion, and shall dedicate myself to their service, by promoting to the utmost of my abilities the trade and commerce of this great metropolis, by which alone it can maintain the first rank it now enjoys, and I hope, with its liberties, will ever enjoy.[27]

After the other candidates had made their speeches, the sheriff called for a show of hands. Wilkes was the clear winner. It being obvious, however, that most of those in the room were not liverymen, and as such not eligible to vote, the rival candidates asked, as expected, for a poll to be taken. At that point the sheriff ordered for the books to be opened and for the liverymen to come forward to cast their vote.

As the voting began, the candidates went to work. Over the next few days, Wilkes, enjoying his newfound status as a leather-aproned man, established an electoral headquarters at the Joiners' Hall in Thames Street. The custom in the City election was for the various livery companies to cast their votes *en bloc* behind their chosen candidate. Arriving late to the election, Wilkes had no chance of swaying the companies, who had long since committed themselves. Instead he sought to pick off single votes, and to do so he called in at the various companies, day after day, to scent out whatever support he could. To enhance the camaraderie, Wilkes arranged for supporters to meet him each morning at the Joiners' Hall, so that he could accompany them to the Guildhall where they were to cast their votes. Before long it became something of a fashion to be seen parading with Wilkes. Those liverymen who gave him their single votes were labeled the "Sons of Liberty" in the press.[28]

All this time Wilkes was at risk. Midway through a dinner at the King's Arms on March 19, he was served with an Exchequer writ by an agent of the Treasury. This warned him that should his outlawry be upheld, his effects would immediately be seized. For now this was as far as the government was willing to go, but their threat was ominous. And still no one was sure whether Wilkes could actually be admitted to the Commons if he were to be elected. To many, the idea that an outlaw would be permitted to sit in the assembly responsible for creating the laws of the kingdom was ludicrous. To reassure people that he had no hostile intentions, Wilkes made public a letter he had written to the solicitor of the Treasury. In it he stated his intention, on his honor as a gentleman, of surrendering to the Court of the King's Bench on the opening day of the next session in

April. He made it clear that whatever the verdict he would abide by the judgment of the court.

This shrewd move quieted the legal arguments and allowed Wilkes's campaign to move forward. By now it was already clear that his return was a masterstroke. The ministry had no idea what to do with him. His supporters had been mobilized, and on March 17 a public subscription was set up at Lee and Ayton's Bankers in Lombard Street to satisfy Wilkes's creditors. On its first day some gentlemen were seen contributing as much as £150 at a time. Wilkes, the argument went, was such a unique champion of English liberty that he could not be left to the mercy of creditors. His commitment to a virtuous cause was sufficient to dispel any worries about his private life. "Does Mr Wilkes's private character injure his public one?" asked one newspaper correspondent.[29] "Remember, the brightest object is the most easily sullied." Another stated:

> Sir, if a man in this country should want to have his transgressions brought to his own or the public recollection, the shortest way to attain that end, would be to put up for a member of parliament, when he need not fear of being reminded of all the sins he ever was guilty of, and some more in addition, lest the weight of his own should not sufficiently sink him. This is exactly the case of poor W——, whose faults are aggravated, but his virtues forgotten.[30]

Scores of pieces like these flooded the papers as the poll books remained open at the Guildhall. They were enough to unsettle Wilkes's enemies in Westminster, as was the news that he had been borne through the streets in an open-top chair behind a jaunty band of musicians. As Wilkes was hoisted high into the air, a man was heard to cry out, "By God Master Wilkes, we'll carry you, whether you carry your Election or not."[31]

It was with some relief, then, that such people received news of the count in the City of London on Wednesday, March 23. Harley, Ladbroke, Beckford, and Trecothick had won the seats. Wilkes, for all the noise, had trailed in a very distant last. In retrospect it seemed mad that anyone had expected anything else. The blocs of votes that determined the City election had been pledged or purchased months before. To turn up and hope for the best at the last moment was no strategy in such a system. But after the result, Wilkes made an announcement that shocked and thrilled in equal measure. Among prominent MPs, especially those who represented competitive constituencies, it was common practice to enter their names in multiple races. There was no law against this, and essentially it meant that if they failed in one preferred constituency then at least they would have a backup that would ensure their political career could continue from another.

During the City vote, people had wondered whether Wilkes would do this. There was every reason for him to keep his campaign going. The one problem he confronted, though, was time. As the days had passed, the papers had carried reports of concluded elections. The count was already over in Westminster. His old seat at Aylesbury had gone too. There was just one obvious place that both fitted Wilkes's list of requirements and which had yet to hold its count. On the hustings in the Guildhall, Wilkes revealed his plan. He was now going to enter the contest for the County of Middlesex.

This was an electrifying move. Middlesex was an ancient county that covered much of London north of the Thames. While it included many rural areas to the west of the capital, it also embraced many of the inner-city areas. The riverside neighborhoods of Wapping, Shadwell, and Limehouse, for instance, were included within Middlesex's eastern division. Here lived scores of small freeholders and upwardly mobile tradespeople who were both ideologically aligned with Wilkes and unsettled after the hard weather of the previous winter. Placed right next to the City of London, these voters would also have felt the force of Wilkes's return and the heat his first campaign had generated. If Wilkes could gather together a coalition of such people, along with the kind of gentlemen that had been supporting his subscription in Lombard Street, and a miscellaneous cluster of others, then he might well have a chance.

JUST FOUR DAYS REMAINED before the polls were due to open on Monday, March 28. But while time was short, Wilkes had several important advantages. The Middlesex election was to be held in the little town of Brentford. Seven miles outside London, on the Bath Road, it was a quaint and comely town on the northern lip of the River Thames, with little more than a collection of houses, some market gardens, and a church. But for Wilkes this church mattered deeply. For, since 1760, the priest of the parish of New Brentford was one of his most ardent supporters: John Horne.

After a final blaze of electioneering in the City over the weekend, Wilkes set off toward Horne's parsonage in Brentford on the eve of the election. The county of Middlesex sent two MPs to the Commons. The incumbent members, Sir William Beauchamp Proctor and George Cooke, had represented the voters of the county for eighteen years. Most of the freeholders were pledged to support one or the other of them, so, until a few days before, they had considered their reelection to be a foregone conclusion. Wilkes's last-minute entry challenged their complacency. He arrived in Brentford to find that Horne had been relentlessly electioneering on his behalf. "Scarcely allowing himself time for the usual refreshments which nature requires," one story went, Horne had spent days, "sometimes on foot, and sometimes on horseback, in canvassing the county, enumerating the merits and the sufferings of Mr Wilkes, palliating his errors, and apologizing for his follies."[32] Horne's enthusiasm for his candidate was astonishing to those who met him. Once, in an intemperate moment, he told one of the freeholders that "in a case so just and so holy, he would dye his black coat red." When Wilkes arrived at Brentford, where he planned to lodge with Horne during the election, he found that his reverend friend had even managed to secure two of the best inns in the town as bases for his election campaign.

At eight in the morning, Wilkes approached the hustings. He came, according to one newspaper, "in a coach drawn by Six long-tail Horses, and was accompanied by a great Number of People."[33] The site of the election was a place called Brentford Butts, where a temporary booth had been erected. Climbing onto the platform, Wilkes gazed over the growing crowd, many of whom were wearing his blue cockades, and waited calmly for his opponents. Some hours passed. It was early afternoon before they appeared. Beauchamp Proctor came first on horseback, with George Cooke following in a coach and six soon afterward. Cooke had evidently spent the morning strategizing. His coach was accompanied by a "great Number of Gentlemen in Carriages and on Horseback." Mingled with these were more of Cooke's supporters on foot carrying large blue flags, on which were written in golden letters the taunting slogan "No BLASPHEMERS, No FRENCH RUNAGATES." Seeing this, Wilkes's supporters attempted to tear the flags down, "and a Scuffle ensued, in which many were greatly Hurt."[34]

By now the candidates were together on the platform. Gazing around him, a sight presented itself that even Wilkes had never witnessed before. "It is impossible to paint the Scenes that presented themselves to a Spectator," wrote an onlooker, who estimated, surely with some exaggeration, that "Fifty Thousand People were collected on the Occasion."[35] Finding an elevated place, he was amazed "to see how warm and rapturous the Mob were in Mr Wilkes's Cause." The arrival of Beauchamp Proctor and Cooke inflamed them, and it seemed only by a stroke of luck that a riot was avoided. Wilkes's colors were blue, but so were those of Cooke and Beauchamp Proctor, which meant that it was very difficult to distinguish who was supporting who. In so chaotic a scene, all the mob could do was roar

"Wilkes and Liberty for ever!" as the candidates stared back at them from the hustings.[36]

The sheriffs nonetheless plowed on with the business of the day. A call of hands was demanded, and almost everyone pledged for Wilkes. The inevitable poll was then requested, and at two in the afternoon the books were opened and voters invited to step forward. An excitable, confused period of time followed. As names gathered in the books, the mob milled expectantly. With little to occupy them, they began to harry the locals. Drivers of coaches entering Brentford were stopped and quizzed as to whether they supported Wilkes. When they were satisfied a coach driver "was loyal to *Wilkes and Liberty, and heartily hated* Cooke *and* Beauchamp," the number 45 was chalked on the outside panels and the coach was allowed to pass. Confronted with such provocation, the hundred or so local constables were left terrified. There was little to protect the voters. To begin with, the candidates formed a lane around the stage, providing a space for the freeholders to come forward, but this soon disintegrated. "For the Mob," wrote one witness, "determining to have Wilkes elected, surrounded the Place, and rent the Air with, *Huzza* Wilkes, *and no* Cooke."[37]

Despite the intimidation, and despite the pledges given to the other candidates, it was clear that Wilkes had supporters pouring in from all directions. Many came on foot, but one party of twenty freeholders came up the Thames in barges. Alighting at Brentford, they processed to the booth in laced hats and jackets, preceded by a band and followed by a group of 130 others. Each cast their votes for Wilkes. As Proctor and Cooke watched nervously, more freeholders continued to appear. At length Cooke vanished. The rumor was that he had dashed into London in the hope of rousing last-minute support. In consequence he was not there at sunset when the flow of voters dwindled and the sheriffs made their customary proclamations, calling any remaining freeholders to come forward. When no one was forthcoming, they ordered the books to be sealed up so the tallies could be checked.

After an anxious night's sleep, the results were announced the following day:

Mr. Wilkes	1292
Mr. Cooke	827
Sir William Beauchamp Proctor	807[38]

A wave of astonishment rolled through the crowd. From a position of utter hopelessness, Wilkes had achieved one of the greatest reversals in political history. Climbing on to the hustings, he was invited to deliver a speech that would have seemed unimaginable just two months before:

> You Gentlemen, have shewn, that you are neither to be deceived nor enslaved. In proving yourselves enemies to ministerial persecution, the eyes of the whole kingdom, of the whole world, are upon you, as the first and firmest defenders of public Liberty. Happy shall I think myself, if, fired by your example, the efforts of my warmest zeal may be deemed an adequate return for the favours you have bestowed on me; but however insufficient my abilities, my will to serve you is as unbounded as it is unalterable.[39]

By the time he made this speech, however, the forces Wilkes had unleashed had taken on a life of their own. Ever since the election had opened in Brentford, a mob had been patrolling the London road. Along this Wilkes's supporters had instigated their own kind of law. The rules of passage stated that every coach had to bear the number 45, while those who rode inside must carry a paper with the words "Wilkes for ever, and no Excise." If anyone was foolish enough to object to this, their coach was smashed to pieces. Meanwhile flags began to appear proclaiming *More Meat and Fewer Cookes*.

Once Wilkes's election was confirmed, all order vanished. Moving back to the capital from Brentford, the mob arrived at the Duke of Northumberland's home at Charing Cross. Hammering at his door, they demanded he place candles in his windows to demonstrate his support for liberty. Terrified, the duke complied, and, in an effort to placate them, he sent out six barrels of beer. This may have been unwise, as the mob was now both encouraged and intoxicated. From Charing Cross one detachment marched toward Pall Mall, demanding that candles be shown in every building that they passed, or they would break all the windows. Soon candles were burning in houses belonging to everyone from the prime minister to the king's younger brothers, the dukes of Gloucester and Cumberland. All the time the streets were filled with cries of *Wilkes and Liberty!*

While this part of the mob frightened the well-to-do in Pall Mall, another marched eastward into the City of London. Arriving at the Mansion House, they managed to force their way inside, where they broke all the lamps and windows they could find. A chandelier, too, thought to be worth a hundred guineas, was smashed. Scrambling to contain the violence, the ministry ordered two companies of soldiers to be sent out from the Tower. Out of the blackness they came toward the Mansion House with their drums beating and their fifes playing "as loud as possible." A dreadful confrontation was only averted at the last minute by the brave actions of an alderman who ordered the soldiers to halt.

> He then came out of the Mansion House great Door with a Candle in each Hand, placed them on the Balustrades, pulled off his Hat, and huzza'd *Wilkes for ever!* And then addressed the Mob on the Impropriety of their zeal for Mr Wilkes's Success, and ordered what Candles could be procured to be immediately set out; He then represented to them that their present Conduct,

instead of serving Mr Wilkes, would irritate his Enemies, and greatly prejudice his Cause: In short, his prudent, resolute, sensible and affable Behaviour, effectually quieted the Mob: After which he quitted his Station with a Huzza for Wilkes and Liberty, which was re-echoed by the Mob, and no Mischief was done afterwards.[40]

That night, as the mob retreated, London's streets glowed with light. Candles, a symbol of English liberty, burned in window after window. When the sun came up the next morning, people saw the number 45 had been chalked across almost every pane of glass in Fleet Street. We can imagine the slogan too, on the fine new windows of the King's Printing House.

"I BELIEVE THERE NEVER was so much Noise and Confusion made about one Man in England before," reflected one Londoner in the days after the Middlesex election.[41] Indeed, if the newspaper's reports were to be believed then Wilkes's name was being sung on street corners and in alehouses across the country. In Wilkes's old constituency of Aylesbury, for instance, news of his victory had been greeted with "inexpressible joy."[42] The town bells had rung for twelve hours without pause, and every inhabitant had worn a blue cockade in their hat. In Newport on the Isle of Wight, a grand celebration had been held for forty-five freeholders, who had forty-five candles placed in the tavern windows while they gave forty-five huzzas. Similar stories came from Bath in the south to Newcastle in the north, and reports of Wilkes's triumph were circulated around the continent too. One young Londoner was given the task of rushing a report to Wilkes's friends in Paris. The story went that he was so desperate to reach his destination that he collapsed in a heap on arrival, with blood seeping through the knees of his breeches.

There were other, marvelous details. Someone pointed out that as the MP for Middlesex, Wilkes was now King George's democratic representative in the House of Commons, as his residence lay in the constituency. Others dwelt on the daring feats performed by the mob, which was playfully referred to as "their High Mightiness." On one occasion they had stopped the French ambassador in his coach and obliged him to drink a pint of porter to Wilkes and Liberty. The ambassador had complied "with the greatest affability."[43] Less sanguine, if the reports were to be believed, was the Austrian ambassador, who was said to have been turned out of his coach before having the number 45 chalked onto the soles of his boots.

But it is easy to overstate things. London was certainly a hotbed of Wilkites. Several other places—Exeter and Aylesbury, for example—were almost equally so. But neither the political nor logistical infrastructure existed to transfer the heady atmosphere of Brentford across all the many shires of England. In many county towns Wilkes had gained a smattering of enthusiastic supporters, but for all their zeal, and for all that their dinners and toasts were reported in the newspapers, their sentiments should not be confused with those of the wider community. Britain in the spring of 1768 was not primed like France in 1789, where the provinces would be just as ready to explode as the capital. Only the orchard counties like Dorset, Herefordshire, and Worcestershire, thanks to the cider tax, were truly restless. While much of the country loathed the idea of Bute's pernicious presence at the heart of government, they had not yet gone so far as to fully embrace a radical alternative.

Even so, for Wilkes's enemies that spring was a disturbing time. It evoked memories of 1763, when events had escalated quickly. If anything, this time it was worse. At least back then there had been a plan to neutralize Wilkes. Now the way forward was much less clear. There were clearly legal questions about what had happened at Middlesex, and there were the charges remaining from 1763, and the matter of Wilkes's outlawry too. But to arrest Wilkes now would be hazardous. In London he was shrouded by the protection of a public who saw deeper meaning in his struggle. Edmund Burke, who was astonished to see Wilkes carry the Middlesex election, was struck by the people's habit of being drawn "from abstract principles to personal attachments."[44] Liberty was all anyone could talk about, and Wilkes had become synonymous with the cause. It was there on every flag and in every toast: "Wilkes and Liberty!" The two had become inseparable. To imprison Wilkes would be an act of treason against the nation.

For many in Britain's elite, this was maddening. Charles Pratt, the judge who had been so helpful to Wilkes in 1763, was horrified. Now ennobled as Lord Camden, he expressed his disgust that such "a criminal should in open daylight thrust himself upon the country as a candidate, his crime unexpurgated." Johnson thought that Wilkes, "of whom no man speaks well," was beyond contempt.[45] King George, too, was said to be incandescent, privately raging that such a situation had been allowed to develop. With Pitt still in poor health and hidden away at his residence at Hayes, no one had grasped control. Politicians left Wilkes to be dealt with by Lord Mansfield, the judge who presided over the Court of the King's Bench. A date for a hearing on Wilkes's outlawry had been set for three weeks' time. Anticipating more disturbance, the ministry ensured that troops were stationed on high alert in the Tower of London, Savoy House, and the Tiltyard in Whitehall. According to the papers, the soldiers had been furnished with "sixteen rounds of ammunition" each.[46]

On April 20, Wilkes, as promised, attended the Court of the King's Bench in the Palace of Westminster to learn his fate. What transpired was underwhelming. Due to a technicality, the case was postponed. For a week the people were left to stew. During that time Wilkes's supporters were further riled to find that his name was not listed in the London Gazette as the returned member for Middlesex, and whispers circulated that Chatham had come to court to attend a grand council for the first time in months.

Such was the mood on April 27 when Wilkes came to court again. This time Mansfield refused Wilkes's application for bail and announced that, until his trial could begin, he was to be held at the King's Bench Prison. It was a predictable outcome. But it was also an inflammatory one. When the crowd outside the court saw Wilkes being escorted into a carriage, tempers began to flare. The prison was just a short distance away in St. George's Fields, on the south side of the river, but as Wilkes's carriage set off across Westminster Bridge toward Surrey, the mob went with it. Soon it was halted altogether. While Wilkes appealed for calm, a voice shouted out: "I tell you, Master Wilkes," it exclaimed, "horses often draw asses, but as you are a man, you shall be drawn by men."[47]

Overpowering the tipstaffs, the mob then unhitched Wilkes's carriage and drew it in the opposite direction, back through Westminster, up Whitehall, and along Charing Cross and the Strand toward the City of London. It was a magnificent, farcical parade that followed the route of Anson's triumph back in 1744. At the center of it, however, was not a returning military hero, but the hugely symbolic figure of Wilkes—the champion of liberty—being carried aloft by his supporters. Having reached the City, the procession kept going, into the streets of Spitalfields. Eventually it came to a stop at a tavern called the Three Tuns, where Wilkes was borne inside through a mass of jostling, shouting, singing bodies. At a top floor window, as once before in Great George Street, Wilkes appeared, to be cheered by the crowds.

Only when night fell was Wilkes able to escape. In disguise he crept through the capital, crossing the bridge to the southern banks of the Thames, before surrendering himself at the gates of the King's Bench Prison. "Many persons had fled disguised out of a *Prison*," one newspaper wrote in astonishment, "but Mr Wilkes is perhaps the first who ever stole disguised *into one*."[48]

Twelve

VOX POPULI

ON THE NIGHT OF Wilkes's election in March, Franklin saw the fury of the mob for himself. Craven Street was just seconds from Northumberland House, where the crowds had amassed. A fortnight later, he remained in disbelief. "'Tis really an extraordinary event," Franklin reflected to his son William, "to see an outlaw and exile, of bad personal character, not worth a farthing, come over from France, set himself up as candidate for the capital of the kingdom, miss his election only by being too late in his application, and immediately carrying it for the principal county."[1]

Franklin had seen much during his long years in the rough and tumble of Pennsylvanian politics, but never anything quite like this. The size of the crowds; their rage; their meaningful embrace of the number 45; their sheer audacity and total disrespect to people even of the highest class—all this was shocking. And not only did they seize control of the principal streets like Piccadilly, St. James's, or the Strand, they roamed through the "small cross streets, lanes, courts, and other out-of-the-way places," demanding everyone signal their support by illuminating their windows. People who blew out the candles too early were ordered to light them again. "Those who refused had all their windows destroyed." The infection, he told William, had spread far beyond London. In early April Franklin had traveled south-west to Winchester. For fifteen miles outside of the capital, "there was scarce a door or window shutter" beside the road that was not marked with *Wilkes and Liberty*. "This continued here and there quite to Winchester, which is 64 miles."[2]

Such a story might have thrilled Franklin in his younger days. Here he was, at the very center of the most important political movement of the day. He had seen one man subdue the might of the British state with nothing more than his personality and his pen. And those who had borne Wilkes through the streets were from Franklin's own leather-aproned class: the smiths, hatters, joiners. This wave of populism seemed like something out of a consular election in the late Roman Republic, not an event that belonged to polite British, enlightened society. Whatever it was, it left Franklin cold. The sight of Wilkes that spring aroused nothing other than disgust in him. In his April letter to William he described the scenes as being truly "horrible."[3]

For Franklin the Wilkes affair was unsettling not only for what it was, but for what it portended. America after the Stamp Act and the Townshend Duties was just as febrile as Britain. Might the same riots happen there? There had been rumors for years that Wilkes was about to migrate. The idea of him living among the austere Puritans in New England might be amusing, but even there he might be treated like a king. It was a long-established fact that what convulsed Britain would reverberate in America. It was like seeing the flash of a cannon and knowing that, after a pause, a boom would follow. Scores of letters would be making their way across the Atlantic, many of them destined to be printed in the newspapers for everyone to read, all of them full of fizz and color about Wilkes's astonishing triumph. What effect they would have when they arrived he could not tell.

Increasingly, in Franklin's eyes, Britain's poisonous politics were spoiling everything good about the country. Already the papers were anticipating another change in the ministry, with Pitt rumored to be making way for a returning Grenville. This was a thought to make Franklin's spirits plunge. Three and a half years had now passed since he had left Philadelphia, and, with his political embassy almost out of steam, he continued to make promises to Deborah about an imminent return. These were only ever half meant. Something always prevented him from packing his things and taking the road to Portsmouth. Part of this was his emotional connection to London, where he had "formed so many Friendships."[4] Another was a desperate hope he had that he might be able, somehow, to rescue the political situation. In the spring of 1768 he had heard from a friend that, with the creation of Hillsborough's new colonial department, he might soon receive some ministerial appointment.

Franklin was now in his early sixties. If he was ever going to attain true power then it had to come soon. Almost two decades had passed since he had introduced himself to European intellectual society with his thrilling work on electricity. Back then he had been at the head of a new generation of enlightened thinkers. Some of this glamour remained in 1768, but he was now undeniably an older man, much heavier than he had been in his working days and prone, too, to painful attacks of gout. More often than not Franklin found himself being used as a travel agent to introduce more energetic, younger colonials to British society.

The most recent case was of a clever medical student from Philadelphia called Benjamin Rush. Still only in his early twenties, Rush had appealed to Franklin for help as he set out to study at Edinburgh's renowned school of medicine. Franklin's influence had brought Rush magical opportunities. He had dined with the philosopher David Hume and the physician Alexander Dick, and he had kept Franklin cheerfully informed of his progress throughout. "It has been a great Pleasure to me to hear," Franklin wrote to Rush in March as Wilkes's election campaign was gaining momentum, "that you were closely engag'd in your Studies, and distinguishing yourself by the Progress you made in them. I promise my self that you will return with such a Stock of useful Knowledge as will render you an Ornament to your Country."[5]

There was an ambiguity to this last statement. Franklin might have marked Rush down to be a doctor. But he also seemed to sense greater abilities in this young man. Rush had an unusually powerful memory as well as a striking capacity for empathy. He was also intensely political. Not so many years before, like many other Philadelphians, he had despised "Dr. Franklin" for his apparent acquiescence in the Stamp Act. "*O Franklin, Franklin,*" he wrote, "thou curse to Pennsylvania and America, may the most accumulated vengeance burst speedily on thy guilty head!"[6] As the facts had become known, Rush had modified his opinion, but when he arrived in London from Edinburgh in 1768, Franklin could see that Rush's warmth in politics remained. One day he visited the House of Commons to see where Pitt had stood when he made his famous denunciation of the Stamp Act. After he was shown to the exact spot, Rush stood in silence for a moment, before he took a breath and started to recite the words of Pitt's speech from memory.

Extraordinary though Rush clearly was, he was also representative of the new generation of educated colonists who were making the journey to the mother country. These were quite different to the Americans of old repute. They were not the uncouth yokels of Swiftian satire. Instead they were cultured, well read, and intensely political. They were also not in awe of Britain as so many of their forebears had been. While Franklin nurtured Rush and watched disapprovingly as Wilkes's election absorbed the nation, he was introduced to another remarkable product of British America. This was a collection of artfully written, deeply researched essays that had started to appear in a new Philadelphian paper called the *Pennsylvanian Chronicle* at the end of 1767. Far better than anything that had come before, they argued that the chartered rights of the colonies were not mere courtesies, bestowed by the mother country. Instead they were the essential right of every British subject and vital to the smooth running of the Empire. The first of the essays opened with a brief character sketch of the author himself, who identified himself only as "the farmer."

> I am a farmer, settled after a variety of fortunes, near the banks, of the river *Delaware*, in the province of *Pennsylvania*. I received a liberal education, and have been engaged in the busy scenes of life: But am now convinced that a man may be as happy without bustle, as with it. My farm is small, my servants are few, and good; I have a little money at interest; I wish for no more: my employment in my own affairs is easy; and with a contented grateful mind, I am compleating the number of days allotted to me by divine goodness.[7]

Franklin's first acquaintance with what would become known as the *Farmer's Letters* must have been a curious one. The author's stance was familiar from *Poor Richard's*. Here was a sage, living a blameless life in an unspecified location on the banks of the Delaware. He is roused out of this Horatian ideal of honest country living by the press of events. This was the exact same device that Franklin had employed all those decades before. But unlike "Richard Saunders," the farmer was not there to poke fun. Nor would he be gazing into the future. Instead, for the greater good of his "beloved countrymen," he was going to coolly evaluate the behavior of Great Britain over the past three years.

Reading the *Farmer's Letters* for the first time, Franklin could be excused for almost hearing his own voice rising from the pages. If he did, he was not alone. On one of his visits to Lord Hillsborough at the colonial office, the letters came up in conversation. Hillsborough had been studying them too. He told Franklin, "they were well written, and he believed he could guess who was the author." As he spoke, Hillsborough gazed deeply into Franklin's face. It was, Franklin told his son William, "as if he thought it was me."[8]

FOR FRANKLIN THE AUTHORSHIP of the *Farmer's Letters* remained a perplexing mystery for several weeks. Having lived in Philadelphia for so long and served in its assembly for much of that time, he knew all the leading characters of the province. But he remained at a loss as to who could have produced such a well-argued and nimbly written series of essays. He had not heard of any of the names suggested by his son William. It was well into spring before Franklin's curiosity was satisfied. The man behind the letters, as it turned out, was someone he had cause to know well.

When he had left Philadelphia in 1764, John Dickinson had been one of the sharpest thorns in his side. An astute, vigorous lawyer in his thirties, Dickinson was one of the most effective members of the Penn family's "Proprietary Party." Although he had only been elected to the Pennsylvania Assembly two years before, he had not been awed by anything—and certainly not by Franklin. Indeed he had been staunch in his opposition to the proposal that Pennsylvania be taken over as a Crown colony, and the arguments became so heated that, once, he even challenged one of Franklin's chief allies to a duel. On another occasion he went after Franklin himself, protesting against his appointment as Pennsylvania's agent in fiery terms, regretting that the happiness of the province "should be sacrificed for the Promotion of a Man, who cannot be advanced but by the Convulsions of his Country."[9]

Words like these had haunted Franklin ever since. It was presumably the force of the invective that made it hard for him to believe, four years on, that Dickinson had written something so restrained, logical, and persuasive. Dickinson, however, was well capable of such a thing. He was an educated man. Like Rush he had undertaken a tour of Britain in the 1750s, studying law and constitutional history with the brightest young scholars at the Middle Temple in London. Ever since his return to America, he had worked with distinction as a lawyer, latterly in Philadelphia, where he was known as one of the most erudite and capable members of his profession.

From the start, his *Farmer's Letters* had a cool analytical quality. It was as if from his spot beside the Delaware the farmer had a better perspective on events than those in the heat of the towns and cities. His first letter examined Parliament's recent suspension of New York's Assembly. This was done in punishment for the colony's failure to fully comply with the terms of the Quartering Act. On what authority, Dickinson asked, was the assembly suspended? He framed the argument in logical terms. Either the assembly had a right to refuse to comply with the Quartering Act, or it did not:

> If they had, and I imagine no American will say, that they had not, then the parliament had no *right* to compel them to execute it.—If they had not *that right*, they had *no right* to punish them for not executing it; and therefore had *no right* to suspend their legislation, which is a punishment.[10]

As it was, it seemed that Westminster believed that New York's Assembly did have the legal right to refuse to comply with the Quartering Act, but in doing so they then placed themselves in opposition to the British Parliament, which, in consequence, punished them. What kind of system was this? Dickinson was worried, too, about the apathy of the other colonies. Since the New York Assembly had been suspended two others had sat and adjourned "without taking any notice," something that boded ill. "For the cause of *one* is the cause of *all*," he pointed out. "*To divide, and thus to destroy*, is the first political maxim in attacking those who are powerful by their union."[11]

Once again this was a sentiment that was bound to appeal to Franklin. Almost fifteen years before, he had agitated for colonial unity in the run-up to war with France. He had asked Hall to print his famous political cartoon, *Join or Die*, which advocated the very thing that Dickinson was arguing for here. The notion of the united colonies all under attack was a theme that ran through the *Farmer's Letters*. Until the 1760s, Dickinson contended, the situation had remained harmonious. Britain provided laws and protection. In return, raw materials flowed back across the Atlantic, generating wealth for the parent country. To maintain the dynamics of this relationship, the British government introduced legislation that sometimes prevented the colonies from developing manufactories of their own, and, from time to time, specific duties on distinct products to regulate the operation of the whole machine. Never before 1765, however, Dickinson stressed, had any tax been levied for the particular purpose of raising a revenue. Throughout the colonial period, Britain had been:

> engaged in fierce and expensive wars; troubled with some tumultuous and bold parliaments; governed by many daring and wicked ministers; yet none of them ever ventured to touch the PALLADIUM of American Liberty. Ambition, avarice, faction, tyranny, all revered it.[12]

This, Dickinson argued, was part of a pact. Britain would grow rich on the raw materials that were sent east across the Atlantic, but American liberty was to be preserved at all costs. This freedom was vital. It was a liberty that was both earned by the "immense emoluments" of the raw materials the colonists delivered to Britain, and inherited by the colonials as part of their birthright as British subjects. The most important part of their liberty was their property. It was every colonist's right, Dickinson elaborated, quoting scripture, "that they should sit *every man* under his vine, and under his fig-tree, and *none should make them afraid*."[13]

To Dickinson's mind, this was a pact that had held until the 1760s. Only with the coming of Grenville and the Stamp Act had it been challenged. Now, "a generous and humane people that so often has protected the liberty of strangers, is inflamed into an attempt to tear a privilege from her own children." If anything the Townshend Duties were worse than the Stamp Act. Whereas Grenville's pet scheme was a brazen violation, the duties that had followed it were sly. Since they were only small levies that applied to a few goods like glass and paper, they were easy for the colonists to accept. Those who did so, however, were being fooled into admitting that the British Parliament had the right to tax them in such a way. Dickinson's point, as ever, was the principle. In a rousing passage, he laid bare the facts of the matter:

> These duties, which will inevitably be levied upon us, and which are now levying upon us, are expressly laid for the sole purpose of taking money. This is the true definition of taxes. They are therefore taxes. This money is to be taken from us. We are therefore taxed. Those who are taxed without their own consent, given by themselves, or their representatives, are slaves. We are taxed without our own consent given by ourselves, or our representatives. We are therefore—I speak it with grief— I speak it with indignation—we are slaves.[14]

Reading this in Craven Street, Franklin was impressed. In his letters to William he retained a degree of caution. He owned himself "not yet the master" of some of Dickinson's arguments. What was the difference, he wondered, between Parliament's "regulating the trade" and "raising a revenue." This was a very lawyerly distinction. That aside, Dickinson had given clarity to his own thinking. For some time Franklin had been turning over the great question of Parliament's supremacy. Since the Stamp Act many views had been expressed, each of them seemingly more complex than the last. By now Franklin was beginning to see the issue in far simpler terms. He explained his reasoning to William: either Parliament was sovereign, as most Britons thought it was, and it had the power to make laws for America. Or it had no power to make any laws in America at all. Overall, he wrote, "I think the arguments for the latter more numerous and weighty than those for the former."[15]

While Franklin approved of Dickinson's logic, he liked his tone still more. In an acrimonious debate, Dickinson had done his best to write reasonably. The letters were filled with the kind of moderation Franklin used himself. "I hope," Dickinson wrote in one essay,

> my dear countrymen, that you will in every colony be upon your guard against those who may at any time endeavour to stir you up, under pretences of patriotism, to any measures disrespectful to our sovereign and our mother country. Hot, rash, disorderly proceedings, injure the reputation of a people as to wisdom, valour and virtue, without procuring them the least benefit. I pray God, that he may be pleased to inspire you and your posterity to the latest ages with that spirit, of which I have an idea, but find a difficulty to express: to express in the best manner I can, I mean a spirit that shall so guide you, that it will be impossible to determine, whether an *American*'s character is most distinguishable for his loyalty to his sovereign, his duty to his mother country, his love of freedom, or his affection for his native soil.[16]

The appearance of this allied voice reassured Franklin. Ever since the Stamp Act, he had often felt marooned in London, as if it was his particular, peculiar destiny to be making America's case alone. Now reports kept arriving in Britain, speaking of Dickinson's newfound popularity in the colonies. In March a collected volume of all twelve letters had been published as a pamphlet in Boston. Heartened, Franklin took it upon himself to see a London edition through the press. On May 8, he wrote a foreword for the first British edition of the *Farmer's Letters*. In it he emphasized the importance of rational debate. "Whenever there is any News of Discontent in America," he reflected, "the Cry is, 'Send over an Army or a Fleet, and reduce them to Reason.'"

> I hope *Britain* is not so choleric, and will never be so angry with her *Colonies*, as to *strike* them: But that if she should ever think it *may be* necessary, she will at least let the *Word* go before the *Blow*; and reason with them.[17]

The publication of the *Farmer's Letters* was a significant moment in Anglo-American relations. For the first time Franklin felt able to step back and let one of his countrymen press the arguments instead. The result was encouraging. The two-shilling pamphlet sold briskly and "quickly circulated through coffee-house and drawing room."[18] It was also notable for another reason. Despite Franklin's involvement, the *Farmer's Letters* were not printed, as might have been expected, by William Strahan at Little New Street.

FOR ALL THE TALK about liberty, it was still a concept that people struggled to adequately put into words. English liberty, for some reason, was something that was far easier to picture than explain. It was the broad open landscape, the mill pond and cider press; the maypole and parish oak, the ale house and the village green. All these things symbolized freedom, longevity, and honest, undisturbed enjoyment. To drift into such a landscape was to escape the eyes of tax collectors and the laws of corrupt politicians. Many Londoners cherished visions like this. Often they were only first- or second-generation urban dwellers themselves, and many had been raised in the countryside or provincial towns. For them, as for Johnson in his much-cherished poem *London*, the city had become a malign, sickening, tyrannical space, at odds with rural England, where true liberty continued to reign free.

There every bush with nature's music rings,
There every breeze bears health upon its wings;
On all thy hours security shall smile,
And bless thine evening walk and morning toil.[19]

Such evergreen thoughts had added meaning in London in early May. For as Franklin worked on his foreword to the *Farmer's Letters* in his Craven Street lodgings, he would have seen out of his window a steady flow of people cutting through his street toward Westminster Bridge. Crossing the Thames, they would follow the New Road to Lambeth Marsh and then down toward St. George's Fields. This was an undeveloped stretch of green countryside, more than a mile across in all directions. For Londoners it was a place of resort in the summer months: somewhere to picnic, to play, to gather flowers or wade in one of the ponds that were dotted here and there. But that spring there was a different reason for crossing the river. For at the eastern edge of St. George's Fields, near the junction of Blackman Street and Dirty Lane, there stood the King's Bench Prison, the latest home of John Wilkes.

The presence of the prison cast a shadow over this otherwise inviting landscape. Recently rebuilt, it stood on the edge of the open fields, a tall brick structure with its outer grounds divided from the neighboring countryside by a great semicircular wall twenty feet high. If the open fields nearby stood for freedom and escape, the King's Bench Prison embodied the absolute opposite. Ever since their hero had arrived here of his own volition on April 27, the prison had been a site of pilgrimage for his supporters. Outside, people chanted "Wilkes and Liberty" and swapped stories about the day of the Middlesex election. Sometimes the euphoria showed itself in striking ways. The papers reported the story of two pregnant ladies, who, "passing the King's Bench Prison, a sudden Fit of *Longing* seized them to see Mr Wilkes!" Gaining access to his cell, they greeted each other, "with a civil Salute, they drank a Glass to *mutual speedy and happy* DELIVERY, and so parted, highly satisfied with each other."[20]

Such levity characterized the mood outside the prison in the early days of May. The scene resembled a fair. Among the laborers, sailors, tailors, porters, and ordinary Londoners of all types were many women and children, all of them running races, singing ballads, and participating in what William Prentice, the prison's turnkey, called "mountebank performances," in the spring sunshine.[21] The size of the gatherings, however, unsettled the authorities. During that first week a military presence began to shadow the civilian one. News came from the Tower of London that two soldiers had been flogged "in a very severe manner" after being seen among the mob. This punishment told a story of its own. Not only were the ministry nervous. The lines between protestor and protector were dangerously indistinct.

As the days wore on, and there was no change in Wilkes's status, the crowds began to grow restless. Several rumors were in currency. One suggested that the ministry had decided to postpone Wilkes's trial for as long as possible, in order to keep him out of the new Parliament, which was due to meet on May 10. "Whether they will succeed or not," pondered one newspaper,

and whether the same System of Politicks will still be pursued, which has already produced such a hideous Train of Evils; and from a prosperous, united and happy People, has filled us with Jealousy,—Discontent,—and Animosity;—reduced us from Affluence to a State of general Poverty, and driven us to the Verge of Ruin and Despair; or whether *this System*, or the *Old English Constitution* shall any longer exist, will greatly depend upon the prevailing Temper of the new Parliament, the Discovery of which is waited for with anxious Solicitude.[22]

This "anxious Solicitude" was not conducive to civil harmony. On Saturday, May 6, Wilkes was returned to the King's Bench Court for another hearing on his outlawry. At this, Mansfield confirmed that no progress could be made until the next appointed day on June 8.

The news of this was taken as a confirmation that the ministry was indeed trying to keep Wilkes out of the new Parliament, which would open in just four days. By now the mood in St. George's Fields was beginning to turn. One night a small mob pulled up a run of wooden rails that enclosed a walkway outside the prison and built a bonfire. On top of this they burned a boot and a bonnet, the symbols of Bute and Augusta. Once the fire had died down, they then toured the neighboring streets and yards, compelling people to illuminate their windows. Along with the ubiquitous cries of "Wilkes and Liberty!" people began to hear a more sinister one: "It's as well to be hanged as to starve."[23]

Throughout the century mobs had risen in London at times of strife, but this sustained show of popular protest was unusual. On May 8, while Franklin was writing his foreword in Craven Street, they seemed ready to test their strength. That day the crowd outside the prison was the largest yet. They roared for Wilkes's release and threatened to pull down the roof of the marshal's house. The people were conciliated to some degree by Wilkes himself, who appeared at the window of his cell. He shouted out, telling the mob to disperse, which they started to do. But at that moment their attention was caught by someone. This person, unlike everyone else, was expensively dressed, and that made him conspicuous. Worse, he was found to have a Scottish accent. At this the mob turned on him. They angrily accused him of speaking offensively of their hero and demanded that he sink down on his knees and shout out, "Wilkes and Liberty!" Satisfied, they then threw him into a nearby pond.

As the opening of Parliament approached, tensions rose further. To prohibit a freely elected MP from taking his seat seemed an almost impossibly outrageous slur on the constitution. Yet for almost three weeks this was what the ministry had been preparing to do. On April 22, the Duke of Grafton, who had become one of the leaders of the government in Pitt's absence, had informed the king that it was their conviction that "Mr Wilkes should not be allowed to sit in

Parliament, if it could be avoided by any means justifiable by Law."[24] George could hardly have been more supportive of this stance. Writing to one of his favorite young ministers, Lord North, he expressed his belief that expelling Wilkes from the House was "highly proper."[25] To the king's mind, Wilkes had dashed every last hope of reprieve on his most recent appearance at the King's Bench. Instead of showing contrition for his behavior in 1763, "he had declared number 45 a paper that the author ought to *glory in*, & the Blasphemous Poem, a mere Ludicrous production."[26] For such a man, the king felt certain, there was no way back.

There was none of this clarity among the crowd outside the King's Bench Prison. As the spring sun rose on the morning of Tuesday, May 10, it was said that St. George's Fields "wore a more military appearance" than "any day since the Revolution."[27] Thousands had gathered there, anticipating some development on the day Parliament was due to open. Once again rumors swirled among the crowd. One suggested that Wilkes was about to be released. Another was that a plan had been hatched to storm the prison and set him free. This, at least, explained the heightened military presence. At least a hundred troops belonging to the Third Regiment of the Foot Guards—a predominantly Scottish regiment—had arrived to keep the peace. This would be a sizeable detachment in normal times, but its numbers were nothing in comparison to the crowds who had come to see Wilkes, which were estimated to be twenty thousand strong. The early morning passed uneasily. While the crowd was irascible, the soldiers were equally prickly. It was later said that they treated the people roughly, "pushing at and wounding them with their bayonets." Eventually a determined few broke through the cordon around the prison and pasted a sheet of paper onto the wall. Signed "Philo Libertatis, No 45," it contained a brief poem that opened:

> *Venal judges & Ministers combine*
> *Wilkes and English Liberty to confine*[28]

As the paper was torn down, the crowd began to jostle. The common chant "Wilkes and Liberty!" gave way to more incendiary language: "Damn the King!" "Damn the government!" Some people later reported hearing the word "Revolution" for the first time.[29] It was now that the delicate truce between Wilkes's supporters and the soldiers, which had just about held for the past fortnight, buckled and broke. Jostling turned into fighting. Stones were thrown, and a justice of the peace ordered the riot act to be read.

This had no effect. Instead of quelling the crowd, the justice himself was struck by a stone that was flung by a man wearing a red coat. In the roar of action, a squad of soldiers set off in pursuit, away from the prison and into Blackman Street, where he vanished into the mill of the traffic. The soldiers ran into the road, catching sight of a red coat as it disappeared into a cow house beside the Horse Shoe Inn. Hurrying inside, the soldiers cornered the man then shot him dead. Whether they realized their mistake at once is uncertain. But the truth dawned quickly enough. The boy they had shot was not the man who threw the stone. He was William Allen, the innkeeper's lad, "a hopeful and very promising Youth of 19 Years of Age."[30]

Back in St. George's Fields a fraught situation had developed. Panicked by the size and temper of the crowd, the soldiers attempted to seize control by force. Guns were fired. Quite who they were aimed at was a mystery. The bullets struck at random. As well as firing into the heart of the mob, they cut down people in nearby fields, and passersby on the high roads. Two dozen fell in the smoke. Most were just wounded, but at least five lay dead. Among these was a man called William Bridgeman who was shot through the chest while he was filling a hay wagon. A lady named Mary Jeffs was killed beside her orange cart. Another, a drayman's wife called Margaret Walters, who was seven months pregnant, was trampled in the melee. Both Margaret and her baby died the next day.

As news of these killings spread through London, it was accompanied by the claim that the violence had been instigated by Scottish guards. It was them, after all, who had pursued Allen and provoked the crowds beside the prison. And while these "North British" soldiers might have been responsible for the murder itself, it was Bute who had managed everything from afar. It was he who had to take responsibility for the events of May 10, 1768, which would pass into history as the "St. George's Fields Massacre." During the week that followed, civil order collapsed.

In Craven Street, Franklin saw it all. Four days after the massacre he wrote a letter to one of his friends in the Pennsylvania Assembly. "This Capital," he lamented in one of the most forceful passages in all his letters:

> the Residence of the King, is now a daily Scene of lawless Riot and Confusion. Mobs are patrolling the Streets at Noon Day; some Knocking all down that will not roar for Wilkes and Liberty; Courts of Justice afraid to give Judgment against him; Coalheavers and Porters pulling down the Houses of Coal Merchants that refuse to give them more Wages; Sawyers destroying the new Sawmills; Sailors unrigging all the outward-bound Ships, and suffering none to sail till Merchants agree to raise their Pay; Watermen destroying private Boats and threatning Bridges; Weavers entring Houses by Force, and destroying the Work in the Looms; Soldiers firing among the Mobs and killing Men, Women and Children, which seems only to have produc'd an universal Sullenness, that looks like a great black Cloud coming on, ready to burst in a general Tempest. What the Event will be God only knows: But some Punishment seems preparing for a People who are ungratefully abusing the best Constitution and the best King any Nation was ever blest with, intent on nothing but Luxury, Licentiousness, Power, Places, Pensions and Plunder. Meanwhile the Ministry, divided in their Counsels, with little Regard for each other, worried by perpetual Opposi-

tions, in continual Apprehension of Changes, intent on securing Popularity in case they should lose Favour, have for some Years past had little Time to attend to great National Interests, much less to our small American Affairs, whose Remoteness makes them appear still smaller.[31]

WILKES LISTENED TO THE confrontation from his cell. Although he was unable to see exactly what was happening, the commotion was clearly audible. The sounds that surrounded the prison in the days before May 10 were like, he told his friends, that of a military encampment. "Such was the din and clashing of arms, such the neighing and trampling of the cavalry." On May 10 itself he had listened to "the marches and counter-marches of the troops, their divisions and subdivisions, the foot advancing, attacking and afterward pursuing . . . the horse at full speed, galloping backwards and forwards." With all the gunshots, it seemed to Wilkes as if it was a day of battle, "and the people the enemies, not the unarmed dutiful subjects of a gracious king at full peace with them . . . Such a day," he wrote in despair, "has not been in England since the accession of the mild house of Brunswick."[32]

The events outside the prison walls inflamed a situation that was, for Wilkes, already extraordinary. Since he had arrived at the prison in late April, he had been half king, half captive. Though his liberty had been taken away, he had lived in more opulent style than for many years past. His old friend Cotes had led the way with the presents, sending a large quantity of fine wines. These had been followed in early May by the delivery of a large turtle, the first to arrive in England that year. Finding his pantry sufficiently stocked and with plenty of visitors wishing to see him, Wilkes had thrown a splendid turtle feast for his closest supporters. Together they toasted English liberty with glasses of burgundy, claret, and Madeira. "[I] was as gay as you ever saw me," Wilkes wrote to a friend.[33]

Wilkes's public life was conducted from his prison cell. This time his conditions were nothing like 1763 when he was kept closely guarded in the Tower of London. Now he had access to whatever he could afford, and chief among his requirements were paper and ink. His first move, as the opening of Parliament approached, was to compose an open letter to his constituents in Middlesex. In this he expressed his intention to represent them as well as he could, in spite of the cruelty of those who wished to silence him. "In this prison, in any other, in every place," he wrote, "my ruling passion will be the love of England and our free constitution. To those objects I will make every sacrifice."[34]

Wilkes's letter soon found its way into the newspapers. It was followed by another piece—anonymous though easily detectable as by the same hand—that condemned the massacre and traced the blame for it back to Bute's office in Westminster, "from whence it is known, that every order of importance, even every hint of what is to be done, has for several years issued." Five years after the *North Briton* ceased publication in the spring of 1763, Wilkes's sentiments about Bute and his pernicious influence on the king were unmodified. Having manipulated the king, Bute had directed the soldiers "to kill the English, like flocks of sparrows, in absolute wantonness, without pity or remorse."[35]

The ferocity of Wilkes's prose belied the delicacy of his situation. While he was a hero to the masses, there was still much for him to fear from English law. He remained in a legally complicated situation. He was concurrently an outlaw and an elected MP. As well as this, Wilkes had yet to be sentenced for the two counts of libel of which he had been found guilty while on the run in February 1764. But as an outlaw Wilkes could not receive these sentences because, in legal terms, he lay outside the bounds of English law. The picture was confused still further by a raft of countermoves on Wilkes's part, since he was still attempting to somehow bring charges against Halifax for his role in the affair of 1763, and had discovered irregularities with the manner in which his outlawry was pronounced the following year.

It was the work of the courts over the late spring and early summer to make sense of such a tangled state. The first problem to be resolved by the Court of the King's Bench was Wilkes's outlawry. On June 8, it was nullified on a technicality. The wording of the proclamation in 1764 had been imprecise, referring only to "the county court," when the full phrase "the county court of the county of Middlesex" was required. Wilkes's supporters were exhilarated by this judgment, which was celebrated by "great illuminations and rejoicings."[36] But the news was not altogether bad for Wilkes's enemies. Now he had been readmitted as a citizen, he could legally receive his sentence for libel. On June 18 he again set out from St. George's Fields on the increasingly familiar journey to court.

While Wilkes was so often bellicose, on this day he seemed nervous. In a report prepared for the king, one member of the ministry recorded that Wilkes was fractious and "indecent" throughout. His attempts to affect "Ease & Indifference by picking his Teeth & talking to those near him" were wholly unconvincing. The reason for this was clear enough. That day Wilkes was fined £500 for producing the *North Briton* No. 45 and £500 more for the *Essay on Woman*. In addition, each of the libels was punished by a year's imprisonment—making a total sentence of twenty-two months, once the two months he had already spent in jail had been taken into consideration. "He was reconducted," explained the king's report, to St. George's Fields, "& by a little Management Things went off quietly, notwithstanding great Pains taken by his Friends to stir up & prepare the Mob for the Event of this Morning."[37]

Wilkes, who had done so much to define this decade, was now to end it in prison. It would be the spring of 1770 before he could walk London's streets again. Despite this, he was not entirely eradicated from political life. With St. George's Fields so close to the Palace of

Westminster, people could always feel his presence. In captivity, he was about as potent a living symbol of English liberty as there could possibly be. Indeed, in a curious sort of way, there was something almost regal about Wilkes's circumstances. He lived in a fortress patrolled by troops. He ate luxurious food, entertained guests, and received petitions from an endless stream of admirers. One that especially caught Wilkes's attention arrived in July. It came from the Committee of the Sons of Liberty in the town of Boston in Massachusetts, and it had been written when the news of his election in Middlesex had reached America.

This "memorial" explained that forty-five friends of liberty had gathered at Boston's Whig Tavern in honor of Wilkes, "the illustrious patriot." They viewed him as an "incomparably honest man reserved by heaven to bless and perhaps save a tottering Empire." It was signed by a list of names that were new to Wilkes—Benjamin Kent, Thomas Young, Benjamin Church, John Adams, and Joseph Warren—and it was full of stirring sentiments:

> That the British Constitution still exists is our Glory, feeble and infirm as it is, we cannot, we will not despair of it.—To a Wilkes much is already due for his strenuous efforts to preserve it. Those generous and inflexible principles which have rendered you so greatly eminent support our claim to your esteem and assistance.—To vindicate America is not to desert yourself.
>
> Permit us therefore much respected Sir to express our confidence in your approved abilities and steady Patriotism. Your Country, the British Empire, and unborn millions plead an exertion, at this alarming Crisis.—Your perseverance in the *good old cause* may still prevent the great system from dashing to pieces.[38]

Enclosed with this was a copy of the *Farmer's Letters*. "His sentiments are ours," the writers laconically explained. Thrilled that his reputation had extended so far, Wilkes replied immediately. He declared his commitment to America, reassuring his friends in Boston that:

> As a member of the Legislature, I shall always give a particular attention to whatever respects the interests of America, which I believe to be immediately connected with & of essential moment to our parent country, and the common welfare of this great political system. After the first claims of duty to England, and of gratitude to the County of Middlesex, none shall engage me more than the affairs of our Colonies, which I consider as the *Propugnacula imperii*, and I know how much of our strength and weight we owe to and derive from them.
>
> I will ever, Gentlemen, avow myself a friend to universal liberty. I hope freedom will ever flourish under your hemisphere as well as ours, and I doubt not from your spirit & firmness that you will be carefull to transmit to your posterity the invaluable rights and franchises, which you receiv'd from your ancestors. Liberty I consider as the birthright of every subject of the British empire, and I hold Magna Charta to be in as full force in America as in Europe. I hope that these truths will become generally known and acknowledg'd thro' the wide-extended dominions of our Sovereign, and that a real union of the whole will prevail to save the whole, and to guard the public liberty, if invaded by despotic Ministers in the most remote equally as in the central parts of this vast empire.[39]

This reply marked a shift in the story. The Wilkes affair had started with a modest objective. In 1762, Lord Temple simply wanted him to rile a political opponent in the *North Briton*. An opportunist, Wilkes had found, when he came under attack himself, that his best mode of defense was to identify himself with the cause of English liberty. Just how honestly and deeply he held the views he championed repeatedly in his speeches and essays is a question that remains tantalizingly open to this day. Was he a true purist? Or did he seek to shield a wretched personal life behind a glorious cause?

Whatever we might decide, the reality is that across the Atlantic Ocean in the 1760s, Wilkes came to be viewed as a hero. His story—the plundering of his house, his imprisonment, his exile and bankruptcy—was interpreted as a cautionary tale. Every twist and turn of his return in 1768 and eventual triumph at Middlesex was enthusiastically followed in British America, where toasts were offered up to him from Boston to South Carolina. As the Harvard professor Bernard Bailyn evaluated it two centuries later:

> John Wilkes's career was crucial to the colonists' understanding of what was happening to them; his fate, the colonists came to believe, was intimately involved with their own. Not only was he associated in their minds with general opposition to the government that passed the Stamp Act and the Townshend Duties, that was flooding the colonies with parasitic placemen, and that appeared to be making inroads into the constitution by weakening the judiciary and bestowing monopolies of public offices on pliant puppets—not only was he believed to be a national leader of opposition to such a government, but he had entered the public arena first as a victim and then as the successful antagonist of general warrants, which, in the form of writs of assistance, the colonists too had fought in heroic episodes known throughout the land. He had, moreover, defended the sanctity of private property against confiscation by the government. His cause was their cause. His *Number 45 North Briton* was as celebrated in the colonies at it was in England, and more generally approved of; its symbolism became part of the iconography of liberty in the colonies.[40]

There was another lesson from the Wilkes Affair. It was that taking risks and standing up to authority could bring great rewards.

There were many examples of this: Wilkes's damages cases against the government officials, the reversal of the outlawry, and, most triumphant of all, the result at Middlesex in March. It was this spirit that was needed, not just in the streets of London, but in the most distant corners of the Empire, if modern Britain was not going to descend like Ancient Rome into a state of tyranny. For those, like John Adams and the Sons of Liberty in Boston, or John Dickinson in Philadelphia, who thought in such terms, it seemed as if a broad and energized movement was rising in defense of the old ideals. This was a movement with a cause (liberty), with a leader (Wilkes), an intellectual figurehead (Macaulay), a set text (the *Farmer's Letters*), a series of martyrs (those killed at St. George's Fields), and some clearly identifiable enemies (Lord Bute and George Grenville).

This was a movement that had not existed with clarity before. And as the letters between Wilkes and the Sons of Liberty in Boston suggested, it was a movement and a cause that transcended national borders. Franklin's protégé, Benjamin Rush, saw the truth of this. Visiting Wilkes in the King's Bench Prison, he found him "one of the most entertaining men in the world," full of enthusiasm for American Liberty. During dinner, Wilkes told Rush that "if you can but preserve an equality among one another, you will always be free in spite of everything . . . He inquired in a particular manner after Mr Dickinson," Rush added. "His *Farmer's Letters*, he says, are superior to anything of the kind that was ever published in any age or country." Rush's evening in the prison ended with a succession of toasts:

"His Majesty and all the Royal Family!"
"Liberty to the British Empire!"
"The Pennsylvanian Farmer!"
"Number 45!"[41]

Happiness

(1771–1776)

Thirteen

A STRANGE DISTEMPER

ON AN AUGUST AFTERNOON in 1771, Benjamin Franklin climbed into a coach outside his home in Craven Street. A short and familiar journey lay before him: up the gentle incline past Northumberland House and Charing Cross, then through Haymarket and Piccadilly before cutting northward into the fashionable neighborhood of Mayfair, toward Berkeley Square.

More than six years had now passed since Franklin's return to England. And despite his many promises to Deborah and all his friends in Market Street, there was little to suggest he was going to bring his third spell in London to an end any time soon. Whereas in Philadelphia this was by now, quite rightly, feeling like a case of abandonment, in London Franklin sought to justify his long-continued residence. For a long time there had been suggestions he was about to be drafted into government in some sub-ministerial position. There were times when this seemed very likely to happen. Nothing, though, had come of it. For all Franklin's undoubted talents, the reality was that he was not trusted by Lord Hillsborough, the secretary for the colonies.

According to William Strahan, the mistrust went further than that, Franklin being "not only on bad Terms with Lord Hillsborough, but with the *Ministry in general*."[1] After all the mixed messages, Franklin had reconciled himself to the situation by 1771. The government was going to do nothing for him. Even so he lingered on in London. Explaining himself, he reflected that he had lived, "so great a Part of my Life in Britain," that to leave it was a melancholy prospect.[2] There was so much activity in London and so much to learn out in the shires whenever he traveled to view some exciting new industry or meet with some learned friend. Britain was only a slight place in comparison to America, Franklin once said. The island was hardly more than "a stepping Stone in a Brook, scarce enough of it above Water to keep one's Shoes dry." But this island, he continued, enjoyed, "in almost every Neighbourhood, more sensible, virtuous and elegant Minds, than we can collect in ranging 100 Leagues of our vast Forests."[3]

That afternoon, Franklin was traveling to Berkeley Square to dine with a group of just such people. His destination was John Pringle's house. Pringle was an old friend. Like Franklin, he was now in his sixties and a veteran of the scientific and political establishments. A Scottish medical man of the highest standing, for the past decade he had been the physician in ordinary to Queen Charlotte. Pringle had come to know Franklin in the 1750s through their shared connection to the Royal Society, the preeminent scientific club which had awarded both of them its prestigious Copley Medal.

Now older men, Pringle and Franklin retained their zest for science. Franklin in particular was still known as an avid follower of the latest fashions as well as remaining something of a tinkerer himself. This part of his personality was most visible in the bamboo cane he carried with him during these years. Secreted inside the hollow upper cavity of this cane Franklin kept a little oil. He had long been interested in the ability of the substance to calm turbulent waters. With the help of the cane he was able to delight his friends with a parlor trick. On finding a pond or lake, he would upend his cane and let the oil trickle out onto its surface. To the uninitiated onlooker, watching as the water stilled, it was as if Franklin had the ability to calm the waves, just as he could snatch lightning from the sky.

John Pringle was too wily a bird to be taken in by such trickery, but it was the sort of thing that would make him smile. For years they had met up to chat about science, politics, and the running of the Royal Society, often over an afternoon's game of chess. But this Sunday was different. As Franklin climbed the steps to Pringle's house he may well have done so with an extra spring of anticipation, for the sages were to be joined by two of the most sought-after guests imaginable: Joseph Banks and Dr. Daniel Solander.

FOR MONTHS EXCITEMENT HAD been mounting in London, as news of an astonishing voyage was reported in the papers. This was an expedition that had started three years before, when everyone was distracted by John Wilkes and St. George's Fields. Back then a ship, the *Endeavour*, had left Britain for the South Seas, as the Pacific Ocean was then known. Its principal objective was to observe and measure a rare solar event, the Transit of Venus, which promised to unlock several secrets of the universe. Because of the voyage's scientific character, the Royal Society was involved in preparations, and in an unprecedented move, the *Endeavour* sailed with a party of naturalists aboard.

Leading this party, and covering the expense, was a young, handsome, Oxford-educated gentleman named Joseph Banks. Banks was known for his mania for botany. He was said to have spent ten thousand pounds equipping his team with instruments that would help with their scientific research. "No people ever went to sea better fitted out for the purpose of Natural History, nor more elegantly,"[4] it was reported. Banks's scientific party was fortified at the last minute by the addition of a Swedish employee of the British Museum, a botanist called Daniel Solander who had previously studied in Upp-sala under Carl Linnaeus.

For years no one had heard anything of the *Endeavour*. But then in the spring tantalizing reports started to surface. After many ad-ventures and despite several near disasters, it seemed that the ves-sel was safe. On July 12, the ship's captain, a Yorkshireman named James Cook, had anchored off the Downs. Ever since, the voyage had been the greatest story in town. The papers were filled with capti-vating tales of emerald islands and coral seas, encounters with un-known peoples and enchanting beasts. Having been faintly involved with the voyage at its outset, through his connection to the Royal Society, Franklin was far ahead of the general tattle. But even for someone like him it was difficult to properly establish the facts of what had happened until he managed to talk to Banks himself. And for weeks Banks's time was entirely consumed with social engage-ments and the unloading of what seemed to be his quite spectacu-lar collections—tens of thousands of pressed plants, animal skins, shields, shells, ceremonial dresses, and books of drawings—which were being transported to his Mayfair house on New Burlington Street. One thing, however, was plainly clear. At twenty-eight, hand-some and appealingly rich, Banks was a new kind of intrepid, scientific hero for modern Britain. Now, at Pringle's house, Franklin had the opportunity to hear the exhilarating stories for himself.

The conversation, predictably, centered on the most enticing places the voyagers had visited. As *Endeavour* was preparing to sail in 1768, the news had arrived of the European discovery of an enchant-ing green island in the very center of the Pacific Ocean. In homage to the young king, the British sailors had soon named it George's Island, and the *Endeavour* had departed carrying orders to make it the location for their observations of the Transit. Banks and Solander confirmed that they had found the island and spent six fascinating weeks there.

To Franklin and Pringle, who had been stuck in smoky, bad-tempered London, this place must have sounded like a utopia. To its people it was called Otaheite.* It was shaped like a figure of eight, with handsome, verdant hills rising up from sandy beaches. Sitting under coconut trees, the voyagers were able to glance up toward the cloud-topped heights or out to the turquoise shallows, which were protected from the ocean by outlying reefs. There, sipping "cocoa-nut milk,"[5] they watched as the islanders splashed and dived in the water with amazing dexterity. This was detail to engage Franklin, whose own aquatic feats were still a matter of pride. Particularly inspiring was the description of an Otaheitean sport, where the is-landers floated on planks of wood in the shallows, waiting for a wave that would propel them triumphantly in toward the shore.

This was delightful to hear, but when Franklin came to write up his account of the dinner, he focused more on the character of the people Banks and Solander had encountered. On Otaheite, the *En-deavour*'s crew camped ashore and lived in close and constant contact with the islanders. Banks had compiled a detailed survey of their manners and customs. He told Franklin he believed them "civilised in a great degree." They lived in a structured, hierarchical society not unlike England's old feudal system with various ranks from royalty at the top to the working people at the bottom. They all lived under one "supreme God" and several "inferior Gods." These divinities had their own temples, built for their convenience "when they happen to come down among Men."[6]

More intriguing still to Franklin was the islanders' behavior. London was already alive with rumors that Banks and Solander—along with many of the common sailors—had enjoyed intense, amorous

---

* Not until after James Cook's second expedition (1772–75) would the voyagers real-ize that the "O" in Otaheite was an article rather than a true part of the island's name, "Tahiti."

relationships. "Their Morals are very imperfect," Banks confirmed, "as they do not reckon Chastity among the Virtues, nor Theft among the Vices." Franklin was particularly struck by one of Banks's more salacious observations. "They had no Idea of Kissing with the Lips," Franklin was told; "it was quite a Novelty to them, tho' they lik'd it when they were taught it."[7]

This detail stayed with Franklin. Like most people who lived in Georgian Britain, he was especially interested in ideas concerning pleasure. And here was a place in which pleasure seemed to abound, a place that brought real meaning to Rousseau's fashionable writing about the human spirit. "MAN was born free, and he is everywhere in chains,"[8] Rousseau had famously written in 1762. But this did not seem to be the case in Otaheite. As Banks explained it, the people there retained a powerful connection to nature. Despite the feudal character of their society, they continued to travel freely. "They have a considerable Knowledge of the Stars," Banks and Solander elaborated, "sail by them, and make Voyages of three Months westward among the Islands." When the Endeavour's crew had shown the islanders all their "Advantages" of art and science, "they were of Opinion after much Consideration that their Condition was preferable to ours."[9]

The people of Otaheite were not the only ones Banks and Solander had met. Over the months and years that followed, Endeavour had charted the two islands of a faraway land called New Zealand, where they had encountered the Māori, "a brave and sensible People." From there, confronted with the dilemma of how to get home, Cook decided to continue west. Soon after they fell in with another uncharted coastline, of a land known only as New Holland. There they were almost wrecked on a tremendous coral reef. Their experiences here were perplexing for Banks. Ashore, they found none of the spirit of Otaheite and none of the proud belligerence of the Māori. In contrast, in the place known today as Australia, the Endeavour's crew were shunned. Their presents were ignored. The people had no interest in the material wealth and technological prowess of the Europeans. Banks recounted one story:

> Finding 4 Children in a Hut on one Part of the Coast, and see-
> ing some People at a distance who were shy and would not be
> spoke with, we adorn'd the Children with Ribbands and Beads,
> and left with them a Number of little Trinkets and some useful
> Things; then retiring to a Distance, gave Opportunity to the
> People to fetch away their Children, supposing the Gifts might
> conciliate them: But coming afterwards to the Hut, we found
> all we had left, the Finery we had put upon the Children among
> the Rest.[10]

Returning to Craven Street, Franklin was left to dwell on this. He lived a minute's walk from the Strand, one of the great marts of the world. This was a street of dreams, its shops filled with prod-ucts that promised to improve life in every conceivable way. And yet the Indigenous people of New Holland, when presented with objects they had never seen before, were indifferent. "We call this Stupidity," Franklin ruminated in his account of the dinner in Berkeley Square. "But if we were dispos'd to compliment them, we might say, Behold a Nation of Philosophers! Such as him whom we celebrate for saying as he went thro' a Fair, *How many things there are in the World that I don't want!*"[11]

Franklin was not alone in this thinking. In the years ahead he would meet James Cook, the impressive lieutenant who had com-manded *Endeavour* on this audacious voyage. Cook was a more low-key character than Banks. He had also puzzled over the behavior of the people they encountered. It was easy in this enlightened age, Cook believed, to deride them as "the most wretched people upon Earth," but there were different ways of interpreting their demeanor. In a passage in his voyaging journal, he speculated that "in reality" he believed them to be far more happier than we Europeans; being wholy unacquainted not only with the superfluous but the necessary Conveniences so much sought after in Europe, they are happy in not knowing the use of them. They live in a Tranquility which is not disturb'd by the Inequality of Condition: The Earth and sea of their own accord furnishes them with all things necessary for life, they covet not Magnificent Houses, Household-stuff &cᵃ, they live in a warm and fine Climate and enjoy a very wholsome Air, so that they have very little need of Clothing and this they seem to be fully sensible of.[12]

ALL THESE YEARS AFTER he had passed on the *Pennsylvania Gazette* to David Hall, Franklin still loved the buzz of a news story. In a puckish mood at the Stevensons' house the previous year, he tried to rekindle some of the old excitement of his Market Street days by launching a spoof title called the CRAVEN STREET GAZETTE. This lampooned the various characters in the household: Margaret, his landlady, Franklin himself, and several assorted others. It distilled into humorously familiar courtly language their comings and goings, their whims and eccentricities:

> This Morning Queen Margaret, accompanied by her first Maid of Honour, Miss Franklin, set out for Rochester. Immediately on their Departure, the whole Street was in Tears—from a heavy Shower of Rain.
>
> It is whispered that the new Family Administration which took place on her Majesty's Departure, promises, like all other new Administrations, to govern much better than the old one.
>
> We hear that the *great* Person (so called from his enormous Size) of a certain Family in a certain Street, is grievously affected at the late Changes, and could hardly be comforted this Morning, tho' the new Ministry promised him a roasted Shoulder of Mutton, and Potatoes, for his Dinner.[13]

Here was the instinct for a story that had driven Franklin for so long during those years in Philadelphia, when the highlight of the week was the arrival of a colorful letter from London with a ship's captain. Decades later in Craven Street, this instinct remained. One can see it in his account of that afternoon at Pringle's in Berkeley Square as he tries, like any determined journalist, to elicit more and more detail about the voyage from Banks and Solander. Here is Franklin at work on a story; determined to tease out the most stimulating, revealing information, and to interpret its meaning before anyone else.

Franklin's report of the dinner would not be released in a newspaper, but it would go into a private letter to his friend Jonathan Shipley, the Bishop of St. Asaph. From this account it is clear that, of all the elements of the *Endeavour* story, Franklin is most interested in the opportunity the voyage has presented for comparing very different modes of living. The three great areas of encounter—the South Sea Islands, New Zealand, and New Holland—had generated three unique chances for Britons to measure their own society against ones that were fundamentally different. Just how old these societies were was anyone's guess, but it appeared from the evidence they were very much established in their ways. Living in contrasting climates at the far side of the world, they were nonetheless biologically the same, or at least similar, creatures to those that strolled around the ring in Hyde Park. They were at once familiar and alien. The question this raised for Franklin was the same one James Cook had driven himself to ask when *Endeavour* was sailing away from the New Holland coast. Were these people happier?

It was a quirk of history that the ship that had borne Franklin's father to Boston in the 1680s was likely called *Endeavour*. Back then, like so many others, the Franklins were escaping religious persecution as they sailed to the sanctuary of New England. For centuries up until that point, the purpose for most people in Christendom was to live a pious and meaningful life according to the directions of Scripture. This was a life pleasing to God that fortified his kingdom on earth and opened the gates of Heaven. But as Josiah Franklin was riding on the Atlantic swell, forces were building deep in English philosophy. John Locke was among the proponents of a new conception of life. Humans, he affirmed in 1677, were creatures adrift in a mysterious, incomprehensible universe. There was a futility to this state. No one could possibly know the nature of the sun or the stars, and even "the consideration of light itself leaves us in the dark." Even if we could know this:

> they would be of no solid advantage to us, nor help to make our lives the happier, they being but the useless employment of idle or over-curious brains, which amuse themselves about things out of which they can by no means draw any real benefit.
>
> So that, if we will consider man as in the world, and that his mind and faculties were given him for any use, we must necessarily conclude it must be to procure him the happiness which this world is capable of.[14]

In passages like this, Locke was representing one of the most profound and consequential shifts in Western thought. While humans lacked the capacity to understand, he argued, they certainly possessed the capacity to enjoy. To look around was to see that God had provided all the raw materials people needed for the better enjoyment of life. Rather than perplexing themselves about "the original frame or constitution of the universe" or "building hypotheses, obscure, perplexed, and of no other use, but to raise dispute and continual wrangling," Locke thought people should "trouble their heads with nothing but the history of nature, and an inquiry into the qualities of the things in the mansion of the universe that hath fallen to their lot." By "directing their thoughts," he argued, "to the improvement of such arts and inventions, engines, and utensils, as might best contribute to their continuation in [the world] with conveniency and delight, they might well spare themselves the trouble of looking any further."[15]

Locke was one of a number of writers to express this argument toward the end of the seventeenth century. The social conditions of the time were such as to make it more powerful. For almost two centuries Europe had been convulsed by conflict between Catholics and Protestants, religious wars that had shattered the unifying clarity of the Christian vision in the West. Meanwhile a series of scientific advances, from Galileo to Newton, Hooke to Harvey, had demonstrated how much progress in knowledge could be attained in the present day. The daily reality of human life really could be improved. Hitherto, hardship had been accepted as a constant feature of temporal existence. Before this time most people had had no access to medical care, and few had enjoyed much leisure. Death frequently came suddenly, through sickness, hunger, accident, or war. Earth was commonly described as a vale of tears, a sordid place that lay beneath the glimmering uplands of the celestial sphere. The very idea of seeking happiness in this life was ludicrous.

By the mid-seventeenth century, these old notions were beginning to be challenged. A decisive shift came in the 1650s, when the English Civil War swept away not only a monarch, but many other certainties about the way life was to be lived. In these years it was possible to find Gerrard Winstanley, leader of the Digger movement, asking, "Why may not we have our heaven here . . . and heaven hereafter too?"[16] Winstanley's argument might well have been laughed at a few decades earlier, but as the century wore on, it became more persuasive. Advances in medicine promised a degree of protection from illness and pain. New agricultural techniques helped to stimulate food production and released people from the backbreaking business of subsistence farming. A new word, "fun," entered the English language as a way to describe a particularly modern sensation that could be experienced at the pleasure gardens or in the theater. As people flocked to the cities from the countryside and global trading networks gathered the produce of the world for sale in shopping streets like the Strand, what Darrin M. McMahon has called the "great reorientation of the human gaze—from the joys of heaven to the happiness of earth," gathered pace.[17] By the time Franklin came to London in the mid-1720s, the old obsession with the afterlife had been to a great degree supplanted by a new ideal, an ideal that was to be the guiding principle for an ever-increasing number over the years ahead: the pursuit of happiness.

When Britons talked of happiness in the eighteenth century, their conception of the word was subtly different to how we understand it today. Happiness was not usually thought of as a transient emotion, experienced intensely for an ephemeral moment or a distinct period of time. Instead it was visualized as a prolonged, settled state of being. In his *Dictionary* Johnson described happiness as the "state in which the desires are satisfied." He expanded this definition with a quotation from the sixteenth-century theologian Richard Hooker:

> *Happiness* is that estate whereby we attain, so far as possibly may be attained, the full possession of that which simply for itself is to be desired, and containeth in it after an eminent sort the contentation of our desires, the highest degree of all our perfection.[18]

There was an amorphous quality to the word, as these desires might vary from person to person. One individual might covet health, another money, a third domestic affection, and a fourth might desire a sense of professional accomplishment. There was none of the prescriptive certainty of religion. This fact stimulated a huge amount of writing throughout the eighteenth century on what constituted true happiness, and how it could best be obtained. Opinions differed wildly. For John Wilkes it meant a maximum of personal freedom, in everything from sex to creative expression, just so long as the body and the bank could keep up. Other gentlemen evoked the ideals of Epicureanism, which promoted a lifestyle in which pleasure was enjoyed in a modest and civilized manner. This was the stance taken by the writer Edward Gibbon, for instance, who liked to repeat a line of the thirteenth-century monarch Alfonso the Wise of Castile: "Old wood to burn, old wine to drink, old friends to converse with and old books to read."[19]

No so long ago the pursuit of happiness had only been a concern of a tiny number at the top of the social hierarchy. Henry Fielding had pointed out as recently as the 1750s that

> To be born for no other Purpose than to consume the Fruits of the Earth is the Privilege (if it may be called a Privilege) of very few. The greater Part of Mankind must sweat hard to produce them, or Society will no longer answer the Purposes for which it was ordained. *Six Days shalt thou labour*, was the positive Command of God in his own Republic.[20]

But as the century wore on, this belief faded. Works like Franklin's *Poor Richard's* and Hogarth's *Industry and Idleness*, for instance, invited people of all classes to think about how they might acquire happiness.

In 1768 the *Annual Review* printed a long report of a boisterous meeting in one of London's great "disputing" clubs. "As these are places where all persons have admittance at a very moderate expence," the *Review* noted, "it is not to be wondered at, if there is a great diversity in the manners and characters of the speakers." The topic of the day was happiness. The question in particular was "If happiness be in our power, in what state of life is it most easily acquired?"[21] The opening speaker made a passionate case for self-reliance. He declared himself a happy man and explained that this happiness came from his heart. It was as simple as that. Another debater maintained that money was the thing that mattered. People should apply themselves to making as much of it as possible so they could lift themselves free of the things—work, sickness, subservience—that create unhappiness.

A third speaker proposed, in true Enlightenment spirit, to apply the power of reason to the question. Taking for his starting point that "the universal passion is the *love of fame*"—an axiom that he believed had been established beyond question in Edward Young's poem of the same name—he theorized that to be happy, a person had to acquire fame. The means of doing so, he continued, differed from one country to another. In warlike nations it meant having military prowess. In more gentle countries fame might come from the polite arts, learning, or success in commerce. In Great Britain, he revealed, there was one particular cause that eclipsed all others:

> What is it that we pant after in this country:—Liberty. What is the favourite wish and solace of our hearts?—Liberty. What is the surest road to fame in this country?—To signalise one's self in the cause of liberty. He, therefore, who has the best opportunity of signalising himself in the cause of liberty, is the likeliest man to be happy in his own mind, and that *particular station in life which gives the greatest and most striking opportunities of signalising one's zeal in that glorious cause, must of course (in this country at least) be the state in which happiness is most likely to be found.*[22]

Following his logic doggedly to the end, the speaker concluded that to have the greatest chance of happiness in Britain, it was best to choose a job as either a printer or a coalheaver, as these were two professions in which it was easiest to "signalise" oneself in the cause of liberty. All a printer needed to do was to dash off a pamphlet championing liberty and a rush of approval would come back their way. A coalheaver, meanwhile, had only to join one of the many marches that his fellows undertook in the name of liberty. A degree of fame would arrive as soon as he was spotted in the street. Happiness would follow.

Skittish pieces like this were bound to amuse Franklin, who, as it happened, had long ago argued in one of his brilliant, trenchant *Gazette* editorials that printers were condemned to a "peculiar Unhappiness," as they were frequently caught in the middle of disputes.[23] This may have been so, but otherwise it was said that Franklin had a particular "talent for happiness." In 1766 he had explained how he attempted to maintain his own contentment, despite all the disturbances and criticism that came his way, in a letter to his sister Jane. His trick, he explained, was to maintain a sense of balance. Writing at the time of the Stamp Act Crisis, he fell back on a meteorological metaphor:

> It sometimes is cloudy, it rains, it hails; again 'tis clear and pleasant, and the Sun shines on us. Take one thing with another, and the World is a pretty good sort of a World; and 'tis our Duty to make the best of it and be thankful. One's true Happiness depends more upon one's own Judgement of one's self, on a Consciousness of Rectitude in Action and Intention, and in the Approbation of those few who judge impartially, than upon the Applause of the unthinking undiscerning Multitude, who are apt to cry Hosanna today, and tomorrow, Crucify him.[24]

There was, of course, much more to Franklin's perspective than Stoic resilience. In the weeks before he had met Banks and Solander at Pringle's house in August 1771, Franklin had spent an enjoyable few weeks in Twyford in Hampshire, at the country residence of the Bishop of St. Asaph. Out of town, in congenial surroundings, and with time to fill, there he had started on something of a voyage of his own. It was not, like the *Endeavour*'s, a voyage across geographical space, but a journey back through linear time. Franklin had decided to write his own story. "Having emerg'd from the Poverty & Obscurity in which I was born & bred," he explained in the opening lines, "to a State of Affluence & some Degree of Reputation in the World, and having gone so far thro' Life with a considerable Share of Felicity," he concluded it was time to commit his story to paper.[25]

So began a piece of writing that would develop over the years to become Franklin's *Autobiography*, a work that is now considered his most famous literary production as well as being the founding classic of American literature.* In those days at Twyford, in a burst of creative energy, Franklin completed twenty-three sheets that took his story from his birth up to the year 1730. Contained within these pages were many magical scenes from his Copperfieldish tale—his austere beginning as a clever, wilful, bookish boy in Boston; his acrimonious and sometimes violent relationship with his brother James; his decision to run away and his memorable entry into Philadelphia when he had strolled blithely up Market Street on a Sunday morning, filthy after his perilous journey, and with a bread roll tucked beneath each arm. It was at this moment, Franklin confirmed, that Deborah Read, his future wife, had laid eyes on him for the very first time.

In the *Autobiography* Franklin was not only developing a new literary form, he was documenting a new approach toward life. Franklin portrayed himself as the star of an Enlightenment story: undertaking more and more complex projects, generating an increasing amount of wealth, and acquiring ever-greater levels of happiness as the years passed. Franklin's was a story of progress, a microcosm of Britain's own history since the Glorious Revolution. In his own picaresque tale, Franklin was demonstrating to everyone who lived under the country's constitution, who enjoyed liberty of conscience and move-

---

* Franklin's *Autobiography* is the opening work to feature in the first volume of Charles W. Eliot's *Harvard Classics* works of literature, speeches, and historical documents (otherwise well known as Dr. Eliot's Five-Foot Shelf of Books), published in 1909. Interestingly, Franklin referred to his book as an "Account of my Life" rather than an "autobiography"—that word only being coined in 1797. Writing in the *Monthly Review* (a title originally printed by Strahan) for December that year, a journalist apologized for using the term "*Self-biography*," explaining, "it is not very usual in English to employ hybrid words partly Saxon and partly Greek: yet *autobiography* would have seemed pedantic." Nevertheless, the term caught on and Jared Sparks, the first great compiler of Franklin's papers in the nineteenth century, saw fit to apply it to his "account."

ment, just what they could achieve with a measure of application and skill. For Franklin the belief that happiness was more easily attained in Britain than anywhere else was central. But as he sketched out the opening pages of his *Autobiography* in the summer of 1771, he had more and more reason to doubt himself.

SOME WEEKS EARLIER, ON June 4, King George had celebrated his thirty-fourth birthday. To mark the occasion the Royal Academy, which had been established by the king in 1768, celebrated with an illumination of the royal coat of arms at Somerset House. This spectacle was ruined, however, when a mob carrying fireworks had set part of the house ablaze. The fire at Somerset House was the latest in a succession of dramas. Earlier in the spring, rotten fruit had been thrown at the king's golden carriage in Westminster. A rowdy crowd had likewise gathered on April 1 at Tower Hill, bringing with them two carts in which were seated effigies of George's mother, Augusta, and Lord Bute. According to Walpole these were "beheaded by chimney-sweepers, and then burnt."[26]

There was something unsettling about all this. Edmund Burke would describe the atmosphere in London as being a "strange distemper."[27] It was strange because so many of the conditions necessary to happiness were present at the time. Most reasonable people regarded King George as a decent, diligent, Christian monarch. He was certainly no tyrant. Equally, following the victories of the Seven Years' War, Britain had become a recognized and wealthy global power, whose future looked bright. And yet there was an unease in London, a restlessness that all too often and all too quickly became violent. Over the years, in his letters to his friend in Philadelphia, William Strahan had sought to explain this perplexing mood. "The Singularity of our present Situation is this," he confided to Hall in March 1770, "that while there is actually no National Dissatisfaction existing, our Newspapers are filled with nothing but the most daring and unprecedented Attacks upon the Ministry and the King himself."

These were the victims of a populist propaganda campaign, Strahan believed, behind which was "an Inconsiderable Junto of Men."[28]

Strahan was by now in a position to make such a claim. As King's Printer he now had complete liberty of the House of Commons *ex officio*, which allowed him to watch any debate he pleased. A wealthy man, he was also invited to dinner parties by politicians who wanted to court him. "I am to dine today," he wrote to Hall a few days after the king's birthday on June 8, 1771, "with some of our Great men, who are in the Secret of Affairs."[29] Strahan blamed four specific groups for the political tensions. First was the people themselves, "the Canaille of this City," who he thought had "grown insolent beyond all Example." They had been driven on by the actions of a second group, made up by powerful politicians like the Lords Temple, Camden, and Chatham, who were all scheming to regain their places.

Strahan's suspicions about Chatham, who he believed to be "playing an Artful and factious Game, in order to push himself into Power,"[30] ran particularly deep, and he saw how the former prime minister manipulated a different tier of politicians. These, the third of Strahan's groups, was made up of those who held power in London's municipal government. They included Catharine Macaulay's brother, John Sawbridge, who had been elected as a sheriff of London; and William Beckford, the old lord mayor, whom Strahan described in explosive terms, as "a bold and ready tool in the Hands of Lord Chatham, equal to the most daring and hazardous Service, whose Assurance could not be daunted, and whose Thirst after political Mischief was unquenchable."[31]

But none of these were in Strahan's eyes as malign an influence as those who met at the London Tavern, calling themselves "the *Supporters of the Bill of Rightes*," and their leader John Wilkes. The damage this one man had done, Strahan thought, was extraordinary. Even jail had not quieted him. In January 1769, while still incarcerated, he had been elected an alderman of the City of London in a move Strahan thought disgraceful. Shortly after, once his expulsion from the House of Commons had been confirmed, he entered himself once again as a candidate for Middlesex. In February 1769 he had been reelected unopposed, upon which he was expelled once again. "I am quite sick of Politicks," Strahan had written to Hall as Britain was thrown into a constitutional crisis. "Whilst the Legislature hath many important Matters to attend to, which require immediate Discussion, the Commons were employed all last Week, night and day (for they sat every Day till 2, 3, or 4 in the Morning, upon that pitiful Fellow Wilkes." As testament to the peculiarity of the situation, Strahan had watched George Grenville voting in Wilkes's favor, dejectedly telling his colleagues that it was better "in order to quiet the Minds of the Public" to let him have his way.[32]

Once again Wilkes's fate had become the dominating issue of public conversation. Even Samuel Johnson, who had tried to ignore him, had ventured an opinion. "THAT a man was in jail for sedition and impiety," he argued, "would, I believe, have been within memory a sufficient reason why he should not come out of jail a legislator."[33] Wilkes was, however, returned for a third time in April 1769, and this time the ministry responded by having him declared "incapable of being elected a member." This done, his seat was surrendered to the second-place candidate, Henry Lawes Luttrell. "With regard to Mr Wilkes," as Strahan relayed the news to Hall,

> and those contemptible Fellows who with the most unheard of Audacity have erected themselves into a Tribunal of Enquiry into the Conduct of all the Branches of the Legislature, I need not repeat to you what all our Newspapers have been stuffed with for many Months past. You will doubtless be astonished at their Boldness, and the Lenity or Forbearance, or Timidity, or—what shall I call it?—of the Ministry. It is indeed equally unaccountable and unprecedented.—However, their Operations seem now to be nearly at an end. Wilkes, as I foretold in my Letter of March 11, is thrown out of the House of Commons,

and Lutterel, tho' he had few votes, declared duly elected in his Stead.[34]

Strahan was of an optimistic cast of mind, and at the close of each of these little episodes he was inclined to think that Wilkes's support was about to fizzle out. He enthusiastically passed on an anecdote to Hall in November 1770, when one of his acquaintances had bumped into the newly liberated alderman, who had told him that he himself was "*pretty well . . . but damnably sick of Wilkes and Liberty.*"[35]

But Wilkes's career was not finished yet. In June 1771, as Franklin was following news of the *Endeavour*'s return, Strahan was informing Hall of Wilkes's latest electoral success as he became one of the two sheriffs of London. This made him responsible, of all things, for the administration of justice in the capital. Strahan was unperturbed. "All this signifies nothing," he told Hall. "The Spirit of Faction must gradually subside for want of Fuel; for in reality we have no Grievances worth naming to complain of."[36] A bigger concern for Strahan was the state of affairs in America. On June 15, 1771, as he composed his latest letter to Hall, he had a copy of the *Pennsylvania Gazette* open before him on his desk. "In the second Page of which," he complained, "there is hardly a Paragraph that is not diametrically opposite to Truth."

> From that and such like Papers, one at a Distance who had no other Means of Information must naturally conclude that we are here in a State of the utmost Distraction, and just at the Eve of some grand Convulsion. Whereas the real Truth is, we are in perfect Peace and Tranquillity, nor any Complaint heard, unless of the present Dearness of Provisions, which nobody lays to the Account of the King or his Ministry.[37]

Here Strahan was engaging with a vital point. The hysterical nature of the newspapers' stories could be countered rationally by someone who was on the spot in London. But in the colonies the more lurid reports of secret meetings in the king's closet or sinister schemes against liberty championed by Bute or Augusta, or the latest prime minister, Lord North, could pass without challenge, and as Strahan realized were widely believed. Reading the *Gazettes* that made their way to Little New Street, filled with reports of unconstitutional taxes, the Wilkes affair, the swarm of placemen that were being sent from England, he could see how all of these were taken as evidence of "a deliberate assault of power upon liberty."[38]

This worried Strahan. Despite all of his hopes, Britain's relationship with the colonies had never returned to the harmonious state of the days before the Stamp Act. He was irritated, too, by the scheming of Edmund Burke, whose speculative writings had served to exacerbate the hostility. Burke's pamphlet *Thoughts on the Cause of the Present Discontents* had been published on St. George's Day the previous year. Rather than scotch the theory of a ministerial conspiracy against liberty, Burke had given weight to it. In Burke's analysis a malevolent cabal that had infiltrated government was responsible for all the strife in contemporary politics. Styling themselves "the King's Men" or "King's Friends," they had subverted the natural flow of power between the monarch and his ministers and, ultimately, undermined the constitution. "The Cabal," Burke explained, thinking not only of Bute but a group of sinister, self-interested operators, "have established a sort of *Rota* in the Court":

> All sorts of parties, by this means, have been brought into Administration, from whence few have had the good fortune to escape without disgrace; none at all without considerable losses. In the beginning of each arrangement no professions of confidence and support are wanting, to induce the leading men to engage. But while the Ministers of the day appear in all the pomp and pride of power, while they have all their canvass spread out to the wind, and every sail filled with the fair

and prosperous gale of Royal favour, in a short time they find, they know not how, a current, which sets directly against them; which prevents all progress; and even drives them backwards. They grow ashamed and mortified in a situation, which, by its vicinity to power, only serves to remind them the more strongly of their insignificance.[39]

Many people in Britain and America were convinced by Burke's diagnosis. One person, however, was not.

A YEAR BEFORE THE *Endeavour*'s return had brought crowds to Deptford docks, another Thames-side spectacle had captured the attention of Londoners. The *Duchess of Gordon* was a transatlantic merchant vessel, the kind of merchant that carried commodities like tea, paint, and glass—the products Charles Townshend had targeted with his duties—from British manufactures to American consumers. On this day in August 1770, though, the *Duchess of Gordon* was a ship transformed. Her commander, Captain Winn, had ordered her to be decorated with flags and streamers, which were slung from mast to mast, across the yards and along the gunwales. On the ensign staff, instead of the usual red flag, Winn had raised one depicting the ancient form of Liberty with her "insignia," supported on one side by the Historic Muse and the other by Fortitude.

That day the *Duchess of Gordon* was to play host to a dinner in honor of Winn's guest, Catharine Macaulay. As she stepped into a barge to be rowed aboard, Macaulay was met by a group of musicians who began to play Handel's *Water Music*. This continued until the barge came under the ship's stern, at which another shipboard band struck up another Handel favorite, *See, the Conqu'ring Hero Comes!* This, in turn, developed into *Rule, Britannia* as the historian climbed aboard. As Macaulay, tall, thin, still not yet forty, reached the captain's cabin, the *Duchess of Gordon*'s cannons were discharged in her honor.[40]

In the summer of 1770 Macaulay's popularity had reached a new peak. Along with the public displays of affection, like the one accorded by Captain Winn, Macaulay was in great favor with the press. The July edition of the *London Magazine* led with a fulsome tribute to "that celebrated Lady":

> for notwithstanding many women may at this day equal her in private excellencies, her literary abilities render her an honour to her sex, and give her that kind of pre-eminence, that is beheld with reverence and acknowledged with delight; for . . . when we find an . . . instance, where to the domestic virtues are superadded the powers of uncommon perspicuity; we place it in the most conspicuous point of view, and unite astonishment to approbation.[41]

This article was preceded with a tender copper-plate print of Macaulay, dressed in the character of a matron, "lamenting," as the accompanying caption put it, "the lost Liberties of Rome." The cause for all this adulation could be found in the spring of 1770, when Burke's *Thoughts on the Cause of the Present Discontents* had appeared. Westminster watchers had marked this down as an important moment. For the first time since the days of the *North Briton*, a high-ranking insider had exposed the corruption that was hobbling British politics. Burke was no ordinary insider, too. Over the past dozen or so years, he had demonstrated his remarkable mind in a series of books, pamphlets, and speeches, combining analysis and eloquence in a way that had led people to think of him as the "modern Cicero."[42] For him to attack the King's Party in a public pamphlet was no small matter.

Burke had brooded over the pamphlet for at least a year and, perhaps wisely, had decided not to put his name on the title page when it was released. His authorship was soon guessed at, however, and soon people were marveling over his elegance, bravery, and incisive mind. Macaulay was not so impressed. Not long after Burke's pamphlet went on sale, Macaulay's own followed. Briskly titled *Observations on a Pamphlet, Entitled, Thoughts on the Cause of the Present Discontents*, Macaulay had no such qualms including her name on the cover. The venom inside was suggested by a Shakespearean quote, aimed squarely at Burke and planted on the title page. "Assume a Virtue, if you have it not." Her conclusion, she explained, was that Burke's was a "baneful" production.

> To the disgrace of human nature, and the plague of society, an able head and an honest heart are but too often separated. The pamphlet in question is written with great eloquence, acuteness, and art; but its fine turned and polished periods carry with them a poison sufficient to destroy all the little virtue and understanding of sound policy which is left in the nation.[43]

To Macaulay's mind, Burke had been insincere. Rather than honestly examine the problems of Britain's political system, he had merely attributed all its shortcomings to a blanket theory of political conspiracy in "the dangerous designs of a profligate junto." Was this really the case, or was Burke trying to oust a set of men for his own political convenience? What about the true evils? The national debt? The soldiers billeted on the people? The corrupted armies of place-men and pensioners, "whose private interest is repugnant to the welfare of the public weal"? The septennial parliaments and the heavy taxes? Burke had nothing to say about any of these. But Macaulay believed that each of them were the hallmarks of a nation ruled not by liberty but tyranny. To Burke these were necessary evils, "rather to be supported than abolished," an attitude that revealed him to be a creature of tyranny just as much as the others. Macaulay had gone further than this. Her attack had not just centered on Burke, but on all conventional Whigs. Their conviction that the Glorious Revolution had produced the greatest political system known to man, she argued, was misguided. Instead it had been flawed from its beginning. Britons had no more perfected politics, she argued, than anyone else.

Macaulay's pamphlet was an audacious performance. In the seven years since her *History* first appeared, she had come to be seen as a purist: uncorrupted, virtuous, and patriotic. People across the country had evoked her spirit with toasts to "Mrs Macaulay,"[44] and newswriters had made it a habit to seek out her thoughts on the story of the day, much like a modern political commentator. The previous year, for instance, when it was said that the ministry were thinking of suppressing the freedom of the press to combat Wilkes's supporters, the *Bath Chronicle* reported that "Upon the above subject Mrs Macaulay makes this very just and sensible observation: 'There is not, says this historian, a more certain mark of an *ill-designing*, or *important administration*, than attempts to *restrain the liberty of speaking or writing.*'"[45]

Moments like this charted Macaulay's transformation from scholarly historian into active political agitator. Both of these states were completely novel for a woman at the time, and although Macaulay no longer had the protection of being married to a wealthy and respected medical man, she continued to benefit as much as anything from the singularity of her status. Everyone knew who she was, and her reputation was not confined to literary circles. Lord Lyttelton, the old chancellor of the exchequer, remarked that pictures of her were on "every print-seller's counter," while one letter to the newspapers, written in dismay at the "INNS and OUTS" at the top of politics, playfully suggested that "Mrs. Macaulay" be given a turn as "First Lady of the Treasury—because she despises money, and has a sufficient resource in her own genius."[46]

In the spring of 1770, her attack on Burke enhanced her standing yet further. Here she was squaring up to the intellectual champion of the day, combating eloquence with reason and insinuations with cold, clear facts. Her pamphlet, however, was not just a critique of Burke. In it Macaulay reassured her readers that a truly moral political system—one that safeguarded the "peace, happiness and dignity of society"—was possible. "The wisdom of man is fully adequate to the subject," she wrote. "It would be unworthy the idea we ought to form of God, to suppose him so capricious a being as to bestow that high degree of wisdom and ingenuity" on people, while not rendering them equal to forming "regulations so necessary to [their] security, happiness, and perfection."[47]

Macaulay's rejoinder to Burke raced through several editions. Copies of it were carried across the Atlantic too, where her *History* had been allowed a "free sale" despite the import ban on British books. It was reported that "the Ladies of America in particular read her History with great Avidity, and speak of her with the greatest Applause."[48] Macaulay had been kept abreast of this by a steady flow of letters from colonial correspondents. From Philadelphia came admiring letters from Franklin's young protégé, Benjamin Rush, and John Dickinson, while in Boston she formed a connection with the lawyer James Otis. Admiring Otis's vigorous campaign against the British governor, Macaulay had sent him a specially bound copy of her *History*. Soon afterward she received an appreciative reply, praising her writing and describing in additional detail the British treatment of the colonists, which he described as being as violent and rapacious as that of the infamous Verres of Sicily, whose prosecution for a rule of plunder and terror in the first century BC had ignited the career of a young lawyer named Cicero.

OVER THE WINTER OF 1769–70, Macaulay's health had started to falter. In the early spring of 1770 she took the decision to leave Berners Street. For Macaulay and her five-year-old daughter, there was to be a complete change. She placed a notice in the newspapers, announcing that all her household possessions were to be auctioned, and that she was, "on account of her Health, retiring into the Country." Among her supporters this ad generated a flutter of disquiet. The news was reported as far away as Charleston, where the *South-Carolina Gazette* clarified that the reason for her leaving town "is entirely from indisposition . . . She means," the paper added, quenching local gossip, "to make her residence at Hampstead, and not in America; though we believe so illustrious, so patriotic, a female would only meet that respect from the noble Americans her merits entitle her to."[49]

The indisposition these reports referred to was not fully explained, though Macaulay's health cannot have been helped by the workload of the last decade. In that time she had been married and widowed; she had become a mother, published four volumes of an immense literary project, and run a political salon at Berners Street. After such a time, the pure, gentle air of Hampstead with its open heaths was bound to appeal. It was perhaps the prospect of such a revitalizing change that filled Macaulay with the spirit to begin her *Observations*.

An even more powerful prompt, however, came into her hands around the start of May. This was a package from Massachusetts. Inside was a pamphlet, *A Short Narrative of the Most Horrid Massacre in Boston*. On Monday, March 5, a party of seven or eight British soldiers, under the command of an officer called Captain Preston, had apparently, "without the least warning of their intention," opened fire upon the people in a central thoroughfare called King Street. It was, the pamphlet explained, a "horrid transaction," that "has occasioned the greatest anxiety and distress in the minds of the inhabitants." Three people had been killed on the spot, another had since died from his wounds and several more were dangerously and "some it is feared mortally wounded."[50]

For anyone who had lived so recently through the St. George's Fields Massacre, it took little imagination to picture the events of that day. Nonetheless the pamphlet was enlivened with a dramatic woodcut of the "murders." It was a dismal scene. The view looked straight down King Street, with shops and elegant townhouses on either side and a church at the end. Here the artist, a man called Paul Revere, had divided the sides in two. To the right were the scowling British soldiers with their guns leveled at the crowd on the left-hand side of the street. Revere had frozen the action a moment after the guns had discharged. A disorientating cloud of smoke was filling the air. Already two men were lying dead and a third was being heaved up from the floor. Even as desperate rescue attempts were going ahead, the commander of the troops—presumably Captain Preston himself—kept his sword raised, urging his men on.

Along with this pamphlet, which had seemingly been produced in haste in the days following the killings, was a frantic letter. Addressed to Macaulay, it was written by three leading Bostonians: Samuel Pemberton, James Bowdoin, and Joseph Warren. Their objective was clear. Everyone was agreed that a crime had been committed. What remained to be decided now was where the fault lay. In the letter, the Bostonians talked of "the designs of certain Men," malevolent characters, who were "plotting the Ruin of our Constitution and Liberties." These figures had already begun a scheme, "to bring an Odium on the Town as the Aggressors in that Affair," by twisting, conflating, and misrepresenting the truth of what had happened. It was vital, the letter declared, that the king's troops should not be reinforced as some might be demanding. Instead, it was the humble and fervent "prayer of the Town, and the Province in General that his Majesty will graciously be pleased, in his great wisdom and goodness, to order the said Troops out of the Province."[51]

This package arrived from Boston as Macaulay was preparing her response to Burke. It came at a time when Macaulay was already thinking about the American problem. She had recently read Dickinson's *Farmer's Letters*, which had fortified her support for the colonists' cause. In her view the Americans had been badly treated by Westminster. She thought there were a dozen measures the ministry could have taken prior to their levying taxes. They might have reduced exorbitant salaries, abolished sinecures, or ended iniquitous pensions.

That they had done none of this was yet more proof of the pernicious forces in Britain's politics. It was worse than Burke's "cabal" or "junto." The problem was not confined to the personalities of those in charge. It was instead a systemic flaw in the way British politics was practiced, which encouraged the expansion of power. How else could one explain the existence of a standing army of the type that had been sent to Boston in 1768? In itself this was "contrary to the very existence of real liberty," she wrote in her *Observations*. Having read the *Short Account of the Horrid Massacre at Boston*, Macaulay passed it to her publishers Edward and Charles Dilly, who would soon reprint it. Seemingly Macaulay then sent a copy of this English edition back to Boston, accompanied by a forthright letter that was addressed to the committee of the town, applauding "the spirit and prudence" of the people and the way in which they had responded to the provocation.

These actions brought Macaulay an unmatched popularity in the colonies. Unlike Wilkes she was not compromised by a disreputable private life or saddled with enormous debts. Instead she was seen as possessing a unique mix of erudition, authenticity, and bravery. Also of importance, in Boston particularly, was the fact that Macaulay was a believing and practicing Christian, something she made very plain in her writings. Not long after, the Philadelphia-based sculptor Patience Wright would cross the Atlantic to make wax figures of the most prominent Britons with the idea of having them brought back to America for display. The three individuals she decided to feature were the heroic Lord Chatham, the admired old chancellor Lord Lyttelton, and the intrepid champion of liberty Catharine Macaulay. For Wright, she was more of a draw than even Wilkes himself.

At about the same time, in August 1770, another letter arrived from Boston. This was from a young lawyer called John Adams. A brilliant, opinionated, and somewhat emotional young man, Adams had recently gained notoriety for defending the British soldiers accused of perpetrating the massacre, a duty which he considered to be separate from his zealous devotion to the cause of liberty. To Macaulay, Adams wrote:

I have read, not only with Pleasure and Instruction, but with great admiration, Mrs Macaulay's History of England. It is formed upon the Plan, which I have ever wished to see, adopted by Historians. It is calculated to strip off the false Lustre from worthless Princes and Nobles and selfish Politicians, and to bestow the Reward of Virtue, Praise, upon the generous and worthy only. No charms of Eloquence can atone for the want of this exact, historical Morality; and I know of no History, in which it is, so religiously regarded.

It was that History, as well as the concurrent Testimony of all who have come to this Country from England that I had formed the highest opinion of the Author, as one of the brightest ornaments, not only of her Sex, but of her age and Country. I could not therefore but esteem the Information given me by Mr Gill, as one of the most agreeable & fortunate occurrences of my Life.[52]

So opened one of the most unusual of friendships. Macaulay and Adams would often correspond over the years before 1776. John's wife Abigail would write too, letters filled with a sense of kinship and common purpose. Reading them today, one senses a topsy-turviness about the writing, as Adams—the fabled Founding Father, the champion of Congress who was destined to succeed Washington as second president—politely addresses Macaulay, a lady who few now remember.

In his first letter, in August 1770, Adams reveals he has heard a rumor of Macaulay's intention to write an American history. "If this is true," he enthuses, "it would give him infinite Pleasure—Whether it is or not, if he can by any Means in his Power, by Letters or otherwise, contribute any Thing to your Amusement, and Specially to your Assistance in any of your Inquiries, he will always esteem himself extremely happy in attempting it."[53]

Fourteen

THOSE WHO RUSH ACROSS
THE SEA

IN THE EARLY 1770S a story about Macaulay started to do the rounds in London. To some it was a funny piece of social tittle-tattle. For Macaulay, however, it was embarrassing. According to the gossip she had been invited to a dinner at which Dr. Samuel Johnson was also present. Everyone knew how loaded a situation this was. Johnson was a dominating presence who was always combative in conversation. Nor was Macaulay one to concede ground in any debate. The dinner started unluckily. Even before the food was served the subject of civil government came up. "Johnson, as usual," the story went, "declared in very strong terms, for monarchy. Mrs M. for a republic."[1] A round of verbal sparring followed, with Johnson recalling quotations from Scripture to support his position, and Macaulay, who knew her Bible equally well, replying with even "more potent" theological arguments. This left Johnson, a man who did not "easily digest contradiction," sour and brooding as they were invited to sit to eat.

The annunciation of dinner occasioned a truce to debate. But the doctor, with more ill manners than I ever heard authentically placed to his account, except in this instance, took occasion, when the company were all seated at table, to renew hostilities with his amiable antagonist. Mrs M's footman was standing, according to custom, at the back of his lady's chair; when Johnson addressed him thus: "Henry, what makes you stand? Sit down. Sit down. Take your place at table with the best of us. We are all Republicans, Henry. There's no distinction here. The rights of human nature are equal. Your mistress will not be angry, at your asserting your privilege of peerage. We are all on a level. Do take your chair, and sit down."[2]

In an age still governed by strict social codes, this was a flagrant breach of etiquette. According to the gossip Macaulay was left humiliated. She "coloured a little, and drew up her head, but made no answer."[3] The silence was Johnson's triumph. Stories of the exchange were spread all over London. In the versions the fine details shifted. The dinner was at someone else's house. Or perhaps it was at Macaulay's. Some said Johnson had spoken so loudly that everyone had listened. Others—later including Macaulay—dismissed this, arguing it had been a quiet, private conversation. Something of the sort, however, certainly did take place. Johnson himself confirmed it to Boswell. "I thus, Sir," he explained, "shewed her the absurdity of the levelling doctrine. She has never liked me since. Sir, your levellers wish to level *down* as far as themselves; but they cannot bear levelling *up* to themselves. They would all have some people under them," he went on, "why not then have some people above them?"[4]

The popularity of the anecdote is almost as instructive as its substance. Here was a classic of British culture, something that could be interpreted either as the forceful destruction of cant or the silencing of a noisy upstart. Certainly, as her enemies noted, Macaulay's private life did leave her open to accusations of hypocrisy. After all, with her dinners and levees, ice cream, and silk damask fabrics, she lived a life which combined celebrity and luxury. All the while she kept thundering into print with criticisms of the society that had made such conditions possible. Equally there is a sense of this story being artfully deployed against Macaulay and all she represented. Johnson was by this point considered the ultimate destructive weapon. An idea or an argument might get past softer critics, but if it did not have true worth then it would be scorched to cinders when it reached Johnson. For those who felt unsettled by the radical turn politics was taking as the 1770s began, or those who disliked the presence of a combative woman in London society, the story of Johnson's triumph was particularly attractive. He had exposed the contradictions of her position, the shallowness and excitability of her thinking.

Johnson was now in his sixties, and the days of struggle in Gough Square were well behind him. He had left that elegant house in 1759 but continued to live around Fleet Street with Anna Williams, Robert Levet, and Francis Barber. Aged about thirty, Barber was by this time as established a part of Johnson's household as Levet and Williams. Apart from a spell in 1768, when Johnson sent him to a school at Bishop's Stortford in Hertfordshire, where he studied Latin and Greek, Barber had lived continuously with his master in Fleet Street. For the stream of callers at Johnson's lodgings, it was common to be greeted by Barber at the door, before they were shown in to meet "Dr. Johnson."

By the 1770s this was part of daily life in Fleet Street. Once he was out of bed, Johnson generally received a "levee of morning visitors." These were predominantly literary characters like John Hawkesworth, Oliver Goldsmith, or Topham Beauclerk. "He seemed to me," wrote a clergyman called William Maxwell, "to be considered as a kind of publick oracle, whom everybody thought they had a right to visit and consult."[5] Another regular caller was the playwright Arthur Murphy, who memorably described Johnson as living "in poverty, total idleness, and the pride of literature."[6]

Murphy's caricature was, however, not quite accurate. Johnson may have been haphazard in his ways and disheveled in his dress, but he was supported financially by the pension Bute had granted him. He also continued to be an active force in cultural life, producing essays and pamphlets on the topics of the day—issues that he also churned over at his famous club with friends like Joshua Reynolds, Edmund Burke, Adam Smith, and Edward Gibbon. Even in such company, on those dimly lit club nights when they met at the Turk's Head Tavern in Soho, it was understood that Johnson was the greatest conversationalist of them all. When engaged he could rise into flights of eloquence or erudition, and to cross him was considered foolish. Like Macaulay an opponent could end up humiliated not just once, but over and over and over again, as the story was repeated all over town.

One person to be cautioned about meeting Johnson at this time was an American called John Ewing. Ewing was no lightweight himself. He was Professor of Natural Philosophy at the College of Philadelphia, where, in the 1760s, he had gained a reputation for his inspiring lectures and insightful papers published in the *Transactions of the American Philosophical Society*. In 1773, at the age of forty-one and with his career established, Ewing had decided to take time out to visit Britain. Despite the fractious political environment, the tour went well. In Scotland his "virtues, general intelligence, and scientific reputation"[7] were much admired, and the University of Edinburgh awarded him an honorary degree. Like Rush before him, Ewing rounded off his visit to Britain with a trip south to London, where he received an invite to dine at the home of Charles Dilly.

Dilly was Macaulay's publisher, and his table was one of the reputed venues of her collision with Johnson. Whether that was so or not, Johnson was certainly going to be there this time. "You will meet the great Dr. Johnson, but you must not contradict him; we never contradict him," Dilly told Ewing. The American had particular cause to mark this advice. Johnson's original mistrust of Americans had solidified into dislike throughout the 1760s, and Ewing knew this well. That night he arrived a little before Johnson, who soon came shambling into the parlor. As the doctor pulled off his coat, Ewing noticed the mood shift from "easy conversation" to "general silence." Johnson seemed very gloomy and disengaged. Throughout dinner, he "attended" to "nothing but his plate," and only when he was finished did he scan the table. Dilly's guests had been questioning Ewing about the political controversy, and he had been seeking to defend the American point of view. Johnson eyed Ewing suspiciously. "*What do you know, Sir, on that subject?*" he demanded.

> Dr. Ewing calmly replied, that, having resided in America during his life, he thought himself qualified to deliver his opinions on the subject under discussion. This produced an animated conversation. Johnson's prejudices against the Americans were strong; he considered them, as he always termed them, rebels and scoundrels, and these epithets were now by no means sparingly used. It is difficult to say how far he might have been provoked, by opposition in argument, if a fortunate turn had not been given to the dispute. Johnson had rudely said, "Sir, what do you know in America? You never read: you have no books there." "Pardon, me, Sir," replied Dr. Ewing, "We have read the *Rambler*." This civility instantly pacified him; and, after the rest of the company had retired, he sat with Dr. Ewing until midnight, speaking amicably and eloquently, and uttering such wisdom as seldom falls from the lips of man.[8]

As with the anecdote about Macaulay, this one seems almost certainly to have been polished up over time. When it was first recorded in the early nineteenth century, Boswell's vision of Johnson as the irascible oracle was firmly established, and it seems to fit that picture far too neatly. It is suspicious, too, that Johnson should be so vulnerable to flattery. In this account just five short words about the *Rambler* were enough to conquer him completely. And yet, for all this, the vignette remains compelling. In the familiar setting of Dilly's bookshop, it takes us into the intriguing relationship between Johnson and

America. This was a relationship that, in turn, has much to tell us about Johnson's ideas regarding happiness.

IN HIS EARLY LIFE, Johnson's roaming mind was drawn east rather than west. From his boyhood reading of the *Spectator* he was introduced to the period convention of the Eastern tale, where the vivid landscapes of Persia, India, or Egypt would be evoked as a backdrop for allegories or stories of moral instruction. When he was at Oxford one of the books that most gripped his imagination was an account of travels in the region of north-eastern Africa known as Abyssinia by a seventeenth-century Portuguese Jesuit called Father Jerome Lobo. A translation of this for a Birmingham bookseller became Johnson's first published work in 1735, and ever since, Lobo's portrayal of the green and flourishing Nile Valley, the vast deserts and mountains, remained strongly with him.

In comparison, Johnson felt a coolness when he looked west. Like everyone who grew up in the first half of the eighteenth century, Johnson heard the stories of colonial progress: of the new harbors, roads, towns, and churches. This was a time when everyone could sense America's potential. Johnson, in particular, connected these stories from Boston, New York, or Philadelphia with something else that had come out of seventeenth-century Portuguese thinking. This was the concept of the "Fifth Empire," an interpretation of human progress that viewed civilization as already having moved through four distinct eras. First came Ancient Greece, then the Roman Empire, which was followed by Christendom and most recently modern Europe. In this interpretation of history, a "Fifth Empire" was destined to rise on the western side of the Atlantic. This would be a place of tremendous power that combined wisdom and learning in ways that would dazzle the world. The Irish bishop George Berkeley played with this concept in his poem *Verses on the Prospect of Planting Arts and Learning in America*, which was published when Johnson was still a boy in Lichfield in the 1720s. It ended:

Westward the seat of empire takes its way:
The four first acts already past;
The fifth shall end the drama with the day;
Time's noblest product is the last.[9]

Beyond this Johnson had little cause to think much about colonial America in his younger life. To him as to most people, it was a wild and bustling* society peopled by a raw population of migrants who spent their days farming or chasing beavers. There was not much evidence in the reports that came back to Britain to suggest that this land was really going to fulfil the vision of the "Fifth Empire." Nevertheless, as Johnson pondered at around the time his *Dictionary* was published, "as power is the constant and unavoidable consequence of learning, there is no reason to doubt that the time is approaching when the Americans shall in their turn have some influence on the affairs of mankind."[10]

The prompt for this reflection was the appearance in London of a compelling American work. By the mid-1750s Johnson knew that a library had been founded in one of the Carolinas and that "some great electrical discoveries" had been made at Philadelphia. Then a beautifully engraved map, along with a fine descriptive treatise, was passed into his hands for review in the English press. The map, given to Johnson during the first years of his acquaintance with Francis Barber, interested him. Entitled *A General Map of the Middle British Colonies in America*, it was made by a friend of Franklin's, a Welsh-born surveyor called Lewis Evans who had spent years ranging across territory that was little known to the colonists, meeting Indigenous peoples, taking measurements, and recording observations. The map was finely detailed and illustrated with the location of historic events and additional notes on the most interesting geographical features,

---

* "Bustle," as Walter Jackson Bate pointed out, was one of Johnson's pet words. He used it often, to indicate "foolish and ill-directed activity carried on for no other purpose than to relieve tedium or "fill up the vacuities of life." (He once defined it as "getting on horseback in a ship.") Bate, *Samuel Johnson*, p. 19.

such as Lake Ontario in the north or the Ouasioto Mountains in the south, "through which there is not yet any occupied Path." In a time of huge territorial expansion, Johnson was as attracted to Evans's work as anyone, seeing it as an expression of true cartographic skill.

Johnson was also drawn to Evans's accompanying treatise. This, he decided, was "written with such elegance as the subject admits, though not without some mixture of the American dialect; a tract of corruption to which every language widely diffused must always be exposed."[11] To read Johnson's review of Evans's work is to evoke a picture of him absorbed—as he was in Oxford years before with Lobo's descriptions of the Nile Valley—with a strange and distant landscape. He extracts sinuous passages on the wood-cloaked hills that extended in all directions about the Mississippi River. "To look from these hills into the lower lands," Evans wrote, "is but as it were into an ocean of woods, swelled and depressed here and there by little inequalities, not to be distinguished, one part from another, any more than the waves of the real ocean."[12] In contrast were the lakes of Erie, Ontario, and Champlain on the northern frontier. These were so vast they shared characteristics with the Caspian Sea or even the Mediterranean, with their own distinct tidal and weather systems. Here was North America, in all its majesty, all its variety, in a way Johnson had never seen before.

This presented Johnson with a new appreciation of America's geography and potential. One thing that he could not gather from Evans's map, however, was that he himself had become an active presence in this distant place. As Strahan heard from Philadelphia decades before, "Your authors know but little of the Fame they have on this Side the Ocean." And since Franklin's first printing of *The Vanity of Human Wishes* in 1749, a Johnsonian readership had begun to grow across the colonies.

In 1757, John Hancock—the merchant whose suave handwriting would sign off the Declaration of Independence—was one of those who eagerly picked up a copy of the *Rambler*. John Adams was reading

Johnson too. Adams knew his poem *London* and *The Vanity of Human Wishes* well enough to quote them in his earliest writings. Indeed, by the 1770s, Johnson's *Rambler* and *Idler* essays were listed as among the most used books at Harvard College Library in Cambridge, Massachusetts. People were relying on his *Dictionary* too. In 1774, Alexander Hamilton would quote from it in his first political writings while a student at King's College, New York. Meanwhile, in Virginia, another bright young reader named Thomas Jefferson was also an enthusiast, including the *Dictionary* on a list of core titles for a friend who was planning to start a private library. In 1770 Jefferson even acquired a copy of Johnson's political pamphlet, *The False Alarm*, which dealt with John Wilkes and the Middlesex Election controversy. As historians have since noticed, in the fourth paragraph of this, Johnson used a favorite phrase of his: "The pursuit of happiness."[13]

Given all this, Ewing would quite plausibly have been able to inform him about the *Rambler*'s popularity. But we know that the meeting between these two was not Johnson's only opportunity to find out about his American success. Not long before the dinner at Dilly's in 1773, he had met another Philadelphian in London. Like Ewing, the Reverend William White was a hugely impressive character. Still in his twenties, he was also connected to the College of Philadelphia. After graduating at the age of seventeen in 1765, White decided his vocation lay with the church. Since then he had studied liberal Anglican theology, and by the time he traveled to England for his ordination as deacon in 1770, he was already being spoken of as a candidate to be the first Anglican bishop in British America. On a second visit to England in 1772, for his ordination as priest, White met Johnson several times. For White this was an exciting opportunity to converse with a writer whose reputation across the Atlantic was formidable. For Johnson the meetings were equally significant. Here, before him, was true proof of American progress. White was the kind of character to explode the stereotype. He was no wild projector, no chancing merchant. Instead he was a paragon of the polite, well-educated, and pious individual Johnson believed was at the core of a virtuous society.

White also turned out to be a dutiful correspondent. In one of his meetings with Johnson, he mentioned that along with his *Dictionary* and *Rambler*, another of his literary efforts had been recently printed in Philadelphia. Arriving home, White set out for Market Street, found the American edition of Johnson's novella, *The History of Rasselas: Prince of Abissinia*, and immediately sent a copy back to London. The book arrived at about the time of Johnson's meeting with Ewing in 1773. On March 4, Johnson sketched out a note of thanks. "I received the copy of Rasselas," he confirmed to White.

> The impression is not magnificent, but it flatters an author, because the printer seems to have expected that it would be scattered among the people. The little book has been well received, and is translated into Italian, French, German, and Dutch. It has now one honour more by an American edition.[14]

AS BEST AS HE could, Johnson tried to live by the maxim "the business of life is to go forward."[15] The past could be, as he well knew, a place of painful reflection and reproach. He carried this belief through into his writing as well, often dashing off material in the heat of creativity before discarding it and moving decisively on to the next project. This was a characteristic that Johnson shared with Franklin, who, when asked by his sister to make a list of his journalistic pieces to the press, held up his hands in defeat. "I could as easily make a Collection for you of all the past Parings of my Nails."[16]

Likewise, Johnson would claim to Boswell that he had hardly seen *Rasselas* since the moment of its composition in 1759. As with his biography of the poet Richard Savage, which had flowed out of him, if the legend was to be believed, in a thirty-six-hour torrent in 1743, *Rasselas* had supposedly been written in haste and then forgotten about until White sent the copy to Fleet Street in 1773. Flicking through this edition fourteen years later, Johnson permitted himself a little nostalgia. *Rasselas* was a singular work in his career. It was a novella, comprising forty-nine short chapters—some only a few paragraphs long—that was set in the landscapes that Johnson had read about as a young man in Father Lobo's *Voyage to Abyssinia*. Coming at the end of what scholars have labeled his decade of moral writing, Johnson's hero is Rasselas, a prince of Abyssinia. And Rasselas undertakes a philosophical quest: to discover how to be happy.

To readers opening the book for the first time, Rasselas's story was at once compelling and perplexing. The simplicity and universality of the desire to be happy was enticing enough, and in the opening pages of *Rasselas* Johnson shows that his central character has everything that he needs for contentment. Born to the rank of a prince, Rasselas has no financial worries. Better still, he lives in a utopian setting called the "Happy Valley," a place that is tightly enclosed and protected on all sides by impenetrable mountains. Johnson describes the valley in lavish terms in his opening chapter:

> The sides of the mountains were covered with trees, the banks of the brooks were diversified with flowers; every blast shook spices from the rocks, and every month dropped fruits upon the ground. All animals that bite the grass, or brouse the shrub, whether wild or tame, wandered in this extensive circuit, secured from beasts of prey by the mountains which confined them. On one part were flocks and herds feeding in the pastures, on another all the beasts of chase frisking in the lawns; the sprightly kid was bounding on the rocks, the subtle monkey frolicking in the trees, and the solemn elephant reposing in the shade. All the diversities of the world were brought together, the blessings of nature were collected, and its evils extracted and excluded.[17]

Aged twenty-six, Rasselas, the fourth son of the emperor, was expected to pass his days in the Happy Valley until the time came for

him to be called to the throne. But rather than basking in the luxuries that were all around him, Rasselas felt restless. Johnson pictured
him sitting at a table filled with dainties, withdrawn and disinter-
ested. Instead of eating, Rasselas would rise "abruptly in the midst
of the song" and leave his company for long, brooding walks around
the valley.[18] When challenged about his behavior by one of the sages,
Rasselas confessed to a yearning. Despite the fact that all his corporal
necessities were fulfilled, his mind, he explained, was "pained with
want." Unlike the animals he saw all around him, the cows in the
meadows or the birds on the branches, he could not find satisfaction
in food and drink, or even music and company. "I fly from pleasure,
said the prince, because pleasure has ceased to please; I am lonely
because I am miserable, and am unwilling to cloud with my presence
the happiness of others."

This was disarming. "You, Sir, said the sage, are the first who
has complained of misery in the *happy valley*."[19] Having considered
this for a moment, the sage continued, "If you had seen the miseries
of the world, you would know how to value your present state." At
this, Rasselas brightened. "Now, said the prince, you have given me
something to desire: I shall long to see the miseries of the world,
since the sight of them is necessary to happiness."[20]

So began Rasselas's pursuit of happiness. In brisk chapters the
plot played out. It began with Rasselas's escape from the Happy Valley, a process that took several years and the support of a wise poet
called Imlac to accomplish. Imlac, who was well traveled, issued
Rasselas with a caution. "The world, which you figure to yourself
smooth and quiet as the lake in the valley," he told Rasselas, "you will
find a sea foaming with tempests, and boiling with whirlpools."[21] But
nothing could stop the prince. Having tunneled through the mountains, he, Imlac, and his sister Nekayah—who joined them at the last
moment with a wish to flee "this tasteless tranquillity"—burst out
into the broad and open world.

Having made their way to Cairo, the trio began their systematic study of society, to see where happiness was best to be found. Everywhere they looked they found disappointment. Rasselas saw the cultivated contentment of a Stoic philosopher shattered by the news of his daughter's death. Out in the countryside they met a wealthy master who lived in a fabulous palace. This man confessed that his happiness had been ruined because he was forced to endure the jealousy of others. Next they met a hermit, living quietly in a cavern shaded by palm trees, safe from the "snares, discord and misery" of the world. This hermit soon admitted that he was bored in his solitude. When Rasselas and his friends offered to take him back to Cairo with them, his eyes shone with excitement. "He dug up a considerable treasure which he had hid among the rocks, and accompanied them to the city, on which, as he approached it, he gazed with rapture."[22]

With his quest growing increasingly complicated and maddening, at one point Rasselas cried out, "What then is to be done? . . . the more we enquire, the less we can resolve."[23] The truth of Imlac's warning was beginning to strike him: "Human life is every where a state in which much is to be endured, and little to be enjoyed."[24] Having seen much, at the end of the novella the characters went their various ways. Rasselas, ever the idealist, decided to form "a little kingdom, in which he might administer justice in his own person." But, as Johnson wearily explains in a final chapter, entitled "*The conclusion, in which nothing is concluded,*" Rasselas, "could never fix the limits of his dominion, and was always adding to the number of his subjects."[25] The reader is left with the vision of the prince walking away from Cairo, his mind as unsettled as ever. "The mind dances from scene to scene," Johnson wrote at one point, "unites all pleasures in all combinations, and riots in delights which nature and fortune, with all their bounty, cannot bestow."[26]

For British readers in 1759, familiar with Johnson's approach to life, *Rasselas* was an entertaining extension of the same seam of thought that was first expressed in *The Vanity of Human Wishes.* Instead of the roaming eye of the poet who surveys mankind "from China to

Peru," all the variety of human experience was condensed into Ras-selas's picaresque journey across the north-eastern corner of Africa. The characters he met were those who frequently raise Johnson's ire, the philosophers, scientists, projectors, and idealists who all live "in idea" rather than reality. All these figures were united in mak-ing what Johnson considered to be the classic mistake of equating a particular vision of life with a state of pure happiness. The reality was far more complicated. While happiness may be obtained, Johnson suggested, it was always fleeting and amorphous, rather than settled and secure. The happiest moments in Rasselas's life came not when he was thinking about his pursuit of it, but when his attention was channeled elsewhere, such as when he was confronted with the chal-lenge of how to escape the Happy Valley.

Here Johnson was framing a central paradox. To pursue hap-piness aggressively and actively was to push it further away. Like a rainbow it would retreat if approached. And yet, as Johnson stated elsewhere, he believed happiness to be "the end of all human ac-tions."[27] It is the combination of these incompatible views that cast humans, like Rasselas, into an endless, adventurous quest that was destined to be filled alternately with hopes and disappointments. Life was to be a journey that would occasionally be lit by beams of sunlight and sometimes darkened by gloomy clouds. To give up the pursuit would be to deny our humanity, but to think it ever had an end would be to deny reason.

On this point one of Johnson's readers, at his hilltop home in Vir-ginia, Monticello, was in agreement. Thomas Jefferson, like Johnson, was familiar with the commonly expressed aspiration "the pursuing and obtaining of happiness." Indeed, this was exactly the formulation of language that would, in a few years' time, be used by George Ma-son in his text for the *Virginia Declaration of Rights*. Jefferson is thought to have studied Mason's writing in June 1776 as he began his draft for the Declaration of Independence, and he followed his wording quite closely. It seems, however, that on this central point, Jefferson accorded with Johnson. People might have an inalienable right to *pursue* happiness, but no one could expect to *find* it.

THE MEETINGS WITH WHITE and Ewing confirmed to Johnson his popularity in the colonies. When the Philadelphian version of *Rasselas* arrived at his home in 1773, this assumed tangible form. The book was the first work printed by a bookseller called Robert Bell on his arrival in the colonies in 1768. Bell, presumably hoping to make a statement, packed the usual two volumes into one and boisterously announced his version of *Rasselas* as being "PRINTED FOR EVERY PURCHASER."[28]

While he was impressed with White and Ewing and pleased to hear that *Rasselas* was finding an audience across the Atlantic, for his part Johnson remained suspicious of the colonists. This mistrust was grounded in his dislike of the imperial project. In 1756, when he looked over Evans's map and read his pamphlet, he was intrigued. But he also bristled. Johnson could see that Evans's chart was as much about power as the art of cartography. In the accompanying pamphlet Evans entreated the British government to intercede in the area known as the Ohio Valley, both to check the expansion of the French and to acquire a portion of land "greater than a fourth part of Europe." Johnson took issue with these "pompous paragraphs." The Ohio, he wrote, might well be "magnificent in prospect, but will lose much of its beauty on a nearer view." Who, for instance, was going to live in this vast area?

It is indeed supposed by our author to receive inhabitants from Europe; but we must remember that it will very little advance the power of the English to plant colonies on the Ohio by dis-peopling their native country. And since the end of all human actions is happiness, why should any number of our inhabitants be banished from their trades and their homes to a trackless desart, where life is to begin anew, and where they can have no other accommodation than their own hands shall immediately procure them? What advantage, even upon supposition of what is scarcely to be supposed, an uninterrupted possession and unimpeded improvement, can arise equivalent to the exile of the first planters, and difficulties to be encountered by their immediate descendants?[29]

Meanwhile back in Britain, Johnson pointed out, fertile land was plentiful, and for all the developments that had taken place in the eighteenth century, there was still much more in the way of raw materials available than was being used. All this was easily accessible, and "by proper regulations we may employ all our people, and give every man his chance of rising to the full enjoyment of all the pleasures of a civilised and learned country." In response to Evans's claim that the Ohio, once colonized, could soon be turned into a fruitful territory for the production of silk, Johnson was withering. "I know not indeed," he confessed, "whether we can at home procure any great quantities of raw silk, which we are told is to be had in so great plenty upon the banks of the Ohio. Away therefore with thousands and millions to those dreadful desarts, that we may no longer want raw silk!"[30]

This was classic Johnson, pulling apart a seductive vision and showing how apt humans were to stake so much on a whim. For such little gain, people were willing to abandon the safety of their home parishes and the comforts of their family for a life of toil. And that was not all. Not only was Evans's proposed project on the Ohio dangerous to the happiness of the untold thousands of migrants that would be tempted to travel there, but what of those who lived there already? These people would inevitably be chased from their ancestral lands, thereby doubling the tragedy. This was an argument Johnson would return to over and over again, most famously in his description of the Seven Years' War. In Johnson's eyes the battle for supremacy on the North American continent between Great Britain and France was nothing more than "the quarrel of two robbers for the spoils of a passenger."[31]

To Johnson's mind this was a collective crime, one in which the expansionist Whigs and the adventurous colonists were both complicit. This belief informed part of Johnson's hostility toward America. Also connected to this were his ideas about human happiness. Johnson had grown up during the years of astonishing colonial development. In Lichfield, Oxford, and London he would have known people who decided, like Hall, to travel in search of a better life. For Johnson, such a course of action was a dangerous hazard. Of all his favorite writers, few ranked higher than Horace the Roman poet, who memorably observed, "They change their sky, not their soul, who rush across the sea."[32]

Time and again Johnson would echo Horace's conviction that happiness was not solely dependent on place. It is one of the central themes of *Rasselas*, where he shows happiness to be as elusive in the Happy Valley as it is in the majestic city of Cairo. If that was the case, what was the chance that it was to be found in the wilds of colonial America? Acknowledging the copy of *Rasselas* sent by White in 1773, Johnson was reminded of this again. "It was long since observed by Horace," he wrote in his reply, "that no ship could leave care behind."[33] This was the same thought Johnson expressed twenty years earlier, in the *Rambler* No. 6:

> THE general remedy of those, who are uneasy without knowing the cause, is a change of place; they are always willing to imagine that their pain is the consequence of some local inconvenience, and endeavour to fly from it, as children from their shadows; always hoping for more satisfactory delight from every new scene of diversion, and always returning home with disappointment and complaints.[34]

A key part of this statement comes toward the beginning. In referring to those "who are uneasy without knowing the cause," Johnson qualifies himself. He is not claiming that *no* link exists between place and happiness. Indeed, his own fondness for London was well known. In 1769 he told Boswell that "The happiness of London is not to be conceived but by those who have been in it," and Johnson found great pleasure in the idea that "there is more learning and science within the circumference of ten miles from where we now sit, than in all the rest of the kingdom."[35] Rather than demolishing the connection entirely, Johnson's argument is that restless people were apt to blame the world around them for their unhappiness rather than themselves.

As the political atmosphere darkened in the 1760s, this conviction began to take on renewed meaning. For Johnson the quarrels over the Stamp Act and the Townshend Duties and the violent confrontations in Boston bore the hallmark of an excitable, restless, inconstant people. These were people who had first abandoned the security of home and were now, as predicted, returning with their "disappointments and complaints." In the American edition of *Rasselas*, the publisher had added a telling quote to the title page. This was a maxim from the seventeenth-century French moralist François de La Rochefoucauld. "For if a Man don't find Ease or Content in *himself*, and his *Rational Employments*, and *Connections,* 'tis in vain to seek it *Elsewhere.*'[36]

WHILE ROBERT BELL'S *RASSELAS* was introducing more readers across the Atlantic, one of the book's true devotees could be found much closer to Fleet Street. By the 1770s James Boswell had become Johnson's admiring shadow, and of the doctor's literary works, *Rasselas* was one of his favorites. Later, in his biography of Johnson, Boswell claimed to re-read the book every year, reveling in its "fund of thinking" and finding the scope for long meditations in "almost every sentence."[37] In this biography Boswell would also give a definitive shape to an astonishing story that had long been circulated about *Rasselas*'s creation. Boswell acquired his version of the tale directly from Strahan, who, as Johnson's printer, was closely involved. As Strahan told it, Johnson simply dashed off *Rasselas* having received news of his mother's death to "defray" the expense of her funeral "and pay some little debts which she had left." According to Joshua Reynolds, a founding member of Johnson's club, the writing came high speed, "in the evenings of one week," during which time it was sent off to Strahan in portions for printing.[38]

Such was the mythology that surrounded Johnson, even in his lifetime, that the circumstances of *Rasselas*'s creation have been, as the literary scholar Thomas Keymer has termed it, "permanently blurred."[39] As with much Johnsoniana, however, the story does contain a good deal of truth. We know this thanks to a letter Strahan preserved from Johnson, written on January 20, 1759, three days before his mother's funeral, and just before he left London for the journey home to Lichfield. In it Johnson elaborates on his new project, which he had told Strahan about during a meeting the night before. "The title will be The choice of Life or The History of . . . Prince of Abissinia," he writes. "I will not print my name, but expect it to be known." The letter gives an intriguing glimpse into Johnson's life at a moment when emotional distress and powerful creativity had combined. His message to Strahan is brisk and pointed. The story as told by Reynolds is borne out by Johnson's eagerness for a quick sale. Having signed off the letter he adds an imploring coda: "Get me the money if you can."[40]

This letter is usually quoted for the insight it brings to *Rasselas*'s genesis. But it also provides a glimpse into the relationship between Johnson and Strahan. Living at close quarters, their regard for each other was not destroyed by the stresses of the *Dictionary* project. Instead, by the end of the 1750s, they had formed a close professional bond. Here was Johnson, in January 1759, thrown into despair at the news of his mother's death. This was an event Johnson had long dreaded. He once confessed to his stepdaughter Lucy Porter it was "one of the few calamities on which I think with terror." When it arrived, Johnson turned to the things he knew and trusted to see him through: his creative and literary abilities, and his facility for producing high-quality work at pace. These talents would have been useless, though, had he not had access to an utterly dependable figure like Strahan, who was able to turn ideas into tangible, profitable, literary material.

In 1759 Johnson made use of Strahan just as Franklin had in the 1740s. To both of these men, and many more besides, Strahan was a fulcrum. He was not the type to shine in public: to issue pamphlets, or make speeches. But his influence as an *éminence grise* outstripped that of many who did. Although Johnson enjoyed making fun of Strahan, belittling him as a tradesman whom he employed to frank his letters, he knew the value of keeping him close. David Hume knew this too. "There is no man of whom I entertain a better opinion," he wrote in 1773, "nor whose friendship I desire more to preserve, nor indeed any one to whom I have owed more essential obligations."[41]

The regard of Hume and Johnson, however, was not the equal of Strahan's relationship with his two closest friends. One of these, Benjamin Franklin, lived nearby, and it was easy for the two to meet socially. With David Hall, however, things were not so simple. It is a testament to the depth of affection between the two that despite the fact that an ocean separated them, their correspondence never let up. New letters were always started as soon as the old ones were sent, and over the years a growing note of personal pride had begun to appear in them too. "It is an agreeable Circumstance, that your two Sons are so far advanced in Life," Strahan wrote to Hall in 1771, still playing the part of older brother, "that the eldest is already fit to assist you, and the other nearly so. There will be room enough in your own Business for them both; and nothing is easier for a young Man than to pursue the Path, which his Father hath chalked out, and successfully trod before him."[42]

Thinking about the enduring link between their families was one of the satisfactions of Strahan's life. Already he had started a separate correspondence with his "namesake," William Strahan Hall, and the prospect of the second-generation meeting or forging business partnerships excited Strahan. As such he kept Hall abreast of his own children's development. His eldest son, William—the "Young Billy" intended as a match for Franklin's Sally—had set out as a printer alone. "He is very clever," Strahan asserted, "has already a good Share of Business, and will, in time succeed to some of the more profit-able Branches of it, as his Seniors drop off." His second son, George, was now in clerical orders, "and will, I am convinced, make a good Figure in that Walk of Life." Only the youngest, Andrew, remained at Little New Street. "His Time is almost totally taken up in the Print-ing house," he told Hall, "in looking after 7, 8, or 9 Presses, which are constantly employed there."[43]

Strahan had built up a handsome business to the north of Fleet Street. Thrice a week there was a *Chronicle* to print, and every four weeks a *Monthly Review*. There was a constant stream of book work, all the official business of the King's Printing House, and the separate matter of the Law Printing House, which was carried on elsewhere. "It is true," Strahan wrote to Hall, "we have distinct Overseers for both these Branches, to take Care of the Conduct of the Business within Doors. But still the general Management, and the Accounts, of all these Branches, falls to my Share."[44] On top of all this, Strahan had taken a share in many new books. This was still a novel thing for a printer, when booksellers traditionally owned the titles they sold. But by the start of the 1770s, Strahan had an interest in more than two hundred books, "which require, every one of them, some Atten-tion." He explained all of this to Hall:

> It is easy to manage one Branch of Business; but nobody in my Way ever before extended it so far as I have done. My Reason was this: I quickly saw, that if I confined myself to mere *print-ing for Booksellers* I might be able to live, but very little more than live; I therefore soon determined to launch out into other Branches in Connection, with my own, in which I have happily succeeded, to the Astonishment of the rest of the Trade here,

who never dreamt of going out of the old beaten Track. Thus I have made the Name of *Printer* more respectable than ever it was before, and taught them to emancipate themselves from the Slavery in which the Booksellers held them.[45]

As well as business and personal matters, political news remained a central theme of Strahan's Philadelphia letters. The agreement was that Hall could have exclusive access to the material for the London column in the *Gazette*, but to anyone who reads the correspondence today it is clear that it far exceeded, in length and detail, what was required for purely professional reasons. Both Strahan and Hall were dedicated politics-watchers. Neither was a natural participant, but both loved to know what was happening, to mull over the merits or otherwise of a policy or a personality. For years Strahan's political writings had been filled with despair, but from 1770 onward they had grown rosier. The reason was Strahan's regard for Lord North, the figure who now combined the post of First Lord of the Treasury with the other central offices of Chancellor of the Exchequer and Leader of the House of Commons. After years of weak leadership, Strahan was impressed. "Lord North acts his Part very well," he confirmed to Hall in November 1772. "Spirited, firm, and cool in his Operations."

> Neither fool hardy nor over-cautious, he proceeds in a way in general unexceptionable, and often praise-worthy. And his private Character is without Blemish. "Tother Day he was unanimously elected Chancellor of the University of Oxford; an Honour very rarely, if ever before, conferred on the Prime Minister. In short, from every Quarter it is apparent that the People are, in general, well satisfied with our present Rulers, and are duly sensible of the many Blessings peculiar to this Country.[46]

Strahan's hope was that with British politics stabilizing, the effect would be replicated in the colonies. This was not a forlorn wish.

Since 1770 there had been something of a *détente* in Anglo-American relations. Only in some quarters had tempers remained high. The most febrile place was New England. In June 1772 there was a violent confrontation in Narragansett Bay, Rhode Island, when a customs schooner called HMS *Gaspée* was seized and burned by furious locals. A commission was dispatched from Britain to investigate the affair, but they had not found anyone willing to testify. Beyond this, more opposition came from Boston, where meetings had been held and a committee of correspondence formed by men with increasingly familiar names: Samuel Adams, Joseph Warren, James Otis, John Hancock.

Strahan loved Hall's letters, and for years he had longed to see him again. The idea of a reunion was one he could never let go. Perhaps it was the prospect of taking Hall on a tour of his Little New Street premises; or of helping him into his carriage before they set out triumphantly into London's streets; or of inviting him into the gallery of the House of Commons so he could watch the action for himself. As the years passed, the likelihood of such things ever happening began to melt away. Occasionally Strahan let his frustrations show. "I wish you were here," he wrote to Hall in 1770. "I have, at your Desire, long forebore to mention your coming here; but I must beg leave to ask you once more, *Do you ever intend to visit your native Country?*"[47]

But something was not right in the early weeks of 1773. No word from Philadelphia reached Little New Street. Strahan began to fret. Over the last year Hall had complained about his health, something he had never done before. This propelled Strahan into one last effort to convince him of making "a Trip to your Native Air."[48] But then, most likely on the same ship that carried White's present of *Rasselas* to Johnson in March 1773, came the dreadful news. David Hall was dead at the age of fifty-eight. "I will restrain myself," wrote a devastated Strahan to Hall's son, "and not more than is necessary recall to your Remembrance the irreparable Loss you have sustained by the Death of one of the best of Parents and of Men."[49]

Fifteen

LETTERS

WHEREAS HIS FRIENDSHIP WITH Strahan was always warm, Hall's relationship with Franklin had long been strained. It never properly recovered from the days of the Stamp Act. Hall wrote to Little New Street of "misunderstandings" that were connected to the expiry of their partnership agreement. Strahan was cast in the role of peacemaker. He scolded Hall that "two such Men as you and he, whom I love and esteem, should love and esteem one another."[1] But Strahan made little progress. Surprised at the depth of Hall's resentment, Strahan advised him: "If you think you have been aggrieved by any part of his Conduct (which I am convinced he never intended) the nobler it will be in you to make the first Step to a thorough Reconciliation."[2] It is doubtful that Hall ever took that step.

Meanwhile Strahan's own friendship with Franklin had sustained its own tensions. While the two were still close and continued to meet to play cards and discuss the latest news, by the 1770s both of them could detect a coldness. The trouble was politics. In earlier years the two had been perfectly aligned. But now they were at odds over the colonial quarrel. "He and I differ widely in our American Politics," Strahan told Hall in 1770, "which I am heartily sorry for, as

I esteem him highly.——But tho' we *differ* we do not *disagree*; and must ever be good Friends, as I trust we aim at both the same End, tho' we differ in the Means."[3]

Looking back, these differences had existed for several years. Even at the time of the Stamp Act crisis, when Strahan acted so decisively to rescue Franklin's reputation, the two men had construed events rather differently. Franklin's main concern was the infringement of the colonists' rights. Since 1766 he increasingly dwelt on the privileges that he believed were rightfully enjoyed by Americans. In the 1770s he compiled a list of these:

1. They make their own laws, provided that their acts do not conflict with those of Parliament.
2. They tax themselves.
3. A Parliamentary statute made after the colonies were founded applies to them only when so stipulated, and even that is disputed, some contending that no British act is in force there, unless expressly adopted by some act of their own.[4]

There was much here to nettle Strahan. Each of these points, whatever convention might have sprung up over time, was a direct challenge to the principle of Westminster's sovereignty. This was an orthodox position, to which Strahan held fast. As Johnson had put it, "in sovereignty there are no gradations."[5] While it was certainly correct to repeal something as poorly thought out as the Stamp Act, Strahan was less supportive of the concessions that had followed. The colonists had been equally hostile to the Townshend Duties, to the point that North was obliged to almost totally abolish them when he became prime minister. This frustrated Strahan. He was not a man to brook dissent, and by the end of the 1760s he had come to the conclusion that Britain was showing a lack of spine. Were the two countries destined to be locked in this endless and repetitive pattern? A policy would be generated in Westminster, only to be growled down in Boston, or wherever else, before the tedious process would begin again.

This was an offense to Strahan's sense of efficiency as much as anything else. As he saw it the colonists were quick to talk about their privileges, but slow to accept their obligations. He sketched out his views in a letter to Hall.

> It is the peculiar Happiness of the British State, That ye Parliament's Power hath hitherto been in general satisfactory to the People, and that they acquiese in its Regulations, which in similar Cases no arbitrary Prince durst risk; To this Power we, in a great Measure, owe our Wealth and Consideration.—Taxes upon Consumption will always follow Properly, and the Parliament are as good Judges as the People what Articles will best bear taxing. If they err in any Case, they seldom fail to alter upon proper Representation. The Americans ought therefore to contribute to the Support *of the whole* in such Proportion as they are able, since they avail themselves of those Laws made by Parliament for the Protection of their Lives and Properties, and enjoy, in common with all British Subjects, the Protection of her Fleets and Armies.[6]

Strahan made his feelings clear to Franklin too. Arriving home at Craven Street one day at the end of 1769, Franklin found a letter waiting for him. It opened with odd formality. "Dear Sir," Strahan wrote, "In the many Conversations we have had together about our present Disputes with North America, we perfectly agree in wishing they may be brought to a speedy and happy Conclusion. How this is to be done is not so easily ascertained."[7] The aim, as Strahan saw it, was twofold. Firstly, "To relieve the Colonies from the Taxes complained of, which they certainly had no hand in imposing." And second, "to preserve the Honour, the Dignity, and the Supremacy of the British Legislature over all his Majestys dominions." To this end, Strahan listed seven questions:

1. Will not a Repeal of all the Duties (that on Tea excepted which was before paid here on exportation, and of course no new Imposition) fully satisfy the Colonists?
2. Your Reasons for that Opinion?
3. Do you think the only efectual Way of composing present Differences, is to put the Americans precisely in the Situation they were in before the passing of the Late Stamp Act?
4. Your Reasons for that Opinion?
5. If this last Method is deemed by the Legislature and his Majisty's Ministers, to be repugnant to their Duty as Guardians of the Just Rights of the Crown, and of their fellow Subjects, can you suggest any other Way of terminating these Disputes, consistent with the Ideas of Justice and Propriety conceivd by the Kings Subjects on both Sides of the Atlantic?
6. And if this Method was actually followed, do you not think it would encourage the Violent and Factious part of the Colonists to aim at Still farther Concessions from the Mother Country[?]
7. If they are relieved in part only, what do you, as a reasonable and dispassionate Man, and an equal Friend to both Sides imagine will be the probable Consequences?[8]

Franklin was sufficiently provoked to answer right away. His response ran to two thousand words. The key to reestablishing relations, he argued, was contained in Strahan's third question. The "only effectual" method of reconciliation was to return to the state of affairs that existed before the Stamp Act. Every other course of action had been tried and had only led to greater strife. To return to the old consensus did not necessarily involve a loss of prestige for Britain,

Franklin pointed out, as the mechanism for doing so could be an act of Parliament, which would in itself assert Westminster's supremacy.

Having stressed this, Franklin conveyed his own ideas about the colonial relationship. His views had changed over the last years. While he still very much believed that the peoples of Britain and America lived under the same Crown, he had decided that, politically, the citizens of each bore allegiance to their local legislatures. For those in the British Isles this was Westminster; in the colonies it meant the various assemblies. "We are free Subjects of the King," he put it, "and that *Fellow Subjects* of one Part of his Dominions are not Sovereign over *Fellow Subjects* in any other Part."[9] To Franklin's mind, if such a conception of the colonial architecture could be agreed on then the dispute might quickly end. There only needed to be a repeal of all duties laid expressly for raising a revenue without the colonists' consent, and "the present Uneasiness would subside; the Agreements not to import would be dissolved, and the Commerce flourish as heretofore."[10]

Given the well-known human proclivity for persisting in error, however, Franklin did not think that this was likely to happen. Having worked his way through Strahan's questions, he explained that, before he finished, he would like to "go a little farther, and tell you what I fear is more likely to come to pass *in Reality*." With the government convinced that Parliament must be supreme over all British dominions, Westminster's politicians would contrive a consoling narrative. They would convince themselves that colonial America was a backward place, filled with people incapable of manufacturing goods for themselves. They would maintain that discontent was emanating from a troublesome few and that the sensible majority would very soon submit to the inevitable. In time:

> farther rash Measures there, may create more Resentment here,
> that may Produce not merely ill advis'd and useless Dissolutions
> of their Assemblies, as last Year; but Attempts to Dissolve their

Constitutions; more Troops may be sent over, which will create more Uneasiness; to justify the Measures of Government, your Ministerial Writers will revile the Americans in your Newspapers, as they have already began to do, treating them as Miscreants, Rogues, Dastards, Rebels, &c, which will tend farther to alienate the Minds of the People here from them, and diminish their Affections to this Country. Possibly too, some of their warm patriots may be distracted enough to expose themselves by some mad Action to [be] sent for Hither, and Government here be indiscrete enough to Hang them on the Act of H[enry].8. Mutual Provocations will thus go on to complete the Separation; and instead of that cordial Affection that once and so long existed, and that Harmony so suitable to the Circumstances, and so Necessary to the Happiness, Strength Safety, and Welfare of both Countries; an implacable Malice and Mutual Hatred (such as we now see subsisting between the Spaniards and Portuguese, the Genoese and Corsicans, from the same Original Misconduct in the Superior Government) will take place; the Sameness of Nation, the Similarity of Religion, Manners and Language not in the least Preventing in our Case, more than it did in theirs.[11]

"I hope," Franklin concluded, "that this may all prove false Prophecy: And that you and I may live to see as sincere and Perfect a friendship establish'd between our respective Countries as has so many years Subsisted between Mr. Strahan and his truly affectionate Friend, B. Franklin."[12]

IT IS EASY TO imagine Franklin in Craven Street, scanning his eyes over Strahan's list of questions at the end of 1769. Two years earlier he was captured in just such a pose by the Scottish artist David Martin. In Martin's portrait Franklin sits at a table. He is locked in concentration, his eyes trained on a sheaf of papers he holds in his left hand. The setting is appealing, with the deep, rich blue of Franklin's coat and the velvety reds of the chair and table, but the portrait is just as suggestive about Franklin's interior world. Martin shows Franklin as a man completely lost in thought. Gazing at the papers before him, he is reasoning, strategizing, plotting. Franklin rests his head on his right hand, and pushes his thumb hard into his chin. It seems as if Franklin is on the verge of breaking into a smile as he finishes his reading and readies himself for his response.

For Franklin, for whom so much of life was a performance, it is at moments like this, when left alone at his writing desk, that he was free to be his most authentic, happiest self. Martin's portrait might show him as an older man in London, but we can easily picture him in a similar pose in the New Printing Office in Market Street in the 1720s, or jotting down his observations about electricity in the 1740s, or composing his letters to the press after his arrival in Britain. At such times one feels that Franklin was in total control. For while he could falter when speaking in public, or could be too reserved in conversation, in the act of writing he was completely at ease. At his desk, with a pen in hand, he was free to concentrate on the matter at hand, his incisive mind working like a great turbine, lifting up the weight of any problem and carrying it on an intellectual journey as it revolved toward its solution.

As the 1770s wore on, Franklin spent an increasing amount of time on his correspondence at Craven Street, compiling reports for the various colonial assemblies he represented, communicating with scientific friends like Joseph Priestley, and keeping up with close family such as William Franklin in New Jersey. As he wrote, one dilemma hung constantly over him. Had the time finally come to return to Philadelphia? Franklin was not much more than fifty in 1757 when he had embarked for London. Now he was sixty-seven. "It seems but t'other Day," he wrote to Deborah in January 1773, "since you and I were rank'd among the Boys and Girls, so swiftly does Time fly!"[13]

There was levity in this statement, but there was guilt too. Franklin's relationship with Deborah had never been straightforward. In the 1720s, after instigating a "Courtship" with her, he abruptly sailed away to London and forgot "by degrees" his "Engagements with Miss Reed." When beginning his *Autobiography*, he dwelt on his behavior to Deborah, "to whom I never wrote more than one Letter, & that was to let her know I was not likely soon to return."[14] Arriving back in Philadelphia he found her deeply unhappy. With Franklin gone she had entered into a rash marriage that soon failed. "I pity'd poor Miss Read's unfortunate Situation," he wrote, "who was generally dejected, seldom cheerful, and avoided Company." Franklin considered his "Giddiness & Inconstancy when in London as in a great degree the Cause of her Unhappiness." He ended the opening section of the *Autobiography* begun in 1771 on an uplifting note, correcting "that great *Erratum*" when he "took her to Wife."[15]

Forty-three years had elapsed since then, but, as he must have reflected, some things had scarcely changed. While "Giddiness & Inconstancy" did not accurately describe his behavior these days, the central dynamic remained the same. Franklin was in London pursuing his passions while Deborah was left to patiently await his return in Philadelphia. It had been this way for a long time now. Over the last sixteen years, Deborah had only seen her husband for two. Even when he was in the colonies in 1762–64, Franklin's time had often been consumed by politics or by long tours away from Philadelphia. And the years since had been littered with broken promises. In 1765, for instance, having just arrived in London, Franklin wrote home signaling his intention "to return about the End of Summer."[16] Receiving this letter shortly after she moved into the house they had planned for their retirement, Deborah was heartened. "I have bin so happey as to reseve severel of your dear letters with in these few days," she replied later that year, "and to see a man that had seen you[. H]e teles me you look well which is next to seeing of you."[17]

Other tender notes had arrived over the years. In 1770, hearing her husband was suffering from gout, Deborah wished she "was near aneuef to rube it with a lite hand."[18] Occasionally Franklin would reciprocate, but her letters were never enough to draw him home. Even when the news reached London that Deborah's health was failing— she had suffered a stroke, and her memory was growing cloudy—he continued to find excuses.[19] All this time Franklin remained comfortable and busy in his lodgings with Mrs. Stevenson at Craven Street. Over the years his range of responsibilities had continued to grow. Along with his work with the postal service and his original assignment as colonial agent for Pennsylvania, since the Stamp Act crisis he had taken on representative roles for Georgia, New Jersey, and Massachusetts too. These, along with his friendships, his interest in politics, and his various publishing projects, had always provided him with a reason for staying in Britain. But as Deborah aged and his interest with the powerful waned, justifying his absence became more difficult.

With the window for crossing the Atlantic closing soon, in August 1773 Franklin confronted on paper the problem of whether he should return. Knowing how much of his future happiness depended on getting this decision right, he attempted to remove emotion from his reasoning. Instead he divided his paper into two columns, labeling one "Stay" and the other "Go." Underneath he listed the competing arguments. He then put into practice a method he had explained to his scientific friend Joseph Priestley the previous year, striking out the arguments of equal weight and seeing which column ended with the greater number.

Franklin's "Prudential Algebra" was a typically idiosyncratic invention. But it also owed much to an increased zest for logical reasoning that was a hallmark of the Enlightenment. Newton had used this power to explain the forces that were at work in the solar system. If he could do that, then should it not be possible to harness the same techniques to improve the circumstances of their own lives and to crack the riddle of happiness? Was there a way, as the Scottish theorist Francis Hutcheson framed it in the 1720s, of accomplishing "the *greatest Happiness* for the *greatest* Numbers?" Thinking along those lines, in a piece of scholarship that aligned with the zeitgeist, Hutcheson had developed a whimsical recipe that he believed would enable people to reach what he called "a Moment of Good."[20] To get to this point, several important factors had to be considered. These were Benevolence (B), Ability (A), Self-love (S), and Interest (I). If these were milled together in the right concentrations, they would lead to the "Moment of Good" (M).

This thinking had led Hutcheson into such labyrinths as $M = B + S \times A = BA + BA$, which were not of great use to the average person in daily life. Franklin, though, toying with the same intellectual impulses, created a system that he thought was more practical. In a complex situation, he theorized, when it was easy to be drawn one way or another by disruptive emotions, a little prudential algebra was useful. Anyone who could write had the ability to divide a page into columns, and a result would soon emerge. Indeed, this is what happened that August. Nine arguments congregated in Franklin's "Stay" column against six in his "Go."[21] Whether this process completely resolved Franklin's dilemma or not, he was soon writing to Deborah once again. "My dear Child, I must, I find, stay another Winter here absent from you and my Family, but positively nothing shall prevent, God willing, my Returning in the Spring."[22]

His decision would have its consequences. For some years the eerie lull in the Anglo-American dispute had continued. Since the concessions that came with North's appointment in 1770, no great, disruptive episode had occurred. Nevertheless the political situation lay primed, and the most likely source of unrest remained Massachusetts. Franklin, along with a clever and fiery young lawyer called Arthur Lee, represented the colony in London, and he knew that if any trouble was to erupt then he would be deeply involved. And trouble was pretty much inevitable. In Boston there was a dangerous mix of personalities. James Otis, Samuel Adams, and the Sons of Liberty had long been active, holding rowdy town meetings that were attended by thousands. Ranged against them were the province's representatives: its governor Thomas Hutchinson, and lieutenant governor Andrew Oliver. There had been acrimony between these two groups for years. Oliver, in particular, was caught up in the troubles of 1765 during his short-lived stint as the stamp officer. Since then the opponents had jostled against each other on numerous occasions. As well as what he could learn from the papers, Franklin was kept informed of the latest disagreements by Thomas Cushing, the speaker of the Massachusetts assembly with whom, as the colony's agent, Franklin was in regular correspondence.

The most recent news Franklin had been relaying to Cushing was about tea. When North removed the Townshend Duties from the statue books in 1770, he had left the duty on tea intact. This, as Strahan pointed out to Franklin, was fair enough. A duty on tea predated anything Townshend had done, and its survival was symbolic as it mollified British politicians by upholding Parliament's supremacy. Strahan nevertheless saw the danger of the move. "This, you will say," he told Hall at the time, "is doing Things by Halves, of all others, in my Mind, the worst Method."[23] But while some Americans might not have liked it, the compromise was accepted at the time. As the majority of the colonies' tea was smuggled anyway, it was hardly a burden. A brittle compromise had been reached. Westminster could keep their principle and the colonists could keep their money.

In the spring of 1773, however, Franklin informed Cushing that this dynamic was poised to change. The catalyst was the East India Company. A lustily commercial, thoroughly amoral joint-stock corporation that had been expanding at a staggering rate for decades, in October 1772 the company sent a shock through British commerce and politics when its chairman revealed to Lord North that it was very nearly bankrupt. There was a range of causes: problems with revenue collection, the price of the annual levy, the shareholders' dividends. To stimulate back into life something that was deemed far too big to fail, a commission was established, which recommended that the company be bailed out with a variety of loans.

In addition to this, North's ministry wanted to allow the East India Company to generate some quick profits by removing the duties on tea being exported to the American colonies. As the company had amassed large stockpiles of the commodity, this seemed to be a sensible move. The Tea Act of May 1773 was calculated to incentivize profitable trade across the Atlantic. The only losers would be the gangs of smugglers who for years had monopolized the colonial tea market. There was a financial logic at play too, Franklin conceded, because with the export duties removed the tea might actually end up being cheaper, even though the ministry had decided to keep the old Townshend Duty in place. But that, he knew, was a blinkered way of evaluating the policy. "They have no Idea," he went on, "that any People can act from any Principle but that of Interest; and they believe that 3*d.* in a Pound of Tea, of which one does not drink perhaps 10 lb in a Year, is sufficient to overcome all the Patriotism of an American!"[24]

AS SUMMER REACHED ITS peak, Franklin left London as usual. At Little New Street there was no such rest. In early August, Strahan had the thrill of seeing *An Account of the Voyages to the South Sea*, with details drawn from Joseph Banks and James Cook's journals, complete its journey through his press. He had gained the contract to print the official account of the voyages due to his connection with government ministers like Sandwich. A marquee production, elegantly produced in three volumes on royal paper, featuring engravings by Giovanni Battista Cipriani and a selection of maps and charts "relative to Countries now first discovered" like Otaheite, New Zealand, and New Holland, for a steep price of three guineas, it was the kind of book that no one but Strahan could have produced.[25]

Meanwhile the more regular work continued. The *Monthly Review* and *London Gazette* had become staples for Strahan, with readerships in the town and country. But just as the capital filled up again after the summer exodus, the public's attention was caught by an article in a rival paper, Henry Sampson Woodfall's *Public Advertiser*. On September 11, a clever, teasing piece appeared, introduced by the sentence "RULES *by which* a GREAT EMPIRE *may be reduced to a* SMALL ONE." Thoroughly Swiftian in tone, it was addressed to "all Ministers who have the Management of extensive Dominions, which from their very Greatness are become troublesome to govern." A list of twenty rules followed, beginning:

> In the first Place, Gentlemen, you are to consider, that a great Empire, like a great Cake, is most easily diminished at the Edges. Turn your Attention therefore first to your remotest Provinces; that as you get rid of them, the next may follow in Order.[26]

For a few weeks these rules were the talk of the coffee houses. An even greater fuss, however, was produced by a second piece, which ran in the same paper on September 22. It began with an announcement:

> *For the* Public Advertiser
> The SUBJECT of the following Article of
> FOREIGN INTELLIGENCE
> Being exceedingly EXTRAORDINARY, is the
> Reason of its being separated from the usual
> Articles of *Foreign News*[27]

There followed the text of an edict that purported to have been issued by the King of Prussia. It was, as Strahan would have recognized immediately, an ingenious device. Frederick II was a well-known figure. Prussia had fought alongside Britain against France in the Seven Years' War, and there was a general feeling that it had been abandoned during the peace talks of 1762–63. Everyone knew that Frederick

was not the type to let such a slur pass. In recent times he had shown
his aggression, bullying the neighboring Poles and issuing belligerent
statements condemning the Dutch. The *Public Advertiser* piece played
on this. But rather than looking east to Poland or west to Holland, it
portrayed Frederick as turning his eyes across the North Sea. Here
lay Britain, a country that, Frederick pointed out, owed everything
to the Germanic peoples who had established it in the first place.

Composed in the high-flown courtly language of the day, the
"edict" claimed that since the peopling of the island, Britain had
thrived under Prussian protection. The time was well overdue that
"a Revenue should be raised from the said Colonies in Britain towards
our Indemnification." According to the edict a levy of 4½ percent
was soon to come into force on "all Goods, Wares and Merchan-
dizes, and on all Grain and other Produce of the Earth exported
from the said Island of Britain . . . *ad Valorem*, for the Use of us and
our Successors."[28] To comply with the terms of this, British merchants were obliged to present themselves at the port of Königsberg
to be "searched, and charged." In Britain itself, meanwhile, all the
mills and forges were to be shut, to eradicate any competition for the
manufactories of Prussia. The export of woolen goods and hats was
also to stop immediately. The "edict" concluded:

> And lastly, Being willing farther to favour Our said Colonies in
> Britain, We do hereby also ordain and command, that all the
> Thieves, Highway and Street-Robbers, House-breakers, Forger-
> ers, Murderers, So[domi]tes, and Villains of every Denomina-
> tion, who have forfeited their Lives to the Law in Prussia, but
> whom We, in Our great Clemency, do not think fit here to
> hang, shall be emptied out of our Gaols into the said Island of
> Great Britain *for the* BETTER PEOPLING *of that Country.*[29]

It would not have taken Strahan long to realize that he was reading the writing of his friend Franklin. Equally clear was the piece's

satirical brilliance. The "edict" turned the bitter colonial quarrel on its head, reimagining the world as a place where it was the British who lived in the shadow of an overbearing parent. As a printer, too, Strahan could appreciate the care with which Franklin and Woodfall had devised the hoax. It was inserted along with the foreign news and framed as a piece of "doubtful" intelligence that had reached London from Danzig. For these efforts, Franklin was rewarded. His identity may have been obvious to someone like Strahan, but others were more comprehensively fooled. Franklin wrote gleefully to his son William that he had been witness to a delightful episode at the home of Francis Dashwood, Bute's chancellor who had since inherited the title of Lord le Despencer. As Franklin stood chatting with him, one of the lord's friends came hurtling into the parlor with a copy of the *Public Advertiser* in his hands. "Here!" he announced, "here's news for ye!"

> *Here's the king of Prussia, claiming a right to this kingdom*! All stared, and I as much as any body; and he went on to read it. When he had read two or three paragraphs, a gentleman present said, *Damn his impudence, I dare say, we shall hear by next post that he is upon his march with one hundred thousand men to back this.*[30]

At this point, Franklin elaborated, the man,

> began to smoke it, and looking in my face said, *I'll be hanged if this is not some of your American jokes upon us.* The reading went on, and ended with abundance of laughing, and a general verdict that it was a fair hit: and the piece was cut out of the paper and preserved in my lord's collection.[31]

As well as framing Franklin as the teasing, knowing manipulator, the story is also revealing of the paranoia Britain was suffering from at that time. People had become defensive and hostile. They were easily inflamed by any story they deemed an insult to national pride. It was this mood Franklin had played upon, and he certainly had a little fun. But would such pieces change anything? Even Franklin was doubtful about that. Instead he saw his satires as part of a broader information campaign that was designed to put across the colonists' point of view. The pieces served another purpose as well. As he wrote in one of his early anonymous contributions to the *Pennsylvania Gazette* in the 1730s, "When the Writer conceals himself, he has the Advantage of hearing the Censure both of Friends and Enemies, express'd with more Impartiality."[32]

It was notable, too, that Franklin had conspired with Woodfall instead of Strahan for these last two pieces. But Franklin certainly still made use of his old friend from time to time. Earlier that year, for instance, Franklin had asked Strahan to print five hundred copies of a pamphlet from Massachusetts. *The Votes and Proceedings of the Freeholders and other Inhabitants of the Town of Boston* was a vehement production. Along with an outline of grievances against Britain, it contained a blunt condemnation of the behavior of the royal governor, Thomas Hutchinson, whose salary they asked to be halted. This was not the kind of sentiment Strahan liked. "Bostonian," as Johnson would soon point out, was becoming a colloquial shorthand for awkwardness and mischief. This quarrel between the colonists and their royal governor was the latest evidence of that. And over the course of the summer, the news that arrived from Boston suggested that the arguments had grown far worse. At the end of July a tantalizing story was reprinted from the *Boston Gazette*. It referred to events from six weeks earlier:

> For several Days past some extraordinary Discoveries have been talked of, which were expected to amaze the whole Province. Hints have been thrown out, that the Characters of some Men in Power would appear infamous in the highest Degree; all seemed to be a general Surmise and Expectation, until Wednesday about Eleven o'Clock before Noon, when the Galleries in the Commons House of Assembly were ordered to be cleared

of all present. This confirmed the general Opinion, and we are well informed that very important Matters will soon transpire, which will bring many dark Things to Light—gain many Proselytes to the Cause of Freedom—make tyrannical Rulers tremble—and give Occasion for the whole People to bless the Providence of God, who causeth the Wicked Man to fall into the Pit he hath digged for another.[33]

The riddle of this was soon laid bare. It turned out that some highly embarrassing political letters had been leaked. Of the ten letters, four had been written by Andrew Oliver, the lieutenant governor of the province. The other six were the work of Hutchinson. Dating to around the time of the Wilkes affair, four or five years before, when Boston was experiencing a similar period of civil strife, they were part of a private correspondence between Oliver and Hutchinson and a British associate of Grenville's called Thomas Whately. Just how the letters had been leaked was unknown. But one thing was plain. Oliver and Hutchinson were mortified by their appearance.

The reason for this was obvious for everyone who read the printed transcripts of the letters (and pretty much everyone did) during the summer of 1773. Oliver and, particularly, Hutchinson had used them as a forum to gossip about politics in Boston. For Hutchinson's opponents, reading them several years on, they were like a passport into a hidden world: a place where the division between the private and public selves evaporated. He wrote scathingly about opponents like James Otis "and his creatures." He described them as modern-day "Catalines," evoking the malevolent rebel who had sought to seize control of Rome. In paragraph after paragraph, it was plain to see where Hutchinson's loyalties lay. Everything connected to the British interest in the province was "ours." Everything else was "theirs."

For his opponents, the most enraging letter of all was one of Hutchinson's from January 20, 1769, in which he urged a policy of intensified firmness toward Massachusetts. He dwelt on "the *depen-*

dence which a colony ought to have upon the parent state," reasoning that if no measures were taken quickly "to secure this dependence, or no thing more than some declaratory acts or resolve, *it is all over with us* . . . I never think of the measures necessary for the peace and good order of the colonies without pain," he confided to Whately, continuing:

> There must be an abridgement of what are called English liber-
> ties. I relieve myself by considering, that in a remove from the
> state of nature to the most perfect state of government, there
> must be a great restraint of natural liberty. I doubt whether it
> is possible to project a system of government, in which a colony
> 3000 miles distant from the parent-state, shall enjoy all the
> liberty of the parent state.[34]

Hutchinson had ended this, the most combustible of all his let-ters, with a plea that his sentiments be kept secret. His alarm in the summer of 1773, therefore, when he heard that they were circulating freely around the colony, can only be imagined. By then it was too late. Hutchinson was forced to confront the gloomy reality. His own words would be used against him. The letters would be quoted in whatever way and for whatever purpose anyone wanted. Well drilled after years of combat, his enemies in the province knew exactly how to extract every drop of political capital from his indiscretions. They could tar him as a cold-hearted authoritarian, a tool of the British government who cared nothing for the happiness of the citizens he was supposed to represent. It was of no surprise to Hutchinson that a petition was drawn up, from the House of Representatives, bound for Franklin in Craven Street, stating that:

> The people of New England had no confidence in their
>   Governor
> That they considered him as an enemy to the Province

That the breach between them and him was so open and
avowed, and the enmity between them so declared and
positive, the public business of the Province was thereby so
essentially hindered and impeded, that it was necessary for
the public service, as well as their happiness to remove him.[35]

By the time the reports made it to London, Hutchinson's fate
seemed sealed. But one puzzle did linger: How had Whately's letters
been leaked? It was clear that they had been sent from Massachusetts to London four or five years before. But how had they returned?
Whately himself was now dead, which added to the mystery. So was
George Grenville, "who was the Centre to which flow'd" all to do
with America.[36] Yet somehow the letters had arrived back in Boston
for their inevitable detonation. The answer to this riddle eluded everyone throughout the autumn. Then, in December, as the initial interest
was beginning to subside, there was a flare of anger in the newspapers.
An accusation was made and a duel was fought between Whately's
brother, William, and an opponent called John Temple. Readers soon
learned the full story. William Whately had publicly insinuated that
Temple was responsible for the leak. Temple had bristled at this, and
there was the familiar exchange of letters. The duel that followed
was a shabby affair. Instead of pistols, Temple and Whately had used
swords. According to accounts, Whately left the field "dangerously
wounded." With the issue still undecided, a second duel was expected.

Whether Strahan knew more than anyone else up till this point
is impossible to say. But shortly before Christmas 1773, it was to
his Scottish friend that Franklin again turned for help. With a life at
risk, Franklin concluded he had no other option. In the edition for
December 23–25, a notice appeared, "To the PRINTER of the London
Chronicle." It began:

Finding that two gentlemen have been unfortunately engaged in
a Duel, about a transaction and its circumstances of which both

of them are totally ignorant and innocent, I think it incumbent on me to declare (for the prevention of farther mischief, as far as such a declaration may contribute to prevent it) that I alone am the person who obtained and transmitted to Boston the letters in question.[37]

TO MARK THE SEASON, William Whitehead, the Poet Laureate, produced a poem: *Ode to the New Year, 1774*. It contained a warning. He depicted Britain as a wronged and angry "Imperial Xerxes," whose "fond eyes" were "suffus'd with tears." Whitehead cast a glance across the globe and foresaw dangerous times ahead:

Pass but a few short fleeting years,
And all that pomp which now appears
A glorious, living scene,
Shall breathe its last; shall fall, shall die,
And low in earth yon myriads lie,
As they had never been![38]

In Craven Street, Franklin also began the year with a sense of foreboding. His forced confession regarding the Hutchinson Letters had left him totally exposed. In an instant he had given credence to the rumors of months, even years, regarding his conduct. Those who had long suspected that Franklin was guilty of nefarious activities—snide pieces in the papers, antagonistic letters to America—now seemingly had proof of it. Here once again were the old claims: of John Webbe's ancient charge that he "bespattered the Characters" of those he did not like, or John Penn's acid description of his "inveterate malice and ill nature."

"I am told by some," Franklin wrote in a letter to Cushing in Boston, "that it was imprudent in me to avow the obtaining and sending those letters, for that administration will resent it. I have not much apprehension of this, but if it happens I must take the consequences."[39]

This was the voice of experience. Franklin had found himself in scrapes before and things always worked themselves out. As he explained to his sister Jane, "One's true Happiness depends more upon one's own Judgement of one's self, on a Consciousness of Rectitude in Action and Intention."[40] This was a point Johnson made in *Rasselas* too. "No evil is insupportable, but that which is accompanied with consciousness of wrong."[41] To Franklin's mind, his conduct when it came to the letters had been, if not quite unquestionable, then at least understandable. Having been made aware of them, what else was he to do?

Franklin's involvement with the Hutchinson and Oliver letters had begun about a year earlier. Someone—Franklin never revealed who—passed them to him after Thomas Whately's death. Quickly realizing that these were, as it was later put, "public letters, to public persons, on public affairs, and intended to produce public measures," Franklin concluded it was his duty as agent for Massachusetts to send them to Cushing, the speaker of the House. This was a somewhat unusual move for Franklin, who rarely placed his faith in the discretion of others. But they were sent in December 1772 with the instruction that they should only be shown to a select few. Cushing had complied with this. He also refused to reveal his source for the letters, even though Franklin had not asked for this directly. Consequently only Cushing and one other person in Boston knew of Franklin's involvement. But many more started to hear about the letters as 1773 progressed. It turned out that Franklin had forgotten his own advice. As *Poor Richard* pointed out, "three can keep a secret, if two of them are dead." In this case Franklin had put the letters into the trust of many more than three. Soon, inevitably, the whole province and, soon after, the whole Anglo-American world knew what Hutchinson and Oliver had written. There would be few worse-kept secrets that century.

Franklin's unflustered attitude in January 1774 might well have been vindicated were it not for the timing. Just as the first volume of Macaulay's *History* would not have caused such a stir had it not been released at such a politically charged moment, and just as Wilkes's return in 1768 would not have instigated such a period of upheaval had it not followed a desperately cold winter, so Franklin's disasters of January 1774 would not have been so extreme had not the news from the colonies been so inflammatory. But, after the long and uneasy lull, the confrontation had finally come.

As the East India ships, laden with tea, had approached the American coast in early winter, the familiar fires were kindled ashore. "We are now in anxious expectation of the tea ship," came a report from Philadelphia. "She will meet a warm reception here, as we are determined the Captain shall not land one Chest of it."[42] In Boston, the temper of the people was even more belligerent. Under Hutchinson's orders the three ships were permitted to anchor. But on December 16, a party of locals disguised as Mohawks boarded and seized control of them, carted a total of 342 chests up onto the deck, and tipped their contents over the gunwales and into the harbor.

The news reached London on January 19. While the perpetrators of the crime were, at least for now, well out of reach in Boston, Franklin was not. It was not just King George who was "much hurt" by the reports, but time-worn friends of America like Chatham too.[43] For Franklin, his lodgings in Craven Street had long felt like a happy enclave at the heart of a fabulous city. Reading the aghast commentary in the papers, he must have felt as if the old reality had vanished and he was instead marooned in some embattled fort far behind enemy lines. That January had already started badly. He had been rattled by the news that William Whately was bringing a chancery suit against him for the theft of the letters.

Something more ominous followed the week after. A series of notes were delivered to his door, requesting his attendance at a meeting at a debating chamber in Whitehall called the Cockpit. The ministry was at last ready to hear the petition for Hutchinson's removal. Thinking this odd—petitions did not usually require committee meetings—Franklin was more disturbed by the sight that greeted him at the Cockpit. There he found Hutchinson and Oliver's London representative—a man named Israel Mauduit—sitting next to the formidable figure of Alexander Wedderburn, the Solicitor General. A tense few hours had followed, during which Wedderburn had questioned the veracity of the letters and then interrogated Franklin about his behavior. With Franklin protesting that he had been cornered, the session had been adjourned for three weeks to allow him to find himself legal counsel.

It was during this intermission that the news of Boston's so-called Tea Party reached London. While Franklin fretted about the best course of action to take, rumors were beginning to be passed around the town that he had been "grossly abused by the solicitor-general at the council board." These were premature, Franklin explained in a letter to Cushing:

> He had only intended it, and mentioned that intention. I heard too, from all quarters, that the ministry and all the courtiers were highly enraged against me for transmitting those letters. I was called an incendiary, and the papers were filled with invectives against me. Hints were given me, that there were some thoughts of apprehending me, seizing my papers, and sending me to Newgate. I was well informed that a resolution was taken to deprive me of my place; it was only thought best to defer it till after the hearing: I suppose, because I was there to be so blackened, that nobody should think it injustice.[44]

There was an indistinctness to all of this. Was there some Philip Carteret Webb figure at work somewhere in the offices of Whitehall? Had Hillsborough or Lord North himself decided that Franklin must be neutralized? Franklin was not sure. But if the anxiety that clung to him during January 1774 were to take a human shape, then that shape must surely have been Alexander Wedderburn's. Wedderburn was the kind of person one hopes never to meet in a courtroom. In one sense he was just another in the never-ending stream of formidable Scots that were springing from the universities of Edinburgh and Glasgow before traveling south to ply their trade. But even among such company, there was an edge to Wedderburn. Still only forty, he was known for his ferocious work ethic, his daring, and his utter lack of deference to figures of authority. One story described the day he quit the Scottish courts in exasperation. Having been chastised by a judge for the asperity of his language, Wedderburn apparently pulled off his gown, set it down before the judge, bowed, and then walked out of court. The same night, so the story went, he took the road south, for London and the Inner Temple.

This was the man whose eyes met Franklin's as the Privy Council resumed the case of the petition at the Cockpit on Saturday, January 29. Appreciating the jeopardy that he was in, Franklin had taken some measures to protect himself. He had hired a lawyer, the former Solicitor General John Dunning, who had instructed him that if he was interrogated on the transmission of the letters, he was not obliged to answer. This was some comfort to Franklin as he came into the Cockpit that day, wearing a suit of spotted Manchester velvet. Gazing around he could see that it was going to be one of those classic Westminster occasions. Like the day of Wilkes's humiliation in the Commons, people seemed to have had advance warning. "There never was such an appearance," wrote Franklin, "of privy counsellors on any occasion, not less than thirty-five, besides an immense crowd of other auditors."[45] Among those watching were Edmund Burke and Joseph Priestley, Lord North and Lord le Despencer, General Thomas Gage, and a young Jeremy Bentham. Surely, though the fact is not recorded, Strahan was there too. If he was then Strahan would have seen two figures who were completely familiar to him. One was his old Philadelphian friend, his "countenance as immovable as if his features had been made of *wood*."[46] Then there was the sight of his countryman, Wedderburn.

The hearing began, as ever, with the formalities. The petition against Hutchinson and Oliver was read. A few remarks then followed from Dunning. Unfortunately for Franklin, his counsel was suffering from a "disorder on his lungs that weakened his voice exceedingly." Wedderburn, who came next, had no such problem. He opened with what he called a "history" of recent events in Massachusetts province. During this, Franklin later told Cushing, he bestowed plenty of abuse on the colony. The most venomous section of his speech, however, was personally reserved for Franklin. Wedderburn's attack was wide ranging, but in essence it was an assault on Franklin's character. He had shown himself for who he was, Wedderburn contended, by his high-handed conduct. "If there be any thing held sacred in the intercourse of mankind," he proposed, "it is their private letters of friendship." Franklin had violated this sanctity, offering them up into public, "for his own private purpose."

> How he got at them, or in whose hands they were at the time of Mr Whately's death, the Doctor has not yet thought proper to tell us. Till he do, he wittingly leaves the world at liberty to conjecture about them as they please, and to reason upon those conjectures.—But let the letters have been lodged where they may, from the hour of Mr Thomas Whately's death, they became the property of his brother, and of the Whately family. Dr Franklin could not but know this, and that no one had a right to dispose of them but they only.—Other receivers of goods dishonourably come by, may plead as a pretence for keeping them, that they don't know who are the proprietors: in this case there was not the common excuse of ignorance; the Doctor knew whose they were, and yet did not restore them to the right owner.—This property is as sacred and as precious to gentlemen of integrity, as their family plate or jewels are. And

no man who knows the Whatelys, will doubt, but that they would much sooner have chosen that any person should have taken their plate, and sent it to Holland, for his avarice, than that he should have secreted the letters of their friends, their brother's friend, and their father's friend, and sent them away to Boston to gratify an enemy's malice.[47]

One point at a time Wedderburn refuted the case for making the letters public.

"But," says the Doctor [Franklin], "they were written by public officers."—Can then a man in a public station have no private friends? and write no private letters? . . .

But "they were written on public affairs." A very grievous offence! But it is a crime, of which probably we all of us have been guilty, and ought not surely for that only to forfeit the common rights of humanity . . .

But "the writers of them desired secrecy." True, they did so. And what man is there, who, when he is writing in confidence, does not wish for the same thing? Does not every man say things to a friend which he would not chuse to have published to other people, and much less to his enemies? Would letters of friendship be letters of friendship if they contained nothing but such indifferent things as might be said to all the world?[48]

Throughout all this Franklin stood stock-still, "the butt of his invective and ribaldry for near an hour."[49] The experience was humiliating, he later confessed to Cushing, but the worst of it was that Wedderburn was permitted to go on. "Not one of their lordships checked and recalled the orator to the business before them, but on the contrary (a very few excepted) they seemed to enjoy highly the entertainment, and frequently burst out in loud applause." As the minutes passed, and Wedderburn sensed the freedom that he was being given, his restraint vanished. Given the codes of the day his insinuations against Franklin, "whose whole conduct in this affair has been secret and mysterious," were scandalous.[50] His theme was not dissimilar to the one Burke put at the heart of his *Discontents* pamphlet several years earlier. Franklin, he suggested, lay at the heart of a malevolent "junto" who were bent on filling the British Empire with division and bringing down figures as irreproachable as the royal governor of Massachusetts.

What would a decent person do, Wedderburn wondered, if they came into possession of private letters? A man whose

> heart was cast in the common mould of humanity, would have been apt to say, These are letters irregularly obtained: the writers desire that everything they write should be kept secret: they belong to Mr Whately, who never injured *me*: I will therefore return them to the right owner.
>
> —Dr Franklin's reasoning is of a very different cast. After having just before told us, These are public letters, sent to public persons, designed for public purposes, and therefore I have a right to betray them; he now says, These are letters which the writers desire may be kept secret, and therefore I will send them to their enemies.[51]

The shock of his experience at the Cockpit was so profound that it took Franklin a fortnight to collect himself to write a full account for Cushing. "It may be supposed that I am very angry on this occasion," he owned, "but indeed what I feel on my own account is half lost in what I feel for the publick." There was no sense left in Westminster's politicians; no mildness and no willingness to understand. All criticism, Franklin wrote, was treated as an affront, "and the messengers punished as offenders." In such a world, "who will henceforth send petitions? and who will deliver them?" For ages past, Franklin elaborated, "it has been thought a dangerous thing in any state to stop up the vent of grief." But this is what had happened. "Where complaining is a crime," Franklin sighed, "hope becomes despair."[52]

Franklin was doing well to appreciate the broader point. After all, what had happened over the past month could easily have been interpreted as simply a personal attack on himself. He was at home recovering from Wedderburn's assault on Sunday, January 30 when the news arrived that he had been relieved from his role of deputy Postmaster General of America. Days later, with a full transcript of Wedderburn's speech before the Privy Council already in print, the papers were reporting that Hugh Finlay, the Surveyor of the Post in America, had been appointed to replace him. By then Franklin knew his British political career was over. And it was likely that the ministry's vengeance would not be restricted to him. "This Line is just to acquaint you that I am well," he started a letter to William at the start of February,

> and that my Office of Deputy-Postmaster is taken from me. As there is no Prospect of your being ever promoted to a better Government, and That you hold has never defray'd its Expences, I wish you were well settled in your Farm. 'Tis an honester and a more honourable because a more independent Employment. You will hear from others the Treatment I have receiv'd. I leave you to your own Reflections and Determinations upon it.[53]

While many enjoyed the stories of Franklin's public disgrace, some clear-eyed commentators saw the folly and the unfairness of it. Hadn't the government, when all was said and done, merely made an enemy of a friend? Hadn't they alienated the most influential American in London? One newspaper article lambasted Wedderburn, describing his attack as "gross, brutal, and vulgar . . . This Clodius of the Bar produced no Fact of Argument; all was Rant, Rhapsody, and Declamation against the Agent, for having done his Duty."[54] But then, who could expect anything better? Another paper weighed in:

> It is a melancholy Reflection, and is daily made by almost every Man, that when the present King ascended the Throne, the whole Empire was in Unanimity, Happiness, and Prosperity; and that now every Part of it is distracted, miserable, and impoverished.— This horrible Reverse is accomplished in a very few Years; first, by the accursed Councils of an ignorant, despotic Scotch Favourite, and is now not only continued, but encreased and aggravated, by a Set of low, upstart Beings, as ignorant and tyrannical as himself; breathing all the Tory Nonsense of Prerogative, and infusing all the Stuart Principles of arbitrary Power; with all his Pride and Weakness, without his Rank and affected Consequence, to give something like Weight to their Proceedings.[55]

This same thought was playing in Franklin's mind too. Having regained his balance, by late February he embarked on a pamphlet-length riposte to the printed version of Wedderburn's speech. He also arranged for his exchange of letters with Strahan on the colonial controversy to be printed—something he hoped would clarify his position. But it soon became clear that the old fight had gone out of him. His rejoinder to Wedderburn never materialized, and while his London life seemingly continued unchanged at Craven Street, something had tilted in his mind. By the summer of 1774, his printing account with Strahan was closed. There would be no more anonymous pieces for the paper, no more earnest political pamphlets. Instead he began to spend more time on letters to friends in America. For the first time in his life, perhaps, news from the western side of the Atlantic appealed more than that from the east. "You will hear before this comes to hand," he wrote to his sister Jane, "that I am depriv'd of my Office. Don't let this give you any Uneasiness. You and I have almost finished the Journey of Life; we are now but a little way from home, and have enough in our Pockets to pay the Post Chaises."[56]

ONE PARTICULAR STORY TO catch his eye arrived in June. It described the mock execution of Wedderburn and Hutchinson in Philadelphia, for the crime of "traducing the American Colonies, and insulting their Agent before his Majesty's Privy Council for doing his duty." The two men were thrown into a cart and conducted through the streets Franklin knew so well. On Wedderburn's breast was fixed a label:

> The infamous
> WEDDERBURNE
> A pert prime Prater, of a Scabby race;
> Guilt in his heart, and famine in his face.[57]

Despite all this, Franklin still found it hard to leave. For William, writing from New Jersey, the continual, illogical delays were maddening. "If there was any Prospect of your being able to bring the People in Power to your way of Thinking, or of those of your Way of Thinking's being brought into Power," he argued,

> I should not think so much of your Stay. But as you have had by this Time pretty strong Proofs that neither can be reasonably expected and that you are look'd upon with an evil Eye in that Country, and are in no small Danger of being brought into Trouble for your political Conduct, you had certainly better return, while you are able to bear the Fatigues of the Voyage, to a Country where the People revere you, and are inclined to pay a Deference to your Opinions.[58]

Though Franklin did not know it, by the time that William wrote these words, one thing at least was certain. Deborah would never see her husband again. She died on December 19. On Christmas Eve William wrote to his father, "I came here on Thursday last to attend the Funeral of my poor old Mother."

> Your old Friend H. Roberts and several other of your Friends were Carriers, and a very respectable Number of the Inhabitants were at the Funeral . . . Her Death was no more than might be reasonably expected after the paralytic Stroke she received some Time ago, which greatly affected her Memory and Understanding. She told me, when I took Leave of her, on my Removal to Amboy, that she never expected to see you unless you returned this Winter, for that she was sure she should not live till next Summer. I heartily wish you had happened to have come over in the Fall, as I think her Disappointment in that respect preyed a good deal on her Spirits.[59]

Separations of all kinds were beginning to crowd in. Soon after the news of the Tea Party reached London, North's government appointed General Gage as Hutchinson's replacement in Massachusetts, and he arrived on May 13, 1774. Four coercive acts had meanwhile been passed through Parliament. These, labeled the Intolerable Acts in America, closed the port at Boston, suspended the province's charter, removed powers from the local courts, and permitted red-coat troops to be billeted in requisitioned—although not private—buildings. The full text of all these acts was produced at the King's Printing House in Little New Street. At a surprise general election, called six months early in September of that year, North's majority was bolstered. Among the incoming MPs who would support the acts that were to bring the colonists to heel was Strahan, who purchased the seat of Malmesbury. "I am entirely for coercive methods with these obstinate madmen," Strahan confessed to his friend David Hume: "And why should we despair of success?—Why should we suffer the Empire to be so dismembered, without the utmost exertions on our part?"[60]

To many people's minds, Franklin had lingered far too long in London. But before his eventual departure in March 1775, he did at least perform one more decisive contribution to the colonial cause. It appeals all the more to historians today, because for once Franklin did not appreciate the gravity of what he was doing. On September 30, the day King George dissolved the Parliament that had sat since 1768, Franklin wrote a letter of recommendation for "an ingenious, worthy young man" who had decided to migrate.[61] Like David Hall thirty years before, Thomas Paine had set his heart on a voyage to Philadelphia.

Sixteen

ATLANTICUS

OF ALL THE TIMES to sail across the Atlantic, late autumn was the worst. In October and November, the atmosphere was at its most charged and capricious. The captains of the packet vessels that shuttled to and fro throughout the year knew the signs well. The western horizon would darken. Low, fast, scudding clouds—known as messenger clouds—would race over the tops of the mainmast. Within hours the wind would be whistling through the rigging and the sea beneath would have turned an iron gray. Suddenly the packet would feel very small and very frail. For captains this was the time to act: to strike the sails, to secure the hatches, and to order the passengers below.

In 1764, Franklin had been so eager to escape Philadelphia that he had embarked in November nonetheless. His crossing had been an exhilarating, high-speed affair. A decade on, with no appetite for a repeat, he remained in London awaiting the gentler winds of spring. Thomas Paine reasoned differently. Once he had obtained Franklin's letter of recommendation, Paine's plans to leave Britain for good went forward at speed. One can imagine him in the early autumn of 1774—tall, willowy, serious, with his flashing dark eyes and a mane of black hair—sitting in a London coffee house, dashing off letters of farewell to his friends in Thetford and Lewes, regretting the nature of the separation but emphasizing the charms of Philadelphia and his hopes for yet another new start.

There is an intensity to this vision. Once Paine was set on a course of action, he was decisive. He was soon down at the docks, trying to secure his berth. Paine discounted the first vessel he saw, "it not having proper Conveniences," but he almost immediately located a second.[1] By the middle of October, Paine was at sea on the *London Packet*, commanded by one Captain Cooke. Now, as the vessel rose and fell beneath his feet, he was free to focus his mind on America.

Paine's crossing turned out to be a grim affair. But it was not the weather that made him miserable, it was the sickness that broke out once he was at sea. Traveling with him on the *London Packet* were 120 other passengers, the majority of them indentured servants from Britain and Germany, eager to find their fortunes in Pennsylvania. Perhaps it was in the luggage of one of these that a mite or a louse had brought aboard the bacteria that caused typhus. Within weeks this disease—Paine called it a "Putrid Fever"—was working its way through the ship's company. For those on board, living in an age where medical efforts were far more hopeful than precise, it was a "dismal and dangerous" time.[2] Everyone knew the symptoms. Once infected a body would grow feverish, perpetual headaches would rage, the pulse would drop, and strength would falter—as would the stability of the mind.

Although there was a doctor aboard, there was very little that medicine could do. Contemporary wisdom recommended a course of "Peruvian bark"—the ground stem and branches of the cinchona plant—with good liquors and cold air. At least Paine, who had paid more for a better berth, was not crowded beneath with the majority of the ship's company. Instead, as he fought the sickness he had at least some conversation to look forward to with the captain. Cooke, in turn, could keep his sick passenger updated with the ship's progress and the state of the wind and the weather, and ply him with stories of Philadelphia. From these conversations, Paine could at least get a sense of perspective. Ship fever was dangerous, but there were worse things that could happen to a vessel that was sailing on the Atlantic so late in the season.

The worst had happened at this very time of year a dozen years before to a slave ship called *Phoenix*. Sailing from London, the *Phoenix* had traveled to the Guinea coast to pick up its cargo of 332 slaves. Its captain, a Mr. McGacher, then turned westward into the Atlantic bound for Chesapeake Bay. On October 20, 1762, the *Phoenix* was caught in a tremendous gale, "with Thunder and Lightning, the Sea running very high."[3] McGacher struck sails and sought to weather the storm with bare masts. But soon water was rising in the hold. A desperate few hours followed. With all hands pumping below, McGacher changed tactics completely. He ordered the sails up and tried to put the ship before the wind. This was more than the *Phoenix* could take. Six hours after the storm struck, the situation was bleak. The foremast had collapsed, the rigging was sprawled across deck, casks were floating on seven feet of water in the hold, and the pumps were choked with sand ballast. McGacher now ordered the guns to be hove overboard, which righted the ship a little. A frantic period of bailing and pumping then began.

The slaves, who till this time had been secured below, were let out of irons and for almost two days they joined the relentless effort to save the ship. But with all the stores spoiled, time was against them. At length the slaves, according to one account, became "very sullen and unruly." It was hardly surprising. They had not been given any food of any kind for two days, "excepting a Dram." Half of the strongest of them were clapped back into irons and fastened below. For two days more, efforts to save the ship continued. But during this time many of the trapped slaves had worked themselves free of their chains and were attempting to break through the gratings. "We were obliged," the account went on, "for the Preservation of our own

Lives, to kill 50 of the Ring-leaders, and [the] stoutest of them." The story then reached its wretched, appalling conclusion.

> It is impossible to describe the Misery the poor Slaves underwent, having had no fresh Water or Food for five Days. Their dismal Cries and Shrieks, and most frightful Looks, added a great Deal to our Misfortunes; four of them were found dead, and one drowned herself in the Hold. This Evening the Ship gained on us, and three Seamen dropt down at the Pump with Fatigue and Thirst, which could not be quenched, though Wine, Rum and Shrub, were given them alternately. On Tuesday Morning the Ship had gained, during the Night, above a Foot of Water, and the Seamen quite wore out, and many of them in Despair. About Ten in the Forenoon we saw a Sail; about Two she discovered us, and bore down upon us; at Five spoke us, being the King George of Londonderry, James Mackey, Master; he immediately promised to take us on board, and hoisted out his Yawl, it then blowing very fresh, the Gale increasing, prevented him from saving any Thing but the White Peoples Lives (which were 36 in Number) not even any of our Cloathes, or one Slave, the Boat being scarce able to live in the Sea the last Trip she made.[4]

The shocking story of the slave ship *Phoenix* did make the pages of the *Pennsylvania Gazette*. But it did not cause any prolonged period of introspection. While almost everyone realized how dreadful the episode was, it was explained away as the kind of thing that occasionally happened on an ocean voyage. Paine's perspective was quite different. To him America was a land of promise. There was no good reason for it to be burdened by the vices of the Old World. When the *London Packet* came to anchor in the Delaware, Paine was still too weak to turn in his bed without help, and he had to be carried ashore. His entrance into America was not auspicious, but a conviction burned inside him. America, like him, might be sick. But with his help, very soon, they would both be well.

THOMAS PAINE WAS THE sort of character Samuel Johnson treated with suspicion. He was drifting, peripheral, restless. Originally from the quiet town of Thetford in Norfolk, where he was born the son of a Quaker staymaker in January 1737, Paine had never demonstrated any ability to stick at things for long. Although he did not like to talk about his past, Franklin had likely gleaned the bones of it. Paine had buried one wife and separated from a second. He had been apprenticed as a staymaker, but he had given this up to work, in two stints, for the excise office. His most recent posting had been at Lewes on the Sussex Downs, but now that had been curtailed too. His offense this time was "having quitted his business, without obtaining the Board's Leave for so doing, and being gone off on account of the Debts which he hath contracted."[5] In the more distant past, at a raw, adventurous age, Paine had sailed on a privateer in the opening phases of the Seven Years' War. For Johnson this would have been the detail to secure his verdict. "Men go to sea," he once commented, "before they know the unhappiness of that way of life; and when they have come to know it, they cannot escape from it."[6] That Paine had survived to return, and return with prize money, was more luck than his judgment deserved.

For Franklin, as well, Paine's history was scarcely cause for optimism. The colonies had long been filled with inconstant, ill-omened characters like him: those whose talents were compromised by some defect in their personality. Franklin had known scores of such people during his younger days in Philadelphia. There was John Webbe, of course, and others rose in his memory as he worked on his *Autobiography* in the early 1770s. One was his first employer, the bearded eccentric Samuel Keimer, who had roared insults at him in the street. Another was a printer called David Harry, who had ruined himself with his lust for luxury. Both Harry and Keimer (and Webbe for all he knew) had ended up the same way—sailing off in ruin to Barbados for yet another new start. Casting his eye over Paine in the parlor of Mrs. Stevenson's in Craven Street, Franklin must have wondered what this man's fault was. Pride? Passion? Drink?

Despite all this there was something, if not quite impressive, then striking about Paine. In Lewes people noticed a glimmer in his eyes. They were "full, brilliant and singularly piercing." He was gracious in public, too, and had a feel for fashion, wearing "his hair cued with side curls and powdered," which made him look "altogether like a gentle-man of the old French school." It was in private, though, that Paine really shone, engaging his friends with his "bold, acute, and indepen-dent" Whiggish views.[7] He was known for his unusual gift for writing as well. Some years before, Paine had been selected, out of thousands of other excisemen, to draft a petition for an increase in their wages. He had made a fine job of it. The skills had always been there. One of the few remaining traces of his early life is a sprightly verse epitaph, written at the age of eight, on the death of a pet crow.

Here lies the body of John Crow,
Who once was high but now is low;
Ye brother Crows take warning all,
For as you rise, so must you fall.[8]

This fragment provides a captivating glimpse. It is written with a knowing humor and a surprising sense of perspective for someone so young. We can imagine the young boy in the country town, the skit-tish crow refusing his approach and darting away to a nearby tree. Then shortly after, the boy looking down at the crow's lifeless body, drawing his lesson from this. Young Tom was struck by the thought that we should all be wary of pride. Fate will, ultimately, level us all.

Thirty years later, in December 1774, Paine still had plenty of cause to ponder the caprice of fate. This time last year he had been married, employed, and seemingly settled in Lewes on England's

South Downs. Now he was in America, with scarcely more than Franklin's letter of recommendation in his pocket and a great gulf of possibilities opening up before him. As he recovered his spirits, he ventured out into the city. In Philadelphia, this was one of the most charming times of the year. At Christmas, when the ground was frozen underfoot and the sky was bright and blue, the people stirred into life. It was a custom for locals to roast oxen on the banks of the Delaware, while braver souls ventured onto the river's "thick ribbed ice." Sometimes the ice "would crack and rend itself by its own weight, without separating, in sounds like thunder."[9]

In the absence of any certain evidence, it is tempting to place Paine in this scene at Christmas 1774, gazing out onto the Delaware, or venturing up Arch Street to the site of the great skating ponds around Seventh and Eighth Streets. During his time in Lewes, Paine had gained a reputation for ice skating, being known as "the Commodore." But there was nothing in all England to compare with what greeted him now. Philadelphians had long learned to take advantage of the cold winter weather, donning skates and woolen coats and heading out onto the ice in their thousands. The best skaters were celebrities. To watch them sweeping across the ponds in vast elegant curves, with their arms folded triumphantly across their bodies, was one of the sights to see. The most cherished part of the spectacle was known as the "Philadelphian Salute." This was executed by simultaneously sliding to a stop, doffing the hat, and sinking to a dignified bow.

On the cusp of 1775, the Philadelphian Salute was an appropriate emblem for a city filled with confidence and style. By the time of Paine's arrival, its population had swelled to an estimated thirty thousand, three times what it had been in the 1740s. Such growth firmly established Philadelphia as the largest city in the colonies. It was the most vibrant too. Exploring its streets in early January, Paine would have been able to see this for himself. Besides the older civic buildings—the State House, Court House, the Gaol—he could look at the new college building at the junction of Arch and Fourth Street, and the Pennsylvania Hospital out in the purer air near the Schuylkill. This was unquestionably the finest medical establishment in America.

The beating heart of commercial Philadelphia, however, remained around Market Street. Everything was for sale here. The well-to-do could buy a coach from Mr. Johnson, designed with the fashionable high wheels and crane necks that were usually seen in London. Crossing Market Street, they could nip into Wright's confectionery store for macaroons, Shrewsbury cake, almond chips, raspberry jam, sugar plums, and citron peel. The range was impressive, but so was the service. Customers could order up Mrs. Wright's highly regarded biscuits "upon an hour's warning." Nearby was a drapery shop, run by the appropriately named Mr. Stretch, who stocked every cut of clothing imaginable in fabrics that ranged from silk to muslin. A more surprising combination of goods was to be found at William Norton's, who specialized in chocolate, ground coffee, and mustard. For someone of bookish tastes like Paine, one obvious destination was John Sparkhawk's London Book-Store, just around the corner on Second Street, where there was also an assortment of other "curious hardware": tea urns, knives and forks, eye-glasses, horse pistols, telescopes, snuff boxes, mathematical drawing instruments, razor cases, and Red Morocco velvet pouches.

For all of the lure of Market Street, however, over the past few months the focus had been directed toward a different part of Philadelphia. From early September to late October, a Continental Congress had convened at Carpenters' Hall, a handsome new brick building on Chestnut Street. Week after week, fifty-six delegates from twelve colonies (Georgia decided against attending) had gathered inside to hammer out the collective response to the Intolerable Acts. The delegates represented a full spectrum of views, from the hawkish John Adams to the conciliatory John Dickinson. In October the Congress had issued a Declaration of Rights and Resolves, which were a response to both the Acts and another loathed piece of legislation, the Quebec Act. This, passed earlier in the year at Westminster, returned to the

Canadians the right to practice Catholicism and live under French Law, causing dismay in the colonies. All this, the Congress declared, was "impolitic, unjust and cruel, as well as unconstitutional."[10]

It seems inevitable that Paine must have strolled up Chestnut Street in early 1775 to have a look at Carpenter's Hall for himself and to think about the events of the last few months. By that point many of the formative events of the revolution to come had already taken place. John Adams had arrived from Boston. Before Adams had left the "happy, peaceful, the elegant, the hospitable and polite city of Philadelphia," he had met Benjamin Rush, along with the tall, silent Virginian George Washington.[11] There was no Thomas Jefferson quite yet, but his cousin, Peyton Randolph, had been here and served as Congress's first president. Along with September's Declaration of Rights and Resolves, yet another petition had just been composed for the consideration of King George in London too.

Almost everything lay primed at the time Thomas Paine first explored Philadelphia. Just one vital element was missing. Very soon he would provide it.

ON JANUARY 2, 1775, an advertisement was printed in the city's newspapers that was bound to catch Paine's eye. In a week's time, "*At the* REQUEST *of a Number of his* FELLOW CITIZENS," Rush was to begin a series of public lectures on chemistry.[12]

This, in all likelihood, was the first that Paine would have heard of the brilliant medic: the young man who had corresponded with Franklin, dined with Wilkes, and discussed politics with Macaulay. For all these reasons, Paine might have thought him a worthwhile person to seek out. Besides this there was Paine's long-standing zest for science. In London in the 1750s he had attended lectures by the charismatic astronomer James Ferguson. Back then Ferguson had promised to make his subject "the sublimest of Sciences familiar and easy to those who will only look and be attentive."[13] Paine was one of those to fall under his spell. At about that time Paine bought a pair of astronomical globes so that he could model the movements of the planets at home. Now, years later, he had the exciting opportunity to immerse himself in a similar manner at Rush's lectures.

On his return from Britain in 1769, Rush had been appointed the first ever professor of chemistry at the College of Philadelphia. Now, beginning on January 10, Rush was going to open up to a public audience his knowledge on a dazzling range of subjects: the effects of heat upon bodies; the natural history of cold; climates; the structure of thermometers; the nature, origin, and use of fixed air; the chemical history of animal bodies. There would be a practical edge to these lectures too. He promised to explain the process behind the manufactories of glass and porcelain, along with the methods by which saltpeter and gunpowder could be produced.

For someone of Paine's disposition, this was temptation indeed. For a guinea each, tickets were on sale at Robert Aitken's Bookshop on Front Street, just next door to Paine's lodgings. This is a tantalizing detail because it was inside this bookshop on around January 10 that Paine had one of his earliest and most significant encounters in the city. This was with Aitken himself. Although he was still relatively new in business, there was a dynamism about Aitken. In an increasingly competitive business environment, he had secured a prime position on Front Street, close to the London Coffee House. Here he sold imported books, and he printed new titles too. Aitken's most recent was a pirated octavo edition of *Domestic Medicine*, an accessible guide by the Scottish physician William Buchan. In time-honored fashion he had tried his hand at an almanac, too, advertising *The Philadelphia Newest Almanack for 1775* over the course of the previous autumn. That January, Aitken was toying with another new project too. This was one to make more seasoned Philadelphians smile. His idea was to launch a magazine.

Thirty-five years had passed since Franklin had concocted this same idea. In the intervening years there had been some attempts to succeed where Bradford's *American Magazine* and Franklin's *General Magazine* had failed. Nothing, however, had lasted much more than a year. Aitken had most probably gathered as much from friends, but he was determined to try nonetheless. Three years had now passed since David Hall's death, and during that time a new wave of printers had appeared in the city. Aitken was part of this. A generation younger than Hall, Aitken otherwise bore quite the resemblance. A fellow Scot, he had been born in Dalkeith near Edinburgh, where he was apprenticed as a bookbinder before making his way to Pennsylvania. Though the political environment was abysmal, business remained brisk. A magazine was just the thing, he reasoned, to make his name. By the end of 1774 he felt bold enough to advertise his plan. The *Pennsylvania Magazine* was to go on sale on the first Wednesday in February 1775.

All this might have sounded ominously familiar to old hands at the London Coffee House. But Aitken had taken some precautions. In his advertisements he had constantly stressed the fact that the magazine would only continue if the numbers of subscribers remained high. His choice of title also suggested a lowering of expectations. Instead of the *American Magazine*, Aitken had opted for a more localized name. To thrive in one colony would be success enough. But even this was looking doubtful when he crossed paths with Paine. In January 1775 Aitken was in a familiar muddle. With a launch date advertised and subscribers waiting, the *Pennsylvania Magazine* was far from complete. Aitken's intention had been to rely on two key contributors: a clever lawyer called Francis Hopkinson and the president of the College of New Jersey, John Witherspoon. But even with their pieces, huge gaps still remained. This was especially perplexing for Aitken, Paine wrote, because while he was a competent printer, he had "little or no turn" in the literary way.[14] What he desperately needed was the same kind of figure that Franklin had looked for in 1740: someone with knowledge, who could write well and could write quickly. Whereas Franklin's hunt had led him to John Webbe, Aitken fared much better. He had no way of appreciating it at the time, but at just the right moment one of the finest writers on the American continent had strolled into his shop.

The proof of this was borne out when the *Pennsylvania Magazine* was published. In a few short weeks Paine had not only supplied its deficiencies, he had also charged the magazine with intent. At the head of the magazine, underneath the motto "Juvat in sylvis habitare" ("Happy it is to live in the woods"), Paine inserted his own purposeful introduction. It contained a quintessentially Franklinian message.

> America has now outgrown the state of infancy: Her strength and commerce make large advances to manhood; and science in all its branches, has not only blossomed but even ripened upon the soil. The cottages as it were of yesterday have grown to villages, and the villages to cities.[15]

Three generations before Ralph Waldo Emerson argued that Americans "have listened too long to the courtly muses of Europe," Paine's introduction to the *Pennsylvania Magazine* conveyed an identical sentiment.[16] America needed to forge its own literary identity. "The British magazines, at their commencement," Paine wrote, "were the repositories of ingenuity: They are now the retailers of tale and nonsense. From elegance they sunk to simplicity, from simplicity to folly, and from folly to voluptuousness." Whatever the state of politics might be, for Paine it was high time that America decided on some kind of intellectual independence from Britain. "I have no doubt but of seeing," he wrote, "in a little time, an American magazine full of more useful matter, than I ever saw an English one. Because we are not exceeded in abilities, have a more extensive field for enquiry. And whatever may be our political state, Our HAPPINESS WILL ALWAYS DEPEND ON OURSELVES."[17]

Here, out of the mists, comes the full earnestness, the full force of Paine's prose. The confidence with which he wrote was matched by his gift for attractive imagery. To him, he explained, a magazine was the perfect forum for featuring a wide range of useful material. "I consider it," he merrily announced:

a kind of bee-hive, which both allures the swarm, and provides room to store their sweets. Its diversion into cells gives every bee a province of its own; and though they all produce honey, yet perhaps they differ in their taste for flowers, and extract with greater dexterity from one than from another. *Thus* we are not all PHILOSOPHERS, all ARTISTS, nor all POETS.[18]

WHEN HE MET FRANKLIN in London, Paine had been unsure about the kind of work he would like to do when he arrived in Philadelphia. He had envisioned being a clerk, a tutor in a school, or an assistant to a land surveyor. But six weeks after his arrival, he found himself doing something quite different. Casually employed as a magazine editor, Paine found, for the first time, that the haphazard course of his life was not a disadvantage. Instead, the fact that he knew a little about science, a little about politics, a little about the function of government, and a little about the adventurous seafaring life, meant that his mind was sufficiently dexterous and sufficiently well stocked for the demands of the literary format.

Energized by his new surroundings, the words flowed from Paine's pen. Aside from his introduction to the *Pennsylvania Magazine*, he contributed a jaunty mathematical puzzle as well as a descriptive review of "a NEW ELECTRICAL MACHINE." By the next issue his output had doubled. Leading the way was a feature article by Paine, written under the pseudonym "ATLANTICUS," titled "USEFUL *and* ENTERTAINING HINTS" on the natural riches of the colonies. The catalyst for this was a trip Paine made to Philadelphia's library, where he found himself gazing into a cabinet filled with fossils. These had been gathered from locations across the colonies, "along with several species of earth, clay, sand, &c," and the sight of them had set Paine's mind in motion. Great work had already been done by settlers who had devoted themselves to tilling the earth. This had demonstrated what the land could produce. But no one yet knew what the land contained. Should progress continue at such a pace, Paine argued, then the discovery of metal and mineral riches would surely follow. "Perhaps a few feet of surface," he wrote, "conceal a treasure sufficient to enrich a kingdom."

> Of the present state we may justly say, that no nation under heaven ever struck out in so short a time, and with so much spirit and reputation, into the labyrinth of art and science; and *that not* in the *acquisition* of knowledge only, but in the happy advantages flowing *from* it. The world does not at this day exhibit a parallel, neither can history produce its equal.[19]

By the March issue, Paine's creative output had reached an even higher peak. He contributed a piece on the life of Alexander the Great, a bright poem called *The Snow-drop and Critic*, and an eye-catching article on a "Method of making Salt-Petre." It seems likely that this was based on material Paine had heard in Rush's lectures.[20]

Drawn together, this journalism presents a portrait of Paine during his early days in Philadelphia. Like Hall all those years before, he had swiftly discovered a streak of patriotic pride. His transformation from Briton to American was already complete. We can glimpse him out and about in the city: peeking into glass-topped cabinets at the Library Company, sitting toward the back of the lecture hall at the college, scribbling notes as Rush speaks. Having spent years as a hated collector of taxes for the Crown in Britain, Paine seems overjoyed to have thrown off his old, suffocating identity. He has little to say about England, and when he does mention the land of his birth his sentiments are scornful. Rather than looking east across the sea for inspiration, one gets the sense that Atlanticus has put the ocean and the Old World firmly to his back. His eyes, and mind, are fixed toward the West.

In his early months in Philadelphia, Paine's experience seems to have challenged Johnson's views about happiness. He had fled a stifling, unhappy existence in Britain, and here in Philadelphia, for a time at least, he was living a more satisfying life. He brought with him the energy of a migrant. But along with this enthusiasm tagged something else. Paine was a quick and agile thinker, but he also suffered from a lack of reserve. This was dangerous in a place like Philadelphia. Writing scathingly about the British was unlikely to lose Paine many friends, but to openly criticize the merchant class and the city's established social practices was a different matter. And yet Paine's sense of moral outrage toward the slavery that he encountered for the first time was something that he could not stifle. Every time he browsed a newspaper in the London Coffee House, he was confronted with ads concerning slaves. Opposite his lodgings on Front Street was the newly built stand where the latest arrivals would be sold off to the highest bidder. Most striking of all, perhaps, would have been the sight of those in bondage themselves, out on errands for their masters, or glimpsed through the windows of properties.

Confronted with all this, Paine decided that he could not keep quiet. Three months after his arrival, a forthright, stringent piece appeared in a paper called the *Pennsylvania Journal* on March 8.

> To Americans. That some desperate wretches should be willing to steal and enslave men by violence and murder for gain, is rather lamentable than strange. But that many civilized, nay, Christianized people should approve, and be concerned in the savage practice, is surprising; and still persist, though it has been so often proved contrary to the light of nature, to every principle of justice and humanity, and even good policy . . .
>
> Our traders in MEN (*an unnatural commodity!*) must know the wickedness of that SLAVE-TRADE, if they attend to reasoning, or the dictates of their own hearts; and such as shun and stifle all these, wilfully sacrifice conscience, and the character of integrity to that golden idol.[21]

In this essay, signed only "JUSTICE AND HUMANITY," Paine's language was unsparing. He branded those involved in the trade "infidel cavaliers," "devils," "monsters." The case against slavery, he declared, was closed. It was against scripture and the laws of nature. Nobody who participated in it had any defense at all.

Reading over the piece today, its emotional intensity is striking. There is none of the polish or flair of his magazine articles. Instead his thoughts spill out in a chain of poorly punctuated sentences, as if the writing was done in an angry half hour and taken, without a second look, to the printing shop. It is only in the second half that Paine's practical instinct takes over. Not only is slavery morally repugnant, he argues. It also harms the colonists' cause in Britain. Why should their petitions about "attempts to enslave them" be taken seriously in London when hundreds of thousands *really* are enslaved in the colonies? For Paine the great question could not be *when* slavery should be abolished. It was, "What should be done with those who are enslaved already?" Having spent his time thinking about this, Paine had come to some conclusions. He believed the colonists had a duty to care for the elderly. The younger slaves, however, should be given their own land on reasonable rent, with every encouragement to build on it. "The family may live together," he explained, "and enjoy the natural satisfaction of exercising relative affections and duties, with civil protection, and other advantages, like fellow men."[22]

Caution was always Franklin's advice. Had someone told him, as Paine stood in Mrs. Stevenson's parlor in 1774, that this man was going to embark at Philadelphia and announce himself with a polemic against slavery, he would have shaken his head. But while caution is usually prudent, there are times in life when the bravest course brings the biggest rewards. So it was with Paine's article. It came at a time when public opinion about slavery was shifting. In a dramatic though somewhat cryptic judgment in the Court of the King's Bench in June 1772, Wilkes's enemy, Lord Chief Justice Mansfield, had ruled that the practice was not supported by English law. Although his ruling carried no weight in America, across the colonies slavery was increasingly becoming a legitimate topic for discussion. In Massachusetts in the 1770s, there had been repeated moves to abolish the slave trade, while at the Continental Congress in September a pledge had been issued, "to discontinue the slave trade everywhere."[23]

Paine's pamphlet caught this moment. It was widely read, and some have since argued that it played a direct part in the establishment in April of the "Pennsylvania Society for the Relief of Negroes Unlawfully Held in Bondage," the first abolitionist society of its kind in the Western world. Another consequence is easier to trace. Writing about the essay forty years later, Benjamin Rush remembered being "much pleased" with it. The vigorousness of the writing left Rush wanting to know Paine better. He sought him out at Aitken's bookshop in the early spring when he "did homage to his principles and pen upon the subject of the enslaved Africans."[24]

A bold stroke, in this case, had served Paine well. He could now count one of the leading intellectual figures in the city as an admirer. For his part, Rush was impressed not only with Paine's prose style and his stance on slavery. He liked the other pieces—his nimble poems and practical articles—that continued to appear each month in the *Pennsylvania Magazine*. Paine's literary talent, Rush decided, had filled Aitken's magazine with a "sudden currency" which few other works had ever had in America.[25] In a letter to Franklin, written at about the same time, Paine was able to deliver a snippet of cheerful news himself. Aitken only had six hundred subscribers for his magazine when he launched, he revealed. "We have now upwards of 1500, and daily encreasing."[26]

From one of these subscribers came a delightful letter, which Aitken printed in the April issue:

SEVERAL attempts have been made to establish a Magazine in different parts of the Continent, all of which, meteor like, have blazed through with different degrees of lustre, and expired. I begin to have other expectations of the present one; for without paying any other compliment than merit is justly entitled to, I look on several of the original pieces which have already appeared in the Pennsylvania Magazine, to be equal in point of elegance, and invention to the best pieces in the English ones.[27]

By way of thanks the correspondent promised any of the "ingenious" contributors to the magazine a place to stay, should they ever venture out into the country. "I have fine fields for the muses to range in," he wrote, "walks dark with the shade of cedars at noon day, and groves of perpetual twilight." It was the kind of vision to make Paine smile. Unlike Johnson, Paine really was a utopian. Everything he wrote was undercut with the idea that a world and a society of true, perfect happiness was possible. Demonstrating this faith, Paine included a poem in the April edition about the island of "Otaheite." "THE adventures of Mr Banks in the island of Otaheite, have caused that island to be so well known," he explained, "as to render any introductory account thereof needless."

> Beneath their shades the gentle tribes repose;
> Each bending branch their frugal feast bestows:
> For them the cocoa yields its milky flood,
> To slake their thirst, and feed their temp'rate blood.[28]

By its April edition, the Pennsylvania Magazine had hit its stride. The opening pages were filled with pieces on practical science and whimsical observations about the human and animal worlds. As the correspondent implied, it was a publication to lift or charge the spirits. Only toward its latter pages did politics creep into the magazine. There, in a section entitled "MONTHLY INTELLIGENCE," an acrimonious story was playing out. In Britain, Parliament remained enraged with America after the Boston Tea Party. The mood of the court party was made worse by the fact that John Wilkes's unlikely career had moved into a new phase. Having first been an alderman and then a sheriff, he had recently reached the zenith of city politics with his election as the Lord Mayor of London.

The king was said to be dismayed at this development. Over the years his loathing of the man he called "that Devil Wilkes" had only intensified.[29] Now he was forced to endure the stories of him riding through London in the Lord Mayor's carriage. Philadelphians, too, kept abreast of Wilkes's movements, as they always had. They also learned from the magazine that Franklin and Arthur Lee had presented Lord Dartmouth, the latest colonial secretary, with the Continental Congress's petition. The reception of this was said to be "more favourable than the hopes of some," and there were other hints of a softening in the British stance too. In Boston, General Gage had been ordered "not to proceed to extremities," if he could help it, but to act upon the defensive."[30]

Then, as the April issue of the *Pennsylvania Magazine* was going to print, breaking news arrived in Philadelphia:

> ON Monday April 24, this city was greatly alarmed by an express arriving about three in the afternoon, with an account of an engagement between the king's troops and the provincials, near Boston. As the exact circumstances of that affair are not yet certainly known, we shall give our readers the expresses and accounts in the order they were received.[31]

What was known of the story was conveyed in a series of letters. A brigade of more than a thousand British soldiers had marched out of Boston to a town called Lexington. There they had encountered a company of the colonial militia and had fired on them "without any provocation, and killed six men."[32] What would be next, no one could tell. But civil war, it seemed, had come to America. "The pent up flame," wrote one of the delegates who was gathering in Philadelphia for the new Continental Congress, "has broke out."[33]

As people digested this disturbing turn of events in early May

1775, something else happened. This time it was more comforting news. The tidings gave "New Spring" to everyone. To the "great joy" of the town, went a letter written in Philadelphia on May 6, "YES-TERDAY evening Dr FRANKLIN arrived here from London."[34]

WRITING TO DEBORAH SEVERAL years before, Franklin had expressed his fear that when he did finally return he would find himself a stranger in his own country. This was the reality that he had to confront in May 1775. The old familiar streets were still there, along with Christ Church, the State House, and the Crooked Billet Tavern—the places he knew so well. But Philadelphia was oddly altered. David Hall was gone. Now David Hall, Jr., was managing his New Printing Office. But even that name had an off-kilter air about it. The New Printing Office was by now one of the oldest businesses in the city, and opposite on Market Street was the "Newest Printing Office" set up by an energetic Irishman called John Dunlap.

Adding to the eerie sense of unreality was the frenzied political atmosphere. Companies of riflemen were marching in the streets, and the city was filled with the sound of drums and fifes. Everyone seemed to be learning the basics of manual exercises and the handling of weapons. Twenty-eight companies of foot, each of sixty-eight men, were now said to be operational, all of them training twice a day. Alien as all this was, after having felt like a prisoner in London for so long, Franklin was at least pleased to see his countrymen planning their response. "You will have heard before this reaches you of the Commencement of a Civil War," he wrote to David Hartley, the newly elected MP for Hull. "I find here all Ranks of People in Arms, disciplining themselves Morning and Evening, and am informed that the firmest Union prevails throughout North America."[35] To another friend he remembered the truth of an old saying: "*Make yourself sheep and the wolves will eat you.*"[36]

There were multiple dimensions to Franklin's letters back to Britain these days. He wanted to convey news to his friends, of course. But as he knew that his mail would be intercepted, opened,

and analyzed when it reached London, he also wrote with the ministry's spies in mind. It did not hurt for them to know the preparations
that were underway. But it was not all propaganda. Franklin had
been genuinely heartened to find a staunchness, a unanimity across
the colonies. News of General Gage's attack at Lexington had been
met with outrage. According to the Virginian Richard Henry Lee,
another of the delegates who had arrived in Philadelphia for the Congress, the act "roused such a universal Military spirit thro out all the
Colonies, and excited such universal resentment against this Savage
Ministry, and their detestable Agents, that now no doubt remains of
their destruction with the establishment of American Rights."[37] On
his arrival Franklin had been delighted to find that New York, whose
allegiance had been uncertain, was now said to be warmly attached
to the patriotic cause. Even Georgia, which had stayed away from
the First Continental Congress, had swung into line. On May 13,
a representative called Lyman Hall had arrived after a long journey
from the town of Sunbury, just outside of Savannah. At last, a week
after his return, Franklin could savor something he had long wanted
to see. East and West Florida, recently acquired by the British in the
Seven Years' War, might not be joining the Congress, but for all of
their differences, thirteen others were represented. And if they were
not *quite* united, then at least they were together.

Franklin, naturally, was instantly admitted as a delegate to this Second Continental Congress too. As the assembly got to work over the
weeks that followed, Franklin was observed to be a quiet, contained
presence. Given the circumstances, this is not surprising. Deborah was
not yet six months dead, and the fine house that they had planned
together high up on Market Street must have seemed heavy with her
presence. From New Jersey, too, came another powerful source of
anxiety. William was the son into whom Franklin had poured all his
hopes. The success of 1762, when he had successfully lobbied Bute to
have him appointed as governor of the colony, had, until now, been
counted as among the triumphs of his life. But what was a triumph in

the 1760s became a tragedy in the 1770s. Faced with a crisis of loyalty, William, it was clear, was going to side with the Crown.

Franklin knew what such a decision meant. On a personal level
their relationship would have to end—for the time being at least.
But this did not dispel the worries Franklin must have had for William's safety. He had seen for himself what had happened to Joseph
Galloway, his closest political ally from his days in the Pennsylvania
Assembly. He had also taken the British side. As Franklin had returned, Galloway's efforts to counter the resolutions of the 1774
Congress were petering out. His actions, by now, had earned him
the enmity of his peers. "By this Step," one delegate explained, "he
has lost the Confidence of all ranks of People." Franklin certainly
heard the tale that one day in May Galloway had taken delivery of a
box at his lodgings. "He opened it before several Gentlemen," went
the story, "and was much surprised to find it contained a Halter with
a note in these words, 'all the Satisfaction you can now give your
injured Country is to make a proper use of this and rid the World of
a Damned Scoundrell.'"[38]

Galloway had since vanished, and Franklin knew that similar
treatment was likely to be heading William's way in New Jersey.
This thought was left to fester in his mind during the spring and
into the summer of 1775. Someone else too was flickering across his
conscience. As the drills went forward in the Philadelphian streets
and rumors grew stronger of a mighty British fleet, Franklin thought
occasionally of his old friend William Strahan.

On many occasions during his previous years in Philadelphia,
Franklin had Strahan on his mind. To begin with it had been a
thrill to hear from the inky-fingered businessman from Wine Office Court. In later years Franklin had thought of Strahan as a vital
source of intelligence and the firmest of all friends. But the Strahan of
1775 was none of these things. Instead his printer friend had become
the MP for Malmesbury, who sat on the government's benches in all
his lace and finery as Parliament passed its coercive measures against

Boston. And Strahan did not just vote these measures through; in a cruel twist, thanks to his professional responsibilities he also produced these acts in their physical form at the King's Printing House.

For Franklin this added an intensely personal dimension to the various proclamations that arrived over the spring and summer. Examining these printed sheets, there was so much about them that was familiar. He knew the Caslon type all too well. He knew the royal paper. He probably knew the press rooms where they were printed, and perhaps he even knew some of the pressmen who had carried out the work. Most of all he must have gazed at the imprint at the foot of the sheet.

LONDON

Printed by *Charles Eyre* and *William Strahan*. Printers to the King's most Excellent Majesty.

For the first two months after his return, Franklin ignored Strahan. He prioritized everything and everyone else. But then, on July 5, 1775, a week after the news of the Battle of Bunker Hill reached Philadelphia, in a burst of rage, a short, furious letter came tumbling out:

> PHILADA. JULY 5. 1775
> Mr. Strahan,
> You are a Member of Parliament, and one of that Majority which has doomed my Country to Destruction. You have begun to burn our Towns, and murder our People. Look upon your Hands! They are stained with the Blood of your Relations! You and I were long Friends: You are now my Enemy, and I am, Yours,
>
> B. Franklin[39]

Written on the same day that John Dickinson's final plea for reconciliation, known as the "Olive Branch Petition," was approved by Congress, this letter is one of Franklin's most famous. Historians over the generations have used it to signify a breaking point, a moment when the force of anger grew to such a degree that it overwhelmed Franklin's massive capacity for restraint. But to truly appreciate its power, one has to know the depth of the friendship; to have seen the printing press in Wine Office Court and the crates of books that arrived every year in Market Street; that moment when Franklin and Strahan first met in the house of Peter Collinson in the summer of 1757; and to have pictured the two of them, a decade afterward, seated in composed silence in the gallery of the House of Commons. It seems that some of this rushed through Franklin's head, too, in the moments after he finished this letter. For instead of sealing it into an envelope, Franklin simply left it. His emotion was expressed. The letter went undelivered.

By coincidence, three thousand miles away, on that very same day, William Strahan was writing to Franklin too. Unmoved in his political opinions, Strahan was nonetheless in as emotionally confused a state as his personality permitted. Where was it all going to end? Did Franklin not see the catastrophe that was inevitably coming? What would happen to America? The colonies might find themselves thrown under "the Dominion of some enterprising Leader" or, worse, "leave themselves a Prey to some ambitious European Power, under whom they may *really* experience all the Evils in the highest Degree . . . *Now*," Strahan implored, was the critical moment, it was time for Franklin to crown his spectacular career by brokering some peace and returning to the mother country to finalize it. Oscillating between threat, hope, and despair, Strahan went on:

> For my own Part, I have no doubt of the Prevalence of this Country in the End, should hostile Measures be pursued for any Length of Time. But, good God! Where does Victory on either Side lead to? To the immediate Destruction of half, and the ultimate Ruin of the whole, of the most glorious Fabric of Civil and

Religious Government that ever existed on this Globe. If after we are both weakened by the Struggle, it terminates in our final Separation, this must unavoidably be the Consequence . . .

I believe the Ministry are quite determined in their Operations, and in the Prosecution of coercive Measures. I see everybody is learning the Use of Arms with You; but surely it will not be attempted to distress You by Land. Our Navy is our great Strength, and sorry shall I be to see it long exerted against You; tho' if no Steps are taken towards a Reconciliation, I am afraid that must be the Case.[40]

Although Franklin's short, passionate letter was not sent, Strahan's long, rambling one was. It reached Philadelphia later in the summer. Several others followed. Franklin set them all to one side.

Only at the start of October did he find the time to respond. "Since my Arrival here," Franklin began, "I have received Four Letters from you, the last dated August 2, all filled with your Reasonings and Persuasions, and Arguments and Intimidations on the Dispute between Britain and America." They were all, Franklin owned, very well written, "and if you have shewn them to your Friends the Ministers, I dare say, they have done you Credit." Despite all the words, though, there was nothing new in the message. Franklin would not be returning to London as Strahan hoped, holding Dickinson's olive branch in his hand. Instead, if Strahan and his friends in Parliament desired peace, then "send us over hither fair Proposals," he suggested, "and no body shall be more ready than myself to promote their Acceptation: For I make it a Rule," he concluded, "not to mix personal Resentments with Public Business."[41]

Seventeen

COMMON SENSE

IN THE SPRING OF 1775, along with Franklin, the Atlantic ships brought a number of political pamphlets from London. These constituted the informal British response to the resolutions of the First Continental Congress. The most welcome of these for the citizens of Philadelphia was a short, pointed tract by Catharine Macaulay, entitled *An Address to the People of England, Scotland, and Ireland.*

Macaulay was as fierce as ever. She announced herself uninterested in the powerful, corrupt few in Westminster, who were "dazzled with the sun-shine of a court," and who were fattening themselves "on the spoils of the people."[1] Instead she appealed to the great masses of people across the islands of Great Britain. It was only those "unjustly debarred the privilege of election" who could prevent the calamity of war by rising up against the government's policies.[2] The time for protest, Macaulay argued, was well since past. The British people, "with an entire supineness," had "seen the Americans, year by year, stripped of the most valuable of their rights; and, to the eternal shame of this country, the stamp act, by which they were to be taxed in an arbitrary manner."[3] The colonists had absorbed the blows with "an almost blameable patience," while "innovations" were continually made against their liberty.[4] To Macaulay the resolves of the Congress at Philadelphia had made it clear that this period had come to an end. America would tolerate it no longer. A civil war was imminent.

For her country, neither of the two possible results were good. Either, "by one great exertion," Britain "may ruin both herself and America." Or the colonists, "by a lingering contest, will gain an independency," in which case the British people would lose all the advantages of the trade that have "hitherto preserved [them] from a national bankruptcy." In the years ahead, while "a new, a flourishing, and an extensive empire of freemen is established on the other side the Atlantic," the British would be "left to the bare possession of [their] foggy islands; and this under the imperious sway of a domestic despot."[5] It was either that, or Great Britain would "become the provinces of some powerful European state." Macaulay concluded her argument with a rallying cry:

> Rouse, my countrymen! rouse from that state of guilty dissipation in which you have too long remained, and in which, if you longer continue, you are lost for ever. Rouse! and unite in one general effort; 'till, by your unanimous and repeated Addresses to the Throne, and to both Houses of Parliament, you draw the attention of every part of the government to their own interests, and to the dangerous state of the British empire.[6]

This was the kind of writing to make those down at the London Coffee House on Front Street draw breath. Despite everything, in 1775 there were still many who desperately hoped that some settlement was possible. If not the politicians, then perhaps it would, as Macaulay suggested, be the British people that came to the rescue of their American cousins, lifting them out of their state of "slavery."

But for every shred of hope, each glimmer of sunshine, the next packet boat seemed to bring an equal amount of gloom. Macaulay's pamphlet was published in early January. At the start of March an

answer appeared in print. Samuel Johnson had spent his life fasci-
nated by words, but in his reply to Macaulay he announced that the
word "slavery" was one that he wished "more discreetly uttered." "It
is driven at one time too hard into our ears by the loud hurricane of
Pennsylvanian eloquence," Johnson declared, "and at another glides
too cold into our hearts by the soft conveyance of a female patriot,
bewailing the miseries of her *friends and fellow-citizens*."[7]

Johnson's polemic *Taxation No Tyranny: An Answer to the Resolutions
and Address of the American Congress*, was written on the urging of Grey
Cooper, the Secretary to the Treasury, and it was one of his finest
pieces of political journalism. It had a briskness to it, along with a
creative playfulness and a dark street-fighting spirit. Like Macaulay,
Johnson revealed that he had looked over the resolutions of the Congress, which he considered "wild, indefinite and obscure." He did
not deny, however, that the resolves had made an impact. From New
England to South Carolina, Johnson admitted,

> there is formed a general combination of all the Provinces
> against their Mother-country. The madness of independence
> has spread from Colony to Colony, till order is lost and govern-
> ment despised, and all is filled with misrule, uproar, violence,
> and confusion. To be quiet is disaffection, to be loyal is treason.[8]

It seemed to Johnson that these intimidations were not only being
heard in America, but in Britain too. Reports held that "the continent
of North America contains three millions, not of men merely, but of
Whigs, of Whigs fierce for liberty, and disdainful of dominion; that
they multiply with the fecundity of their own rattle-snakes, so that
every quarter of a century doubles their numbers."[9] In such a world,
what was to be done?

Johnson conceded that the colonists' story was filled with romance. People with tender hearts could easily be swayed by tales of
men "who fled from tyranny to rocks and desarts" and gradually built

up a magnificent new world around them.[10] But what really were the terms of colonization? In a passage reminiscent of *Rasselas*, Johnson reasoned:

> it sometimes happened that by the dissensions of heads of families, by the ambition of daring adventurers, by some accidental pressure of distress, or by the mere discontent of idleness, one part of the community broke off from the rest, and numbers, greater or smaller, forsook their habitations, put themselves under the command of some favourite of fortune, and with or without the consent of their countrymen or governours, went out to see what better regions they could occupy, and in what place, by conquest or by treaty, they could gain a habitation.[11]

In distant ages this pursuit of happiness was unregulated and therefore very dangerous. But as the centuries wore on and human societies developed, a new system of formalized colonization developed. This was not a haphazard affair, but whether one agreed with it or not, it was a regulated way of securing a conquest. A colony would be planted, a territory would be occupied and settled, and it would be kept flourishing by the "radical vigour" of the mother country.[12]

A British colony, in particular, was a clearly defined thing. It was "a number of persons, to whom the King grants a Charter permitting them to settle in some distant country, and enabling them to constitute a Corporation."[13] This, Johnson argued, is how the British had long thought of their colonies. However distant, they were a part of the whole. "The inhabitants incorporated by English Charters, are intitled to all the rights of Englishmen. They are governed by English laws, entitled to English dignities, regulated by English counsels, and protected by English arms; and," he drily added, "it seems to follow by consequence not easily avoided, that they are subject to English government, and chargeable by English taxation."[14]

Having framed his view of the colonial superstructure, Johnson commenced his attack. By denying the British government the right of taxation, the Americans had shown their greed to the world. The colonists wanted it both ways. They wanted Britain to have dominion without authority, and for them to be subjects without subordination. But this was impossible. "He that will enjoy the brightness of sunshine," Johnson wrote,

> must quit the coolness of the shade. He who goes voluntarily to America, cannot complain of losing what he leaves in Europe. He perhaps had a right to vote for a knight or burgess: by crossing the Atlantick he had not nullified his right; for he has made its exertion no longer possible. By his own choice he has left a country where he had a vote and little property, for another, where he has great property, but no vote.[15]

There was little good that representation would do them anyway, Johnson reasoned. Give America twenty-three MPs in the House of Commons, half as many as Scotland, he pondered. "What will this representation avail them?"[16] The laws would still pass, the taxes would still be due. But what of their complaint that Britain has never taxed them before? "To this we think it may be easily answered," Johnson wrote, "that the longer they have been spared, the better they can pay."[17]

Having dealt with the resolves of the Congress, Johnson then embarked on an attack of his own. Some, he acknowledged, made the argument that the colonies should be granted their independence. This would save the cost and bloodshed of war. But why had someone not suggested this in the years before the war against France? "By letting them loose before the war, how many millions might have been saved?" He declared that one "ridiculous proposal" should be met with another. "Let us restore to the French what we have taken from them. We shall see our Colonists at our feet, when they have an enemy so near them."[18]

Maybe the British, too, should enact another law that the liberty-loving colonists "cannot but commend," Johnson added. An act should be passed through Westminster to set all the slaves free. "If they are furnished with fire arms for defence, and utensils for husbandry, and settled in some simple form of government within the country, they may be more grateful and honest than their masters."[19] For, after all, he stated, in the latest pamphlet to appear off the press at William Strahan's printing house in Little New Street, "how is it that we hear the loudest yelps for liberty among the drivers of negroes?"[20]

OVER THE SUMMER OF 1775 the work continued at the *Pennsylvania Magazine*. For all its commercial success, however, the atmosphere at Aitken's shop was tense. While Aitken had cause to be thankful to Paine, there was a clash of personalities between the shrewd businessman and the gifted but impetuous writer. It made life difficult.

Aitken was of a cast of character, shared by his countrymen Strahan and Hall, that valued neat professionalism. Paine, meanwhile, was unpredictable, and he had the writer's usual disregard for deadlines. In later years a story would be told describing the moment when the harassed Aitken lost patience with Paine's tardiness and decided to confront him at his lodgings. It makes for a lively picture, the stern Scotch printer marching along Front Street and rapping on Paine's door. Opening it up, the story went, Paine listened as Aitken demanded his finished articles for the press. He coolly replied, "You shall have them in time." As Aitken had no faith in this, he insisted Paine accompany him to the printing office, where he was to write the pieces while the pressmen awaited. Now, perhaps for the first time, Aitken had the opportunity of watching Paine in the act of composition. He was soon

seated at the table with the necessary apparatus, which always included a glass, and a decanter of brandy. Aitken observed, "he would never write without that." The first glass put him in a train of thinking; Aitken feared the second would disqualify him, or render him intractable; but it only illuminated his intellectual system; and when he swallowed the third glass, he wrote with great rapidity, intelligence, and precision; and his ideas appeared to flow faster than he could commit them to paper. What he penned from the inspiration of the brandy, was perfectly fit for the press without alteration, or correction.[21]

This is a fascinating glimpse of Paine at work, but one has to treat it with care. The portrait of the restless genius, unwillingly propelled into magical action, was a recurring trope at the time. More commonly stories like this were ascribed to Johnson himself, who was famously said to have written the *Rambler* No. 134—all about the perils of idleness and procrastination—while the printer's boy waited at his door. In essence, though, Aitken's recollection does capture something of Paine. At first he comes across as slothful, obstinate, and wildly idealistic. It is easy to see how a man like this would have failed repeatedly back in Britain. But he is nonetheless stimulated into brilliance by Aitken's stern, Midlothian manner. Inside the press room, surrounded by precision technologies, Paine becomes the most efficient machine of all. A conspicuous role is played by the bottle of brandy, without which he appears to be unable to work. It would be a common charge laid against him in later years. Paine's was a mind that needed stimulation. The brandy was a symbol of this. Paine was at his best, people said, when he was close to danger: both physical and intellectual.

While his relationship with Aitken was strained, Paine otherwise relished his work at the magazine. The variety of the content suited him. One day he might be scanning the text for an article on "The Military Character of Ants." The next he may be examining a map of Boston. In between all this he worked on his own original pieces. As well as his prose articles, Paine continued with his forays into verse. One admired effort was *The Death of General Wolfe*. In the July edition of the magazine, writing again as Atlanticus, another fine work materialized. This was his song-poem, *Liberty Tree*. Set to the popular tune "The Gods of the Greeks," it opened,

In a chariot of light from the regions of day,
The Goddess of Liberty came;
Ten thousand celestials directed the way,
And hither conducted the dame.

A fair budding branch from the gardens above,
Where millions with millions agree,
She brought in her hand, as a pledge of her love,
And the plant she named, Liberty Tree.[22]

There was only one part of the magazine that irritated Paine, and this might well have contributed to the tensions with his employer. For all the *Pennsylvania Magazine*'s virtues, it suffered—as so many colonial publications did—from what he thought was a subservient obsession with Britain. Large portions of every issue would be given over to extracts from the latest British books. In the May and June issues, for instance, pages had been consumed by excerpts from Samuel Johnson's *Journey to the Western Isles of Scotland*. This fixation was demonstrated even more clearly in the "Monthly Intelligence" section, which always led with the latest lines out of the court at St. James's or the debates in Parliament. Having so recently escaped Britain and having so fully embraced the spirit of potential in the New World, Paine was forced to read passages of mindless puffery that recounted, for instance, the fact that King George had sat down on his golden throne at two o'clock on May 26, for the meeting with the gentleman usher Black Rod.

Nor was this obsession confined to the magazines or newspapers. During his first six months in Philadelphia, Paine saw how people would pore over pamphlets like Macaulay's and Johnson's. To Paine this was pathetic and demeaning. The people should think better of themselves, he argued, than hanging on every word from each new packet. These were views Paine's friend Benjamin Rush agreed with. It seems, from what can be pieced together from the surviving accounts, that by the late summer of 1775 the two of them had become close. Both fervent patriots, they were trusting enough of each other to be able to discuss politics openly. In Philadelphia at the time, this could be a perilous thing. While military preparations were going forward in plain view in the streets, there was still a timorousness when it came to the issue of independence. When Rush greeted John Adams on the eve of the Congress in August 1774, he had quietly cautioned him to "not utter the word "Independence," nor give the least hint or insinuation of the idea, neither in Congress or any private conversation . . . If you do, you are undone."[23]

Paine himself later recollected:

> It cannot at this time a day be forgotten that the politics, the opinions and the prejudices of the country were in direct opposition to the principles contained in that work. And I well know that in Pennsylvania, and I suppose the same in other of the then provinces, it would have been unsafe for a man to have espoused independence in any public company.[24]

And yet both Paine and Rush were wary of the silence. While some elegant and neatly reasoned pamphlets like Thomas Jefferson's *Summary View of the Rights of British America* had appeared over the last year, there was still something wanting. What was needed, Rush thought, would go "beyond the ordinary short and cold addresses of newspaper publications."[25] It was the kind of thing that usually arrived from Britain—a fiery, pulse-raising polemical pamphlet written in pugnacious style by the likes of Wilkes, Macaulay, or Johnson. Having read Paine's work in the *Pennsylvania Magazine*, Rush had started to form an idea.

In his own account, he explained that he called on Paine "and

suggested to him the propriety of preparing our citizens for a perpetual separation of our country from Great Britain, by means of a
work of such length as would obviate all the objections to it." Paine
did not recall such a meeting himself, but he did remember that 1775
was "a point of time full of critical danger to America." The central
point on which its future well-being depended, he believed, "was in
changing the sentiments of the people from dependence to independence and from the monarchical to the republican form of government." If America had split on this question, Paine wrote, "or entered
coldly or hesitatingly into it, she most probably had been ruined."[26]

According to Rush, Paine "seized the idea" for a pamphlet "with
avidity." For him Paine's enthusiasm could be interpreted easily
enough. Here was the chance for him to test his literary skills against
the political issue of the day. But there was no way Rush could have
truly known how long Paine had been in preparation for this moment.

Back in 1762, when Britain's political scene had split into the
fiery factions around Lord Bute and William Pitt, Paine was embarking on one of the most divisive of careers, as an excise officer
in Lincolnshire. As Wilkes's *North Briton* exposed, satirized, and
ridiculed the tyrannies of a corrupt minister, and Francis Dashwood
enraged the orchard counties with his Cider Tax, Paine was sent out
on horseback as the king's representative officer, riding over the wet
marshes and windy Wolds, charged with gauging casks, inspecting
storehouses and record books, and keeping watch for any sign of
smugglers. Here Paine was the hated insider, a subject of derision for
the liberty-loving English. The excise was, after all, as Johnson had
defined it: "A hateful tax levied upon commodities, and adjudged not
by the common judges of property, but wretches hired by those to
whom excise is paid."[27]

Paine had continued with his work through the tax riots of 1763,
and he doubtless read the *North Briton* along with everyone else. He
knew the power of the written word. In a meditative piece published
in the first issue of the *Pennsylvania Magazine*, he observed:

Wit is naturally a volunteer, delights in action, and under proper discipline is capable of great execution. 'Tis a perfect master in the art of bushfighting; and though it attacks with more subtlety than science, has often defeated a whole regiment of heavy artillery.[28]

Here were the words of someone who had lived through 1763 and 1768, years when Wilkes's pen seemed to be equal to all the military might of the crown. Later at a debating society in Lewes known as the Headstrong Club, Paine gained practice at marshaling his arguments. Now, in 1775, with all the rage of the convert, Paine took the opportunity of bringing all this experience to bear in a forum to which he was perfectly suited. As the historian Bernard Bailyn has noted, the so-called "daring impudence" and "uncommon frenzy" that filled the pamphlet that Paine now began "had been nourished in another culture, and was recognized at the time to be an alien quality in American writing."[29] Wilkes, for all his promises, had never set foot in America. But Paine had come. And with him he brought an evolution of the *North Briton* style. It was sharper, emotive, more serious, and, as events were soon to prove, a good deal more explosive.

PAINE WAS NOT SIMPLY the inspired, emotional writer Aitken later described. As well as the heat of his heart, he also brought to his work a cooler, analytical eye. Along with the poems and prefaces in the *Pennsylvania Magazine*, Paine had written several fine-combed descriptive pieces on electrical machines or new methods for building frame houses. In contributions like these Paine demonstrated an ability to step back and dispassionately, almost Franklin-like, evaluate something from a distance.

Over the past years Paine had brought this same structured mode of thinking to bear on politics. Reflecting on the formation of human communities, he decided that they all shared two key features.

The first of these he termed "society," which, he argued, was the inevitable product of human needs. It was a binding force, formed out of the rational and instinctive human desire for safety, efficiency, and companionship. This drew people into community, out of which a collective was born. But as human groups were delicate, combustible things, soon after the creation of "society" people realized their behavior needed to be regulated by a system. The result was "government." In his view "society" and "government" were therefore the two fundamental, opposing forces. It called to mind Franklin's division of electricity into positive and negative charges. Paine thought of society as a positive, creative force; government as a negative, restrictive one. Both were milled together, and in the correct proportions they created happiness. They did this, however, in different ways. Society "promotes our happiness *positively* by uniting our affections," Paine wrote. Government operated "*negatively* by restraining our vices. The one encourages intercourse, the other creates distinctions. The first is a patron, the last a punisher."[30]

This was an appealing appraisal. Just as in Franklin's scientific writing, where the positive and negative charges were in a constant state of flux, attempting but never managing to find the ultimate balance, Paine saw a similar dynamic in human communities. Too much freedom could be countered by more government. Too much regulation could be balanced by an increase of social liberties. To correctly administer these forces was the business of politicians, although it was not an easy task to do so. Paine remembered a line from Giacinto Dragonetti, the Italian theorist, whom he considered a "wise observer on governments." According to Dragonetti, "the science of the politician consists in fixing the true point of happiness and freedom. Those men would deserve the gratitude of ages," Dragonetti had asserted, "who should discover a mode of government that contained the greatest sum of individual happiness, with the least national expense."[31]

It was with a discussion of all of this that Paine began his political pamphlet in the autumn of 1775. Opening with a section on the *"Origin and Design of Government in General"* may not seem the most promising way of starting the pamphlet Rush had suggested, but it was a shrewd move. Paine sensed that it was important for him to demonstrate his rationality, before he unleashed his passion. Franklin and Dickinson had used similar devices. Paine wanted to portray himself as the careful scrutineer. He was a mechanic analyzing a machine. And the machine that was set before him in the autumn of 1775 was the political system of Britain.

For years everyone had heard about Britain's much-vaunted constitution, with its clever series of checks and balances that stopped power from being concentrated in dangerous places. But like Macaulay before him, Paine was suspicious of this. Was it not the case, he pointed out, that simple things were the least likely to become disordered? That they were the easiest to repair? But what could be more complex than Britain's political constitution? It was so complicated that, if there was a problem, "the nation may suffer for years together without being able to discover in which part the fault lies." Some will point here, and some there, "and every political physician," Paine wrote, "will advise a different medicine."[32]

The careful observer, however, could find some clarity. Britain's politics consisted of three constituent parts, Paine explained. There was the remains of monarchical tyranny in the person of the king; the relics of aristocratic tyranny in the House of Lords; and then some "new republican materials," in the House of Commons, "on whose virtue depend the freedom of England."[33] But was this actually such an inspired system? It was true, he admitted, that the House of Commons had the power to restrain the Crown by refusing the funds that were needed for its upkeep, but why should the Crown be empowered in the first place, with its ability to reject all the bills that came before it? Does this not, Paine wondered, suppose "that the king is wiser than those [in Parliament] whom it has already supposed to be wiser than him?" What kind of contradictory arrangement was that? "A mere absurdity!"[34] Although "we have been wise enough to shut and lock a door against absolute monarchy," he elaborated, "we at the same time have been foolish enough to put the crown in possession of the key."[35]

It was at this point, around a dozen pages in, that Paine settled on his target. Until the autumn of 1775 the king had remained above the criticisms that the colonists had leveled at politicians like Lord North or George Grenville. Most people regarded King George as a pious, devoted, and serious figure at the heart of the nation. It was much easier, as Burke had, to blame "cabals" for the disenchantment. Even Catharine Macaulay stopped short of any direct attack on the Crown. What had happened to John Wilkes in 1763 was a warning. And, after all, what did King George have to do with something that was essentially a political dispute between the House of Commons and the colonists? For Paine, however, the Crown was no innocent bystander. It was simultaneously all-powerful and completely ignorant of the reality of life for ordinary people. "There is something exceedingly ridiculous," he observed, "in the composition of monarchy":

> it first excludes a man from the means of information, yet empowers him to act in cases where the highest judgment is required. The state of a king shuts him from the world, yet the business of a king requires him to know it thoroughly; wherefore the different parts, unnaturally opposing and destroying each other, prove the whole character to be absurd and useless.[36]

Having found his theme, Paine dropped his reserve. Mankind had been created equal. How had it come to pass then that people had been divided into "KINGS AND SUBJECTS"?

> Male and female are the distinctions of nature, good and bad the distinctions of heaven; but how a race of men came into the

world so exalted above the rest, and distinguished like some new species, is worth enquiring into, and whether they are the means of happiness or of misery to mankind . . .[37]

It is more than probable, could we take off the dark covering of antiquity, and trace them to their first rise, that we should find the first of them nothing better than the principal ruffian of some restless gang, whose savage manners or pre-eminence in subtlety obtained him the title of chief among plunderers.[38]

In Britain, where the royal line traced its heritage to the days of William the Conqueror, the story was hardly a glorious one. "A French bastard landing with an armed banditti, and establishing himself king of England against the consent of the natives, is in plain terms a very paltry rascally original.——It certainly," Paine added, nearing the end of a rhetorical point that would have made even John Wilkes wince, "hath no divinity in it."[39]

Paine was not quite finished yet. Although he had vowed to restrict his arguments to the "doctrine" and not the man, he could not spare George III entirely. "In England," he wrote,

a k——g hath little more to do than to make war and give away places; which in plain terms, is to impoverish the nation and set it together by the ears. A pretty business indeed for a man to be allowed eight hundred thousand sterling a year for, and worshipped into the bargain! Of more worth is one honest man to society, than all the crowned ruffians that ever lived.[40]

His argument established, at last Paine felt free to turn his attention to America. In words that would soon echo across the continent, he issued his call to arms:

The sun never shined on a cause of greater worth. 'Tis not the affair of a city, a country, a province, or a kingdom, but a continent—of at least one eighth part of the habitable globe. 'Tis not the concern of a day, a year, or an age; posterity are virtually involved in the contest, and will be more or less affected, even to the end of time, by the proceedings now. Now is the seed time of continental union, faith and honour. The least fracture now will be like a name engraved with the point of a pin on the tender rind of a young oak; the wound will enlarge with the tree, and posterity read it in full grown characters.[41]

From the carefully analytical, Paine's language grew fierce and urgent. "Now," he repeated over and again, was the time to act. The affair had progressed from argument to arms. That shameful moment on April 19 when the first shot rang out at Lexington had opened a new era in politics. It was time for "a new method of thinking . . . All plans, proposals, &c prior to the nineteenth of April," he declared, "are like the almanacs of the last year, which, though proper then, are superseded and useless now."[42] Before that date it may have been correct for the colonists to petition the king and patiently await an answer. "There was a time when it was proper, and there is a proper time for it to cease."[43]

But what of those colonists who argued for reconciliation? Paine believed that they could be divided into four distinct categories of people. The first three were the interested, the weak, and the prejudiced. Numbered among them were lamentable figures like William Franklin and Joseph Galloway, those who owed either their wealth or their social status to the present corrupted system. Either such people were not to be trusted, or they were to be pitied. To the weak-willed who argued that America had flourished only because of her connection to Britain, and that the continuance of this connection was everything to her future happiness, Paine had a simple answer. "We may as well assert, that because a child has thrived upon milk, that it is never to have meat; or that the first twenty years of our lives is to become a precedent for the next twenty."[44] A fourth group, however, engaged Paine's attention far more. These were a "certain set of moderate men, who think better of the European world than it deserves." It was with such people that the truest danger lurked.

> Men of passive tempers look somewhat lightly over the offences of Britain, and, still hoping for the best, are apt to call out, *"Come we shall be friends again for all this."* But examine the passions and feelings of mankind. Bring the doctrine of reconciliation to the touchstone of nature, and then tell me, whether you can hereafter love, honour, and faithfully serve the power that hath carried fire and sword into your land? If you cannot do all these, then you are only deceiving yourselves, and by your delay bringing ruin upon posterity.[45]

For those still wavering, Paine was contemptuous:

> Hath your house been burnt? Hath your property been destroyed before your face? Are your wife and child destitute of a bed to lie on, or bread to live on? Have you lost a parent or a child by their hands, and yourself the ruined and wretched survivor? If you have not, then are you not a judge of those who have. But if you have, and can still shake hands with the murderers, then are you unworthy the name of husband, father, friend, or lover, and whatever may be your rank or title in life, you have the heart of a coward, and the spirit of a sycophant.[46]

Reading these words, a picture of Paine rises up through the centuries. He sits in the warm, glossy light of an early autumn evening, glancing out from his lodgings toward the flow of people on the street, measuring their mood. In his prose, Paine was a master of the psychological trick. He had a talent for making people feel alternately vulnerable and powerful. One moment he would remind readers that it was not twelve months since a common pirate "might have come up

the Delaware, and laid the city of Philadelphia under instant contribution, for what sum he pleased."[47] The next he would tell them that
America's future lay entirely in their hands. "And history sufficiently
informs us, that the bravest achievements were always accomplished
in the nonage of a nation."[48] Now, he repeated, was the time to declare independence. The opportunity that lay before them may well
have vanished in half a century's time. They had a moral duty, a rare
opportunity, to act:

> These proceedings may at first appear strange and difficult,
> but, like all other steps which we have already passed over, will
> in a little time become familiar and agreeable; and, until an
> independence is declared, the Continent will feel itself like a
> man who continues putting off some unpleasant business from
> day to day; yet knows it must be done, hates to set about it;
> wishes it over; and is continually haunted with the thoughts of
> its necessity.[49]

As the pages of copy accumulated, Paine fell into the habit of visiting
Rush to read to him his latest work. With the draft almost finished in
December, Rush took on the role of informal literary agent. With a
fair copy of about one hundred pages worked up, he started to think
about publication. He understood that Paine's relationship with Robert Aitken had soured. He also knew that Aitken, like Hall before
him, was keen to stay out of the political fray. The city, however, was
now teeming with ambitious printers.

Rush soon approached one of them, the same Robert Bell who
had started his career in Philadelphia eight years before with an
American issue of Johnson's *Rasselas*. Warily, Bell took on the job.
He agreed to print a thousand copies, so long as Paine stood the risk
of financial loss. The bargain struck, the final task was to settle on a
name for the pamphlet. Paine had intended to call it *Plain Truth*, but

Rush was not convinced. A better title, he reckoned, was *Common Sense*.

A THICK, DARK FOG shrouded Philadelphia in the middle of December. On the nineteenth it lifted, and the old, familiar north-west wind began to blow again. For Franklin, at his house on Market Street, it was the kind of weather to stir ancient memories, with Christmas just a week away.

Exactly a year had passed since Deborah had died in this house. Then, Franklin had still been living in Craven Street; that phase in his life was now definitively closed. Instead of philosophy lessons with Polly Stevenson or chess games with John Pringle, he had been propelled into a life of almost constant activity, of letter writing and committees. Much of this was centered at the State House, where the Second Continental Congress had been in session since the spring, but occasionally he was obliged to travel too. In October he had made an arduous trip as part of a three-man delegation from Congress to Washington's encampment in Cambridge, near Boston. Washington had been stationed there since July, tasked with the challenge of keeping the British troops penned inside the city.

The situation was unpromising. While the British expected to be reinforced by sea at any time, Washington's makeshift army was in a ragged condition. There were few uniforms, little structure of command, hardly any weaponry or ammunition, and wretchedly poor morale. At the age of almost seventy, Franklin was thrown into the middle of discussions about rations, pay, and munitions. There did not seem to be any end to it. Back in Philadelphia more letters were waiting for him: from the aggressive General Charles Lee who was eager to set to work; from the cautious Brigadier General Horatio Gates; from persons unknown, soliciting patronage or a position in one of the newly formed battalion groups.

Among all this, on the final packet to reach the city before the service was suspended, came another letter from Strahan. It would be the last Franklin was likely to hear from him for some time. Once again, Strahan's tone was urgent. He had read the reports in the London papers that Franklin had accepted from Congress the position of postmaster for the colonies. This was evidence enough of the way events were heading. A separation, Strahan saw, was clearly going to take place. In his letter, Strahan cast his mind back to the series of questions he had proposed to Franklin in 1769. It was striking, he wrote, that Franklin's prophecy had been so completely fulfilled.

> But I am greatly afraid you have carried Things too far, and I am persuaded you will find it so ere long. You are now, I am very sorry to see it, in the Evening of Life embark'd in the most arduous, most dangerous and most uncertain Task that ever Man engaged in, where Difficulties will of course succeed Difficulties; where various Interests will clash against one another, perhaps unseen; where the Humours of a great Body of People are to be attended to, and if possible, reconciled to the great Plan of Operations; and where the Ambition of a single Individual may, at length, in one Moment overturn that System of Liberty you are now contending.[50]

In London, meanwhile, Strahan had seen "many worthy Men" over the past few months "who have been forced to abandon their Homes in almost every part of the Continent, to avoid Confinement, Confiscation of Goods, and even Corporal Punishment." It was something he never thought he would witness. His pity was with these industrious people, who had been chased from their homes and livelihoods. But this was still nothing when compared with what he felt about his old friend. To Strahan, Franklin's personal involvement in the rebellion was an aberration. While he could have been passing the remainder of his days "in the Exercise of those Studies" or "in the Company of such Men, as best suit your Philosophical Turn of Mind," he had embroiled himself in a reckless conflict. "I own," Strahan repeated, "I wish your great Talents had found other Employment."[51] If he had had the chance, had the packet been turning around as usual for its return voyage to London, Franklin might well have conveyed the same message to his Scottish friend.

As the new year, 1776, began, the sense lingered for Franklin that nature was disordered. Philadelphia was outwardly the same city that he had always known. But now it seemed decisively changed. His wife was dead. His son William was estranged. Joseph Galloway, his political ally, had left the city and the Congress. David Hall, Jr., was at least one link with the past, but even he was a difficult figure for Franklin to confront. Part of Franklin's old life, when he had been one of the chief royalists in Pennsylvania, continued in Hall's hands. It was his duty to reprint the proclamations and speeches from the throne as they arrived in Philadelphia. On January 10, 1776, another of these arrived. It was the most vehement expression yet of George's fury. It accused the colonists of promoting a desperate conspiracy. A set of rebels had inflamed the people, infusing "into their minds a system of opinions repugnant to the true constitution of the colonies."

> They have raised troops, and are collecting a naval force; they have seized the public revenue, and assumed to themselves legislative, executive, and judicial powers, which they already exercise in the most arbitrary manner, over the persons and properties of their fellow-subjects. And altho' many of these unhappy people may still retain their loyalty, and may be too wise not to see the fatal consequence of this usurpation, and wish to resist it, yet the torrent of violence has been strong enough to compel their acquiescence till a sufficient force shall appear to support them.[52]

The king made it plain that his patience was at an end. It was now, he stated, the time "to put a speedy end to these disorders, by the most decisive exertions." Before long a British Army would begin its work on the American continent.

The King's speech, it was clear, was intended to strike terror into the people. Given the accumulated might of Britain's military force, the prospect of what might happen to Philadelphia, to New York, to Boston or Charleston, and everywhere else in between, was disturbing enough. But before anything more could happen, George's words were met by some others even more forceful.

> THIS DAY IS PUBLISHED, and now selling, by ROBERT BELL, in Third-street, PRICE TWO SHILLINGS, COMMON SENSE; addressed to the Inhabitants of America, on the following interesting Subjects. 1. Of the Origin and Design of Government in general, with concise Remarks on the English Constitution. 2. Of Monarchy and Hereditary Succession. 3. Thoughts on the present State of American Affairs. 4. Of the present Ability of America, with some miscellaneous Reflections.
>   Man knows no Master save creating HEAVEN,
>   Or those whom choice and common good ordain.
>
>   Thomson

Paine would soon reflect that, "had the spirit of prophecy directed the birth" of *Common Sense*, "it could not have brought it forth at a more seasonable juncture, or a more necessary time." The "bloody mindedness" of the King's speech showed "the necessity of pursuing the doctrine" of *Common Sense*.[53] "Men read by way of revenge. And the Speech, instead of terrifying, prepared a way for the manly principles of Independence."[54]

Franklin had witnessed many literary sensations over his time. There was Wilkes's *North Briton* and Dickinson's *Farmer's Letters*. He had enjoyed the rush of adulation with his own *Experiments and Obser-*

vations on Electricity and in more distant times with *Poor Richard's Alma-nack*. But what followed with *Common Sense* during the early months of 1776 eclipsed absolutely everything that went before.

Rush wrote that it burst from the press "with an effect which has rarely been produced by types and paper in any age or country."[55] Aitken's bookshop, just one of thirty such stores trading in Phila-delphia at the start of 1776, was said to have sold seven dozen in a fortnight, and in the same space of time new editions had appeared across the colonies. By January 24, General Charles Lee had finished it at Stamford, Connecticut. He wrote to Washington in Boston.

> Have you seen the pamphlet *Common Sense?* I never saw such a masterly irresistible performance. It will, if I mistake not, in concurrence with the transcendent folly and wickedness of the Ministry, give the *coup-de-grace* to Great Britain. In short, I own myself convinced, by the arguments, of the necessity of separation.[56]

In Cambridge, General Washington was reading *Common Sense* too. He decided its reasoning was "unanswerable."[57] Not far away in New England a minister called Ashbel Green described the pamphlet in more poetic terms. It "struck a string," Green wrote, "which required but a touch to make it vibrate. The country was ripe for Independence, and only needed somebody to tell the people so, with decision, boldness and plausibility."[58] In Virginia its effect was just as powerful. According-ing to the young lawyer Edmund Randolph, it charged the minds and spirits of everyone that read it. "The public sentiment which a few weeks before had shuddered at the tremendous obstacles, with which independence was environed, overleaped every barrier."[59]

While *Common Sense*'s effectiveness was instantly apparent, people were left to guess at the identity of the author. Because it had ap-peared in Philadelphia, it was only natural that some concluded it was Franklin's work. As for Paine himself, he remained tight-lipped. In an updated introduction to a new edition, he explained, "who the Author of this Production is, is wholly unnecessary to the Public, as the Object for Attention is the *Doctrine itself*, not the *Man*." All he would reveal is that, "he is unconnected with any Party, and under no sort of Influence public or private, but the influence of reason and principle."[60] But anonymity was too much to expect in such a case. Franklin, writing to General Lee in February, described Paine as "the reputed, and I think the real Author of *Common Sense*." This was enough to appease Lee, who in turn passed the hint on to Adams, explaining that Paine was "a gentleman about two years from England" and that he was a man who had "genius in his eyes."[61]

As so often with Franklin, his involvement in the pamphlet is difficult to pin down. According to Rush, he played a more active role in its composition than he was willing to admit. In a later account, Rush explained that before publication Paine gave Franklin a copy of the manuscript for inspection. Franklin did not change anything, but he did strike one passage out. It was the following, Rush remembered—"A greater absurdity cannot be conceived of, than three millions of people running to their sea coast every time a ship arrives from London, to know what portion of liberty they should enjoy." Amid all the other inflammatory material—about the king, about the British government—Rush was surprised that this sentence, which he thought was one of the "most striking," should be deleted.[62] But had he known Franklin better, then perhaps it would have not seemed quite so mysterious. It was a line, after all, that captured something of Franklin's own life experiences. For him it was, perhaps, just a little too close to home.

This aside, *Common Sense* made its way into the world with no further editorial interventions. Paine's rich, irresistibly quotable language would reach, according to the estimate of one scholar, between 150,000 and 250,000 readers across America and Europe in 1776 alone.

A long habit of not thinking a thing *wrong*, gives it a superficial appearance of being *right*.

———

Time makes more converts than reason.

———

We have it in our power to begin the world over again.

———

Small islands not capable of protecting themselves, are the proper objects for kingdoms to take under their care; but there is something very absurd, in supposing a continent to be perpetually governed by an island. In no instance hath nature made the satellite larger than its primary planet.[63]

By the spring of 1776 it was another of Paine's passages that was commanding attention. Toward the end of *Common Sense* he had argued that it would be in the colonies' interests to produce a manifesto that could be "dispatched to foreign courts,"

> setting forth the miseries we have endured, and the peaceable methods we have ineffectually used for redress; declaring, at the same time, that not being able, any longer to live happily or safely under the cruel disposition of the B——sh court, we had been driven to the necessity of breaking off all connection with her; at the same time assuring all such courts of our peaceable disposition towards them, and of our desire of entering into trade with them: Such a memorial would produce more good effects to this Continent, than if a ship were freighted with petitions to Britain.[64]

On June 7, 1776, this is just what Congress decided to do. Following a motion from Richard Henry Lee, a committee of five delegates was formed to prepare a declaration of independence. Benjamin Franklin, as ever, was among the five, as was John Adams. And as was another Virginian, called Thomas Jefferson.

Eighteen

PLODS

A LITTLE BEFORE FOUR o'clock in the afternoon of Wednesday, May 15, 1776, James Boswell settled himself down beside Samuel Johnson in a hackney carriage. As it lurched forward and they began their short journey from 8 Bolt Court, Fleet Street, to the Poultry, off Cheapside in the City of London, Boswell felt a pang of satisfaction. "I exulted as much as a fortune-hunter," he recalled, "who has got an heiress into a post-chaise with him to set out for Gretna-Green."[1]

Boswell had formed his plan a week or so earlier. He had been with his friends Edward and Charles Dilly, who kept a book and printing shop on the Poultry. This was a social as well as a commercial space. Over the years the Dillys had built up a reputation for hospitality, throwing generous parties for the leading literary figures of the day. One of their prized guests was Catharine Macaulay, whose pamphlets the brothers printed and whose Whiggish opinions they shared. Although Macaulay had left London behind for the restorative atmosphere of Bath, the Dillys maintained their connection to radical politics through their fondness for John Wilkes.

While visiting the brothers, Boswell learnt that they were planning a dinner for Wilkes and some other gentlemen. Would Boswell like to come? Boswell thanked the brothers for their offer and asked if Johnson could join their party too. "What, with Mr. Wilkes? Not for the world," replied Edward Dilly. "Dr. Johnson would never forgive me." Amused by the idea, Boswell persisted. At length an agreement was struck. Boswell would manage everything—the invitation, collecting Johnson, the ride home—and would be answerable for anything that went wrong along the way. "Nay, if you will take it upon you," Dilly conceded, "I am sure I shall be very happy to see them both here."[2]

Social gatherings like these were a much-cherished part of life. As the sun dipped in the sky, Londoners would climb into their coaches or chairs or set out on foot to where conversation and company awaited. For those of a high or distinguished rank, it often signaled one of the prominent club or society meetings. London abounded with such dining clubs. There was the Beefsteaks who met in Covent Garden, for instance, and the Royal Society or "Royal Philosophers" who congregated weekly at the Mitre on Fleet Street. Johnson himself belonged to the most notable, which met at the Turk's Head tavern and included, among others, the artist Joshua Reynolds, actor David Garrick, and writer Edward Gibbon. "Our Club, Madam," Johnson would crow to his friend Hester Thrale, "is a society which can scarcely be matched in the world."[3] Franklin also loved London's clubbable atmosphere. "I find I love Company, Chat, a Laugh, a Glass, and even a Song," he told a friend in the 1760s, "and at the same Time relish better than I us'd to do, the grave Observations and wise Sentences of Old Men's Conversation."[4] Enjoyment was a central part of it. But the conversation had other qualities too. When the like-minded were drawn together, a club became a forum for exchanging news, hatching plans, and scrutinizing the latest events.

Dinner parties like the ones thrown by Joshua Reynolds or the Dilly brothers were an extension of this. They were formal, lavish, tastefully curated affairs. The guests would be carefully selected and the menu specially tailored to suit them. With the guests having all they needed, there would be nothing to distract them from the conversation. The Dillys, who were adept operators in the social life of literary London, knew the rules and expectations well. And of all the unwritten rules in existence, one must have been nagging them as they fretted over their preparations in May 1776. Never mix the irascible Samuel Johnson with the provocative John Wilkes. Something far more explosive than the Macaulay–Johnson episode was bound to result.

In the spring of 1776 Wilkes's term as Lord Mayor of London had recently come to an end, and he had been replaced in the role by Macaulay's brother, John Sawbridge. Wilkes's mayoralty was generally regarded as a success. A natural showman, he had brought considerable flair to the post, stage-managing his ceremonial duties with élan. His generous banquets at the Guildhall in particular were the talk of the town. Wilkes's political agenda was popular too. He had been progressive, winning admirers for his attempts to regulate food prices as well as his schemes for extending charity to prisoners. As ever Wilkes had little concern for budgets, overspending his allowances by almost double. Unabashed, he carried on with the same energy he had shown during the days of his tussles with the ministry in the 1760s. Apart from his busy private life, he managed to combine his mayoralty with other duties in the House of Commons, to which he was reelected as one of the members for Middlesex in 1774.

Returned to the green benches, Wilkes believed he had gone some way to correcting the wrongs of the past. He continued to seek redress, however, for a number of issues, and he also cautioned Lord North's government over its policies toward the American colonies. "Men are not converted," he argued, "by the force of the bayonet at the breast." Otherwise he approached his Parliamentary duties with his usual mix of seriousness and humor. According to the diarist Nathaniel Wraxall: "he was an incomparable comedian in all he said or did; and he seemed to consider human life itself as a mere comedy . . . His speeches were full of wit, pleasantry, and point; Yet nervous, spirited, and not at all defective in argument."[5] No amount of humor seemed likely to endear him to Johnson, a man who could hardly have forgotten the attack Wilkes made on him in the *North Briton*, when he ridiculed him as "Pensioner Johnson." Although the two had corresponded through intermediaries in the past, they otherwise stayed clear of one another. Boswell knew as much, but the prospect of seeing them together was irresistible. His first challenge, though, was to get Johnson to commit to attending the dinner. He knew Johnson would almost certainly avoid it if he knew in advance who was going to be there. But Boswell had formed a plan. Visiting Johnson at his lodgings, he casually mentioned that the Dillys were organizing a dinner party, to which he was invited.

> JOHNSON. "Sir, I am obliged to Mr. Dilly, I will wait upon him—" BOSWELL. "Provided, Sir, I suppose, that the company which he is to have, is agreeable to you." JOHNSON. "What do you mean, Sir? What do you take me for? Do you think I am so ignorant of the world, as to imagine that I am to prescribe to a gentleman what company he is to have at his table?" BOSWELL. "I beg your pardon, Sir, for wishing to prevent you from meeting people whom you might not like. Perhaps he may have some of what he calls his patriotick friends with him." JOHNSON. Well, Sir, and what then? What care *I* for his *patriotick friends*? Poh! BOSWELL. "I should not be surprized to find Jack Wilkes there." JOHNSON. "And if Jack Wilkes *should* be there, what is that to *me*, Sir? My dear friend, let us have no more of this. I am sorry to be angry with you; but really it is treating me strangely to talk to me as if I could not meet any company whatever, occasionally." BOSWELL. "Pray forgive me, Sir: I meant well."[6]

Boswell was delighted with this. He knew that having committed himself Johnson would be too proud to withdraw. On the day of the dinner, half an hour before the appointed time, Boswell called at Johnson's at Bolt Court. Inside, as usual, Boswell was served by Francis

Barber. Boswell knew and liked Barber, who was now in his thirties and married to a lady called Elizabeth Ball. With Barber's help, after a little difficulty, he was able to get Johnson into a fresh shirt and then a hackney carriage. Soon they were entering the Dillys' front door, where Johnson was surprised to find himself in unfamiliar company.

Boswell watched Johnson keenly. Once inside the drawing room he whispered to one of the brothers, "Who is that gentleman, Sir?" He was told that it was Arthur Lee, the American diplomat who, with Franklin, had been representing Massachusetts in London for the past years. Johnson was alarmed at this, murmuring "too, too, too" under his breath, "which was one of his habitual mutterings." A sterner shock followed. "And who is the gentleman in lace?" Johnson enquired. "Mr Wilkes, Sir," replied Dilly. Johnson "had some difficulty" restraining himself. He picked up a book, "sat down upon a window-seat and read, or at least kept his eye upon it intently for some time, till he composed himself."[7]

Only when they were called to dinner did the company congregate. Boswell was shocked to see that Wilkes placed himself next to Johnson. In a life of audacious action, this was another of Wilkes's bold moves. The strangest thing, however, happened next. Johnson was at his happiest in company. He once memorably declared, "a tavern chair was the throne of human felicity,"[8] and Boswell well knew that there was no one who, as he put it, ate "more heartily than Johnson, or loved better what was nice and delicate." Wilkes seemed to have identified this weakness.

Mr. Wilkes was very assiduous in helping him to some fine veal. "Pray give me leave, Sir:—It is better here—A little of the brown—Some fat, Sir—A little of the stuffing—Some gravy—Let me have the pleasure of giving you some butter— Allow me to recommend a squeeze of this orange;—or the lemon, perhaps, may have more zest."—"Sir, Sir, I am obliged to you, Sir," cried Johnson, bowing, and turning his head to

him with a look for some time of "surly virtue," but, in a short
while, of complacency.[9]

From this point, the evening grew convivial. Rather than being divided by their differences, Johnson and Wilkes started to hold forth
on subjects of common interest. They talked about the best actors
of the day; about the Roman poet Horace, and Shakespeare's plays.
Wilkes made Johnson laugh with the observation that, "among all
the bold flights of Shakespeare's imagination, the boldest was making Birnamwood march to Dunsinane; creating a wood where there
never was a shrub; a wood in Scotland! ha! ha! ha!"[10]

Here was a topic that they could both rally behind. Boswell
was forced to sit for an hour and endure their delight in abusing his
home country. "You have now been in Scotland, Sir," he eventually
protested, "and say if you did not see meat and drink enough there."
To this Johnson replied, "Why yes, Sir; meat and drink enough to
give the inhabitants sufficient strength to run away from home."
Johnson then turned to Wilkes with a smile:

JOHNSON. (to Mr. Wilkes,) "You must know, Sir, I lately took
my friend Boswell and shewed him genuine civilised life in an
English provincial town. I turned him loose at Lichfield, my native city, that he might see for once real civility: for you know he
lives among savages in Scotland, and among rakes in London."
WILKES. "Except when he is with grave, sober, decent people like
you and me." JOHNSON. (smiling,) "And we ashamed of him."[11]

The high spirits continued for some hours. Johnson told Wilkes the
story about Macaulay and her footman, which he asserted proved the
"ridiculousness of the argument for the equality of mankind." Wilkes
then brought up the *North Briton* and Lord Bute. Had Bute stuck to
Scotland only, he told Johnson, he would not have taken the trouble
to write his eulogy. "Sir," declared Johnson, as the night drew to an

end, "it is not so much to be lamented that Old England is lost, as that the Scotch have found it."

When the story of the evening began to circulate, people could scarcely believe it. Edmund Burke credited Boswell with a quite majestic triumph, pleasantly observing, "that there was nothing to equal it in the whole history of the *Corps Diplomatique*."[12]

WHILE TALES OF BOSWELL'S unexpected success were left to spread around town, one person's perspective was omitted. In all his lengthy descriptions of Johnson and Wilkes's repartee, Boswell overlooked the brooding presence of Arthur Lee at the table. Lee was a fiercely political creature. Born to a wealthy family in Virginia, he was brought over to Britain to be schooled at Eton and the University of Edinburgh. Proud and intense, during the 1760s Lee had been one of the most stringent and energetic writers on the colonial dispute. Along with essays attacking slavery, he wrote ten unsparing pieces in support of Dickinson's *Farmer's Letters*, training his fire on Townshend's assault on America's rights. Based in London since 1768, Lee became friendly with radicals like Macaulay, Wilkes, and Joseph Priestley, and writing under the pseudonym "Junius Americanus" he joined Burke and others in producing searing attacks on the "King's Men" at court. Over the last years Lee had worked with Franklin as an agent for Massachusetts, and he was at the Cockpit in January 1774 to see his colleague's humiliation. Hotter by temperament than Franklin, he had nonetheless survived longer. In the spring of 1776, he was one of the most senior American diplomats to remain in the British capital.

None of this forceful personality is captured by Boswell in his famous account of the dinner at the Dillys'. It is Wilkes and Johnson who hold court, as if the rest of the party looked on in silent awe. There is something jarring about this. Lee was not the kind of person to stay quiet. And to reframe the dinner party from his perspective is to see it quite differently. Rather than the triumph described by

Boswell and enjoyed by London's literary society, for Lee and those interested in politics the night must have been much more of a disappointment. For as they sat down to eat in the Poultry, a dramatic story was unfolding on the south coast. The papers had been full of it all week. The most recent issue of the *Chronicle*, printed by Strahan at Little New Street, carried the latest dispatch in a letter from Plymouth: "Yesterday passed by this place all the fleet, amounting to upwards of 120 sail, with the Hessian troops and guards, and train of artillery on board, bound to America, and the *Tartar* man of war, Capt Ommaney, that was here, joined them."[13]

This was the culmination of a story that had been building for months. A massive invasion force, bolstered by European troops that had been purchased from various rulers by King George, was gathering in Portsmouth. Now, in the last week, they had weighed anchor and begun their passage across the Atlantic. This was a fleet bigger than any known before. It numbered hundreds of ships, carrying tens of thousands of troops and hundreds of tons of stores and ammunition. No one could quite be sure what its destination was. But everyone knew that when it did arrive in Boston, Newport, Philadelphia, or New York, a bloody contest would ensue. To Britons the outcome of this seemed a foregone conclusion. It would not be long—the end of the summer perhaps—before the rebellion was neutralized. That would leave the only remaining question: What to do with the ringleaders? Should General Washington, Adams, Franklin, and all the rest of them be brought back to England? Or should they be tried by their own people in America?

That such a developing story could be passed over in silence must have seemed perverse to Lee. The fate of his country was at stake, along with the fortunes of the British Empire, and neither Johnson nor Wilkes had anything to say. Was this delicacy? Did his fellow diners not want to offend Lee? Or was it complacency?

Over the last few weeks the British papers had been filled with fiery extracts from the Philadelphian pamphlet *Common Sense*. No one had yet had the courage to print it in its entirety, as it was considered to be too full of treason and rebellion. Nevertheless everyone was talking about it. To one newspaper correspondent—someone who had managed to read the whole work—it was essential that it be made available as quickly as possible. It was not that they agreed with the author, "whoever he is," but that it was vital that the British be animated by *Common Sense* just as the Americans had plainly been. Only by reading the pamphlet could the British grasp the gravity of the situation. "It might tend to open the eyes of many well-meaning, though deluded people," cautioned the correspondent, "who have been led to believe, by the abettors of rebellion in this country, that the *poor distressed Americans* have never had any other view than a redress of the grievous burdens imposed on them by the British Parliament." *Common Sense* disproved that. It advocated independence and nothing else. And for those who said the pamphlet was the work of a madman, it was best to consider "that it has gone through three editions, the two first published under the nose of the Congress, and the last by their own printer."[14]

Sitting at the same table as two of the greatest political writers in Britain, Lee must have expected to hear some commentary on all this. Yet Johnson had nothing at all to say. Nor did Wilkes, a figure with a distinct interest in political pamphleteering, mention *Common Sense* at all. In addition to this, nothing was said about the invasion fleet that King George had personally helped to assemble, with promises to the Hessians of bounties for American blood. Nor was any word uttered about the other shocking news that had recently arrived in the capital. General Howe, with all of his advantages of troops and firepower, had been forced to abandon his military headquarters in Boston after the cleverest and most intrepid tactical maneuvers by Washington. Everyone was wondering how on earth such a thing could have happened.

As Boswell describes it, Lee did attempt to raise the subject of America at one point. He told Wilkes and Johnson that a community of Scottish immigrants had settled in a barren part of America, "and wondered why they should choose it." Johnson swiftly shut this topic down. "Why, Sir, all barrenness is comparative. The *Scotch* would not know it to be barren."[15] This was humor, but it was also evasion. Sitting there listening to the old jokes and hackneyed stories, to Lee the pair can only have looked like figures marooned out of time. Across the Atlantic something extraordinary was happening. As Edmund Burke would soon put it in a manuscript note, "A great revolution has happened":

> A revolution made not by chopping and changing of power in existing states, but by appearance of the new state among mankind, of a new species, in a new part of the earth. It has made as great a change in all the relations and balances and gravitations of power, as the appearance of a new planet would in the system of our solar world.[16]

As Lee followed Johnson, Boswell, and Wilkes out of the Dillys' bookshop and into that spring night, the picture is one of changing times. Once, not so long ago, Wilkes and Johnson had been at the forefront of political culture. Now, as far as America went, they seemed too comfortable, too satisfied, too complacent. The important words that were being written about society now, the words that were being written about life and liberty and happiness and the Enlightenment vision of an improved world, were not those coming from the garrets of Fleet Street or the town houses around Westminster or St. James's. Neither Wilkes nor Johnson seems to have grasped it, but in Philadelphia a new generation of scholars, journalists, lawyers, soldiers, figures of genius, had begun to speak.

IN A FEW WEEKS' time Jefferson would start to draft the text for the Declaration of Independence in his lodgings on Seventh and Market Street. Resting on the idiosyncratic writing desk of his own design that he used when traveling, Jefferson cast his mind around for words that fitted the task at hand. Jefferson had an extraordinary gift, Bernard Bailyn noted, "for supple and elegant if abstract expression."[17] He was not grand like Johnson, teasing like Franklin, or waspish like Wilkes. Instead he had an ability to condense so much experience into brief, dignified statements. As he set down his draft, he brought shape to the story, clarity to the arguments, and passion to his vision. "Life, Liberty, and the pursuit of Happiness."

As Jefferson circulated his draft with Franklin and Adams at the end of June 1776, another writer was also busy at his desk in Philadelphia. It might seem that Thomas Paine had played his part already. But as Paine would explain it himself, in words that would ring throughout the ages, "When my country, into which I had just set my foot, was set on fire about my ears, it was time to stir. It was time for every man to stir."[18]

For Paine, as for Franklin, Johnson, Strahan, Wilkes, and Macaulay, the most effective medium remained the pen. On June 29, 1776, it seems that it was him, writing under the pen name "Republicus," who called for this new nation to be given the dignity of a name. Published as John Adams prepared to confront John Dickinson in the State House, and as Jefferson steeled himself for the debate on his draft text to begin, the piece did away with "the colonies" and instead conferred a name upon them. It was a name by which they would be known forever after:

For the PENNSYLVANIA EVENING POST.

EVERY moment that I reflect on our affairs, the more am I convinced of the necessity of a formal Declaration of Independence. Reconciliation is thought of now by none but knaves, fools and madmen; and as we cannot offer terms of peace to Great-Britain, until, as other nations have done before us, we agree to call ourselves by some name, I shall rejoice to hear the title of the UNITED STATES OF AMERICA.[19]

Epilogue

CROSSINGS

ON JULY 15, 1784, Catharine Macaulay Graham looked out at the coast of the United States of America for the first time. As she sailed into Boston harbor, just months after the war had come to a formal close, Macaulay became one of the very first British supporters of the revolution to clap eyes on the country she had long dreamed about.

For someone of Macaulay's tastes, Boston was a suitable first point of contact. Like Rome, it was a town built on hills. Due to the events of the war, the names of these had become almost as familiar to Britons as those of the Esquiline or the Palatine. There was Bunker Hill, where the fighting properly began in June 1775, and Dorchester Heights, where Washington had outflanked General Howe the following spring to bring the Continental Army an important strategic victory. Then, trending to the south, was a chain of hillocks that fed down to Penn's Hill and a region rich in wildlife and agriculture. This was the home of Macaulay's American friends, Abigail Adams and her husband John, whose efforts during the Second Continental Congress had been decisive. As John had written in 1778:

If human Nature could be made happy by any Thing that can please the Eye, the Ear, the Taste or any other sense, or Passion or Fancy, this Country would be the Region for Happiness: But, if my Country were at Peace, I should be happier, among the Rocks and shades of Pens hill: and would chearfully exchange, all the Elegance, Magnificence and sublimity of Europe, for the Simplicity of Braintree and Weymouth.[1]

By 1784 John and Abigail Adams were traveling yet again. This time they were in Europe, where they were consolidating the United States' new position among the old powers. But they would soon hear about Macaulay's arrival, along with her second husband, William Graham. According to Mercy Otis Warren, a common friend, Macaulay and her husband were "treated in Boston and its Environs with every mark of Respect. She is a Lady of most Extraordinary talent," Warren added, with, "a Commanding Genius and Brilliance of thought."[2]

This was rather gentler treatment than Macaulay had experienced in Britain in recent times. When she had married William in December 1778, he had been twenty-one, to her forty-seven. Worse than that, he was a mere assistant to a ship's surgeon. Fashionable society in Bath had been scandalized. No longer was Macaulay talked about as a celebrated female historian; Catharine Macaulay Graham was recast as a temptress, a destroyer of conventions, a lurid stain on the polite world.

While the marriage itself was wounding enough to her reputation, what really proved fatal was the rumor that Macaulay had previously conducted a sexual affair with her second husband's older brother, the notorious quack doctor James Graham. The elder Graham's interest was treating nervous conditions, which he combatted with a lively range of treatments, from milk baths to electrified chairs. Adding particular spice to the stories was Graham's invention of the "celestial bed," fitted with electrical wires and magnets, and engraved with the motto "Be fruitful, multiply and replenish the earth."[3] A night in the bed, Graham claimed, was enough to cure sterility or impotence.

For Macaulay's enemies, all this was irresistible ammunition. Throughout the years of war she continued to write, but the gossip about her private life had eclipsed the old interest in her scholarship and political views. Sometimes she was ignored altogether. When he heard the news that another volume of her *History* was being published in 1781, Horace Walpole jibed, "I believe England will be finished before her 'History.'"[4] A tour of America, then, would give Macaulay some respite from the sneering. As people who had long been disdained by England's social elite, the Americans were primed to feel an affinity with the lady they encountered in the summer of 1784. But Macaulay was more than someone to be pitied. Memories of the war were still raw, and people well remembered Macaulay's unswerving, vociferous support during the daunting events of 1775. For years before that, too, Macaulay had championed the American cause in Britain, condemning Grenville and Townshend's duties as assaults on the colonists' liberties and constantly reminding her readers of the insidious nature of power.

For Americans the real heroism of Macaulay lay in the fact that she had not been corrupted, unlike so many others. The 1760s, the decade of Macaulay's emergence, was widely regarded in the colonies as having seen the beginning of the plot against liberty. By the end of the war this narrative had been refined. The conspiracy had begun at about the time of George III's accession; it was instigated by Augusta and Lord Bute, who, years after he had stopped exerting real political influence, was still being condemned in Boston as "the seven headed beast mentioned in the 13th Chapter of Revelation."[5] For many the plot had been carried forward by the likes of George Grenville and Lord North. Given the power these men held it was difficult to resist their influence. Only a few, including William Pitt, John Wilkes, and Benjamin Franklin, had truly stood firm. And among these, few had stood with as unwavering a conviction as Macaulay. That liberty had survived this latest assault to flourish anew in the New World was an achievement to which she had contributed and something for which she should be honored.

Over the next year Macaulay undertook a grand tour of the country she had once foreseen as "a new, a flourishing, and an extensive empire of freemen,"[6] from the misty banks of the Piscataqua River in the north, to the wind-scoured bays of Rhode Island, and south to the vast sunburned plains of Virginia. Along the way she met James Monroe, the future president; Henry Knox, a decorated general in the Continental Army; Richard Henry Lee, the politician who had proposed the motion for independence in June 1776; and, in Philadelphia, Benjamin Rush. Twenty years before, Rush had been a politically engaged medical student at Macaulay's salons in London. He was now a signee of the Declaration of Independence, and one of the republic's foremost citizens. Rush, like everyone else, was pleased to meet Macaulay, although to some Philadelphians, seeing her walking the streets may have been an eerie experience. Seven years earlier, at the height of the war, Patience Wright's waxworks of Chatham, Macaulay, and others had gone on display in the city. When John Adams had seen them, they gave him a fright. "I seemed to be walking among a group of corpses," he wrote home to Abigail.[7]

While Macaulay retained her strong mind and staunch heart in 1784, there was a frailty to her too. "Slow-pacing time begins to shed, / Its silver blossoms o'er her head," one newspaper wrote as she rolled in her coach through the post roads of the east coast.[8] Catching sight of Macaulay on the road south out of New York, the *Delaware Gazette* noted she had no "vain pomp in dress or equipage," favoring instead "a plain, yet elegant stile."[9] In this fashion, Macaulay reached Mount Vernon for her most prized visit of all. There she spent a week with Washington, discussing the plans for a future constitution and browsing the general's wartime correspondence. One newspaper recorded that she left, "satiated with the happiness she anticipated in viewing that great and good man."[10] This was too much for those at home in Britain. Sour reports in the columns in early 1785 divulged the news that she had spent Christmas with Washington, Lafayette, and Nathanael Greene. "What a pity," sneered one newspaper, "the celebrated Dr. Franklin was not likely to return from France to be present at this constellation of patriotism, the like of which has not been seen for many ages!"[11]

One person that Macaulay did not see during her tour was Thomas Paine. During the war, Paine had remained an active participant, following *Common Sense* up with his motivational *Crisis Papers*, then serving as an aide-de-camp to the star general Greene. At the time of Macaulay's arrival he had been rewarded for his contribution to the cause with the gift of a confiscated farm in New Rochelle, New York, and a payment of £500. Had Macaulay and Paine met it would have made for a curious scene. They were perhaps the two most prominent English republicans of the age, and they would certainly have had much to talk about.

They also had the idea of a project in common. Since 1777, Paine had been collecting materials for what he intended to be a history of the American War. After years of haphazard work it seemed that those who believed Paine was not suited to the discipline of book writing were correct. More hopes, though, were put in Macaulay. The idea that she should be the person to write the history of the conflict had gained ground over the course of her tour. Her plan, she elaborated to friends, was to start in the year 1744 and then trace all the ideological developments that ran through the quarrels of the 1760s to the conflicts of the 1770s. A subscription was underway, Mercy Otis Warren told Adams, and "it fills very fast."

With this in mind Macaulay and her husband had boarded a vessel in New York in July 1785 for their return to Britain. Excited by what she had seen in America, Macaulay was nonetheless wearied by her travels. Her health had been wretched for fifteen years, and in fact she had only six more to live. Perhaps deep down, as her ship cut loose from its moorings and drifted out into New York's spectacular harbor, she knew that she would never set foot in the United States again. Her book would never be written.

AS MACAULAY WAS BEGINNING her Atlantic crossing, on July 24, 1785, Benjamin Franklin was disembarking at Southampton. Sixty-one years after he had first arrived in London as a footloose boy of eighteen, he was getting one last, unexpected look at Great Britain.

A year and a half had passed since the British ministry and United States Congress had finally ratified the peace agreement that had been brokered in Paris. This was where Franklin had lived and worked for much of the past decade. His task, throughout the long, bitter years of war, consisted, as the writer Stacy Schiff described it, of "appealing to a monarchy for assistance in establishing a republic."[12] Subtly, teasingly, artfully, he had achieved his aim. The French had provided what the colonies did not have. In monetary terms their contribution to the American war effort ran to about 1.3 billion livres, about $13 billion today. "France was crucial to American independence," Schiff explained, "and Franklin was crucial to France."[13]

Though his presence still struck those who met him as powerful, at nearly eighty Franklin's body was nonetheless failing him. He continued to suffer attacks of gout, and, worse, since the summer of 1783 it was clear that a stone was growing in his bladder. "I feel the infirmities of age coming on so fast," he said toward the end of his time in France, "and the building to need so many repairs that in a little time the builder will find it cheaper to pull it down and build a new one."[14] As he set out on the long trip home to Philadelphia from Passy, on the edge of Paris, he was carried on King Louis XVI's royal litter, drawn by mules, all the way to Le Havre on the Channel coast. From there he crossed to Southampton, where he waited for a ship to take him westward.

Over the days that followed, a number of people came to see him.

One notable meeting was with his estranged son William, whose days as the royal governor of New Jersey were now long gone, and who was living in London. The father and son had not met since 1776. Another to make the journey to Southampton was Jonathan Shipley, affectionately known to Franklin as the "good Bishop" of St. Asaph, with whom he had been staying in the summer of 1771 when he began his *Autobiography*. Shipley had remained a constant correspondent during the years of war, and had stayed a staunch friend to America throughout. Franklin valued this. From Paris he had watched Westminster carefully, seeing the mood of the Parliament change during the course of the war, from a confident haughtiness, to vengefulness, to a state of bemusement, then alarm, and, finally, to resignation.

Another of the friends to America in Westminster in these years was John Wilkes. Having cautioned North not to embroil himself in a violent confrontation, Wilkes's efforts to salvage the colonial relationship continued longer than almost anyone's. After hearing of Lieutenant General John Burgoyne's surrender at Saratoga in 1777, Wilkes proposed the repeal of the 1766 Declaratory Act—the legislation that asserted Parliament's supremacy in the colonies—but without success. Within a year of this he was urging the ministry to accept the inevitable, by recognizing American independence. "A series of four years disgraces and defeats," he told the House, "are surely sufficient to convince us of the absolute impossibility of conquering America by force."[15] Reading reports of this, Franklin must have been left feeling off-balance. Here was the infamous "outlaw and exile" who was "not worth a farthing," displaying more sense than the rest of Westminster put together.

In an age of change and confusion, at first glance there was something familiar about the British general election of 1784. Running his eyes down the list of constituencies, Franklin would have seen Wilkes's name next to the seat of Middlesex. But appearances were deceiving. It was not at all like 1768. The word from Westminster was that Wilkes now supported the impressive new prime minister, William Pitt the Younger, and that his rebellious days were at an end. This might have been so, but as Wilkes took his seat in the safety of the political pack, he could dwell on the changes that his career had brought. In 1782 he had managed to finally overturn the disqualification of his 1769 election, enshrining in English law the principle that voters could pick any candidate they chose. More law had been created by the dramatic events connected to the *North Briton*, after which no secretary of state could issue general warrants at a whim. Wilkes could take pride in this division of political and judicial power, and in a few years' time he would be able to see the influence of 1763 when the Fourth Amendment of the United States' Constitution affirmed the "right of the people to be secured in their persons, houses, papers, and effects, against unreasonable searches and seizures."[16]

Sitting down with Jonathan Shipley, Franklin had the chance to hear about Wilkes and Westminster. But of one old friend, William Strahan, he knew there would be nothing more to say. After the collapse of their friendship in 1775, the old connection between Market Street and London fell silent. Only when he had arrived in Paris, in January 1777, did a note reach Franklin from Strahan. "This is a Letter of Friendship, not of Politicks," he explained, vowing to "not say a Word on the Subject; but only to express my Wish and Hope that Peace, Unity and Happiness may be quickly restored."[17] Franklin decided that these terms were fair enough. Somewhat stiffly, somewhat coldly, occasionally prickly, their correspondence rose into life again. During Franklin's years at Passy, letters would turn up—maybe three or four times a year—from Little New Street. With politics excluded as a topic, Franklin was left to admire the ever-improving state of Strahan's fortunes. After all, 1776 may have been a disastrous year for him politically, but professionally it had been his *annus mirabilis*. In that year Strahan had printed and published two books that would define the age: Edward Gibbon's *The Decline and Fall of the Roman Empire* and Adam Smith's *The Wealth of Nations*.

Adam Smith's production, in particular, seemed appropriate for Strahan. It was a clever, rational, insightful evaluation of the developing mercantile world. This was the world that had brought Strahan and Franklin together in the first place. It was a place of promise and progress, excitement and dynamism. But whereas they had once thought, plotted, and worked as one, it was clear to Franklin in hindsight that they had deliberately chosen different paths. As Franklin had put it to Strahan, in a letter written just a year earlier, on August 19, 1784:

> we have risen by different Modes. I, as a Republican Printer, always lik'd a Form well *plaind down*; being averse to those *overbearing* Letters that hold their Heads so *high* as to hinder their Neighbours from *appearing*. You, as a Monarchist, chose to work upon *Crown* Paper, and found it profitable; while I work'd upon *Pro-patria* (often indeed call'd *Fools-Cap*) with no less advantage. Both our *Heaps hold out* very well, and we seem likely to make a pretty good day's Work of it.[18]

Franklin was being kinder about Strahan's politics here than many others would have been. From the time Strahan entered Parliament in 1774, he consistently voted with North's ministry. Those who saw him in the Commons remembered that he generally sat two or three rows up, directly behind the treasury bench. More of a watcher than a speaker, Strahan displayed none of the dexterity of mind that he demonstrated in his letters while in the chamber. His one recorded speech in the House came in April 1781, during a debate about a proposed tax on almanacs. Apart from this, he was only ever heard to speak with the braying multitudes, crying "Aye" or "No" at the allotted moments, and always at the beck and call of his masters.

In 1780 Strahan swapped his seat at Malmesbury in Wiltshire

(which he had represented along with a young Charles James Fox) for neighboring Wootton Bassett. During this time he saw the American war implode, the fall of Lord North, and the revitalizing appearance of Pitt the Younger. When Strahan stood down in 1784, Britain was attempting to put the disasters of the last decades behind it, and the air was full of talk of reform. By that time, with the conflict over, Franklin was bold enough to touch on politics again. He did so playfully, though, shrouding his criticism in a form of language that Strahan would have appreciated:

> Those Places, to speak in our own old Stile (*Brother Type*), may be *for the good of the* CHAPEL, but they are bad for the *Master*, as they create constant Quarrels that hinder the Business. For example, here are near two Months that your Government has been employ'd in *getting its Form to Press*, which is not yet fit to *work on*, every Page of it being *squabbled*, and the whole ready *to fall into Pye*. The Founts too must be very scanty, or strangely *out of Sorts*, since your *Compositors* cannot find either *Upper-* or *Lower-Case* Letters sufficient to set the Word ADMINISTRATION, but are forc'd to be continually *Turning for them*.[19]

This was a passage to raise a smile in Little New Street. Franklin knew that Strahan, like him, was a printer at his core. Indeed it was printing and not politics that would be Strahan's legacy. His third son, Andrew, would continue to build the business, which after his death passed into the family of his sister Margaret. In 1779 Margaret Strahan had married a man called John Spottiswoode, and it was under his name that Strahan's New Street establishment would endure throughout the Victorian and Edwardian Ages, as one of Britain's greatest printing houses. What it became by the beginning of the twentieth century, Franklin would have loved to see. By then the New Street complex would be filled with 950 workers; the buildings would be protected from fire by alarms and sprinkler systems; while all the machinery would be powered by diesel oil, steam, and, best of all, electricity.

But Franklin would have no chance of speculating on the future with Strahan. On July 9, 1785, a fortnight before Franklin reached the south coast of England, Strahan died in London. He left to his family a fortune of £100,000, all the buildings in New Street, his half shares in the King's and Law Patents, and his interests in the *London Chronicle* and *Public Advertiser*. It was commonly agreed that Strahan had built "the greatest printing house in London."[20] This verdict had been issued a few years earlier by Samuel Johnson, who was well placed to judge. Johnson's relationship with Strahan was of almost equally long standing as Franklin's, and like the Philadelphian, Johnson had had his disagreements with the printer over time. Tellingly, after a sharp quarrel in 1778, it had been Johnson who had sought to mend the breach. "It would be very foolish," he reflected, "for us to continue strangers any longer."[21]

Their friendship restored, Strahan stayed with Johnson to the end. In his final days, in December 1784, Johnson had frequently appealed to Strahan for assistance, and it was the printer's second son, the Rev. George Strahan, who comforted him at his last. Also there as Johnson took his final breaths was Francis Barber. The man who had once been a slave boy in Jamaica had now been with Johnson for more than three decades. The fate of the Barbers had been much on Johnson's mind in his last weeks. Most of what he owned, he had decided—his belongings, books, and papers—would be left to the boy who had come to him with nothing. For his part Barber signaled his affection for his master in his own way. The year before Johnson's death, Barber and his wife welcomed a baby into their family. They named him Samuel.

With these deaths there was, even at the time, the sense that a period in history was closing. On July 28, 1785, Franklin boarded a vessel called, appropriately enough, the *London Packet*. He would soon be back in Philadelphia, his travels finally at an end. "I am now," Franklin wrote to his friend John Jay, "in the Bosom of my Family, and find four new little Prattlers, who cling about the Knees of their Grand Papa, and afford me great Pleasure." He was, Franklin confirmed, "very happy."[22]

Notes

ABBREVIATIONS

BFP: Leonard W. Labaree et al. (eds.), *Papers of Benjamin Franklin*, 43 vols to date (New Haven, CT: Yale University Press, 1959–).

PROLOGUE: THE FOURTH OF JULY
1. Paul H. Smith, "Time and temperature: Philadelphia, July 4, 1776," *The Quarterly Journal of the Library of Congress*, Vol. 33, No. 4 (Washington: Library of Congress, 1976), p. 296.
2. Thomas Jefferson Randolph (ed.), *Memoirs, Correspondence, and Private Papers of Thomas Jefferson, Late President of the United States*, Vol. 4 (London: Henry Colburn and Richard Bentley, 1829), pp. 451–52.
3. David McCullough, *John Adams* (New York: Simon & Schuster, 2001), p. 126.
4. Edmund Burke, *Speech . . . on moving his resolutions for conciliation with the colonies, March 22, 1775*, 2nd ed. (London: J. Dodsley, 1775), p. 31.
5. Jefferson's "original Rough draught" of the Declaration of Independence, Library of Congress: loc.gov/exhibits/declara/ruffdrft.html (accessed August 2022).
6. Carl Becker, *The Declaration of Independence: A Study in the History of Political Ideas* (New York: Peter Smith, 1933), p. 5.
7. Timothy Pickering, *A Review of the Correspondence between the Hon. John Adams, Late President of the United States, and the late Wm. Cunningham, Esq* (Salem: Cushing and Appleton, 1824), p. 187.
8. The finished text listed twenty-seven.
9. Smith, "Time and temperature," p. 296.
10. Nicole Hodges Persley, *Sampling and Remixing Blackness in Hip-Hop Theater and Performance* (Ann Arbor: The University of Michigan Press, 2021), p. 233.
11. "The Virginia Declaration of Rights," National Archives: archives.gov /founding-docs/virginia-declaration-of-rights (accessed August 2022).

12. Johnson used the phrase "pursuit of happiness" on at least five occasions before 1776. It appears in the *Rambler*, No. 29; the *Dictionary of the English Language* (under "*preferable*"); in the thirty-eighth chapter of *Rasselas*; the *Idler*, No. 62; and his political pamphlet *The False Alarm* (1770).

13. Catharine Macaulay, *A Short Sketch, &c. Addressed to Signior Paoli* (London: T. Davies, 1767), p. 2.

14. John Locke, *Two Treatises of Government*, new ed. (London: Whitmore and Fenn, 1821), p. 259.

15. William B. Willcox (ed.), *The Papers of Benjamin Franklin*, Vol. 22 (New Haven, CT: Yale University Press, 1982), p. 88.

16. Charles Henry Hart (ed.), *Letters from William Franklin to William Strahan* (Philadelphia: privately published, 1911), p. 13.

17. Bernard Bailyn, *The Ideological Origins of the American Revolution*, 50th anniversary ed. (Cambridge, MA: The Belknap Press of Harvard University Press, 2017), p. 95.

18. Darrin M. McMahon, *Happiness: A History* (New York: Atlantic Monthly Press, 2006), p. xiv.

1. A NEW MAN

1. Benjamin Franklin, *The Autobiography and Other Writings with an Introduction by Jill Lepore* (New York: Knopf, 2015), p. 27.

2. *The Pennsylvania Gazette*, December 11, 1740.

3. Ibid.

4. All of these from Paul Leicester Ford (ed.), *"The Sayings of Poor Richard": The Prefaces, Proverbs, and Poems of Benjamin Franklin* (New York: The Knickerbocker Press, 1890), p. 29; p. 54; p. 53.

5. Bailyn, *Ideological Origins*, p. 191.

6. Sally Schwartz, "William Penn and toleration: Foundations of colonial Pennsylvania," *Pennsylvania History*, Vol. 50, No. 4 (University Park: Penn State University Press, 1983), p. 294.

7. John W. Reps, "William Penn and the planning of Philadelphia," *The Town Planning Review*, Vol. 27, No. 1 (Liverpool: Liverpool University Press, 1956), p. 29.

8. Gary B. Nash, "Slaves and slaveowners in colonial Philadelphia," *The William and Mary Quarterly*, Vol. 30, No. 2 (Williamsburg, VA: Omohundro Institute, 1973), p. 227.

9. Ford (ed.), *"The Sayings of Poor Richard,"* p. 23.

10. Ibid., p. 24.

11. Ibid., p. 25.

12. Ibid., p. 35.

13. Franklin, *Autobiography*, p. 106.

14. Ford (ed.), *"The Sayings of Poor Richard,"* p. 27; p. 52; p. 54; p. 39; p. 54.

15. Franklin, *Autobiography*, p. vii.

16. *The Works of Dr. Benjn. Franklin; consisting of essays, humorous, moral and literary; with his life, written by himself* (London: J. Limbird, 1823), p. 6.

17. Examination before the Committee of the Whole of the House of Commons, February 13, 1766, *BFP*, Vol. 13, p. 135.

18. *The Gentleman's Magazine: or, Monthly Intelligencer,* Vol. 1 (London: F. Jefferies, 1731), n.p.

19. Benjamin Franklin to William Strahan, November 27, 1755, *BFP*, Vol. 6, p. 278.

20. Franklin, *Autobiography*, p. 112.

21. *The American Magazine or a monthly view of the political state of the British colonies, reproduced from the original edition Philadelphia, 1741, with a bibliographical note by Lyon N. Richardson* (New York: The Facsimile Society, 1937), n.p.

22. Ford (ed.), "*The Sayings of Poor Richard,*" p. 53.

23. *The Pennsylvania Gazette*, November 13, 1740.

24. John Webbe: The Detection, November 17, 1740, *BFP*, Vol. 2, p. 266.

25. Ibid., p. 266.

26. Ibid., p. 269.

27. Ford (ed.), "*The Sayings of Poor Richard,*" p. 114.

28. Franklin, *Autobiography*, p. 30.

29. Ibid., p. 67.

30. For a broader look at the interesting life of Andrew Bradford, see: J. Willard, William Tailer, John Clark, and Anna Janney de Armond, "Andrew Bradford," *The Pennsylvania Magazine of History and Biography*, Vol. 62, No. 4 (Philadelphia: University of Pennsylvania Press, 1938), pp. 463–87.

31. John Webbe: The Detection, November 17, 1740, *BFP*, Vol. 2, p. 267.

32. Franklin, *Autobiography*, p.64.

33. John Webbe: The Detection, November 17, 1740, *BFP*, Vol. 2, p. 267.

34. Gordon S. Wood, *The Radicalism of the American Revolution* (New York, Vintage Books, 1993), p. 27.

35. Gordon S. Wood, *The Americanization of Benjamin Franklin* (New York: Penguin Books, 2005), p. 19.

36. *The Champion: Containing a series of papers, humorous, moral, political and critical*, Vol. 1 (London: J. Huggonson, 1741), p. 9.

37. Carl Van Doren, *Benjamin Franklin* (New York: The Viking Press, 1938), p. 91.

38. *The Pennsylvania Gazette*, December 11, 1740.

2. THE RACE

1. John F. Watson, *Annals of Philadelphia, being a collection of memoirs, anecdotes, & incidents of the city and its inhabitants from the days of the Pilgrim Fathers* (Philadelphia: E. L. Carey and A. Hart, 1830), p. 62.

2. *The Pennsylvania Gazette*, January 8, 1741.

3. Watson, *Annals*, p. 119.

4. I have been able to reconstruct the cold winter of 1740–41 in Philadelphia with accuracy thanks to a weather diary that was kept by someone in the city. This descriptive journal of snow, ice, drizzling rain, clouds, and the aurora borealis (which was seen over the city on March 26, 1741) was printed in the final issue of the *American Magazine*, and it can be found in *The American Magazine . . . with a bibliographical note by Lyon N. Richardson*, pp. 115–20.

5. *The Tatler and The Guardian Complete in One Volume* (London: A. Wilson, 1814), p. 171.

6. *The Lubrications of Isaac Bickerstaff Esq*, Vol. 3 (London: Charles Lillie, 1711), p. 259.

7. For more on the context of this, see: Brian William Cowan, "Mr. Spectator and the coffeehouse public sphere," *Eighteenth-Century Studies*, Vol. 37, No. 3 (Baltimore: Johns Hopkins University Press, 2004), p. 353.

8. Henry Fielding, *An Enquiry into the Causes of the Late Increase of Robbers, &c.* (London: A. Millar, 1751), p. xiii.

9. Sir Stephen John Sedley, "New corn from old fields: Ministerial government, history and the law," The Denning Lecture 2012: lincolnsinn.org.uk/wp-content/uploads/2018/11/THE-DENNING-LECTURE-Sedley-2012.doc (accessed August 2022).

10. Franklin, *Autobiography*, p. 53.

11. Philip Dray, *Stealing God's Thunder: Benjamin Franklin's Lightning Rod and the Invention of America* (New York: Random House, 2005), p. 7.

12. Franklin, *Autobiography*, p. 89.

13. The pamphlet in question is called *A Dissertation on Liberty and Necessity, Pleasure and Pain*. For an analysis of Franklin's beliefs at this time, see: Nick Bunker, *Young Benjamin Franklin: The Birth of Ingenuity* (New York: Alfred A. Knopf, 2018), pp. 174–78.

14. Voltaire, *Letters Concerning the English Nation* (London: C. Davis, 1741), p. 41.

15. Jared Sparks (ed.), *The Works of Benjamin Franklin*, Vol. 1 (Philadelphia: Childs and Peterson, 1840), p. 568.

16. Bunker, *Young Franklin*, pp. 258–59.

17. A Proposal for Promoting Useful Knowledge, May 14, 1743, *BFP*, Vol. 2, p. 380. Franklin expressed this view repeatedly throughout the 1740s.

18. *The Pennsylvania Gazette*, December 4, 1740.

19. James L. Clifford, *Young Samuel Johnson* (London: Heinemann, 1957), p. 186.

20. *The Pennsylvania Gazette*, December 4, 1740.

21. Ibid., February 19, 1741.

22. Ibid., January 8, 1741.

23. Ibid., January 29, 1741.

24. Ibid., February 5, 1741.

25. Ibid., February 12, 1741.

26. Advertisement in *The General Magazine*, February 16, 1741, *BFP*, Vol. 2, p. 301.

27. *The General Magazine and historical chronicle for all the British plantations in*

America, reproduced from the original edition Philadelphia, 1741, with a bibliographical note by Lyon N. Richardson (New York: The Facsimile Society, 1937), p. 72.

28. *The Pennsylvania Gazette*, February 26, 1741.

29. Ibid.

30. Ibid., April 9, 1741.

31. Watson, *Annals*, p. 600.

32. For a broader look at the design of Franklin's "fireplace," see: An Account of the New Invented Pennsylvanian Fire-Places, 1744, *BFP*, Vol. 2, p. 419.

33. For more about James Read, see: J. Bennett Nolan, *Printer Strahan's Book Account: A Colonial Controversy* (Reading, PA: The Bar of Berks County, 1939).

34. James Aikman Cochrane, *Dr. Johnson's Printer: The Life of William Strahan* (Cambridge, MA: Harvard University Press, 1964), p. 60.

35. Benjamin Franklin to William Strahan, July 10, 1743, *BFP*, Vol. 2, pp. 383–84.

3. NORTH STAR

1. *Derby Mercury*, June 15, 1744.

2. Sylvanus Urban, *The Gentleman's Magazine and Historical Chronicle for the year 1744*, Vol. 14 (London: F. Jefferies, 1744), p. 336.

3. *Caledonian Mercury*, July 10, 1744.

4. *Newcastle Courant*, July 7–14, 1744.

5. Voltaire, *Letters*, pp. 58–59.

6. *The history of the minority; during the years 1762, 1763, 1764 and 1765. Exhibiting the conduct, principles, and views, of that party* (London: privately printed, 1765), p. 10.

7. William Strahan, "Correspondence between William Strahan and David Hall, 1763–1777 (concluded)," *The Pennsylvania Magazine of History and Biography*, Vol. 12, No. 2 (Philadelphia: University of Pennsylvania Press, 1888), pp. 248–49.

8. Gabriel Thomas, *An historical and geographical account of the province and country of Pennsilvania; and of West New-Jersey in America* (London: A. Baldwin, 1698), p. 7.

9. Benjamin Franklin to William Strahan, July 10, 1743, *BFP*, Vol. 2, p. 384.

10. For a deeper investigation into the beginning of Strahan's relationship with Franklin, see: Nick Wrightson, "'[Those with] great abilities have not always the best information': How Franklin's transatlantic book-trade and scientific networks interacted," *Early American Studies*, Vol. 8, No. 1 (Philadelphia: University of Pennsylvania Press, 2010), p. 109.

11. Cochrane, *Dr. Johnson's Printer*, p. 65.

12. Nolan, *Printer Strahan's Book Account*, p. 20.

13. Cochrane, *Dr. Johnson's Printer*, p. 65.

14. Ibid., p. 64.

15. Ibid., p. 66 .

16. Ibid., p. 67.

17. Ibid., p. 65.

18. Ibid., p. 66.
19. Ibid., p. 67.
20. K. I. D. Maslen, "William Strahan at the Bowyer Press 1736–8," *The Library*, Vol. 15, No. 3 (Oxford: Oxford Academic, 1970), pp. 250–51.
21. *A modest proposal for preventing the children of poor people from being a burthen to their parents or the country, &c* (London: Weaver, Bickerton, 1730), p. 10.
22. Benjamin Franklin to William Strahan, July 31, 1744, *BFP*, Vol. 2, p. 412.
23. James Logan (trans.), *M. T. Cicero's Cato Major, or his Discourse of Old Age* (Philadelphia: B. Franklin, 1744), p. vi.
24. Benjamin Franklin to William Strahan, July 4, 1744, *BFP*, Vol. 2, pp. 410–11.
25. Nolan, *Printer Strahan's Book Account*.
26. Benjamin Franklin to William Strahan, January 4, 1747, *BFP*, Vol. 3, p. 108.
27. Benjamin Franklin to William Strahan, July 4, 1744, *BFP*, Vol. 2, p. 411.
28. Ibid.
29. Ibid.
30. Ibid., p. 418.
31. Benjamin Franklin to William Strahan, February 12, 1745, *BFP*, Vol. 3, p. 14.
32. Ibid., p. 13.
33. *The Critical Review: Or, annals of literature*, Vol. 45 (London: A. Hamilton, 1778), p. 186.
34. Edw[ard] Chamberlayne, *Angliae notitia: Or the present state of England* (London: T. H., 1704), p. 347.
35. James Boswell, *London Journal* (Mineola, NY: Dover Publications, 2018), p. 5.
36. Jerry White, *London in the Eighteenth Century: A Great and Monstrous Thing* (London: The Bodley Head, 2012), p. 94.
37. *The Scots Magazine*, July 1745.
38. *Derby Mercury*, August 16, 1745.
39. Ibid., August 30, 1745.
40. Ibid., November 8, 1745.
41. *The Scots Magazine*, October 4, 1745.
42. White, *London*, p. 95.
43. *Supplement to the Pennsylvania Gazette*, July 5, 1746.
44. Benjamin Franklin to William Strahan, April 26, 1746, *BFP*, Vol. 3, p. 75.

4. SPARKS

1. Nolan, *Printer Strahan*, p. 20.
2. William Strahan, "Correspondence between William Strahan and David Hall, 1763–1777 (concluded)," *The Pennsylvania Magazine of History and Biography*, Vol. 12, No. 2 (Philadelphia: University of Pennsylvania Press, 1888), p. 248.
3. See: John Fisher (ed.), *Industry and Idleness: Exemplified in the conduct of two fellow apprentices in twelve moral and instructive prints by William Hogarth* (London: Guildhall Library, 1978).
4. *The Effects of Industry and Idleness Illustrated* (London: C. Corbett, 1748), p. 3.

5. Franklin, *Autobiography*, p. 141.
6. Cochrane, *Dr. Johnson's Printer*, p .7.
7. Silence Dogood No. 4, May 14, 1722, *BFP*, Vol. 1, p. 17.
8. Franklin, *Autobiography*, p. 64.
9. Ernest Barker, *Oliver Cromwell and the English People* (Cambridge: Cambridge University Press, 1937), p. 104.
10. See: Wrightson, "[Those with] great abilities have not always the best information," pp. 101–107.
11. Plain Truth, 1747, *BFP*, Vol. 3, p. 199.
12. Ford (ed.), "*The Sayings of Poor Richard*," p. 164.
13. Voltaire, *Letters*, p. 95.
14. "An extract of a letter from James Logan, Esq; to Sir Hans Sloane, Bart R. S. Pr. concerning the crooked and angular appearance of the streaks, or darts of light'ning in thunder-storms," *Philosophical Transactions*, Vol. 39, No. 440 (London: T. Woodward and C. Davis, 1738), p. 240.
15. Dray, *God's Thunder*, p. xlv.
16. *The Gentleman's Magazine*, April 1745.
17. "A Letter to Cromwell Mortimer, M. D. Secr. R.S. containing several experiments concerning electricity; by Mr. Stephen Gray," *Philosophical Transactions*, Vol. 37, No. 417 (London: W. Innys and R. Manby, 1733), p. 40.
18. *The Gentleman's Magazine*, April 1745.
19. Ibid.
20. Benjamin Franklin to Peter Collinson, March 28, 1747, *BFP*, Vol. 3, pp. 118–19.
21. Dray, *God's Thunder*, p. 45.
22. "An extract of a letter from Mr. John Henry Winkler, Græc. & Lat. Litt Prof. publ. Ordin. at Leipsick, to a friend in London; concerning the effects of electricity upon himself and his wife," *Philosophical Transactions*, Vol. 44, No. 480 (London: C. Davis, 1748), pp. 211–12.
23. "Part of a letter from Mr. John Browning, of Bristol, to Mr. Henry Baker, F.R.S. dated Dec. 11. 1746. Concerning the effect of electricity on vegetables," *Philosophical Transactions*, Vol. 44, No. 482 (London: C. Davis, 1748), p. 375.
24. *The Gentleman's Magazine*, January 1750.
25. Benjamin Franklin to Peter Collinson, April 29, 1749, *BFP*, Vol. 3, pp. 364–65.
26. Benjamin Franklin to William Strahan, October 23, 1749, *BFP*, Vol. 3, p. 394.
27. Franklin, *Autobiography*, p. 121.
28. A Proposal for Promoting Useful Knowledge, May 14, 1743, *BFP*, Vol. 2, p. 380.
29. *Pennsylvania Gazette*, August 24, 1749. The letter referred to is Pliny IV.13.
30. Proposals Relating to the Education of Youth in Pensilvania, 1749, *BFP*, Vol. 3, p. 402.
31. Ibid.
32. Ibid., p. 404.

33. Ibid., p. 417.
34. George W. Boudreau, "'Done by a tradesman': Franklin's educational proposals and the culture of Eighteenth-Century Pennsylvania," *Pennsylvania History*, Vol. 69, No. 4 (University Park: Penn State University Press, 2002), p. 529.
35. I. P. Fleming (ed.), *Dr Johnson's Satires: London and The Vanity of Human Wishes with Notes, Historical & Biographical, & a Glossary* (London: Longmans, Green, and Co., 1888), p. 39.
36. Ibid., p. 42.

5. THE *RAMBLER*

1. *The Gentleman's Magazine*, May 1750.
2. *The Rambler*, Vol. 1 (London: J. Payne, 1752), p. 209.
3. Ibid., pp. 209–10.
4. Ibid., pp. 210–11.
5. Clifford, *Young Johnson*, p. 135 .
6. Madame D'Arblay, *Memoirs of Dr Burney* (Philadelphia: Key and Biddle, 1833), p. 103.
7. Michael Bundock, *The Fortunes of Francis Barber: The True Story of the Jamaican Slave Who Became Samuel Johnson's Heir* (New Haven, CT: Yale University Press, 2015), p. 4.
8. Victor Hugo, *Les Misérables* (New York: Carleton, 1862), p. 74.
9. Richard Holmes, *Dr Johnson and Mr Savage* (London: Harper Perennial, 2005), p. 27.
10. Henry Hitchings, *Dr Johnson's Dictionary: The Extraordinary Story of the Book That Defined the World* (London: John Murray, 2005), p. 56.
11. Hesther Lynch Piozzi, *Anecdotes of the Late Samuel Johnson, LL.D.* (London: T. Cadell, 1786), p. 237.
12. Samuel Johnson, *A Dictionary of the English Language in which The Words are Deduced from their Originals* (London: W. Strahan, 1755), n.p.
13. Voltaire, *Letters*, p. 91.
14. Samuel Johnson, *The Idler with Additional Essays* (London: C. Cooke, 1799), pp. 242–43.
15. Bailyn, *Ideological Origins*, pp. 86–87.
16. Clifford, *Young Johnson*, p. 101.
17. *The Rambler*, Vol. 1, p. 164.
18. *The Plan of a Dictionary of the English Language; Addressed to the Right Honourable Philip Dormer, Earl of Chesterfield* (London, J. and P. Knapton, T. Longman and T. Sherwell, C. Hitch, A. Millar, and R. Dodsley, 1747), p. 10.
19. James Boswell, *The Life of Samuel Johnson* (London: Penguin, 2008), p. 29.
20. Katharine C. Balderston, "Doctor Johnson and William Law," in *Publications of the Modern Language Association (PMLA)*, Vol. 75, No. 4 (Cambridge: Cambridge University Press, 1960), p. 382.

21. William Law, *A Serious Call to a Devout and Holy Life* (London: William Innys, 1729), pp. 1–2.
22. Benjamin Franklin, *Autobiography*, p. 90.
23. James Boswell, *The Life of Samuel Johnson, LL.D.* (Philadelphia: Claxton, Remsen & Haffelfinger, 1868), p. 156.
24. Bundock, *Fortunes*, p. 39.
25. James L. Clifford, *Dictionary Johnson: The Middle Years of Samuel Johnson* (London: Heinemann, 1979), p. 41.
26. *The Life of Samuel Johnson with Maxims and Observations* (Boston: Marsh, Capen and Lyon, 1833), p. 243.
27. John Gay, *The Present State of Wit, in a Letter to a Friend in the Country* (London: privately printed, 1711), pp. 206–207.
28. Bate, *Samuel Johnson*, p. 352.
29. *The Rambler*, Vol. 1, p. 10.
30. Ibid., p. 12.
31. Ibid.
32. Ibid., p. 10.
33. Ibid., p. 15.
34. Ibid., p. 68.
35. *The Rambler*, Vol. 8, p. 173.
36. Ibid., p. 89.
37. Ibid., p. 181.
38. Walter Jackson Bate, *Samuel Johnson* (London: Chatto & Windus, 1978), p. 109.
39. *The Rambler*, Vol. 1, p. 62.
40. Ibid., p. 145.
41. Leo Damrosch, *The Club: Johnson, Boswell, and the Friends who Shaped an Age* (New Haven: Yale University Press, 2019), p. 39.
42. *The Rambler*, Vol. 1, p. 181.
43. Clifford, *Dictionary Johnson*, p. 78.
44. W. J. Bate and Albrecht B. Strauss (eds.), *Samuel Johnson: The Rambler* (New Haven, CT: Yale University Press, 1969), p. xxvi.
45. Charles Francis Adams (ed.), *The Works of John Adams*, Vol. 4 (Boston: Charles C. Little and James Brown, 1851), p. 31.
46. Fielding, *Enquiry*, pp. xxxi–xxxii.
47. Clifford, *Dictionary Johnson*, p. 79.
48. Ibid., p. 80.
49. Anna Laetitia Barbauld (ed.), *The Correspondence of Samuel Richardson*, Vol. 1 (London: Richard Phillips, 1804), p. 247.
50. *The Gentleman's Magazine*, February 1749.
51. Clifford, *Dictionary Johnson*, p. 55.
52. R. W. Chapman (ed.), *The Letters of Samuel Johnson*, Vol. 1 (Oxford: Clarendon Press, 1952), pp. 38–39.

53. Cochrane, *Dr. Johnson's Printer*, p. 102.
54. William Strahan: Letters to David Hall, BL. RP 1279.
55. I. Bernard Cohen, *Benjamin Franklin's Science* (Cambridge, MA: Harvard University Press), p. 70.
56. *The Rambler*, Vol. 4, p. 164.
57. *The Rambler*, Vol. 8, p. 174.
58. *The Rambler*, Vol. 1, p. 120.
59. Boswell, *Life of Johnson* (2008), p. 66.
60. Holmes, *Dr Johnson*, p. 25.
61. Damrosch, *The Club*, p. 30.
62. Clifford, *Dictionary Johnson*, p. 298.

6. ESCAPE

1. Clifford, *Dictionary Johnson*, p. 102.
2. George Birkbeck Hill (ed.), *Boswell's Life of Johnson*, Vol. 1 (New York: Harper and Brothers, 1889), p. 322.
3. Piozzi, *Anecdotes*, p. 83.
4. Bundock, *Fortunes*, p. 26.
5. Ibid.
6. For more on the knotty legal context surrounding baptism and freedom, Ibid., p. 34.
7. Hill (ed.), *Life*, p. 4.
8. Ibid., p. 290.
9. Ibid.
10. Ibid., p. 282.
11. Ibid.
12. Ibid.
13. Bundock, *Fortunes*, p. 47.
14. Hitchings, *Dr Johnson's Dictionary*, p. 58.
15. Johnson, *Dictionary of the English Language*, n.p.
16. Bate, *Johnson*, p. 240.
17. Allen Reddick, *The Making of Johnson's Dictionary 1746–1773* (Cambridge: Cambridge University Press, 1996), p. 67.
18. James Walvin, *The Trader, The Owner, The Slave: Parallel Lives in the Age of Slavery* (London: Vintage Books, 2008), p. 126.
19. Walvin, *The Trader*, p. 107.
20. Ibid., p. 113.
21. Olaudah Equiano, *The interesting narrative of the life of Olaudah Equiano or Gustavus Vassa, the African. Written by himself* (London: privately published, 1794), p. 40.
22. Trevor Burnard and Kenneth Morgan, "The dynamics of the slave market and slave purchasing patterns in Jamaica, 1655–1788," *The William and Mary Quarterly*, Vol. 58, No. 1 (Williamsburg: Omohundro Institute of Early American History and Culture, 2001), p. 212.

23. For many years Barber remained as an enticing but marginal character in the broader story of Johnson's life. In 2015, this lacuna was filled by Michael Bundock's *The Fortunes of Francis Barber*, which shed much new light.

24. Bundock, *Fortunes*, p. 11.

25. Equiano, *Narrative*, p. 62.

26. Ibid., p. 67.

27. Ibid., pp. 71–72.

28. Bundock, *Fortunes*, p. 54

29. For more on this, see: Gordon Turnbull, "Samuel Johnson, Francis Barber, and 'Mr Desmoulins' Writing School,'" *Notes and Queries*, Vol. 61, No. 4 (Oxford: Oxford University Press, 2014), pp. 483–86.

30. I. P. Fleming (ed.), *Satires*, p. 32.

31. Walvin, *The Trader*, p. 20.

32. John Immerwahr, "Hume's revised racism," *Journal of the History of Ideas*, Vol. 53, No. 2 (Philadelphia: University of Pennsylvania Press, 1992), p. 481.

33. *Doubts on the abolition of the slave trade; by an old Member of Parliament* (London: John Stockdale, 1790), pp. 21–22.

34. Valentine Low, "George III called slavery 'repugnant,'" *The Times*, December 23, 2021: thetimes.co.uk/article/george-iii-called-slavery-repugnant -pmmdd0tq3 (accessed September 2022).

35. Bundock, *Fortunes*, p. 26.

36. Samuel Johnson, "[Review of] *Geographical . . . essays . . . containing an analysis of a map of the middle British colonies in North America . . . By Lewis Evans*," *Literary Magazine*, vol. 1 (London: 1756), p. 468.

37. *The Idler*, p. 224.

38. Ibid., p. 240.

39. O. M. Brack, Jr., and Robert DeMaria, Jr. (eds.), *Johnson on Demand: Reviews, Prefaces, and Ghost-Writings* (New Haven: Yale University Press, 2018), p. 438.

40. Ibid., p. 441.

41. Ibid.

42. Ibid., p. 442.

43. Benjamin Franklin to Peter Collinson, May 9, 1753, *BFP*, Vol. 4, p. 486.

44. Such advertisements were printed in newspapers across the country. This one is taken from *The Manchester Mercury*, April 29, 1755.

45. Clifford, *Dictionary Johnson*, p. 138.

46. Ibid.

47. Bundock, *Fortunes*, p. 64.

48. Ibid., p. 69.

49. Ibid., p. 71.

50. Kevin J. Hays, "New light on Peter and King, the two slaves Benjamin Franklin brought to England," *Notes and Queries*, Vol. 6, No. 2 (Oxford: Oxford University Press, 2013), p. 208.

51. Bailyn, *Ideological Origins*, p. 22.

52. This was supposedly first printed in the *Public Advertiser*; see: Clifford, *Dictionary Johnson*, p. 143, and for the broader context, Herman W. Liebert, *The Bear and the Phoenix: John Wilkes' Letter on Johnson's Dictionary Newly Reprinted in Full* (Lunenburg, VT: Stinehour Press, 1978).
53. Bundock, *Fortunes*, p. 93.

7. SCRIBBLERS AND ETCHERS

1. Benjamin Franklin to William Strahan, January 31, 1757, *BFP*, Vol. 7, p. 116.
2. Benjamin Franklin to Deborah Franklin, March 5, 1760, *BFP*, Vol. 9, p. 33.
3. For more on this singular episode, see: Maurice J. Quinlan, "Dr. Franklin meets Dr. Johnson," *The Pennsylvania Magazine of History and Biography*, Vol. 73, No. 1 (Philadelphia: The Historical Society of Pennsylvania, 1949), pp. 34–44.
4. William Strahan to David Hall, August 10, 1762, *BFP*, Vol. 10, p. 141.
5. Ibid.
6. Benjamin Franklin to Deborah Franklin, March 5, 1760, *BFP*, Vol. 9, p. 32. The original manuscript is torn, leaving some words missing, which are supplied editorially in the Yale edition of Franklin's papers. For simplicity's sake I have omitted the editorial square brackets. The text in the Yale edition reads as follows: "Mrs. Strahan a sensible [and] good Woman, the Children of amiable [char]acters and particularly the young Man, [who is] sober, ingenious and industrious, and a [desirable] Person. In Point of Circumstance [there can] be no Objection, Mr. Strahan being [in so thriving] a Way, as to lay up a Thousand [Pounds] every Year . . ."
7. William Strahan to David Hall, August 10, 1762, *BFP*, Vol. 10, p. 141.
8. Benjamin Franklin to William Strahan, August 23, 1762, *BFP,* Vol. 10, p. 149.
9. *The European Magazine and London Review*, Vol. 75 (London: James Asperne, 1819), p. 226.
10. Alexander Stephens, *Memoirs of John Horne Tooke*, Vol. 1 (London: J. Johnson and Co., 1813), p. 48.
11. *The London Magazine*, November 1761.
12. Andrew Roberts, *George III: The Life and Reign of Britain's Most Misunderstood Monarch* (London: Allen Lane, 2021), p. 32.
13. *The Letters of Horace Walpole, Earl of Orford, to Sir Horace Mann*, Vol. 1 (London: Richard Bentley, 1843), p. 2.
14. George Goodwin, *Benjamin Franklin in London: The British Life of America's Founding Father* (London: Weidenfeld & Nicolson, 2016), p. 139.
15. Franz A. J. Szabo, *The Seven Years War in Europe* (Abingdon: Routledge, 2008), p. 79.
16. Bailyn, *Ideological Origins*, p. 124.
17. Roberts, *George III*, p. 34.
18. Ibid., p. 55.
19. Adrian Hamilton, *The Infamous Essay on Woman or John Wilkes Seated between Vice and Virtue* (London: Andre Deutsch, 1972), p. 32.

20. Kate Hotblack, "The Peace of Paris, 1763. Alexander Prize Essay, 1907," *Transactions of the Royal Historical Society*, Vol. 2 (Cambridge: Cambridge University Press, 1908), p. 253.

21. For more on the circumstances of William Franklin's appointment as the royal governor of New Jersey, see: R. C. Simmons, "Colonial patronage: Two letters from William Franklin to the Earl of Bute, 1762," *The William and Mary Quarterly*, Vol. 59, No. 1 (Williamsburg, VA: The Omohundro Institute of Early American History and Culture, 2002).

22. Jeremy Black, *Eighteenth-Century Britain 1688–1783* (Basingstoke: Palgrave, 2001), p. 250.

23. *The History of the Minority, during the Years 1762, 1763, 1764, and 1765. Exhibiting the Conduct, Principles and Views of that Party* (London: s.n., 1764), p. 78.

24. Arthur Cash, *John Wilkes: The Scandalous Father of Civil Liberty* (New Haven, CT: Yale University Press, 2006), p. 63.

25. Hamilton, *Essay on Woman*, p. 14.

26. *The North Briton from No. 1 to No. 44 Inclusive* (London: W. Bingley, 1769), p. 3; p. 4; p. 9.

27. Hamilton, *Essay on Woman*, p. 52.

28. *The North Briton*, p. 13.

29. Edward H. Weatherly (ed.), *The Correspondence of John Wilkes and Charles Churchill* (New York: Columbia University Press, 1954), p. 8.

30. Joseph Hone, *The Paper Chase: The Printer, the Spymaster, and the Hunt for the Rebel Pamphleteers* (London: Chatto and Windus, 2020), p. 203.

31. *The North Briton*, p. 1.

32. Ibid., p. 35.

33. Ibid.

34. Hamilton, *Essay on Woman*, p. 45.

35. Ibid., pp. 54–55.

36. Richard Thomson (ed.), *A Faithful Account of the Processions and Ceremonies Observed in the Coronation* (London: John Major, 1820), p. 63.

37. *The North Briton*, p. 37.

38. *A Complete Collection of the Genuine Papers, Letters, &c. in the Case of John Wilkes, Esq.* (Berlin: s.n., 1769), p. 3.

39. *The Leedes Intelligencer*, May 6, 1760.

40. *Complete Collection of the Genuine Papers*, p. 7.

41. Ibid., p. 11.

42. Ibid., p. 12.

43. Ibid., p. 14.

44. Ibid., p. 16. In Wilkes's long account of this episode he does not use the words "I wrote the *North Briton*," although they are implied. He stated: "Both our fires were in very exact time, but neither took effect. I walked up immediately to his Lordship, and told him that now I avowed the paper."

45. Weatherly (ed.), *Correspondence*, p. 23.

46. Ibid., p. 19.
47. *The North Briton*, p. 52.
48. Ibid., p. 88.
49. John Almon, *Anecdotes of the Life of the Right Honourable William Pitt, Earl of Chatham*, Vol. 1 (London: J. S. Jordan, 1793), pp. 438–39.
50. State of Facts Relative to Mr. Wilkes, BL. Add MS 22132 (4).

8. NO. 45

1. *The North Briton*, p. 85.
2. Leonard W. Levy, "Origins of the Fourth Amendment," in *Political Science Quarterly*, Vol. 114, No. 1 (New York: The Academy of Political Science, 1999), p. 80.
3. Bailyn, *Ideological Origins*, p. 81.
4. Thomson (ed.), *Faithful Account*, p. 61.
5. *The North Briton*, p. 125.
6. "Correspondence between William Strahan and David Hall, 1763–1777," *The Pennsylvania Magazine of History and Biography*, Vol. 10, No. 1 (Philadelphia: University of Pennsylvania Press, 1886), p. 89.
7. *The North Briton*, p. lxiii.
8. J. Heneage Jesse, *Memoirs of the Life and Reign of King George the Third*, Vol. 1 (London: Tinsley Brothers, 1867), p. 166.
9. *The North Briton*, p. 141.
10. *The North Briton*, p. 143.
11. Cash, *John Wilkes*, p. 93.
12. *The Kentish Post, or Canterbury News-Letter*, April 27, 1763.
13. Horace Bleackley, *Life of John Wilkes* (London: The Bodley Head, 1917), p. 89.
14. Roberts, *George III*, p. 98.
15. *History of the Minority*, p. 92.
16. *The North Briton*, p. 85.
17. Hamilton, *Essay on Woman*, p. 81.
18. Ibid., pp. 79–85.
19. State of Facts Relative to Mr Wilkes, BL. Add MS 22132 (24).
20. Ibid. (31).
21. *History of the Minority*, p. 138.
22. *The North Briton*, p. 157.
23. State of Facts Relative to Mr Wilkes (28–29).
24. Cash, *John Wilkes*, p. 103.
25. State of Facts Relative to Mr Wilkes (49).
26. *The North Briton*, p. xxx.
27. *The Works of Charles Dickens: Pickwick Papers, Barnaby Rudge, Sketches by Boz* (New York: D Appleton and Company, 1874), p. 23.
28. "Wyndham, Charles, second earl of Egremont," in *Oxford Dictionary of National Biography* (oxforddnb.com, accessed September 2022).

29. *The North Briton*, p. xxx.
30. State of Facts Relative to Mr Wilkes (51).
31. Ibid.
32. *The North Briton*, p. xxx.
33. State of Facts Relative to Mr Wilkes (56).
34. Ibid. (47).
35. *The North Briton*, p. xxxi.
36. Ibid., p. xxxi.
37. Ibid., pp. xxxi–ii.
38. State of Facts Relative to Mr Wilkes (15).
39. Cash, *John Wilkes*, p. 109.
40. Benjamin Franklin to William Strahan, May 9, 1763, *BFP*, Vol. 10, p. 261.
41. Benjamin Franklin to Lord Kames, June 2, 1765, *BFP*, Vol. 12, p. 159.
42. Ibid., p. 160.
43. *The Maryland Gazette*, June 30, 1763.
44. *The South-Carolina Gazette*, July 16, 1763.
45. Benjamin Franklin to John Whitehurst, June 27, 1763, *BFP*, Vol. 10, pp. 302–303.
46. Benjamin Franklin to William Strahan, June 28, 1763, *BFP*, Vol. 10, p. 304.
47. *The Pennsylvania Gazette*, July 14, 1763.
48. Ibid.
49. *Observations upon the authority, manner and circumstances of the apprehension and confinement of Mr. Wilkes* (London: J. Williams, 1764), p. 2.
50. William Strahan to Benjamin Franklin, August 18, 1763, *BFP*, Vol. 10, p. 326.
51. Ibid., pp. 324–25.
52. *The Pennsylvania Gazette*, June 30, 1763.
53. Ibid., August 11, 1763.
54. Ibid., July 7, 1763.

9. INFAMOUS

1. *The Aberdeen Journal*, November 14, 1763.
2. Hamilton, *Essay on Woman*, p. 104.
3. Roberts, *George III*, p. 122.
4. *The London Chronicle*, November 3–5, 1763.
5. Ibid.
6. Ibid.
7. Ibid.
8. William James Smith (ed.), *The Grenville Papers*, Vol. 2 (London: John Murray, 1852), p. 155.
9. Ibid., p. 160.
10. *The North Briton*, p. xxxii.
11. Cash, *John Wilkes*, p. 98.
12. Smith (ed.), *Grenville Papers*, p. 72.

13. Hamilton, *Essay on Woman*, p. 87.
14. Ibid., pp. 212–13.
15. Ibid., p. 97.
16. State of Facts Relative to Mr Wilkes (291).
17. Ibid. (292).
18. Smith (ed.), *Grenville Papers*, p. 161.
19. Hamilton, *Essay on Woman*, p. 114.
20. *The Manchester Mercury*, November 22, 1763.
21. *The Scots Magazine*, Vol. 25, p. 629.
22. *The Athenaeum*, August 19, 1893.
23. *The Scots Magazine*, Vol. 25, p. 629.
24. "Cust, Sir John, third baronet," in *Oxford Dictionary of National Biography* (oxforddnb.com, accessed September 2022).
25. *The Scots Magazine*, Vol. 25, p. 628.
26. Ibid., p. 628.
27. Smith (ed.), *Grenville Papers*, p. 73.
28. *The Scots Magazine*, Vol. 25, p. 628.
29. *The North Briton*, p. 132.
30. Cash, *John Wilkes*, p. 153.
31. Horace Walpole, *Memoirs of Reign of King George the Third* (London: Richard Bentley, 1845), p. 312.
32. *The North Briton*, p. xi.
33. Mr Martin's Answer, BL. Add MS 41,354 (79).
34. Narrative of the Affair between Mr. W & Mr Martin, November 16, Ibid. (82–85).
35. Claire Gilbride Fox, "Catharine Macaulay, an eighteenth-century Clio," *Winterthur Portfolio*, Vol. 4 (Chicago: University of Chicago Press, 1968), p. 134.
36. *The North Briton*, p. xii.
37. A. Barrister (ed.), *The Speeches of The Rt. Hon. The Earl of Chatham* (London: Aylott and Co., 1853), p. 64.
38. *Cato's Letters; or, Essays on Liberty, Civil and Religious*, Vol. 1 (London: W. Wilkins, 1737), p. 192.
39. *The Monthly Review*, November 1763.
40. Karen Green (ed.), *The Correspondence of Catharine Macaulay* (Oxford: Oxford University Press, 2020), p. 29.
41. Mary Hays, *Female Biography; or, Memoirs of Illustrious and Celebrated Women*, Vol. 5 (London: Richard Phillips, 1803), p. 289.
42. Ibid., pp. 289–90.
43. Bridget Hill, *The Republican Virago: Life and Times of Catharine Macaulay, Historian* (Oxford: The Clarendon Press, 1992), p. 40.
44. Ibid.
45. Ibid., p. 41.
46. *The Monthly Review*, November 1763.

47. Ibid.
48. Ibid.
49. Ibid.
50. Smith (ed.), *Grenville Papers*, p. 78.
51. *The Manchester Mercury*, December 13, 1763.
52. Hamilton, *Essay on Woman*, p. 122.
53. *The Manchester Mercury*, December 13, 1763.
54. John Brewer, "The misfortunes of Lord Bute: A case-study in eighteenth-century political argument and public opinion," *The Historical Journal*, Vol. 16, No. 1 (Cambridge: Cambridge University Press, 1973), p. 7.
55. Roberts, *George III*, p. 129.
56. John Almon, *The Correspondence of the Late John Wilkes, with his Friends, Printed from the Original Manuscripts*, Vol. 2 (London: Richard Phillips, 1805), p. 49.
57. *The Derby Mercury*, December 23, 1763.
58. *The Monthly Magazine, and British Register, for 1796*, Vol. 2 (London: R. Phillips, 1796), p. 576.
59. Almon (ed.), *Correspondence*, p. 54.
60. Stephens, *Memoirs*, p. 54.
61. Ibid.
62. Ibid., p. 63.
63. *The London Chronicle*, December 11, 1764.

10. NEWS-WRITERS

1. Benjamin Franklin to William Strahan, June 25, 1764, *BFP*, Vol. 11, p. 242.
2. Richard Arthur Austen-Leigh, *The Story of a Printing House: Being a Short Account of the Strahans and the Spottiswoodes* (London: Spottiswoode, 1912), p. 22.
3. Hill (ed.), *Life*, p. 291.
4. Austen-Leigh, *The Story*, p. 32.
5. Wrightson, *"Great Abilities,"* p. 109.
6. Strahan, "Correspondence between William Strahan and David Hall," Vol. 10, No. 2, p. 218.
7. Ibid., Vol. 10, No. 1, p. 93.
8. Ibid., p. 99.
9. "The Spectator": The Duke of York's Travels, May 15, 1765, *BFP*, Vol. 12, pp. 123–24.
10. Hart (ed.), *Letters*, p. 22.
11. Walter Isaacson, *Benjamin Franklin: An American Life* (New York: Simon & Schuster, 2003), p. 213.
12. J. Philip Gleason, "A scurrilous colonial election and Franklin's reputation," in *The William and Mary Quarterly*, Vol. 18, No. 1 (Williamsburg, VA: Omohundro Institute of Early American History and Culture, 1961), p. 76.
13. Ibid., p. 77.
14. Hart (ed.), *Letters*, p. 29.

15. "A Traveller": News-Writers' Nonsense, May 22, 1765, *BFP*, Vol. 12, p. 135.
16. Ibid., pp. 134–35.
17. Ibid., p. 134.
18. *Stroud Journal*, April 2, 1870.
19. Strahan, "Correspondence between William Strahan and David Hall," Vol. 10, No. 1, p. 97.
20. Ibid., Vol. 10, No. 2, p. 220.
21. Ibid., Vol. 10, No. 1, p. 95.
22. Benjamin Franklin to David Hall, January 12, 1765, *BFP*, Vol. 12, p. 19.
23. Benjamin Franklin to David Hall, February 14, 1765, *BFP*, Vol. 12, p. 66.
24. David Hall to Benjamin Franklin, June 20, 1765, *BFP*, Vol. 12, p. 189.
25. Ibid.
26. Some of Hall's letters to Franklin during the crucial months of June and July 1765 have been lost. This line appears in one of the lost letters. We know this because Franklin quoted Hall's writing back to him, in a letter written on September 14. "You tell me 'you should have been glad if I could have done anything to prevent the Stamp Act, as nothing could have contributed so much to have *removed the Prejudices* of many of the People against me . . .'" See: Benjamin Franklin to David Hall, September 14, 1765, *BFP*, Vol. 12, p. 267.
27. Benjamin Franklin to David Hall, June 8, 1765, *BFP*, Vol. 12, p. 171.
28. David Hall to Benjamin Franklin, September 6, 1765, *BFP*, Vol. 12, p. 257.
29. Ibid., p. 258.
30. Ibid., p. 259.
31. John Hughes to Benjamin Franklin, September 1765, *BFP*, Vol. 12, pp. 264–66.
32. Deborah Franklin to Benjamin Franklin, September 22, 1765, *BFP*, Vol. 12, p. 271.
33. Benjamin Franklin to Deborah Franklin, November 9, 1765, *BFP*, Vol. 12, p. 360.
34. Benjamin Franklin to David Hall, November 9, 1765, *BFP*, Vol. 12, p. 366.
35. Verner W. Crane (ed.), *Benjamin Franklin's Letters to the Press 1758–1775* (Chapel Hill: The University of North Carolina Press, 1950), p. 36.
36. Ibid.
37. Ibid., p. 37.
38. Ibid.
39. Damrosch, *The Club*, p. 301.
40. Strahan, "Correspondence between William Strahan and David Hall," Vol. 10, No. 1, p. 91.
41. Examination before the Committee of the Whole of the House of Commons, February 13, 1766, *BFP*, Vol. 13, p. 129.
42. Ibid., pp. 129–30.
43. Ibid., pp. 133–34. The assertion that these questions were Grenville's is made by Franklin himself, in an annotated copy of the Examination that he later sent to friends. In this he identified each of the questioners from memory. It deserves

to be mentioned that of these three questions—27, 28, and 29—Franklin wrote, "I think these were by Mr. Grenville, but am not certain."

44. Ibid., p. 125.
45. Strahan, "Correspondence between William Strahan and David Hall," Vol. 10, No. 1, p. 92.
46. Ibid.
47. Ibid., pp. 96–97.
48. Benjamin Franklin to William Strahan, November 27, 1765, *BFP*, Vol. 12, p. 385.
49. Strahan, "Correspondence between William Strahan and David Hall," Vol. 10, No. 2, p. 221.
50. Ibid., Vol. 10, No. 1, p. 96.
51. Ibid., p. 93.
52. Watson, *Annals*, p. 677.
53. Basil Cozens-Hardy, *The Diary of Sylas Neville 1767–1788* (Oxford: Oxford University Press, 1950), p. 20.
54. *The Public Advertiser*, April 7, 1770.
55. Peter Cunningham (ed.), *The Letters of Horace Walpole*, Vol. 5 (London: Richard Bentley and Son, 1891), p. 146.
56. Cozens-Hardy, *Diary*, p. 20.
57. "Macaulay [née Sawbridge; other married name Graham], Catharine," in *Oxford Dictionary of National Biography* (oxforddnb.com, accessed September 2022).
58. Cozens-Hardy, *Diary*, p. 31.
59. Lucy Martin Donnelly, "The celebrated Mrs. Macaulay," in *The William and Mary Quarterly*, Vol. 6, No. 2 (Williamsburg, VA: Omohundro Institute of Early American History and Culture, 1949), n.p.
60. Catharine Macaulay, *Loose remarks on certain positions to be found in Mr. Hobbes's Philosophical Rudiments of Government and Society, with a short sketch of a democratical form of government* (London: T. Davies, 1767), p. 31.
61. Ibid., p. 29.

11. A SEVEN-YEAR LOTTERY

1. Austen-Leigh, *The Story*, p. 12.
2. Ibid.
3. *The Annual Register, or a View of the History, Politics, and Literature, for the Year, 1768* (London: J. Dodsley, 1780), p. 57.
4. Strahan, "Correspondence between William Strahan and David Hall," Vol. 10, No. 2, p. 221.
5. Stephen Fried, *Rush: Revolution, Madness, and the Visionary Doctor Who Became a Founding Father* (New York: Crown, 2018), p. 44.
6. Strahan, "Correspondence between William Strahan and David Hall," Vol. 10, No. 2, p. 222.

7. William Hague, *William Pitt the Younger* (London: Harper Perennial, 2005), p. 21.
8. Robert Middlekauff, *The Glorious Cause: The American Revolution 1763–1789* (Oxford: Oxford University Press, 2005), p. 153.
9. Strahan, "Correspondence between William Strahan and David Hall," Vol. 10, No. 3, p. 322.
10. To the Printer of the Gazeteer, January 6, 1768, *BFP*, Vol. 15, p. 13.
11. Causes of the American Discontents before 1768, January 5–7, 1768, *BFP*, Vol. 15, pp. 12–13.
12. Strahan, "Correspondence between William Strahan and David Hall," Vol. 10, No. 3, p. 331.
13. Ibid., p. 329.
14. Cash, *John Wilkes*, p. 186.
15. BL. Add MS 30870.
16. "Wilkes, John," in *Oxford Dictionary of National Biography* (oxforddnb.com, accessed September 2022).
17. *The North Briton*, p. xxviii.
18. Cash, *John Wilkes*, p. 198.
19. Ibid., p. 201.
20. *The Newcastle Courant*, February 27, 1768.
21. *The Scots Magazine*, March 7, 1768.
22. Ibid.
23. Strahan, "Correspondence between William Strahan and David Hall," Vol. 10, No. 3, p. 332.
24. Benjamin Franklin to Joseph Galloway, March 13, 1768, *BFP*, Vol. 15, pp. 79–80.
25. *The Derby Mercury*, March 18, 1768.
26. James P. Holcombe, *Literature in Letters: Manners, Art, Criticism, Biography, History, and Morals* (New York: D Appleton and Company, 1866), p. 330.
27. *The Scots Magazine*, April 1, 1768.
28. *The Pennsylvania Gazette*, June 2, 1768.
29. *The Scots Magazine*, March 7, 1768.
30. Ibid.
31. *The Pennsylvania Gazette*, June 2, 1768.
32. Stephens, *Memoirs*, p. 94.
33. *The Derby Mercury*, April 1, 1768.
34. Ibid.
35. *The Pennsylvania Gazette*, June 9, 1768.
36. Ibid.
37. Ibid.
38. *The Derby Mercury*, April 1, 1768.
39. *The Scots Magazine*, April 1, 1768.
40. *The Oxford Journal*, April 2, 1768.

41. *The Pennsylvania Gazette*, June 9, 1768.
42. Ibid.
43. Ibid.
44. George Rudé, *Wilkes and Liberty: A Social Study of 1763 to 1774* (Oxford: Clarendon Press, 1962), p. 46.
45. [Samuel Johnson,] *The False Alarm* (London: T. Cadell, 1770), p. 6.
46. Cash, *John Wilkes*, p. 214.
47. Ibid., p. 217.
48. *The Newcastle Courant*, May 7, 1768.

12. VOX POPULI

1. Benjamin Franklin to William Franklin, April 16, *BFP*, Vol. 15, pp. 98–99.
2. Ibid.
3. Ibid.
4. Benjamin Franklin to Lord Kames, February 25, 1767, *BFP*, Vol. 14, p. 69.
5. Benjamin Franklin to Benjamin Rush, March 22, 1768, *BFP*, Vol. 15, p. 86.
6. Fried, *Rush* (New York: Crown, 2018), p. 44.
7. John Dickinson, *Letters from a Farmer in Pennsylvania, to the Inhabitants of the British Colonies* (Frankfurt: Outlook, 2020), p. 34.
8. Benjamin Franklin to William Franklin, March 13, 1768, *BFP*, Vol. 15, p. 75.
9. Gleason, "A scurrilous colonial election," p. 75.
10. Dickinson, *Letters*, p. 35.
11. Ibid., p. 36.
12. Ibid., p. 51.
13. Ibid., p. 24.
14. Ibid., p. 63.
15. Benjamin Franklin to William Franklin, March 13, 1768, *BFP*, Vol. 15, p. 76.
16. Dickinson, *Letters*, p. 44.
17. The English Editor to the Reader [of John Dickinson's *Letters from a Farmer*], May 8, 1768, *BFP*, Vol. 15, p. 111.
18. Dickinson, *Letters*, p. 6.
19. Fleming (ed.), *Dr Johnson's Satires*, p. 35.
20. *Jackson's Oxford Journal*, May 14, 1768.
21. Cash, *John Wilkes*, p. 222.
22. *The Pennsylvania Gazette*, June 30, 1768.
23. Cash, *John Wilkes*, p. 221.
24. J. Fortescue (ed.), *Correspondence of King George III 1760–1783*, Vol. 2 (London: s.n., 1927–28), no. 612.
25. Ibid., no. 613.
26. Ibid.
27. *The North Briton*, p. lxxviii.
28. Rudé, *Wilkes and Liberty*, p. 50.
29. Ibid.

30. *Jackson's Oxford Journal*, May 14, 1768.
31. Benjamin Franklin to John Ross, May 14, 1768, *BFP*, Vol. 15, p. 129.
32. *The North Briton*, p. lxxviii.
33. Cash, *John Wilkes*, p. 218.
34. *The Pennsylvania Gazette*, July 21, 1768.
35. *The North Briton*, p. lxxviii.
36. *The Pennsylvania Gazette*, August 25, 1768.
37. Fortescue (ed.), *Correspondence*, no. 630.
38. BL. Add MS 30870.
39. Ibid.
40. Bailyn, *Origins*, pp. 110–11.
41. Lyman Henry Butterfield (ed.), *Letters of Benjamin Rush*, Vol. 1 (Princeton, NJ: Princeton University Press, 1951), p. 72.

13. A STRANGE DISTEMPER

1. Wood, *Americanization*, p. 138.
2. Benjamin Franklin to Lord Kames, February 25, 1767, *BFP*, Vol. 14, p. 69.
3. Benjamin Franklin to Mary Stevenson, March 25, 1763, *BFP*, Vol. 10, p. 232.
4. Beaglehole, J. C. (ed.), *The Endeavour Journal of Joseph Banks 1768–1771* (Sydney: Angus and Robertson, 1962), Vol. 1, p. 30.
5. Sydney Parkinson, *Journal of a Voyage to the South Seas, in his Majesty's Ship The Endeavour* (London: privately printed, 1773), p. 14.
6. Benjamin Franklin to Jonathan Shipley, August 19, 1771, *BFP*, Vol. 18, p. 209.
7. Ibid.
8. Jean-Jacques Rousseau, *The Social Contract* (London: Penguin Books, 2004), p. 2.
9. Benjamin Franklin to Jonathan Shipley, August 19, 1771, *BFP*, Vol. 18, p. 210.
10. Ibid.
11. Ibid.
12. J. C. Beaglehole (ed.), *The Voyage of the Endeavour 1768–1771* (Cambridge: Cambridge University Press, 1955), p. 399.
13. "The Craven Street Gazette," September 22–26, 1770, *BFP*, Vol. 17, p. 220.
14. [Peter,] Lord King (ed.), *The Life and Letters of John Locke* (London: Henry G. Bohn, 1858), p. 88.
15. Ibid.
16. *Gerrard Winstanley: Selections from his Works* (London, Cresset Press, 1944), p. 101.
17. Darrin M. McMahon, *Happiness: A History* (New York: Atlantic, 2006), p. 190.
18. Johnson, *Dictionary*, n.p.
19. Damrosch, *The Club*, p. 327.
20. Fielding, *Enquiry*, p. 11.
21. *Annual Register*, p. 187.
22. *Annual Register*, p. 190.

23. Apology for Printers, June 10, 1731, *BFP*, Vol. 1, p. 194.
24. Benjamin Franklin to Jane Mecom, March 1, 1766, *BFP*, Vol. 13, p. 188.
25. Franklin, *Autobiography*, p. 3.
26. Horace Walpole, *Memoirs of the Reign of King George the Third*, Vol. 4 (London: Richard Bentley, 1845), p. 307.
27. [Edmund Burke,] *Thoughts on the Cause of the Present Discontents* (London: J. Dodsley, 1770), p. 5.
28. Strahan, "Correspondence between William Strahan and David Hall," Vol. 11, No. 2, p. 233.
29. Ibid., Vol. 11, No. 4, p. 489.
30. Ibid., Vol. 11, No. 2, p. 231.
31. Ibid., Vol. 11, No. 3, p. 353.
32. Ibid., Vol. 11, No. 1, p. 101.
33. [Johnson,] *False Alarm*, p. 7.
34. Strahan, "Correspondence between William Strahan and David Hall," Vol. 11, No. 1, p. 103.
35. Ibid., Vol. 11, No. 3, p. 354.
36. Ibid., Vol. 12, No. 1, p. 118.
37. Ibid.
38. Bailyn, *Ideological Origins*, p. 117.
39. [Burke,] *Thoughts*, p. 31.
40. *The South-Carolina Gazette*, August 9, 1770.
41. *The London Magazine*, July 1770.
42. *The Public Advertiser*, September 11, 1770.
43. Catharine Macaulay, *Observations on a Pamphlet, Entitled, Thoughts on the Cause of the Present Discontents* (London: Edward and Charles Dilly, 1770), pp. 6–7.
44. *Rind's Virginia Gazette*, April 20, 1769.
45. *The Bath Chronicle*, August 31, 1769.
46. *The Leeds Intelligencer and Yorkshire General Advertiser*, November 7, 1769.
47. Macaulay, *Observations*, pp. 10–11.
48. *The Derby Mercury*, November 17, 1769.
49. *The South-Carolina Gazette*, May 17, 1770.
50. John Doggett, Jr. (ed.), *A Short Narrative of the Horrid Massacre in Boston* (New York: John Doggett, Jr., 1849), p. 8.
51. Ibid., p. 107.
52. Ibid., p. 115.
53. Ibid., p. 116.

14. THOSE WHO RUSH ACROSS THE SEA
1. Karen Green, *Catharine Macaulay's Republican Enlightenment* (Abingdon: Routledge, 2020), p. 44.
2. Ibid., pp. 44–45.
3. Ibid.

4. Womersley (ed.), *Life*, p. 236.
5. Bate, *Samuel Johnson*, p. 351.
6. Damrosch, *The Club*, p. 95.
7. *American Quarterly Review*, p. 17.
8. Ibid., p. 18.
9. Johnson, "Review," p. 455.
10. Ibid.
11. Ibid.
12. Ibid., p. 460.
13. James G. Basker, *Samuel Johnson in the Mind of Thomas Jefferson* (Charlottesville: University of Virginia, 1999), p. 6.
14. Malone (ed.), *Life* (1827), p. 203.
15. *The Life of Samuel Johnson with Maxims and Observations* (Boston: Marsh, Capen and Lyon, 1833), p. 243.
16. Franklin, *Autobiography*, p. vii.
17. Samuel Johnson, *The History of Rasselas, Prince of Abissinia*, ed. Thomas Keymer (Oxford: Oxford University Press, 2009), p. 8.
18. Ibid., p. 10.
19. Ibid., p. 12.
20. Ibid., p. 13.
21. Ibid., p. 35.
22. Ibid., p. 51.
23. Ibid., p. 59.
24. Ibid., p. 32.
25. Ibid., p. 108.
26. Ibid., p. 94.
27. Ibid., p. x.
28. Ibid., p. ix.
29. Johnson, "Review," p. 468.
30. Ibid.
31. John A. Vance, *Samuel Johnson and the Sense of History* (Athens: University of Georgia Press, 2009), p. 114.
32. The original quote is, "Caelum, non animum mutant, qui trans mare currunt" (Horace, *Epistles* I.XI.27). See: Edward Mendelson, *Early Auden, Later Auden: A Critical Biography* (Princeton, NJ: Princeton University Press, 2017), p. 304.
33. Malone (ed.), *Life* (1827), p. 203.
34. *The Rambler*, Vol. 1, pp. 46–47.
35. Womersley (ed.), *Life*, p. 300.
36. [Samuel Johnson,] *The History of Rasselas, Prince of Abissinia*, Vol. 1 (Philadelphia: Robert Bell, 1768), title page.
37. Womersley (ed.), *Life*, p. 183.
38. Ibid., p. 182.
39. Johnson, *Rasselas*, p. xiii.

40. Ibid., p. xiv.
41. Austen-Leigh, *The Story*, p. 31.
42. Strahan, "Correspondence between William Strahan and David Hall," Vol. 12, No. 1, p. 116.
43. Ibid.
44. Ibid., p. 117.
45. Ibid., p. 117–18.
46. Ibid., Vol. 12, No. 2, p. 245.
47. Ibid., Vol. 11, No. 3, p. 352.
48. Ibid., Vol. 11, No. 4, p. 484.
49. Ibid., Vol. 12, No. 2, p. 248.

15. LETTERS
1. Strahan, "Correspondence between William Strahan and David Hall," Vol. 11, No. 3, p. 350.
2. Ibid., p. 349.
3. Ibid., p. 357.
4. Franklin's Contribution to a History of the British Colonies in America, Before May 20, 1773, *BFP*, Vol. 20, pp. 208–209.
5. Samuel Johnson, *Taxation No Tyranny; An Answer to the Resolutions and Address of the American Congress* (London: T. Cadell, 1775), p. 24.
6. Strahan, "Correspondence between William Strahan and David Hall," Vol. 11, No. 3, p. 356.
7. William Strahan to Benjamin Franklin, November 21–22, 1769, *BFP*, Vol. 16, p. 233.
8. Ibid., p. 234.
9. Benjamin Franklin to William Strahan, November 29, 1769, *BFP*, Vol. 16, pp. 246.
10. Ibid., p. 247.
11. Ibid., pp. 248–49.
12. Ibid., p. 249.
13. Benjamin Franklin to Deborah Franklin, January 6, 1773, *BFP*, Vol. 20, p. 16.
14. Franklin, *Autobiography*, p. 46.
15. Ibid., pp. 75–76.
16. Benjamin Franklin to Deborah Franklin, February 9, 1765, *BFP*, Vol. 12, p. 42.
17. Deborah Franklin to Benjamin Franklin, October 8, 1765, *BFP*, Vol. 12, p. 42.
18. Deborah Franklin to Benjamin Franklin, August 16, 1770, *BFP*, Vol. 17, p. 205.
19. Many historians have sought to explain Franklin's behavior toward Deborah during these years. The orthodox explanation is that theirs was an uneasy match. Franklin's drive, intellect, and ambition far outstripped Deborah's, and, while there were many practical advantages to their union in the short term, these subsided as time wore on. Franklin's desire to be in London, matched

with Deborah's determination not to travel, made their separation inevitable. There is much truth here. Another theory has recently been proposed by the author Stephen Cross, who traces the difficulties in the Franklins' marriage back to the death of "Frankie" from smallpox in 1736. This argument is set out in Stephen Cross, "What led Benjamin Franklin to live estranged from his wife for nearly two decades?": smithsonianmag.com/history/benjamin-franklin -estranged-wife-nearly-two-decades-180964400 (accessed September 2022).

20. Ritchie Robertson, *The Enlightenment: The Pursuit of Happiness* (London: Allen Lane, 2020), p. 7.
21. Franklin's Use of "Prudential Algebra," Before August 3, 1773, *BFP*, Vol. 20, p. 337.
22. Benjamin Franklin to Deborah Franklin, October 6, 1773, Ibid., p. 436.
23. Strahan, "Correspondence between William Strahan and David Hall," Vol. 11, No. 2, p. 231.
24. Benjamin Franklin to Thomas Cushing, June 4, 1773, *BFP*, Vol. 20, p. 228.
25. *The Ipswich Journal*, August 14, 1773.
26. Rules by Which a Great Empire May Be Reduced to a Small One, September 11, 1773, *BFP*, Vol. 20, p. 391.
27. An Edict by the King of Prussia, September 22, 1773, Vol. 20, p. 414.
28. Ibid., p. 415.
29. Ibid., pp. 417–18.
30. Benjamin Franklin to William Franklin, October 6, 1773, *BFP*, Vol. 20, p. 438.
31. Ibid., pp. 438–39.
32. On Literary Style, August 2, 1733, *BFP*, Vol. 1, p. 328.
33. *The Derby Mercury*, July 30, 1773.
34. *The Scots Magazine*, August 1773.
35. *The Leeds Intelligencer*, February 8, 1774.
36. Benjamin Franklin to Thomas Cushing, July 7, 1773, *BFP*, Vol. 20, p. 272.
37. Franklin's Public Statement about the Hutchinson Letters, December 23–25, 1773, *BFP*, Vol. 20, p. 514.
38. *The Scots Magazine*, January 1, 1774.
39. Benjamin Franklin to Thomas Cushing, January 5, 1774, *BFP*, Vol. 21, p. 6.
40. Benjamin Franklin to Jane Mecom, March 1, 1766, *BFP*, Vol. 13, p. 188.
41. Johnson, *Rasselas*, p. 75.
42. *The Derby Mercury*, January 21, 1774.
43. Roberts, *George III*, p. 232.
44. Benjamin Franklin to Thomas Cushing, February 15–19, 1774, *BFP*, Vol. 21, pp. 89–90.
45. Ibid., p. 92.
46. The Final Hearing before the Privy Council Committee for Plantation Affairs, January 29, 1774, *BFP*, Vol. 21, p. 41.
47. *The Scots Magazine*, January 1774.
48. Ibid.

49. A Letter from London, April 25, 1774, *BFP*, Vol. 21, p. 81.

50. *The Scots Magazine*, January 1774.

51. Ibid.

52. Benjamin Franklin to Thomas Cushing, February 15–19, 1774, *BFP*, Vol. 21, pp. 93–94.

53. Benjamin Franklin to William Franklin, February 2, 1774, *BFP*, Vol. 21, p. 75.

54. *The Hibernian Journal*, February 7, 1774.

55. Ibid.

56. Benjamin Franklin to Jane Mecom, February 17, 1774, *BFP*, Vol. 21, p. 103.

57. *The Leeds Intelligencer*, June 14, 1774.

58. William Franklin to Benjamin Franklin, December 24, 1774, *BFP*, Vol. 21, pp. 403–404.

59. Ibid., p. 403.

60. G. Birkbeck Hill, *Letters of David Hume to William Strahan* (Oxford: The Clarendon Press, 1888), pp. 304–305.

61. Benjamin Franklin to Richard Bache, September 30, 1774, *BFP*, Vol. 21, p. 325.

16. ATLANTICUS

1. Thomas Paine to Benjamin Franklin, March 4, 1775, *BFP*, Vol. 21, p. 516.

2. Ibid.

3. *The Pennsylvania Gazette*, November 11, 1762.

4. Ibid.

5. "Paine, Thomas," in *Oxford Dictionary of National Biography* (oxforddnb.com, accessed September 2022).

6. Womersley (ed.), *Life*, p. 498.

7. "Paine, Thomas," in *Oxford Dictionary of National Biography*.

8. John Keane, *Tom Paine: A Political Life* (London: Bloomsbury, 2009), p. 25.

9. Watson, *Annals*, p. 241.

10. Roberts, *George III*, p. 249.

11. McCullough, *John Adams*, p. 87.

12. *Dunlap's Pennsylvania Packet, the General Advertiser*, January 2, 1775.

13. A. Q. Morton, "Lectures on natural philosophy in London, 1750–1765," *The British Journal for the History of Science*, Vol. 23, No. 4 (Cambridge: Cambridge University Press, 1990), p. 421.

14. Thomas Paine to Benjamin Franklin, March 4, 1775, *BFP*, Vol. 21, p. 517.

15. *The Pennsylvania Magazine; or, American Monthly Museum*, January 1775.

16. Joel Porte and Saundra Morris (eds.), *The Cambridge Companion to Ralph Waldo Emerson* (Cambridge: Cambridge University Press, 1999), p. 208.

17. *The Pennsylvania Magazine; or, American Monthly Museum*, January 1775.

18. Ibid.

19. Ibid., February 1775.

20. For more on Paine's journalism after arriving in Philadelphia, see: Frank Smith, "New light on Thomas Paine's first year in America, 1775," *American*

Literature, Vol. 1, No. 4 (Durham, NC: Duke University Press, 1930), pp. 347–71.

21. Michael Foot and Isaac Kramnick (eds.), *The Thomas Paine Reader* (London: Penguin Books, 1987), p. 52. Also, see peter-moore.co.uk/paine-slavery.

22. Ibid., p. 55.

23. Bailyn, *Ideological Origins*, p. 245.

24. James Cheetham, *The Life of Thomas Paine, Author of Common Sense, the Crisis, Rights of Man, &c. &c. &c.* (New York: Southwick and Pelsue, 1809), p. 35.

25. Ibid., p. 36.

26. Thomas Paine to Benjamin Franklin, March 4, 1775, *BFP*, Vol. 21, p. 517.

27. *The Pennsylvania Magazine; or, American Monthly Museum*, April 1775.

28. Ibid.

29. This quote became the title of a fine twentieth-century biography of Wilkes. See: Raymond Postgate, *"That Devil Wilkes"* (London: Constable and Co., 1930).

30. *The Pennsylvania Magazine; or, American Monthly Museum*, January 1775.

31. Ibid., April 1775.

32. Ibid.

33. Paul H. Smith (ed.), *Letters of Delegates to Congress 1774–1789*, Vol. 1 (Washington: Library of Congress, 1976), p. 334.

34. Extract of a Letter from Philadelphia, May 6, 1775, *BFP*, Vol. 22, p. 30.

35. Benjamin Franklin to David Hartley, May 8, 1775, *BFP*, Vol. 22, p. 34.

36. Benjamin Franklin to Humphry Marshall, May 23, 1775, *BFP*, Vol. 21, p. 51.

37. Smith, *Letters*, p. 337.

38. Ibid., p. 342.

39. Benjamin Franklin to William Strahan, July 5, 1775, *BFP*, Vol. 21, p. 85.

40. William Strahan to Benjamin Franklin, July 5, 1775, *BFP*, Vol. 21, p. 87.

41. Benjamin Franklin to William Strahan, October 3, 1775, *BFP*, Vol. 21, pp. 218–19.

17. *COMMON SENSE*

1. Catharine Macaulay, *An Address to the People of England, Scotland, and Ireland on the Present Important Crisis of Affairs* (London: Edward and Charles Dilly, 1775), p. 10.

2. Ibid., p. 7.

3. Ibid., p. 8.

4. Ibid., p. 10.

5. Ibid., pp. 28–29.

6. Ibid., p. 31.

7. [Samuel Johnson,] *Taxation No Tyranny; An Answer to the Resolutions and Address of the American Congress* (London: T. Cadell, 1775), p. 79.

8. Ibid., p. 55.

9. Ibid., p. 7.

10. Ibid., p. 4.

11. Ibid., p. 17.
12. Ibid., p. 23.
13. Ibid., p. 25.
14. Ibid., p. 29.
15. Ibid., p. 38.
16. Ibid., p. 53.
17. Ibid., p. 62.
18. Ibid., p. 84.
19. Ibid., p. 85.
20. Ibid., p. 89.
21. Craig Nelson, "Thomas Paine and the making of 'Common Sense,'" *New England Review*, Vol. 27, No. 3 (Middlebury, VT: Middlebury College Publications, 2006), p. 232.
22. *The Pennsylvania Magazine; or, American Monthly Museum*, July 1775.
23. Fried, *Rush*, p. 2.
24. Nelson, "Thomas Paine," p. 236.
25. Cheetham, *Life of Thomas Paine*, pp. 36–37.
26. Nelson, "Thomas Paine," p. 236.
27. Johnson, *Dictionary*, n.p.
28. *The Pennsylvania Magazine; or, American Monthly Museum*, January 1775.
29. Bailyn, *Origins*, p. 18.
30. Thomas Paine, *Common Sense* (London: Penguin Books, 2004), p. 5.
31. Ibid., p. 43.
32. Ibid., p. 9.
33. Ibid.
34. Ibid., p. 10.
35. Ibid., p. 11.
36. Ibid., p. 10.
37. Ibid., p. 13.
38. Ibid., p. 19.
39. Ibid., p. 20.
40. Ibid., p. 24.
41. Ibid., p. 25.
42. Ibid.
43. Ibid., p. 35.
44. Ibid., p. 26.
45. Ibid., pp. 32–33.
46. Ibid., p. 33.
47. Ibid., p. 51.
48. Ibid., p. 54.
49. Ibid., p. 60.
50. William Strahan to Benjamin Franklin, October 4, 1775, *BFP*, Vol. 21, pp. 221–22.

51. Ibid., p. 223.
52. William Bell Clark (ed.), *Naval Documents of the American Revolution*, Vol. 2 (Washington: US Navy Dept, 1966), p. 777.
53. [Thomas Paine,] *Common Sense; Addressed to the Inhabitants of America* (Philadelphia: W. and T. Bradford, 1776), p. 77.
54. Woodrow Wilson, *A History of the American People*, Vol. 5 (New York: Harper & Brothers, 1918), p. 181.
55. Cheetham, *Life of Thomas Paine*, p. 38.
56. Nelson, "Thomas Paine," p. 245.
57. Ibid.
58. Foot and Kramnick (eds.), *The Thomas Paine Reader*, pp. 9–10.
59. Ibid., p. 10.
60. [Paine,] *Common Sense*, p. 5.
61. Nelson, "Thomas Paine," p. 245.
62. Cheetham, *Life of Thomas Paine*, p. 37.
63. Paine, *Common Sense*, p. 3; p. 69; p. 35; p. 52; p. 54; p. 39; p. 54.
64. Ibid., pp. 59–60.

18. PLOTS

1. Womersley (ed.), *Life*, p. 554.
2. Ibid., p. 553.
3. Damrosch, *The Club*, p 134.
4. Benjamin Franklin to Hugh Roberts, February 26, 1761, *BFP*, Vol. 9, p. 280.
5. "Wilkes, John," in *Oxford Dictionary of National Biography* (oxforddnb.com, accessed September 2022).
6. Womersley (ed.), *Life*, pp. 553–54.
7. Ibid., p. 555.
8. Damrosch, *The Club*, p. 130.
9. Womersley (ed.), *Life*, p. 555.
10. Ibid., p. 557.
11. Ibid., p. 560.
12. Ibid., p. 561.
13. *The London Chronicle*, May 11–14, 1776.
14. *The Caledonian Mercury*, May 13, 1776.
15. Womersley (ed.), *Life*, p. 560.
16. Damrosch, *The Club*, p. 306.
17. Bailyn, *Origins*, p. 16.
18. Michael Foot and Isaac Kramnick (eds.), *The Thomas Paine Reader* (London: Penguin Books, 1987), p. 7.
19. *The Pennsylvania Evening Post*, June 29, 1776. There is broad consensus that Paine was responsible for this letter, although his authorship has not been proved conclusively. The question of who first named the country has engaged various scholars and journalists over the centuries. References to the "united

states of America" appear in several manuscript letters as far back as January 1776, and this same formulation of language was printed in the *Virginia Gazette* of April 6. "Republicus," however, remains the first to have seen the "United States of America" into print. See: nyhistory.org/blogs/coined-phrase -united-states-america-may-never-guess (accessed September 2022).

EPILOGUE: CROSSINGS

1. Margaret A. Hogan and C. James Taylor (eds.), *My Dearest Friend: Letters of Abigail and John Adams* (Cambridge, MA: The Belknap Press of Harvard University Press, 2010), p. 206.
2. Hill, *Republican Virago*, p. 127.
3. "Graham, James," in *Oxford Dictionary of National Biography* (oxforddnb.com, accessed September 2022).
4. Cunningham (ed.), *Letters*, Vol. 7, p. 509.
5. Brewer, *Misfortunes*, p. 10.
6. Macaulay, *An Address*, p. 28.
7. Charles Francis Adams (ed.), *Letters of John Adams, Addressed to his Wife*, Vol. 1 (Boston: Charles C. Little, 1841), p. 224.
8. Gilbride Fox, *Catharine Macaulay*, p. 141.
9. Ibid.
10. Ibid.
11. *The Belfast Mercury or Freeman's Chronicle*, January 21, 1785.
12. Stacy Schiff, *A Great Improvisation: Franklin, France, and the Birth of America* (New York: Henry Holt and Company, 2005), p. 2.
13. Ibid., p. 5.
14. Charles F. Jenkins, "Franklin returns from France—1785," *Proceedings of the American Philosophical Society*, Vol. 92, No. 6 (Philadelphia: American Philosophical Society, 1948), p. 418.
15. "Wilkes, John," in *Oxford Dictionary of National Biography* (oxforddnb.com, accessed September 2022).
16. Levy, *Origins*, p. 79.
17. William Strahan to Benjamin Franklin, January 23, 1777, *BFP*, Vol. 23, p. 227.
18. Benjamin Franklin to William Strahan, August 19, 1784, *BFP*, Vol. 43, p. 29.
19. Benjamin Franklin to William Strahan, February 16, 1784, *BFP*, Vol. 41, p. 573.
20. Austen-Leigh, *The Story*, p. 26.
21. Ibid., p. 29.
22. Elizabeth M. Nuxoll, *The Selected Papers of John Jay*, Vol. 4 (Charlottesville: University of Virginia Press, 2015), p. 187.

Selected Bibliography

PRINCIPAL SOURCES

Franklin, Benjamin, *The Autobiography and Other Writings with an Introduction by Jill Lepore* (New York: Knopf, 2015).

[Johnson, Samuel,] *The Rambler*, 8 vols. (London: J. Payne, 1752).

Labaree, Leonard W., et al. (eds), *Papers of Benjamin Franklin*, 43 vols. to date (New Haven: Yale University Press, 1959–).

The Pennsylvania Magazine: or, American Monthly Museum, 2 vols. (Philadelphia: R. Aitken, 1776).

State of Facts Relative to Mr. Wilkes, BL. Add MS 22132 (4).

[Strahan, William,] "Correspondence between William Strahan and David Hall, 1763–1777," *The Pennsylvania Magazine of History and Biography*, Vols. 10–12 (Philadelphia: University of Pennsylvania Press, 1886–88).

ADDITIONAL READING

Adams, Charles Francis (ed.), *Letters of John Adams, Addressed to his Wife*, 2 vols. (Boston: Charles C. Little, 1841).

Almon, John, *The Correspondence of the Late John Wilkes, with his Friends, Printed from the Original Manuscripts*, 2 vols. (London: Richard Phillips, 1805).

The American Magazine or a monthly view of the political state of the British colonies, reproduced from the original edition Philadelphia, 1741, with a bibliographical note by Lyon N. Richardson (New York: The Facsimile Society, 1937).

Austen-Leigh, Richard Arthur, *The Story of a Printing House: Being a Short Account of the Strahans and the Spottiswoodes* (London: Spottiswoode, 1912).

Bailyn, Bernard, *The Ideological Origins of the American Revolution*, 50th anniversary ed. (Cambridge, MA: The Belknap Press of Harvard University Press, 2017).

Balderston, Katharine C., "Doctor Johnson and William Law," in *Publications of the Modern Language Association (PMLA)*, Vol. 75, No. 4 (Cambridge: Cambridge University Press, 1960).

Basker, James G., *Samuel Johnson in the Mind of Thomas Jefferson* (Charlottesville: University of Virginia, 1999).

Bate, W. Jackson, *Samuel Johnson* (London: Chatto and Windus, 1978).

Bate, W. J., and Albrecht B. Strauss (eds), *The Yale Edition of the Works of Samuel Johnson*, Vol. 3: *The Rambler* (New Haven, CT: Yale University Press, 1969).

Beaglehole, J. C. (ed.), *The Voyage of the Endeavour 1768–1771* (Cambridge: Cambridge University Press, 1955).

Becker, Carl, *The Declaration of Independence: A Study in the History of Political Ideas* (New York: Peter Smith, 1933).

Bennett Nolan, J., *Printer Strahan's Book Account: A Colonial Controversy* (Reading, PA: The Bar of Berks County, 1939).

Black, Jeremy, *Eighteenth-Century Britain 1688–1783* (Basingstoke: Palgrave, 2001).

Bleackley, Horace, *Life of John Wilkes* (London: The Bodley Head, 1917).

Boswell, James, *The Life of Samuel Johnson* (London: Penguin, 2008).

Boswell, James, *London Journal* (Mineola, NY: Dover Publications, 2018).

Boudreau, George W., "'Done by a tradesman': Franklin's educational proposals and the culture of eighteenth-century Pennsylvania," in *Pennsylvania History*, Vol. 69, No. 4 (University Park: Penn State University Press, 2002).

Brack, O. M., Jr., and Robert DeMaria, Jr. (eds), *Johnson on Demand: Reviews, Prefaces, and Ghost-Writings* (New Haven: Yale University Press, 2018).

Brewer, John, "The misfortunes of Lord Bute: A case-study in eighteenth-century political argument and public opinion," in *The Historical Journal*, Vol. 16, No. 1 (Cambridge: Cambridge University Press, 1973).

Bundock, Michael, *The Fortunes of Francis Barber: The True Story of the Jamaican Slave Who Became Samuel Johnson's Heir* (New Haven, CT: Yale University Press, 2015).

Bunker, Nick, *Young Benjamin Franklin: The Birth of Ingenuity* (New York: Alfred A. Knopf, 2018).

[Burke, Edmund,] *Thoughts on the Cause of the Present Discontents* (London: J. Dodsley, 1770).

Burnard, Trevor, and Kenneth Morgan, "The dynamics of the slave market and slave purchasing patterns in Jamaica, 1655–1788," in *The William and Mary Quarterly*, Vol. 58, No. 1 (Williamsburg, VA: Omohundro Institute of Early American History and Culture, 2001).

Butterfield, Lyman Henry (ed.), *Letters of Benjamin Rush*, Vol. 1 (Princeton, NJ: Princeton University Press, 1951).

Cash, Arthur H., *John Wilkes: The Scandalous Father of Civil Liberty* (New Haven, CT: Yale University Press).

Chaplin, Joyce E., *The First Scientific American: Benjamin Franklin and the Pursuit of Genius* (New York: Basic Books, 2006).

Cheetham, James, *The Life of Thomas Paine, Author of Common Sense, the Crisis, Rights of Man, &c. &c. &c.* (New York: Southwick and Pelsue, 1809).

Clifford, James L., *Dictionary Johnson: The Middle Years of Samuel Johnson* (London: Heinemann, 1979).

Clifford, James L., *Young Samuel Johnson* (London: Heinemann, 1957).

Cochrane, James Aikman, *Dr. Johnson's Printer: The Life of William Strahan* (Cambridge, MA: Harvard University Press, 1964).

Cohen, I. Bernard, *Benjamin Franklin's Science* (Cambridge, MA: Harvard University Press).

A Complete Collection of the Genuine Papers, Letters , &c. in the Case of John Wilkes, Esq. (Berlin: *s.n.*, 1769).

Cowan, Brian William, "Mr. Spectator and the coffeehouse public sphere," in *Eighteenth-Century Studies*, Vol. 37, No. 3 (Baltimore: Johns Hopkins University Press, 2004).

Cozens-Hardy, Basil, *The Diary of Sylas Neville 1767–1788* (Oxford: Oxford University Press, 1950).

Crane, Verner W. (ed.), *Benjamin Franklin's Letters to the Press 1758–1775* (Chapel Hill: The University of North Carolina Press, 1950).

Cunningham, Peter (ed.), *The Letters of Horace Walpole*, 9 vols. (London: Richard Bentley and Son, 1891).

Dalrymple, William, *The Anarchy: The Relentless Rise of the East India Company* (London: Bloomsbury, 2019).

Damrosch, Leo, *The Club: Johnson, Boswell, and the Friends who Shaped an Age* (New Haven: Yale University Press, 2019).

Dickens, Charles, *The Works of Charles Dickens: Pickwick Papers, Barnaby Rudge, Sketches by Boz* (New York: D Appleton and Company, 1874).

[Dickinson, John,] *Letters from a Farmer in Pennsylvania, to the Inhabitants of the British Colonies* (Philadelphia: William and Thomas Bradford, 1769).

Doggett, John, Jr. (ed.), *A Short Narrative of the Horrid Massacre in Boston* (New York: John Doggett, Jr., 1849).

Donnelly, Lucy Martin, "The celebrated Mrs. Macaulay," in *The William and Mary Quarterly*, Vol. 6, No. 2 (Williamsburg, VA: Omohundro Institute of Early American History and Culture, 1949).

Dray, Philip, *Stealing God's Thunder: Benjamin Franklin's Lightning Rod and the Invention of America* (New York: Random House, 2005).

The Effects of Industry and Idleness Illustrated (London: C. Corbett, 1748).

Equiano, Olaudah, *The interesting narrative of the life of Olaudah Equiano or Gustavus Vassa, the African. Written by himself* (London: privately published, 1794).

Fielding, Henry, *An Enquiry into the Causes of the Late Increase of Robbers, &c.* (London: A. Millar, 1751).

Fisher, John (ed.), *Industry and Idleness: Exemplified in the conduct of two fellow apprentices in twelve moral and instructive prints by William Hogarth* (London: Guildhall Library London, 1978).

Fleming, I. P. (ed.), *Dr Johnson's Satires: London and The Vanity of Human Wishes with Notes, Historical & Biographical, & a Glossary* (London: Longmans, Green, and Co., 1888).

Foot, Michael, and Isaac Kramnick (eds), *The Thomas Paine Reader* (London: Penguin Books, 1987).

Ford, Paul Leicester (ed.), "*The Sayings of Poor Richard": The Prefaces, Proverbs, and Poems of Benjamin Franklin* (New York, The Knickerbocker Press, 1890).

Fortescue, J. (ed.), *Correspondence of King George III 1760–1783*, Vol. 2 (London: s.n., 1927–28).

Fox, Claire Gilbride, "Catharine Macaulay, an eighteenth-century Clio," in *Winterthur Portfolio*, Vol. 4 (Chicago: University of Chicago Press, 1968).

Fried, Stephen, *Rush: Revolution, Madness, and the Visionary Doctor Who Became a Founding Father* (New York: Crown, 2018).

Gleason, J. Philip, "A scurrilous colonial election and Franklin's reputation," in *The William and Mary Quarterly*, Vol. 18, No. 1 (Williamsburg, VA: Omohundro Institute of Early American History and Culture, 1961).

Goff, Frederick R., *The John Dunlap Broadside: The First Printing of the Declaration of Independence* (Washington, DC: Library of Congress, 1976).

Goodwin, George, *Benjamin Franklin in London: The British Life of America's Founding Father* (London: Weidenfeld and Nicolson, 2016).

Green, Karen, *Catharine Macaulay's Republican Enlightenment* (Abingdon: Routledge, 2020).

Green, Karen (ed.), *The Correspondence of Catharine Macaulay* (Oxford: Oxford University Press, 2020).

Hague, William, *William Pitt the Younger* (London: Harper Perennial, 2005).

Hamilton, Adrian, *The Infamous Essay on Woman, or John Wilkes Seated between Vice and Virtue* (London, Andre Deutsch, 1972).

Harlan, Robert D., "William Strahan's American book trade, 1744–76," in *The Library Quarterly: Information, Community, Policy* (Chicago: University of Chicago Press, 1961).

Hart, Charles Henry (ed.), *Letters from William Franklin to William Strahan* (Philadelphia: privately published, 1911).

Hawkins, Sir John, *The Life of Samuel Johnson, LL.D* (London: J. Buckland, J. Rivington and Sons, 1787).

Hay, Carla H., "Catharine Macaulay and the American Revolution," in *The Historian*, Vol. 56, No. 2 (London: Taylor and Francis, 1994).

Hays, Kevin J., "New light on Peter and King, the two slaves Benjamin Franklin brought to England," in *Notes and Queries*, Vol. 6, No. 2 (Oxford: Oxford University Press, 2013).

Hill, Bridget, *The Republican Virago: Life and Times of Catharine Macaulay, Historian* (Oxford: The Clarendon Press, 1992).

The History of the Minority, during the Years 1762, 1763, 1764, and 1765. Exhibiting the Conduct, Principles and Views of that Party (London: s.n., 1764).

Hitchings, Henry, *Dr Johnson's Dictionary: The Extraordinary Story of the Book that Defined the World* (London: John Murray, 2005).

Holmes, Richard, *Dr Johnson and Mr Savage* (London: Harper Perennial, 2005).

Hone, Joseph, *The Paper Chase: The Printer, the Spymaster, and the Hunt for the Rebel Pamphleteers* (London: Chatto and Windus, 2020).

Hotblack, Kate, "The Peace of Paris, 1763. Alexander Prize Essay, 1907," in *Transactions of the Royal Historical Society*, Vol. 2 (Cambridge: Cambridge University Press, 1908).

Immerwahr, John, "Hume's revised racism," in *Journal of the History of Ideas*, Vol. 53, No. 2 (Philadelphia: University of Pennsylvania Press, 1992).

Isaacson, Walter, *Benjamin Franklin: An American Life* (New York: Simon and Schuster, 2003).

Jenkins, Charles F., "Franklin returns from France—1785," in *Proceedings of the American Philosophical Society*, Vol. 92, No. 6 (Philadelphia: American Philosophical Society, 1948).

Johnson, Samuel, *A Dictionary of the English Language in which The Words are Deduced from their Originals* (London: J. Knapton; C. Hitch and L. Hawes; A. Millar; W. Strahan; R. and J. Dodsley; and M. and T. Longman, 1755).

[Johnson, Samuel,] *The False Alarm* (London: T. Cadell, 1770).

Johnson, Samuel, *The History of Rasselas, Prince of Abissinia*, ed. Thomas Keymer (Oxford: Oxford University Press, 2009).

[Johnson, Samuel,] *The History of Rasselas, Prince of Abissinia*, Vol. 1 (Philadelphia: Robert Bell, 1768).

Johnson, Samuel, *The Idler with Additional Essays* (London: C. Cooke, 1799).

[Johnson, Samuel,] *Taxation No Tyranny; An Answer to the Resolutions and Address of the American Congress* (London: T. Cadell, 1775).

Keane, John, *Tom Paine: A Political Life* (London: Bloomsbury, 2009).

King, [Peter,] Lord (ed.), *The Life and Letters of John Locke* (London: Henry G. Bohn, 1858).

Law, William, *A Serious Call to a Devout and Holy Life* (London: William Innys, 1729).

Lepore, Jill, *New York Burning: Liberty, Slavery, and Conspiracy in Eighteenth-Century Manhattan* (New York: Vintage Books, 2006).

Levy, Leonard W., "Origins of the Fourth Amendment," in *Political Science Quarterly*, Vol. 114, No. 1 (New York: The Academy of Political Science, 1999).

Lincoln, Margarette, *London and the Seventeenth Century: The Making of the World's Greatest City* (London: Yale University Press, 2021).

Locke, John, *Two Treatises of Government*, new ed. (London: Whitmore and Fenn, 1821).

Logan, James (trans.), *M. T. Cicero's Cato Major, or his Discourse of Old Age* (Philadelphia: B. Franklin, 1744).

Macaulay, Catharine, *An Address to the People of England, Scotland, and Ireland on the Present Important Crisis of Affairs* (London: Edward and Charles Dilly, 1775).

Macaulay, Catharine, *The History of England from the Accession of James I. to that of the Brunswick Line*, Vol. 1 (London: J. Nourse, 1763).

Macaulay, Catharine, *Loose remarks on certain positions to be found in Mr. Hobbes's Philosophical Rudiments of Government and Society, with a short sketch of a democratical form of government* (London: T. Davies, 1767).

Macaulay, Catharine, *Observations on a Pamphlet, Entitled, Thoughts on the Cause of the Present Discontents* (London: Edward and Charles Dilly, 1770).

McCullough, David, *John Adams* (New York: Simon and Schuster, 2001).

McMahon, Darrin M., *Happiness: A History* (New York, Atlantic Monthly Press, 2006).

Maslen, K. I. D., "William Strahan at the Bowyer Press 1736–8," in *The Library*, Vol. 15, No. 3, (Oxford: Oxford Academic, 1970).

Middlekauff, Robert, *The Glorious Cause: The American Revolution 1763–1789* (Oxford: Oxford University Press, 2005).

Moore, Peter, *Endeavour: The Ship and the Attitude That Changed the World* (Chatto and Windus, 2018).

Moritz, Carl Philip, *Journeys of a German in England* (London: Eland Books, 1983).

Morsley, Clifford, *News from the English Countryside 1750–1850* (London: Harrap, 1979).

Moxon, Joseph, *Merchanick Exercises: Or, The Doctrine of Handy Works. Applied to the Art of Printing* (London: Joseph Moxon, 1683).

Myles, Paul, *Rise of Thomas Paine and the Case of the Officers of Excise* (Lewes: The Thomas Paine Society, 2018).

Nash, Gary B., "Slaves and slaveowners in colonial Philadelphia," in *The William and Mary Quarterly*, Vol. 30, No. 2 (Williamsburg, VA: Omohundro Institute, 1973).

Nelson, Craig, "Thomas Paine and the making of 'Common Sense,'" in *New England Review*, Vol. 27, No. 3 (Middlebury, VT: Middlebury College Publications, 2006).

The North Briton from No. 1 to No. 44 Inclusive (London: W. Bingley, 1769).

Observations upon the authority, manner and circumstances of the apprehension and confinement of Mr. Wilkes (London: J. Williams, 1764).

Paine, Thomas, *Common Sense* (London: Penguin Books, 2004).

Philip, J. R., "Samuel Johnson as antiscientist," in *Notes and Records of the Royal Society of London* Vol. 29, No. 2 (London: Royal Society, 1975).

Piozzi, Hesther Lynch, *Anecdotes of the Late Samuel Johnson, LL.D.* (London: T. Cadell, 1786).

Postgate, Raymond, "*That Devil Wilkes*"(London: Constable and Co., 1930).

Quinlan, Maurice J., "Dr. Franklin meets Dr. Johnson," in *The Pennsylvania Magazine of History and Biography*, Vol. 73, No. 1 (Philadelphia: The Historical Society of Pennsylvania, 1949).

Randolph, Thomas Jefferson (ed.), *Memoirs, Correspondence, and Private Papers of Thomas Jefferson, Late President of the United States*, 4 vols. (London: Henry Colburn and Richard Bentley, 1829).

Reddick, Allen, *The Making of Johnson's Dictionary 1746–1773* (Cambridge: Cambridge University Press, 1996).

Reps, John W., "William Penn and the planning of Philadelphia," in *The Town Planning Review*, Vol. 27, No. 1 (Liverpool: Liverpool University Press, 1956).

Richardson, Lyon N. (ed.), *The General Magazine and historical chronicle for all the British plantations in America, reproduced from the original edition Philadelphia, 1741, with a bibliographical note by Lyon N. Richardson* (New York: The Facsimile Society, 1937).

Roach, Hannah Benner, "Benjamin Franklin slept here," in *The Pennsylvania Magazine of History and Biography* Vol. 84, No. 2 (Philadelphia: University of Pennsylvania Press, 1960).

Roberts, Andrew, *George III: The Life and Reign of Britain's Most Misunderstood Monarch* (London: Allen Lane, 2021).

Robertson, Ritchie, *The Enlightenment: The Pursuit of Happiness* (London: Allen Lane, 2020).

Roger, N. A. M, *The Insatiable Earl: A Life of John Montagu, Fourth Earl of Sandwich 1718–1792* (New York: W. W. Norton and Company, 1994).

Rudé, George, *Wilkes and Liberty: A Social Study of 1763 to 1774* (Oxford: Clarendon Press, 1962).

Schiff, Stacy, *A Great Improvisation: Franklin, France, and the Birth of America* (New York: Henry Holt and Company, 2005).

Schwartz, Sally, "William Penn and toleration: Foundations of colonial Pennsylvania," in *Pennsylvania History*, Vol. 50, No. 4 (University Park: Penn State University Press, 1983).

Simmons, R. C., "Colonial patronage: Two letters from William Franklin to the Earl of Bute, 1762," in *The William and Mary Quarterly*, Vol. 59, No. 1 (Williamsburg, VA: The Omohundro Institute of Early American History and Culture, 2002).

Smith, Frank, "New light on Thomas Paine's first year in America, 1775," in *American Literature*, Vol. 1, No. 4 (Durham, NC: Duke University Press, 1930).

Smith, Paul H. (ed.), *Letters of Delegates to Congress 1774–1789*, Vol. 1 (Washington, DC: Library of Congress, 1976).

Smith, Paul H., "Time and temperature: Philadelphia, July 4, 1776," in *The Quarterly Journal of the Library of Congress*, Vol. 33, No. 4 (Washington, DC: Library of Congress, 1976).

Smith, William James (ed.), *The Grenville Papers*, Vol. 2 (London: John Murray, 1852).

Smythe, Albert H., *The Philadelphia Magazines and their Contributors 1741–1850* (Philadelphia: Robert M. Lindsay, 1892).

Stephens, Alexander, *Memoirs of John Horne Tooke*, Vol. 1 (London: J. Johnson and Co., 1813).

[Swift, Jonathan,] *A modest proposal for preventing the children of poor people from being a burthen to their parents or the country, &c* (London: Weaver, Bickerton, 1730).

Szabo, Franz A. J., *The Seven Years War in Europe* (Abingdon: Routledge, 2008).

Thomas, Gabriel, *An historical and geographical account of the province and country of Pennsilvania; and of West New-Jersey in America* (London: A. Baldwin, 1698).

Turnbull, Gordon, "Samuel Johnson, Francis Barber, and 'Mr Desmoulins' writing school,'" in *Notes and Queries*, Vol. 61, No. 4 (Oxford: Oxford University Press, 2014).

Van Doren, Carl, *Benjamin Franklin* (New York: The Viking Press, 1938).

Voltaire, *Letters Concerning the English Nation* (London: C. Davis, 1741).

Walpole, Horace, *Memoirs of the Reign of King George the Third*, 4 vols. (London: Richard Bentley, 1845).

Walvin, James, *The Trader, the Owner, the Slave: Parallel Lives in the Age of Slavery* (London: Vintage Books, 2008).

Watson, John F., *Annals of Philadelphia, being a collection of memoirs, anecdotes, & incidents of the city and its inhabitants from the days of the Pilgrim Fathers* (Philadelphia: E. L. Carey & A. Hart, 1830).

Weatherly, Edward H. (ed.), *The Correspondence of John Wilkes and Charles Churchill* (New York: Columbia University Press, 1954).

Wecter, Dixon, "Thomas Paine and the Franklins," in *American Literature* Vol. 12, No. 3 (Durham, NC: Duke University Press, 1940).

White, Jerry, *London in the Eighteenth Century: A Great and Monstrous Thing* (London: The Bodley Head, 2012).

[Wilkes, John,] *A Letter to his Grace the Duke of Grafton, First Commissioner of His Majesty's Treasury* (London: J. Almon, 1767).

Wilkinson, Hazel, "Benjamin Franklin's London printing 1725–26," in *The Papers of the Bibliographical Society of America* (Chicago: University of Chicago Press, 2016).

Willard, J., William Tailer, John Clark, and Anna Janney de Armond, "Andrew Bradford," in *The Pennsylvania Magazine of History and Biography*, Vol. 62, No. 4 (Philadelphia: University of Pennsylvania Press, 1938).

Williams, Glyn, *The Prize of All the Ocean: The Triumph and Tragedy of Anson's Voyage Round the World* (London: Harper Collins, 1999).

Wood, Gordon S., *The Americanization of Benjamin Franklin* (New York: Penguin Books, 2005).

Wood, Gordon S., *The Radicalism of the American Revolution* (New York, Vintage Books, 1993).

Wrightson, Nick, "'[Those with] great abilities have not always the best information': How Franklin's transatlantic book-trade and scientific networks interacted," in *Early American Studies*, Vol. 8, No. 1 (Philadelphia: University of Pennsylvania Press, 2010).

Acknowledgments

BOOKS ARE LONG IN the making. There are parts of this one that take me right back. Almost my first memories are of tottering walks with my mother around Beacon Park in Lichfield, Staffordshire, and of chatter about someone called "Dr. Johnson." After this, Johnson haunted my childhood. People said that his father, the bookseller Michael Johnson, used to set up shop at an ancient structure called the Butter Cross in our village. Afterward, at the local high school in Uttoxeter, we marked Johnson's birthday by walking through the September drizzle to the Market Place. There we stood in imitation of the famous penance he once performed for having, when young and swollen with pride, refused to help on the family stall. Later still, when we were teenagers and growing fast, we filled ourselves up with baked potatoes of epic Johnsonian proportions, which were sold from a kiosk inside the Johnson Memorial. Writing about Johnson over these last few years has often stirred these memories, particularly of those walks around Lichfield with my mother. She died as this book was going to press, and it is to her, for encouraging my love of history from the very beginning, that I owe my deepest debt.

Some decades on, with lots of writing to do and a home filled with yapping infants, Nadia Fontaine threw me a lifeline when she allowed me the use of a quiet room in her beautiful house. For this kindness I am incredibly grateful, and this book is immeasurably better. To the artist Paul Wuensche, too, for his great generosity, company, and knack for always knowing another book on just about any subject, I am extremely thankful. For even more guidance, encouragement, and great good cheer, I am indebted to my friends the authors Mike Jay and Sarah Bakewell, both of whom excel in what Franklin once termed "grave Observations and wise Sentences" in the pubs of London. My thanks, too, to Professor Simon Schaffer for some hints about Franklin and science, to Dr. Julie Wheelwright for reading parts of an early draft, to Andy Patterson for valued support, to the wonderful Vicky Dawson and everyone at Buxton, and to all my students and colleagues at the University of Oxford for the many discussions about the craft of writing.

As ever, a word for those who expertly run the Rare Books and Music Reading Room at the British Library, and the always helpful staff at the London Library in St. James's Square. The London Library's decision, during the first lockdown of the COVID-19 pandemic, to post up to fifteen books to stranded members has rightly been described as the literary equivalent of the Berlin Airlift of 1948–49. As one of those marooned on the ground back then, now is the time to return my thanks.

In March 2022 I was honored to be asked to give the Johnson Society's annual lecture, which presented me with the chance to test some of the material in this book. Thank you to Phil Jones for the invitation, to John Winterton, to Marty Smith, and to Joanne Wilson for an interesting snippet about electricity. For his provoking work on Francis Barber and for taking the time to tell me a little bit more, I also want to express my gratitude to the biographer Michael Bundock.

My exceptional publisher Becky Hardie has championed this book from the very start. To her, Clara Farmer, Asia Choudhry, Rose Tomaszewska, Anna Redman Aylward, and the whole team at Chatto & Windus and Vintage, I'm hugely grateful. Also to my brilliant agent Annabel Merullo, Rebecca Wearmouth, and Daisy

Chandley at Peters, Fraser and Dunlop; to Ileene Smith, Molly Grote, Stephen Weil, Hillary Tisman, and the perceptive Ian Van Wye at Farrar, Straus and Giroux; and to Juliet Brooke and Greg Clowes, who both encouraged me at the very beginning, my warmest thanks. Working on this book editorially with Dr. Henry Howard has been a tremendously enriching experience. It is one that has given me, by turns, an insight into what it must have been like to have been cross-examined by Alexander Wedderburn, printed by William Strahan, and amused by John Wilkes. I am lucky to have an editor who has engaged so deeply and intelligently with the story.

Away from the eighteenth century, Maria Nolan, Violet Moller, Artemis Irvine, Jordan Lloyd, and John Hillman have kept me on my toes with our continuing, always fascinating series of recordings at www.tttpodcast.com. My father has remained a huge support right throughout too. But as ever, my last and most heartfelt thanks must go to my wife, Claire, who has now lived through my successive obsessions with cirrus clouds, oak trees, and all the rest of it. I am indebted to her for all she has done to aid this book's creation and to our two wonderful children, Thomas and Tess, who, for all their yapping, really do light up our days—each and every one.

PM, Palliser Road, London. October 2022

Index

A Note About the Author

Peter Moore is a writer, historian, and lecturer. He is the author of *Endeavour* and *The Weather Experiment*, both of which were *Sunday Times* bestsellers in the UK. *The Weather Experiment* was also chosen by *The New York Times* as one of the 100 Notable Books of 2015. Moore teaches at the University of Oxford, has lectured internationally on eighteenth-century history, and hosts a history podcast called *Travels Through Time*.